I Come From A Place Called Home

(1882–1929)

ELIZABETH BURR MARQUARD

Liz Marquard
2015

The people and experiences presented in this book reflect the observations and interpretations of the author. Some of the names have been changed to protect the privacy of certain individuals.

ISBN-10:1514398567
ISBN-13:978-1514398562

Dedicated to the Seibel siblings
who lived this story,
and
to my mother who encouraged
me to tell it.

I hear ethereal whispers,
persuasive,
soft and still.
"Daughter, if you don't
remember us,
who will?"

Dot Stutter

Family Tree

Wilhelm & Kathrina (Scheldt) Seibel
had four children:
Wilhelmine, George, Lisetta, & **William**

John Frederick & Katherine (Schaefer) Gasteier
had ten children:
Maggie, Fred, **Sophie,** Libby, Katie, Charles, Will, Emma, Henry, & Louise

William "Papa" Seibel & Sophie "Mama" Gasteier
had eight children:
Ada, Ella, Flora, Hermine, Margaret, Martha, Minola, & Bill

Ada Seibel & Albert Gfell
had four children:
Mildred, Roberta, Russell, & **Martha Jane**

Martha Jane Gfell & Mark Burr
had three children:
Stephen, Matthew, & **Elizabeth**

Elizabeth Burr & Robert Marquard
had two children:
Seth & Ashley

Chapter 1
Monroeville, Ohio
May 1985

A LARGE SEMI TRUCK blasted its horn in angry staccatos as Minola Seibel slowly exited the highway. She eased the Buick onto the brick-paved access road, the tires *rum-tumming* on the uneven surface, then nosed the car between the wrought iron pillars supporting the arch that announced "Riverside Cemetery." Just past the third gravel crossroad, Minola pulled the car onto the grass under a massive oak and released a long, slow breath. Her hands clenched the steering wheel, fingernails digging into her palms. Her right leg quivered involuntarily as she continued to depress the brake.

"Old fool!" she chastised herself. "When Dr. Bailey said 'Your eyesight is getting worse and will continue to fail,' he didn't mean 'Take one last road trip, old girl, and see if you can get yourself killed'!"

Even though she had taken the lesser-traveled highways from her home on the west side of Cleveland, Minola found the traffic daunting. Other drivers seemed impatient with her slow, cautious speed and made liberal use of their horns. On more than one occasion, the menacing grill of a hulking semi truck had filled her rearview mirror. So much urgency, such preoccupation with getting somewhere quickly.

Minola stabbed the gearshift into park and flexed the fingers of both hands, releasing the tension. Smoothing her palms down her lap, she wiped away the moisture generated from gripping the wheel for an hour, then absentmindedly straightened the pleats of her skirt as she watched a tractor pull a planter across the flat expanse of the field just beyond the row of pine trees marking the cemetery's east edge. Spring had come early this year, and many of the fields she had passed on her trip were dotted with farmers taking advantage of the warm weather to plant their corn. Even though Minola had left the farm over sixty years ago, she still understood the urgency that came with spring: the renewed hope that this year's crop would be bountiful so that bills could be paid, debts retired, food placed upon the table, and maybe, just maybe, a small improvement made in the family's quality of life. At least that was the way she remembered farm life in the early 1900s. She didn't suppose things had changed much, other than the size of the farms, the equipment, and the subsequent debt.

Minola opened the car door and slowly swung her legs out. Grabbing the car's armrest for support, she pulled herself to her feet and stood there a moment. The long, tense drive had left her achy. With one hand on the side of the car for balance, she walked toward the trunk and popped the lid. A flat of geraniums greeted her, their cheery red heads crowded together. Minola selected a dozen of the pots and placed them in a wicker basket alongside a trowel. With the basket in one hand and a dented tin watering can in the other, she crossed the gravel drive.

Minola stopped in front of a low granite headstone: William J. Seibel, July 29, 1861 to Nov. 9, 1939; Sophia K. Seibel, Feb. 17, 1866 to Jan. 20, 1938. A strong shaft of sunlight washed across the inscription on Papa's side of the headstone, but Mama's side was dappled with both shade and sun. Minola shook her head slightly.

"How typical of you, Mama," she murmured. "Always with a dark side." Minola set the wicker basket and watering can beside the headstone and slowly crouched, gingerly dropping to one knee, then both. She brushed some grass clippings and bird droppings from the surface of the marker, then spaded a shallow trench along its front. She shook the geraniums loose from their individual pots, spaced them evenly in the trench, and pressed the soil firmly over their roots. Minola sat back on her heels to admire her work.

Her legs ached from the crouching position, but as she attempted to shift her weight, she lost her balance and toppled sideways onto the grass, upsetting the wicker basket and watering can in her fall. Empty plastic pots spilled onto the grass, and the trowel made a heavy *clink* as it came to rest against the corner of the headstone.

Minola lay on her side in the grass. She waited for the piercing pain of a broken hip or a fractured vertebra. To her astonishment, nothing seemed damaged except her pride and her nylon stocking, which had a gaping hole in it after snagging on the jagged seam of the watering can. Now, here was a dilemma she hadn't conceived: an eighty-year-old woman, sprawled in the grass at a rural cemetery, who must get back on her feet unassisted. At the far end of the cemetery, the sexton and his assistant were mowing and trimming the grass. Calling for help was futile—they would never hear her over the loud whine of their equipment. She supposed she could lay here until they took a lunch break—*if* they took a lunch break—and then flag them down.

She studied the blades of grass just inches from her nose and wondered how many years it had been since she'd had such an intimate relationship with grass. Probably not since she was a child and had been flung across the grass of the Plank Road schoolyard in a game of "Crack the Whip." That game had ended disastrously, too, with her sleeve ripped at the shoulder and grass stains marring the entire left side of her dress. On the walk home from school that afternoon, she and younger brother Bill had stopped at the little creek that split the neighboring fields. There, they attempted to scrub the stain out of her dress with handfuls of wet gravel. Instead of diminishing the grass stain, the muddy creek gravel had added its own dark smear.

Fearing Mama's wrath at the damaged dress, she and Bill had avoided the house until nearly suppertime. They climbed the haystack in the horse barn, inspected the pigeon cotes for eggs, then slid down the stack and nestled into the sweet-smelling hay. When at last they'd slipped into the summer kitchen, they ran smack into Mama, who was replacing the weighting stone on a crock of sauerkraut. For one long moment she stared at the wisps of hay in their tousled hair. Then, spying the torn and stained dress, Mama flew into a rage.

"*Sieh Dich an! Warum kannst Du nicht ordentlich und sauber sein?* (Look at you! Why can't you be neat and tidy?)," she shouted and began hitting both Minola and Bill about the head and shoulders with a wooden spoon.

The children fled into the kitchen, to the refuge of their six older sisters. Ada and Ella were preparing supper, Hermine was setting the table, and Flora was in the adjacent pantry, skimming cream from the day's milk. Margaret was helping Martha with her homework at the long table between the kitchen and living room.

Minola and Bill threw themselves at Ada, burying their faces in her apron. Hearing the commotion, Flora quickly stepped from the pantry and diverted Mama by efficiently steering her toward the stove with a request to fry up some potatoes and onions for supper. Ada whisked the two distraught youngsters to the back porch, where they were joined by Margaret.

Ada tipped Minola's chin upward. "Tell me what happened."

Minola sobbed out the story of the "Crack the Whip" tumble, the stop at the creek, the hideout in the barn, and Mama's angry outburst. Meanwhile, Margaret plucked errant strands of hay from Minola and Bill's hair and smoothed their tousled heads.

Ada examined the torn dress. "I can mend the sleeve later," she said. "It's ripped on the seam—hain't that bad. I seen worse." Using the edge of her apron, she wiped Minola's tear-stained cheeks.

"I'm sure I can get those stains out with some softsoap and rainwater," Margaret assured.

"Just stay out here on the porch, out of harm's way for a little while. Mama's German is up," Ada cautioned over her shoulder as she slipped back inside to resume her kitchen chores.

Mama usually spoke German-peppered English, but it was never a good sign when she reverted solely to her native tongue. "Her German is up" was an indication that Mama was under the siege of another spell.

"I'll stay out here with you for a while," offered Margaret. "Martha's got the hang of that math now anyway," and she sat down on the weathered top step. Bill and Minola took their places on either side of her, and Margaret wrapped her arms around their shoulders, pulling them closer to her. "Mama's just being Mama," she offered by way of explanation.

* * * * *

"Well, Mama, nothing *ordentlich und sauber*—neat and tidy—about me right now!" Minola muttered to herself in disgust as she whipped her pleated skirt over the torn stocking. "And no sisters to rescue me, either."

Minola had always prided herself on her independence, and she was determined to use her ingenuity to resolve this predicament, too. With her knee, she nudged the toppled watering can closer to her hand. Rolling over onto her stomach, she pushed herself up onto all fours, then to her knees. By placing the watering can on top of Mama's side of the headstone and bracing both hands on the can's curved handle, Minola was able to lean heavily on the makeshift support until she had both feet under her and was again erect.

She smoothed the pleats on her skirt, brushed off her hands, and chuckled to herself. Imagine that—leaning on Mama for support!

Minola carried the watering can to the nearby water pump and filled it, then rinsed off her hands. She returned to the freshly planted row of geraniums and gave them a soaking, then retrieved the scattered plastic pots and trowel and placed them in the basket.

Her plans to plant a row of geraniums at Flora, Ella, and Margaret's headstones now appeared overly ambitious, just as the drive here had been. She returned the watering can to the car trunk, then placed the remaining geraniums in the wicker basket and retraced her steps to the family plot. She stood before Ella and Margaret's side-by-side headstones. Bending carefully, she situated four geraniums in a cluster in front of each marker.

"Sorry about the slipshod placement of the flowers, girls. I'm just not willing to risk another tumble," Minola offered apologetically. With a sigh and a cock of the head, she grew quiet, thinking of how inadequate her gesture seemed.

Minola turned and walked a short distance down the gravel drive, then stepped off into the grass until she came to Flora and Phil Burrer's headstone. There, she centered the remaining geraniums in front of the headstone. Stepping back, Minola assessed her work. Something about it was unsettling. With a sidelong glance at Phil's name, she nudged the flowers until they were clustered on Flora's side of the plot. "Much better," she thought to herself.

At last, Minola approached an upright headstone close to the pine tree boundary. Ada and Albert Gfell. She knew there would already be flowers here; the Gfell children saw to it that attractive bedding flowers or seasonal arrangements were always in place on their parents' plot.

Ada had done more mothering to her seven younger siblings than Mama had. In fact, Minola's earliest memory involved Ada. Minola had curled her small toddler fingers over the rim of a hot skillet on the stovetop. Almost simultaneously, she could hear and feel the sizzle of burning flesh. She recoiled in pain, instinctively jamming the burned fingers into her mouth and clutching for the comfort of Mama's skirts. But with one swift, fluid motion, Mama routed the howling child toward Ada, just as deftly as if she were flipping a fried egg. Ada plunged Minola's burned fingers into the kitchen water bucket and murmured soothingly. After the throbbing stopped, she applied a dab of homemade butter to the blistered flesh, then slipped a fat sugar cookie into Minola's other fist. Mama had shown no reaction, no concern.

Even after Ada and Albert married, Minola and Bill had followed like lost ducklings. At the close of school on Fridays, she and Bill walked the mile north of town to spend their weekends with the young couple in "the honeymoon cottage," as everyone referred to Ada and Albert's first home. Albert never protested their presence nor their hearty attacks on Ada's cookie jar. With his slow, shy smile and deep-set blue eyes, Albert kindly accepted the "package deal" that Minola and Bill represented.

Minola stood with her hands clasped before her, thinking of her six older sisters and younger brother Bill. How could it be that she was the last surviving sibling? Blinking rapidly, she turned and walked back to the car.

Minola set the wicker basket inside the trunk beside the now-empty flat and closed the lid. Sliding into the front seat, she pulled a brown paper bag and thermos of coffee from the passenger's side. As she ate her lunch, she thought about her initial intent to visit each of her siblings' headstones one last time. However, the difficulty of the drive and the tumble in the grass had proved to her how overly ambitious that plan had been. Hermine, Martha, and Bill were buried in various cemeteries in the Cleveland suburbs. Driving in unfamiliar territory, especially those Cleveland suburbs that had recently mushroomed in growth, was not a good idea, given her diminishing eyesight. Maybe one of the attendants at the assisted-living facility where she was moving next month would drive her to those three cemeteries—for a fee, of course. The transition from independence to dependence came with many price tags, Minola was ruefully discovering.

There was one place left on her list that she wished to visit: home. Minola could no longer remember how many years had passed since she had been to the homestead. Nor did she know who lived there now, but she did not intend to bother them with an unexpected visitor. Instead, she would park in the drive for a moment, satisfy her curiosity that the old place still stood, and then be on her way back to Cleveland. She neatly folded the waxed paper that had wrapped her sandwich, replaced the cup on the top of the thermos, and took a deep breath before turning the key in the ignition.

The cemetery drive looped around the back of the property before rejoining itself at the entrance. Minola carefully navigated the narrow gravel passageway and exited onto the brick roadway. Her tires drummed their cadence on the uneven surface until turning onto a paved road that led to Monroeville. At the only stoplight, she turned left onto Monroe Street and proceeded west, where the tiny village soon opened into vast farmland dotted by tractors. Plank Road was no longer the rutted, hard-packed dirt byway of her youth. In fact, it was no longer even called Plank Road but went by the thoroughly bland designation of Route 547.

Up ahead, a rural road snaked off to the left: Townline Road 32, separating the townships of Lyme and Ridgefield. Minola turned onto the narrow road, barely the width of one car. Over a low rise and at a small bend in the road, she spotted the old family burial ground. During her youth, the plot was wildly overgrown with grape hyacinths and riddled with woodchuck holes. As children, she and Bill had often climbed over the fence and explored the lot. Their interest was not in the relatives buried beneath the tilted and sinking headstones with German inscriptions. Rather, their curiosity involved woodchuck habitats and whether the creatures really did maintain front and back entrances to their passages. On one occasion, Bill tossed a kerosene-soaked rag into the opening of a tunnel and then joined Minola by the "back door" to wait expectantly for the offended woodchuck to emerge. Instead, a very disgruntled skunk had trundled forth. The children fled, but in their hasty retreat, Bill lost half the sole of his shoe. Papa kept a small tack hammer and little nails for such cobbling repairs in his workroom on the second floor of the cornbarn. However, Papa was an unapproachable fellow. His tolerance was nil for such foolishness as losing the sole of one's shoe while taunting a skunk. He would surely dole out a stern reprimand and probably an additional odious chore or two as punishment. On the other hand, Bill was equally reluctant to attempt a retrieval of the missing half-sole, thereby risking a second encounter with the malodorous critter. Instead, he elected to wear one half-soled shoe for a week until he could summon the courage to face both the skunk and Papa.

Across the road from the little cemetery stood a stately white farmhouse. It looked very much as Minola remembered it from her youth. When Papa and Mama had married on Christmas Day, 1888, it was understood that they would inhabit this house upon their return from the honeymoon trip to Columbus. However, during their absence, Papa's brother George and his wife Bertha had moved there from the homeplace on the adjoining farm, bringing with them everything of value, including the cupboards from the kitchen walls. Papa and Mama were left with the much older and now barren homestead house, a fact that Mama remained bitter about for the rest of her life. Even during her spells, when nothing she said or did seemed rational, she complained quite coherently about the unexpected house shuffle. Would Mama's life have turned out differently had she lived in the longed-for house? Probably not—but in times of agitation, she blamed Papa for the loss and berated him with accusations such as "*Nur ein schwacher Mann gibt oben Land ohne einen Kampf* (Only a weak man gives up land without a fight)."

Just to the south of the coveted property was the Seibel homestead. Minola blinked several times and slowed the car to a crawl. If she had not known that this was the location of the homeplace, she would not have recognized what lay before her. All but one of Papa's many barns were gone. The apple, pear, cherry, and mulberry trees, the grape arbor, the lilac and snowball bushes, and the massive yellow rose bush that should be in full bloom by the front corner of the house—gone as if they had never existed. The yard looked as though it had recently been brushhogged as a means of weed control. The only foliage that she recognized was the clematis vine that had overgrown the front porch in an apologetic attempt to conceal the sad state of the house. An eaves trough dangled freely from the roof line, and the clapboards were nearly devoid of paint. The house had a hollow-eyed appearance, and as Minola drew closer, she realized that all of the windows had been removed.

A dusty red pickup truck sat in the driveway, and Minola pulled in behind it and parked the car. This aroused the attention of a mixed-breed dog that had been stretched across the toolbox in the bed of the truck. The dog jumped to its feet and began barking, running first to one end of the toolbox, then to the other. The tailgate of the truck was down, and Minola spotted several old window frames stacked neatly in the bed. The house was being cannibalized, she realized, and she did not care to stay and watch the feast.

Minola was fumbling to put the car in reverse when she heard a man's voice yell "Buster!" A stocky young man carrying a window frame stepped from the back porch and walked toward the vehicles.

"Quiet, Buster!" he called again. The dog wiggled from head to tail in obvious delight at seeing the young man and gave one more bark as it leaped from the toolbox into the bed of the truck.

The young man stacked the frame on top of the others while the dog licked at his face. "Ought to call you 'Bluster' instead of Buster—you're all bark and no bite," he pretended to scold as he scratched the dog behind the ears.

"Can I help you?" he asked as he approached Minola's car.

Minola rolled down the car window and stammered, "I . . . well, I. . ."

"Are you lost? Do you need directions?" asked the young man, tilting his baseball cap toward the back of his head and scratching his hairline.

Minola regained her composure at the poignancy of his question. "Yes, I guess you could say I'm a little bit lost. I used to live here many, many years ago, but, well, I hardly recognize the place now."

"Yeah, she's lookin' a little rough. In fact, the house is a goner—has been since before my family started farming the place. Now my wife and me are going to move over here."

"Oh," Minola brightened, "so you're fixing up the house for you and your wife?"

"Fix this place?!" the man guffawed. "Naw, it's beyond hope. I've just been pulling out anything that can be used—like these windows." He waved his arm toward the bed of the truck. "My wife likes to vegetable garden, so I'm going to make her some cold frames—let her get a little head start on the growing season."

"But I thought you said you and your wife were moving onto the property. Are you building a new house?" Minola craned her neck to look around the property for signs of construction.

"Nope. Can't afford to build. The Monroeville Fire Department's coming next week to do a controlled burn on the house. That's why we had to get out here and brushhog the place. The firemen don't want to hassle with shrubs and stuff up close to the house. Then we'll backfill the cellar. You know those old fieldstone cellars; they're wet and have radon gas and always smell bad. When that's all done, we're going to put a double-wide mobile home right over there," he said as he pointed to the area that Minola and her siblings had used as a croquet grounds in their youth.

Minola felt as though a fist had punched her in the chest. This lovely old farmhouse, full of so many memories—good and bad—was fated to be burned to the ground. She couldn't help but note the irony. The first time Minola had learned that the neighbors regarded Mama as "different" came as a result of one of Mama's escapades with flames.

Mama had learned the phrase "apple-pie order" during her teen-aged years when she worked as a domestic for the Wrights, a wealthy Yankee family. She quickly adopted the term, taking her already Germanic tidiness to obsessive levels. However, on occasion, she confused her apple dishes, barking out, "Girls! I want this house in apple-*sauce* order!" Mama's vigilant march toward apple-pie order spilled over into the yard. No weeds were tolerated around the foundations of the house and outbuildings. Any twig or fallen branch was immediately seized and added to a growing pile between the woodshed and the outhouse.

One day, during a particularly dark mood, Mama decided the pile itself violated her sense of order. She grabbed the tin container of kerosene from the summer kitchen, where it was kept for the weekly chore of cleaning and refilling the kerosene lamps, and tucked a handful of matches in her apron pocket. With purposeful strides, she returned to the pile and began liberally splashing the dry kindling with kerosene. Mama struck a match on the sole of her brogan, and with a *whoosh!* the kerosene ignited. Flames danced higher and higher, sending sparks into the air and licking outward into the dry grass where Mama had spilled kerosene. Soon, the fire raced across the yard, pushed along by a light westerly breeze. It consumed the dry grass and leaves until only one structure stood before it: the outhouse. Flames licked at the sides of the building, and smoke poured through the cracks of its plank roof. A hen that had been nesting in the corncob box in the corner of the outhouse shot out of the partially opened door, flapping its wings and protesting loudly as it sped off toward the chicken house.

Ada was rinsing the last section of the cream separator when Mama slammed through the door of the summer kitchen. Grabbing her chipped ironstone mug, Mama poured herself a cup of coffee from the enamelware coffeepot on the back of the stove. "*Benutzen Sie den Outhouse nicht für eine Weile* (Don't use the outhouse for a while)," she commanded.

"Why?" Ada asked. "Are the hornets riled up again?"

"*Ja*," Mama barked and stomped out of the summer kitchen, across the porch, and into the house.

At that moment, Ada heard a man's frantic shouts of "Fire! Fire!" She looked out the kitchen window just in time to see Mr. Moss, their neighbor to the south, dash across the backyard. He grabbed the wet rag rugs that she and Ella had washed and hung on the clothesline that morning and ran toward the outhouse.

Ada plucked up the bucket of rinse water and banged through the summer kitchen door, yelling "Girls, help me! There's a fire!"

The girls and Bill spilled out of the house like ants from a hill. Mr. Moss was already beating the flames with the wet rugs in a valiant attempt to save the structure. He had been plowing his field just south of the Seibel place when he spotted the conflagration. Wheeling his horses toward the scene, he had plowed a furrow around the area to contain the flames.

Ada flung the rinse water on the fully engaged outhouse and ran for the well, where Bill and Minola furiously pumped water. Flora gathered up the remaining wet rugs and joined Mr. Moss in the vain attempts to snuff out the flames. Ella had plucked up the empty milk pail as she exited the summer kitchen, and Margaret ran to the barn to retrieve as many buckets as she could quickly gather. Martha frantically pulled on the rope that sounded the old school bell on the top of the summer kitchen. It was the signal to Papa that he was urgently needed at the house. Martha joined Minola and Bill in taking turns at the pump handle while Ada, Ella, Hermine, and Margaret ran a bucket brigade.

Despite their efforts, the outhouse was gone. Acrid wisps of smoke curled into the air. In the ashes lay one very hard-cooked egg.

The school bell alarm had attracted the attention of the neighbors. Uncle George arrived, out of breath from his run across the fields, and Mr. Ordmann, who lived across the road from the Mosses, galloped in on horseback. Across the field from the south ran Mr. Moss's teenaged daughter Edith, eager to see the cause of the commotion. All were surveying the ruins and asking questions about how the fire had started, when Papa arrived from the back field atop Davey the workhorse, who was still dragging the harrow.

Papa leaped to the ground and rushed toward the crowd of

onlookers, then saw the tendrils of smoke curling up from the ashes where the outhouse had once stood. Spying the kerosene can, he wheeled and grabbed young Bill by the collar, pulling him close to his angry face.

"D-D-Did you do this?" Papa bellowed. In times of agitation, Papa stuttered, which only made him more intimidating. "T-T-Tell me the truth!" and he gave Bill a small shake.

Bill's blue eyes grew huge with fear as he stared up into Papa's crimson face. He tried to speak, but his throat closed. Ada quickly stepped between the two. In a low voice so that the neighbors wouldn't hear, Ada said, "No, Papa, it wasn't Bill. He was playing upstairs with Minola when this happened." Lowering her voice even more, she whispered, "It was Mama."

Papa released Bill, who buried his face in Ada's soot-stained apron.

As if on cue, Mama emerged from around the corner of the house, her coffee mug still in hand. She spotted Mr. Moss, who was standing beside the smoldering ashes, picking up and examining the scorched rugs.

Mama stopped short, then rushed at him. "*Ach! Sie haben meine Wolldecken ruiniert! Gehen Sie nach Hause! Nach Hause, gehen Sie Teufel!* (Ach! You've ruined my rugs! Go home! Go home, you devil!)" She cocked back her arm and hurtled the ironstone mug at Mr. Moss.

While Mr. Moss could not interpret German, he did understand the meaning of a coffee mug sailing toward his head. He quickly dropped the rugs and ducked. The mug flew over his head and bounced on the ground with a *thump,* its handle spinning off in another direction.

"Jesus!" Mr. Moss exclaimed. "What'd you do that for, Sophie?!"

Mama steamed off toward the barns, barking snatches of incoherent German and completely disregarding the stunned onlookers.

"Jesus, Bill," Mr. Moss said to Papa, "you've really gotta get her under control!"

Throwing up his hands, Papa turned and walked back to the waiting workhorse, shaking his head and muttering his frustrations under his breath. He grabbed Davey's halter and led the horse back to the field where he had been working. Uncle George and Mr. Ordmann exchanged glances, then turned toward their homes. Mr. Moss wiped his sooty hands on his pants and walked out into the field to retrieve his horses, stepping over the glistening black firebreak he had plowed earlier.

Edith Moss sidled up to Ada, who now had both Minola and young Bill clinging to her skirts. Minola felt Ada's body tense.

"What's wrong with your Mama?" Edith asked in mock concern.

"She has spells," Ada replied tersely.

"No, that's not it. Your Mama is just plain *crazy*!" hissed Edith. "Everybody says so!"

Minola saw Ada's lips tighten into a straight line. "I told you—she has spells," Ada repeated emphatically.

"People with spells stay in bed all day. *Crazy* people burn down outhouses," declared Edith as she lifted her chin in superiority.

Ada turned on her heel and ushered Minola and Bill toward the house. The other five sisters followed, their eyes downcast.

At every step, the word *crazy* crashed through Minola's brain. "*Crazy, crazy ... your Mama is crazy ... everybody says so ... crazy ...*"

* * * * *

"Ma'am ... ma'am?"

Minola jolted from her reverie as she realized the young man was addressing her. "Are you alright?" he queried.

"Yes, yes, I'm sorry. You probably think I'm *crazy* or something," she smiled weakly and fumbled through her purse for a tissue. "It's just that, well, there are so many memories here."

"Yeah, I suppose so," he replied. He pulled his cap down on his forehead and studied Minola as she dabbed at the corners of her eyes. "Say, I probably shouldn't do this—liability issues and all—but would you like to go in and take a look around one last time?"

Minola drew in her breath. Such finality to those words *one last time*. But wasn't that the theme of this trip? She was visiting the graves of her siblings *one last time*. Why not go home *one last time*? She pulled the keys from the ignition, sniffed lightly, and replied, "Yes, I think I would."

The young man opened Minola's car door. "My name is Jim Weiss," he said as he offered his hand. Realizing how dirty his hand was from the window work, he quickly withdrew it and wiped it on his pant leg before offering it again.

Minola smiled at this gesture. "Weiss. That sounds like a good German name," she said. "This farm started off in a German family; it's nice to know it's back in German hands. My name is Minola Seibel." She grasped his hand, and he helped her to a standing position.

"Seibel." Jim said thoughtfully. "I think I remember seeing that name on the title search we had done when my folks bought this place. But that name goes way, way back."

"Indeed it does," Minola proudly responded. "My father's family bought this farm in the 1840s. It stayed in our family for almost one hundred years."

"A hundred years! What happened? Why did you sell out?" inquired

Jim as they began walking toward the back of the house.

"Oh, many reasons. Hard times, poor health. I guess the biggest reason was lack of manpower. My folks had seven girls before they finally had a boy. You know how it is with farming, Jim; you need strong young men, especially back then when so much of the work was physical. But, that's not to say my sisters and I didn't do our share of farm work. Believe me, Papa saw to it that we spent plenty of time in the fields. I sometimes think he didn't realize just how difficult the labor was for us girls. And by the time they finally had a son, well, it really didn't matter anymore," Minola shrugged, her voice trailing off.

"How could it not matter?" inquired Jim. "Every man wants a son."

Minola chuckled. "Well, my brother Bill claimed that until he was nine years old, Papa thought he was just another one of the girls."

They had reached the steps to the back porch, which joined the house to the summer kitchen. Minola stopped and looked up toward the summer kitchen's roofline. The cupola that had housed the school bell sagged precariously.

"Is the old school bell still there?" Minola asked, shielding her eyes against the sun and trying to get a better angle.

"School bell!?" exclaimed Jim. "Why would there be a school bell on this run-down thing?"

"Because this section of the house *was* an old school house—the first in this community. I think my father attended school in it, although I can't tell you where it was located at the time. Somehow, it came into my father's family's possession after a larger school was built. We used it for a summer kitchen. And, yes, it did have a school bell on top, but we only rang it in case of emergencies."

"Hmmph!" responded Jim. "I'd have never guessed." Turning toward the truck, he slapped his leg and called, "C'mon, Buster."

The dog leaped from the bed of the truck, tail wagging furiously, and dashed toward the house.

"He'll go crazy in here with the scent of all them raccoons," Jim advised. "They've made a pretty bad mess in here, so be prepared."

"Mama didn't allow dogs in the house," Minola stated absentmindedly as she eyed Buster. When she noticed Jim's raised eyebrows, she offered, "Just one more disruption in a house that already had too much commotion for her to handle."

"She was a nervous sort, huh?" Jim asked as he scratched Buster's back.

"Nerves or what we called 'spells.' I think she probably had bipolar disorder or some other emotional affliction; but of course, back then those kinds of things weren't diagnosed or treated. In fact, those kinds of things weren't even talked about. Seems like we spent most of our time avoiding Mama, trying not to agitate her. But no matter what, eight children were just too much for her," Minola said with finality.

Jim pulled open the summer kitchen screen door, which squealed on its only hinge. The ripped screening lolled like a tongue. Buster charged ahead, his nose working the floor and air for the raccoon scent.

"How many times did we slam through this back door?" Minola wondered aloud. She recalled seeing Mama flinch each time the door banged shut.

The summer kitchen was in worse condition than Minola had imagined. Crumbled plaster, raccoon feces, shredded fast-food wrappers, and old newspapers littered the floor. A gaping hole in the wall indicated where a sink had been removed. It was the same location where the wellwater pump had stood—the pump that had frozen in the winters and required a teakettle of hot water be poured down its stalk before the mechanism creaked to usefulness. An imprint on the wall indicated where the *Mehlfach* was once attached. In an earlier day, this bin had held flour, but Minola remembered it containing old newspapers for the daily fire-starting needs.

"Hard to believe we used to cook, put up preserves, and do laundry out here all summer long," mused Minola. "In the winter, we used it like an icebox, since it was unheated. But no matter what the season brought—rain, snow, mud—there was always clothing out here in various stages of drying." She could still see Flora bringing in armloads of frozen-stiff long underwear from the outdoor clothesline and standing the garments in a row along one wall. As they thawed and drooped onto the floor, Flora removed them to clothes bars in the house to finish drying. Flora was fastidious about ensuring that the long johns were thoroughly dry. Family lore had it that Papa's sister Wilhelmine suffered an untimely death as the result of wearing damp underwear.

"This room may look bad now, but believe me, Jim, it was nothing fancy back then either. The walls were covered in newspaper, and it smelled of sauerkraut year-round because the crocks of kraut were kept here."

Minola pointed to a spot on the floor near where the sink had been removed. "When my older sister Hermine was a little girl—probably about four years old or so—she fell right through a hole in the floor over there and landed in the crawl space by the cistern."

"Fell through the floorboards?!" exclaimed Jim. "Why did your kitchen floor have a hole big enough to swallow a child?"

Minola chuckled at Jim's astonishment. "Well, that's a good question. I suppose fixing it was one of those things on Papa's 'to-do' list, but it didn't get bumped up in priority until after the incident. As Hermine told it in later days, the floorboards had a rotten spot, which everyone knew they were supposed to avoid. But one day, Ada, my oldest sister, had baked a küchen—that's a type of coffeecake, you know—and for some reason, it wasn't reserved for Sunday. You see, we only had desserts on Sundays back in those days. So, there was great excitement about this rare treat. The children were galloping about the summer kitchen, clamoring for a piece of küchen, when *whoomp!* Hermine disappeared through the floorboards. She landed in the crawl space next to the cistern, where it was dark and she was surrounded by cobwebs. When she looked up, she saw the faces of her three older sisters gathered around the rim of the hole, peering down at her. And that's when the tears started."

"So, how did they get her out of the crawl space?" inquired Jim.

"Remember that school bell I told you about?" Minola pointed toward the roof. "One of the girls rang it to summon Papa from the field. He pried up a few of the rotted boards to make a bigger opening, then lowered a rope, which Hermine clung to so he could pull her back up through the hole. Is it any wonder Hermine had a life-long dislike of spiders?"

Jim whistled. "Whew, can you imagine if an agency like Social Services had existed back then and they heard about your sister falling through rotten floorboards in the kitchen? All of you would have ended up in foster care!"

Minola nodded thoughtfully. "We were borderline-motherless children as it was, but the saving grace was that we always had each other."

Crossing the porch, Jim opened the door to the main kitchen. Buster squirmed past his legs and dashed into the room, his tail wagging wildly.

Minola looked around the summer kitchen one more time. She could almost smell Ada's rich küchen baking. Ada used the back of a spoon to make deep valleys in the pillowy dough, which she then filled with cream—Ada had a generous hand when it came to the cream. She topped the creation with a thick coating of cinnamon and sugar, then baked it to perfection. Minola felt her mouth start to water. "I'd gladly fall through the floor right now for a piece of Ada's küchen," she said wistfully before following Jim.

Buster had bounded through the kitchen, into the pantry, and down the cellar steps. Jim stood at the top of the steps, calling "Buster! Buster! Get back up here!"

Minola looked aghast at the skeleton of the kitchen before her. It bore no resemblance to the room that had served as the heart of their home. Mama had been particularly demanding that the kitchen be *ordentlich und sauber*—neat and tidy—but the room was now in disarray and smelled of mice and rotten potatoes. Cheap, torn linoleum covered the wooden floors that Ada, Ella, and Flora had scrubbed every Monday with the water left over from washing clothes. Where the drysink had once stood, a gaping hole in the plaster revealed the wooden lathe behind. All of the cupboards had been ripped from the walls. Minola shook her head. "This house sure has a hard time hanging on to its cupboards," she said under her breath.

A cast iron register stood where the old wood-burning cookstove had squatted, its insatiable hunger fed by cord after cord of firewood chopped by Papa. He chose this labor-intensive form of fuel rather than spend precious money on coal. The children's nightly chore—and a hated task it was—involved filling the woodbox beside the cookstove with chunks of firewood as well as bringing in a basketful of corncobs to use as kindling. The task was repeated for the heating stove in the parlor. As detestable as the chore was, having the kindling and firewood handy was not only a convenience but a necessary precaution. On more than one occasion, Mama's impatience with a scant amount of fire-starting material had led her to pour on a steady stream of kerosene. Only the kitchen water bucket had averted tragedy.

Minola picked her way across the curled and littered linoleum and entered the small room where Jim stood at the top of the cellar steps.

"C'mon, Buster. There's nothing down there for you," Jim implored.

"For us, it was a root cellar," commented Minola as she gazed down into the dark cavity. The musty smell of an earthen-floored basement wafted up, bringing with it memories of vinegar barrels and root crops.

"We kept bushel baskets of apples down there in the winter, and every evening, one or the other of us would bring up a big pan of apples for a snack," Minola reminisced. "Some of the apples kept better than others, so, of course, Papa wanted us to eat the poor-keepers first, which we did begrudgingly. Well, one night, my older sister Margaret volunteered to bring up the pan of apples. After she'd been gone a while, I began to wonder what was taking her so long. I opened up the cellar door, and there she sat on the steps, crunching away on the crispest, juiciest apple you'd ever seen—certainly not one of the poor-keepers."

"Sounds like something my sister would do, too," chuckled Jim.

"Yes, Margaret had her mischievous side, but she was very generous too," continued Minola. "She went like this"—Minola held her index finger up to her lips to make the "Shhh" signal—"and then she winked and motioned me to join her. So, we sat together on the cellar steps crunching away on one crisp apple after another. At one point, Margaret held up a perfect apple on her flattened palm and after examining it from all sides, she whispered, 'Just remember, Minola: If you always eat the best apple first, you've always had the best apple.' I've never forgotten that—'always eat the best apple first.'"

"And do you? Eat the best apple first, I mean?" asked Jim.

Minola's smile faded. "To this day, I can't eat an apple without thinking of Margaret. In many ways, *she* was the best apple," Minola sighed, her eyes welling with tears.

"So, did the rest of your family begin to wonder why it was taking so long for the pan of apples to make it upstairs?" Jim inquired.

Minola rapidly blinked back her tears and chuckled in spite of herself. "Well, yes they did, and leave it to Ada to figure out that something was amiss. Margaret and I were in mid-chew when the cellar door flew open, and there stood Ada. She had her hands on her hips, and as she shook her head from side to side, she exclaimed, 'The I-dacity!' That was her favorite expression whenever one of us had done something she found pretty offensive—'the I-dacity!'" Minola threw back her head and laughed at the memory.

"Did you two get a lickin'?" asked Jim, a smile creeping across his face.

"From Ada? Oh, my no. Ada would scold but she very rarely raised a hand to any of us. I do remember getting a spanking from her once—I don't remember the reason for it, but I'm sure it was well deserved—and I bellowed out, 'I feel sorry for your children when you marry!' Wasn't I a threatening thing, though?" Minola shook with laughter and dabbed at her eyes.

Buster charged up the cellar steps, his whiskers laced with cobwebs.

"Looks like you found the only thing left down there, Buster," Jim said as he knelt to pet the dog's face and brush away the cobwebs.

"Never a shortage of cobwebs in a country home, that's for sure," commented Minola as she eyed the narrow shelves that lined both of the walls leading to the cellar steps.

It seemed strange to see the pantry's shelves empty. They had always been filled with jars of pickles and tomato juice, a narrow-necked jug of molasses, crocks of apple butter and lard, and the cookie kettle with its noisy lid that alerted Ada to a small hand on a stealthy mission. In this room, Flora skimmed the cream from the milk and added it to a crock in the cellar until she had enough to churn into butter. There was never a sufficient supply of butter to satisfy the demands of cooking, baking, and everyone's preference for it as an *Aufstrich* (spread) on their slices of homemade bread. Flora took this insufficiency personally, as though she alone was responsible for the amount of cream that the cows produced. This was Flora's nature: always eager to please others, while subjugating her own needs and desires.

Given that type of personality, it had been easy for Mama to drill into Flora a work ethic of the highest Germanic order. Once, when Flora was about ten years old, Mama had found her absorbed in reading a book at the long table between the kitchen and living room. Mama reached over Flora's shoulder and slammed the book shut.

"No man wants a woman who neglects her *Haushalt* (housekeeping) for such *Dummheit* (foolishness) as reading!" she had commanded.

Thereafter, Flora, being the obedient type, had suppressed her love of books and made herself indispensable in shouldering the family workload, both in the house and around the farm. In fact, Papa, whose praise came sparingly, proudly referred to her as his "right-hand man."

Jim and Minola stepped back into the kitchen, with Buster squeezing between them and dashing off to explore the rest of the house.

"Ah! Stegmiller's stairs!" exclaimed Minola, pointing toward a narrow set of stairs that began in the southwest corner of the kitchen and made a sharp curve to the left. "I *have* to go up Stegmiller's stairs!"

"Why do you call them 'Stegmiller's stairs'?" asked Jim, with a puzzled look on his face. "I've never heard of naming a stairway."

"I'll tell you in a minute. Can you help me up the stairs, Jim? There's no railing, and I already took one tumble this morning," said Minola as she cocked her head to peer up the stairwell.

Jim bounded up the first several steps, then turned and extended his hand toward Minola. Grasping Jim's hand firmly in hers and using the other hand to steady herself against the wall, Minola gingerly progressed up the steep pitch, while Jim ascended the steps backwards ahead of her.

"To think I used to dash up and down these steps while carrying things in my hands," commented Minola ruefully.

The stairs opened into a small single room with sloping ceilings.

There were no doors connecting the room to the rest of the upstairs.

"Not much up here," commented Jim as he helped Minola up the last step.

"There never was," replied Minola as she caught her breath and looked around. "A couple of old *Kisten,* or trunks, that contained some out-of-date clothing, and that was it. But to us children, this was a sanctuary. We came up here to play and to escape Mama. She would never climb those narrow, winding stairs. Now, I can see why."

Minola pointed to the window frame still in place at the top of the stairs overlooking the backyard. "You missed one, Jim."

"Yeah, I've got a few more windows to pull yet," he replied as he flexed his fingers.

Suddenly Minola realized the intrusion she had made in this young man's day. Her cheeks flushed at the thought of how she had rambled on with family stories when all he probably wanted to do was return to his work. She detested the self-absorption exhibited by so many of her elderly peers, and she was chagrined to find herself doing the same.

"I'm sorry," Minola apologized. "I've interrupted your work with my silly little trip down memory lane." She turned toward the stairs. "If you'll just help me back down these stairs, I'll release you from your tour-guide duties and you can get on with your day."

"Nonsense, Miss Seibel!" cried Jim. "I have until next week to get everything out of this house. It doesn't have to be done today. Anyway, you didn't tell me why these were called Stegmiller's stairs."

Jim smiled disarmingly, and Minola debated whether he was simply humoring an old woman or he was truly being sincere. She hated to be intrusive or dependent, and right now, she felt she was both. But because she was standing at the top of a stairway that she couldn't descend without assistance, she chose to believe he was being genuine.

"Well, long, long before I was born—in fact, it was probably when my father was a little boy—the family had a hired man by the name of Stegmiller, and this was his room," Minola explained. "As you probably noticed, the room doesn't connect with the rest of the upstairs, so it was perfect for the hired help."

"And your family only used this room for a play room? That seems like a waste of space with a large farm family," Jim responded.

"Oh, we stored some foodstuffs on the steps, mostly baskets of hickory nuts and crocks of honey. When my younger brother Bill got a little older, this became his bedroom. Prior to that, he shared a room with seven sisters. You can imagine how a growing boy must have needed a little space to himself. But I can't begin to tell you the importance of this room for us children who needed a haven away from the unpredictability of Mama."

Minola remembered happy hours spent up Stegmiller's stairs, cutting paper dolls with Martha or a flurry of paper snowflakes with Bill. They had fashioned a tiny family out of old wooden spools and acorns, then used a piece of chalk to sketch the floorplan of a little house on top of one of the trunks. There had been games of school, and silly poems scribbled on the walls with a piece of charred wood from the cookstove. It had been a refuge from Mama, a place where children could simply be children.

And yet, one of the two trunks in that room had held a touch of intrigue that involved Mama. Nestled in yellowed newspaper inside the smaller trunk was a heavy black fur cape. It had a high, tight collar with a frog clasp and low, narrow slits for the arms to pass through. The cape belonged to Mama's sister Libby, who was one year younger. The garment was said to have been a contributing factor in Libby's accidental death. One winter afternoon in 1890, Libby and another sister, Katie, had been traveling homeward in their buggy after making a call in the neighborhood. The shrill whistle of a passing steam train caused their horse to bolt in fright. Libby, who was at the reins, struggled mightily to control the horse, but her arms were constrained by the limiting slits in the cape. The buggy pitched wildly from side to side before careening into the ditch, crushing Libby. Why had Mama chosen such an odd keepsake as the death cape? It was but one more puzzling element about the dark and fragmented world that Mama inhabited. Sometimes, Libby was even intertwined in Mama's spells.

"*Libby versteckte die Eier vor mir! Wo sind sie?* (Libby hid the eggs from me! Where are they?)," Mama muttered as she ransacked the pantry, overturned the corncob basket next to the cookstove, then proceeded into her bedroom where she dumped the dresser drawers, searching for the missing eggs. The girls quietly restored order in her wake.

Once, when Minola had fumed that her new shoelaces were missing, Bill opened his blue eyes wide and innocently announced, "Libby hid them!"

* * * * *

Minola looked down the Stegmiller stairs, eyeing their steep pitch, narrow steps, and lack of handrail. A sense of vertigo overtook her and she swayed momentarily. Jim noticed her unsteadiness and quickly descended the first few steps, then turned and extended his hand. With a twinkle in his eye, he asked, "May I have this dance down Stegmiller's stairs?"

Minola smiled and nodded, "You certainly may, and I'll try to be a good dance partner and not step on your toes or tumble down on top of you."

With Jim's assistance and one hand braced against the opposite wall, Minola slowly edged sideways down the stairs. After years of living in a single-story dwelling, she realized how out of practice she was with stairs and stair climbing. Like the drive from Cleveland and the geranium planting at the cemetery, the climb up Stegmiller's stairs had been a lesson in her limitations.

When they reached the bottom of the steps, Minola smoothed her skirt and drew a deep breath. Buster bounded into the kitchen from the living room, his tail beating happily at the sight of Jim.

"Watch your step in these next rooms," cautioned Jim over his shoulder. "A couple from Monroeville came out and got all the wooden moldings from around the doorways and windows. They're gonna use it to renovate their house. But they left a lot of nails and plaster all over the floor."

"So, the trim in the house is being recycled?" asked Minola as she stepped around several large chunks of plaster and empty boxes in the living room.

"Oh, more than just the trim," replied Jim. "Next Monday, a restoration company from Cleveland is coming out to get the doors and even the old cast iron registers. I guess people who are restoring their homes go crazy for these old doors and glass knobs and such."

Minola shook her head in amazement. "It wasn't enough that the family left; now pieces of the house are leaving, too," she observed quietly.

As they passed through the wide doorway into the parlor, Minola stopped and looked up. "We used to have a portiere hanging here," she motioned toward the width of the passageway.

At Jim's puzzled expression, she explained, "It was a type of beaded curtain that we made out of little rolled strips of wallpaper threaded onto strings. Papa bought several books of wallpaper samples at an auction one day, and then he rigged up a little mechanism to tightly roll the strips of paper. Gosh! He was the king of making gizmos out of spare parts! Anyway, we sat for hours at the table in the living room, cutting, rolling, then dipping the little wallpaper beads in a glue mixture. It was one of the few projects I remember Mama working on with us, but I suppose it appealed to her because it was a form of work. Always had to keep the hands occupied," Minola's voice trailed off.

With a smirk, she continued, "Of course, we didn't realize it at the time, but if Papa could buy the wallpaper samples at an auction, then portieres were already out of style." She shrugged, "But, we thought they were elegant. And Bill and I used to love to dash through them and feel the little beads hitting our faces like rain."

"Well, you won't find things like wallpaper at farm auctions around here these days," commented Jim as he hooked his thumbs in the back pockets of his jeans. "It's mostly tools and equipment—once in a while some household stuff."

"We just never knew what Papa would bring home from an auction. Sometimes it was pure junk—or at least it was to us kids, but Papa would find a way to make it useful through his endless tinkering."

"Sounds like a true farmer," observed Jim, "Able to make do with the makeshift."

"Sometimes, Papa surprised us with an auction find that was really nice. The most wonderful was a piano, which sat here in the parlor," Minola said as she motioned toward one wall. "Most of us girls took piano lessons from Mrs. Knopf down at the corner. The most hideous thing he brought home was a set of steer horns that he fitted with a velvet forehead and insisted on mounting on the wall in the living room."

"Steer horns!" hooted Jim. "Sounds like you were living in the Wild West, not just *west* of Monroeville!"

Minola chuckled and shook her head. "Oh, Jim, you have no idea what an embarrassment those steer horns were to us girls. Our neighbors, the Mosses and the Ordmanns, were better off than us, and they had nice furnishings, like velvet settees with matching chairs in their parlors. We had the odd assortment of family hand-me-downs, auction items, and those ghastly steer horns. One time, Bill hooked his wet socks over the ends of the horns, just to get Papa's attention."

"And did he?" asked Jim with a smile.

"Well, as it turned out, it wasn't Papa's attention that he caught," confessed Minola. "Mrs. Moss from next door stopped by. She was a rather haughty woman, and the whole time she was carrying on a conversation with you, her eyes would be roving around the room, sizing things up. Anyway, she was chatting with Ada about one thing or another, and all of a sudden her eyes landed on those drippy socks dangling from the ends of the steer horns. She lifted her chin and snidely asked, 'Strapped for drying space on laundry day, are we?' Ada was mortified and muttered some explanation about Bill and boys being boys, but we knew Mrs. Moss would share the incident with the other neighbors. We always suspected there was a lot of neighborhood gossip about that *crazy* Seibel family."

Their footsteps echoed in the small, empty parlor. A rusty stain crept down one parlor wall, a remnant from an overhead leak. This had been Ada and Albert's courting room. For seven years, Albert had patiently waited for Ada to satisfy her obligations at home before marrying him and starting a family of their own. While patience was necessary, despair often crept into their young hearts. Minola remembered galloping into the parlor one rainy afternoon to find all five of her older sisters clustered around Ada, who was sitting on the black leather couch. Minola elbowed into their midst and was surprised to see Ada, face buried in her hands, sobbing uncontrollably.

Looking at the solemn faces around her, and knowing that it was rare for Ada to cry, Minola asked, "What's wrong with Ada?"

Ella and Flora exchanged glances, then Ella offered, "It's just that Ada and Albert can't get married because … well, because … Albert's Catholic, that's why."

Minola had no knowledge of what "Catholic" meant, but given the gravity of Ella's pronouncement and the looks of concern on her sisters' faces, she was sure a "Catholic" must be the equivalent of a horse thief or a leper. But, if Albert was that bad, why hadn't Papa run him off? Everyone knew Papa had the highest standards for honesty and certainly wouldn't allow his eldest daughter to take up with an outlaw, nor would he tolerate a disease-ridden suitor.

Minola was puzzled, but she wanted to comfort Ada, just as Ada had always soothed the bumps and upsets of her young life. Minola wrapped her small arms around Ada's slumped shoulders and cooed, "Don't worry. You'll always have Bill and me."

Had Minola just imagined it, or did Ada sob harder at hearing those words?

* * * * *

Minola quietly clucked her tongue at the memory. Many years later, she realized the truth of that day. Albert's religion was not the obstacle—*they* were: an incapable mother, a father seeking a household manager, and seven youngsters needing maternal guidance. Ada had ably and conscientiously fulfilled the role of mother and manager, even though it meant postponing her own dreams. Minola's cheeks flushed at the thought of how little gratitude she had expressed to Ada for her years of sacrifice. It was one of her deepest regrets in life.

A doorway, stripped of its molding, opened from the living room into a room behind the parlor. Mama and Papa's bedroom. Here, each of the eight Seibel children had been born. And here, Mama would sleep for days after one of her spells, in an almost hibernation-like slumber. After a siege of ranting and raving and causing mayhem, her sleep brought a palpable sense of relief to the house. Another storm weathered. On those days of sleep-induced calm, the children tiptoed about the house, caught the screen door before it slammed, took care not to drop the cutlery or rattle the pans in the drysink, refrained from playing the piano—any means of preserving the peace was worth the extra effort.

Motioning to the wall just inside the door, Minola said, "Mama and Papa had a tall cherry bookcase that stood right here. Papa kept his farm ledgers in the top section and the tickets from the strawberry pickers in the bottom part."

"You grew strawberries here?" inquired Jim, his eyes widening.

"Fields and fields of them. About eighteen acres," replied Minola. "Folks used to call my father 'Strawberry Bill.' People came out from Monroeville to pick berries here—some for their own consumption and others to earn money. The pickers received a ticket for each quart they picked, then Papa would settle up their accounts and pay them on Saturdays."

Jim pushed his cap back, scratched his forehead, and let out a low whistle. "This is almost too weird to be a coincidence, but my wife and I were thinking of planting a couple of self-pick strawberry patches here after we get settled. A little extra income, you know?"

Minola clasped her hands and brought them up to her chin. "Really?" she beamed in disbelief. "This place will be a strawberry farm again?"

"Well," hesitated Jim, "I don't think people will be calling me 'Strawberry Jim,' but on a small-scale basis, yeah, I'd like to give it a try."

"The soil here is certainly right for strawberries, but as you know, Jim, it's the weather that plays havoc with berries," cautioned Minola. "Too wet and the berries rot and are tasteless; too dry and the yield is down. My father was a natural-born pessimist, and every spring, as soon as the first strawberry blossoms appeared, he'd predict a killing frost that would wipe out the entire crop."

"Did that ever happen?" asked Jim.

"No, although at times we girls secretly wished for it," Minola chuckled. "But we knew those berries were a very important source of income—they were second only to potatoes as our cash crop. I don't recall that we ever had a total crop failure, but it was the work we dreaded, Jim—hot, back-breaking. You'll find out," Minola wagged her index finger at him. "It's all stoop work."

"Yeah, that's one of the reasons we decided to start out small—see if this is something just my wife and me can handle by ourselves," Jim replied.

* * * * *

Minola could still see Papa, tense and agitated throughout the berry season. If he wasn't fretting about the weather, he was grousing about the pickers—claiming they trampled over the strawberries like cattle. He stayed nervous and edgy until the last berry was picked and sold.

Although the picking season was brief, the preparation had begun months earlier. Papa spent the winter in his workroom on the second floor of the cornbarn, crafting quart containers out of thin strips of pressed wood. Since no experienced berry picker picked by the single quart, he also made rectangular berry carriers with bentwood handles that held six of the quart containers. Twenty-four of the filled quarts were placed into a slatted shipping crate, also made by Papa, and transported to market.

On a day in mid-April, when the sun shone promisingly but the winds still blew a chill across the open fields, Papa would stride purposefully toward the house, calling "Girls! Girls!" (He had become so accustomed to this unisex call to work that even after the birth of Bill, Papa continued to use the one-gender refrain.) Every heart sank.

Papa assigned several daughters to bundle up runners from last year's strawberry plants and place them in a wheelbarrow. Minola and Bill were in charge of staking a string from one end of the field to the other to act as a planting guide, which they moved as the planting progressed. When the wheelbarrow was full of bundled runners, the girls pushed it to the designated field, where Papa loaded his shoulder pouch. Papa worked quickly and liked a speedy helper as well, so he usually chose Flora as his assistant. He handed Flora a bundle of runners from his shoulder pouch, and the planting began at one end of the string guide. Papa pressed his spade into the soil, and Flora dropped a runner into the shallow hole. Papa withdrew the spade and used the toe of his brogan to press the soil around the roots of the new planting. The two progressed across the length of the field in a wordless duet of *spade, drop, withdraw, tamp, spade, drop, withdraw, tamp.* When the wheelbarrow had been emptied of its runner bundles, the girls and Bill returned to the barn for load after load of bright golden straw to spread between the rows of berries. This field would not yield fruit for the coming season, but the prime field, which was in its second season, and the waning field, in its third and final year, would soon be filled with the rubied harvest.

By early June, the berries started to ripen, and Papa went into Monroeville to spread the word that pickers were needed. On the appointed day, men, women, and children arrived—some walked the three miles, others biked, and a few caught rides on vehicles heading west out of town. If the season started early, school was still in session. Many boys cut classes and came out to pick just enough berries to earn money to purchase Fourth of July firecrackers. Others, like the Burrer brothers, were dedicated pickers, known for their speed and the light-hearted fun they brought to the drudgery of berry picking. Phil Burrer was the champion berry picker, challenging anyone to a picking duel and easily besting them. When the berries were at their peak, Phil achieved one hundred quarts of berries in a day and liked to fan his fistful of tickets as though they were playing cards.

Papa was a busy man during the berry season, and the pressures of marketing such a highly perishable crop caused him to walk briskly and talk rapidly, often to the point of stuttering. On the few occasions that a picker dared to resort to such horseplay as throwing berries at another picker, Papa pointed a stern finger at the troublemaker and barked, "D-D-Don't you throw my b-b-berries!" Papa was up at four o'clock each morning, driving his spring wagon loaded with strawberries to the railroad town of Willard, which was then known as Chicago Junction. Upon his return, he ate breakfast, tended the horses, and patrolled the berry patch, giving out orders and picking up the berries on hand to ferry to Zipfel's general store in Monroeville. At noon on Saturday, he tallied the tickets for the number of quarts picked that week, paid the pickers, and drove into Bellevue, where he peddled the remaining berries up and down the streets, calling out "Strawberries! Strawberries!"

Inevitably, the relatives who never came to visit throughout the year chose berry season as the opportune time for renewing family ties. They arrived, jovially slapped Papa on the back, chatted with Mama, patted all the children on their heads and inquired of each, "Now, which one are you?," and then left with the object of their visit: free strawberries.

During the height of berry-picking season, Papa roused the children from their sleep with a 4 a.m. wake-up call, "Girls! There's berries to be picked!" The dewbath and dim light of early morning were preferable to the unrelenting sun and heat of midday, so they stumbled sleepy-eyed to the packing house in the middle of the strawberry field, grabbed their containers, and crawled between the rows, filling quart after quart before the sun had crested the horizon.

This was the routine for everyone in the family, except for Mama. As a girl, Mama had had to pick strawberries with her nine siblings on the family farm. She so detested the work that one day, when she reached the end of her assigned row, she flopped down, crossed her arms in her lap, and refused to pick any further. Mama's temper and stubbornness were legendary. Even her old-world German father bowed to her tantrum and allowed her to sit while her siblings bent to the berry picking. Mama enjoyed retelling this story of her liberation from field work, but never suggested that her own daughters likewise be excused from the heavy manual labor. If Mama had assumed the duties of cooking, or even mowing the lawn, during the busy berry season, her exemption from field work may have been forgiven. Instead, no housework was done, and the lawnmower awaited the tired girls at the end of a long day in the fields. Because the older daughters were not in the house to cook or bake, meals were scant and of almost starvation quality. The nightly supper became what Bill referred to as "measles soup"—the day's milk poured over the strawberries that were overripe or too small for sale.

At one point during berry season, while Mama was alone at the house, the junk peddler came by. Always eager for company, Mama had enticed the peddler to linger by offering up bits and pieces of the household belongings. When the girls returned from the fields, they discovered that the copper wash boiler and the milk pail had been given to the junk peddler. From then on, it became an unspoken rule that someone was always to remain at the house with Mama.

* * * * *

Minola shook her head. "Hmmph! Just talking about strawberries makes me think I can smell them in here. It's a fragrance you never forget," she mused. "Do you know that one time I was walking along a crowded street in lower Manhattan, and suddenly I smelled strawberries? It was such an unexpected aroma there in the middle of all that concrete and hustle and bustle. Turns out, the smell was coming from a street vendor who had strawberries for sale. But for just a moment, my world stopped and I was back here on the farm, on my hands and knees in the berry fields with Bill and my sisters. As a child, I never would have dreamed that someday I'd *fondly* remember berry picking, but I do … I do."

Jim and Minola picked their way around the debris in the living room and walked toward the staircase leading to the second floor. Buster bounded ahead of them and galloped up the steps.

"Well, my hope is that the money from the self-pick fields will provide a little extra spending money. Maybe allow us to buy something we couldn't afford otherwise," Jim explained.

"That's the way Papa handled the end-of-the-season berries. He sold what we picked from the waning fields and used the money to buy something we ordinarily wouldn't have," commented Minola.

"Like what? New clothes or shoes?" inquired Jim.

"Oh no, not clothing," responded Minola. "Two of my sisters, Ada and Flora, were excellent seamstresses and kept us well-clothed, thank goodness, and Papa cobbled our shoes, even though we hated the rough, homemade appearance of them. No, much to Papa's credit, he actually used that money to purchase things that brought us enjoyment. One year it was a croquet set with bright-colored stripes painted around the balls and on the handles of the mallets and stakes."

Minola stepped onto the landing of the stairs and turned toward Jim. "And, the croquet set was *varnished*, too," she emphasized, toggling her eyebrows.

Jim smiled at Minola's dancing eyebrows and crossed his arms over his chest. "Okay, I'll bite. What was so special about a varnished croquet set?"

"Ohhh, don't you know?" Minola asked in mock astonishment. "Only the rich had varnished croquet sets back then. At least that was the perception. The neighbor girl, Edith Moss, came down to play croquet one Sunday afternoon. When she saw that new set with its bright colors and varnish, she accused us of putting on airs. I guess families as humble as ours weren't ever supposed to have something nice, even though we'd certainly worked hard for it."

Minola cocked her head. "But Papa bought other things too, like a set of Charles Dickens volumes, which we read over and over and over again. Especially Ella, my second-oldest sister. She so *loved* books."

* * * * *

Ella read while she churned butter, snapped beans, stirred the apple butter, fried potatoes, and boiled the wash. Not even Mama's dogged chastisement that reading was *Dummheit* could discourage Ella from delving into a book and being mentally transported far away. On cold winter nights, Minola and Martha liked to crawl in bed beside Ella, who would lie on her side and bend her long legs into a chair shape for Minola to nestle into her lap, with Martha tucked up in a similar posture at her back. By propping the book on Minola's shoulder, Ella could catch just the right angle of light from the kerosene lamp, and she read to them from *A Tale of Two Cities*, *Bleak House*, *David Copperfield*, and *Oliver Twist.* Minola would close her eyes and imagine the streets of London, the shrill fishwives, the squalor of an orphanage. Soon, the comforting cadence of Ella's voice and the enveloping warmth of their combined body heat would overtake her. Despite her valiant efforts to stay awake and listen to the story, Minola was soon drifting into a contented sleep.

Minola knew she owed her own love of literature to Ella. Every time she checked out a book on tape from the library, she thought of Ella. Wouldn't Ella have appreciated the convenience of going about her housework with both hands free, while still able to absorb a story that carried her far away from those mundane chores?

* * * * *

Clapping her hands together, Minola said, "Jim, I know just what you should buy with your first strawberry money—bananas!"

"Bananas!?" Jim exclaimed. "We buy those at the grocery store every week. They're nothin' special."

"Oh, to us they were!" Minola replied. "You see, sometimes after Papa sold the berries at Zipfel's store in Monroeville, he'd come home with treats, and the best treat of all was bananas, which we just didn't get very often. I suppose he took them in trade for the berries, but oh mercy, how we loved those bananas. Feasted on them as if we were Polynesian royalty. We'd sit on the overturned apple butter kettles behind the summer kitchen and pass around a banana. You can imagine how many bites of banana you got when you were sharing it eight ways!" Minola had a far-away look as she remembered the banana feast. "Mmm, yes, bananas are special indeed."

"Did your father ever bring home any treats besides bananas?" inquired Jim.

"Oh, once in a while, he might bring a small bag of licorice twists or hard candies, and I suppose that's what I thought I'd found one day when the treat turned out to be more of a trick."

"What do you mean?" asked Jim.

"Well, when Papa drove in, we children would swarm his empty spring wagon, looking for the spoils from his trip. As often as not, we'd be disappointed, but one day, all of my older sisters had passed over this small brown pouch lying on the wagon seat. I thought I was really in luck, so I eagerly reached inside, took a generous sample, and got quite a vile surprise."

"What was it?" Jim inquired.

"Chewing tobacco!" exclaimed Minola, her eyes widening. "I turned several shades of green, and oh boy, did I start retching. Finally, my sister Margaret led me by the hand to the well in front of the barn. She pumped me a tin cup full of cold water and got me settled down. Ugghh!" Minola gave an involuntary shudder at the memory.

Jim smiled and held his hand up as if taking an oath. "I promise: it'll be bananas, not chewing tobacco, that I buy with my first strawberry money."

The drumming of Buster's tail against the wall at the top of the stairs interrupted them.

"Oh gees, Buster! Not again," cried Jim as he looked up the stairs. The tail and hindquarters of a mouse dangled from Buster's mouth.

Minola gasped and clasped her hands to her chest as she flattened herself against the stairway wall.

Jim excused himself as he rushed past her, taking two steps at a time. "Sorry, Miss Seibel. The upstairs walls are full of mouse nests."

"That's about all the insulation these old walls ever had," she responded. As Minola slowly climbed the steps, she remembered waking up on winter mornings to a thin dusting of snow on the bedroom floor, blown in by the strong west winds around the ill-fitting windows.

Jim reappeared at the top of the steps, wiping his hands on a red bandana he'd pulled from his back pocket. Buster was by his side, looking a bit sheepish, but tail still wagging.

Jim extended his hand to assist Minola up the steps, then quickly withdrew it. "Uh, maybe you'd rather not hold hands with a mouse handler?"

"Remember, Jim: I'm an old farm girl. If I survived eating tobacco, I think I can survive a few mouse germs," she grinned and grabbed Jim's offered hand again.

Two bedrooms lay before them, the first room opening into the second.

"It was unheated up here, so in the winters, we closed that room off," Minola pointed to the far room, "and all of us slept in here. Seven girls, three beds, one room. Cozy, huh?"

Jim whistled. "Kinda tough to heat a room with body heat alone!"

"Indeed!" exclaimed Minola. "Sometimes, we'd heat up a flatiron and wrap it in newspaper and a flannel cloth to slip between the sheets. That helped immensely, but once in a while, the flatiron would be too hot and it would scorch the underside of the blanket. In retrospect, it's a wonder we didn't go up in flames, given that we were sleeping on straw-filled bed ticks." Minola clucked her tongue and shook her head.

* * * * *

Filling the bed ticks from the large strawstack in the barnyard was the last chore after the wheat had been threshed. The ticks were overstuffed, to last through the winter, and so those first few nights, it seemed as though one could almost touch the ceiling while lying in bed.

Threshing began with Bill's gleeful shout, "Here they come! The threshers are coming!" as he pranced through the summer kitchen door and out again, eager for the excitement of mechanized gadgetry and the male camaraderie that came with this neighborhood event. The threshing machine and crew always proceeded north up the road, stopping to harvest the wheat at Mosses' and Ordmanns' farms first—the unwritten pecking order of Townline Road. The girls grumbled that the threshers seemed to arrive at Seibels' just in time for the noonday meal. Ada, Ella, Flora, and Hermine toiled all morning to prepare the bountiful meal: platters of meat, bowls of gravy and fried potatoes, green beans fried in bacon grease, sauerkraut, tomato slices, several loaves of bread to be topped with fresh-churned butter, and always blackberry pie for dessert. Margaret, Martha, and Minola set the table, pumped pitchers full of cold well water, and set basins of warm washwater, bars of soap, and several towels on the porch just outside the summer kitchen door.

Mama was of little assistance in preparing the meal, but at the sound of the men laughing and talking as they washed up on the back porch, she tied on a clean apron and bustled about the kitchen. Her blue eyes flashed as she chattered endlessly, giving orders to the girls and demanding perfection in the presentation of the food.

Bill seated himself at the table of threshers and beamed at the sea of all-male faces around him—a novel sight in his predominantly female world. He was oblivious to Mama's steady stream of chatter, but Mr. Ordmann had heard enough. He caught Mr. Moss's eye across the table and made a fanning motion next to his ear as if he were waving off an annoying mosquito. Mr. Moss grinned and nodded, then resumed forking in the bountiful meal.

After the threshers had finished scraping the last bit of flaky pie crust from their plates, they pushed back their chairs and contentedly patted their distended bellies while the girls began clearing the table.

"Fine meal, girls … Sophie," they complimented as they rose from the table and headed toward the summer kitchen door.

Mama stopped babbling long enough to acknowledge their

comment with "*Ach!* My girls, they did nothing." In the uncomfortable silence that followed, the girls exchanged glances but knew not to intrude on Mama's moment of stolen glory.

*****

Minola walked to the spot between the two west windows of the bedroom. Here had stood the tall bureau shared by Ada, Ella, and Flora. She remembered quietly carrying a stool up from downstairs so that she could peer over the top edge of the bureau and inspect the items kept there: a tortoise shell brush and comb set with matching hand mirror, a hair receiver, the button hook for fastening all those pesky buttons on their high-topped shoes, a tall rectangular tin of talcum powder, and a shallow round tin of white rice face powder. But the real object of her fascination was Ada's small wooden jewelry box.

Minola never lost interest in opening the lid and carefully removing each of the few treasured items. There was a ring with a deep red stone that Ada had received upon her confirmation at church, a gold bracelet with an engraved filigree design, and a gold locket suspended from a slender chain. The locket's tiny clasp opened to reveal a picture of Albert, his dark hair slicked down from a just-off-center part, and his shy smile curling up one corner of his mouth.

Minola enjoyed sliding the confirmation ring on her finger and the gold bracelet over her slender wrist, then holding her arm out to admire the warm gleam of the gold bands against her skin. She'd fasten the slender chain around her neck and pat the locket as it lay against her flat chest.

Ada's jewelry fascinated Minola as much as her relationship with Albert. He was a weekly visitor and seemed to tolerate Mama's unpredictable behavior. However, all of the other sisters discouraged even school friends from paying visits to their home, for fear of what Mama might say or do. This was especially so after Ella brought home pretty and popular Pauline Mueller to spend the night. Mama had shaken a wooden spoon at Pauline and warned, "Don't ever drop your bloomers for any man!" Pauline was aghast and sputtered a sudden need to go home. Ella, humiliated and in tears, walked her there. Even at a young age, Minola knew that Ada's courtship was special, but that she herself would never risk bringing a beau here.

Minola looked out the vacant windows into the side yard. The lack of trees within view was jarring. Papa had planted many mulberry trees around the house, and as they grew, they had circled the house in a leafy embrace. In the summer, the soft patter of raindrops on leaves had signaled a reprieve from the strawberry fields. In autumn, the golden leaves curtsied in their final dance before the winter winds caused the barren branches to claw at the windows as if trying to gain entrance. Spring brought the verdant buds and Papa's renewed hope for an abundant mulberry crop. In reality, only the mulberry tree by the chicken yard yielded a crop of any consequence. He would walk round and round beneath that tree, stooping to pick up the purplish-black berries and pop them into his mouth.

Those berries had carried a painful lesson as well, remembered Minola. It was the day before the Gasteier reunion—Mama's side of the family. There would be Mama's parents, her eight surviving siblings and their spouses, and all manner of cousins, young and old, gathered at the Gasteier homestead. This was a social outing worthy of great anticipation, since the Gasteier clan was outgoing and fun-loving.

But the greatest anticipation was reserved for the ice cream that Mama's younger brother Will would make. Each of the children sat in the grass at Uncle Will's feet and took turns cranking the churn on the ice cream maker until their young arms tired and they begged for a break. Uncle Will, his brown eyes twinkling, teased them good-naturedly.

"Give it just a couple more turns," he'd suggest, then busy himself preparing the serving cups, all the while whistling and pretending to have forgotten the tired child.

"Uncle Will, my arm's gonna fall off!" the child would cry plaintively.

At that, Uncle Will would turn around and open his eyes wide. "*Ach!* Without arms, you won't be able to lift a spoonful of ice cream to your mouth. Guess I'll have to eat your share!" He'd pat his stomach for emphasis.

Besides the ice cream, there would be a bountiful smorgasbord of food spread on planks supported by saw horses. Everyone brought their best dishes, and Mama demanded that the Seibels be well represented. Therefore, Ada, Ella, Flora, Hermine, and Margaret had been set to the task of preparing the food for the next day's event: deep-fried buttermilk chicken, potato salad, a crock of pickled beets bobbing with hard-boiled eggs, a tall jug of lemonade, and some of Ada's molasses cookies. With all the bustle in the summer kitchen, Ada shooed Martha, Minola, and Bill outdoors.

Martha had read the book *Two Little Indians* that summer and had developed an Indian fascination. She suggested they play Indians, but to add an air of authenticity, they would gather mulberries, crush them, and use the juice to paint themselves a deeper hue. Minola and Bill eagerly agreed, and the three busied themselves with the transformation while seated on the apple butter kettles behind the summer kitchen. They used milkweed fluff dipped in the purple mulberry juice and daubed each other's faces and arms. Martha was quite pleased with the effect, until Mama rounded the corner of the summer kitchen on her way to gather eggs.

"*Ach! Mein gott!* What have you done?" she stormed toward the children who were too frightened to scatter.

Grabbing Bill's face in one hand, Mama turned it side to side, examining the deep-purple stain. She wetted one corner of her apron in her mouth and tried rubbing at the dark pigment, to no avail.

Spying the juice-soaked milkweed fluff still in Martha's hand, Mama lashed out. "How could you be such a *Dummkopf?* You will all look like hobos for the reunion tomorrow," she said, stomping her foot for emphasis. "Stupid, stupid children!" she chastised all of them. Then, to punctuate her anger, she slapped Martha across the cheek.

"In the house! *Jetzt!*" Mama barked. She firmly grasped Minola and Bill by the arm and marched them into the kitchen, while Martha obediently followed behind, one hand clasped to her stinging cheek.

Mama halted them beside the drysink, where she banged a wash basin into the sink and filled it with warm water from the teakettle on the back of the stove. She added some of the slimy brown softsoap, which was usually reserved for the laundry. With a stiff-bristled brush, Mama went to work on their arms and faces, scrubbing vigorously at the offending stain. She scrubbed until their skin grew raw and red, all the while muttering about how shameful they would look for tomorrow's reunion and how her children caused her nothing but trouble. Bill whimpered as the scrubbing became painful, but Mama clutched his arm tighter and persisted with her attack on the mulberry dye. And still the stain remained. Occasionally, the older girls peered sympathetically through the kitchen doorway.

The next day, the baskets of food and the children were settled into the wagon for the long ride to the reunion. Martha, Minola, and Bill were a shade of violet, with red abrasions from Mama's vigorous scrubbing.

The reunion was held in the shade-dappled backyard of the Gasteier homestead. Everyone ate picnic-style on blankets spread on the ground, or balanced a plate of food in their lap as they dangled their legs from the back porch. Rocking chairs had been carried out from the house for Grandpa and Grandma Gasteier to sit on. After the meal, the adults laughed and carried on conversations in German, while the children played games of croquet and hoops. Finally, Uncle Will pulled out the ice cream maker, and the children instantly congregated around him, eager to assist with making the long-awaited treat.

"Martha, I've heard of *green* with envy, but what are you?" he teased as he assessed her stained face and arms when she took her turn at the ice cream crank.

"I was pretending to be an Indian, but Mama says I'm a *Dummkopf*," she replied solemnly, her soulful blue eyes meeting his. Uncle Will raised his eyebrows, remembering Sophie's temper from his own childhood and surmising that she had not taken kindly to this bit of youthful whimsy.

At last, the handle of the churn could be pushed no further, and Uncle Will announced that the ice cream was ready to be enjoyed. The children gathered around, eager for their taste of the cold treat.

Martha, Minola, and Bill stood in line with their cousins and held their cups out to Uncle Will for a scoopful of ice cream. Suddenly, a hand appeared overtop of their cups. It was Mama.

"*Nichts* for them, Will," she said, pointing to the three children. She spoke in German to Uncle Will, explaining their transgression. Then she motioned them out of the line.

Eyes downcast, the three drifted away from the group of cousins gathered for ice cream. Bill's disappointment could not be contained, and tears spilled down his cheeks. They shuffled forlornly around the corner of the house and found Hermine and Margaret seated on the front porch, enjoying their cups of ice cream.

"Where's your ice cream?" asked Hermine, as she licked her spoon.

Martha told of Mama's last-minute decree and their exile from the ice cream line. "Why does she hate us so much?" Martha asked, her chin quivering and tears welling up in her eyes. Disappointment overcame her, and she buried her face in her arms.

Margaret put her arm around Martha's shoulders. "Here, have some of mine," she said as she offered her cup of ice cream. "I've had my share. Really."

Martha lifted teary eyes. "But what about Bill and Minola? They didn't get any either."

"They can have some of mine, too," Hermine quickly responded. She pulled Bill onto her lap and placed the half-eaten cup of ice cream in his hand, motioning Minola to scoot closer for a taste.

The front porch door squeaked open and Uncle Will stepped out. He set down the ice cream canister and churn paddles, which were still covered in ice cream. From his shirt pocket, he pulled three spoons and gave them to Bill, Minola, and Martha.

"Even Indians need ice cream," he said as he winked and stepped back through the door.

* * * * *

Minola turned away from the window and walked into the second bedroom, her footsteps echoing in the empty upstairs. Buster busily snuffled along the edges of the floorboards, tantalized by the scent of mice. Pink wallpaper hung in tatters in this room. A border of hearts and angels still rimmed the walls close to the ceiling.

It was obvious to Minola that a recent family had used this room as a nursery or a little girl's bedroom. She shook her head at the thought that no more little girls would grow up in this room. In fact, this house would never again shelter a family; never echo with the sounds of laughter, voices, music, a ticking clock, the whistle of a teakettle; never harbor the aromas of baking bread, burning wood, drying laundry, or frying meat. Minola felt herself overcome with melancholy, and she removed her glasses to rub at her eyes. Was it just the stinging of long-held-back tears, or were her eyes feeling more tired, just as Dr. Bailey had predicted?

Jim spotted her, standing in the center of the room with shoulders slumped. She looked very weary, and suddenly very small and alone.

"Miss Seibel, are you okay?" he asked as he hurried to her side.

"I think it's time for me to go, Jim," she whispered, wiping at her eyes again.

Jim led her to the top of the stairs. He whistled for Buster.

"C'mon, Buster. Get on downstairs so you don't knock us down." He snapped his fingers and pointed, and the dog thumped down the stairs ahead of them.

Turning toward Minola, Jim held out his hand and smiled. "Ready?"

Minola nodded weakly and placed her hand in his. Together, they slowly descended the stairs. When they reached the bottom, Minola sighed and steadied herself against the living room wall.

"You're not ready to drive yet, not like this," Jim admonished. "Why don't you sit and rest a few moments on the landing of Stegmiller's stairs while I finish pulling the windows up there? If you need me, I'll be close by."

Minola nodded her agreement, and Jim led her to the kitchen and seated her on the second step of Stegmiller's stairs. "I'll be right up here," he said, pointing up the crooked stairway.

Minola leaned her head against the doorframe and smoothed her skirt over the run in her stocking. She watched Buster nose about the bare room, his tail wagging at the unfamiliar smells he detected in every crack and corner. How odd it was to see a dog in Mama's kitchen! Minola felt equally out of place here. Perhaps she should have left the image of home as it was in her mind's eye: bustling with activity, filled with comforting sounds and smells, and inhabited by those she loved. But all had been carried away on the river of time, and now, the house was about to meet the same fate. This place called home would no longer exist.

Chapter 2
The Seibel Homestead
1882

PAPA WAS A FATHERLESS CHILD. In September of 1861, when Papa was only two months old, a cholera epidemic swept through the Monroeville community. In two days' time, the disease claimed his father Wilhelm and Wilhelm's brother Friedrich. The two brothers were buried side-by-side in the little family cemetery across the road from the homestead.

Wilhelm's widow Kathrina was left with four small children and a farm to manage. In a few short years, she made a marriage of convenience to the neighbor, Wilhelm Scheidt. Papa always referred to his stepfather as "Old Man Scheidt."

Old Man liked his hard cider, and he showed a decided favoritism toward Papa's older brother George, whom he regarded as the more industrious of the two. George was a methodical worker who often spent hours on a task, while Papa worked quickly, accomplished his chores, and moved on to the next duty. Nevertheless, Papa grew to young manhood as the object of Old Man's ridicule.

One fall day in 1881, when Old Man and the two brothers were cutting corn in the field behind the barn, George stopped to sharpen the blade on his corn knife and lingered over the task. Old Man, who was leaning against the wagon, took a long draw from his cider jug and eyed Papa.

"*Warum kümmerst Du Dich nicht so gut um mein Werkzeug, wie dein Bruder George?* (Why don't you take good care of my tools, like your brother George?)" Old Man asked with a sneer.

"*Ich schärfe mein Klinge bevor ich anfang zu schneiden* (I sharpened my blade before I started cutting)," explained Papa as he continued to work.

"*Möglicherweise würde Deine Mutter Dir glauben, aber ich nicht* (Maybe your mother would believe you, but I don't)," taunted Old Man, taking another swig from the cider jug.

George continued to slowly rub the blade of his corn knife along the whet stone, watching the confrontation unfold before him.

"*Du denkst nichts Gutes über micht, aber wer hat mehr Mais geschnitten—George oder ich?* (You don't believe anything good about me, but who has cut more corn today—George or me?)" Papa stopped cutting and pointed his blade toward the mounting pile of corn in the back of the wagon.

"*Sich immer mit andere Leute Federn schmücken, auch wenn es nicht passend ist, William? Die Wahrheit ist, Du bist nicht ein habs so guter Arbeiter, wie Dein Bruder* (Always taking credit when it's not due you, aren't you, William? Truth is, you're not half the worker your brother is)," Old Man snorted as he replaced the corncob stopper in the neck of the cider jug. "*Glaubst Du nicht, daß wir diese Arbeit auch ohne Dich getan haben könnten* (Don't think that we couldn't have done this work without you)."

Old Man turned to tuck the cider jug under the wagon seat as Papa came crashing through the rows of dry corn stalks.

"*Er-Er-Erkläre mir nicht, ich hätte nicht meine ganze Kraft auf diesem Bauernhof verwendet!* (D-D-Don't tell me I don't pull my weight on this farm!)" Papa stammered in outrage, as he charged to within inches of his stepfather, still brandishing the corn knife. Papa could smell the sour odor of hard cider on Old Man's breath. The two stared at each other with vehemence, Papa's face flushed crimson in anger.

George had been enjoying the war of words, but Papa's charge toward Old Man with a weapon in hand had escalated the tension to a dangerous point. George waved the blade of his own corn knife between the two men and announced, "*Das genügt!* (That's enough!)"

Papa stomped back to his row of corn. For the rest of the afternoon, the words of Horace Greeley, "Go West, young man," bounded through his brain, and he began to formulate a plan to escape his unhappy home life. After all, he was twenty years old and ready for an adventure.

William Seibel

A few months later, on a Sunday afternoon in January when all was quiet, Papa walked away from the house, strolled down the lane to the back end of the farm, then picked his way through the thicket that served as a fenceline between the Seibel farm and that of their neighbor to the east. The ground was frozen, making it easy to cut across fields as he angled his way toward Monroeville, then on toward Norwalk.

Once in Norwalk, Papa secured lodging at a modest boarding house. As luck would have it, a severe sleet storm hit, leaving miles of damaged telegraph lines. A repair crew was formed, and word went out that workers were needed, so Papa joined up with a section gang. After several weeks, the repairs were complete, and Papa now had money in his pocket to finance his travel out west.

He returned home to report his plans and pack his few belongings in an old valise. His mother Kathrina was kneading dough for biscuits. Old Man sat close by the warmth of the cookstove, his cider jug within easy reach on the floor next to his rocking chair.

"*Wann sehen wir Dich wieder?* (When will we see you again?)" Kathrina asked, her voice tinged with concern.

"*Zu früh* (Too soon)," muttered Old Man from his corner of the kitchen.

Kathrina shot him a withering glance as she rolled out the dough and made neat circles with a tin biscuit cutter.

"*Ich weiß nicht, aber ich habe bestimmt viel Abenteuer, zu erzählen, wenn ich zurückkomme* (I don't know, but I'll have plenty of adventures to tell you when I return)," Papa replied, arranging his few belongings in the bottom of the valise.

The next morning, Kathrina slipped Papa a bundle of biscuits tied up in a dishtowel. Her hand lingered for a moment on Papa's coat sleeve as he turned toward the back door, then waved goodbye as he strode across the lawn and down the road toward the railroad town of Chicago Junction, fifteen miles away.

Once in the bustling town, Papa made his way toward the rail yards and searched for a freight train. He was not able to locate one heading west, and soon darkness fell. Papa became anxious and paced about, then sat on the ground outside the ticket office. He retrieved the bundle of biscuits from his valise and slowly savored one flaky baked good as he pondered his options. It was too dark and too late to return home, and besides, what was there in Monroeville for him but a life of servitude and endless ridicule from Old Man? At worst, he could find an out-of-the-way building to take shelter in for the night, then try his luck again in the morning.

The whistle of an arriving train caught Papa's attention, and he watched the trainmen's twinkling lanterns as they inspected the running gear and ushered passengers on board.

"All aboard!" called the conductor before disappearing into the train, which had slowly begun to move west.

Papa rose to his feet, brushing the crumbs from his hands and grabbing up the valise. He took three quick steps and leaped for the passenger car stairs where the conductor had recently stood.

The cold, stiff winds that came with the train's increasing speed made Papa's hands numb as he clung to the handrail and his valise. He ducked his chin down into the collar of his coat to protect it against the biting chill and occasional cinder.

Inside the passenger car, the conductor made his way down the aisle, punching tickets and making small talk with the passengers. As he reached the back of the car, he glanced toward the outer door and was astonished to see a young man clinging to the handrail on the opposite side of the glass.

"You fool!" the conductor barked as he opened the door and pulled Papa inside. "You could have been killed! Is a free ride worth risking your life?"

Papa was too cold to reply. He collapsed into the nearest seat, and with hands that could barely move, he fumbled in his pocket for train fare to the next station.

When Papa stepped off the train in Fostoria, he had thawed out enough to feel chagrin and discouragement at his greenhorn ways. As he milled about the rail yard, a fellow about his own age approached.

"Where you headed, Chappy?" the young man called out good-naturedly.

Papa shrugged his shoulders and responded, "Out west." The vagueness of his travel plans and destination began to dawn on him.

"Well, Chappy, how 'bout hookin' up with me and we'll head west together?" the young man asked as he slapped Papa on the back.

"The name's William, not 'Chappy,'" replied Papa.

"Anything you say, Sport," the fellow responded. "Name's Henry." He extended his hand to shake Papa's. "C'mon," he tilted his head toward an idling freight train. "Don't want to miss our ride." With his hands in his pockets, Henry began ambling toward the train.

"Don't we need to stop at the ticket office first?" protested Papa, remembering his earlier experience.

Henry turned and looked in bemused astonishment at Papa. "Are you rich, Sport? Gonna *buy* your way west?"

"I, well, I…," Papa sputtered and then thought better of exposing his inexperience. He silently followed Henry.

Henry strolled along nonchalantly, trailed by Papa clutching the valise. When he reached the train, Henry took a quick look about, then scrambled up the back ladder to the top of the boxcar.

Papa stood rooted to the gravel beside the train, looking wide-eyed up at Henry. The memory of his brief but miserable ride outside the passenger train was still vivid.

"What you waitin' for, Sport?" Henry called down. "Think a conductor's gonna give you a hand with your bag?" he chuckled.

Papa looked about. "It's just that, well, we're gonna ride on *top* of the car?" Papa swallowed hard.

"Sure, stay low, keep your head down when we pass under bridges and through tunnels, and you'll be fine. Best view in the world from up here. Hurry up, Sport, before the railroad bulls see us," Henry said with impatience.

Papa scrambled up the ladder. The height was dizzying, and he knew he'd want full use of both hands to hang on. Using his belt, he secured his valise to his pants, then flattened himself on the boxcar roof.

The train slowly pulled from the rail yard. Papa hung onto the catwalk support bars crossing the top of the boxcar until his knuckles turned white. To his surprise, the freight train did not pick up the speed that the passenger train had. While cold, the ride was not disagreeable, and as the sun came up, Papa began to agree with Henry that the view was indeed spectacular.

The train finally pulled into the massive rail yards in the city of Chicago. The two young men scrambled down from the top of the boxcar and began walking.

"Gees, I could eat a horse!" exclaimed Henry as they crossed several sets of tracks.

Papa remembered the biscuits in his valise. He offered two to Henry and took one to munch himself. Only two biscuits remained wrapped in the dishcloth, and Papa knew he'd have to find more substantial sustenance soon.

Henry seemed to have a familiarity with the city, and he led Papa to a second-rate hotel on South Clark Street. They passed charred wreckage and molten glass that stretched for blocks.

"What's all that?" Papa inquired as he pointed to the rubble.

"That's what's left from the Great Chicago Fire," replied Henry with a mouth full of biscuit. "Still waiting to be cleared away, and it's been over ten years."

After they had secured a room, Henry advised Papa that he had some business to attend to, but upon his return they would go out for supper.

Papa set his valise on the only chair and looked about the drab little room. It wasn't much, but it was affordable and better than sleeping outdoors. He patted the slim packet of money in his coat pocket and hoped that Henry knew a cheap place to eat.

Soon, Henry returned. "C'mon, Sport. Let's dine like kings!" and he led the way to a restaurant several streets from the hotel.

Once seated, Henry ordered a plate of steak and eggs for each of them and mugs of hot coffee.

Concerned for his finances, Papa leaned forward and whispered, "Henry, I was planning to eat a little … cheaper. I've got to watch my funds if I'm gonna make it out west."

"Don't worry, Sport," Henry smiled, "The meal's on me!"

Papa felt relieved at his friend's generosity, and a bit smug at having made acquaintances with a man of means so early in his travels. He enjoyed every mouthful of the hearty meal.

When it was time to settle up the bill, Henry produced a dollar bill, then caused so much confusion over the amount of change due him that he managed to leave the restaurant with two dollars in change. Papa was confused by the transaction. As they stepped into the street, Papa turned to question Henry about the dealings, but Henry grabbed Papa's arm and dragged him along in a full sprint down the street, around the corner, and through several alleys.

"What was all that about?" panted Papa when they finally slowed to a walk.

"That's called workin' it, Sport, just workin' it," Henry responded, looking over his shoulder. Papa was still confused.

Several days later, Henry attempted one of his schemes unsuccessfully, and they exited town in such haste that Papa didn't have time to return to the hotel for his valise. They hopped atop a boxcar, and during the ride, Papa had time to reflect upon his relationship with Henry. He finally concluded that he was in the company of a flimflam man.

The train chugged into the rail yards of Milwaukee, and the two climbed down from the boxcar.

"I've gotta get some grub," Henry announced as they approached a small store near the tracks. "Wait out here," he instructed Papa.

"B-b-but, Henry," Papa protested, "what you're doin' is dishonest."

Henry glanced over his shoulder at Papa as he opened the store's door. "Are you rich, Sport?" he grinned, then disappeared inside the store. The bell on the door merrily announced his entrance.

Papa stood on the sidewalk, wrestling with the uncertainty of his situation. If he stayed with Henry, he would never reach the west; in fact, he'd probably end up in jail somewhere after one of Henry's schemes ran afoul of the law. On the other hand, it was nice to have companionship, particularly of someone so knowledgeable about the ways of the world.

Papa's reverie was broken by the clanging of the bell on the store door. Out dashed Henry, with the store's proprietor a few steps behind.

"Follow me, Sport!" Henry yelled as he galloped past Papa, but Papa stood rooted to the spot and watched the pursuit. Henry leaped for the last car on a slow-moving freight train and scrambled up the ladder.

The store proprietor waved his fist in the air and shouted, "Don't ever show your face in my business again, you scalawag!"

Papa thought it best to move on before the store owner returned, so he ambled down the sidewalk, crossed the street, and bought an apple from a vendor before returning to the rail yard.

A passenger train headed west for Janesville, Wisconsin, was slowly starting to pick up steam on its departure from the rail yard. Papa clamored up behind the tender and settled in to watch the countryside pass as he crunched his apple.

Soon, Papa grew quite warm and removed his jacket. Smoke billowing backward from the train's engine burned his eyes and caused him to cough. He swatted at an uncomfortable burning on the back of his neck, then another and another. To his horror, Papa realized that he was being showered with cinders due to his proximity to the smokestack. He covered his head with his jacket and crouched as low as he could. The ride was stifling and Papa grew damp with perspiration. Falling cinders burned his hands and scorched holes in his clothing. He longed for a conductor to once again rescue him, but his position behind the tender was not visible to the train crew. For sixty long miles, Papa endured a painful ride.

When at last the train pulled into the rail yards of Janesville, Papa leaped down from the tender and surveyed the damage to his clothing. His coat, shirt, and pants were peppered with burn holes. In places, the cinders had burned through the clothing and left welts on his skin. He was covered with a dusting of black soot, and he reeked of smoke.

With the last of his funds, Papa rented a room at a modest boarding house and purchased a new set of clothes. Once again out of money, it was necessary to inquire about local work opportunities.

The owner of the boarding house steered Papa toward some of the other boarders, who were members of a construction crew building a bridge. Papa signed on and was glad for the work, which lasted until torrential rains began to fall, causing widespread flooding. Unbeknownst to Papa, he had elected to go west during the year of one of the most devastating floods ever experienced on the Mississippi River.

With the bridge work suspended, Papa rode the rails down to Davenport, Iowa, where he picked up an assortment of odd jobs. He made the acquaintance of an agreeable young fellow named Birchard. One day, while the two bagged grain at a mill, Birchard shared his dream with Papa.

"I wanna see the ocean, Bill. I been stuck in the middle of this country all my life. I wanna see one end or the other of it, and seems to me that the Pacific is calling my name."

Papa opened his arms wide and in a falsetto voice warbled, "Come to me, Birch. I am the Pacific Ocean. I been callin' you, callin' you. Where are you, Birch?"

Birchard chuckled and poked Papa in the ribs. "I thought you said you wanted to go west, too, Bill. Or is Davenport, Iowa, west enough of Ohio for you?"

Papa thought for a few moments. Birchard was right—he had been stalled in Iowa for too long.

"Well then, let's go, Birch. Me and you. Let's head out west and see that ocean that's callin' your name," replied Papa.

With their next pay, they bought a supply of food, which they stuffed into their coat and pants pockets until their garments bulged. At the rail yards, they hunted about for suitable travel accommodations. A brakeman inspecting the wheels of a grain car spotted them.

"Where ya headed, boys?" he called out.

"Goin' west. Gonna dip our toes in the Pacific Ocean," responded Birchard with a lift of his chin. Papa thought he saw Birchard's chest puff out a bit.

"It'd be a nice, easy ride, sittin' on top of this load of grain," offered the brakeman, patting the side of the boxcar.

Birchard and Papa exchanged glances, then scrambled aboard.

"Now, you boys just holler when you're ready to get out, and I'll open 'er up," the brakeman said before sliding the boxcar door closed and securing the latch on the outside.

In the pitch black, Birchard and Papa settled into a comfortable recline on the mountain of grain. Papa tucked his hands behind his head and laughed out loud, "Birch, my friend, we are two lucky lads! This is so much better than ridin' on the roof."

Before long, the train slowly chugged out of the rail yards. As the train picked up speed, the gentle sway of the boxcar lulled the two young men to sleep.

Papa awoke when he felt the train start to slow. "Wonder where we are?" he commented to Birchard.

They sat in silence, not hearing the shouts and clatter that would signal their arrival in a rail yard.

"Don't know our whereabouts," said Birchard, "but I do know I'm hungry." He rummaged in his bulging pants pockets and retrieved some beef jerky. Papa pulled out an apple and the two ate in contented silence.

"I tell you, Birch," commented Papa, "this is the way to go west—ridin' in comfort."

"You'd be the one to know, you old hobo," chided Birchard. "Only gripe I've got is that it's so darn stuffy in here. Makes me thirsty."

The train sat idle for a long time, then slowly moved on. This sequence of moving and stopping for long periods was repeated several more times. The two young men dozed and dined, and before long, the food that was to last them to the end of their journey had all been consumed, leaving them with a powerful thirst. Their discomfort made time drag. Had they been locked in this dark prison for hours or days?

Finally, the train came to a long halt, and Papa and Birchard could hear the chuffing of steam engines, the squealing of brakes, and the clanging of locomotive bells close by. It was obvious they had reached a rail yard. Papa knocked on the side of the boxcar as a signal for the kindly brakeman to flip the outside door latch and release them.

They sat in darkness and waited. "He should be comin' by on his inspection pretty soon," assured Papa. They waited.

Papa knocked again, and again there was no response. Birchard joined Papa, and together they banged on the side of the boxcar, then tried yelling for help. They alternated pounding and shouting until their fists hurt and their parched throats ached. Still, there was no response.

"Bill, that brakeman is the only one who knows we're in here," Birchard said with growing alarm. He began clawing at the seam of the locked sliding door. "Either he forgot about us, or this is his idea of a joke."

"Or he switched trains at one of those layovers," added Papa.

The grain that had made such a comfortable bed now acted like quicksand as the two young men frantically thrashed about, searching in the darkness for a way out. Papa carefully ran his hands over the walls of the boxcar, feeling for rivets or a weld that would indicate a portal. His fingers finally bumped into a seam, which he followed upward on the boxcar wall. There, he found a small panel. With great effort, he slid the panel to the left, and a bright shaft of sunlight streamed in, causing him to wince and fall back onto the mountain of grain.

Birchard and Papa were overcome with relief. The opening was small, but it was their only means of escape. Birchard shed his coat, and with a boost from Papa, he folded his shoulders and pulled his upper torso through the portal. By twisting his body to the side, he managed to grasp the rung of the outside ladder, but his legs kicked so wildly in the process that Papa had to lay back on the grain to avoid being struck. Soon Birchard's boots disappeared over the lip of the panel. Papa passed his coat out to Birchard, who then extended his hand through the opening to give Papa an assist. With a mighty heave and a generous amount of twisting, Papa pulled himself free of the dark grain prison and descended the boxcar ladder.

The two shook the grain from their coats and slapped the dust from their pant legs.

"If I'd eaten one more apple on that trip, I don't think I could have squeezed through that opening," commented Birchard as he sat on a rail and dumped the grain from his boots. "Where are we, Bill? Must be pretty far west by now, huh?"

Papa looked about him. There was something familiar about these rail yards. He spotted an engineer descending the ladder of a locomotive several tracks over.

Papa cupped his hands to his mouth and called out, "Hello! Sir! What city is this?"

The engineer gave Papa a peculiar look. "It's Chicago, boy!"

"Chicago!" cried Papa and Birchard in unison.

Birchard leaped to his feet. "I rode all that way, nearly suffocated to death, and I went *east* instead of *west*?!" His arched eyebrows nearly touched his hairline, and he held a boot in each of his outstretched hands.

Papa felt equally deflated. The long ride had merely circled him back to the city he had left over a month ago.

"This ain't the life for me, Bill," Birchard huffed as he flopped down onto the rail and jammed his feet back into his boots. "If I ever hear that ocean voice callin' my name again, you know what I'm gonna do?"

Papa shook his head.

"I'm gonna stuff cotton in my ears. I'll pretend I got a hearing problem," Birchard grumbled as he yanked at his shoe laces. "I'm goin' home, and I'm *stayin'* there," he said with finality as he stood up.

"I don't blame you, Birch. C'mon, I'll ride the rails with you back to Davenport," offered Papa.

"Nope!" Birchard responded emphatically. "I'm buying me a ticket and ridin' in a passenger car like a human being. You can do what you want, Bill. Go west without me. I've had enough of this hoboin'." Birchard stepped over several tracks and marched toward the ticket office.

Papa was alone once again. He absentmindedly swatted at his dusty hair and clothing as he pondered what to do next. Slowly, he walked to the South Clark Street hotel, where he settled the unpaid bill left by his hasty departure over a month ago. He retrieved his old valise and walked around the neighborhood that he had so recently left, avoiding the restaurant and other establishments where Henry had plied his shady transactions.

Finally, Papa formed a plan. He made arrangements for his valise to be sent to St. Louis, Missouri, where he hoped to eventually pick it up, and he started walking, following the rails out of town.

Papa walked many miles of track, at one point following a rail spur that took him off his course. Late in the day, a drizzly rain settled in. Papa pulled the collar of his coat up to offer a measure of protection and trudged onward. Eventually, he spotted a string of empty boxcars sitting idle on a siding, so he climbed aboard, glad for the shelter. In one corner, a board had been propped up, making a good head rest. Papa removed his coat, folded it into a pillow, and reclined against the board. In no time, he had drifted into a deep sleep.

Papa awoke with a start. The rain had stopped, and night had fallen. He blinked several times, trying to get his bearings. Then he realized what had awoken him. Someone had climbed into the boxcar. Framed in a patch of moonlight from the doorway was a large shadow, and it was coming directly toward him.

The shadow stumbled over Papa's outstretched legs and, after recovering from this surprise, grumbled, "Get out of here! This be my bed!"

Papa grabbed his balled-up coat and scrambled to the opposite end of the boxcar, hoping that his quick surrender of the board would appease the shadow. He held his breath, listening for trouble in the darkness. After a series of grunts and moans, the shadow settled down against the inclined board and was soon deep into a rhythmic snore, punctuated by an occasional snort.

Papa slept fitfully for the rest of the night. When the earliest light appeared, he crept to the boxcar door and quietly slipped out. He retraced his steps of the previous day, back to where the spur had taken him off course.

Papa spent long solitary days, alternately walking and riding the rails southwest toward St. Louis. One evening, he approached a small knot of men huddled about a campfire not too far from the rails. He hailed them and was invited to join their group. The conversation turned toward their destination.

"Join us," the leader of the bunch urged. "Plenty of work to be had harvesting grain around Belleville, Illinois, right now."

"You'll earn every penny of your pay, no doubt about that, but the farmwives sure know how to feed the hired hands," another chimed in.

Papa had been subsisting on what he could forage along the way. Once, after several days of slim rations, he had found a grove of mulberry trees and was overjoyed to have a meal of ripe berries. The thought of a thresherman's dinner was indeed enticing. Papa accompanied the group to Belleville, but thought he may have better luck finding employment if he wasn't part of a pack, so he journeyed on to Washington County, Illinois. He'd heard there was a large German farming community there. Certainly none of the German farmers could be as difficult to work for as Old Man.

Papa arrived in the small town of Okawville and stopped at the lumberyard near the tracks to inquire about work. He was given the name of a threshing crew foreman, Mr. Sliter, and directions to his house.

The Sliter hound dogs met Papa on the road and set up a racket, announcing his arrival.

"Hep! Hep! Git back here, dogs!" yelled Mr. Sliter from his front yard. He placed his thumb and index finger into his mouth and emitted a shrill whistle. The dogs bounded back to the yard and stood on either side of Mr. Sliter, but still issued an occasional bark.

"Where's your manners?" Mr. Sliter addressed the dogs as he caressed their long ears. "We got company, and you're behaving mighty rudely."

Papa reached the yard and extended his hand. "My name's Bill. I'm lookin' for Mr. Sliter. Might that be you?"

"Guilty as charged. And you've already met my hounds," Mr. Sliter responded as he nodded toward the dogs. "This here is Cleopatra. Ain't she a looker?" Mr. Sliter asked with obvious pride.

Papa glanced down at the female hound. Her drooping eyelids, flopping jowls, and long, dangling ears made Papa question Mr. Sliter's notion of beauty.

"And this is her brother Vesuvius," Mr. Sliter motioned to the other hound.

"Ve … ve … what?" stumbled Papa.

"Vesuvius. He just ain't got the digestive tract of a hound. Erupts a lot, you know, like the volcano that buried the ancient city of Pompeii," Mr. Sliter offered by way of explanation.

Papa wasn't quite sure what sort of erupting the dog was prone to do, but made a mental note to avoid Vesuvius' proximity.

"Well, you're a couple days early for the harvest, young man," Mr. Sliter commented, "but the farms around here will be needin' all the hands I can round up soon enough. Where you staying?"

"I … well … I," Papa shrugged his shoulders.

"You can stay here." Mr. Sliter motioned Papa to follow as he turned toward the small house, the hounds at his heels. Mr. Sliter held the door open for the dogs and patted their backs as they passed inside.

Mrs. Sliter was in the kitchen cooking supper. The smell of frying meat almost made Papa's knees buckle. He couldn't remember the last time he'd eaten a real meal. After the two men washed up, Mr. Sliter indicated Papa's seat at the table and eased himself into the chair opposite Papa. Cleopatra and Vesuvius took their positions on either side of Mr. Sliter, and their woeful eyes watched intently as each forkful of food passed from Mr. Sliter's plate to his mouth. Long strings of drool hung from the dogs' jowls.

Out of consideration for his hosts, Papa ate with restraint. When Mrs. Sliter offered him the last piece of meat on the platter, he politely declined. Mr. Sliter shrugged, then forked the remaining meat onto his plate. He carefully cut it into two equal portions and held the meat out to Cleopatra and Vesuvius. The dogs practiced much less restraint than Papa. As they gobbled down the meat, their flapping jowls sent the long strings of drool flying about the kitchen.

That evening, Mr. Sliter suggested Papa bed down on the carpeted living room floor. Papa was glad for the comfortable shelter, even if

Cleopatra and Vesuvius were sharing his sleeping quarters. He folded his coat into a pillow for his head and was just drifting off to a contented sleep when he detected a foul odor. Papa burrowed his nose deeper into his pillow, but the smell permeated every fold in the fabric. Obviously, Vesuvius was erupting! Then Papa felt a tiny bite on his arm, followed by one on his leg, and then the sensation of little legs running across his forehead. He sat up and swatted at his hair and beat at his clothing. Fleas! The carpet was alive with fleas!

Papa exited the house. He knew that if the inside of the house was flea-ridden, the grass would be just as infested. Leaning against the back of the house was a long board that the Sliters used for a section of footpath between the house and outhouse when the mud was deep. By the light of the moon, Papa wedged the board into a horizontal position between two trees, and then he stretched out for a night of sleep beneath the stars.

Mr. Sliter spent the next day in town rounding up a harvesting crew, then visited the farmers who had contracted with him for threshing services. When he had secured about fifteen young men and lined up the threshing order, he returned home to oil and prepare his steam engine and threshing machine. Papa was fascinated by the gadgetry and eagerly assisted Mr. Sliter with the preparations. That evening at the supper table, Mrs. Sliter offered Papa the last piece of meat. He accepted it and ate with gusto, under the baleful watch of Cleopatra and Vesuvius.

The threshing began the next morning on the Zettel farm, after the sun had dried the dew from the wheat. While Mr. Sliter monitored the steam engine, the rest of the crew fed bundles of wheat into the threshing machine, stacked straw, and loaded wagons with cleaned grain to be hauled away.

At noontime, the farmer's wife and young daughters drove a spring wagon to the edge of the field and tied the horses in the shade of some large elm trees. While Mrs. Zettel arranged the bountiful dinner on the tailboard of the wagon, her daughters placed buckets of water, several bars of soap, and some towels under one of the trees. The hot, hungry men washed the itchy chaff from their faces, necks, and arms, then stood in line at the wagon to help themselves to the tempting buffet. They ate picnic-style under the elms. As Papa neared the wagon, he spotted a crock of sauerkraut among the comestibles. He felt a wave of homesickness come over him. There was always a crock of sauerkraut in the summer kitchen back home.

"*Es ist lange her daß ich Sauerkraut gegessen habe* (It's been a long time since I've eaten sauerkraut)," Papa said wistfully.

Mrs. Zettel overheard his comment, and the two began to converse in German. Several members of the threshing crew were eating their dinner in the shade of the spring wagon, and they exchanged glances as Papa and Mrs. Zettel carried on a lively conversation in a foreign language.

"Hey, Dutch," one of them called out to Papa. "Don't go sparkin' the farmer's wife—she's already taken." Loud guffaws erupted from those seated under the wagon.

Papa blushed crimson to his hairline and joined the threshers who were dining beneath the elms.

After dinner, Mr. Sliter asked Papa to monitor the steam engine while he drove the water wagon to the next farm where they would thresh.

"Well, Dutch, you sure have found a way to be the favorite on this crew," sniped Jake, the fellow who had previously poked fun at Papa's conversation with Mrs. Zettel. Jake's teasing only intensified when one of Mrs. Zettel's young daughters appeared at the edge of the field as the crew was preparing to move on to the next farm. She handed Papa a small cloth bundle containing a souse sandwich and a piece of küchen.

"*Mutter sagte ich soll Dir das geben* (Mother said to give this to you)," the little girl said, her eyes cast shyly downward.

"*Sage Deiner Mutter vielen Dank* (Tell your mother thank you)," called Papa as the girl sped off down the long lane toward the farm house.

"Ain't you just the lady's man, Dutch? First the farmer's wife, and now his little girl. Guess I'll have to learn to talk the same gibberish as you if I wanna eat well around these parts," Jake groused.

Papa didn't want any trouble with Jake and his friends, and he kept his distance from them for the rest of the day.

The harvest season flew by in a blur of sweat, sore muscles, and exhausted sleep on the plank between the trees in Mr. Sliter's backyard. On Saturdays, Mr. Sliter met the crew in town to pay them for their week of work. Papa had been earning extra money by chopping the wood needed to fuel the steam engine, and he banked most of his earnings. One Saturday toward the end of August, Papa was accosted by Jake and his friends as he exited the bank.

"Where you been gettin' all that money, Dutch? You don't work no harder than the rest of us," Jake sneered as he stepped within inches of Papa's face. Jake's friends clustered around the two men.

"I've earned it threshin', and I've been choppin' wood for Mr.

Sliter," explained Papa.

"I ain't never seen you chopping no wood," spat Jake. "I'm missin' some money, and I think you stole it. That's how come you're so flush with cash."

"S-S-Stole it!" shouted Papa, his temper rising. "I earned every cent!"

Over Jake's shoulder, Papa spotted Mr. Sliter exiting the grain mill.

"Mr. Sliter! Mr. Sliter!" Papa called.

Mr. Sliter turned and saw the knot of men gathered in front of the bank. He crossed the street to see why he was being summoned.

Papa explained the accusation against him, and Mr. Sliter vouched for Papa's extra earnings. Jake and his men grumbled and moved on down the street where they found a fellow thresher, Lawson Cray, and his teenaged son Lee. Jake peppered the Crays with the same accusation. Mr. Sliter followed and broke up that confrontation as well.

Papa had had enough of Jake's teasing, and now the accusation of dishonesty made Papa uncomfortable about continuing to work with this crew. Such men were known to conveniently cause "accidents" to happen around the dangerous threshing machinery. In addition, the harvest season was almost over and it would be time to find work elsewhere. Papa approached the Crays and suggested the three of them ride the rails to St. Louis. Lawson and Lee were equally eager to part company with Jake and his buddies. Papa withdrew his money from the bank and thanked the Sliters for their hospitality. The next morning, he met the Crays at the rail yards, where they jumped aboard a train headed west.

In St. Louis, there was much talk about the Cotton Exposition that would be held in New Orleans. The Crays and Papa thought New Orleans sounded like a promising destination, and by pooling their funds they were able to buy a rowboat, several guns, some ammunition, a tent, blankets, cooking utensils, dishes, and a supply of food for the long float down the Mississippi River. Papa picked up his valise that he had sent on ahead from Chicago, and Lawson stopped by the stockyards to select some steer horns to hold gunpowder.

The day of departure dawned clear and warm. Papa steered the rowboat out into the current, then took turns with Lee manning the oars. The novelty of being on the water and having such an easy ride kept their spirits high. They bobbed along on the earthy waters, enjoying the scenery of passing towns, farms, and open country. Lawson sprawled against their baggage in the prow of the boat and passed the hours by polishing the steer horns to a high gleam.

As evening came, they rowed toward shore and tied up, then pitched their tent on a suitable patch of land. At daybreak, they threw back their blankets and began breakfast preparations. Lawson suggested he tend the campfire and start a pot of water to boil while Papa and Lee went hunting for game in the surrounding thickets.

Day after day passed in this pleasant manner. When they found a spot that had abundant game, they stayed for as long as they pleased; there was no urgency to reach New Orleans. Eventually, curiosity about what lay around the next bend in the river beckoned them on.

After a number of weeks, Papa began to realize that he and Lee were doing all the heavy work around the camp—hunting, fishing, and gathering firewood. Since Lee was but a lad of seventeen, the initiative to get the work done fell to Papa. Lawson preferred to lounge around the camp. He tended to the camp fire and occasionally baked sweet potatoes or some corn pone in the cooking pot lid, but his greatest endeavor was continual polishing of the steer horns.

The trio had been camping near Columbus, Kentucky, for several weeks when Lee and Papa went out hunting one day and discovered some large pecan trees. Using the gunny sack they had brought along for carrying game, they gathered as many nuts as the bag would hold. The two young men hauled their harvest into the town of Columbus, where they sold the pecans for a very good price.

Upon their return to camp, Lee related their good fortune to his father, who was seated by the campfire, poking the coals with a stick. Lawson's small black eyes quickly shifted toward Papa.

"You owe me half of your share of the pecan money, Bill," he demanded. "We're partners. Half of everything you got is mine."

"Why ain't you askin' Lee for half of his money?" Papa responded.

Lawson grew belligerent. "Lee's kin. You're a business partner. I told you: half of what you got is mine. Now, hand it over!" Lawson prodded the stick menacingly at Papa.

Papa looked at Lee, expecting some rebuttal, but Lee would not meet his gaze. Feeling outnumbered, Papa counted out half of his pecan money and threw it on the ground at Lawson's feet. Lawson greedily clawed the money together and stuffed it into his pants pocket.

Later that night, Papa awoke with a chill. He wrapped his blanket tightly around him but still could not warm up. He slept fitfully. By morning, he was burning with fever. Papa tossed aside the blanket and unbuttoned the front of his shirt to allow the cool morning air access to his bare skin. His clothing was soaked through with sweat. Lee was in a similar cycle of chills and fever.

"You boys got the river fever, I 'spect," announced Lawson. "Won't be goin' nowhere for a while."

Lawson made a feeble attempt at nursing the two, but his greater efforts were expended on Lee. When Lee was chilled, Lawson draped his own blanket over the shivering boy. During Lee's episodes of profuse sweating, Lawson held a cup of cool water to his son's lips. Despite his father's ministrations, Lee frequently called out for his mother as he tossed and turned in fitful sleep. Papa endured fevered dreams of trickling streams of water, frosty pitchers of lemonade, and snowflakes caught on his outstretched tongue. He awoke with a parched throat and cracked lips. Occasionally, Lawson would offer him a cup of water; other times he laid there unable to muster the strength to crawl over to the water bucket and dip a cup for himself. When the chills overtook him, he covered himself with his coat, blanket, and the gunny sack used for carrying game, and stuck his feet inside his old valise. Still, he shuddered uncontrollably.

After several weeks, the two young men recovered enough that Lee announced he was through with river life. He struck out on foot for home and his mother in Kentucky. Lawson and Papa continued on downriver, although the zest for adventure was now at low ebb.

About thirty miles below Memphis, Tennessee, they stopped at the camp of a friendly fisherman named Millard Young. Papa's strength had not returned, so it was easier to stay put for a while rather than continue on.

One day, Millard told them about the great flocks of ducks to be found at a lake about seven miles into the backwaters. The next morning, while Lawson lagged around the campfire, Papa took his gun and went in search of the lake. He walked all morning before finally locating it. After he shot a few ducks, he attempted to wade out and retrieve them, but he soon realized that the water was too deep. Without a boat, Papa had no means of recovering the downed birds. Dejected, he turned back toward camp.

Papa walked and walked for hours, battling his way through the thick, dense growth along the ridges between the bayous. At times, the brush was impossible to penetrate, causing him to change direction. The day began to wane, and Papa still had not reached the river. Night fell, and now he realized he was hopelessly lost. Papa began to panic, and his pace became more frantic. He stumbled into pools of black water. The tangled undergrowth caught at his boots and gun. As he wrestled the gun free from the brambles, it exploded in an accidental discharge.

Papa sat down on a fallen log and laid the gun across his knees. The night sounds were strange and frightening. Weird trills, howls, yelps, and screams emanated from all parts of the wilderness around him. Papa thought of the bears, wildcats, and poisonous snakes known to inhabit the area. Chills went down his spine as he realized that he had always been the hunter; would he now become the hunted?

The noise of rustling underbrush startled him. He swung his gun to the left and stared down its barrel into the inky blackness. Papa listened intently, but the only sound he could hear was the roar of his own heartbeat. He waited, half expecting to feel the claws of a catamount tear into his shoulder, or the jaws of a bear clamp down on his throat. Nothing happened, and soon his heartbeat slowed to a mild pounding in his ears. He slowly lowered the gun back to his lap, but kept his hands gripped firmly around the barrel and stock. The night was overcast, and Papa could not get his bearings from the moon or stars.

After a sleepless night, the gray dawn of morning crept over the backwaters of the bayou. Papa breathed a sigh of relief: he had survived a night in the wilderness. He searched in his coat pocket for the handful of pecans he had brought along, then used a nearby rock and the heel of his wet boot to crush the shells. Munching on the pecans, Papa felt renewed hope, and he started out again.

The day was a continued struggle against the brambles and thick undergrowth. At noontime, Papa propped his gun against a tree, then sat at its base and pulled a piece of dried fish from his pocket. He tired easily in his weakened condition from the river fever, and the lack of food left him feeling shaky. Papa leaned his head against the tree and closed his eyes. He thought wistfully about the succulent taste of a roasted duck dinner.

Papa awoke with a start. He blinked hard, trying to clear his vision and get his bearings. In his exhausted state, he had slept away the afternoon, and now his second night in the jungle of the backwaters was upon him. Papa leaped to his feet and crashed onward, not sure if the direction he was heading would take him toward or away from the river. He flailed against the tangled brambles, his heart thumping at the thought of his plight. Surely Lawson had questioned his lengthy absence and had begun searching for him by now. Papa stopped and called out a forlorn "Hallooo!" then listened for a response. Only the eerie sounds of the backwater filled the evening air. Papa thought about home. If he perished in this bayou, no one back in Monroeville would ever know his fate. They would simply say he had gone west and was never heard from again.

Just when Papa feared that this nightmare would never end, the moon rose above the ragged edge of the swampline. Using it to set his bearings, Papa stumbled all night in the direction of the river. He emerged in Millard Young's camp at midmorning to find Lawson lounging beside the campfire, tugging on a bottle of whiskey.

"Well, well, well. Look who's back after their big adventure," Lawson sneered. "I been workin' up a powerful hunger for some roast duck while you was gone."

Papa collapsed beside the fire. "Where's Millard?"

"Out fishin'. But I'm tired of fish; where's the ducks?" Lawson queried.

"Didn't get none," Papa replied, his head cradled in his hands.

"What!?" exploded Lawson. He pushed himself up on one elbow and glared at Papa. "You been gone for two nights and you return empty-handed!?"

"Halloo, Bill! Glad to see you made it back," called Millard as he climbed the river bank toward camp, a line of buffalo fish tossed over his shoulder. "Must of been *some* hunting to keep you out that long."

Papa related the whole story of being unable to retrieve the downed ducks, then becoming hopelessly lost in the bayou wilderness. Lawson's response was to belch loudly.

"You look like your stomach's about to touch your backbone. Help me fillet these fish, and we'll have 'em cookin' in no time," Millard motioned Papa toward the river.

When Papa and Millard were crouched beside the river, out of earshot of the camp, Millard leaned toward Papa. "Look, Bill, I don't know what kind of partnership you got there with Lawson, but I'm tellin' you, the man ain't to be trusted."

"What's he done?" asked Papa as he slit the belly of a buffalo fish and gutted it out.

"The first night you didn't come back, I says to Lawson that maybe he ought to do something about findin' you, and he only laughed and said it would be a good joke if you never did find your way out of that wilderness," confided Millard. "He didn't seem none too concerned about you, Bill."

Papa jammed his knife into the ground and stormed up the embankment toward the camp. Millard hurried after him.

"L-L-L-Lawson! I'm done with you, you lazy d-d-drunk!" shouted Papa, his face flushed with anger as he charged into camp and stood over Lawson. "Our partnership is over, r-r-right now!"

Lawson finished draining the whiskey bottle and threw it aside. "You're done with *me*?" Lawson asked in mock disdain. "After all I done for you, *you're* callin' for an end to the partnership?"

"W-W-What have you done for me?" Papa shouted. "You took half of the money *I* earned sellin' pecans, you never did a lick of work around camp, and then you didn't bother to come lookin' for me when I was lost in the wilderness." Papa motioned angrily toward the bayou. "That ain't my idea of a partnership. I never shoulda struck up with you, Lawson. You're nothin' but a lazy, drunken cheat."

"Nobody calls me a cheat, leastways some green-as-corn farm boy from Ohio," growled Lawson as he rolled to his side and reached for his gun.

Millard stepped between the two men. "Now look, boys, ain't no use for this to come to violence. Seems to me this partnership can be peaceably dissolved and the two of you go your separate ways."

With Millard acting as referee, Papa and Lawson divided their property. Lawson took ownership of the boat and a gun, and the remainder of the goods belonged to Papa. Lawson tucked the steer horns in beside him as he set off in the boat down the Mississippi.

With no means of conveyance to continue his travels, Papa stayed on with Millard and helped with his fishing enterprise. In the fall they harvested buffalo fish, which weighed about twenty-five pounds and were only worth two cents at the market. In the spring, they set their lines for catfish, which were worth twice as much and generally weighed about seventy-five pounds. Three times a day they checked their half-mile-long lines, harvesting the fish and re-baiting the hooks. The fish were stored in a large wooden crate anchored in the river to keep the catch fresh. When about a ton of fish had been harvested, Millard and Papa enlisted the aid of Grady, a local black man, to help them row the heavily-loaded boat upriver to Memphis.

Aside from the efforts of rowing against the current, the men also were challenged by whirlpools that sometimes stretched from one side of the river to the other. The outer rim moved slowly, with the speed increasing as it neared the center, which dished down toward the bottom of the river. Papa and Grady walked along the bank and used a rope to pull the boat safely along over the danger zone while Millard stayed on board to steer.

During one trip upriver, the three were confident that they could skirt the edge of a whirlpool without the necessity of towing from on shore. To their horror, the boat swung into the outer rim of the rushing water and began circling the vortex.

Grady panicked and began pushing their load off the back of the boat.

"No, Grady, no!" shouted Millard. "We got to stay as heavy as possible to slow us down. Grab them oars and row, boy, row!"

The three frantically plied their oars against the circling waters and managed to pull the boat free of the downward spiral. To avoid other whirlpools in their upriver trip, they cut across the river and circled around President's Island, which lay opposite of Memphis. The trip that normally took six hours turned into a twenty-four-hour marathon of rowing and vigilance. Their tired muscles screamed as they unloaded the fish at the dock in Memphis and hauled on their return cargo of low-grade flour, cornmeal, and blocks of spoiled cheese to be mixed into marble-sized balls of bait.

During the winter, Millard and Papa trapped beaver and raccoon. River mink were plentiful, but their hides were nearly worthless. Raccoon hides brought fifty cents, while beaver skins were worth four to six dollars, depending on the grade. The two men poled along the river bank and bayous, digging into the embankments to set their traps.

At the end of one winter, Millard announced that the trapping season was over, and he began preparing the fishing gear for the upcoming season. Papa wanted to make one more trapping run, and he finally convinced Millard that he could handle a trip into the backwaters by himself.

"I'm not easy with this, Bill. You had one scare in the backwaters; you don't need another," Millard frowned. "Leastways, take some grub with you this time. You got a better chance of survivin' if you got a supply of food."

Millard wrapped a couple of roasted raccoons in a sack and set them in the small boat, while Papa loaded in about fifty traps, his gun and ammunition, some cooking supplies, and his blanket. With a tip of his chin, Papa signaled goodbye to Millard and set off on one final run.

He set traps at all of their regular places on Cuckleberry Lake, then portaged the boat to South Horn Lake, a bayou about ten miles long, then portaged on to North Horn Lake.

Papa was busy setting traps when an ominous rumbling of thunder alerted him to a change in the weather. Glancing at the boiling black clouds overhead, Papa hurried to set the few traps that remained. The storm broke with a fury before he could finish his task. The rain lashed in great white sheets across the bayou and clawed at his face. Papa rowed to a nearby fallen willow tree and hastily tied his boat to a branch. The trunk of the downed tree formed a bridge between the bayou and a spit of wooded land. Papa grabbed his gun, blanket, and sack of roasted raccoons and hurried across the log, his boots slipping on the wet bark.

In the woods, the trees swayed and groaned in the stiff wind but offered a measure of shelter from the pelting rain. It was the best Papa could hope for, until he spotted a woodchopper's shanty in a small clearing. The cockeyed door squealed on its hinges, revealing a dark, dank, one-room interior, but it was a refuge from the storm. Papa carefully inspected the room for snakes, then settled down on the sleeping bench that hugged one wall.

He removed his wet shirt and pants and hung them to dry on nails protruding from the wall, then wrapped himself in his blanket and feasted on some roasted raccoon meat. As darkness fell, he stretched out on the sleeping bench and listened to the steady drum of the rain on the sheet metal roof. He worried about his small boat. Had he lashed it securely enough to resist the driving winds? If it had floated away or been submerged, how would he escape these backwaters?

The rain pounded down through the night and up until noon of the next day. When Papa emerged from his shanty, he found a watery world awaited him. The spit of land that had provided his sanctuary was now even smaller. Splashing down to the bayou, he found the willow log bridge nearly submerged, but to his great relief, the boat still bobbed at the end of the branch. By bear-hugging the log, Papa slowly inched his way along the slippery bark and out to the boat. Several inches of rainwater filled the bottom of the boat, and his cooking supplies floated in the murky drink. Using his cooking pot, he bailed out the water, then returned to the shanty to retrieve his gun and blanket.

The swift current carried the little boat along. There was no need to portage now, since water covered the land and transformed it into one continuous stream. The traps Papa had set along the way were not worth salvaging, because their springs had been damaged from being in the water too long. The trip had been a complete failure; the trapping season was indeed over.

In the summers, when there was no fishing or trapping, Millard and Papa hunted about for any kind of work they could find. Papa tried his hand at picking cotton but found the heat too intense. He never made more than seventy-five cents a day in the cotton fields, but he marveled at the sing-song manner of the black cotton pickers who seemed impervious to the heat.

A sorghum mill was being built on a nearby sugar plantation, and Millard and Papa made arrangements to furnish the clapboards for the roof. They searched up and down the river for a suitable cypress log and finally found a large one that was partially submerged along the bank. With great effort, they floated it out into the river. Papa climbed up onto the front end of the log and used his river pole to guide it downstream. Millard went on ahead in the skiff to locate a sandbar where the tree could be beached and cut up.

The two men worked for weeks cutting the log into clapboards and stacking the planks. When the work was done, they notified the plantation owner that his roof material was ready. Several weeks later, a boat docked at the sandbar one night. A crew of about twelve black roustabouts came ashore to haul away the clapboards. When they could not produce any money to exchange for the boards, Millard and Papa sent them away empty-handed. The boards sat for the rest of the summer before a plantation owner who needed material for repair work on his buildings struck a deal with Millard and Papa.

One morning, following a heavy storm, a thick mist hung over the river. Millard and Papa set out in the skiff to inspect their fishing lines. Papa looked upriver and saw something he couldn't quite make out in the mist.

"What is that, Millard?" Papa asked, squinting in the direction of the mysterious object.

"Don't know. Let's go have a look-see," Millard replied, and they swung their skiff upriver.

As they neared the dark hulk, Papa whistled, "It goes from one side of the river to the other."

"Jesus!" squealed Millard as he recognized the dangerous situation before them. He frantically paddled to turn the skiff downriver.

The river was filled with hundreds of log rafts that had broken loose from their moorings. The storm the night before had ruptured the boom which held them in at the mouth of the Wolf River near Memphis, where there was a new mill.

Papa and Millard paddled rapidly to the safety of their camp's embankment and pulled the skiff ashore. They watched as the great mass of rafts passed before them. Some rafts snagged on sandbars or along the edges of the river, and the two men decided to capture those. They managed to round up five of the forty-feet-long, thirty-feet-wide crafts, which were difficult to maneuver due to their size.

Millard suggested they lash the rafts together and float them downriver to a sawmill in Greenville, Mississippi, where they could be sold. With the help of Grady, their black assistant, and Pat, an Irishman who had appeared on the river that spring, the rafts were merged into one big flotilla. Before they could depart, the rafts snagged on a submerged log and broke apart. They again set to work fastening the rafts, and when the craft was deemed ready for the trip, they secured a supply of food and firewood, constructed a mud fireplace in the front section of the raft, pitched a tent in the center of the expanse, and loaded a rowboat onboard for the return trip. Millard elected to remain in camp to run the fishing lines while Grady, Pat, and Papa made the trip downriver.

The three men poled the massive armada into the main current. Spirits were high at being aboard this unique conveyance.

"Whoo-hoo," shouted Pat, grinning from ear to ear. "Just let the other river traffic beware of us! We're a force to be reckoned with, we are."

Passing boats gave them wide berth. Folks stood on the shore and waved, and children ran along the embankment in a footrace with the barge. Papa waved his hat in a friendly salute to the onlookers.

"You's the king of the river, Mr. Bill," Grady teased Papa as he poled near the front of the raft.

At night, the men took turns keeping the fire burning as a beacon for other barges. It was peaceful on the river at night, and Papa didn't mind serving as sentinel. When he wasn't watching for other river traffic, he admired the stars and tested his ability to identify the constellations. It was hard to believe that the same stars that twinkled at him were also shining down on his mother, Old Man, and brother George on the farm in Monroeville.

One night, the rhythmic rocking of the boat and the gentle slap of the waves lulled Pat to sleep during his turn at sentinel. Without additional fuel, the neglected fire burned down and then winked out. The darkened barge continued to drift down the river.

A deafening blast jolted the three men from their deep slumber. As they shot upright from their pallets, a powerful searchlight swept the barge.

"Glory! It's a steamboat!" screamed Pat from the front of the craft.

Shielding his eyes against the steamer's blinding searchlight, Papa shot out of the tent and scrambled to his station. He threw all of his energy into rowing furiously to route the barge out of the path of the steamer. Grady stumbled to the oars, his blanket still wrapped around one foot, and pulled with all his might as the steamer bore down on them.

The steamer continued to blast its warning horn, drowning out the panicked commands of the three men on the barge as they frantically plied their oars and river poles. The steamer swung to the right, narrowly averting a collision with the corner of the flotilla. As it passed by, Papa could see the ship's pilot illuminated in the wheelhouse. He was frantically cranking the wheel, and his jaws were moving at a rapid pace. Papa had no doubt the man was spewing a stream of curses at their negligence.

The remainder of the trip passed without incidence. Then, without warning, they found themselves upon the city of Greenville and gliding past it in the swift current. Their raft was still riding in the middle of the river, and it would take many miles before they could bring it to shore. Their opportunity to sell the rafts at the Greenville sawmill was gone.

Pat snatched off his hat and threw it down. "Mother Ireland! All this way, and we miss our market!" He paced angrily at the edge of the raft, watching as the last buildings of Greenville passed out of sight.

"Let's just ride downriver and try to find another sawmill," suggested Papa.

"Do you know where the next sawmill be?" Pat barked as he whirled around and confronted Papa.

"Well . . . no, I don't," conceded Papa.

"Same thing's gonna happen to us again, Bill. With a boat this large, we can't hug the shoreline. We'll be past the next sawmill, and the next and the next, before we can bring this beast to shore. I say we forget this whole blarney thing!"

"What?!" Papa exclaimed. "You wanna throw away this chance to make good money?"

"Don't you see, Bill? We can't keep floatin' this rig down the river, spottin' mills when it's too late to stop. We'll end up in the Gulf of Mexico, and I've already crossed one ocean in me lifetime, thank you." Pat folded his arms across his chest in a defiant stance.

Grady, who had been watching and listening, quietly added, "Mr. Bill, we cain't keep a'goin'. We's about outta firewood, and our supplies is runnin' low. Tain't no sense in spendin' money when we ain't sure we's gonna make any."

Papa reluctantly agreed to begin the return journey upriver. They landed the flotilla long enough to slip the rowboat into the water, then loaded the smaller vessel with their meager possessions. As Papa lowered himself into the rowboat, he turned for one last look at the raft. It had begun to nudge itself back into the current. Papa watched forlornly as the abandoned armada floated downriver toward the gulf, carrying with it his dreams of fortune.

Papa continued to be plagued by recurring bouts of river fever. Millard was a more attentive nurse than Lawson Cray had been, and he carefully tended to Papa during his sieges of fever and chills.

One day, when Papa was recovering from a recent attack, Millard announced, "Bill, I believe you'd shake off this river sickness if you'd just get away from the river for a spell. Head on down to Cow Island. There's farmin' land there. Maybe some time on land is what'll cure you."

Papa was willing to try anything to rid himself of the river fever, so he made arrangements to rent twenty-five acres of tillable land, a mule, a plow, and other farming tools for twenty-five dollars for the growing season. He loaded the skiff with his gun, some ammunition, a 150-year-old coin he'd found, corn and cotton seed, a few cooking utensils, and some dried fish. He tossed in his valise, which held his extra clothing, and a blanket. Papa floated downriver three miles to the thousand-acre Cow Island.

Once there, he found the only existing cabin was occupied by another island farmer. Papa foraged for building materials. Using salvaged logs, planks, and driftwood from the river, he hastily erected a small shack that provided meager shelter.

Papa set about preparing the ground to plant ten acres of corn and ten acres of cotton. It was miserable work. Gert, the rented mule, was an obstinate beast who knew only two speeds: breakneck and stopped. During Gert's gallops across the field, Papa wrestled the plow to keep its blade engaged in the soil. When the mule made an abrupt stop, it nearly hurtled Papa over the crossbar between the handles of the plow. No amount of cajoling or threats could persuade Gert to resume plowing, that is, until she was sure Papa had stepped away from the plow. Then, she was off like lightning, the unattended plow bouncing behind her until Papa could catch up. At the end of each day, Papa surveyed the few furrows he had managed to plow in this stop-start fashion. They did not aim arrow-straight across the field, as they did when he plowed on the farm back in Monroeville. Instead, these furrows snaked along in a drunken zigzag. Papa was privately relieved that no one from back home—Old Man, in particular—was here to witness this random attempt at plowing.

To add to the misery, huge swarms of buffalo gnats descended on Papa and Gert. While the gnat lifespan was short, its annoyance factor was long. Gert's flesh rippled in constant irritation from the biting. She flung her head first to one side, then the other as she attempted to nip at the stinging hordes amassed on her flanks. Field work that was already slow due to Gert's obstinacy now became even more erratic due to her misery. Papa used a stick to scrape the mounds of gnats from the mule's sides and back. He swabbed her flesh with fish oil to repel the insects. Papa kept himself well covered with a long-sleeved jacket, a hat pulled low, and a handkerchief wrapped around his neck. His beard provided a measure of protection for his lower face. Papa tore strips of cloth from the seed bags and tied them just above and below his eyes, so that only a narrow slit remained to peer through, and to shield his nose from inhaling the pests. Likewise, he wrapped his hands in strips of cloth. Papa had never experienced such adverse farming conditions.

At the end of one long day, Papa led Gert across the field toward the shanty. The mule snorted and stopped, refusing to take another step. This was typical behavior when work was expected, but Gert never balked when leaving the field. Papa tugged at the reins and swatted at her rump, but the mule stood her ground and shook her head, making her harness jingle.

Exasperated, Papa stood with his hands on his hips and gazed across the field toward the shanty. His eyes grew wide and an electric charge surged through him when he noticed a man exiting the shanty.

"Hey! Hey, you there!" Papa shouted as he dropped the reins and charged across the field. Gert chose that moment to abandon her root-bound stance. She dashed pell-mell toward the shanty, kicking up her back hooves as she ran in a zigzag pattern in front of Papa.

The intruder turned and spotted Papa and the free-wheeling mule racing toward him. He rounded the corner of the shanty, broke into a run, and disappeared in the direction of the river. Papa reached the open door of the shanty and conducted a quick assessment of its contents. His gun, ammunition, and the old coin were gone, along with a few pieces of cookware. Papa sped out of the shanty, rounded the corner, and raced toward the river. The thief had outdistanced Papa and was paddling a canoe toward the swift current in the center of the river.

Papa stood at the river's edge, his hands clasping his knees and his chest heaving with every ragged breath. "Damn mule," he sputtered.

When Papa's corn had finally reached the roasting ear stage, bears, raccoons, and squirrels emerged from the nearby woods and feasted until the crop was destroyed. At about the same time, Papa realized that the expense of harvesting the cotton crop would be greater than its worth at market. He left the unharvested cotton in the field, returned Gert and the farming equipment to the other island farmer, and slowly paddled his skiff upriver to rejoin Millard. His experiment with southern farming had been an utter failure.

By now, the mosquitoes were in high season. Even though Millard and Papa strung up mosquito netting to sleep under, the insects still gained entry. The incessant high-pitched whine followed by their stinging bites tormented the two men to the point of sleeplessness. One night, Papa decided he could stand it no longer. He rowed his skiff out into the middle of the river and dropped anchor. The mosquitoes did not pester over the moving water. In his exhausted state, Papa fell into a deep and undisturbed slumber.

The sun was high the next morning before Papa awoke. He rubbed his eyes and blinked until the surrounding scenery came into focus. Nothing looked familiar. As Papa sat up, he noticed the skiff was drifting slowly downstream. Quickly examining his anchor rope, he discovered a piece of driftwood had caught on it during the night, dragging the skiff along in its downstream journey. Papa untangled the rope from the floating wood and began paddling upstream. It was a five-mile row before camp came into sight.

Millard hailed him from shore where he was repairing some fishing line. "You been out checkin' the lines, Bill?"

Papa sheepishly recounted his deep slumber and inadvertent travels downstream.

Millard shook his head. "I'm warnin' you, Bill, the river's no place to sleep. I wouldn't go back out there tonight if I was you."

But Papa was determined to get a good night's rest, so he returned to the river again that night. This time, he anchored his skiff just below a sandbar. Feeling confident that he had found a secure place, he settled down for a peaceful slumber.

In the middle of the night, Papa bolted upright at the shrill blast of a river steamer, which had chosen that hour to cut around the sandbar to save time. Its searchlight blinded him as he fumbled for his knife, and the skiff rocked precariously as Papa frantically sawed at the anchor rope. Once the tether was cut, he paddled furiously to escape the oncoming steamer's path. The next night found Papa sleeping—or trying to—on shore.

Although there were other fishermen living along the river, Papa and Millard kept mainly to themselves. However, gossip did travel up and down the waterway, and that is how they learned about a couple named Big Tom and Geneva who were hiding out in the wilderness several miles upriver. While serving as the marshal of Columbus, Kentucky, Big Tom had quarreled with a man. During the brawl, Big Tom had sunk his knife deep into the man's belly. He and Geneva skipped town, seeking refuge in the anonymity of river life.

One afternoon in early fall, Big Tom's hired man, Zeb, rowed over. He was sporting some abrasions on his cheek, and his tousled hair was strewn with leaf litter. Zeb seated himself on a tree stump by the camp fire and watched as Papa spooned cornbread batter onto the lid of the hot cooking pot.

"Bet some honey'd taste mighty good on that corn pone," Zeb commented while gingerly touching the contusions on his cheek.

"That it would," agreed Papa, "but I hain't seen a bee tree around here in all the huntin' I've done. Have you, Millard?"

Millard wiped his fillet knife on his pant leg and skewered a gutted buffalo fish with a green willow branch. "If I'd seen one, I'd a been on it like a bear," Millard growled for emphasis and made a clawing motion with his hands.

Papa chuckled and shook his head.

"Well, I know where there's a whole hive full of honey, free for the takin'," Zeb boasted.

Millard snorted. "When it comes to bees, 'free' has a pricetag."

"Beestings ain't nothin'," Zeb commented as he fingered the rising welt on his cheek.

Papa's interest was piqued. "Where's this hive at?"

"Across the river. In a thicket. I'll show you after supper," Zeb offered, inviting himself to the feast Millard and Papa were preparing.

After the meal, Zeb threw some green willow branches onto the fire and instructed Papa and Millard to stand downwind until their clothes were thoroughly smoky. He grabbed a bucket to carry the honey, and the three men rowed across the river. Zeb led the way through the thicket, motioning for Papa and Millard to follow quietly. At the hive, he worked quickly to extract the honey-laden combs and drop them in the bucket. The bees buzzed around their heads but did not light due to the smoky scent.

Back at camp, Millard sliced off a corner of the comb and slipped it into his mouth. A wide smile split his face, and his eyes rolled upward in delight. Papa retrieved the leftover corn pone and dribbled some honey on it, then passed a piece to Zeb. They chewed in contented silence. As darkness fell, the three men sat around the campfire, taking turns dipping their fingers into the bucket of honey and enjoying the sweet treat.

"Won't Big Tom be missin' you?" asked Papa as he licked the honey from his hand.

"I quit him," Zeb replied. His fingers instinctively flew to his face, where they gingerly touched the black-and-blue lump rising from his cheekbone.

Millard and Papa exchanged glances.

For the next few days, Zeb helped Millard and Papa run the fish lines. One morning, as they were gathering in the lines, a rowboat appeared upstream. It was Big Tom and Geneva, and they were steaming toward the three men. Big Tom leaned into his oars with angry intent, and Geneva, who was not a small woman, also plied her paddles with gusto.

"You thievin' son-a-bitch," Big Tom roared as they pulled alongside Papa's skiff. He thrust out a meaty paw and grabbed Zeb by the collar, yanking the smaller man over the edge of the skiff and onto the floor of Big Tom's rowboat. Geneva held firmly to the lip of the skiff with one hand and wielded her paddle as a weapon in the other.

Zeb's feeble resistance was met with repeated blows from Big Tom's huge fist, interspersed with whacks from Geneva's paddle.

"Teach … you … to steal … mah … honey!" Geneva enunciated with each whack of her paddle.

"What's this all about?" Millard shouted indignantly as he and Papa tried to stabilize the precariously rocking skiff.

"My beehive's been raided, and it weren't by no bear! That thievin' son-a-bitch is the only one 'sides Geneva and me who knowed its whereabouts!" Big Tom bellowed as he pointed to Zeb, who cowered in the bottom of the rowboat. "You two in on it too?" Big Tom asked menacingly as his gaze shifted between Papa and Millard.

Papa noticed Big Tom's hand poised over the hilt of his large hunting knife, which protruded from a leather sheaf attached to his belt.

"W-W-W-We didn't know it was your beehive, Big Tom. Honest!" stammered Papa. "We hain't thieves!"

Big Tom whipped the knife from its sheaf and shook it at Papa and Millard. The sun glinted off its polished blade. "Don't cross me agin, you hear? I won't be so pleasant next time."

Geneva released her grip on the edge of the skiff, and she and Big Tom rowed their boat across the river. From time to time, Geneva pulled her paddle from the water and delivered a whack to poor Zeb, who still lay in the bottom of the boat.

Millard let out a low whistle. "Jesus, Bill. That was a close shave. I'd a never gone near that honey if I'd knowed it was Big Tom's. Don't need to get my throat slit over bee juice."

Papa sat silently and watched as the rowboat disappeared. He tucked his hands between his knees so Millard wouldn't see how they were shaking.

In February, word traveled up and down the river that an unusually large flood was coming their way. Papa and Millard had already noticed the river was rising and realized that their camp near the embankment would soon be washed away. They built a platform five feet above ground in a cluster of old willow trees. Recent sleet storms had downed a considerable number of tree limbs, which they used in addition to some salvaged planks in the construction of a sixteen-foot-wide living space. They fashioned a mud fireplace for cooking and topped the scaffold with their tent. Next, they hoisted all of their possessions onto the platform and tied their skiffs to the tree.

They didn't have long to wait for the floodwaters to arrive. In no time, the muddy waters were lapping just below the level of the platform. Papa and Millard hastily disassembled their living quarters and moved it ten feet higher in the tree. The waters continued to rise, and the two men soon realized they were not high enough. Using their skiffs, they gathered up planks and other building material that floated by and rebuilt their platform another ten feet higher. The water rose to within two feet of their treetop sanctuary before cresting.

Shanties, dead livestock, and uprooted trees floated by and sometimes endangered the stability of the platform. During the day, they could spot an oncoming threat and use their river poles to divert the obstacle before it slammed into their scaffold. In the night, however, they were often awakened by a jolt that shook the trees and caused the cobbled-together boards to groan. In the darkness, they fumbled to dislodge the dangerous debris without falling into the floodwaters themselves. The winds blew fiercely for days and tore at their tent covering and thin blankets.

Before long, Millard and Papa had exhausted the easily accessible supply of raccoons and squirrels that had taken refuge in the treetops. They continued to trap along the river, but the flooding had disrupted the yield. An occasional roasted beaver was an especially welcome treat. Otherwise, rations became slim and consisted of baked sweet potatoes or corn pone. Sometimes, fuel could not be found, and cold meals of dried fish and cracked pecans provided meager sustenance.

One night, a levee broke about eight miles downriver. The water roared like cannons and washed away houses in the overflow district. A few days later, Papa and Millard floated their skiff into the backwater area to view the devastation. Dead livestock and fowl bobbed in the waters. On any available high ground, horses and cattle stood, the waterlogged flesh on their legs rotted to the bone. Starvation was certain. From the roofs of floating shanties, from the tops of trees, and from floating logs, stranded people cried out for help. Papa and Millard ferried as many of them to safety as they could reach.

It was the middle of May before the waters finally receded and Millard and Papa were able to return to the ground. Papa stretched his arms and legs—it felt wonderful to extend one's limbs without fear of knocking something off the platform into the floodwaters. The ground was still spongy, and everything was coated in dried mud, but it was a relief to be back on land.

Several weeks later, a portly man by the name of Cyrus pulled his skiff up at the edge of the river and huffed and puffed as he climbed the embankment to Millard and Papa's camp.

"Gentlemen," he said, tipping his hat as he seated himself on a nearby log, "I'll get straight to the object of my visit. I've got a houseboat tied up about ten miles downriver that I'm lookin' to sell. Would you folks be interested?"

"A houseboat?" Papa exclaimed. He looked at Millard and raised his eyebrows.

"How big is it?" inquired Millard.

"The gunwale's about forty foot long and six foot wide," Cyrus replied as he pulled a handkerchief from his back pocket and mopped at his brow. "Lordy, it gets humid down here so early. That's why I'm sellin' out. Can't take this weather. I'm goin' home to St. Paul."

"How much you want for it?" inquired Papa.

"It's worth two hundred dollars," Cyrus stopped mopping his brow and eyed Millard and Papa for their reaction to his price. When he saw them flinch, he countered with, "Make me an offer, boys, and we'll see if we can negotiate."

"Forty bucks is all we got 'tween the two of us," Papa replied.

Cyrus frowned thoughtfully and resumed patting at his brow and neck.

"Let's go have a look-see before we get any further in these negotiations," suggested Millard.

The two men followed Cyrus downriver to the place along the Arkansas shore where the houseboat was tied up. They were pleased to find a well-constructed boat that sported a cabin with two bunk rooms and a kitchen with a woodburning stove and a folding table and benches. Satisfied by their inspection, Millard and Papa agreed to buy the houseboat.

"You boys are gettin' a bargain at forty dollars," commented Cyrus as he folded their money into his pocket. "If I weren't so darn anxious to get outta this part of the country, I'd drive a harder deal." Cyrus eased himself into his skiff and nosed out into the current, still mopping at his brow and neck between strokes of his paddle.

Millard and Papa grinned at each other.

"A roof over our heads. Imagine that, Millard," smiled Papa as he looked about the cabin.

"Might be too civilized for a couple of old river rats like us," joked Millard as he nudged Papa with his elbow.

The two men returned upriver in their skiff to break up their camp, then transported their possessions to the houseboat. They ventured into the Arkansas canebrake and filled the bunk ticks with reeds. All was satisfactory with their new living accommodations, except for its location. Before long, Millard and Papa realized that the fishing was not good here. They decided to move the houseboat upriver to their old site.

They collected all the rope they owned or could find. Unraveling the larger ropes, they spliced in the smaller ones until they had about two hundred feet of strong anchor cord. Carrying the stout tether upriver as far as it would stretch, they dropped the anchor. Back on the boat, both men pulled in the rope until the anchor was reached. They repeated this cycle again and again, inching the boat upriver until they had finally reached the familiar shore of their original encampment.

The houseboat was a decidedly better home, but strong winds and heavy current often shoved it onto a sandbar. One day, while Millard and Papa were busily dislodging the vessel, a packet boat made a sharp turn within a few rods of them and washed a huge wave over Papa. The skiff, which was chained to the houseboat, bobbed up and tilted the board that Papa stood upon. The sudden shift in his footing catapulted Papa into the river, and he went under the side of the houseboat. Papa emerged, sputtering river water and gasping for air. He grabbed wildly for the skiff's chain, but a second wave submerged him before he could secure a handhold. In all of his time on the river, Papa had never learned to swim. Now, he was sinking under the murky waters.

Millard, who had been struggling on the opposite side of the boat to free it from the sandbar, began to wonder why Papa was no longer pushing with his river pole. He came around to Papa's side of the boat just in time to witness Papa's frantic thrashing as he sank below the water's surface. Groping in the muddy waters, Millard felt the fabric of Papa's shirt. He grabbed a handful of cloth and pulled Papa to the surface, then dragged the nearly drowned man on board. Papa lay on the deck, retching river water and gasping for air.

In the meantime, the packet boat had gotten into trouble as well. While turning toward a deeper channel, it had run aground on a sandbar. The crew called over to Millard and Papa for assistance, but Papa, who was still coughing, turned to Millard and rasped, "To hell with them!"

One night as the two men sat opposite each other at the folding table in the houseboat cabin, Millard announced that he would be leaving the river to marry Isabelle, a widow he had been courting.

"Bill, you oughta find yourself a good woman like Isabelle," urged Millard. "She's just as sweet and mild as they come."

Papa thought for a moment and gazed over Millard's shoulder. "I want a woman with some spunk," he commented. "Someone with delicate white skin, but a spark in her eyes."

"Careful what you wish for, Bill. You might not be able to handle such a spitfire," Millard chuckled as he rolled onto his reed-filled bunk cushion. "Besides, where you gonna find a woman like that?"

"I don't know. I hain't been looking," replied Papa, "but I'll know she's the one when I see her."

At the end of the fishing season, Millard and Papa split their joint possessions. Millard gave Papa his share of the houseboat in return for one of the skiffs. With a handshake, the two men bid goodbye.

Millard maneuvered his skiff toward the center of the river, then turned and waved his hat in a final salute. Papa raised his hand in farewell and watched as the skiff floated out of sight. He had partnered with Millard for over two years, but now he was on his own once again.

For several weeks, Papa lived alone, running the trapping lines and leading a solitary existence. One day, a shabbily dressed man pulled up to the houseboat and hallooed for permission to board.

"Name's Philo Hawk out of Kentucky," the man said, extending a thin hand that quivered slightly. "I'm a mite down on my luck and wonder if I could put up here for a spell."

Papa had missed the companionship he enjoyed with Millard, and so he agreed to the man's request. He soon realized that Philo was not the kind of person he wished to keep company with. Philo was never far from his liquor flask. He liked to prop himself against the cabin wall with his legs stretched out on the bench before him and methodically sharpen the blade of his pearl-handled knife. At one point, he held the tip of the blade up to an ugly scar that snaked along the edge of his jaw.

"See this?" Philo asked, tapping the scar. "Got it in a gamblin' brawl in Kansas. See this?" He waved the blade menacingly back and forth, then suddenly thrust it forward. "The other guy got *this*!" He laughed a loud, raspy chuckle that ended in a prolonged coughing spell.

One day, Papa returned from running the trapping lines with the weak, feverish sensation of the river sickness descending upon him. He collapsed on his bunk, draped his arm across his aching eyes, and fell into a fitful sleep. He dreamed of shimmering icicles dripping into his parched mouth and could hear the sound of ice skates scraping across the frozen surface of the Huron River back home. When he awoke, he realized the scraping sound was Philo's knife blade being dragged against the whet stone.

Papa raised his head. "Philo! Philo! Bring me a cup of water … please," he whispered hoarsely.

"I ain't your nurse-maid!" Philo barked.

Papa's head fell back on his bunk cushion. He ran his hands through his hair and closed his eyes.

After the bout of river fever had passed, Papa resumed trapping. One afternoon when he tried to enlist Philo's aid in preparing the beaver and muskrat hides for sale, Philo replied bluntly, "I ain't no trapper."

Papa stormed over to the bench where Philo reclined and slammed his fist on the folding table. "W-W-What do you do, Philo, besides sit around all day and drink and sharpen that knife?" exploded Papa. "Only time you leave the boat is to get more liquor."

"You don't like my ways, maybe you the one ought to be leavin' this boat," sneered Philo as he jabbed the point of his knife blade into the surface of the table near Papa's fist.

Papa angrily returned to bundling the hides. As he worked, Philo's comment resounded in his head, and he decided that leaving the boat was the best option. He was weary of Philo's lazy, quarrelsome nature.

The next morning, Papa loaded the skiff with the hides, tent, cookware, his new gun and a supply of ammunition, a couple of roasted beaver wrapped in burlap, and the valise, which held his meager personal effects. Philo was sprawled in his usual spot on the bench, methodically rubbing his knife blade over the whet stone. Neither man said a word. Papa slipped the skiff into the current and headed downstream. He stopped in Greenville to sell the hides, then continued on toward Vicksburg, where he fell in with an old trapper and fisherman named Isaac Moore.

Isaac and Papa trapped the Yazoo River during the rest of the winter, using a lightweight dugout that was easy to portage in the backwaters. One day, Papa trapped an especially large raccoon, clubbed it, and tossed it in the back of the boat. He continued to run his trap line and had just laid down his paddle to reach for a trap when a sudden blow from behind pitched him forward. The raccoon had merely been dazed, and when it awoke, it launched itself onto Papa's back. Its claws sank into his coat, and its jaws clamped onto his collar. The animal's high-pitched *cac-cac-cac* shrieked in Papa's ear. The sudden weight of the animal and the surprise attack almost hurtled Papa into the water. His dugout pitched precariously, and he tried to stabilize it with one hand while grabbing for the raccoon with the other. Papa finally managed to use two hands to wrestle the animal from its lock on the back of his coat, and he flung it out into the water. The raccoon surfaced and swam for the nearest cypress tree, while Papa paddled a hasty retreat in the opposite direction.

In the spring, Isaac and Papa followed the fish out of the Yazoo and up the Mississippi River about ten miles. All along the shore, the Mississippi River Commission was busy erecting flood-control measures, following the massive destruction of the flood of 1882. Isaac and Papa watched as great barges arrived, carrying willow trees that had been wired together. These barricades were placed along the banks of the river and weighted down with rocks.

"Think that'll hold back the river?" Papa asked, pointing his chin at the construction.

Isaac snorted. "Not the river *I* know!"

Isaac and Papa paddled on until a man wearing a suit flagged them down from the dock of an old plantation.

"You fellas headin' to Vicksburg?" the man called anxiously.

Papa looked at Isaac and shrugged. "Could be," he replied. Isaac and Papa rowed over to the dock.

"I'm with the River Commission," the man explained, "and I've got paperwork that has to be filed at the courthouse in Vicksburg today. I'll pay you five dollars if you take me down there."

"Five dollars!" exclaimed Papa. "Climb in!"

The trip downriver was easily accomplished, and when they reached Vicksburg, the man asked Papa to accompany him to the courthouse on the top of the high bluff above the river. There, he could obtain his payment.

Papa waited on the courthouse steps and struggled to catch his breath from the long climb up the steep bluffs. He looked around at the city that lay before him and the river below him. Ordinarily, he would have enjoyed the view and the opportunity to take in the sights of a new town, but he felt unusually weak in the legs and plopped down onto a step.

The government agent returned with Papa's payment. "Young man, you don't look so good," the man said with concern as he bent over to peer into Papa's face.

"Don't feel so good neither," Papa mumbled, rubbing his hand over his eyes. He rose and stuffed the five dollars into his pocket.

"You want to lie down inside?" called the agent as Papa waved him off and staggered down the bluff.

By the time Papa reached Isaac and the skiff, he was sweating profusely and wobbling as he walked. He crawled into the skiff and lay down.

"River fever again?" Isaac asked.

Papa just nodded.

"It's comin' on you all too frequent, Bill. You need to get away from the river. Time you head on home to Iowa," Isaac urged.

"Ohio," mumbled Papa, "I'm from Ohio."

"Ohio, Iowa ... same difference," shrugged Isaac as he began rowing the skiff upriver.

The river fever kept Papa so miserable that he finally agreed with Isaac: it was time to head for home. Papa sold what little he owned, including the valise, which provided him with just enough money to buy the lowest-level fare on the steamer *Sherlock Holmes* from Vicksburg to Cincinnati. Deck passage entitled Papa to the use of the lower deck only; it was up to him to furnish his own food and find a place to sleep.

Papa hid his small bundle of dried fish and pecans between some bales of cotton on deck. He strolled about the lower level of the boat and watched the river scenery pass by. That night, he stretched out on top of the cotton bales and slumbered peacefully as the steamer plied the waters northward.

The next morning, he slipped his hand between the bales to retrieve his food parcel. Nothing but cotton and burlap greeted him. Surely, he was not mistaken about the spot where he had tucked his bundle. He plunged his hand into the next seam and the next. Each time, he came up empty-handed. Papa paced about on the deck. He could smell the aroma of frying bacon and brewing coffee as breakfast was being prepared for the first- and second-class passengers. His stomach rumbled and gnawed. Spying burlap sacks of peanuts stacked on deck, Papa looked left and right for any authority who may be overseeing the shipment. When he was sure he was alone, he quickly untied the string on one bag and filled his pockets with handfuls of peanuts.

On the third day, a man about to disembark turned his job over to Papa. He chopped wood, helped in the kitchen, and served as cabinboy when necessary. In return, Papa was entitled to any food left over after the first- and second-class passengers had eaten. Papa gobbled up the scraps with gusto.

When the steamer arrived in Cincinnati, Papa disembarked and sought directions to the rail yard. There, he milled about until he found an open boxcar on a train that was heading north. Papa sat in the open doorway of the car and watched as the Ohio countryside rolled by. It was late spring 1885, and the fields were lined with rich, dark furrows ready for planting. Probably brother George and Old Man Scheidt were busy with plowing and planting back home.

In Findlay, Papa hopped an eastbound boxcar and rode the rails to Chicago Junction, where he leaped off the train and started walking north. As he left the small rail yard, he smiled and shook his head slightly, remembering his greenhorn experiences on the initial leg of his journey out west. It had been a little over three years since he'd begun his trek, and now he was homeward bound. Home! Papa was overcome with a longing to be back home. His footsteps turned into a run, then an exhausted walk as he covered the last fifteen miles toward home.

It was twilight by the time Papa crossed the yard of the homestead and climbed the back porch steps. As he reached the top step, he could hear the rattle of crockery from the kitchen. The aroma of sauerkraut wafted through the open summer kitchen door. Papa's knees buckled, and he collapsed on the porch floorboards.

Kathrina heard a loud thump and turned toward the door. Cocking her head, she hurried across the kitchen and gasped when she saw the crumbled form of a man lying on the back porch.

"*Wilhelm! George! Dieser Mann benötigt Hilfe!* (This man needs help!)"

she shouted.

Kathrina bent over the fallen man and peered into the bearded face. Her hand flew to her breast as she screamed, "*Es Ist William! Es Ist William! Mein Gott! William ist nach Hause gekommen!* (It's William! It's William! My God! William has come home!)"

Old Man Scheidt and George rushed onto the porch. Old Man carried the kerosene lamp and held it high over Papa's form. He announced solemnly, "*Sieh ihn an! Er ist nach Hause gekommen, um zu sterben.* (Look at him! He's come home to die.)"

Papa's eyes blinked open, and he gazed in confusion at the concerned faces huddled above him. It had been so long since Papa had heard or spoken fluent German that their words swam in a jumbled stream through his head.

Old Man passed the kerosene lamp to Kathrina, and he and George lifted Papa to his feet. They walked him into the kitchen, where they eased him into the rocking chair. Kathrina bustled about, heating up the leftover meat and gravy from the evening's meal. Papa tilted his head against the back of the rocker, closed his eyes, and listened to the sounds of home.

The Seibel homestead—summer kitchen & back porch on the left

Papa's trip out west had taken a physical toll. When he'd left home, his hair was black, but upon his return, it was mostly gray. On three different occasions during his westward journey, he had used his fillet knife to poke a new hole in his belt, each one to cinch the belt tighter around his shrinking waistline. Despite Kathrina's hearty meals and generous portions, Papa did not regain the lost weight. For the rest of the summer, he languished. Finally, a doctor was summoned. Papa responded to the medical treatments and was at last free of the river sickness.

That fall found Papa in the fields behind the barn, harvesting corn alongside George and Old Man.

Chapter 3
The Gasteier Homestead
Oxford Township, Erie County
1885

OF THE TEN CHILDREN born to John Frederick and Katherine Gasteier, all embodied the Germanic custom of obedience, except for Mama. She was a willful child given to fierce displays of temper. Even her Old World father grew exasperated with attempts to control her. When she flopped down at the end of a strawberry row and refused to pick any further, he threw up his hands in frustration. One evening, while she gathered the eggs, brother Fred crept up and latched the chicken house door, imprisoning her inside. His laughter infuriated her, and when she finally freed herself, she hurtled every egg at him in retaliation. Consequently, there were no eggs for breakfast or for baking. When sister Libby borrowed Mama's good pair of black hosiery without asking permission, Mama carried Libby's shoes outside to the well and pumped them full of water. Her parents punished and threatened, but Mama's outbursts could not be tamed.

Sophie Gasteier

While her temper set her apart from the others, she was very much like her siblings in her social aptitude. The Gasteier offspring were lively young people who laughed easily, participated in the community's events, and were well liked by all. They attended the local Lutheran school where only German was spoken. At about the age of confirmation at the Oxford Evangelical Church, the children quit school and sought employment. For the daughters, this meant "working out," or serving as domestics in the homes of the local English families, or "Yankees" as the German families referred to them.

The English families had been in America longer than the German settlers and therefore enjoyed greater prosperity and education. Mama was impressed by the gracious manner of living that she noticed in the Yankee homes, and she felt disdain for the lack of refinement in her own home life. When she pointed out to her father that the Yankee families traveled to church in buggies or carriages, but the Gasteier family arrived in a spring wagon, he responded curtly, "*Sie können auch zu Fuß zur Kirche gehen, wenn der Lastwagen solch eine Schande ist.* (You may use your own legs to walk to church if the wagon is such an embarrassment.)"

In 1885, when Mama was nineteen, her friend Anna Wetzel secured work as a domestic in the new brick manor house built by John Wright on the Ridge Road in Lyme Township. At Anna's urging, Mama soon followed. She was awed by the twelve-foot-high ceilings, which were centered with ornate plaster decorations and gas-burning chandeliers. The newel post at the foot of the grand staircase was topped by a brass lantern that was lit by acetylene gas made on the premises. Equally impressive were the fine furnishings, thick carpets, two indoor water closets, and the floor-to-ceiling cupboards in the formal dining room that housed the Wright's fine English china and sparkling crystal. Mama shuddered as she thought about the chipped ironstone dishes, the thin carpets, the kerosene lamps with their soot-blackened chimneys, and the well-worn path to the outhouse back home.

Anna and Mama's chores at the Wright mansion were demanding. They scrubbed floors, dusted the fine furnishings, applied lemon oil to the woodwork, washed the massive French plate glass windows, boiled and ironed the laundry, carried out the ashes from the many fireplaces, swept the miles of thick carpeting, and hauled the heavy rugs outside to be beaten. They assisted with the cooking and cleanup under the watchful eye of Mrs. Dowd, who reigned supreme in the kitchen. Mrs. Dowd insisted upon perfection. Each day, Mama was required to dip a rag into the wood ashes from the cookstove and rub the cutlery until a high gleam was achieved. Mrs. Dowd inspected each piece, and if she could see herself in the silverware without a spot of tarnish marring the reflection, the job was considered acceptable.

Mama picked up rudimentary English from her experiences in the Yankee homes. Mrs. Dowd, in particular, left a lasting impression. She would stand with her hands on her hips and command, "Now girls, I want this place in apple-pie order!"

"Apple-pie order, apple-pie order," Mama repeated to herself under her breath as she tidied up. The words sounded strange to her ear, and as she scrubbed, she sometimes corrupted them into a rhythmic English-German chant: "Apple sauce *Auftrag*, apple sauce *Auftrag*."

When Anna heard her, she'd chuckle and nudge Mama. *"Wie kannst Du sagen 'Apfelmus' Auftrag? Was soll das sein!* (Do you know you are saying 'apple sauce' order? That would be a mess!)" The two young women dissolved in giggles.

"Get a hustle on your bustle" was another of Mrs. Dowd's admonitions. When Mrs. Dowd wasn't looking, Mama coiled up the dishtowel and snapped it at Anna's backside. "*Hustle dein bustle, Fräulein!* (Hustle your bustle, miss!)" Mama's blue eyes sparkled with mischief, and Anna bit her lower lip to keep from laughing out loud.

Saturdays were payday. The hired hands who cared for the livestock and those who tended the crops lined up at the side entrance door to the library. Mrs. Dowd let them in, and Anna and Mama joined the others in a long line that snaked around the room. The library's dark walnut trim smelled of lemon oil, and the workers could see their reflection in the banks of glass-fronted bookcases that lined the walls from floor to ceiling. The employees shuffled their feet and waited in silence for Mr. Wright to appear. Finally, the massive door from the east parlor opened, and Mr. Wright entered. He stood before his desk and lifted his chin. Clearing his throat, he solemnly read each person's name from an envelope that held their pay. As the employee stepped forward, Mr. Wright folded his hands behind his back and stared past the worker. Each employee was required to walk behind Mr. Wright to receive their pay envelope from his clasped hands.

The first time Mama watched this ritual unfold, her blue eyes grew wide and she flushed red to her hairline. When Mr. Wright called her name, Mama glared straight into his unseeing eyes as she marched toward him, then snatched her pay envelope from behind his back. After she and Anna returned to the kitchen, Mama hissed, "*Warum gibt Herr Wright uns unsere Bezahlung in solch einer Weise?* (Why does Mr. Wright make us accept our pay in such a manner?)"

Anna shrugged and responded, "*Das ist, wie es immer hier getan wird, Sophie.* (That's how it's always done here, Sophie.)"

Mama's eyes glinted. "*Er behandelt uns, wie Diener.*" (He treats us like we are servants.)"

At Anna's puzzled look, Mama stomped her foot and snapped, "*Ich bin kein Diener!* (I am not a servant!)"

The Wrights were a socially prominent family and often entertained other well-connected guests. Mama enjoyed these occasions because it afforded her an opportunity to handle the fine linens and delicate crystal and china that were used on the tables in the formal dining room. Mama and Anna wore stiff white aprons and dainty pleated lace caps pinned to their upswept hair as they carried dish after dish between the kitchen and the dining room. While Mama could not always translate all of the snippets of conversation she overheard, she enjoyed the elegant atmosphere and the perfumed guests. One night, the wine had flowed and the guests had lingered longer than usual at the table. At last, Mr. Wright suggested that they adjourn to the west parlor, and Anna and Mama were finally able to clean up the dining room.

Anna carried a tray of wine goblets into the kitchen while Mama used a wooden-handled brush to whisk the crumbs from the tablecloth into her cupped hand. Muffled laughter and soft notes from the piano wafted in from the parlor at the front of the house. Mama looked up when one of the gentlemen guests returned to the dining room. He had left his monogrammed cigar case on the dining table. As he slipped the slim container into his inner coat pocket, he nodded at Mama and said something in English, which Mama could not translate. She responded with a polite smile and returned to brushing the linen. Suddenly, the man was beside her, with his arms around her waist and his lips brushing the back of her neck. Mama whirled about and smacked the man in the jaw with the back of the wooden-handled brush. He reeled backward and his hand flew to his jaw.

Mama shook the brush at him and scolded, "*Berühren Sie mich nicht! Sie haben kein Recht, mich zu berühren! Ich bin nicht diese Art von Mädchens!* (Don't touch me! You have no right to touch me! I am not that kind of girl!)" Brandishing the brush, she angrily stepped toward the man, who retreated, bumped into the doorway, then fled to the parlor as Mama unleashed a torrent of German invectives.

Hearing the commotion, Anna stepped from the kitchen and watched in horror as Mama chased the man from the dining room.

"*Sophie, ist er ein Gast!* (Sophie, he is a guest!)" she gasped.

"*Gast oder nicht, er hat nicht das Recht, mich zu anzutatschen* (Guest or not, he doesn't have the right to paw at me)," Mama replied angrily and proceeded to tell Anna about the man's transgression. Anna's eyes grew wide and she clasped her hand over her open mouth.

Mama and Anna shared a small room off the third-floor ballroom. On dance evenings, they lay awake and listened to the three-piece orchestra play as the Wrights and their guests waltzed across the ballroom floor. The guests laughed and chatted merrily, and the girls envisioned the fancy ball gowns they could hear swishing across the floor outside their door. The violin music made Mama tap her toes under the covers.

On one such evening, Mama turned to Anna as they lay side-by-side in their narrow bed. "*Warum laden sie uns niemals ein zum Tanzen?* (Why don't they ever invite us to dance?)"

Anna raised herself up on one elbow and looked with astonishment at Mama's profile in the moonlight. "*Verstehst Du Deine Rolle hier nicht, Sophie? Du bist Bediensteter, nicht einer ihrer Gäste.* (Don't you understand your place here, Sophie? You're a servant, not one of their guests.)"

When there was no reply from Mama, Anna plucked at the sleeve of Mama's flannel nightgown and teased, "*Außerdem trägst Du nicht das eleganteste Tanzkleid.* (Besides, you're not wearing the most elegant ball gown.)" Anna collapsed beside Mama and the two young women giggled. Waving their hands above them in the darkness, they pretended to conduct the orchestra or demurely flutter fans before their faces the way the wealthy ingénues did.

After the guests had gone, Anna tugged Mama from the bed and cautiously opened the door from their room to the darkened ballroom. Leading Mama by the hand, she tiptoed out to the center of the ballroom floor. Bowing deeply, Anna whispered "*Darf ich diesen Tanz haben, Fräulein Gasteier?* (May I have this dance, Miss Gasteier?)"

Mama curtsied, holding her flannel nightgown out to the sides, and the two clasped hands for a barefoot waltz across the ballroom floor. Neither girl was an accomplished dancer, and there were plenty of fumbles and stepped-on toes.

Mama whispered, "*Oh, Fräulein Wetzel. Ich trete auf den Boden und Sie können auf meinen Füßen tanzen.* (It's alright, Miss Wetzel. I will walk on the bottom of my feet, and you may walk on the top.)" Anna threw back her head and laughed.

Mama clapped her hand over Anna's mouth and pointed to the

other small bedroom adjoining the back of the ballroom. She whispered, "*Shhh. Du weckst Frau Dowd auf.* (Shhh. You'll wake up Mrs. Dowd.)"

Anna shook off Mama's hand and replied, "*Ach! Sie schnarcht wie ein Bär.* (Oh! She sleeps like a bear.)" Anna made a deep snoring noise. The two young women doubled over with barely contained laughter.

Mama was an early riser, but her first priority of the day was not starting a fire in the cookstove or beginning breakfast preparations. Mama's first obligation was to brush her long chestnut hair. As a young teenager, she had vowed this would be the first ritual of her day, and she had stuck to this commitment. Mrs. Dowd clucked her tongue in disapproval as she passed Mama and Anna's open bedroom door and spied Mama's personal grooming regime each morning.

"That is vanity, just plain vanity," Mrs. Dowd chided as she descended the narrow third-floor stairs.

Mama did not understand Mrs. Dowd's words, but she comprehended the disapproval. She rolled her eyes at Anna, who had hastily braided and pinned her hair in a knot at the back of her head and was now using the button hook to fasten the long row of buttons on her shoes. Mama continued brushing her hair. When she was satisfied with its glossy appearance, she tied it with a broken shoe lace at the nape of her neck and swung the long mane over her shoulder to braid it.

"*Wirklich, Sophie, gibt es wichtigere Sachen als Dein Haar* (Really, Sophie, there are more important things than your hair)," chided Anna.

"*Nichts ist wichtiger als ordentlich und sauber zu sein* (There is nothing more important than being neat and tidy)," Mama responded as she coiled the braid into a bun at the back of her head. She eyed the wisps of hair that had already escaped from Anna's braided knot. "*Ordentlich und sauber, Fräulein* (Neat and tidy, miss)," Mama admonished as Anna wrinkled her nose and dashed down the third-floor steps.

Mr. Wright's daughter Josephine was unexpectedly widowed, and she and her young son Walter moved into the manor house. Little Walter often wandered into the kitchen and sat on a stool, watching Mrs. Dowd, Anna, and Mama bake and prepare meals. He was an inquisitive boy and asked many questions. He quickly comprehended that the language barrier kept Mama from understanding him. One day, as Mama removed a pan of sugar cookies from the cookstove, little Walter pointed at the cookies, then at himself. Raising his eyebrows, he asked, "Cookie?" Mama replied "Cookie" as she tapped her floured finger on his nose and passed him a still-warm cookie.

Mama adored young Walter. Whenever he entered the kitchen, the two would point at each other and simultaneously shout "Cookie!" Mama would then press a cookie into his small hand and pat him on his head as he perched on the stool and ate his treat.

Anna chided her for spoiling Walter, but Mama was unrepentant. She announced that she liked little boys and that someday she would have a son, whom she would name Walter.

"*Du kannst den Namen wählen, aber nicht ob es ein Junge oder ein Mädchen wird* (You can choose the name, but I don't think you can choose whether you have a boy or girl)," responded Anna as she peeled potatoes.

"*Ich möchte einen Jungen* (I will have boys)," insisted Mama, smiling at Walter.

In the late summer of 1887, Mr. Wright gave the staff a weekend off to attend the Huron County Fair in Norwalk. He was exhibiting some of his horses there, and the grooms had trotted the selected show horses to the fair earlier in the week.

Anna and Mama had talked about the fair for days, and on Saturday morning, they took turns pinning up each other's hair, brushing their dresses, and polishing their shoes. The groundskeeper and his wife were also heading to the fair and agreed to take the two young domestics along. Mama and Anna chatted happily as the miles rolled beneath the buggy wheels.

Sophie Gasteier

The two young women strolled the fairgrounds, stopping to pick some wild daisies that grew on a grassy embankment just outside the horse barn. Mama removed her hat and tucked the daisies into her chestnut crown of hair.

Papa had chosen that weekend to also attend the fair. He purchased a paper cup of boiled peanuts and nibbled on them as he ambled through the exhibits. He entered the horse barn and admired the fine stable of horses belonging to Mr. John Wright. In the center of the aisle, he spied his friend Emil Stotz, who worked as a groom for Mr. Wright. Emil was leaning on a pitchfork and chatting with two attractive young ladies. Papa stood and watched. One of the young women had flowers in her hair, and as she talked, she tipped her head to the side in an animated fashion. Soon, the women moved off toward the end of the barn.

Papa strode up the aisle toward Emil. The two men shook hands and slapped each other on the back.

"*Bill, ich habe dich lange nicht gesehen. Wo warst du?* (Bill, it's been a long time since I've seen you. Where've you been?)" asked Emil.

"*Ich war auf dem Mississippi Fluß für einige Jahre* (I was on the Mississippi River for a few years)," Papa replied, keeping his eye on the two young ladies at the end of the barn.

Emil whistled softly. "*Irgendein Abenteuer!* (Some adventure!)"

"*Ja, ja,*" Papa replied absentmindedly. "*Wer ist die junge Dame mit den Blumen in ihrem Haar?* (Who's the young lady with the flowers in her hair?)" Papa asked, pointing with his chin in Mama's direction.

Emil looked toward the end of the barn, then back at Papa with a bemused expression on his face. "*Sophie Gasteier? Sie arbeitet im Haus für Herr Wright.* (Sophie Gasteier? She works in the house for Mr. Wright.)"

"*Stellst du mich ihr vor?* (Will you introduce me to her?)" requested Papa, never taking his eyes off Mama.

Emil chuckled. "*Ja, aber pass auf. Sie ist eine Wildkatze. Ich hörte, daß sie fast einem Mann den Kopf abriss, als er was von ihr wollte.* (Yes, but beware. She's a wildcat. I hear she almost took off a man's head when he got fresh with her.)"

Papa smiled. A girl with spunk. Emil grabbed Papa's elbow and they approached Anna and Mama.

"*Sophie, das ist mein Freund, Bill Seibel, und er möchte das Mädchen mit dem Unkräuter im Haar treffen* (Sophie, this is my friend, Bill Seibel, and he's asked to meet the girl with the weeds in her hair)," Emil teased.

"E-E-Emil!" Papa sputtered in embarrassment.

Mama's blue eyes flashed, and she punched Emil in the arm. "*Ich mag kein Unkräuter in meinem Haar.* (I don't like weeds and I would never put them in my hair.)" She tossed her head as she lightly touched her hair.

Mama turned to Papa and offered her hand. Papa took it, expecting to receive only a light touch of the fingertips, as so many women did. To his surprise, she grasped his hand in a firm handshake while saying, "*Schön sie kennengelernt zu haben, Herr Seibel.* (Pleased to meet you, Mr. Seibel.)"

Cocking her head, Mama looked quizzically at Papa's graying hair beneath the rim of his hat. She furrowed her brow and inquired, "*Wie alt sind sie, Herr Seibel?* (Just how old are you, Mr. Seibel?)"

Taken aback, Papa stammered, "*I-I-Ich bin Sechsundzwanzig.* (I-I-I'm twenty-six)."

"*Er muß nicht mehr geweidet werden!* (He's not ready to be put out to pasture yet!)" hooted Emil.

"*Ach, dachte ich sie wären älter. Ich bin einundzwanzig* (Oh, I thought you might be older. I'm twenty-one)," Mama replied matter-of-factly.

"Sophie!" squealed Anna, gasping in disbelief at her friend's straightforwardness and revelation of her age.

Papa was thoroughly smitten. He could not take his eyes off this attractive young woman. Her fair complexion, clear blue eyes, and chestnut hair were striking, but it was her sass that electrified him. For a woman of that time, her demeanor was slightly bold, which he found disarming and undeniably alluring. Papa was jolted from his trance when he realized that she was speaking to him.

"*Würden Sie mir einige jener Erdnüsse anbieten, Herr Seibel, oder planen Sie sie zu pflanzen?* (Are you going to offer me some of those peanuts, Mr. Seibel, or do you plan to grow them?)" Mama asked coyly, her head tilted to the side and her chin slightly raised.

Papa looked down at the paper cup of peanuts that he still clutched in his hand. He had completely forgotten about them. He hastily thrust the cup toward Mama and watched in horror as some of the peanuts jolted from the cup and rolled down the front of Mama's dress, landing at her feet in the dust of the barn floor.

Mama gazed momentarily at the fallen peanuts, then winked at Papa as she scooped a few peanuts from the cup into her hand. "*Ich denke beides—anbieten und pflanzen.* (I guess you're doing both—offering and planting.)" Her eyes sparkled and Papa laughed nervously.

For the rest of the afternoon, the four young people walked about the fairgrounds. Papa bought Mama a lemonade and told her about some of his adventures on the Mississippi. When it was time for Mama and

Anna to meet the groundskeeper and his wife for the return trip to the Wright estate, Papa asked if he could pay a visit sometime.

Mama cocked her head and stated emphatically, "*Morgen. Zwei Uhr.* (Tomorrow. Two o'clock.)"

Papa was stunned that she had agreed to see him again so soon, but he quickly confirmed the day and time. He watched as the buggy rolled away from the fairgrounds. She was the one.

The next day, Mama and Anna spent an hour arranging Mama's hair, inspecting her best dress for soiled areas or needed repairs, and polishing the dust of the fairgrounds from her shoes. Anna snuck the bottle of vanilla extract from the kitchen, and Mama patted a small amount behind each ear.

Shortly before two o'clock, they climbed the steep stairs behind the orchestral stage in the ballroom until they had reached the top of the tower that crowned the manor house. From there, windows afforded a view in all directions. On a clear day, they could see Lake Erie to the north, the growing town of Bellevue to the west, and a young suitor named Bill arriving from the east.

Papa had hurried through his morning chores and spent the rest of the time curry-combing his horse's coat to a high gleam, polishing his boots, and making sure he had a clean starched collar. Kathrina and Old Man Scheidt had retired from farming and moved into a small house in Monroeville, leaving Papa and his brother George to live together in the homestead house and tend to the two adjoining farms. George was courting Bertha Loew, so he was also busily preparing for an afternoon visit. Papa's rush through chores and his sudden attention to his appearance did not go unnoticed by George.

"*Wo willst du so schnell hin, William?* (Where are you off to in such a hurry, William?)" asked George as he seated himself in a kitchen chair and slid his feet into his boots.

Papa was standing in front of the small shaving mirror on the kitchen wall, his cheek pulled tight as he razored it smooth. "*Ich habe jemand spezielles getroffen* (I've met someone special)," he replied, then flinched as the razor bit a small gash in his chin. "*Ach!*" He charged across the kitchen to retrieve a towel to apply to his chin. His loose suspenders banged against the back of his legs.

George chuckled and continued lacing up his boots. "*Speziell, eh?* (Special, eh?)"

"*Ja. Das ist sie* (Yes. She's the one)," announced Papa from around the towel.

George reeled back in his chair. "*Das ist sie? Wie willst du dsa wissen? Du hast noch keine Frau gehabt, es sei denn auf der Mississippi-Reise, was du uns aber nicht erzählt hast.* (The one!? How do you know? You haven't even looked at any women, unless you were doing something on your trip down the Mississippi that you didn't tell us about.)"

"*Sie ist die Eine. Ich weiß es* (She's the one. I just know)," replied Papa with finality.

George shook his head. "*Daß Flußfieber muß dir was angetan haben.* (That river fever must have done something to you.)"

Because it was not acceptable for an unmarried couple to spend unchaperoned time together, Anna accompanied Papa and Mama on their walk through the apple orchard, the fruit tree grove, and around the pond on the Wright estate that Sunday afternoon. Mama and Anna showed Papa the self-sufficient little community. Papa, with his bent for gadgetry, was in awe.

Soon, Papa became a regular Sunday afternoon caller. Their visits were spent in long walks, with Emil sometimes joining the young couple and Anna. Emil liked to tease, and he knew he could rouse a reaction from Mama with a little needling. One afternoon as they strolled through the apple orchard, Emil broke off a cattail from the nearby ditch and suggested Mama would like to adorn her hair with it. Mama waved him off, but Emil persisted. He broke the cattail in two and blew the feathery contents close to Mama's face. The cattail fluff floated about Mama's head like a cloud, catching on her eyelashes, in her hair, and on the frilly rows of ruching on the front of her dress. Mama clawed at the whispery fluff that adhered to her lips.

Emil doubled over in laughter at Mama's predicament. Then he felt the sting of an apple slamming into the side of his head. He straightened up to see another apple aiming straight toward his chest. Mama was charging toward him, stopping only long enough to pick up more ammunition and discharge it in a wicked overhand throw. She harangued Emil verbally as well.

Papa watched in stunned amazement. Mama reminded him of an angry hornet. Anna turned toward Papa, her eyebrows raised.

Papa shrugged. "*Sie hat Feuer.* (She has spunk.)"

The following spring, Mr. Wright, who had been widowed early in Mama's tenure, decided to remarry. He and his new wife left for a one-year honeymoon trip to Europe. Parts of the manor house were closed off until the newlyweds' return. With less work to be done in the house and no entertaining scheduled for the coming year, Mrs. Dowd informed

Mama that her services were no longer necessary. Mama returned home to Oxford Township.

Papa continued to pay visits every Sunday, depending on the weather. However, by the fall, it was apparent that the long buggy drive to the Gasteier homestead was becoming untenable. In October, Papa's brother George married his sweetheart Bertha, and the three were living together in the Seibel homestead house. Papa felt like an unwanted guest in their home. Finally, Papa spoke what was in his heart. He asked John Frederick Gasteier for his daughter's hand in marriage.

John Frederick & Katherine Gasteier

John Frederick liked the quiet William Seibel, but he silently wondered if this young man—or any man, for that matter—was the match for his daughter Sophie. Either Sophie had kept her temper in check during their courtship, or William was too blinded by love to see the dual nature of his daughter's personality. John Frederick set aside his personal reservations and gave his blessing to the union.

He offered Mama a choice of wedding gifts. He would either pay to have a new coat tailor-made for her, or he would give her and Papa a fine cow. Mama did not hesitate in her selection. She chose the coat.

The wedding was scheduled for Christmas Day, 1888, followed by a brief honeymoon trip to Columbus. Upon their return, it was agreed that the young couple would move into the farmhouse just north of the Seibel homestead, while George and Bertha would remain on the homeplace. Mama had expressed her preference for this larger, newer house and was quite pleased that George and Bertha had agreed to the arrangement.

Wedding picture of William & Sophie Seibel

The 30th of December was warmer than usual, and the sun shone brightly. The day matched Mama and Papa's mood as they chatted happily on their return from the honeymoon trip. Mama smoothed her hand over her new three-quarter length plush wedding coat.

Papa turned the horse and buggy into the drive of their new home. Mama smiled and shielded her eyes against the sun as she admired the house. Her smile vanished and she stiffened when she noticed clothes flapping on the clothesline in the backyard.

"*Warum ist da Wäsche auf der Wäscheleine?* (Why is there laundry on the clothesline?)" she asked warily.

"*Möglicherweise kam Bertha vorbei und hat etwas sauber gemacht für Ihre Ankunft. Das ist nett von ihr?* (Maybe Bertha came over and did some cleaning for your arrival. Wasn't that nice of her?)" Papa assured.

Mama was not so easily dissuaded. These were not linens and towels drying on the line after a good housecleaning. These were men's workshirts and pants.

Mama did not wait for Papa to come around to her side of the buggy and help her alight. She scrambled down and made a beeline for the back porch, where she pounded fiercely on the kitchen door.

Bertha opened the door, and Mama barked, "*Was tun Sie in meinem Haus?* (What are you doing in my house?)" Behind Bertha, Mama could see a checked tablecloth covering the kitchen table, and the smell of baking bread wafted through the open door.

"*Ihr Haus? George und ich leben hier jetzt* (Your house? George and I live here now)," Bertha replied sternly, placing her hands on her hips.

"*Nein! Das ist mein Haus. Es wurde vereinbart. Mein Haus!* (No! This is my house. It was agreed. My house!)" Mama shouted and stamped her foot for emphasis.

By this time, Papa had secured the horse and was nearing the two arguing women. George had also heard the commotion and approached from the tool shed.

Mama looked around in exasperation. She spied a bucket of washwater that Bertha had set by the kitchen door to use in scrubbing the porch floorboards. Mama reared back her leg and gave the bucket a hearty kick. The bucket ricocheted off the porch pillar and rolled back and forth in a narrow arc across the porch floor, sending soapy washwater splashing against the house and running in small rivulets off the side of the porch.

Bertha retreated inside the kitchen door, with just her nose and one eye peering out.

"*Jesus, William! Was hast du nach Hause gebracht?* (Jesus, William! What did you bring home?)" cried George.

Papa rushed toward his angry wife, shouting "*Sophie! Sophie! Anhalte!* (Sophie! Sophie! Stop!)"

Mama could not be stopped. She stormed down the porch steps and pounded toward the clothesline. As she angrily marched along the line, she ripped down the clean laundry and threw it on the ground.

This elicited a cry of outrage from Bertha, who burst from behind the shelter of the kitchen door. "*Meine ganze harte Arbeit!* (All my hard work!)" shrieked Bertha as she ran to collect her laundry from the ground where Mama had tossed it.

Mama steamed out the front yard and turned down the road toward the homestead place. Papa ran a few steps after her, shouting "*Sophie! Sophie! Komm zurück!* (Sophie! Sophie! Come back!)" When she did not heed him, he returned to settle things with George.

"*W-W-Was machst Du und Bertha hier, George? Wir vereinbarten, daß Sophie und ich diesen Platz haben würden* (W-W-What are you and Bertha doing here, George? We agreed that Sophie and I would have this place)," Papa demanded, his face flushed crimson.

"*Alter Mann Scheidt sagte, daß er mir das Haus gibt. Der Bauernhof gehört ihm, weißt Du. Es ist seine Entscheidung* (Old Man Scheidt said he wanted me to have this place. The farm does belong to him, you know. It's his call)," George explained with a shrug.

Papa shook his head in disgust and shoved his hands into his pockets. Old Man, again. He sighed and looked down the road at the small form of Mama about to reach the yard of the homestead. He hastily unhitched the horse and leaped into the buggy. Wheeling the horse around, Papa galloped down the road and into the driveway of the homestead.

Mama was crossing the yard, her back stiff and every stride a purposeful stomp. She pounded up the back porch steps and slammed open the kitchen door.

Papa hitched the horse and hurried across the yard, taking the porch steps two at a time. "*Sophie, hör zu. Ich kann es erklären. Alter Mann Scheidt hat das Ganze verursacht* (Sophie, listen to me. I can explain. Old Man Scheidt caused all of this)," Papa called out.

As he entered the kitchen behind Mama, she stopped and emitted a low guttural scream. "*Sie nahmen alles! Alles! Sogar die Schränke!* (They took everything! Everything! Even the cupboards!)" she wailed.

Papa was aghast. His eyes flashed around the room. It was true; everything of value was gone. They had taken the furniture, the cupboards, and even the shaving mirror from the kitchen wall.

"*Sophie, lass mich erklären. Alter Mann gab George den Bauernhof. Bitte versteh; da konnte ich nichts Machen.* (Sophie, let me explain. Old Man gave the farm to George. Please understand; there was nothing I could do.)" Papa wrapped his arms around Mama to comfort her.

Mama slammed the palms of her hands against Papa's chest and pushed him away from her. "*Nur ein schwacher Mann gibt Land auf ohne einen Kampf* (Only a weak man gives up land without a fight)," she spat at him.

Papa looked for a long moment at his new wife. She held her arms stiff at her side, and her hands were balled into fists. Her blue eyes glared at him with a malevolence he had never seen in anyone before—not even any of the many characters he had met on the Mississippi. He lifted his hands in a helpless gesture, then let them collapse at his side.

Papa turned slowly toward the door, descended the porch steps, and led the horse to the barn. His head hung between his shoulders. He muttered his frustration, gesturing to no one as he spoke. The horse pricked its ears forward and looked at him curiously.

Eventually, Mama calmed down about the unexpected house shuffle, and the young couple settled in. Papa fashioned a few crude pieces of furniture in his workshop on the second story of the cornbarn. He attended local farm auctions, where he picked up an occasional furnishing at a reasonable price.

Mama threw herself into the task of tidying the house by scrubbing walls, floors, windows, and doors. She scolded that the housekeeping had been neglected by Papa's mother, who would readily ignore her housework if a good book was at hand. "*Keine Frau die was auf sich halt würde den Haushalt fürs Lesen lernen vernachlässigen* (No woman of worth would neglect her housekeeping for such foolishness as reading)," Mama chided as she rasped the scrub brush across the kitchen floorboards. Papa looked about the house with pride. Although sparsely furnished, it had never looked better. Together, they were making it their home.

* * * * *

The following spring, Papa was plowing the field closest to the road when Mr. Moss, the neighbor to the south, drove by on his way to Monroeville to buy seeds. Mr. Moss reined his horse and spring wagon to a stop and called out a "halloo" to Papa. The two men chatted over the fence about the weather, the price of seeds, and the likelihood for a good harvest. Tipping his head toward the house, Mr. Moss asked, "Everything alright at your house, Bill?"

Papa was taken aback and turned to look at the house, then at Mr. Moss. "W-w-well, yes. Why do you ask?"

"Well, the other night, me and Emmaline was in town visitin' her folks and playin' cards. I had a pretty hot hand, so we got a later start than usual comin' home. Musta been close to midnight when we come past your place. We could see lantern light comin' from the upstairs windows, and not just the light from one lantern. It had to be every lantern you own was burning up there, Bill."

Papa felt his face flush. He knew exactly what night Mr. Moss was questioning. Three nights ago, Papa had awoken to the sound of a rhythmic thumping and a far-off woman's voice. He lay in the darkness, rubbing his hand over his eyes and trying to discern if he had just awoken from a vivid dream or if he really had heard something. He reached his arm across Mama's side of the bed and found it empty. Alarmed, Papa threw back the covers and bolted from the bed. He stepped quickly from the bedroom, then cocked his head and listened until he determined that the sound was coming from the empty upstairs bedrooms. Papa hurried to the stairwell in the corner of the living room and looked up the stairs. A pool of light bathed the top steps in an amber glow, and he could hear Mama talking to someone up there. Taking the stairs two at a time, Papa burst into the upstairs bedroom.

The room was illuminated in a bright glare from three kerosene lanterns—all they owned—clustered in the center of the floor. Their wicks were fully extended, producing smoke and soot that blackened a spot on the interior of each of the lantern chimneys. Mama was on her hands and knees near the east wall. She dipped her scrub brush into a nearby bucket, then slammed it onto the floorboards as she vigorously scoured the wooden planks. Her nightgown was soaked where it had wicked up the pool of water that she was kneeling in. With each stroke of her arm, the scrub brush rammed into the mopboard, and she chanted "Apple-pie *Auftrag*, apple-pie *Auftrag*."

Papa rushed across the room and grabbed Mama by the elbow, attempting to lift her to her feet. "*Sophie! Sophie! Was ist los?* (Sophie! Sophie! What's the matter?)"

Mama looked up at him with unseeing eyes. "*Ich erklärte bereits, ich kann jetzt nicht jetzt tanzen.* (I told you, I can't dance now.)" She wrested her elbow from his hand and resumed her scrubbing and chattering.

"*W-W-Warum tust Du das?* (W-W-Why are you doing this?)" Papa asked in alarm.

"*Anna hilft mir nicht. Sie ist in der Küche mit Walter* (Anna won't help me. She's in the kitchen with Walter)," Mama replied, continuing to scrub.

"*Anna? Walter? Über was sprecht ihr?* (Anna? Walter? What are you talking about?)" Papa begged.

"Hustle your bustle, *Fräulein!* Apple-pie *Auftrag*, apple-pie *Auftrag*," Mama chanted.

Papa tried again to lift Mama by the elbow. "*Sophie, das kann bis*

Morgen warten. Jetzt komm zurück ins Bett (Sophie, this can wait until morning. Come back to bed now)," he implored.

"*Nein!*" Mama barked, again yanking her arm free of Papa's grip but not stopping her scrubbing long enough to look up at him.

Papa watched Mama for a few moments, and then a smile crossed his face and he chuckled softly. "*Ich weiß, was das Problem ist. Du schlafwandelst! Komm zurück ins Bett, mein Liebes* (I know what the problem is. You're sleepwalking! Now, come back to bed, my dear one)," Papa gently urged, feeling relieved to have arrived at a plausible reason for his wife's strange nocturnal behavior.

Mama stopped scrubbing and sat back on her heels. She scowled up at Papa. "*Ich kann nicht schlafen, William, und gehe von meinem sauberen Fußboden bevor du den ganzen Dreck reinschleppst!* (I am not sleeping, William, and get off my clean floor before you track mud in!)" Mama scolded, motioning with her scrub brush for him to exit.

"*Dreck reinschleppen?* (Track mud in?)" Papa asked in bewilderment as he looked down at his bare feet.

Mama did not answer. She had returned to scrubbing and chattering. "*Können Sie sehen wie es glänzt, Frau Dowd?* (Can you see your reflection now, Mrs. Dowd?)" *Slosh, slam, scrub-thump, scrub-thump, slosh, slam, scrub-thump, scrub-thump.*

Papa stepped back and watched Mama. Her beautiful chestnut hair tumbled around her. The ends of it were wet from dragging through the washwater. A loud *pop!* startled him, and he hurried over to the three lanterns, where one of the chimneys had cracked from the intensely focused heat. Papa dialed down all of the wicks, then sagged against the north wall and ran his hands through his hair. Mama showed no signs of slowing down in her committed task, nor did she seem to acknowledge his presence. He watched for a while longer, then slowly exited the room, walked heavily down the stairs, and returned to his empty bed. For a long time, he lay awake, listening to the thumping of the scrub brush and Mama's distant chatter.

The next day, Mama continued to scrub, and then she slept for the entire following day. This morning, she had awoken, combed her hair as usual, and then sat, dull and lifeless, in the rocking chair in the kitchen. She showed no interest in cooking breakfast and would not speak. Papa was hesitant to leave her, but he had put off plowing for several days so that he could remain in proximity to the house. If he didn't get the field work done, the entire growing season would be in jeopardy.

Papa was embarrassed that a neighbor had noticed something

unusual at his house. He cleared his throat. "It, ah, it was Sophie. She was upstairs cleaning."

"Cleaning!? At midnight?!" exclaimed Mr. Moss. "Why couldn't it wait till morning?"

Papa shrugged and looked toward the house. "She's not feeling well today. Just wants to sit. Guess all that cleaning tuckered her out." Papa shook his head.

"Maybe she needs a spring tonic," suggested Mr. Moss, resting his elbows on his knees. "Emmaline takes a tonic every now and then. Says it lifts her spirits."

"A tonic! Yes, that's it. I-I-I'll get her a tonic the next time I'm at Zipfel's store," replied Papa, brightening.

"Or maybe she's feeling blue about that baby George and Bertha are expecting pretty soon," grinned Mr. Moss. "Bet you could do something to remedy that situation, too." He winked and slapped the reins on the horse's rump as he clattered off toward town.

Chapter 4
The Seibel Homestead
1890

PAPA LEANED against the bedroom door frame, a mug of hot coffee in his hand. He loved this ritual of the early morning, watching Mama comb her long, glossy hair in the glow of the kerosene lamp. From a crib in the corner of the bedroom, baby Ada gurgled and waved her arms and legs. Papa set his coffee mug on top of the bureau and scooped up the baby from her crib.

It was understood that if the baby had been a boy, Mama wanted to name him Walter. However, Papa had assumed that since they'd had a girl, she would be named after Mama's sister Libby, who had been killed in a buggy accident only six weeks before the baby was born. The shrill whistle of a passing steam train had spooked Libby's horse, causing it to bolt wildly. It was felt that the restrictive arm openings in Libby's cape had limited her ability to control the reins, leading to her death. Mama had been deeply affected by this tragic loss, but because it was not considered appropriate for a woman in the late stages of pregnancy to travel or to attend something as emotionally wrenching as a funeral, she had stayed home. Her only request was that she be given the cape that Libby had been wearing when she was killed. John Frederick Gasteier found the demand heartbreakingly strange, but as usual, he acquiesced to his daughter's wishes.

Libby Gasteier

For days, Mama had sat in the rocking chair in the kitchen with the cape cradled in her lap. She ignored Papa's pleas to eat or sleep. Finally, Papa entered the kitchen one day and discovered Mama asleep. When he gently lifted the coat from her lap, Mama's sewing scissors tumbled onto the floor. Mama startled but did not awaken. As Papa folded the coat, he noticed that Mama had used her scissors to cut elongations to both of the restrictive arm slits. Papa gazed for a long moment at the tranquil face of his sleeping wife, then, shaking his head, he tucked the coat under his arm and quietly stepped into the summer kitchen. He wrapped the cape in some old copies of the *Monroeville Spectator*, then carried the small bundle up Stegmiller's stairs and placed it in Mama's trunk. Mama never asked about the coat, nor did Papa mention the alterations she had made.

Papa smiled as he looked into the large solemn eyes of, not Elizabeth Ada or Ada Elizabeth, but baby Ada Emma, born on April 1. Cradling the baby in one arm, Papa used his other hand to flip open the lid of a small box on top of the bureau. He took out a tiny gold band encircled with a raised cloverleaf design and slid the ring onto the baby's finger.

Tossing her long mane over her shoulder, Mama's nimble fingers quickly plaited the hair into a thick braid. "*Ach! Sie verwöhnen bereits jetzt dieses Baby, William* (Ach! You're already spoiling that baby, William)," Mama clucked, but she couldn't suppress her own smile. It was true, the crib and the baby ring had been indulgences on Papa's part, but he was so pleased with the arrival of this brand-new life.

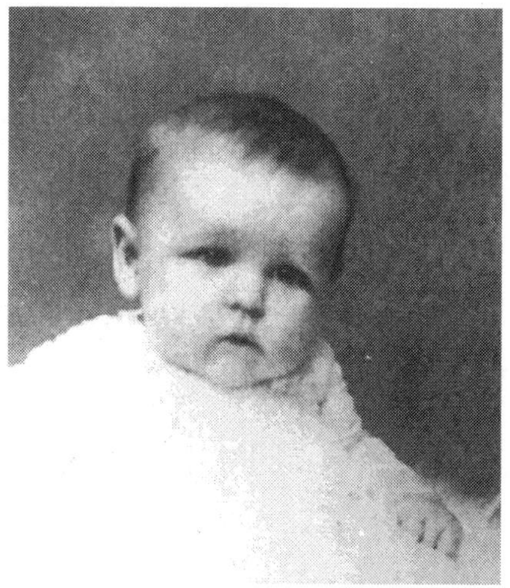

Ada

* * * * *

Papa decided to diversify his crops by planting a variety of fruit trees, which he intended to nurture into a thriving commercial orchard. He knew it would take several years before he saw a return on his investment, but he was certain that the sale of peaches, plums, pears, apples, and cherries would be an asset to his farm income. In order to purchase the nursery stock, he would have to take out a sizeable loan. Mama's younger sister Katie had married into a prominent Monroeville family, and Papa arranged to borrow money from Katie's father-in-law, who made cash loans at six percent interest.

Papa purchased his stock from a commercial nurseryman and spent that spring planting the young trees, some of which were no bigger than a twig. He carefully staked the trees to provide support against the west winds. All summer long, he and Mama carried bucket after bucket of water to the new plantings, tenderly nurturing their investment, while baby Ada waved her little arms and legs from where she lay on a blanket in the shade of the barn. Because Papa was so fond of mulberries, he also purchased some young mulberry saplings to add to the stately old mulberry trees that ringed the house. His next investment was a number of beehives to provide pollination when his trees reached fruit-bearing age.

One summer evening after they had watered the last of the nursery stock, Mama and Papa stood admiring their young orchards. Papa looked toward the barn and made a broad sweeping motion with his hand. "*Eines Tages werde ich 'Seibel Obstgarten' über die Frontseite dieses Stalles malen* (Someday, I will have 'Seibel Orchards' painted across the front of that barn)," he announced.

"*Nein, nein, nein! Es wird 'Seibel und Söhne Obstgarten'* (No, no, no! It will say 'Seibel and Sons Orchards')," corrected Mama, cocking her head as she smiled up at Papa.

"*Ja, 'Seibel und Söhne Obstgarten.' Klingt gut* (Yes, 'Seibel and Sons Orchards.' I like the sound of that)," Papa murmured as he gazed at the blank face of the barn.

* * * * *

That fall and winter, Papa trapped rabbits. While Mama used the meat for stew, Papa tanned the rabbit furs and made little Ada a soft hat. In his workshop above the cornbarn, he crafted a heavy wooden sled that he used to pull Ada on rides over the snow drifts.

George and Bertha's family was growing. In the fall of 1891, their third child in as many years arrived to join little Rosie and Elmer. They named the new baby Walter William. Mama flew into a black rage. It was well known that this was the very name she intended to give to her own son someday. While she would not confront George or Bertha about the purloined name, she berated Papa endlessly. "*Du läßt dir alles stehlen—die Farm, das Haus, und jetzt den Namen von deinem Sohn. Was für ein Kerl bist Du?* (You let them steal from you—the farm, the house, and now the name for your own son. What kind of man are you?)" she thundered as she slammed the cast iron skillet onto the surface of the cookstove.

The loud noise frightened little Ada, who had been playing with a wooden spoon and bowl on the floor. Her eyes grew wide and then filled with tears. The corners of her mouth turned down in a frown as she wailed and toddled toward Mama, arms outstretched.

"*Lass mich in Ruhe!* (Get away from me!)" Mama barked, and she deflected the crying child with a sweep of her arm.

Papa scooped up Ada and carried her outdoors, soothing her with "Shh, shh." He set her down beside the well, and she clung to his pant leg as he pumped cold water into the tin cup that was always hooked over the pump handle. Kneeling next to the sobbing child, Papa held the cup to her lips and encouraged her to sip. Finally, Ada's sobs gave way to hiccups. Rising, he extended one finger to her, which she grasped in her chubby hand. Papa led little Ada on a slow walk down the lane behind the barn. He knew it was best for both of them if Mama had time to cool down.

* * * * *

In May of 1892, baby Ella Katherine arrived. Mama alternated between apology and acceptance that she had not had a boy. Papa responded by building a two-seated tree swing for the girls and bringing home a small black-and-white-spotted puppy from a litter that the owner had placed in a box in the corner of Zipfel's store. A handmade sign saying "Free" had been tacked to the side of the box. They named the puppy "Schwarzweiss," for its black-and-white spots, but shortened the name to "Schwarzie." Papa nailed together a crate for Schwarzie and set it beside the cookstove.

"*Nein! Ich will keinen Hund in meinem Haus* (No! I will not have a dog in my house)," stated Mama emphatically when she entered the kitchen and spotted the crate. "*Besonders nicht in meiner Küche. Schaff ihn rausauf das Portal.* (Especially not in my kitchen. Put that out on the porch.)"

"*Aber Sophie, der Hund muß nachts im Warmen bleiben* (But Sophie, the dog will need to stay warm at night)," protested Papa.

"*Nein!*" repeated Mama, stamping her foot and pointing toward the kitchen door.

Muttering under his breath, Papa picked up the crate and carried it to the porch. Ada followed with the squirming pup in her arms.

Ella & Ada

*****

The winters of the 1890s were exceedingly cold and harsh. The well stalk in the summer kitchen was frozen every morning, forcing Papa to battle the wind and drifting snow to reach the outdoor pump, which inexplicably never froze. Three times a day, Papa carried buckets of water to the house and to the animals in the barn. The full water buckets banged up against his legs as he clambered over the drifted snow, causing cold water to slosh down his legs and into his boots, where it quickly turned to ice. By the time he finished his chores, he could no longer feel his feet.

Papa's peach trees were the first complete casualty of the harsh winters. The cherry, pear, apple, and plum trees suffered partial losses. In addition, the panic of 1893 drove down the market price of most agricultural goods. While unemployment was rampant across the nation, Papa knew that he could at least feed his family as long as he had the farm, but he worried about defaulting on his loan. It was all he could do lately to keep up with the interest payments while making no headway on the principal.

During the winter of 1894-1895, Mr. Moss took advantage of the thick ice on Frink's Run, the Huron River tributary at the south end of Townline Road, to stock his icehouse with huge blocks of ice. Ice cream parties were all the rage in the 1890s, and Emmaline Moss, who liked to be a trendsetter, decided to host a community party featuring the popular treat one warm August evening in 1895.

Papa and Mama and their little family walked down the road to the Mosses'. Mama proudly carried a platter centered with her best white cake. She had spent hours in the kitchen that morning, carefully separating the eggs so that not a drop of yolk would taint the pristine whiteness of the cake. Papa carried the wicker basket that contained their third daughter, Flora Margaret, born early in the bitter cold month of January 1895. Ada and Ella skipped along behind their parents and chased grasshoppers that sprang into the tall grass that lined the dusty road.

Lanterns hanging from trees and situated around the stone patio illuminated the Mosses' backyard. The men and boys took turns cranking the Mosses' brand-new ice cream churn and compared notes on crops and the financial outlook. Heber Grau mentioned that he'd heard of men going to Florida for the winter to earn extra money by harvesting the orange and grapefruit crops. Heber acknowledged that his back was against the wall, financially, and he intended to give it a try this coming winter. Papa was intrigued by the possibility of earning some much-needed money during the slow winter months.

Meanwhile, the women gathered in the kitchen to cut the variety of cakes that had been brought to the party. Mama acknowledged Bertha's presence with a curt nod of the head. Emmaline produced her cake with a great flourish. Mama leaned in for a closer look.

"*Es hat Sauerkraut obendrauf* (It has sauerkraut on top of it)," Mama commented with a puzzled look on her face.

"Oh, you silly Germans think everything is sauerkraut," replied Emmaline, who in actuality was half-German but preferred to identify herself with the English side of her ancestry. "It's the newest thing in baking—it's shredded coconut!"

Mama had to ask Mrs. Ordmann for a translation of Emmaline's comments, and she flushed crimson to her hairline when she understood the put-down.

While they waited for the men to finish cranking the ice cream, Emmaline displayed her brand-new vanity set. "My mother sent all the way to England for it, just in honor of my birthday," she fluttered. Mama was immediately enamored of the set. It was sterling silver and had a low powder receptacle with removable celluloid liner and a soft powder puff, a hair receiver, button hook, fingernail buffer, clothes brush, perfume spritzer, elegant hand mirror with beveled edges, a matching brush and comb, and an engraved tray to hold everything. Mama thought it an injustice that such thin, mousy hair as Emmaline's should be treated to such an expensive and high-quality brush. Imagine the luster that could be produced by such a brush in her own thick hair!

Next, Emmaline had her daughter Edith show the women what had arrived in the England shipment just for her. It was a fancy doll with a bisque head and big blue eyes that closed when the doll was laid on its back. The women oohed and aahed appreciatively, and the little girls looked on in wonderment. Certainly, there was no topping the Mosses when it came to style, although Mrs. Ordmann from across the road did her best to come in a distant second.

After everyone had enjoyed the cake and ice cream, Heber brought out his fiddle and played some selections. He was not an accomplished musician, but toes tapped and couples danced nonetheless. Ada placed her bare feet on top of Papa's shoes and he stepped her around the stone patio, followed by a turn with Ella. The girls laughed and clapped as he took Mama in his arms and swayed side to side.

Papa looked down at Mama's upturned face. Her eyes sparkled as she tipped her head to the side and asked, "*Haben sie eine gute Zeit, Herr Seibel?* (Are you having a good time, Mr. Seibel?)"

"*Bestens, Frau Seibel. Bestens* (The best, Mrs. Seibel. The best)," Papa smiled.

* * * * *

In early December of 1895, after the harvest was in and preparations had been made for the winter ahead, Papa left for the citrus groves of Florida. He had instructed Mama that she was to summon George if she needed help in the coming months. Mama tossed her head at that suggestion. She assured Papa that she and the girls would be just fine, and besides, she would never turn to George and Bertha for help.

Papa met Heber Grau at the end of the road, and the two men cut across the frozen fields toward the rail yard at Chicago Junction. Papa felt a slight sense of exhilaration at this adventure, so reminiscent of leaving home thirteen years ago to head out west. The distinguishing difference, however, was that his financial future depended on the success of this trip. Due to the recent railroad bankruptcies and strikes brought about by the panic of 1893, Papa wasn't sure if it would be as easy to ride the rails as it had been in his previous journeys, but he and Heber had few other options. Neither could afford to pay for transportation, and both desperately needed to earn some money during these winter months.

Mama was now in charge of trips into town to buy necessary supplies and to pick up the mail. Occasionally, there would be a letter from Papa, telling about the balmy weather of Florida and the hard work of picking grapefruits and oranges from the top of a very tall ladder. He related how frugally he and Heber were living, and how they often elected to work seven days a week to make as much money as they could during this short employment opportunity.

One day in late February of 1896, Mama bundled all three girls and tucked them into the buggy for the trip to Zipfel's store. She tied Schwarzie to a rope by the barn. The dog was so devoted to the girls that he would follow the buggy all the way into town if he was not tethered at home. Mama felt on top of the world; ideas raced through her head like shooting stars, and she chattered happily all the way into Monroeville about the items she needed to purchase. First on the list was some fabric to make an extension for the waistband of her skirt, which was growing too tight. She had been using a broken shoe string tied between the top button and the buttonhole to allow some extra room. She hadn't written Papa with the news, but there would be a new baby this summer. She cocked her head to the side and chattered for a few minutes about how nice new wallpaper would look in the kitchen. Yes, she would add wallpaper to her list.

Once in Zipfel's store, Mama was easily distracted by all of the inventory. Mr. Zipfel grew weary from Mama's nonstop chatter. She jumped from one selection to another before finally choosing the wallpaper for the kitchen, some fabric for her skirt extension, and then asked Mr. Zipfel to weigh out a small amount of coffee beans as well as place a sack of chicken mash in the back of the buggy. The girls followed Mama's skirts as she bustled from one side of the store to the other.

Finally, Mr. Zipfel pulled out his big black ledger book and began tallying the amount of the purchases to be charged to Papa's account. As he was ciphering, Mama spotted a silver-plated comb, hairbrush, and hand mirror in the glass-topped display cabinet. She was riveted.

"*Kann ich die sehen? Wieviel kostet das? Sind sie kostspielig?* (Can I see those? How much are they? Are they expensive?)" The questions tumbled out of Mama's mouth in one rapid-fire sentence.

Mr. Zipfel pulled the vanity set from the display case. "*Es ist sieben Dollar für den Satz* (It's seven dollars for the set)," he said wearily, knowing the amount was out of reach of the financially strapped Seibel family.

Mama fingered the set longingly. It wasn't nearly as grand as Emmaline Moss's sterling silver set, but it was better than the comb with the broken teeth and the brush with the bent bristles that Mama was currently using. She held up the hand mirror and looked at her reflection, turning her head from one side to the other. She ran her hand over the soft bristles of the brush, chattering about how much her husband enjoys watching her brush her hair every morning. Mr. Zipfel smiled and raised his eyebrows at this unexpected peek into the intimate life of the Seibels.

"*Ja, ich muß den Satz haben. Fügen Sie ihn unserem Konto hinzu* (Yes, I must have the set. Add it to our account)," Mama instructed.

Mr. Zipfel blinked in surprise. "*Sind Sie sicher, Frau Seibel?* (Are you sure, Mrs. Seibel?)"

The three girls watched transfixed from near Mama's elbow. Ada's nose barely grazed the top of the display cabinet, and she clumsily jostled little Flora from hip to hip. The tips of Ella's fingers grasped the edge of the cabinet as she strained to stand on tiptoes and gaze upon the marvelous vanity set.

"*Kann ich Flora runterlassen, Mutter? Sie wird schwer* (Can I put Flora down now, Mama? She's getting heavy)," begged Ada.

"*Nein! Sie bringt alles durcheinander. Lassen mich einfach meine Transaktion fertig machen* (No! She'll get into everything. Just let me do my transaction)," Mama snapped at Ada. Mama looked about impatiently and spotted the glass candy jar sitting atop the counter. Her hand quickly darted into the jar and withdrew three peppermint sticks.

"*Ja, Herr Zipfel, bin ich. Und fügen Sie das unserem Konto hinzu* (Yes, Mr. Zipfel, I'm sure. And add these to our account)," Mama instructed as she shoved the peppermint sticks toward Ada.

Mr. Zipfel blinked again and ran his finger down the lengthy debit column next to Papa's name. He sighed heavily and penciled in the vanity set and the candies.

Ada passed a peppermint stick to Ella and one to Flora. They popped the treats in their mouths and looked at each other in wide-eyed wonderment. It was fun to shop with Mama!

Mr. Zipfel wrapped the vanity set in brown paper and tied the package with string. He loaded the sack of chicken mash, the wallpaper, material, and package of coffee in the back of the buggy as Mama laid the wrapped vanity set on the seat beside her. The girls clambered into the buggy, and Ada tucked the blankets around them. On the trip home, Mama frequently switched both reins to one hand so she could lovingly pat the vanity set with her free hand. She chattered nonstop about her purchases until the horse turned into the drive of the homestead. Schwarzie barked excitedly and strained at the end of his rope. Ada jumped out of the buggy and untied the dog, which leaped happily to lick at her face.

In the barn, Mama brusquely ordered Ada and Ella to help her lift the heavy sack of chicken mash from the back of the buggy. While the girls fed and watered the horse, Mama removed its harness and hastily curry-combed its sides and back.

"*Füttere die Kühe und die Hühner, und denke daran die Eier einzusammeln* (Feed and water the cows and chickens, and remember to gather the eggs, too)," Mama ordered over her shoulder as she tossed the curry-comb in a box by the barn door and scurried toward the house, clutching her purchases to her chest.

Ella pulled Flora out of the grain box, where she was sifting the oats through her fingers, and held her by the arm as Ada scooped grain into the cows' manger. The two older girls made several trips to the well to pump buckets of water, which they struggled to carry between them to the animals in the barn. Water sloshed over the rim of the bucket and into their shoes. Little Flora toddled after them, stomping her feet in the slushy trail left behind. Schwarzie padded along after the girls, his tail wagging.

Next, they gathered the eggs. There were too many to carry, so they tucked them into their coat pockets. When they were done with the chores, Ada secured the barn door, and the three girls headed for the house, with Schwarzie running ahead to take his usual post just outside the kitchen door.

As the girls climbed the porch steps, little Flora's shoes, which were ice coated on the bottom, slipped on the top step, and she fell, smashing the eggs in her pocket as she tumbled. Blood trickled from the split in Flora's lip, and she wailed in pain and indignation. Ada pulled Flora to a standing position and inspected her lip, then wrapped her arms around the howling child and cooed, "*Sie sind gut, kleines.* (You'll be alright, little one.)"

Ella held the kitchen door as Ada ushered the sobbing child into the kitchen. "*Mutter, Flora fiel und schnitt sich in die Lippe. Sie hat auch Eier in ihren Taschen zermatscht* (Mama, Flora fell and cut her lip. She also has smashed eggs in her pockets)," Ada called.

"*Nimm dir das an* (Take care of it)," Mama ordered from the bedroom.

Ada sat Flora on a kitchen chair, and Ella removed the toddler's wet shoes and placed them beside the cookstove. She retrieved the egg crock from the pantry and added what remained of their egg collection to the bowl. Ada had seen Papa use a crock of snow to plunge his hand into after he'd smashed his finger with the hammer, so she went out in the backyard and filled the kitchen washrag with snow. She instructed little Flora to hold it against her lip. Soon, the child stopped whimpering and Ada was able to remove Flora's coat with the smashed eggs in the pockets. Using the kitchen dishtowel and water from the pail in the drysink, Ada cleaned the broken shells and slimy egg yolks from Flora's coat pockets. She hung the coat to dry behind the cookstove.

"*Mutter, das Feuer im Ofen ist fast aus* (Mama, the fire in the cookstove is almost out)," called Ada.

Mama appeared in the kitchen doorway, her hands on her hips and her long glossy hair flowing down her back.

"*Mutter, Du hast Dein Haar unten und es ist noch nicht Bettzeit* (Mama, you have your hair down, and it's not even bedtime)," observed Ella in awe.

Ignoring the child's comment, Mama stomped across the kitchen floor to the stove. "*Muß ich alles tun?* (Do I have to do everything?)" she barked. She opened the door to the stove's firebox and tossed in a handful of corncobs and some crumpled newspaper. She tapped her foot impatiently as she waited for the fire to catch. Mama started toward the summer kitchen to retrieve the kerosene can when a promising tongue of flame arose from the bottom of the firebox and cast a glow in the dimly lit kitchen. She returned to the stove, added some lengths of oak firewood, and slammed the cast iron door closed.

"*Ich bin hungrig, Mutter. Werden Du Abendessen machen?* (I'm hungry, Mama. Are you going to start supper now?)" asked Ada.

Mama let out a small frustrated grunt. She ducked into the pantry and emerged with the enamel cookie kettle, which she plopped on the kitchen table with such firmness that the kettle lid jumped and rattled. "*Hier, das ist für das Abendessen* (Here, have this for supper)," she commanded as she headed back to her bedroom and the silver-plated vanity set.

Ada removed the lid of the kettle and passed a molasses cookie to Ella and one to Flora before taking one for herself. The girls looked at each other and smiled. Peppermint sticks in the afternoon and molasses cookies for supper—what an unusual day it had been!

A few days later, Mama began wallpapering the kitchen. She cleared the kerosene lamp, spoonholder, salt cellar, small jug of molasses, and the checked tablecloth from the center of the kitchen table and used the flat expanse as a work area for smearing paste on the cut strips of wallpaper. Mama pushed one of the wooden kitchen chairs up against the south wall and, by standing on her tiptoes, was able to just reach the top of the wall where it met the ceiling. She slid a pasted strip of wallpaper into place, then stepped down from the chair to retrieve a rag from the nearby bucket of water. After wringing out the excess water, she climbed back onto the chair and smoothed out any wrinkles or bubbles in the wallpaper. Over and over Mama climbed up and down on the chair until she had finished the south wall by Stegmiller's stairs.

She stepped back to admire her work. Cocking her head to the side, Mama chattered to herself about how pretty the new wallpaper looked and how delighted Papa would be to see the home improvement she had made in his absence. She kneaded her fists into the nagging cramp in her lower back and dragged the kitchen chair over to the west wall.

Across the room, Ada stood on a wooden chair at the drysink and swished the dish rag over the last of the breakfast dishes. For as long as Ada could remember, washing dishes had been part of her daily chores. It wasn't such a bad task, as long as she was careful and did not break anything. Once, an ironstone mug had slipped through her soapy fingers and crashed to the floor. Mama had cuffed her for her carelessness and ordered her to pick up the broken shards. But today, Mama was preoccupied with the wallpapering project, so Ada had time to daydream while she created soapy bubble mounds in the dishwater.

Ella and Flora played on the floor near the cookstove. They had pulled a couple of corncobs from the basketful kept for firestarting and were pretending the cobs were dolls. Ella pranced her corncob character along the rim of the basket, chattering softly as she created a make-believe world. Flora squatted beside Ella, repeating snatches of her sister's dialogue.

Ada had just poked her finger into an especially large soap bubble when she heard a groan behind her. She turned around on the kitchen chair and saw Mama leaning with both forearms against the west wall, her hands wringing the wet rag so tightly that a river of water cascaded down the wall and pooled at her feet. A shudder started in Mama's shoulders and progressed through her body, causing her knees to buckle.

Her elbows slid down the wall, pulling the newly placed strip of wallpaper with them. Mama leaned her forehead against the wall between her arms and groaned again.

Ella and Flora stopped their play and watched as Mama slid into a half-crouch against the wall. The water from the wallpapering rag had mixed with a pool of blood at Mama's feet, and the edge of her skirt was soaked with the dark fluid.

Ada cautiously climbed down from her chair and slowly crossed the room. "*Mama?*" she asked as she approached, "*Ist alles gut?* (Are you alright?)"

Mama did not answer. She remained in a tense ball, leaning against the wall. When the grip of pain had finally passed, she straightened slowly and turned toward the girls. Ada could see that Mama's face was flushed and damp, the way it looked when she made jelly on a hot summer's day.

"*Nein, es ist nicht gut* (No, I'm not alright)," snapped Mama between gritted teeth. She held on to the back of the chair she'd been using for wallpapering and dug her fist into her lower back. Mama swayed momentarily, then staggered toward her bedroom, the wet hem of her skirt leaving a bloody trail behind her. She stopped and looked down at the dark smear on the floor.

"*Ada, mach den Dreck weg* (Ada, clean this mess up)," she said in a wavering voice, then wobbled on toward her bedroom.

Later that afternoon, as Ada was spreading molasses on slabs of bread for Ella and Flora, Mama's thin, weak voice called "Ada! Ada!"

Ada stepped quickly into Mama's bedroom, with Ella and Flora trailing behind her. Mama lay on her back on the bed, her right arm draped across her eyes and her loose hair in a tangle around her head. Her left hand trembled as it pointed toward a small bundle at the foot of the bed.

"*Schafft es in den Garten und begrabt es* (Take that out to the garden and bury it)," Mama whispered.

"*Was ist das?* (What is it?)" asked Ada.

Mama made a small choking sound in her throat.

"*Was ist das?* (What is it?)" Ada asked again.

"*Es ist … mein Junge. Mein Baby Junge* (It's … my boy. My baby boy)," Mama croaked, and her chest heaved with sobs.

Ada looked from Mama to the tiny bundle and back again. "*Ein Baby?* (A baby?)" she asked in disbelief. When Flora was born last winter, Mama's older sister Maggie had come to help with the birth and tend to the household tasks. But none of Mama's sisters were here now, yet a baby had arrived. Ada was perplexed. She asked in astonishment, "*Ein Baby? Du willst dass ich das Baby begrabe?* (A baby? You want me to bury a baby?)"

"*Baby!*" Flora squealed around a mouthful of molasses-covered bread, and she pulled back the blanket that covered the premature infant.

Ada thought the baby resembled the bisque-headed doll that Edith Moss's grandmother had ordered for her from England. The tiny body was covered in wrinkled translucent skin, and his eyes were closed, just the way Edith's doll closed its eyes when laid on its back.

"*Mein Junge. Mein Junge. Mein Seibel und Söhn* (My boy. My boy. My Seibel and son)," Mama continued to whisper. Soon her sobs gave way to wails and she clasped both arms across her chest and rocked from side to side.

Mama's wailing frightened Ella and she stepped back from the bed. Her small brow knit in concern as she watched Mama's hands dig into her scalp and pull at her hair. Spying Mama's dresser set, Ella picked up the silver-plated hairbrush and approached the bed, where she tentatively began brushing the ends of Mama's hair. Mama wiped her hands over her wet cheeks and shuddered as she drew in a deep breath, then turned on her side with her back to the girls.

Ella continued to gingerly brush the ends of Mama's hair as Ada replaced the blanket over the infant. She lifted the tiny bundle from the bed.

Mama raised her head slightly from the pillow. "*Ada, gibt mit meinem Jungen acht* (Ada, be careful with my boy)," she choked out. "*Lassen ihn nicht fallen. Hör mich? Sei gut zu meinem Jungen.* (Don't drop him. Do you hear me? Be good to my boy.)"

Ada nodded solemnly and carried the tiny bundle to the summer kitchen. Ella returned the hairbrush to the dresser and led Flora by the hand to the summer kitchen. Ada pulled their coats from the nails on the wall, and Ella pushed Flora's chubby arms into her coat sleeves, buttoned the front, and pulled a knit hat onto her head.

When the three girls opened the summer kitchen door, Schwarzie greeted them with a wagging tail and quick licks of their faces. He sniffed curiously at the bundle in Ada's arms. Ada brushed him away, and the girls proceeded to the barn to find one of Papa's shovels. Schwarzie grabbed a stick from the yard and bounded after them.

Inside the barn, Ada selected one of Papa's shovels that had a short handle, and Ella dragged it behind her as the girls crossed the yard to the garden. The snow had receded in one corner of the garden, revealing a soft patch of earth. Ada passed the small bundle to Ella, inserted the point of the shovel into the ground, and pushed on the top of the blade with her foot, as she had seen Papa do when he planted potatoes. Schwarzie nosed about the garden and dug randomly in the exposed topsoil.

Ada labored clumsily over her task. Sometimes her foot slipped from the blade and the shovel toppled sideways. Because the ground was still frozen several inches below the surface, she was only able to create a shallow hole. Ella handed the blanket-covered baby to Ada. Mama's words—"*Lass ihn nicht fallen. Sei gut zu meinem Jungen.* (Don't drop him. Be good to my boy.)"—rang in her head, and she clutched the baby to her chest as she carefully dropped to one knee, then the other beside the open hole. She tenderly laid the small bundle in the makeshift grave and began pushing dirt over the blanket. Ella joined her, and Flora grabbed up fistfuls of earth and tossed them about the garden. Schwarzie sniffed inquisitively at the fresh mound as the girls patted the last of the dirt in place.

They returned the shovel to the barn, and Schwarzie trotted after them, once again carrying the stick from the yard. The girls fed and watered the chickens, horses, and cows and gathered the eggs. They returned to the house and added the day's eggs to the egg crock in the pantry.

Ada tiptoed to Mama's bedroom door and peeked in. Mama was lying on her back, staring blankly at the ceiling. Ada approached the bed and stood quietly by Mama's elbow. Finally, Mama's blue eyes rolled toward Ada and she studied her eldest daughter's face for a long moment before asking, "*Was willst du?* (What do you want?)" Mama's words were slow and slurred.

"*Es ist Zeit die Kühe zu melken* (It's time to milk the cows)," Ada advised.

Mama blinked several times and furrowed her brow. "*Wir haben keine Jungen.* (We don't have any boys.)"

"*Was?* (What?)" Ada asked, perplexed by her mother's statement of the obvious.

"*Du mußt es machen* (You'll have to do it)," Mama stated slowly.

Ada was alarmed at Mama's response. "*Aber Mutter, habe ich nie die Kühe vorher gemolken* (But Mama, I've never milked the cows before)," she protested, her heart thumping at the thought of sitting on the little three-legged milking stool beside the massive beasts.

Mama looked puzzled. "*Wir haben keine Jungen* (We don't have any boys)," she slurred with finality. Mama rolled onto her side with her back toward Ada and closed her eyes.

"*W-Was ist mit Abendessen?* (W-What about supper?)" Ada asked tentatively.

There was no response from Mama.

Ada returned to the kitchen and informed Ella that they had to milk the cows. Ella's brow knit. "*Aber Mutter macht es* (But Mama does that)," she protested.

"*Mutter ist zu krank* (Mama's too sick)," Ada explained as she picked up the milk pail from the bench by the kitchen door. Her stomach churned with dread at the thought of the task that lay before them. She waited as Ella retrieved Flora's coat from the kitchen floor where the toddler had shed it and again dressed the child for the outdoors.

Ada swung open the kitchen door, and Schwarzie leaped up to greet them. Ada gasped and recoiled in horror. At the dog's feet lay the unearthed baby boy. No longer bundled by the blanket Mama had wrapped him in, the tiny baby sprawled naked and dirt-smeared on the porch floorboards. Mama's admonishment, "*Sei gut zu meinem Jungen* (Be good to my boy)," rang in Ada's head. She dropped the milk pail, which clattered down the porch steps, and her hands flew to her open mouth. She backed away from the scene.

Hearing the banging of the milk pail, Ella peered around Ada's rigid body in the doorway. When she spotted the baby lying at Schwarzie's feet, Ella began to scream.

Ada whirled around and clapped her hand over Ella's mouth. "*Shh! Shh! Weck Sie Mutter nicht auf!* (Shh! Shh! Don't wake up Mama!)" Ada cautioned, her eyes wide with thoughts of the punishment she'd receive if Ella's screams brought Mama to the porch and the scene of the unburied baby.

"*Baby!*" squealed Flora, and she tried to squirm past her sisters toward the infant on the porch.

Ada pushed Ella and Flora back into the kitchen and quickly shut the door behind her. Her heart was racing and she felt as breathless as if she had just run the entire length of their farm lane, from the ridge at the back of the farm all the way up to the barn. Tears were close behind her eyelids as she squeezed her eyes shut and tried to think of what to do.

When she opened her eyes, Ella's upturned face was in front of hers. "*Wir müssen das Baby wieder begraben?* (We have to bury the baby again, don't we?)" Ella asked quietly, her lower lip trembling.

Ada nodded. "*Und wir müssen Schwarzie anbinden, sonst gräbt er das Baby wieder raus.* (And we have to tie up Schwarzie so he won't dig up the baby again.)"

Ada quickly wiped at her eyes with her coat sleeve. She opened the *Mehlfach* and pulled out some old issues of the *Monroeville Spectator* that were saved for fire-starting needs. Swallowing deeply, she opened the kitchen door and stepped out onto the porch. Ella cautiously followed, holding little Flora by the arm.

Ada placed the newspapers beside the still form of the baby and slapped her hand against her leg, the sign for Schwarzie to follow, as she descended the porch steps. Schwarzie eagerly tagged along, but his tail stopped wagging and his trot slowed when he realized that Ada was walking him toward the rope tether by the barn. He tucked his tail between his back legs and slunk low to the ground. Ada cajoled and scolded and finally managed to secure Schwarzie to the rope. The dog immediately began to whimper and bark.

Ada returned to the porch and spread several newspapers on the floorboards, then carefully placed the baby on them. "*Sei gut zu meinem Jungen* (Be good to my boy)" pounded through her head as she hastily wrapped the baby. Her tongue felt glued to the roof of her mouth. A sudden *thump* startled her and she froze in place as her eyes darted upward to the kitchen door, expecting to see Mama's angry face. But the door remained closed. It was only Flora, who, in swinging around Schwarzie's stick, had struck the side of the house. Ada's hands trembled as she returned to her task.

Once again, the small burial crew rounded the corner of the house and entered the garden. They lowered the tiny bundle into the shallow grave for the second time and scooped the dirt that Schwarzie had scattered back into a mound. The sun was sinking as they patted the last of the earth onto the grave and returned to the house.

In the aftermath of the baby's reburial, all thoughts of milking the cows had vanished. The milk pail lay on its side at the bottom of the porch steps through the night.

Early the next morning, George stood on his back porch and cocked his head. The sound of cows bellowing in distress reached his ear, and a dog barked and howled in the distance. The noise was coming from his brother William's farm to the south. George resolved to investigate the source of the commotion after he finished his own morning chores.

Ada had tossed and turned all night, listening to the bellowing of the cows and Schwarzie's mournful howling. She arose early, dressed, and looked in on Mama. In the early morning darkness, it was hard to tell if

Mama was asleep or lying in mute silence. Usually, Mama was up and bustling about the kitchen by the time Ada came downstairs. In Papa's absence, Mama would start the fire in the cookstove, set the coffeepot on, and head out to the barn to do the morning chores. By the time the girls were up, the kitchen was filled with the brisk aroma of coffee, and Mama would return with pails of warm milk, which she used to make their porridge. Sometimes she'd fry some slices of scrapple or heat up the fried potatoes left over from the previous night's supper and stir in an egg or two.

Ada's stomach growled at the thought of breakfast foods. The slabs of bread spread with molasses that she and her sisters had eaten as their dinner and supper the day before had not been adequately filling. Ada gazed at the outline of Mama's still form on the bed and wished that she'd get up, wished that she'd fix breakfast, wished that today would be the way every day had been … up until yesterday.

Ella padded up behind Ada, followed by Flora, who was rubbing her eyes and whimpering for food.

"*Ich bin auch hungrig* (I'm hungry too)," whispered Ella, her fists digging into her stomach. "*Was gibts zum Frühstück?* (What's for breakfast?)"

Ada entered the kitchen and lit the kerosene lamp. She carried it into the pantry to survey their breakfast options. Ella and Flora followed. The cookie kettle was now empty. Two loaves of bread, wrapped in linen cloths, sat on the carving board, but the thought of another molasses sandwich was unappealing. Ada spotted the egg crock. Mama had shown her how to stir the eggs in the fry pan until they set up into a soft, scrambled form. Ada was confident she could make scrambled eggs for breakfast, if she could get the fire in the cookstove started.

Ella and Flora retrieved old newspapers from the *Mehlfach* and sat on the kitchen floor as they crumpled them into balls. Flora did more shredding than crumpling, but they soon had a small mountain of fire-starting material. Ada created a teepee of corncobs in the belly of the stove and stuffed it with newspaper shreds and balls, as she had seen Mama do. Ella and Flora huddled close to Ada's shoulder as she struck the wooden match, but before she could move it toward the newspaper, Flora puckered her lips together and blew, extinguishing the small flame.

"Flora!" both older girls exclaimed in exasperation. Flora's chin dropped to her chest.

Ella pulled Flora back from the cookstove, and Ada struck another match. She held it to the corner of the paper, and the blaze glowed brightly for a moment, then winked out. Ada sighed. She struck another match and touched it to the edge of the paper, then to another edge and another until the paper was consumed. Patiently, Ada coaxed the flame, adding more newspaper balls and corncobs until a promising fire had started. Soon, she was able to add kindling, followed by lengths of oak from the firewood box. She closed the door on the firebox and retrieved the heavy cast iron skillet. Ada pushed one of the kitchen chairs up to the cookstove and climbed onto it. Ella carried the lard crock from the pantry, and Ada spooned a generous amount of lard into the black fry pan. The girls watched as the white dollop slowly melted and slipped across the bottom of the pan.

Ada selected three eggs from the egg crock and cracked them smartly on the edge of the skillet, just as she'd seen Mama do. A portion of the first egg skidded down the outside edge of the skillet and sizzled on the hot cookstove surface. Fragments of the eggshells were swept into the skillet with the eggs. Ada reached in to retrieve the bits of shells but burned her finger on the hot pan. She decided to leave the eggshells. Ada directed Ella to fill the teakettle and set it on the cookstove so there would be hot water to wash the breakfast dishes.

When the eggs had reached a soft, fluffy consistency, Ada jumped down from the chair and retrieved a plate from the pantry. She scooped the eggs onto the plate and handed Ella and Flora spoons. The three girls gathered around the single plate at the kitchen table and shared their breakfast. Flora looked puzzled when she crunched the eggshells in a mouthful of soft scrambled eggs. While they ate, Ada listened to the bellowing of the cows and knew that she would have to attempt milking them this morning. Her stomach churned at the thought.

After breakfast, Ella took Flora upstairs to dress her, and Ada pushed the kitchen chair over to the drysink. She scooped some softsoap into the wash basin and added hot water from the teakettle. If there was one chore she knew how to do—with or without Mama—it was washing dishes.

As she rinsed the last of the breakfast dishes, Schwarzie's barking reached a crescendo. Ada peered out the kitchen window and saw George open the barn door and disappear inside. Hopping down from the chair, she ran to Mama's room and stood beside the bed. Mama was lying on her side, facing Ada but staring at the window across the room.

"*Mutter, Onkel George ist hier* (Mama, Uncle George is here)," Ada whispered.

When Mama did not respond, Ada repeated her statement, this time a little louder. Mama blinked but did not acknowledge her daughter.

Ada turned to leave but Mama's hand shot out and caught her arm. Ada jumped and emitted a startled cry.

"*Sag ihm nichts von meinem Jungen. Hören Du? Halt den Mund* (Don't tell him about my boy. Do you hear? Hold your mouth)," Mama admonished, her eyes boring into Ada's.

Ada swallowed and nodded her head. Mama released Ada's arm, and she sped out of the room.

George picked up the milking pail at the bottom of the porch steps and turned to look at the barking dog tethered to the corner of the barn. He did not relish the thought of dealing with Sophie, but the engorged condition of the cows indicated that something was amiss in his brother's absence. He climbed the porch steps and knocked on the kitchen door.

Ada opened the door and looked up at him with her large solemn eyes. Ella and Flora stood by the living room doorway. Beside them, a strip of puckered wallpaper sagged from the wall. The girls were dressed, but none of them had had their hair brushed. Balls of crumpled newspaper lay on the floor in front of the cookstove. Although George did not interact much with Sophie, he knew she was a stickler for neatness. Something wasn't right.

"*Wo ist deine Mutter?* (Where's your Mama?)" George asked.

"*Sie ist krank* (She's sick)," responded Ada.

"*Wie lange ist sie schon krank?* (How long has she been sick?)" George inquired.

"*Seit gestern* (Since yesterday)," Ada replied, afraid that she had already revealed more than Mama would like.

"*Zu krank die Kühe zu melken?* (Too sick to milk the cows?)" George asked.

Ada nodded slowly, unsure of her ability to lie to Uncle George if his inquiry became much more pointed.

"*Und wann wurden sie gemolken?* (And when were they milked?)" George probed.

"*Gestern früh. Aber ich wollte sie heute morgen melken* (Yesterday morning. But I was going to milk them this morning)," Ada replied earnestly.

George let out a long, slow breath and muttered "*Ach!*" as he ran his hand over the stubble on his chin. He knew that in their present agitated condition, the cows likely would have injured or killed the little girl if she had attempted to milk them.

George tipped his head toward Schwarzie. "*Warum ist der Hund oben angebunden?* (Why's your dog tied up?)"

Ada shifted uneasily from foot to foot and looked over her shoulder toward the doorway to Mama's bedroom. "*E-Er war böse* (H-He's been bad)," she offered.

George sighed again and shook his head. "*Wo ist der Rest von den Milcheimern?* (Where's the rest of your milk pails?)"

Ada led him to the summer kitchen and gave him the remaining buckets.

"*Ich melke die Kühe bis sich Mutter wieder gut fühlt, aber ihr must euch um den Rest des Viehs kümmern* (I'll milk the cows until your Mama is well again, but you girls will need to take care of the rest of the livestock)," George stated.

Ada nodded and watched as George descended the porch steps and crossed the yard toward the barn. She slipped her coat from the nail on the wall and went outside to feed and water the chickens, horses, and Schwarzie and to bring in an armful of wood for the cookstove.

Inside the barn, George led a bawling cow into an empty horse stall. He snubbed the cow to a barn beam and tied a rope tightly around the cow's middle, just in front of her udder, to discourage kicking. The cow rolled her big brown eyes and edged away as George pulled the three-legged stool close to her side. He set the milk pail under her udder and grabbed a teat in each hand. The cow bellowed and heaved her bulk against him. George toppled backward off the stool, his own boot upsetting the milk pail.

"*Jesus!*" muttered George as he righted himself and retrieved the bucket. "*Verfluchter Dummkopf William, läßt Frau und drei kleine Mädchen allein und gehst zur Orangenernte.* (Damn fool William, leaving that woman and three little girls to go off and pick oranges.)"

By the time George was done milking the balky cows, he had worked himself into a sweat. His only consolation was that the evening milking would be easier. He latched the barn door behind him and looked at the barking dog tethered at the other end of the barn. "*Dieser Hund muß etwas wirklich schlechtes gemacht haben wenn er Tag und Nacht angebunden ist* (That dog must have done something pretty bad to be tied up day and night)," George thought to himself as he grasped the handles on the full milk pails and headed toward the back porch.

* * * * *

The harsh winters of the 1890s had affected the citrus crops in Florida. Heber and Papa had expected to work until almost April, but the harvest was over in early March. It was time to head home. Their earnings for the winter's work were not as large as they had hoped, due to the shortened season, but Papa felt that at least he would be able to make a good-faith payment toward the principal of his loan instead of only meeting the monthly interest. The two men hopped a slow-moving northbound train, and Papa thought about Mama and the girls as he dangled his legs from the open boxcar doorway.

By the time they reached Chicago Junction, Papa was so filled with anticipation at seeing his little family that he would have run the fifteen miles to Monroeville if he could. Instead, he and Heber were slowed by having to stick to the roads rather than cut across the muddy, thawing fields. They walked along briskly, each anxious to return to the embrace of their respective families.

At the intersection of Townline and Everingen Roads, Heber and Papa shook hands and parted company, with Heber heading due east to his home on Everingen and Papa turning north on Townline. Papa's pace quickened into a trot, and he strained for the first sight of home. Over his panting breath, he could hear the sound of a dog howling in the distance.

When Papa neared home, he realized the howling was coming from his own place. Crossing the yard toward the back porch, he was puzzled to see Schwarzie tied to the corner of the barn. Perhaps Sophie and the girls had gone into town and had tethered the dog to keep it from following the wagon. Schwarzie's howls turned into staccato barks and yips as Papa took the porch steps in two long strides.

Flora was standing by the living room doorway, absentmindedly picking at the puckered strip of wallpaper that drooped from the wall. Ada and Ella were in the pantry, skimming the cream from the two pails of milk that Uncle George had left outside the kitchen door that morning.

When Papa burst through the kitchen door, Flora screamed at the sight of this unfamiliar man and ran toward the security of her sisters in the pantry. Ada poked her head around the pantry doorway to see what had frightened Flora.

"Papa!" Ada shouted and ran toward him, with Ella close behind. Papa knelt down and wrapped an arm around each of the two older girls. Flora peeked from around the pantry doorway, but quickly disappeared when Papa beckoned to her.

Papa reached into his coat pockets and pulled out four plump oranges. He handed one to Ada and one to Ella.

"*Was ist das?* (What's this?)" Ada asked, turning the bright orange orb over in her hands.

"*Eine Orange. Iss* (It's an orange. You eat it)," explained Papa.

Ella bit into her orange as if it were an apple. Her eyes immediately squeezed shut, her face wrinkled, and she shuddered at the bitter taste.

Papa chuckled, "*Nein, nein, nein. So.* (No, no, no. Like this)." He dug his fingernail into the orange rind and pulled away the peel, revealing the flesh inside. Separating the segments, he gave a piece to Ella and one to Ada. Their eyes widened at the first taste of the juicy, sweet fruit. He held out a piece to Flora, who was again peering around the corner of the pantry doorway. As soon as they made eye contact, she ducked back into the pantry. Papa grinned and shook his head.

Papa's smile began to fade as he noticed the unkempt condition of the girls. Their hair was uncombed, their faces and hands looked unwashed, and their clothing was soiled. Papa looked over at the half-finished wallpaper project and the drooping strip of wrinkled wallpaper.

"*Wo ist Mutter?* (Where's Mama?)" Papa asked cautiously as he straightened to a standing position.

Ada stopped in mid-chew and looked up at Papa for a long moment. "*Mutter ist krank gewesen* (Mama's been sick)," she replied softly.

"*Krank? Was meinst du?* (Sick? What do you mean?)" Papa asked apprehensively.

Ada searched Papa's face for clues as to how she should proceed. Mama's warning of "Hold your mouth" was firmly implanted in her brain. Finally, she swallowed and said, "*Mutter hatte ein Baby, aber es starb, und sie bat mich es im Garten zu begraben.* (Mama had a baby, but it died, and she told me to bury it in the garden.)"

"*Ein Baby?* (A baby?)" Papa asked in bewilderment.

Ella nodded and added, "*Und Schwarzie grub es aus und legte es auf die Veranda und wir mußten es wieder begraben.* (And Schwarzie dug it up and brought it up onto the back porch and we had to bury it again.)" Her chin began to tremble at the memory of the traumatic event.

"*Mein Gott!* (My God!)" Papa gasped.

Ada grabbed Papa's coat sleeve. "*Sags Mutter nicht. Bitte?* (Don't tell Mama. Please?)" she asked beseechingly. "*Sie bat mich gut zu ihrem Junge zu sein.* (She told me to be good to her boy.)"

"*Ein Junge?!* (A boy?!)" Papa exclaimed, then exhaled slowly. He tilted his chin toward the ceiling and closed his eyes. The story the girls had told him was almost more than he could absorb. After a long moment he looked at the upturned faces of the girls and asked, "*Ist das warum Schwarzie oben angebunden ist?* (Is that why Schwarzie's tied up?)"

Both girls nodded.

"*Und wer hat sich um dich gekümmert?* (And who's been taking care of you?)" he asked.

Ada and Ella looked at each other. Ada shrugged and replied, "*Wir kümmern uns um selbst.* (We take care of ourselves.)"

"*Und der Hof? Wer hat die Arbeit gemacht?* (And the chores? Who's been doing the chores?)" Papa inquired.

"*Onkel George melkt die Kühe, und Ella und ich tun den Rest* (Uncle George milks the cows, and Ella and I do the rest)," Ada replied matter-of-factly.

Papa rubbed his hand over his eyes and then over the stubble on his chin and neck. He felt a mixture of pride in the resiliency of his young daughters, and deep regret at what they had experienced in his absence. And then there was the matter of Mama and the long-awaited baby boy.

Papa placed the two remaining oranges on the kitchen table and walked slowly toward the bedroom.

Mama was out of bed, rummaging through the dresser drawers. Papa stood for a moment in the bedroom doorway, watching her.

"Sophie," he said softly and held his arms out to her.

When she heard Papa's voice, Mama turned and rushed toward him. "*William, helf mir meinen Jungen zu suchen. Wo ist er, William? Wo ist mein Junge?* (William, help me search for my boy. Where did they put him, William? Where did they put my boy?")

Papa's arms dropped to his side as Mama crossed the room and began clawing at the bedcovers. She pulled the quilt and sheets onto the floor, then stopped abruptly and turned to Papa. "*Hat Libby ihn? Ist er bei Libby?* (Did Libby take him? Is he with Libby now?)" she asked, perplexed.

Papa swallowed and nodded his head as he crossed the room toward her. "*Ja, Sophie. Er ist bei Libby. Shhh, shhh* (Yes, Sophie. He's with Libby now. Shhh, shhh)," he soothed as he put his arms around her.

"*Aber ich habe ihr nicht gesagt, daß sie meinen Jungen nehmen könnte! Dieses ist wie, als sie meine besten Strümpfe nahm, ohne zu fragen. Ich will meinen Jungen zurück!* (But I didn't tell her she could take my boy! This is just like the time she took my best stockings without asking. I want my boy back!)" Mama shouted and stamped her foot for emphasis.

She squirmed loose from Papa's embrace and began pacing back and forth, kneading her hands into her hairline and complaining between gritted teeth, "*Dieser Hund! Dieser Hund! Ich kann das Gebelle nicht aushalten! Jemand muß ihn stoppen!* (That dog! That dog! I cannot stand the sound of that barking dog. Someone make it stop!)"

Papa watched helplessly as Mama chattered on, protesting the barking dog and Libby's acquisition of the baby boy. He picked up the strewn bedcovers from the floor and pushed the open dresser drawers back into place. As he did so, he spotted the silver-plated vanity set lying atop the dresser. Papa's brow furrowed. "*Woher kommt das?* (Where did this come from?)" he asked, picking up the handmirror and turning toward Mama.

Mama stopped pacing and rushed to the dresser. She picked up the hairbrush and clutched it to her breast. "*Libby kriegt es nicht. Es ist meins. Ich kaufte es von Herr Zipfel.* (Libby can't have this. It's mine. I bought it from Mr. Zipfel.)"

"*G-G-Gekauft? Mit welchem Geld? Mit Kredit? Dieses und die Tapete, nicht Du?* (B-B-Bought it? With what money? You placed it on credit, didn't you? This and the wallpaper, didn't you?)" Papa asked, his voice rising and his face flushing.

Mama made no response and resumed her pacing, continuing to clutch the hairbrush to her chest.

"*Wieviel kostete es?* (How much did it cost?)" he demanded.

"*Sieben Dollar, zehn Dollar. Ich weiß nicht. Er macht nichts* (Seven dollars, ten dollars. I don't know. It doesn't matter)," Mama muttered as she waved one hand in the air. "*Libby sollte ihn genommen haben, ohne zu fragen mich.* (Libby shouldn't have taken him without asking me.)"

"*Es habe eine Woche gearbeitet für dieses Geld, und du gibst es für … für das aus?* (It took me over a week to earn that much money, and you spent it on … on this?)" Papa thundered. "*Das Geld war für die Rückszahlung des Bauernhof Kredis, und nicht für dieses Zeug!* (The money I earned was to repay the farm debt, not to buy pretties!)" Papa slammed the handmirror onto the dresser top.

The sound of the mirror smacking the dresser surface jolted Mama from her pacing and chattering. She whirled and glared at Papa, shouting, "*Wenn Du mich nicht verlassen hättest, würde ich meinen Jungen noch haben!* (If you hadn't left me, I'd still have my boy!)"

Papa threw his hands up in the air in exasperation and wheeled toward the door.

"*Du hast ihn! Du hast meinen Jungen!* (You took him! You took my boy!)" Mama screamed. Cocking back her arm, she hurtled the hairbrush at Papa's back. It barely missed the heads of the three little girls huddled by the door. The hairbrush bounced off the doorframe, leaving a small gouge in the woodwork.

For the rest of the night, Mama paced, complaining about the barking dog, ransacking the house for the lost baby, and occasionally howling in her grief and confusion.

*****

When the ground thawed that spring, Papa privately reburied the premature baby boy in the family cemetery across the road from George and Bertha's house. At last, Schwarzie was released from his tether by the barn. However, the months of confinement had altered the farm dog's nature. He was now prone to fits of barking and long nights of lonesome howling.

Mama's nature had changed too. Following the death of the baby boy, she was more easily agitated. She flinched each time the kitchen door slammed or a piece of cutlery rattled into the wash basin in the drysink. She lashed out at each minor agitation, and the girls quickly learned to avoid her. Mama began having more frequent spells, too, beginning with a buildup in irritation and exploding into incessant talking and her own strange yells and howls as she wandered about the house. Yet she found Schwarzie's barking and howling unbearable. Before long, she demanded that Papa get rid of the dog.

To soothe his wife's jangled nerves, Papa acquiesced. He found a farmer south of Monroeville who was willing to take the dog. On the day of Schwarzie's scheduled departure, Papa called the girls together near the spring wagon in the yard and told them that Schwarzie's howling upset Mama, so the dog was going to a new home. The girls cried out in protest and outrage.

"*Aber Papa, Mutter heult auch. Warum kann sie bleiben und Schwarzie nicht?* (But Papa, Mama howls too. Why can she stay and Schwarzie can't?)" Ada asked in bewilderment.

Papa merely shook his head in response. He watched sadly as the girls wrapped their arms around Schwarzie's neck and buried their faces in his black-and-white fur. They caressed his ears and stroked his back, their tears spilling onto his coat. Schwarzie responded by licking their faces and nuzzling his nose into their hands.

Papa climbed into the wagon and patted the wagon bench, and Schwarzie leaped aboard, his tail wagging at this rare invitation. Papa slapped the reins on the horse's rump, and the wagon rattled down the driveway.

The girls sobbed and raised their small hands to wave goodbye to their beloved dog.

Chapter 5
The Seibel Homestead
1896

IN THE SUMMER OF 1896, Papa noticed a new schoolhouse being built on the Plank Road about a mile northeast from home. He monitored the progress of its construction when he traveled to Monroeville, and he made up his mind that it was time for Ada to start her formal education.

When he mentioned his plans to Mama, she protested that she needed Ada's help at home, and besides, Ada could learn everything she needed to know working side-by-side with her in the kitchen. Mama firmly believed that an education did not increase a woman's worth. Indeed, a woman whose nose was firmly planted in a book was obviously neglecting her housework. Mama never failed to point out to Papa that his own mother indulged in too much reading and not enough scrubbing.

Papa quietly held to his resolve. After breakfast one September morning, while Mama was seated at the kitchen table braiding Ella's hair for the day, Papa disappeared into the pantry. There, he removed the linen wrapping from one of the loaves of bread that sat on the carving board. He sliced off two thick slabs, spread one with butter, then topped it with the other slab of bread and cut the sandwich down the middle. Papa carefully lifted the lid from the cookie kettle and slipped his hand in to retrieve a molasses cookie. The lid rattled slightly as he replaced it.

Mama heard the sound of the lid settling into place on the enamel cookie kettle. She scolded from the kitchen, "*William, was willst du schon an der Keksdose? Du hattest gerade Frühstück*. (William, it's very early to be getting into the cookie kettle. You just finished breakfast.")

"*Ja, Sophie* (Yes, Sophie)," Papa replied. Placing the butter sandwich and molasses cookie on the bread cloth, he tied up the corners into a neat package.

Ada was standing on a wooden chair at the drysink, washing the breakfast dishes, when Papa swooped her from the chair with one arm and set her on the floor.

"*He Ada. Es ist Zeit für die Schule* (Come on, Ada. It's time for school)," Papa announced as he strode toward the back door with Ada's wet hand in his.

Bewildered, Ada looked over her shoulder at Mama, Ella, and Flora as she was propelled toward the door.

Mama leaped from her seat at the kitchen table, shoving Ella aside in her haste to reach the back door.

Papa and Ada were halfway to the spring wagon when Mama slammed open the kitchen door. "*William, hör mir zu! Sie braucht keine Schule. Ich benötige sie hier, mir zu helfen, Trauben zu gelieren. William, es gibt viel Arbeit hier!* (William, listen to me! She doesn't need school. I need her here to help me make grape jelly today. William, there's work to be done!)

Papa set the cloth-wrapped lunch on the wagon bench and motioned for Ada to clamber in. He climbed onto the wagon bench beside her and slapped the reins on the horse's rump. The wagon lurched forward, causing Ada to grab onto the wagon seat to avoid tumbling backward. She looked over her shoulder at Mama, who was standing on the porch with her fists nested on her hips and an angry scowl clouding her face.

Mama stamped her foot as the wagon turned onto the road, then she threw open the door and stormed into the kitchen. Ella and Flora stood rooted beside the kitchen table and stared wide-eyed at Mama's angry face. Mama's eyes flashed as she surveyed the kitchen, then pointed at Ella and barked, "*Mach deine Schürze ran und mach das Geschirr.* (Get your apron on and finish those dishes.)"

Mama sat down in the kitchen chair where she had previously been braiding Ella's hair. She whirled Flora around and clamped her between her knees, then started to vigorously brush Flora's hair. Flora winced as the brush banged the sides of her head and tugged through the tangles in her hair. Mama's strong fingers rapidly plaited Flora's hair, and the little girl blinked back tears at the rough hairdressing.

"*He komm. Da ist Arbeit zu tun* (Come along. There's work to be done)," Mama commanded as she grabbed a pan and knife and headed out the kitchen door toward the grape arbor.

As the horse trotted north on Townline Road, Ada wiped her wet hands and forearms on her skirt and looked up at Papa's profile. "*Warum konnten Ella und Flora nicht auch kommen?* (Why couldn't Ella and Flora come too?)" she asked in bewilderment.

Papa continued to stare straight ahead and didn't answer. Ada looked over her shoulder one more time at the receding sight of home.

At a curve in the Plank Road, Papa guided the horse into the yard in front of the schoolhouse. Children chased after each other in the schoolyard, while small knots of older students clustered by the fence that separated the schoolyard from a shallow creek at the back of the property.

As Papa climbed down from the spring wagon, Miss Dunn, the schoolteacher, stepped out from one of the two front doors of the schoolhouse. She carried a large schoolbell in her hand and waved it in an arc over her head. At the sound of the bell, the children scrambled to form two lines, the boys tumbling and jostling in a ragged line in front of the east door, and the girls ordering themselves before the west door. Ada watched in amazement; she had never seen so many children in one place.

Papa nodded his head to the schoolteacher and said, "*Guten Morgen. Ich bin Herr Seibel, und das ist mein Tochter Ada.* (Good morning. I'm Mr. Seibel, and this is my daughter Ada.)" Papa offered Ada his hand to help her dismount from the wagon.

Miss Dunn shook her head slightly. "I … I don't speak German," she said as she shrugged her shoulders.

Papa's brow furrowed as he switched from his native tongue to English, "But this is a German community. Most of the children around here speak only German."

Miss Dunn repeated her plea, "But I speak only English."

Papa turned to Ada. "*Du kannst ein wenig Englisch, Ada?* (Do you know any English, Ada?)" he asked.

Ada looked from Papa's face to Miss Dunn's. She knew only two English phrases, so she repeated them in the same brusque command that Mama always used: "Apple-pie order! Hustle your bustle!"

"Oh my!" exclaimed Miss Dunn, as her hand flew to her throat.

Papa's face flushed crimson, and he stammered, "Uh … her M-M-Mama likes things neat and tidy."

"Indeed!" exclaimed Miss Dunn as she blinked rapidly. "Well, come along, Ada," she said as she motioned Ada to join the girls' line. "We'll teach you some other English words that will be … um … more appropriate."

Papa grabbed Ada's shoulder as she took her place at the end of the girls' line. "*Geh nach Hause mit Rosie und Elmer* (Walk home with Rosie and Elmer)," he instructed, pointing toward Ada's cousins. He pushed the cloth-wrapped lunch parcel into her hands.

Ada nodded and watched as Papa climbed into the spring wagon and guided the horse onto the Plank Road. Papa didn't turn the horse toward home, but headed in the direction of Monroeville. He'd decided to take the long way home to allow Mama some time to cool off. Ada watched Papa and the wagon grow smaller and smaller as they headed eastward. She looked down at the familiar red-and-white check of the bread cloth in her hands and thought of Mama, Ella, and Flora. She held the package to her nose. It carried the aroma of yeast bread and the softsoap Mama used to wash clothes. It smelled like home. Tears welled in Ada's eyes and spilled down her cheeks. When she noticed some of the other children staring at her, she ducked her head and quickly wiped her eyes with the back of her hand.

Miss Dunn stood on the stone step between the two lines of children. She opened the cover on a small gold watch that hung by a thin chain from an ornate bar pinned to her blouse. After checking the time, she clicked the cover closed. Ada was mesmerized by the tiny watch. Mama didn't wear jewelry, except for a plain gold circle that she pinned to the neck of her dress on Sundays or special occasions. And neither Mama nor Papa used a watch; they told time by the sun or their own internal senses. Miss Dunn also wore her hair piled high on her head in a soft, billowing arrangement. This wasn't at all like Mama, either, who kept her hair knotted in a tidy bun at the nape of her neck.

Miss Dunn motioned the children to enter the one-room schoolhouse. Ada followed the girls ahead of her and placed her lunch packet on the shelf beside round agateware or tin lunch pails, rectangular cardboard boxes, and other cloth-wrapped parcels. Below the shelf was a row of nails for winter coats and scarves.

The one-room schoolhouse was divided by a low partition, with the boys remaining on the east side and the girls on the west. Children scrambled into their assigned seats, and Miss Dunn guided Ada to an empty seat toward the front of the room.

Miss Dunn stepped up onto the platform at the front of the room and set the black-handled school bell on the corner of her desk. She turned toward the American flag that hung from a wooden standard in the corner of the room. The children rose, placed their right hands across their hearts, and recited something in English that Ada could not understand. She stood and mimicked their posture, then returned to her seat when the others did. The students then folded their hands in their laps, bowed their heads, and recited what Ada assumed was a prayer. She bowed her head and clasped her hands, watching out of the corner of her eye for the next cue.

When the prayer was concluded, Miss Dunn pulled a small round object from her pocket, held it to her lips, and blew into it. A thin note filled the room, and Ada's eyes opened wide. She had heard Heber Grau play his fiddle, and of course there was the reed organ at church, but she had never witnessed someone playing a musical instrument with their mouth! Miss Dunn hummed the note, then began waving her right hand from side to side as the students sang. Ada sat and listened to the strange words of the song. She looked across the room at cousin Elmer in the boys' section. Elmer was the same age as she, so he was also seated toward the front of the room. Elmer was singing along and certainly gave every appearance that he had command of the English words. Ada knew that Uncle George and Aunt Bertha spoke German at home. So, how did Elmer know English? Maybe Rosie, who attended school last year, had taught him.

When the students finished singing, Miss Dunn slipped the pitchpipe back into her pocket and chose two of the older boys, who rose from their seats with smiles on their faces. They were proud to have been selected to carry the common water bucket, which was kept in the boys' entryway, to the neighbor's well. There, they would pump the day's supply of fresh water. Once a week, the neighbor's wife would be asked to wash the bucket. An agateware cup hung from a nail above the water bucket and was used by all the students and the teacher. On occasion, the boys remembered to carry along the cup and ask for it to be washed as well. Ada watched the two boys through the window as they sauntered toward the neighbor's house, swinging the bucket on a stout stick between them.

Ada gazed about the unfamiliar room. It smelled of new lumber and whitewash. A large coal-burning stove stood in the center of the room. Ada's eyes followed its stovepipe as it rose straight toward the roof, then bent and ran suspended along the ceiling until it joined the chimney behind Miss Dunn's desk. A slateboard stretched across the wall. Above it, pictures of brightly colored birds, animals, and flowers marched around the perimeter of the room. Ada studied each one. Other than the family Bible, there were no books at home, and certainly no colored pictures.

Ada heard the jingle of a harness, the rattle of wagon wheels, and the steady clip-clop of a horse approaching on the road in front of the school. She hoped that it was Papa returning to take her home. She listened for the school door to open and the sound of Papa's footsteps striding up the aisle. But the clatter of the wagon wheels and the drumming of the horse's hooves receded into the distance. No one came for her. She thought of Mama, Ella, and Flora and what they were doing at home. Tears welled in her eyes.

Ada's reverie was broken by the sound of Miss Dunn calling her name. The teacher was motioning Ada to a spot next to cousin Elmer on the recitation bench in front of her desk. Ada slid from her desk and took a seat next to Elmer, who held a small slate on his knees. The teacher pointed to some letters on a flipchart, and Elmer dutifully repeated the letter aloud, then copied its form on his slate. When the teacher approved his efforts, he leaned forward, spit on the center of the slate, and used his shirtsleeve to wipe away his markings before proceeding to the next letter. At Miss Dunn's urging, Ada repeated the strange-sounding letters, but she did not have a slate to practice writing them.

Before long, Miss Dunn dismissed the two small students, and Ada watched from her seat as older students took their places on the recitation bench and read aloud from a book. When Miss Dunn tapped the reader on the shoulder, the student passed the book to his neighbor on the bench, and that child read until Miss Dunn repeated the shoulder tap. Other students stood in front of the large slateboard on the wall and copied down numbers that Miss Dunn called out, and later, some pupils stood in a row before Miss Dunn and recited in unison as she clapped a steady rhythm with her hands.

For the rest of the morning, Ada watched and imitated the others, but most of all she kept her eyes on Miss Dunn's beautiful gold watch. When the teacher slipped open the watch cover to check the time, Ada listened for the soft snick of the hasp as the case closed. Just when Ada's tummy started to rumble and her thoughts turned to the contents of her cloth-wrapped lunch packet, Miss Dunn checked her watch. She clasped her hands before her, bowed her head, and led the children in a prayer. Ada offered her own silent prayer of thanks in German that apparently it was time to eat.

The children rose and filed through their separate entryways, grabbing their lunch containers before scattering in the schoolyard. The boys raced to the back of the property, climbed over the fence, and gobbled their lunches on the banks of the little creek. Some used a bent pin on a stick to fish for bullhead, and others used a long, sturdy tree branch to catapult themselves from one bank to the other. An occasional splash and laughter marked the unsuccessful attempts.

The girls gathered in clusters under a tree or along the shady side of the schoolhouse. Ada sat down next to her cousin Rosie and opened the cloth-wrapped parcel Papa had handed her that morning. The sight of the molasses cookie caused her throat to swell with longing for home, and she blinked back tears. She took a bite of her butter sandwich and struggled to swallow around the lump in her throat. The other girls chattered in a combination of English and German. Ada could understand snippets of the conversation, and occasionally Rosie spoke to her in very welcome German. Ada noticed that Mary Della Fox, who spoke only English, also had a butter sandwich, but it was cut into two triangles, unlike the two rectangles of Ada's sandwich. Ada was impressed by this novel sandwich shape and wanted to ask Mary Della if her sandwich tasted better when it was cut that way, but she didn't know the English words to use.

After lunch, Ada whispered in Rosie's ear, and Rosie led her behind the school to the girls' outhouse on the west side of the property. Rosie pointed out that there were two outhouses, but the other one was for the boys, and she wrinkled her nose in disgust. Afterward, they stopped at the water bucket in the boys' entryway. Rosie removed the agateware cup from its nail, plunged it deep into the bucket, and took a long drink before passing the cup to Ada. They joined the other girls who were playing "Pump-Pump-Pullaway" in the schoolyard. Miss Dunn and the older girls ambled along the edge of the grounds, picking purple gentians and Queen Anne's lace, which they fashioned into nosegays.

Miss Dunn checked her watch and returned to the schoolhouse. She reappeared on the stone steps and again swung the schoolbell in a wide arc over the soft billow of her hair. The scene of the morning was repeated, with the boys and girls ordering themselves into two separate rows. Ada gave a small sigh and took her place in line. She had hoped the school day was over. As she mounted the stone steps, she turned and looked east and west along the Plank Road. She longed for Papa to come and take her home, but the road was empty. She filed through the girls entryway, placed the folded red-and-white checked bread cloth on the lunch shelf, and returned to her seat.

The afternoon seemed interminably long to Ada. There were more sessions on the recitation bench with Elmer, and the two took a turn at the large slateboard on the wall, with Ada imitating the numbers that Elmer painstakingly formed. She watched and listened as the others recited their school work or sang songs in a language she did not understand.

Late in the afternoon, Miss Dunn opened the cover on her beautiful gold watch, nodded as she closed it, and then selected a book from the small upright assortment on her desk. She walked up and down the aisles of the school, reading aloud and holding the book out to show the children the illustrations. The pictures were interesting, but Ada could not understand a word of the story. The day had been long, and the sing-song cadence of Miss Dunn's voice made her sleepy. She longed to lay down on the soft bed she shared with Ella, cover herself with the patchwork quilt that Grandma Gasteier had made, and drift into a contented slumber.

A sudden flurry in the classroom startled Ada from her drowsiness, and she realized that the students were exiting. The school day was over at last. Ada slid from her seat and hurried out the door to find Rosie and Elmer.

"*Papa bat mich, mit dir nach Hause zu gehen* (Papa told me to walk home with you)," Ada told them.

"*Kennst du den Weg?* (Don't you know the way?)" asked Elmer. "*Es ist einfach. Ich zeigs dir.* (It's easy. Come on, I'll show you.)" He self-importantly skipped ahead of Rosie and Ada.

The three children walked west a short distance on the Plank Road, descended the embankment by the bridge, and followed the creek south. Elmer pointed to a shallow pool where minnows darted about. He pulled his bent-pin fishhook from the waistband of his trousers and pressed its point into a stick. The three children squatted beside the creek while Elmer tried unsuccessfully to hook a fish. Finally, he abandoned the fishing pole, and they attempted to scoop up the minnows with their cupped hands. When the children grew tired of this game, they gathered small pebbles and tossed them into the water, seeing who could create the highest splash.

Elmer led them along the footpath beside the creek, showing Ada where it was necessary to jump from stone to stone in the water to avoid the thorny hedges that grew down to the water's edge and obstructed the path. Grasshoppers sprang out of the tall grass ahead of them, and the children ran after them, laughing and shouting if they caught one.

At one point, Elmer whirled around in the path and put his finger to his lips. "*Es gibt eine Waldmurmeltierbau da vorn* (There's a woodchuck hole up ahead)," he whispered. Elmer crouched low and stealthily moved forward. Ada and Rosie copied his movements. They peered over the embankment toward Uncle George's hay field and the mound of dirt that marked the entrance to the woodchuck's den. The rodent was nibbling the grass at the fenceline. From time to time, it sat up on its haunches and swiveled its head about, surveying the area for possible threats.

Elmer looked at the girls and smiled mischievously. Suddenly, he popped up over the embankment, shouting and waving his arms wildly over his head. The woodchuck scrambled for its hole, and the girls laughed at the sight of its short tail raised in alarm.

The children crossed the stile that Uncle George had built over the fence at the edge of his field, then followed the lane until it joined the open farmyard behind Uncle George and Aunt Bertha's house. The back door of the house flew open, and Rosie and Elmer's younger brother Walter raced down the porch steps and across the yard to meet them.

"*Bis morgen* (See you tomorrow)," Rosie waved goodbye as she neared the porch.

"*Morgen? Du meinst wir gehen wieder zusammen?* (Tomorrow? You mean we go to school again tomorrow?)" asked Ada, crestfallen at the news.

"*Ja, warum nicht? Wir gehen jeden Tag außer Samstag und Sonntag* (Yes, don't you know? We go every day but Saturday and Sunday)," replied Rosie, climbing the porch steps.

"*Aber nicht an den Tagen wenn das Wetter schlecht ist. Oder wenn Ma oder Pa uns benötigen, hier zu Hause zu arbeiten* (But not on days when the weather is bad. Or when Ma or Pa need us to work here at home)," clarified Elmer.

Arbeit (Work)! The word jolted through Ada's brain and made her think of Mama. She remembered Mama's angry objection when Papa spirited her away to school that morning: "*Es gibt Arbeit zu tun!* (There's work to be done!)" Ada bolted for home. She sped down the driveway, turned onto the road, and ran as fast as her legs could pump. She crossed the yard and could smell the aroma of cooking grapes before she reached the back porch steps.

Ada threw open the summer kitchen door and saw Mama, Ella, and Flora gathered around the work table in the center of the room. The door slammed behind her, and she caught her breath as Mama flinched. Mama was ladling the last of the hot grape jelly into glass preserve jars. She looked up from her work and scowled. Mama's face was hot and flushed, and tendrils of loose hair were trapped in the perspiration along her forehead. It reminded Ada of how Mama had looked the day she was wallpapering and the premature baby boy was born. Ada swallowed hard.

Ella and Flora stood on wooden boxes beside the table. Flora dropped the cloth she was using to wipe the jelly jar rims and jumped down from her box. She ran to Ada and threw her arms around her sister. Ella smiled at Ada and continued to place the glass tops on the jelly jars and secure them with the wire bails.

Mama lifted the cloth bag of cooked grapes from the sieve. She dipped a pan beneath the bag to catch any drips and brushed past Ada and Flora on her way out the summer kitchen door. "*Mach deine Schürze ran. Es gibt viel Arbeit* (Get your apron on. There's plenty of work to be done)," she snapped.

Ada retrieved her apron and pushed a wooden box next to the table across from Ella. She picked up a cloth towel and began wiping the rims of filled jelly jars. Ella peered at Ada from under her eyelashes and said quietly, "*Du warst lange weg. Ich habe dich vermißt.* (You were gone a long time. I missed you.)"

"*Ich vermißte dich auch. Und Flora* (I missed you too. And Flora)," responded Ada. Then she began telling Ella and Flora all about the new experiences she had had that day at school.

Mama returned in time to overhear Ada's glowing description of Miss Dunn's beautiful gold watch and her billowing hair. "*Dummheit und Eitelkeit. Das ist alles was du von ihr lernen kannst* (Foolishness and vanity. That's all you'll learn from her)," chided Mama. "*Jetzt mach den Tisch, Ella.* (Now, set the table, Ella.)"

Ella hopped down from the work table and went into the kitchen. At each place setting, she laid the cutlery in an "X," then inverted the plate over it. She finished by setting an ironstone mug at each of the girls' places, and an ironstone cup and saucer at Mama and Papa's places. At mealtimes, Mama and Papa drank their coffee the German way—by pouring some into their saucer and sipping it as it cooled.

Mama emerged from the pantry with the carving board and the partial loaf of bread that Papa had uncovered that morning while making Ada's lunch. "*Wo ist das Brot Tuch, Ada?* (Where is the bread cloth, Ada?)" Mama asked.

Ada froze as she placed a half-filled jar of grape jelly on the kitchen table. In her haste to catch up to Rosie and Elmer after school, she had forgotten to retrieve the red-and-white checked bread cloth from the shelf where the lunch containers were kept. Her throat constricted and she looked up at Mama. "*Ich vergaß es* (I forgot it)," she offered meekly.

"*Du hast es vergessen?* (You forgot it?)" growled Mama. She slammed the carving board down on the kitchen table with such force that the partial loaf of bread bounced from the board, rolled, and fell off the table edge at Ada's feet.

Mama grabbed Ada's arm and gave her a hard shake. "*Wie kannst du sowas vergessen? Wie kannst du?* (How can you forget such a thing? Tell me! How can you?)"

Ada had no defense. She looked up at Mama's angry face with wide eyes. Ella, who was witnessing the exchange from the opposite side of the table, backed away. She bumped into Flora, grabbed the younger child's hand in her own, and the two clambered up Stegmiller's stairs to sit on the top step, away from Mama.

"*Du bekommst kein neues Tuch bevor du nicht das alte heimgebracht hast. Verstehst du, du sorgloses Kind?* (You won't get another cloth until you bring that one home! Do you hear me, you careless child?)" barked Mama, giving Ada another shake.

Ada nodded quickly.

"*Heb das Brot auf* (Pick up that bread)," Mama commanded as she crossed the room and began stirring the sliced potatoes in the frying pan on the stove.

That night over a supper of fried potatoes, cottage cheese, tomato slices, and still-warm grape jelly on bread, Mama berated Papa for Ada's attendance at school. She scolded that he had deprived her of her best helper just when it was time for making sauerkraut, apple butter, and molasses as well as cracking walnuts and hickory nuts out of their shells.

Papa waved his fork at Ella and Flora seated across the table from him and said, "*Aber die zwei hast du noch.* (But you still have those two.)"

"*Ach! Sie sind keine Hilfe!* (Ach! They're no help!)" Mama scoffed.

Ella cast her eyes downward at Mama's assessment.

"*Sophie, ich habe niemand der mir bei der Arbeit hilft* (Sophie, I don't have anyone to help me with my work, either)," Papa pointed out as he spread grape jelly on a slice of bread.

Mama leaned forward in her chair and hissed, "*Das ist weil wir keine Söhne haben!* (That's because we don't have any sons!)"

After supper, while Ada washed the dishes, she watched through the window as Papa walked out to the barn to finish his chores. He shook his head vigorously, shrugged his shoulders, and at times raised his hands in the air in a gesture of frustration. It was obvious he was still carrying on the argument, and maybe this time he would win it.

As Elmer had stated, the children did not attend school when the weather was bad. On those days, after Ada, Ella, and Flora had finished their chores, they scurried up Stegmiller's stairs and played school. Ada had found some large pieces of river slate behind the barn, and she carried them upstairs to be used in their make-believe schoolhouse. She had also fashioned a pretend gold watch out of a button suspended from a string, which she pinned to the front of her dress. From time to time, she checked it, just as Miss Dunn did.

One afternoon, Mama called the girls to come downstairs and help her in the kitchen. Ada scurried down the steps, forgetting to unpin the button watch and leave it on top of the trunk in their playroom. Mama spotted the button dangling from its string on the front of Ada's dress.

"*Was ist das?* (What is this?)" she frowned as she poked a finger at

Ada's chest.

Ada looked down at her dress. "*Es ist eine Uhr, wie sie Fräulein Dunn trägt* (It's a watch, like the one Miss Dunn wears)," replied Ada.

"*Ach! Dummheit und Eitelkeit! Das alles was du lernst. Dummheit und Eitelkeit!* (Ach! Foolishness and vanity! That's all you're learning. Foolishness and vanity!)" scolded Mama, and she held out her open hand, gesturing for the button watch to be placed in her palm.

Ada reluctantly unpinned the pretend watch while Mama thrust her open hand impatiently in front of Ada's chest. Mama snatched the button and string from Ada's fingers and returned it to her sewing box.

As time went on, Ada began to understand more and more of the English spoken at school. Some of the words found their way into her everyday conversation at home. Ella and Flora soon picked up the English words that Ada carried home, and before long, their German was peppered with English. Papa easily flowed back and forth between German and English, but Mama resisted, even though her two favorite commands were the English "Apple-pie order!" and "Hustle your bustle!"

That December, Papa stopped at Zipfel's store and selected a school slate with a curved-cornered wooden border as well as a slate marker. This would be Ada's Christmas gift. No longer would she have to use a piece of river slate and the stub that Elmer had broken off of his marker and given to her. For Ella, he selected a child-sized teacup decorated with a pink rose, and for Flora there was a small cloth doll with yarn hair. He watched solemnly as Mr. Zipfel added the purchases to the long debit column next to his name in the ledger book.

Just before Christmas, Mama received word that her old friend Anna Wetzel, whom she had worked with as a domestic at the home of John Wright, would be coming for a visit. Anna had "married up," wedding a "Yankee" businessman by the name of Alan Birdsey and moving to the Toledo area. Mama flew into action. She kept Ada home from school to help her scrub the already tidy house from top to bottom. On the day before their visit, Mama baked and frosted a cake, then topped it with shredded coconut. She still thought the coconut resembled sauerkraut, but if Emmaline Moss was baking with coconut, then it must be the latest culinary technique, and Mama wanted to impress Anna.

Before Anna, Alan, and their two small boys arrived, Mama put on her best dress and a long white apron of lawn worked with dainty stitches and drawn threads. She piled her hair in a loose arrangement on the top of her head. Her final preparation was to admonish the girls that they were to be seen but not heard.

When the Birdseys arrived, Mama greeted Anna in German but was surprised when Anna responded in English. Anna explained that Alan did not speak German, and thus she rarely spoke in her native dialect. In fact, her two boys, Arthur and Ellis, knew only a few words in German. Papa, Alan, and Anna conversed freely in English, with Mama able to understand snippets of the conversation. Anna recognized Mama's lag in comprehension and switched over to German as they reminisced about their days as domestics at the Wright home.

"*Kämmst du dir immer noch als erstes die Haare jeden Morgen?* (Do you still comb your hair the first thing every morning?)" Anna asked with a grin.

Mama touched her hair proudly and responded that she did. Papa smiled from his rocking chair across the room. He watched as the auburn highlights in her chestnut hair danced with each nod of her head.

Mama was transfixed by Anna's two little boys. She bounced Ellis on her knee and patted his blond curls.

"*Nein 'Walter' nicht für dich, eh?* (No 'Walter' yet for you, eh?)," Anna asked as she fawned over the girls.

Mama's face clouded as she tersely replied that the name Walter was no longer available. "*Aber ich will einen Sohn!* (But I will have a son!)" she said emphatically, and she continued stroking Ellis' hair.

"*Du bist so glücklich, Töchter zu haben* (You are so fortunate to have daughters)," commented Anna. "*Sie müssen solch eine Hilfe für dich sein.* (They must be such a help to you.)"

"*Mädchen sind für das Kochen und den Haushalt gut* (Girls are good for cooking and cleaning)," sighed Mama, "*Aber Jungen ... Jungen sind ein Gold-Schatz.* (But boys ... boys are a treasure like gold.)" She looked wistfully at young Arthur, who was building a tower out of wooden blocks on the floor with Ada, Ella, and Flora.

When it was time to serve refreshments, the girls couldn't help but notice that Mama gave bigger slices of cake to Arthur and Ellis than to them.

After the Birdseys' visit, Mama made two resolutions: she would learn English, and she would have a son.

* * * * *

On a cool October morning in 1897, Mama gave birth to her fourth daughter, Hermine Christine. The baby favored the Gasteiers in her looks, with a dark complexion, black hair, and clear blue eyes. Mama wept bitter tears that she had been denied a boy once again.

Chapter 6
The Seibel Homestead
1898

PAPA BACKED UP JIB to the cutter in the cornbarn. His fingers were numb with the cold, and he worked slowly to fasten the harness. Jib shook his shaggy head and snorted, his breath hanging in frosty clouds in the frigid January air.

When Papa finished securing the traces, he stomped his feet to restore circulation to his toes, then led Jib and the sleigh across the farmyard toward the house.

Papa slipped his gloved hand inside one coat pocket and felt the slim fold of money. On today's trip into Monroeville, he would stop at Mr. Scheid's house to make a payment on the loan he had taken out eight years ago to buy the nursery stock. Mr. Scheid was "relation"—his daughter-in-law Katie was Mama's younger sister—but despite those family ties, there was no forgiving of debts, even when farm prices were low and the best Papa could do was to cover the monthly interest.

The warmth of the kitchen was inviting. Papa stood close by the cookstove, flexing his outstretched hands. He lifted the coffee kettle from the back of the stove and tipped its spout to his lips for a long drink of the hot liquid, then wiped his coat sleeve across his wet moustache.

Mama bustled about the kitchen, chattering happily as she stacked a pile of folded quilts on the kitchen table and directed the girls to don their winter coats, hats, scarves, and mittens. She wrapped baby Hermine in several blankets, placed her in the wicker carrier, and covered the infant with another blanket, tucking the edges securely under the basket's rim.

Mama pulled a heated soapstone from the interior of the cookstove and wrapped it in an old copy of the *Monroeville Spectator*, then did the same with two flatirons that were heating on the top of the stove.

Ada, Ella, and Flora clambered into the back seat of the cutter, and Papa placed the baby's basket on top of the soapstone at their feet. He covered the four children with layers of quilts, and the girls giggled as they nestled down inside their dark cave. Mama and Papa each had a heated flatiron for their feet, and they shared the thick woolen laprobe.

Mama felt on top of the world. While Papa conducted business with Mr. Scheid, she and the girls were going to Zipfel's store to buy fabric. Hilde Bekker, a young unmarried woman who worked as an itinerant seamstress, was coming to their house. She would stay for about a week, sewing the needed garments for the family, then move on to the Mosses' and the Ordmanns', where she would perform the same service.

Mama felt she had scored a neighborhood coup by making arrangements for Hilde to come to the Seibel house first. In the usual pecking order on Townline Road, the Mosses and the Ordmanns took precedence in everything, but this time, Mama had managed to maneuver the Seibel family to the head of the line.

Not only was Mama pleased about her small victory, but she was also looking forward to having the companionship of another woman in the house. Hilde spent time in all the area homes, and if plied with enough gingersnaps and sweetened tea, she'd gladly share gossip, observations, and news from throughout the neighborhood.

The horse-drawn cutter flew across the icy roads, and soon Papa had delivered Mama and the girls to Mr. Zipfel's store. He slowed Jib to a walk on the way to Mr. Scheid's house. Papa drew a deep breath and rapped at the Scheids' back door.

Mr. Scheid sat close by the fire in his parlor and tapped his pipe against the chimney bricks as Papa counted out a slim stack of money onto the chair-side table. Papa stepped back and waited nervously for Mr. Scheid to acknowledge his payment.

Tamping a fresh wad of tobacco into his pipe, Mr. Scheid eyed the money and then looked up at Papa. "Not a good year, Bill?"

Papa swallowed hard and shook his head. "Crop prices been down a while," he offered as his meager defense.

Mr. Scheid struck a match and held it to the bowl of his pipe, then drew deeply and puffed a blue cloud of smoke into the air between him and Papa. "And more mouths to feed, I hear. What'd you have—another girl?"

Papa nodded. "*Ja.*"

Mr. Scheid slowly tapped the stack of bills with his index finger, then leaned back in his chair and studied Papa. "Girls ain't gonna get you outta debt, Bill."

Papa shifted his weight uneasily.

At Zipfel's store, Mama circled the long wooden table stacked with bolts of cotton, linen, and wool textiles, carefully selecting fabric for the work clothes, undergarments, and nightshirts that Hilde would sew for the family.

Ada sat on the floor next to the woodstove, bouncing the wicker baby basket on her knees. Ella and Flora trailed Mama around the table, occasionally ducking under the table's edge when Mama shot them a disapproving look for fingering the bolts of cloth.

Mama chattered to no one in particular as she pondered a thick wool for a new coat for Ada, whose arms were quickly outgrowing her present garment. Mama stopped in mid-sentence when she spied the remains of a bolt of plaid taffeta.

The sudden halt in Mama's conversation caught Mr. Zipfel's attention from behind the counter, where he leaned on his elbows, balancing his ledger book. He glanced over the rim of his glasses and noticed Mama fingering the fine taffeta fabric.

"You have *ein gutes Auge* (a good eye) for *feinen Stoff* (fine fabric), Mrs. Seibel. Just like Mrs. Gilman, Mrs. Bessel, and Mrs. Daniels," he complimented unctuously, linking Mama's taste to that of the women from Monroeville's leading families. "Those ladies had the Weber girls make them *Abendkleider* (fancy dresses) from that *Stoff* (fabric)," he stated as he jabbed his pencil in the direction of the bolt.

"*Die Weber Mädchen* (The Weber girls)," Mama whispered to herself as she stroked the taffeta. Even though the Weber sisters were middle-aged spinsters, they were known throughout Monroeville as the Weber "girls," the best seamstresses in town. Mama had employed them several years ago to remake her bridal coat to fit her postpartum shape, a task that she did not trust to Hilde, whose sewing skills were adequate for common workshirts and housedresses.

Mama's mind raced. The cost of the cloth was outside her budget, but the better families in Monroeville were wearing it—why shouldn't the Seibels have the best as well? After all, hadn't Mr. Zipfel commented on her ability to recognize fine fabric? There was not enough of the taffeta to make a skirt for herself, but she calculated that two children's dresses could be fashioned from the remaining yardage. And such fine fabric should really be entrusted only to the hands of an expert seamstress.

Mama made a quick decision. She must have the fabric, and she would enlist the Weber girls to make fancy dresses for Ella and Flora. The Weber girls lived just a short walk from Zipfel's store; she could be there and back before Papa returned from Mr. Scheid's.

Mama flew around the long wooden table, gathering up the fabrics she had selected for Hilde and adding the bolt of taffeta to the top of the stack. She dumped the bolts on the counter in front of Mr. Zipfel, who sputtered indignantly as the fabrics tumbled across his ledger book and obscured the lengthy tally next to Papa's name. Mama instructed Mr. Zipfel to wrap up all that remained of the taffeta and to cut the necessary yardage from the other bolts.

Ella and Flora stood on tiptoe at the edge of the counter and watched as Mr. Zipfel tucked his ciphering pencil behind his ear and unrolled a bolt of dark brown wool that would become Ada's new coat. The bolt bounced along the countertop with a muffled *thump, thump, thump* until the fabric stretched the required length along a yardstick tacked to the edge of the counter. Mr. Zipfel lifted the large black-handled scissors that dangled from a string behind the counter and placed the bottom blade in a groove in the counter's surface. With an exaggerated *sn-n-ip, sn-n-ip, sn-n-ip,* he ran the scissors along the groove, making a clean, straight edge across the width of the fabric. The two girls occasionally lifted their eyes from the fabric to study Mr. Zipfel's face as he concentrated on the task before him.

The bell above the store's door jangled as Mama threw it open. She impatiently called over her shoulder, "*Kommt, Mädchen.* (Come, girls.) Mr. Zipfel, I'll be back *für den Rest vom Stoff* (for the rest of the fabric)."

Ella and Flora reluctantly left the mesmerizing textile scene to scamper after Mama, who was clutching the paper-wrapped taffeta to her chest as she descended the steps in front of Zipfel's store.

Ada scrambled up from the floor next to the woodstove and hastily covered baby Hermine with the blanket. She snatched up the basket and flew to the door. Mr. Zipfel scowled at the cold draft that flooded through the open front door.

Ada gingerly picked her way down the icy steps in front of the dry-goods store, using both hands to balance the wicker baby basket in front of her. When she reached the sidewalk, she shifted the basket to one hand and hurried to catch up to Mama and the girls, who were about a half-block ahead. Mama had the package of taffeta tucked under one arm and had grasped Ella and Flora's hands so that she could hasten them along. Ada labored to hurry, but the baby basket was cumbersome, and the uneven sandstone sidewalk was treacherous with snow and ice.

"*Mama, warte auf mich!* (Mama, wait for me!)" Ada called, but the scarf wrapped around the lower portion of her face muffled her plea. She transferred the baby basket to her other hand to relieve her aching arm, but the shift of weight caused Ada's feet to fly out from under her. She landed on one hip on the icy sidewalk, and the basket bounced precariously before settling in the snow. The blanket that had covered the baby was dislodged, and tiny Hermine's eyes blinked in surprise as she gulped frosty air.

Ada rubbed her painful hip as she retrieved the blanket and tucked it securely over little Hermine. "There, there, *liebes Kleines* (little dear one)," Ada soothed the whimpering baby. When she looked up, Mama and the girls were turning the corner. Ella looked back over her shoulder as Mama propelled them along, and then they disappeared down Chapel Street.

Ada limped along, clutching the baby basket with both hands in front of her. It was cumbersome and slowed her progress, but she did not want to fall again and risk spilling the baby from the basket.

Mama marched Ella and Flora up the sidewalk of a little cottage-style house, the third from the corner. She rapped a staccato pattern at the side porch door, her foot drumming impatiently while she waited for a response.

The Weber girls—Mariah and Esther—emerged from the sewing room to see what had brought such an urgent pounding at their door on a frigid January day. Mama thrust forward the package of taffeta and poured out her sewing request in a rapid-fire mix of English and German.

The Weber sisters ushered Mama and the two girls into their sewing room at the front of the house. Large, curtainless windows spanned the wall facing the street, allowing the maximum input of light. A treadle sewing machine occupied a place of prominence in front of the windows, while a sewing form and bolts of fabric crowded one corner. A low bureau filled with paper patterns was topped by neatly labeled boxes storing assorted ribbons, laces, and other trims. Above it, a large pegged board held spools of thread and strings of matching buttons sorted by color.

Mariah pulled a wooden chair into the center of the sewing room and instructed Ella to stand on it. She used the worn tape measure that was always draped over her ample bosom to take Ella's measurements, which Esther jotted down on a pad of paper.

Mariah lifted one eyebrow and shot Esther a quizzical glance, while Mama chattered a constant stream of half-thoughts as she selected notions for the dresses. Mama decided that both dresses should have lace collars, but Flora's would have an additional lace band across the yoke. Next, she selected shiny jet buttons for the cuffs and to run in a long row down the back of the dresses. There would be no scrimping on trims for dresses made from such fine taffeta by the best seamstresses in town.

By the time Ada reached the corner and turned down Chapel Street, Mama and the girls had disappeared. The street was empty, except for a man who was shoveling coal from a wagon into a wheelbarrow. Would he know where Mama, Ella, and Flora had gone? Ada shifted the baby basket in her hands while she thought of what to do. Her arms and shoulders ached from carrying the heavy basket, and her hip hurt from the tumble on the ice. In addition, her leggings had gotten wet from the fall, leaving an icy patch of fabric adhered to her skin. Ada looked at the unfamiliar houses that lined the street. Her chin quivered as she walked slowly toward the man who was shoveling coal.

From her perch on the chair in the sewing room, Ella saw Ada pass by the front windows. "There's Ada!" she cried, pointing toward the window.

"Keep your arms down, child," admonished Mariah. "Impossible to measure children," she muttered, sucking on a lemon drop. "Really ought to charge more for it."

Mama made a frustrated sound in her throat as she dropped the boxes of notions and rushed to the door. "*Ada, kommen her! Wo warst du?* (Ada, come here! Where have you been?)" she scolded as she leaned out the front door and called after the child.

"I fell, and when I looked up, *Sie wurden gegangen* (you were gone)," Ada explained, carefully climbing the porch steps to the Weber girls' house.

"*Ach!*" Mama responded as she lifted the baby basket from Ada's weary arms and returned to the sewing room.

Ada followed and stepped close to the coal stove, extending her numb hands and feet toward its glowing warmth. She was awash with relief at having found Mama, which made her forget about the stinging in her hands and feet as they regained their feeling.

Ada watched as Flora stepped up onto the wooden chair to be measured by Esther. She was fascinated by Esther's tape measure, which retracted into a small tin housing suspended from her belt. It was almost as novel as the watch that Miss Dunn wore pinned to her blouse.

After the arrangements had been made for the completion of the dresses, Mama hurried the girls out the door and back toward Zipfel's store. This time, Mama carried the baby basket, and her pace was not quite so rapid.

Ada snapped an icicle off the back of a shed along their path, and the three girls took turns sucking on its frozen form as they trailed behind Mama.

The taffeta dresses.
Ella, Ada, & Flora

*****

Upon her arrival at the Seibel home, Hilde Bekker knew almost immediately that there was something peculiar about Mama. During her past visits, she had found Mama to be like most of the rural women who employed a seamstress—they sat at the table and offered refreshments while she stitched and shared morsels of gossip. But this time, Mama was a whirlwind of activity. She scrubbed and swept and cooked at a frantic pace, often dashing from one unfinished chore to another, all while talking a little too fast. When Hilde spoke to her about one of the sewing projects, Mama interrupted with fantastic claims about a woman named Libby that stole babies. Mama confided that she would protect baby Hermine by placing her in the cupboard that night, and she admonished Hilde not to reveal the hiding place. When Hilde tried to engage her with a tantalizing bit of neighborhood news, Mama repeated the gossip like a rapid echo but gave no indication that she recognized the names Hilde was dropping. And worst of all, there was no offering of cookies or tea. Instead, Hilde was left to pour herself a cup of overbrewed coffee and listen to her stomach rumble as she thought of the rich küchen she had enjoyed here on her last visit. The seamstress bent to her work, keeping a curious eye on Mama's unusual behavior.

Papa's saw rasped as it bit into a freshly fallen tree in the small grove of pin oaks near the ridge at the back of the farm. The kitchen cookstove and the Round Oak stove in the living room had insatiable appetites, and keeping their woodboxes filled was a full-time task in the winter. Papa spent many long days felling trees, hewing them into logs, splitting the wood into stove-sized chunks, and loading the firewood onto the bobsled. When a sufficient pile had been created, he flicked the reins and made a clicking noise with his tongue. Jib and Davey lurched forward and plodded through the knee-high snow to the woodshed. There, Papa unloaded the bobsled and stacked the firewood in neat rows that reached the ceiling. Over and over he repeated the task until it was dusk and time to start the evening chores.

As he guided the horses toward the barn, Papa spotted Ella emerging from the chickenhouse where she was gathering eggs. Reining in the horses, he called to her, "How's everything *im Haus* (in the house)?"

Ella shrugged, "Hilde's *näht* (sewing) and Mama's *spricht* (talking)."

Papa's brow furrowed with thought while he curry-combed the horses and dried them with an old blanket. He wiped down and oiled the harnesses and hung them on the barn wall, then fed and watered the animals and milked the cows. He carried the steaming pails of milk to the house and set them by the back door, then returned to the outdoor pump for two buckets of water for the supper dishes and the morning's needs. He carried in several armfuls of firewood for the stoves and propped the shovel by the back door, ready for clearing paths to the barn, water pump, chickenhouse, and outhouse in the morning.

After a sketchy supper, Papa eased into the rocking chair beside the cookstove and gave a weary sigh as he removed his wet boots. He stretched his feet toward the heat of the stove, leaned his head against the back of the rocker, and watched Mama buzz around the kitchen. She was indeed wound up and showed no signs of slowing down. Hilde and the girls soon retired to the upstairs bedroom, and Hermine was settled in her crib in the corner of her parent's bedroom. The warmth of the cookstove coupled with the fatigue from the day's timbering overtook Papa. He struggled to keep his eyes open but at last gave in and headed for bed.

Papa drifted between sleep and wakefulness. The smell of woodsmoke and baking bread tickled at the fringes of his consciousness. He slipped back into slumber and dreamed he was once again in camp with Millard Young on the banks of the Mississippi River. A faint smile crossed Papa's face as he split a fresh-baked biscuit, its steam rising skyward in wispy tendrils. His mouth watered at the golden loops of honey he drizzled onto its hot, fluffy surface. Just as he raised the biscuit to take a bite, a baby's cries roused him from his slumber. Papa moved his foot over to nudge Mama and alert her to the baby's needs, but Mama's side of the bed was empty. His eyes fluttered open and he blinked several times, trying to orient himself between the dream state and reality.

The smell of baking bread was not a dream. Its distinct aroma filled the room, and the glow of a lantern slanted across the bedroom doorway. Papa threw back the covers and rushed toward the kitchen, stopping long enough to peer into the empty crib in the corner of the room.

Mama's long hair was loose and tumbled forward over her shoulder as she removed two loaves of bread from the open cookstove. Papa caught a quick whiff of singed hair and leaped forward to grab Mama's long tresses and pull them away from the open flames.

"*Was machst du, Sophie!?* (What are you doing, Sophie!?)" he asked in bewilderment.

Mama shook her hair free of Papa's grasp and crossed the room to place the two freshly baked loaves on the kitchen table beside four other loaves that cooled there. She sprinkled her hands with flour and began kneading a mound of bread dough.

"*Die Threshers kommen morgen, William. Ich muß bereit sein* (The threshers are coming in the morning, William. I have to be ready)," Mama stated with urgency.

"Threshers!?" Papa cried in disbelief. "*Es ist Januar!* (It's January)! I haven't even *den Weizen schon gesät!* (planted the wheat yet!)"

Mama shook her head and grumbled about the lack of help in preparing for the harvest dinner. She continued to work the dough.

"Where's *das Baby?*" Papa demanded as he followed the sounds of the crying child. He opened the bottom door of the pantry cupboard and discovered tiny Hermine lying on a shelf. Her flailing arms and legs had scattered the blankets that once covered her. Papa wrapped the cold and howling infant securely in the blankets and scooped her into his arms.

Hilde was awoken by the sounds of angry voices and a baby's cries. She eased herself out of bed, careful not to wake Flora who slumbered beside her, tiptoed across the plank floor, and crept down the stairs, where she crouched on the landing. Her perch gave her a clear view of the kitchen. Hilde tucked the bottom of her flannel nightgown under her feet to protect them from the cold wooden floors and settled in to watch and listen.

Papa emerged from the pantry with the crying baby and demanded to know why she was in the cupboard. He settled himself into the rocking chair beside the cookstove and tried to calm the distraught child.

At the site of the infant in Papa's arms, Mama became extremely agitated. Pointing a floury finger at him, she commanded, "*Leg sie wieder hin! Leg sie wieder hin gleich jetzt!* (Put her back! Put her back right now!)"

"Sophie, the child belongs *in ihrer Krippe* (in her crib), not *in den Schrank* (in the cupboard)," Papa replied angrily.

Mama cocked her fists upon her hips. "*Leg sie zurück bevor Libby sie findet!* (Put her back before Libby finds her!)" she barked.

When Papa did not heed her commands and continued to rock the child, Mama whirled about and grabbed an empty bread pan, which she hurtled at Papa.

Papa dodged the flying pan and covered the baby's head with his hand as he bolted from the rocking chair and exited the room. Mama flew to the kitchen doorway and threw another bread pan in Papa's direction. It hit the wall beside the bedroom door and clattered loudly to the floor. Hilde gave a little gasp and shrank back into the shadows of the landing so she would not be detected.

"*Es ist deine Schuld. Die Threshers kommen morgen, und ich habe keine Zeit nach ihr zu sehen* (It will be your fault if Libby takes her! The threshers are coming in the morning, and I won't have time to look for her)," Mama shouted. Then her knees buckled and she collapsed. Mama laid on her back on the floor, her arms and legs jerking violently and her eyes wide and unseeing. Guttural noises emerged from her throat.

For several days, Mama slept, then she lay in bed too listless to do more than stare out the window. She thought about swinging her feet over the edge of the bed, but couldn't muster the energy to command the movement. One afternoon, Papa pulled a chair beside the bed and took Mama's hand in his. He stroked the soft white flesh over her wrist and searched her face for answers.

"*Was ist falsch, Sophie?* (What's wrong, Sophie?)" he asked softly.

When Mama didn't reply, he probed, "Is it *die Mädchen?* (the girls?)"

Mama slowly rolled her clear blue eyes in Papa's direction and studied his face. Papa dropped his head between his shoulders and stammered, "*O-O-Oder ist es … ich? Bist du mit mir unglücklich?* (Or-Or-Or is it … me? Are you unhappy with me?)"

Papa looked up when he felt Mama's hand tighten around his. "*Ich bin es* (It's me)," she whispered hoarsely. A tear slid out of the corner of Mama's eye and trickled down her cheek. "*Aber warum?* (But why?)"

*****

Hilde sewed at a furious pace, occasionally casting a wary eye over her shoulder at the bedroom where Mama lay. She finished the assigned sewing projects, accepted her payment from Papa, and declined his offer of a ride to Mosses'—she would walk, thank you.

Emmaline Moss poured a stream of freshly brewed tea into Hilde's cup. She had purposely set the table with the good bone china tea set, its cups so transparent that their delicate pink floral design seemed to float in place. The Mosses may not have been first on Hilde's sewing list this year, but they would certainly set the standard for refinement. And Emmaline was confident that Hilde would share this fact at the other homes she visited on her travels.

Emmaline seated herself across the table from Hilde and used the sterling silver tongs to drop a sugar cube into the seamstress' tea. She offered Hilde a gingersnap, then slowly stirred her own tea while sweetly inquiring about Hilde's mother's health, whether her father had had a successful harvest, and if any of her vast rabble of younger siblings had had the grippe this winter.

Hilde plied her needle slowly, stopping often to nibble on a cookie and sip her tea. She sprinkled their conversation with news of the neighborhood, which Emmaline responded to with a cocked eyebrow and an occasional cluck of the tongue. Then, Hilde paused and tapped her thimbled finger on the table. "You know, I just come from the Seibel place, and..." She shrugged her shoulders and gave a pained expression, then gazed pointedly at the bottom of her empty tea cup while clearing her throat.

Emmaline whipped the quilted tea cozy off the china teapot and refilled Hilde's cup. "And?" she coaxed, reaching over with the silver tongs to deposit two sugar cubes in Hilde's cup.

"Well … things is mighty strange there," Hilde hinted, shaking her head and resuming her sewing.

Emmaline pushed the plate of gingersnaps toward Hilde and leaned closer. "What do you mean?" she breathed, eyes intent on Hilde's face. "What's so strange?"

Hilde told all about Mama's bizarre behavior and odd conversations, from claiming a baby-snatching woman would try to steal Hermine, to baking loaf after loaf of bread for threshers that she thought were coming on a January morning. She recounted how Papa had found baby Hermine in the pantry cupboard, and Mama had hurtled bread pans at him. By the time Hilde related how Mama had had a fit on the floor, then spent days in bed, Emmaline's jaw was slack and her eyes as large and round as the gingersnaps she continued to ply Hilde with.

Emmaline sat dazed for a moment as she digested all that the seamstress had relayed. Then, sitting back in her chair, she cocked her head and announced, "Sophie's crazy! No doubt about it! Just a crazy German!"

Hilde looked up from her sewing and scowled at the insult to her own German heritage, then helped herself to another gingersnap.

* * * * *

In the spring of 1898, Papa walked up and down the rows of orchard stock he had planted eight years earlier. He stopped at each tree and used his thumbnail to scrape back a bit of the bark. Tree after tree showed dry, dead tissue underneath. Many of the plum and pear trees revealed a promising green, but he now realized that the pears were of an undesirable variety, and there was no market for plums. The peach trees had been an early fatality, frozen out by the first harsh winter. Enough apple trees had survived to provide apples, cider, and apple butter for the family's use, and maybe he could find a market for the cherries.

Papa thrust his hands deep into his pockets and pondered the dismal orchard before him. He was paying money on a loan that had yielded nothing but debt, no added farm income. Papa knew he did not have the option of leaving the farm to make extra money, as he had done with the citrus crop in Florida several years ago. It didn't make financial sense to hire someone to do the farm chores while he was away, and Mama's spells were too unpredictable. Mr. Scheid's words, "Girls ain't gonna get you outta debt, Bill," rang in his head. Papa stared at the barn and recalled his dream of having "Seibel and Sons Orchards" painted across its front. He shook his head in disgust, then picked up a clod of dirt from the orchard and hurtled it at the barn.

Papa decided he would have to try a less risky form of crop diversity. He would move the potatoes out of the garden and expand them into a field crop. In addition to serving as a staple in the family diet, they would become a cash crop, along with the grain. But he could not shoulder the additional workload alone.

Ada and Ella joined Papa at the kitchen table, where they sliced the seed potatoes into quarters, making sure each section had at least one eye. They dipped the cut surfaces into wood ashes from the cookstove to callous the potatoes for planting. Flora scooped up the cut potato sections in her small hands and transferred them to bushel baskets on the floor.

After all of the potatoes had been cut, Papa plowed long furrows in the field. The girls dragged the bushel baskets behind them as they dropped potato sections at evenly spaced intervals in the furrows. Papa followed behind with a shovel and scooped dirt over what he hoped would germinate into a bountiful crop.

When the girls finished the outdoor work, Mama enlisted their aid in spring housecleaning. There were heavy rugs to be carried outdoors, hung over the clothesline, and beaten with the wire rug beater. The kitchen chairs were moved outside and washed with softsoap, and the plank floors were given a vigorous scrubbing. The cookstove and Round Oak stove in the living room were swept clean of ashes and their surfaces blacked. All of the dishes were removed from the cupboards, washed, and returned to the freshly scrubbed shelves. Mama's few good pieces of china were kept on the top shelf, out of reach of young hands. Only Mama was allowed to handle those pieces. The broom was inverted to chase cobwebs from the ceiling corners, then turned right-side up for sweeping the steps. Walls and windows were washed, and the lace curtains that hung in the living room and parlor were boiled and carefully pressed with the sad iron. All of the furniture was polished with lemon oil, and the mattresses turned and fluffed. Ada missed two weeks of school for the spring ritual, but Mama insisted a clean house trumped book learning. And in Mama's "book," a house could never be too clean.

Papa turned his shovel to digging roots in the spring. He harvested horseradish that grew wild along the sides of the road and ground it into a pungent condiment. He dug a huge pan of dandelion greens, which Mama served seasoned with bacon drippings and vinegar. From the ridge at the back of the farm, Papa brought sassafras root, which he boiled for a tea. He had heard that sassafras tea thinned the blood and was a tonic for the nerves. He encouraged Mama to drink cupful after cupful, watching hopefully for signs of improvement. But Mama's spells continued, now climaxed by the dramatic seizures that had begun that winter.

Chapter 7
Monroeville, Ohio
1900

PAPA RAPPED ON THE KITCHEN DOOR of his mother's small brick house on the River Road south of Monroeville. He carried a basket filled with a dozen brown eggs, a large chunk of rich, golden butter, and a ring of sausage links from the hogs he had recently butchered. Papa's visits to his mother's house were infrequent and brief, due to Old Man Scheidt's unpleasantness, but he always came bearing some produce from the farm. Papa silently hoped his step-father would not be home today. Old Man frequently ambled down the road to the creamery, where he sat for long hours on a corner stool, visiting with the creamery workers and the area farmers who brought in their excess milk to sell. However, given the frosty February weather, it was likely that Old Man would be hugging the parlor stove and not straying far from his cider jug.

Mama carried the wicker baby basket that held six-month-old Margaret Louise, their fifth daughter, born during the height of the threshing season in August 1899. When the threshers had arrived at the Seibel homestead, Mama had been confined to bed as part of the "lying-in" of childbirth. A young woman by the name of Clara had been hired to help, but she quickly found herself overwhelmed with the care of Mama, a newborn, four little girls, and the chores of a busy farm house. Consequently, Clara had been hard pressed when it came time to prepare the noon dinner for the neighborhood threshers. With the help of nine-year-old Ada and seven-year-old Ella, she had served headcheese sandwiches, pickles, cottage cheese, and elderberry pie. It was not the hearty meal the harvesters had come to expect. Mama knew that word of the slim repast would be carried home by the disappointed men. It only added to her feelings of melancholy over the birth of yet another daughter.

Old Man Scheidt answered the knock at the door. When he saw that it was Papa, he grumbled, "*Ach, du bist es nur* (Oh, it's only you)," and turned back toward the parlor and his warm chair beside the stove. "*Kathrina, dein Junge ist hier* (Kathrina, your boy is here)," he called, emphasizing the word "*Junge* (boy)," even though Papa was thirty-eight years old.

Papa entered the kitchen and set the basket of farm products on the table. Mama turned to the girls and commanded, "Stomp your shoes and don't track any *Schnee im Haus* (snow into the house)." The girls complied by stomping their feet in place and kicking their shoes against the bottom stone step before entering the kitchen.

Kathrina hurried in from the parlor, still carrying the book she had been reading. Mama noticed the breakfast dishes piled in the drysink and the broom that was propped against one of the kitchen chairs, as if abandoned in mid-sweep. It was obvious that Kathrina was deep into another book and couldn't be distracted by the important work of housekeeping. Mama shuddered inwardly.

Kathrina slid the book into her apron pocket and carried the broom to the pantry, where she retrieved the cookie jar. She offered raisin-studded oatmeal cookies to each of the girls, then took the baby basket from Mama and followed Papa into the parlor. Mama pulled four wooden chairs into a circle in the center of the kitchen and told the girls to sit there and eat their cookies. Before she joined the others in the parlor, Mama admonished, "Not a peep out of you. And don't drop *eine Krume* (a crumb)." She punctuated her words by pointing her index finger at each of the girls. They nodded earnestly that they understood.

Old Man reached for his cider jug on the floor beside his rocking chair and inquired about last fall's harvest. Papa replied that the potato yield had been good and he intended to devote even more fields to the crop this year.

"*Kartoffelwirtschaft!* (Potato farming!)" Old Man snorted as he twisted the corncob stopper from the neck of the jug. "*Ich dachte du hast einen Obstgärten. Oder kennst du das Geheimnis Kartoffeln auf Bäumen anzubauen?* (I thought you were going to have orchards. Or did you find a way to grow potatoes on trees?") He chuckled at his own joke and took a long draw from the cider jug.

"*Die harten Winter töteten die meisten meiner Obstbäume* (The hard winters killed most of my fruit trees)," Papa replied quietly as he studied the carpet between his feet.

Old Man wiped the back of his hand across his mouth and shook his head. "*Möglicherweise sollte George dir Lektionen in Farmwirtschaft geben. Er kann mehr als Kartoffeln … und auch Mädchen* (Maybe George ought to give you farming lessons. He knows how to raise more than potatoes … and girls)," Old Man scoffed and waved his jug at little Margaret, whom Kathrina was bouncing on her knee.

Mama's back stiffened and a crimson flush crept up her neck and into her cheeks. She did not enjoy being reminded of Papa's failed nursery stock or their lack of male offspring. The mention of George only freshened her resentment over the house shuffle. She leaned forward and opened her mouth to give Old Man a long-overdue piece of her mind.

"*Oh, dieses Mädchen ist anders* (Oh, but this girl is different)," interrupted Kathrina as she smiled down at Margaret. "*Sieh sie an! Sie ist etwas besonderes, ich weiß das.* (Just look at her! There's something special about this one, I can tell.)" Kathrina smoothed her hand over the auburn curls that ringed the baby's head.

It was true. There was something special about little Margaret. Even Mama, who had been so disappointed to have another girl, couldn't help but be drawn to this child with the infectious smile and outgoing personality. Of the five girls, Margaret was the most like the sociable Gasteier side of the family. Mama often wondered if her dead sister Libby had been reincarnated into the body of baby Margaret.

In the kitchen, the girls nibbled their oatmeal-raisin cookies. Two-year-old Hermine swung her short legs back and forth, striking her hard-soled shoes on the rung of the chair with a staccato *tap-tap.*

"Stop that! Do you want Mama to come?" whispered Ella.

Hermine's eyes grew wide and she quickly shook her head "no," but continued the rhythmic beating of her shoes against the chair rung.

Five-year-old Flora reached over and tried to hold the child's legs still, which only made Hermine giggle and swing her legs harder. Her shoes banged out a loud *knock-knock* each time they connected with the chair rung.

Ella cast a wary eye toward the parlor door, expecting to see Mama's angry face at any moment. She lifted Hermine onto her lap and allowed the child to swing her legs freely, the hard-soled shoes battering Ella's shins. It was painful, but at least it muffled the noise and averted a punishment from Mama.

Ada spotted the cookie crumbs that had cascaded to the floor when Ella moved Hermine to her lap. She quickly knelt and pressed her finger against each crumb, then deposited them in her dress pocket, leaving the kitchen floor clean, as Mama had commanded.

Ada heard movement in the parlor. She slipped back onto her chair just as Mama marched stiffly through the parlor door, clutching the baby basket in front of her. Her face was clouded by a scowl. The girls quickly donned their winter coats, and Ella tied the ribbons of Hermine's knit hat under her chin. They followed Mama and Papa out the kitchen door and climbed into the back seat of the cutter.

Mama whipped the lap robe over her legs, squared her shoulders, and turned toward Papa, her blue eyes flashing. "Why do you let him speak to you that way? He's nothing but an *alter Dummkopf* (old fool)!"

Papa took the reins between his gloved hands and stared straight ahead. "I don't go lookin' for a fight."

"*Ja*, and it's a *schwacher Mann* (weak man) who doesn't fight for himself, or for *das Haus und Land* (the house and land) that were his," Mama snapped, still smarting from renewed thoughts of George and Bertha in the house that was supposed to be hers.

Papa slapped the reins on the horse's rump with unaccustomed force. The cutter lurched forward, jostling the girls in the rear seat.

Ada & Ella
Flora & Hermine

* * * * *

June brought a fierce thunderstorm that matched Mama's agitation. When the winds finally abated, the yard was strewn with twigs and leaves, which violated Mama's sense of order. She bustled about the yard all morning, sometimes gathering the twigs into a pile and other times returning to the kitchen to peel potatoes in rapid-fire succession. That task was soon abandoned when she noticed muddy footprints on the porch steps, and she sailed out the kitchen door with a scrub brush and bucket of sudsy water. Many chores were started, but none were completed before Mama moved on to something else. The only constant was her steady stream of chatter.

The girls knew that when Mama was in one of her moods, it was best to quietly go about one's chores and stay out of her path. Ella and Flora refilled the kerosene lanterns, washed and dried their glass chimneys, and trimmed the wicks at the work table in the summer kitchen. Hermine played with an old ragdoll beneath the work table, while little Margaret babbled happily as she stood on wobbly legs and held onto the corner of the *Mehlfach* (flour bin).

Ada lifted a freshly baked küchen from the cookstove, which had been moved out to the summer kitchen for the warmer months. Ever since Mama had taught Ada how to bake, she had gradually assumed the twice-weekly task of making bread and the Saturday chore of baking a cake, küchen, or pie for Sunday's dessert. The küchen's valleys of thick, rich cream bubbled through its coating of cinnamon and sugar. Ada pulled a straw from the broom that leaned beside the summer kitchen door and plunged the clean end into the center of the coffeecake. The straw emerged without batter clinging to it, signaling that the küchen was baked to perfection. Ada carried it into the kitchen and set it on the table to cool.

Papa assessed the hay field behind the barn. The timothy was too wet from the previous night's storm to be cut, but in a few days, the field would dry out and the haying season could begin in earnest. Papa loaded the hay mower's cutter bar knife into the back of the spring wagon. He normally used a file to sharpen the blade himself, since a dull blade clogged easily and overburdened the horses pulling the mower, but a few of the blade's teeth were badly gouged from hitting rocks in the field. Papa planned to take the cutter bar knife to the blacksmith's shop in Monroeville, where the smithy would use a water grindstone to hone the cutting edges.

Papa led Jib and the spring wagon to the hitching post in the backyard, then cocked his head and listened. He heard a woman's voice singing snatches of "Silent Night" in German. Mama emerged from around the south side of the house. She was pulling weeds at a furious pace while singing and carrying on a confused conversation with no one. Papa sighed and shook his head slowly, then crossed the yard and climbed the porch steps. He noticed the abandoned scrub brush and bucket of water where Mama had left them.

In the summer kitchen, Papa pumped a tin cup of cold water from the wellstalk and watched as Ella and Flora reassembled the cleaned kerosene lanterns. Little Margaret released her hold on the corner of the *Mehlfach* and took a few tentative steps toward him. Papa scooped her up in his arms and crossed to the kitchen, where he found Ada washing the dishes. Ten-year-old Ada only needed to stand on a Montgomery Ward's catalog now to reach the dishes in the drysink.

"I'm going into town," Papa told her as he set Margaret down beside a kitchen chair. He tousled the little child's curls, and a smile played about his lips. "Anything we need from Zipfel's?"

Ada wiped her wet hands on the front of her apron and took a quick inventory of the pantry. "Yes, we're almost out of yeast cakes," she replied. "And the coffee's getting low."

Papa retrieved some cash from the tin box in the cupboard. As he headed out the kitchen door, he paused and turned toward Ada. "Keep an eye on your Mama while I'm gone."

Ada nodded and watched through the kitchen window as Papa and the spring wagon rattled down the driveway.

* * * * *

Galen Pierce checked the clipboard on the buggy seat beside him. When he'd agreed to serve as an enumerator for the 1900 census, he had assumed he would be canvassing his neighborhood of "New England," an English community along Plank Road on the western edge of Monroeville. However, he had been dismayed to learn that his assignment was the outlying German settlements. He had already encountered several families that spoke only German, and his inability to communicate with them made him feel as though they were suspicious of his intentions. Galen sighed and affixed a blank census sheet to the top of the stack on his clipboard. In the summers, he usually supplemented his teaching salary by working as a farm hand. At least the job of a census enumerator was cleaner, less physically demanding, and slightly more interesting. Another perk of the profession was the generous servings of baked goods that the German farmwives served upon his arrival. He chuckled to himself as he realized that part of his summer earnings might be used to pay the Weber girls to sew him larger pants. Galen turned his horse and buggy out of George and Bertha's driveway and headed south to the next farmhouse.

Mama had progressed around the north side of the house in her weed-pulling frenzy. She straightened when she heard a horse and buggy approaching on the road, and a wide smile lit her face when the stranger pulled into the drive and up to the hitching post. Mama's sociability went into overdrive. She wiped her hands on the front of her apron and hurried toward the stranger.

Galen was relieved at the warm reception and Mama's apparent command of the English language. He followed her up the porch steps and into the kitchen, where Ada was drying the dishes. Little Margaret slapped her hands happily on the seat of a kitchen chair and squealed in delight at the sight of the stranger.

Mama motioned to Galen to have a seat at the table. She scooped up Margaret and plopped her in Ada's arms. Ada tossed the dish towel over her shoulder and shifted little Margaret to one hip. Visitors were a rarity at the Seibel house, and Ada was well aware of Mama's rule that children be seen and not heard, particularly when adults were conversing. She carried the baby over to Stegmiller's stairs and seated herself on the bottom step, tucking Margaret into her lap. Ella and Flora overheard Mama's conversation with the stranger, and they peered around the corner of the kitchen door. Spotting Ada and Margaret on Stegmiller's stairs, they quietly entered the kitchen, leading Hermine by the hand. All five girls nestled on the two bottom steps of Stegmiller's stairs and watched with large eyes and solemn faces as Mama bustled about, chattering gaily to the stranger at their kitchen table.

Galen ran one finger down the column on the census sheet and began asking Mama the required questions: name, age, month and year of birth, marital status, number of years married, relation to head of household. Mama rattled off the answers as she cut a piece of Ada's freshly made küchen and placed it on a plate in front of the census taker. Galen looked down in surprise at the offering. While he had grown accustomed to the generous portions served by the German farmwives, this piece was huge, fully one-quarter of the pan of küchen. Mama whirled about to retrieve a fork from the pantry, still answering questions and sharing other bits of unrelated information. She briefly seated herself opposite the census taker and answered a few more questions: place of birth, place of father's and mother's births. She watched Galen savoring his first few mouthfuls of the still-warm küchen, then jumped up and hurried to the summer kitchen. She returned with a tin cup of cold well water, which she set in front of her guest.

Mama seated herself once again and smiled brightly at Galen. He nodded politely at her to indicate his appreciation of the refreshments, even though he knew he could not eat the enormous portion on his plate. He returned to his census sheet and the next question, but when he looked up again, Mama was headed toward the pantry and the cellar steps beyond. He had never seen a woman with this much nervous energy, nor one who chattered so continuously. Galen swung his bewildered gaze to the faces of the five little girls on Stegmiller's stairs. They stared silently back at him, except for little Margaret who smiled and babbled as she waved the dishtowel pulled from Ada's shoulder.

Margaret

Mama returned, bearing an ironstone mug of buttermilk, which she set next to the tin cup of water in front of Galen. His eyes shifted between the two beverages and Mama's face, searching for signs that a joke was being played on him. Mama was beaming and chattering happily. Galen looked to the little girls for a clue. They stared back at him with round, solemn eyes.

Galen cleared his throat and took another bite of küchen, a sip of each of the beverages, and proceeded with the next questions: occupation of head of household, home owned or rented, home free of mortgage. He bent over the census sheet to record Mama's answers.

Mama's face clouded slightly. She responded that Papa was a farmer but he wasn't home right now. In fact, he was in Florida harvesting grapefruit. Galen's head snapped up and he looked at Mama with raised eyebrows. Mama grew agitated and kneaded her hands along the edge of the checked tablecloth. Her words tumbled out about a house that had been stolen, a *schwacher Mann* (weak man) who would not fight, and Seibel and Sons Orchards. Mama's blue eyes were wide as she leaned forward to confide, "And William is going to lose his skirt."

Galen's brow furrowed at Mama's reference to such unusual apparel for a farmer. He knew that some immigrants clung tenaciously to their native country's traditions, but in all of his interactions with the German community, he had never encountered a skirt-wearing man. Then his brow relaxed and he nodded knowingly. "Oh, you mean he's going to lose his shirt."

"*Ja*, that too," replied Mama earnestly, not understanding that she had mangled her translation of the phrase about being deep in debt. Galen held his pencil in mid-air, pondering Mama's confusing jumble of information, then decided to leave blank that section of the census form. He proceeded to the next questions: mother of how many children, number of these children living.

Mama rattled off the girls' names, then jumped up and began to pace about the kitchen. She crossed to the summer kitchen and filled an ironstone mug with coffee from the kettle at the back of the cookstove. Galen stopped writing when she set the mug of coffee in front of him, next to the still-full cup of water and the mug of buttermilk. He looked again at the girls on the steps, but no explanation was forthcoming.

Galen gave his head a small shake and returned to recording the girls' names. He asked off-handedly, "So, no boys?"

Mama stopped her pacing and looked puzzled. "*Ja, ja,* we have a boy." She whirled about and exited the kitchen. Galen could hear Mama opening and closing dresser drawers in the nearby bedroom and muttering about a boy named Walter. He tapped his pencil on the census form as he looked at the five little girls clustered on the steps. Jabbing his thumb in the direction of the bedroom, he asked, "You got a little brother in there?"

Ada slowly shook her head "no."

Mama returned to the kitchen and cocked her head in puzzlement. "What did you want to know?"

Galen looked again at the girls and detected an almost imperceptible shake of Ada's head. He decided to move on to other questions: number of months of school attendance, able to read and write, can speak English.

Mama paced about the room, muttering about housework and reading, then lifted her chin and stated proudly, "*Ja*, we speak English here. Always I have spoke English."

Galen raised one eyebrow at Mama's thick accent and liberal sprinkling of German words throughout her conversation, but dutifully recorded that this was an English-speaking household. He doubted the accuracy of any of the information he had received during his visit. Perhaps if he moved on to the next house on the road, the neighbors could help him fill in the blanks about the very puzzling Seibel household. Galen gathered his papers and clipboard, took one more bite of the delicious küchen, and thanked Mama for her time and hospitality. He nodded to the girls and stepped quickly through the kitchen door, greatly relieved to be ending this strange encounter.

Little Margaret waved the dishtowel in her hand and chattered, "Bye-bye, bye-bye." The other girls watched the stranger leave, then turned their eyes toward Mama, who cocked her head and furrowed her brow as if still trying to remember what she had been searching for in the bedroom. Looking about the kitchen, she spotted the remains of Galen's uneaten küchen and the three beverages on the table. Mama grabbed the plate and dashed out the kitchen door and down the porch steps. "Wait! Wait! You must *essen Sie* (eat) your küchen!"

Galen had unhitched the horse and buggy and was proceeding down the drive when Mama came running across the yard, carrying the plate of küchen in front of her. She trotted alongside the buggy, holding the plate up toward the census taker and imploring him to eat the remains of the huge piece.

Galen looked at Mama with alarm. Her unusual behavior suggested that she might try to climb into the buggy with him, and he had no idea how he would rid himself of her if that happened. He snapped the reins, and the horse picked up its pace as it turned south out of the Seibel driveway. Mama quickened her step, splashing through the mud puddles in the drive as she tried to keep up with the fleeing buggy.

After he'd reached the road and the horse had settled into a comfortable trot, Galen turned to look over his shoulder. Mama stood in the center of the road in front of the Seibel house, holding the plate in her outstretched hands. Her mouth was moving, and Galen knew that she was still chattering. He exhaled in relief, shook his head at the odd experience, and proceeded down the road toward the Mosses' house.

*****

In August, the neighborhood threshing on Townline Road was drawing to a close. Mosses', Ordmanns', Knopfs', and Papa's fields had already been harvested, and now threshing commenced on George's wheat. Until his own crop was threshed, Papa remained anxious, fretting that the machinery would break down or a sudden summer storm would flatten the wheat just before harvest. But when the last bundle of his wheat had been fed into the gaping maw of the threshing machine and the last section of twine tied around the filled grain sacks, he relaxed and enjoyed the experience. The well-oiled machinery, the aroma of the freshly cut wheat, the golden yellow of the straw, and the feel of the wheat kernels cascading through his fingers reminded him of his years on the Mississippi, when he had threshed grain as he traveled west. Papa often thought of those years and his youthful optimism.

Bertha and eleven-year-old Rosie served the threshers a noon meal of beefsteak, mashed potatoes, gravy, green beans, pickles, applesauce, freshly baked bread, and apple pie. After the men had finished eating and returned to the fields, Bertha and Rosie dropped wearily into chairs at the kitchen table and helped themselves to the remaining food. Bertha's beloved pet dog, Bunda, sat beside her chair, his soulful eyes watching each forkful of food that passed from Bertha's plate to her mouth. As she ate, Bertha lovingly stroked Bunda's soft brown ears and occasionally passed him a piece of gravy-soaked meat.

When the meal was over and the cleanup had begun, Bunda trotted to the kitchen door and whimpered. Bertha patted the dog's flank as he shot through the opened door, down the porch steps, and across the yard toward the men working in the wheat fields at the back of the farm.

Bunda nosed about the bundles of cut wheat, diving after mice that darted between the stacks. His tail wagged furiously, and the men joked that George's dog was a better mouser than all of his farm cats.

Papa lifted a pitchfork full of cut wheat and carried it toward the separator. As he leaned forward to toss the bundle of wheat into the threshing cylinder, Bunda darted after a mouse just in front of Papa's feet. He stumbled over the dog, dropping his pitchfork and falling toward the open mouth of the threshing machine. The serrated bars of the beater caught the fingers of Papa's outstretched right hand, neatly severing the tip of his middle finger and badly crushing and mangling the end of his index finger.

George was working on the opposite side of the thresher and saw Papa stumble. He dropped his own pitchfork and rushed forward. Grabbing the back of Papa's shirt, George pulled him from the mouth of the thresher while yelling for Mr. Ordmann to disable the steam engine. Mr. Moss, who had been bagging the cleaned grain at the opposite end of the thresher, ran toward them with an empty grain sack, which he quickly wrapped around Papa's bloody hand and applied pressure. The men eased Papa to a sitting position, and Mr. Knopf poured him a cup of cold switchel from the ironstone jug they kept in the shade of the thresher. Papa's left hand trembled as he raised the cup to his lips.

George offered to hitch up the buggy and drive Papa into Monroeville to see Dr. Gilman, but Papa refused—only an equipment failure or severe weather should keep a man from his field during harvest. The men helped Papa to his feet, and he slowly headed across the fields toward home, clutching his bundled hand to his chest. At times, the pain was blinding, causing him to sweat profusely and feel woozy. After he had crossed behind the hedge row that separated the two farms, Papa bent forward and wretched repeatedly. When the wave of nausea passed, he staggered up the lane toward home.

Mama sent Ella and Hermine out to the grape arbor to pick grape leaves, which would be added to each crock of freshly made pickles to preserve their crispness. Mama brought the pickling brine to a boil on the cookstove in the summer kitchen, while Ada scrubbed the cucumbers in a pan of water at the worktable and removed their blossom ends. The heat in the kitchen was stifling, and Ada wiped her rolled-up dress sleeve across her forehead. Flora sat across the worktable from Ada, plucking heads of dill from their stalks and dropping them into a pan at her feet. Little Margaret napped on a pile of blankets in the corner of the room, her auburn curls damp against her forehead.

Ella reached the end of the arbor and dropped the last grape leaf into her pan. She turned to inspect the leaves in Hermine's pan when she saw Papa stagger around the corner of the barn. Spotting the bloody cloth clutched to his chest, Ella dropped the pan of grape leaves and raced toward the house, screaming "Mama, Mama! Come quick! Papa's hurt!"

Hermine stood paralyzed with fear in the grape arbor. Her lower lip trembled, then she dashed for the house, crying "Papa's dying! Papa's dying!" as she scattered her pan of grape leaves across the yard.

Mama rushed down the porch steps, trailed by the girls, and met Papa on the footpath to the well pump. She carefully unwrapped Papa's injured hand and inspected the damage as he winced and choked out the story between clenched jaws.

Hermine burst into tears at the sight of Papa's mangled fingers. "Hush!" Mama snapped at the crying child. "I cannot think with your *heulen* (howling)!" She pressed her hands to her head as if holding together fragmented pieces. Ada pulled the crying child toward her, and Hermine buried her face in Ada's apron.

It was agreed that Mama would harness Jib to the wagon, but Ada would drive Papa in to see Dr. Gilman so that Mama could return to the pickling process, which was at a critical stage.

Ada settled herself on the wagon bench, took the reins into her hands, and swallowed deeply. She had sat next to Papa or Mama many times when they drove the wagon, but she had never been in control of the reins before. She looked up at Papa, who was slumped beside her on the seat. His tan face was blanched white with pain. When he nodded, Ada gave the reins a slap. Jib started off with a jolt, which caused Papa to groan. Ada pulled in on the reins, slowing Jib to a walk.

"Faster," Papa urged between clenched teeth. He reached over with his left hand and gave the reins an expert tap. Jib settled into a trot, and Ada leaned forward with her elbows on her knees, the reins clutched tightly in her hands.

At each rut in the road, the wagon lurched, causing Papa to groan. Ada looked up at him, wondering if she should slow Jib to a walk, but Papa gave no indication that she should alter the horse's pace.

Dr. Gilman sewed up the tip of Papa's severed middle finger, but declared the end of his index finger beyond repair. The portion from the first knuckle to the fingertip was amputated. The doctor wrapped Papa's hand in layers of clean white gauze, gave him some elixir for pain, and sent him home with an admonition to take it easy for a while.

Papa's threshing season was over, but the work at home could not be ignored. He would need the girls to help him with the daily farm chores, such as milking the cows, feeding and watering the livestock, carrying in firewood for the cookstove, and hoeing the garden. Of course, Mama insisted the girls not neglect their household tasks during that time.

* * * * *

In September of 1900, Flora joined ten-year-old Ada and eight-year-old Ella in attending the Plank Road School. After years of playing school up Stegmiller's stairs with her older sisters as the teacher, Flora was well versed in what to expect. In fact, Ella, who was a bright and capable pupil, had begun to teach her how to read. Ella could not get enough of reading. She read Papa's current issues of the *Monroeville Spectator* that he kept folded in a basket by his rocking chair. She even read the old issues that papered the summer kitchen walls.

For Ada, the best part of school was having her sisters there with her. Each morning, she prepared lunches for three: thick slices of the bread she had baked, spread with butter and sometimes topped with a sprinkling of sugar. To this, she added a cookie, usually oatmeal, sugar, or molasses, and sometimes an apple from Papa's orchards. Ada knotted linen bread cloths around the lunches and handed them to Ella and Flora as they left the house.

On school mornings, Harry and Stella Knopf, from the house at the corner of Everingin and Townline Roads, and Edith Moss and her twin brother Edwin met the Seibel girls on the road in front of their house. They progressed north on Townline Road and turned down George and Bertha's drive, where they were joined by Rosie, Elmer, and Walter. The group of children walked the lane to the end of George's property, crossed the stile over the fence, and followed the creek to Plank Road.

At Edwin's instigation, the boys often tossed large field stones into the creek, creating giant geysers that splashed the girls. Sometimes the little group became so absorbed in trying to scoop up minnows or catch frogs that they completely forgot about their destination, until they heard the sound of Miss Dunn ringing the school bell to signal the start of the school day. Then, they ran pell-mell along the narrow footpath bordering the creek and leaped from stone to stone in the water to dodge the thorny hedges that grew along the bank. Invariably, one of the children missed a stepping stone while crossing the creek and arrived at school with one or both shoes squirting out creek water at every step.

Mama had grown more accepting of her daughters' education, although she still kept one or more home from school on laundry days or to help with heavy cleaning or when extra hands were needed, such as during butchering, soapmaking, putting up preserves, making sauerkraut, or harvesting the potato crop. When Mama's spells raged, one of the older girls stayed home to keep an eye on the younger siblings.

A member of the Plank Road school board took note of the growing Seibel family and asked Papa to serve on the school board. Papa readily accepted this opportunity to support education, and he dutifully fulfilled his role by securing coal for the schoolhouse stove, building an extension to the platform at the front of the schoolroom for staging plays, and obtaining a large Ansonia wall clock. Papa was so enamored of the pleasant *tick-tock* of the school clock that he bought a small shelf clock for Mama's thirty-fifth birthday. It was the first timepiece to grace the Seibel household.

*****

In September of 1901, the Gasteiers decided to hold their first formal family reunion at the homestead of John Frederick and Katherine Gasteier. All eight of Mama's surviving siblings would be there, along with their spouses and children. Mama was bubbling with anticipation. The normal Saturday chores of cleaning the kitchen, scrubbing the plank floors, and moving the kitchen chairs outside for a good washing had been forsaken. Instead, Mama's attentions were turned to food preparation. While she knew that her siblings were aware of the debt Papa carried, she refused to appear destitute by showing up with a slim offering of food. Mama bustled about the kitchen, singing snatches of songs and directing Ada, Ella, and Flora in their duties. There were eggs to hard boil and add to the pickled beets, chicken to dip into buttermilk and deep fry in lard, cucumbers to slice into a cream and vinegar mixture, and apple slices to be sprinkled with cinnamon and sugar and baked between flaky pie crusts.

Early on the Sunday morning of the reunion, all of the food was nestled into baskets in the bed of the spring wagon, and the five girls clambered in beside it. Between Mama and Papa on the wagon seat rested the basket that contained baby Martha Ida, born in late June of 1901. It was Mama's only regret this day, to be showing up at the reunion with six daughters and no sons.

Little Martha was a beauty, with her black hair, dark complexion, and blue eyes. Strangers frequently commented on the child's remarkable attractiveness, which was somewhat of a balm to Mama's disappointment at having another girl.

After a while, Papa guided Jib and the spring wagon off the side of the road at Root Springs, the halfway point between the Gasteier and Seibel residences. The girls tumbled out of the back of the wagon and ran to a small frame shanty built into the hillside. Its dark, cool recesses sheltered a pipe that emerged directly from the hillside and trickled a steady stream of cold spring water to a bed of pebbles below. The girls took turns cupping their hands beneath the tap and sipping the refreshing cold water. When Mama wasn't looking, they held one finger tightly over the opening of the spigot and sprayed each other, or dipped their hands in the water and flicked their fingers, sending droplets of water at an unsuspecting sister.

Papa pulled a bucket from the bed of the wagon and filled it with spring water for Jib. Next, he set a large ceramic jug in the pebbles below the tap. Papa had read that mineral water soothed the nerves, and he hoped the Root Springs water would help Mama's condition. While the jug filled, he called "Girls! Girls!" to gather the sisters from the roadside, where they had scattered to pick bachelor's buttons and Queen Anne's lace. He then helped Mama climb back onto the wagon seat.

Flora ran to the front of the wagon and held up a handful of flowers that she had picked for Mama. Plucking a few bachelor's buttons from the bouquet and inserting them into her upswept hair, Mama turned to Papa and asked coquettishly, "Do you still like it when I wear *Unkräuter* (weeds) in my hair?"

Papa smiled at her. "I do," he replied, giving the reins a tap. "Always have. Ever since the first time I saw you."

The shade-dappled backyard of the Gasteier homestead was bustling with relatives. Mama greeted her parents and siblings and their spouses with hugs, while everyone cooed over beautiful baby Martha. Before the girls could run off with their cousins, Mama directed them to help her carry the food to the two long planks that rested on sawhorses along the stone sidewalk. Mama's spirits soared when she overheard two of her sisters-in-law comment on the abundance of food brought by the Seibels.

Blankets were spread in the shade of the trees for dining picnic-style, while Grandma and Grandpa Gasteier sat in rocking chairs that had been carried out from the house. Plates were piled high with food, and everyone commented on the tempting assortment. After the meal, the children played croquet or walked along the nearby railroad tracks. The women cleaned up the dishes and carried on conversations in German about babies, recipes, and neighborhood gossip, while the men gradually drifted off to examine the field crops.

Mama's younger brother, Will, who still lived on the Gasteier homestead with his parents, pointed out the newest strawberry field, which wouldn't be ready for picking until the following season.

"*Es gibt gutes Geld mit Erdbeeren, Bill. Du solltest es versuchen* (There's good money in strawberries, Bill. You ought to try it)," Will advised Papa.

Papa thrust his hands in his pockets and pondered the neat rows of strawberry plants stretching out before him. He inquired about the markets and prices and how quickly one could expect a return on their investment.

Will answered all of Papa's questions and ended with, "*Selbstverständlich benötigst du eine Menge Arbeiter, Erdbeeren anzubauen, besonders wenn die Frucht reift. Aber es ist die Art der Arbeit die Mädchen machen können, obgleich Sophie es nie mochte.* (Of course, you need a lot of laborers to grow strawberries, especially when the fruit ripens. But it's the kind of work girls can do, although Sophie never liked it.)" Will winked and gave Papa a good-natured nudge with his elbow as he turned back toward the farmhouse. Mama's vehement dislike of field work and her resultant displays of temper were no secret in the Gasteier family, and Will surmised that Papa had frequently been on the receiving end of similar outbursts during his marriage.

Papa cocked his head and continued to gaze at the strawberry field while the other men ambled back toward the farmhouse. He walked down the tidy rows, closely examining the strawberry plants and inspecting a handful of soil.

Mama's younger brother, Will Gasteier

By the time Papa returned to the backyard, Will had carried an ice cream maker out of the house and enlisted all of the youngsters in taking a turn at its crank. They eagerly complied, and when the handle of the churn could be pushed no further, Will scooped the cold treat into small cups. Everyone savored their ice cream and agreed that the first Gasteier reunion had been so enjoyable, they should make it an annual event.

Papa sat in the grass with his back against a tree and his legs outstretched in front of him. He ate his ice cream while deep in thought about strawberries.

First Gasteier reunion—September 1901

Chapter 8
Monroeville, Ohio
1903

ON A SUNDAY MORNING IN APRIL, thirteen-year-old Ada sat with the other confirmands in the front pew of the Emmanuel Evangelical Church in Monroeville. She smoothed the tucks of her white linen skirt and nervously twirled the gold ring with its deep red stone that had been her confirmation gift. Papa had driven all the way to a jeweler's in Norwalk to select the ring, and Ada had been both surprised and pleased to receive her first piece of jewelry.

The sanctuary was packed to capacity. Some of Ada's fellow confirmands came from the more socially elite families in Monroeville—the Bessels, Danielses, and Gilmans—who were all present to see their sons and daughters join the church. Ada's neighbors, the Mosses, Ordmanns, Knopfs, and the George Seibels, were also in attendance. Before services began, Emmaline Moss had been busy encouraging a friendship between her daughter Edith and Mrs. Bessel's daughter Laurinda. When it came to social climbing, Emmaline never missed an opportunity.

Ada looked over her shoulder at her family, who were seated on the opposite side of the aisle, about midway back in the sanctuary. Papa sat at the far end of the pew next to the wall. In his lap was little Martha, not quite two years old. Papa had taken the clean white hankie out of his coat pocket and folded it to resemble a cradle that contained twin babies. Martha held the ends of the hankie and pretended to rock the infants. Next to Papa sat three-year-old Margaret, whose head was in Ella's lap, then Flora and Hermine, with Mama fidgeting in her seat on the aisle. Ada winced to think how Margaret was crushing the sausage curls in her hair that she and Ella had worked so hard to create.

On Saturday evening, Ada and Ella had set the big wooden washtub on two kitchen chairs that faced each other in front of the cookstove. From the wellstalk in the summer kitchen, they pumped bucket after bucket of water, which they carried into the kitchen and poured into the copper boiler on top of the stove. When the water was hot, they transferred bucketsful of steaming bathwater to the washtub, tempering it with just the right amount of cold water. After Ada and Ella had bathed, they added more hot water to the now-tepid bathwater and summoned their four younger sisters into the kitchen. One by one, Ada bathed her siblings and washed their hair with a bar of homemade soap, her fingers briskly scrubbing their scalps and working the lather through to the ends of their long tresses. Flora sputtered as the rinse water momentarily cascaded over her face; Hermine whimpered when the soap stung her eyes; Margaret's only interest was in creating castles of soap bubbles; and Martha splashed so much water that Ada ended up mopping the kitchen floor, which she, Ella, and Flora had scrubbed earlier that day.

Ella was in charge of drying the freshly bathed children and wrapping their hair in a towel, which she twisted to wring out the excess water. Ada and Ella combed each sister's long hair until it was free of tangles, then wound sections of hair around white strips of cloth, which they tied close to the head. Little Martha shook her head so vigorously that they quickly abandoned the hair treatment and allowed her hair to dry into its normal raven waves.

After breakfast the next morning, Ada donned her black lisle stockings, cotton drawers with the lace-trimmed ruffle at the knees, muslin underskirt, gauge vest, white blouse with its lace insertions and tucks, and her long white skirt, trimmed with more lace, tucks, and ruffles. Around her waist she tied a white satin ribbon. She pulled on her polished black shoes and quickly worked the button hook to fasten the long row of shiny buttons. Ada braided her waist-length hair into a thick cord and fastened a big white bow at the nape of her neck.

Ella dressed in her Sunday whites, tied a pale blue ribbon around her waist, and caught her braid in a loop with a stiff bow. When Ada finished with the button hook, Ella bent over the row on her own shoes.

Next, the two sisters dressed the younger girls in black ribbed stockings, ferris waists, and knee-length white dresses. They tied pastel satin ribbons around each girl's waist, then set to work fastening four pairs of button shoes. They carefully removed the white cloth strips from the girls' hair and arranged the sausage curls. Big satin bows were clipped at the side of their heads to finish the effect. Ada cautioned the girls not to shake their heads, or the sausage curls would be reduced to limp strands.

And now, after all that work, Margaret was lying with her head in Ella's lap, crushing the curls. Ada gave a small shrug and consoled herself with the thought that at least they had made a nice impression when they arrived at church.

She returned her attention to Rev. Keppel, who stood behind the altar and broke the loaf of bread for communion. The golden crust made an appealing crackle as it parted, and a shower of crumbs cascaded to the white linen altar cloth. Ada closed her eyes and ran her finger around the inside of her stiff lace collar, where the whalebone inserts were poking into her neck. She thought longingly of the cake and punch that the church ladies would serve at the confirmands' reception after services.

A muffled gasp swept through the congregation, and Ada's eyes flew open. She could not believe what she saw. There stood Mama beside Rev. Keppel behind the altar. She was sweeping the bread crumbs from the altar cloth into her open palm, while muttering "apple-pie order" and "*ordentlich und sauber* (neat and tidy)." Reverend Keppel overcame his surprise and gently took Mama's elbow, intending to usher her back to her pew. Mama jerked her arm free and continued tidying up the altar, oblivious to anything but her need for order.

By this time, Papa was on his feet, crawling over his daughters' legs and depositing little Martha in Flora's lap as he struggled to reach the end of the pew. He strode up the aisle and clamped one strong hand around Mama's upper arm. Papa's face was flushed and his jaw clenched as he wordlessly propelled Mama down the aisle toward the church doors. Mama shrieked, "*Ordentlich und sauber, William, ordentlich und sauber!*" as she slapped at Papa with her free hand.

The sanctuary doors banged shut behind them, but Mama's loud protests could still be heard over the rattle of the wagon as it exited the church yard. A wave of whispering and barely concealed tittering rippled through the congregation.

The girls sat frozen in their pew. Ada's head hung between her shoulders, her cheeks burning and hot tears threatening to spill over her eyelids.

"Where'd Mama and Papa go?" Margaret whispered to Ella, searching her older sister's face for answers.

Ella held her fingertips over the child's lips and shook her head, blinking back tears and wishing she could leave instead of enduring this humiliation.

Reverend Keppel regained his composure, cleared his throat, and resumed the service. When it was Ada's turn to step before the altar for communion, she could feel all eyes upon her and hear a few lingering whispers among the congregation. As she reached for the cube of bread offered by Rev. Keppel, Ada felt the minister's hand rest momentarily on hers and give it a reassuring pat. She looked up and detected sympathy in his kind brown eyes. Ada could barely swallow the communion bread around the lump of shame in her throat. She returned to her pew with eyes downcast.

At the conclusion of the church service, Ada quickly exited her pew and worked her way down the aisle, past tight clusters of church people who stood with their heads close together, sharing whispered opinions about the unusual behavior they had witnessed that morning. When Ada neared, they stopped talking but followed her with their eyes, then resumed their furtive conversations. She finally reached the pew where her sisters sat in uncomfortable silence.

"Let's go home," Ada said quietly as she lifted little Martha onto her hip.

Ella reached for Margaret's hand, and the four sisters followed Ada down the aisle, out the doors, and across the church yard.

"Aren't you staying for the reception?" Edith Moss called mockingly from the front steps of the church. "The least you could do is take a piece of cake home to your mother. She must be hungry after all that tidying up!" Edith turned to Laurinda Bessel and they dissolved in giggles.

Ada's cheeks burned and she quickened her pace. The girls hurried down Baker Street, then turned onto Monroe Street and headed out Plank Road for the three-mile walk home. If the ground hadn't been so muddy from the spring thaw, Ada would have led them across the fields to avoid contact with any of her neighbors, whom she knew would eventually overtake them in their buggies on their way home from church.

The girls walked along in silence until five-year-old Hermine asked innocently, "Why was Mama up there by the altar with Rev. Keppel? Was she being God's helper?"

Ada shifted Martha to her other hip and answered tersely, "No, Mama was just being Mama. That's all."

The sound of a horse and buggy approaching behind them made Ada's heart sink, but she drew in a deep breath and straightened her shoulders.

"You girls need a ride home?" Mr. Moss asked as he reined the horse to a stop next to them. Emmaline Moss's neck stretched around her husband's shoulder, and she peered at the girls suspiciously, as if she expected them to burst into outrageous behavior at any moment. Edwin and Edith leaned forward from the back seat of the buggy and stared at them with barely concealed smirks.

"No, thank you. We'll walk," Ada replied, even though her shoes pinched her feet, her arms were sore from carrying little Martha, and she knew Hermine and Margaret were tiring from the long trek.

Mr. Moss nodded and tapped the reins. When the buggy pulled away, Edwin leaned out of the back of the carriage and made an exaggerated circling motion with his finger next to his ear, the universal childhood symbol for "crazy."

Ada's confirmation

* * * * *

In June of 1903, Papa walked the long rows of the strawberry field, stopping frequently to inspect the rubied fruit that was now ready for picking. This would be his first crop of strawberries, and he had carefully monitored its progress ever since the cold, overcast day in the spring of 1902 when he, Ada, Ella, Flora, and Hermine had planted the field.

On that day, Papa had filled the wheelbarrow with strawberry plants and pushed it to the field he had prepared for his new crop. He thrust a stick knotted with a piece of twine into the ground, then marched a straight course across the length of the field, where he tied the end of the twine to another stick and inserted it into the soft earth. Flora and Hermine were stationed by the stakes and charged with moving the planting guide as the planting progressed.

Papa filled his shoulder pouch with young strawberry plants, and he handed a bundle to Ada and Ella. They began at one end of the twine, working their way down the lengthy row, with Papa slicing his spade into the soil and the girls carefully setting a plant into each hole, with the roots fanning outward. Papa used the toe of his brogan to quickly press the soil around the crown of the roots, then took two steps and dug the next hole. As they became more accustomed to the task, their pace quickened. When the field had been planted, the girls helped Papa carry load after load of golden straw from the barn to spread under the plants and between the rows.

Throughout the months that followed, Papa and the girls prowled the field, pulling weeds by hand and pinching off any white strawberry blossoms to prevent fruit set, thus promoting root and runner development and producing a sturdy plant. When the summer weather turned dry, he and the girls rose early in the morning and carried bucket after bucket of water to the field. In the fall, they covered the plants with more straw to protect against the long winter ahead.

Through the winter months, Papa had busied himself in his workshop above the cornbarn, where he tacked together pieces of pressed wood into quart baskets. He created six-quart carrying containers out of scrap wood, with bent tree bark for handles, and made multi-leveled crates that held twenty-four quart baskets for transporting the fruit to market. He cobbled together a flimsy packing house, which was a three-sided shanty that could easily be knocked down and moved as the harvesting progressed.

By mid-spring, the strawberry field was a sea of white blossoms, and Papa fretted that a killing frost would wipe out his maiden crop. It had been an anxious year awaiting the outcome of his new venture, and Papa knew he could not afford another failed investment. But now it was June, and the bright red berries hung from every plant, waiting to be picked.

At four o'clock the next morning, Papa roused his daughters from their sleep with the call, "Girls, girls! It's time to pick berries."

Ada, Ella, Flora, Hermine, and even Margaret, who was not quite four, dressed in the dark, stumbled sleepy-eyed down the stairs, ate a hasty breakfast of leftover biscuits spread with molasses, and headed out to the strawberry field just as the sun crested the horizon. Papa showed them how to check for ripeness and the proper way to pick a berry, by grasping the stem just above the berry and pulling with a slight twisting motion. He cautioned them to handle the fruit carefully to prevent bruising or crushing and instructed them to top off each quart basket with large, perfect berries. Each girl took a carrier that contained six quart baskets and started at the end of a row, while Papa left the field to milk the cows and attend to the other morning chores.

Soon, the girls' legs, backs, and necks ached from the stoop work. They tried different picking postures: sitting cross-legged, lying on their stomachs, and crouching in a duck walk. Margaret frowned at the few berries that lay in the bottom of her quart basket. She picked up one berry and popped it into her mouth. Her eyes widened at the sweet flavor, and she followed it with another berry and another. At the sight of Papa rounding the corner of the barn, she swallowed quickly and returned to berry picking. Papa grabbed a carrier from the packing house and set to work on his own row. With both hands, he parted the tops of the strawberry plants and plucked the ripened fruit from their stems. He piled handfuls of berries into the quart baskets and quickly outdistanced the girls as he progressed down the length of the field.

Every filled six-quart carrier was taken to the packing house, where the baskets were placed into the larger shipping crate. When a crate was filled, Papa transported it to the cool recesses of the barn for storage. Over and over, the process was repeated as the sun crept higher into the sky.

When the girls took a break for the noon meal, they hoped that Mama would have a hearty lunch waiting for them. However, Mama was pulling weeds around the outbuildings and could not be distracted from her mission. Two-year-old Martha was nowhere in sight.

When Ada entered the summer kitchen, she found little Martha seated in the midst of a sea of flour. Mama had left the child in the house alone, where she had amused herself by scooping flour out of the big metal bin in the summer kitchen and scattering it about the floor. Ada muttered an exasperated "*Ach, himmel!* (Oh, heavens!)" and pulled Martha to her feet. Ella grabbed the broom that leaned beside the summer kitchen door and swept up the mess, while Flora wiped off Martha's hands and dusted the flour from her clothing.

Ada bustled about the kitchen, scratching together a hasty meal of molasses on bread, *Hüttenkäse* (cottage cheese), and a jar of pears that they had preserved last fall. She eyed the loaves of bread on the cutting board in the pantry and calculated that they would soon run out if she did not find time to do the usual midweek baking. The last of the biscuits had been eaten for breakfast, and the cookie kettle was almost empty.

While the girls returned with Papa to the strawberry field, Ada heated some water on the cookstove and washed and dried the lunch dishes. If Mama wandered in and found dirty dishes in the drysink or a crumb on the kitchen table, the punishment would be swift and severe. When the kitchen was tidied, Ada bent over the wellstalk in the summer kitchen and splashed some cold water on her face, then returned to the berry field.

The girls picked while keeping an eye on little Martha, plying her with strawberries to keep her close by. Eventually, the little child laid down in a shady corner of the packing house and fell asleep.

At the end of the long day, the berry crew headed for the house, tired, aching, and hungry. Ada sniffed the air as they approached the back porch, hoping to pick up the aroma of Mama cooking potatoes or frying meat for supper. Nothing but the scent of the sauerkraut crock in the summer kitchen greeted her nose.

Ada started a fire in the cookstove and ladled a generous dollop of lard into the cast iron skillet, then began peeling potatoes. She sent Hermine, Margaret, and Martha outside to gather the eggs, while Flora set the table. Ella went to the cellar to retrieve an onion from the few bundles that still hung from the rafters after last year's harvest. She stopped to fill a pitcher with milk from the pails Papa had set on the cellar steps in the morning. After supper, she and Ada would have to separate the cream from both the morning and evening milking, then store the dairy products in crocks in the cool cellar until they could find time to churn butter and make cottage cheese.

Papa brought in two quart baskets of berries he had deemed too small for sale. Flora hulled one quart of berries into a bowl and poured milk over them, reserving the other quart for their breakfast. Ada stirred the eggs into the fried potato slices and rings of onions. They ate the remains of a loaf of bread with their supper, leaving two loaves that Ada knew would be consumed long before baking day on Saturday.

Mama, fueled by mugs of cold black coffee, continued to tidy the lawn long after sunset, ignoring the needs of the household or the children.

Early the next morning, after Papa had started the girls in the field again, he loaded the crates of berries onto the spring wagon and headed into Monroeville to market them. He and Mr. Zipfel hammered out a trade that would reduce his long-standing debt at the store. While Mr. Zipfel tallied the credit next to Papa's name in his ledger book, Papa wandered to a shelf that contained hats. He fingered the edge of a straw hat and thought of the girls. Porcelain skin was the sign of a lady, so he picked up several straw hats for the girls as well as a pouch of chewing tobacco for himself and told Mr. Zipfel to deduct the items from his berry trade.

As the daily strawberry picking continued, Mr. Zipfel became overwhelmed with the inventory of berries. Papa drove fifteen miles to the rail station in Chicago Junction to market his crop, then peddled the remaining berries in Bellevue, where he drove the wagon up and down the streets, calling "Berries! S-t-r-a-w-berries!" Before long, people started referring to Papa as "Strawberry Bill."

Papa became tense and impatient under the stress of harvesting and marketing his highly perishable crop. Consequently, the girls tended to refrain from conversation or laughter when Papa was near them in the field, feeling sure that he was aggravated by anything but serious berry picking. As soon as he outdistanced them with his rapid picking, they returned to talking, laughing, and teasing each other while they worked their way down the long rows.

The berry picking lasted five weeks. Sometimes Mama was lucid and in command; other times, all meal preparation and household tasks awaited the girls at the end of a long day in the field. As they dropped into bed each night, they commiserated over their sore muscles and fatigue.

When the berry season drew to a close, Papa assessed his experiment. The berries had ripened in such volume that he and the girls could not keep up with them; he had lost a percentage of the crop to over-ripeness and subsequent rot. Nevertheless, Papa considered his venture a success. He intended to add another field next year but knew the future berry-picking demands would be beyond the capacity of his family; he would have to hire pickers. Papa smiled to himself. His brother-in-law Will had been right: there was good money in strawberries.

* * * * *

Late that August, the soaring temperatures and steamy humidity made everyone uncomfortable. Mama and the girls canned tomatoes and green beans in the summer kitchen one morning. Even with the windows propped open, the heat in the room was oppressive. Mama's back ached, which made her more irritable than usual. She lashed out at Ada when one of the glass quart containers cracked in the boiling water bath, and she barked at Flora for not snapping the beans fast enough. Mama kneaded her fists into the small of her back and ordered the three youngest girls out of the summer kitchen.

After a quick lunch of tomato slices on bread served with the leftover green beans, Papa announced he was taking the wagon down to Frink's Run to dig up river gravel. He used the stone to line the paths to the outbuildings as a means of cutting down on the quagmire of mud that resulted from heavy rains and spring thaws.

As Papa pushed his chair away from the kitchen table, Mama wearily propped her elbows on the table's edge and cupped her forehead in the palms of her hands. "Take them with you," she said without looking up. "*Ich muß ausruhen.* (I need to rest.)"

The girls glanced at each other with smiles on their faces. The opportunity to wade in the waters of the shallow tributary was a welcome treat on such a beastly hot day. They quickly cleaned up the kitchen and scrambled out the screen door, being careful to catch it before it slammed.

The girls climbed into the back of the spring wagon beside Papa's shovel. He gave the reins a tap, and Davey reluctantly leaned into the harness. Davey was a strong horse but as lazy as the day was hot. His favorite speed was a leisurely stroll, and the girls regretted that Papa hadn't chosen Jib, who liked to trot and would have generated some air movement on their trip to the river.

When they reached the end of Townline Road, Papa turned Davey west on Everingin Road along the high bluff that overlooked the tributary. The girls stood up in the wagon box to catch a glimpse of the sparkling water below. After a short distance, the wagon reached the point where Everingin abutted Sand Hill Road. Papa turned south, then guided Davey off the road just before they reached the bridge. He drove along the river bank until he found an area where the water was shallow and the horse could easily descend to the river. Davey splashed into the water, and the girls squealed with laughter and held on to the sides of the wagon bed as it rocked precariously from side to side.

After Papa had reined Davey to a stop, the barefoot girls tumbled out of the back of the wagon and into the cool, refreshing water. Papa removed his brogans and socks and rolled up his pant legs, then waded around to the back of the wagon to retrieve the shovel. He smiled as he watched his six daughters splash about in the river. Digging his shovel into the gravel, he began to load the back of the wagon.

The girls waded in the river, holding hands so that no one would lose their footing on the slippery slate that lined the bed of the stream.

They gathered small pieces of slate from the bank and had contests to see who could skip a stone the farthest and who could achieve the most skips before the stone sunk beneath the water's surface. Ella was the undisputed champion, coaxing multiple skips from each toss of a stone. When they grew tired of the game, they scrambled up the bank and dropped pebbles from the bridge, exclaiming over each *plick!* and *ploop!* that the stones made upon entry into the water. The sisters sat on the edge of the bridge deck, swinging their legs and watching the river flow beneath them. When the heat became uncomfortable, they clambered down the bank and took refuge in the shade beneath the bridge, enjoying the mossy coolness of the massive stones that supported the bridge deck.

Soon, the desire to be back in the water overcame them, and the sisters waded east in the stream, toward a high embankment that was littered with old cans and bottles. Folks from the neighborhood often used the area as a dump. The girls stopped frequently to pick up interesting stones in the clear water and found pretty pieces of green, blue, and brown broken glass.

As Ada bent over to examine some glass that sparkled beneath the water's surface, she felt a sharp pain in the sole of her foot. She hobbled to the river bank and found a nasty puncture in the flesh. Ada winced as she squeezed the wound, trying to force the piece of imbedded glass to the surface for removal. The sisters gathered around her and offered sympathy. Finally, Ada gave up, and with Flora and Ella on either side to offer support, and the three younger girls splashing along behind, she limped downstream. Papa inspected the puncture and advised Ada to walk home and use one of Mama's sewing needles to extract the glass. "If you don't get it out," he warned, "it could poison your blood." He pulled a hankie from his pocket and knotted it around Ada's foot.

Ella offered to walk home with Ada, but Ada asserted that she could manage by walking on just the toes of that foot. Besides, she didn't want to pull any of her sisters away from the cool recesses of the river, only to return to the hot house and Mama's irritability.

Ada advised Ella to keep the girls away from the dump, then hobbled up the bank. The walk home was slow, hot, and painful. When Ada reached the back porch, all was quiet. She hoped Mama was napping so that she would not have to explain what had happened. Mama could dole out punishment over the most minor things. Ada intended to retrieve Mama's sewing basket from her bedroom, then sit out on the porch, where the light would be optimal for working on her foot. After the glass was removed, she would retrieve a piece of salt pork from the smokehouse and tie it to the bottom of her foot to draw out any infection.

Ada tiptoed across the porch and quietly closed the screen door behind her. As she crossed toward Mama's bedroom, she stopped and stifled a gasp. A long pool of blood clots and tissue trailed across the kitchen floor. Ada felt an involuntary gag reflex well up from the pit of her stomach, and she clasped her hands over her mouth and squeezed her eyes tight to keep from throwing up.

She skirted around the puddle on the floor and stepped through the kitchen doorway, noticing a trail of bloody fluid that led toward Mama's bedroom. Ada swallowed hard and peered toward Mama's room, where she could see Mama's still form lying on her back on the bed.

"Mama?" Ada called softly, tiptoeing to the foot of Mama's bed. "Are you alright?"

Mama's face was ashen and damp with sweat. For a long moment, she didn't answer but continued staring at the ceiling. Finally, she lifted both trembling hands to her face and rubbed her fingers in slow circles over her eyes. "I lost the baby," she said in a whisper.

"A baby?" Ada replied in astonishment. She had not known that Mama was pregnant.

"Maybe it would have been a boy this time," Mama croaked, her shoulders shaking with sobs. "Why do the *Baby mädchen* (baby girls) always have to survive?"

The comment stung Ada like a slap on the cheek. She stood for a long moment watching Mama sob. She did not know what to do to comfort her mother. The room was stifling, and the smell of blood filled Ada's nostrils. She choked back a rising gag reflex and limped out to the summer kitchen, where she pumped water to heat on the cookstove, then pulled some rags from the bag that hung in the corner cupboard.

When the water was hot, Ada filled a bucket and carried it to the kitchen. She barricaded the kitchen door with a chair so that if the girls arrived home, they would not walk in and find the scene that had greeted her. Ada swallowed deeply, then set to work cleaning up the clotted blood and tissue on the kitchen floor. At times, she could not refrain from violent fits of gagging, which caused her throat to burn with the acrid taste of bile. Tears ran down her face, and she choked back sobs of her own. When the floor was clean at last, she removed the barricade and scooped softsoap into another bucket of hot water. Ada vigorously scrubbed the plank floors, determined to remove all trace of the smell and stain of blood.

She hung the washed and rinsed rags on the clothesline and was just dumping the washwater on the yellow rose bush at the corner of the house when Papa and the girls rattled into the driveway with the load of river gravel.

While Ella, Flora, and Hermine scrambled off the load of stone, Papa helped Margaret and Martha down from the wagon seat. He peered at Ada's tear-streaked face. "Your foot hurt you that bad?"

Ada took Papa aside and told him what had happened, leaving out Mama's cutting remark about the survivability of baby girls. Papa closed his eyes and his head dropped to his chest. He slowly crossed the yard and climbed the porch steps.

While Papa comforted Mama, Ada laid on the back porch with her arm draped over her eyes and her foot in Ella's lap. She winced but did not cry as Ella probed for the piece of glass with the sewing needle.

* * * * *

In the fall of 1903, Papa and the girls uprooted runners from the parent strawberry plants and placed them in crates, along with enough soil to keep the roots moist. Papa carried the crates to the cool cellar for storage through the long winter months. In the spring, he and the girls would set out the runners in another prepared field, which would begin the cycle of planting a new field each year. In time, Papa hoped to have four fields in a constant rotation of strawberries: the newly planted field, the first-year field, the second-year field in its prime, and the waning or third-year field.

Another fall chore was harvesting sorghum cane for molasses. Armed with corn knives, the older girls followed Papa through the cane field. While he lopped the seed heads off the standing cane, the girls stripped the leaves so the syrup would be sweeter and more bountiful. On a return pass through the field, they cut and bundled the cane, which Papa tossed onto the bed of the nearby wagon. When they paused for a break, he showed the girls how to twist a section of cane over their open mouths to catch the juice. The girls quickly learned to avoid the sharp outer covering of the cane, which cut their lips. After the field was harvested, Papa drove the wagon to Heber Grau's house on Everingin Road, where Heber and his sons pressed, strained, and boiled the green juice into molasses in exchange for a jug or two of the dark amber syrup.

The last crop to be harvested in the fall was the potato fields. The work could not be completed in a weekend, so the girls stayed home from school for several days. While Ada, Ella, and Flora thrust their potato forks into the mounded dirt, Hermine, Margaret, and even little

Martha gathered up the unearthed potatoes and carried them to nearby crates. Papa stored a generous supply of potatoes in the cellar, since they were a major staple of the family's daily diet. The rest of the crop was sold for cash.

*****

Hermine, now six years old, had joined her three older sisters on the walk to school that fall. Miss Dunn, the teacher with the billowing hair and the fascinating watch pinned to her blouse, had married and therefore was no longer eligible to teach school. Her replacement was Miss Marian Belle Slade, who believed in improving the children both academically and socially. Under the window in the front of the schoolroom, she set up a sand table for the younger students. For the older students, there were lessons in dancing the Virginia Reel. Miss Slade organized spelling bees, brought her own books to the school to promote a lending library, and planned variety shows that the students staged for their parents and neighbors.

With all of the activity at school, the girls hated to be absent. When they were kept home due to work or weather, their conversations always turned to what they were missing. For Ada, it would be her last year of school. Educating a girl beyond the eighth reader was unnecessary, according to Mama. Papa, however, was giving some thought to Ada's future.

Chapter 9
The Seibel Homestead
1904

WHEN ADA HAD COMPLETED her education at the Plank Road school in late May of 1904, Papa arranged for her to take sewing lessons from the Weber girls, Mariah and Esther. The sisters' initial reluctance to take on a fourteen-year-old apprentice was overcome by Papa's barter. He would provide them with as many fresh strawberries as they could eat during the berry harvest, plus other goods from the farm, including eggs, butter, cream, and seasonal garden produce. In exchange, they would teach Ada the sewing skills necessary to become an itinerant seamstress. By appealing to the Weber girls' gastronomical needs, Papa had secured Ada an apprenticeship with the finest seamstresses in Monroeville.

When the weather and her workload at home permitted, Ada walked the three miles into town, bearing a quart or two of strawberries, a canning jar of thick cream, or a basket of eggs. Once, she had brought the spinster sisters a jar of sauerkraut, but they quickly rejected it, citing delicate digestive tracts and a desire for less Germanic fare. Their sharp eyes inspected every food offering that Ada brought, and they were impossibly hard to please. Their comments ranged from "Hmmm, a lot of seeds in these berries. Are you bringing us the culls?" to "These eggs are smaller than the ones you brought last week," or "This butter certainly looks sweaty. Did you dawdle on your way here?"

The sisters' demand for quality carried over to their sewing. They taught Ada how to sew by having her perform a technique until it was perfect, even if it meant repeatedly ripping out her work and starting over. Thanks to Mama's demands, Ada was used to meeting high expectations. In addition, she had a natural aptitude for visualizing how a garment should be cut and constructed. The Weber girls were pleased with Ada's progress, but their praise was limited to a slight nod of the head and an occasional "Fine" as they inspected her work. Ada was not accustomed to receiving praise at home, so the lack of feedback from the Weber girls did not bother her.

That summer, a special commission kept the seamstresses working diligently. Mrs. Bessel and her daughter Laurinda would be accompanying Mr. Bessel to the national hardware convention in Philadelphia in August, and they had ordered an entire trunk of new clothes to be sewn for the trip. Mariah sucked her lemon drop in rhythm with the *snip, snip, snip* of her scissors as she cut out silk dresses for Mrs. Bessel. Esther sat at the sewing machine by the front window, her feet working the treadle as she stitched intricate tucks into a crepe de chine blouse or secured a delicate band of cutwork lace into the bodice of a linen day dress for Laurinda. Ada was kept busy ripping out rows of basting, pressing seams, and counting the number of tiny stitches per inch as she hemmed numerous garments.

When Mrs. Bessel and Laurinda came for periodic fittings, Ada watched and listened as Mrs. Bessel and the Weber girls debated the merits of cloth-covered buttons versus contrasting buttons for the front of Mrs. Bessel's dresses. While Laurinda flipped through pages of the latest fashions in the *Delineator* magazine, her mother and the Weber girls fussed over the proper length for Laurinda's walking skirt. Sometimes, work that had been completed only the day before had to be ripped out and altered to meet Mrs. Bessel's changing tastes. Ada was receiving a tutorial in human nature along with her sewing lessons.

When the late afternoon heat in the sewing room became oppressive, the sisters retired to the shade of the apple tree in their backyard, glasses of lemonade in hand. Before Ada could be dismissed, she returned the bolts of fabric to the corner of the room where they were kept, folded the patterns and tucked them into the bureau drawers, tidied the cutting table, and swept the sewing room floor. Then, she started the long walk home, eager to see her own sisters and to teach them her newly acquired sewing skills. Flora, in particular, was adept with a needle and demonstrated a rapid mastery of the techniques. In many ways, the Weber girls had more than one apprentice.

* * * * *

The berrying season had been a busy but successful one. The day before picking was to commence, Papa had ridden into town to spread the word that workers would be paid two cents a quart to pick berries at his farm. On the designated day, men, women, and children walked, biked, or caught rides, bringing their lunches with them and working alongside the Seibel girls, who had been in the field since daybreak.

When Papa was in the berry patch, he maintained discipline with his stuttered commands and the menacing shake of his shortened index finger. In his presence, no one dared to initiate such mischief as throwing berries, although Papa had no rules about the amount of strawberries a worker could consume. Serious pickers, however, refrained from eating and worked intently to fill up their baskets, with some picking as many as one hundred quarts in a day. When a picker had filled their six-quart carrier, they took it to the packing house and received a ticket for each quart. At noon on Saturdays, the tickets were exchanged for cash.

Strawberry pickers by the packing house at the Seibel farm. At far left: Papa, Flora, & Ada (wearing straw hat)

Papa continued to market his berries at Zipfel's store as well as in Chicago Junction and on the streets of Bellevue. He sometimes received as much as twenty-five cents a quart, and his long-standing debt at Zipfel's was slowly being erased. Papa also started to make headway on repaying the loan he had taken out to buy nursery stock back in 1890. As the season waned and the berries grew smaller, fewer pickers made their way out from town. Then, the girls picked the remaining berries and made them into jam, or Papa marketed them and bought something to reward his daughters, such as stems of bananas, some hard French candies, or a small bag of brightly colored marbles.

When the berry season was over, Papa indulged in one of his favorite outlets: attending auctions. One afternoon, he rattled into the drive with a major acquisition in the back of the spring wagon. He had purchased an old upright piano at an estate sale. The girls could not believe their eyes. Up until this point, their only exposure to music had been the reed organ at church, a pitch pipe at school, and an occasional fiddle that accompanied the dancing parties organized by Miss Slade. The girls scrambled into the back of the wagon and looked at each other in amazement as they took turns depressing the yellowed ivories and listening to the slightly off-key notes.

Loading the piano into the back of the wagon at the auction had been relatively uncomplicated, due to the abundance of men in attendance. However, unloading it and moving it into the house with just the aid of the girls was going to be a difficult matter. Papa disappeared into the barn and emerged with a rope and two stout planks used during butchering. He placed the equipment into the back of the wagon beside the piano and tapped the reins on Davey's back. The big horse slowly turned the wagon around, and Papa maneuvered Davey until the bed of the wagon was backed up to the open north end of the front porch. He laid the heavy planks across the chasm between porch and wagon and strained to lift the front end of the piano until its castors were on the ends of the planks. Next, he secured the rope around the piano.

The girls ran into the house and pushed aside the furniture in the parlor to make room for the new piano, then propped open the front door. Three-year-old Martha danced between the parlor and porch while her five sisters took their positions behind the piano. Papa stood on the porch and pulled on the end of the rope. His face turned red from the exertion, and the girls braced their feet against the back of the wagon bed and pushed with all their combined might. The piano slowly inched its way up the planks.

Mr. Ordmann passed by on the road and paused to watch as Papa and the girls struggled to move the piano out of the wagon and into the house. He shook his head and muttered, "What don't he have them girls do?!"

When the piano was finally situated in the parlor, Papa took out his hankie and mopped his brow. As Hermine and Margaret plucked out a duet of random notes, Papa cautioned, "Now, be mindful of your Mama's nerves."

Soon, Ella, Flora, and Hermine began taking piano lessons from Mrs. Knopf at the corner of Everingin and Townline Roads. Their practice times were spotty, depending on Mama's ability to tolerate the noise. At other times, she seemed to enjoy the music and commented on the orchestra that used to play for the ballroom dances at the Wright Mansion, where she had worked as a domestic before her marriage. This recollection always ended with Mama furrowing her brow and saying in a puzzled tone, "But they never asked me to dance."

* * * * *

With the berry picking over, Papa allowed the girls to sleep until sunup. One morning, he sat alone at the kitchen table, tying his brogans, while Mama leaned against the living room doorway. She hummed as she brushed her long chestnut hair. Papa looked up at her, and she cocked her head and smiled at him, then asked, "Do you still like to watch me *mein Haar kämen* (brush my hair)?"

Papa nodded, a slight smile on his face, before draining his coffee mug. Mama placed the hairbrush on the table and circled around Papa until she stood behind his chair. She wrapped her arms around his shoulders, her long tresses cascading over his chest, while she nuzzled his neck and whispered in his ear. Papa stood up abruptly, but Mama wrapped her arms around his waist and pressed herself close to him. Her blue eyes sparkled mischievously as she looked up at him.

Papa unclasped her hands from behind his back and gently pushed her away, holding her wrists in his hands. He looked into her upturned face and stated emphatically, "I don't want no more children, Sophie. Six girls is enough."

"But *ein Sohn* (a son), William. *Ein Sohn* (a son)," Mama cooed. "Seibel and Sons Orchards, remember?"

"No. No more children," Papa replied firmly as he dropped Mama's wrists and headed out the kitchen door. Mama watched him walk down the gravel path toward the barn, gesturing as he carried on his argument with no one.

*****

After lunch, five-year-old Margaret noticed the cows congregating around the stone water trough behind the barn. She had watched Papa and her older sisters milk the cows, and she decided this noontime gathering was her opportunity to try her hand. She grabbed the milk pail from the bench in the summer kitchen and returned to the barn, where she picked up one of Papa's three-legged milking stools.

Margaret climbed over the fence into the barnyard and chose Old Bess, the most placid cow in the herd. She set the milking stool beside the cow and the pail below her udder. Grabbing a teat in each hand, Margaret sawed away with deliberation, just as she had seen Papa do, but she was perplexed by the lack of success. She switched to the other two teats, but still the milk pail remained empty. Old Bess chewed her cud in a languid roll of her lower jaw and ignored the assault on her udder.

However, this curious display of noontime milking did not go unnoticed by the rest of the cows in the herd. They began to gather around Old Bess and Margaret, snorting and stretching their long necks toward the scene. Margaret stopped her futile milking and looked around at the cluster of huge bodies that encircled her. Slowly, she stood and began backing away from Old Bess. One cow, which was particularly offended by the unusual activity, lowered its head and charged toward the little girl. Margaret screamed and raced for the fence, with the cow thundering after her. The other cows scattered, their tails raised in alarm.

With tears streaming down her face, Margaret sped to the house, where she related her experience to her older sisters. The girls laughed at her folly, and Flora chided, "Don't you know, silly? Cows only get milked in the morning and night—not at noon! They ain't like the wellstalk, where you pump the handle and get water any time of day." Flora dried Margaret's tears, then took her hand and walked out to the barnyard with her to retrieve the toppled milk pail and stool.

* * * * *

In late March of 1905, the winds were incessant, which added to Mama's growing irritation. Every time a shutter banged against the house or a window whistled in the steady gale, Mama jumped and lashed out at whichever child was close at hand. She roamed the house day and night, talking, singing, or making her own strange yips. This buildup in tension usually culminated in a seizure, which was disconcerting enough, but now Mama was far into her ninth month of pregnancy.

On April 1, Ada's fifteenth birthday, Papa sent for Dr. Gilman to deliver the baby. Mama had been pacing the bedroom and carrying on disjointed conversations with herself, punctuated by agonizing howls of birthing pain. The girls huddled in the kitchen, looking at each other in frightened silence. Hermine and Margaret crawled beneath the kitchen table and clapped their hands over their ears to muffle Mama's groans. Martha climbed into Flora's lap and sobbed quietly, while Ada and Ella heated water in the copper boiler on top of the cookstove and found some clean cloths for the doctor to use. Papa, who had been unhappy about the entire pregnancy, retreated to the barn.

Dr. Gilman did a quick assessment of Mama, then gave her a dose of laudanum to calm her agitation. The drug soothed her nerves, but it also slowed the birthing process. He poked his head out of the bedroom doorway and summoned Ada and Ella. Positioning the girls on either side of the bed by Mama's shoulders, he told them to restrain her if she struggled. From his medical bag, the doctor pulled a silver forceps.

After the baby had been delivered, Dr. Gilman washed up at the drysink in the kitchen, while Ada and Ella changed Mama's bed linens and tended to the newborn infant. The doctor asked where Papa was, and ten-year-old Flora silently pointed toward the barn.

Dr. Gilman placed the medical bag in his buggy, then crossed the farmyard and opened the barn door. He found Papa leaning on the wall of the grain bin, his forehead buried in his folded arms.

"Well, Bill, you've got yourself another girl," the doctor announced. "Now, I've lost track—does that make five or six?"

Papa sighed heavily. "Seven," he muttered into his coat sleeves. "Seven girls."

The doctor gave a low whistle. "I've given Sophie something to make her rest for a while, and the older girls are looking after the baby," Dr. Gilman said. Clearing his throat, he added, "I know every man wants a son, particularly you farmers, but really, Bill, don't keep after your wife till you have a boy."

Papa whirled around to face the doctor. "B-b-but it ain't me!" he protested, his face crimson. "Sophie's the one who wants a boy! Sh-sh-she's the one keeps after me!"

Dr. Gilman chuckled and patted Papa on the shoulder, "Well then, most men would envy you that problem, Bill. You shouldn't complain." Still chuckling, he shook his head and turned toward the door. "I'll tally up your bill when I get back to my office," he called over his shoulder.

Papa slumped against the grain bin wall and slid to the earthen floor of the barn. He picked up the three-legged milking stool beside him and hurtled it against the opposite wall. Propping his elbows on his knees, Papa cradled his head in his hands and ran his fingers through his hair.

It took Mama a few days to recover from her laudanum-induced haze. When she comprehended that she had had another girl, she plunged into deep despair. For a week, the infant went unnamed, being referred to as "Baby" by her sisters who rocked, changed, and bathed her. Mama's only contact with the child was in feeding her. Finally, Mama's mood leveled and she decided on a name for her seventh daughter: Minola Clara.

* * * * *

Papa's success with strawberries had bolstered his confidence in small-fruit diversification. In late April, he drove a wagon loaded with black raspberry and blackberry roots to the patch he had prepared for their planting. Like a new strawberry bed, the brambles would not produce fruit until the following year. The raspberries and blackberries would ripen after the strawberry harvest, and by keeping the plantings to a half acre apiece, Papa reasoned that he and the girls could handle the crop without relying on outside pickers.

An old man by the name of Peter Essendorf came to help Papa with the planting. Peter was an alcoholic who usually stayed with the Lantz family next door to the Plank Road school. He did occasional day labor in the neighborhood in exchange for a ration of hard cider. Papa's experiences with Old Man Scheidt and his ever-present cider jug had made him quite intolerant of alcohol and those who used it. However, the cider barrel in the cellar always had a measure that turned hard before it could be used. Papa felt no qualms about exchanging it for some much-needed manpower about the farm.

Papa and Peter started on opposite sides of the wagon at one end of the field, digging holes about two feet apart. Into each hole, they dropped the root of a bush, pressed the soft soil around the crown, then cut back the canes to a few inches above the ground to force new growth for the following season. As they progressed across the field, Papa made an occasional soft clicking noise with his tongue that signaled Jib to move forward a few paces with the wagon, thus ensuring that a steady supply of planting material was always close by.

The bramble roots that awaited planting were covered with damp burlap bags on the wagon deck. Seven-year-old Hermine was given the task of periodically removing the sun-dried burlap sacks, dampening them in a tub of water that sat in the center of the wagon, and replacing the bags on the roots. The task was not demanding or frequent, so she amused herself by gathering old milkweed pods from the hedgerow and floating them like little boats in the tub of water. When she tired of that, she removed her hair ribbon and held it by one end, watching as the ribbon fluttered in the light breeze.

Papa clicked for Jib to move forward, and the wagon lurched ahead. Hermine quickly reached out to stabilize herself, which caused her to drop the ribbon. She jumped down to search for it and found the ribbon beneath the wagon. There, she stretched out on her stomach and traced roadways with her fingers through the loose soil. She dug miniature lakes and created mountains and valleys, populating the scene with small, smooth stones to represent houses.

Hermine was lost in play when Papa signaled Jib onward. The horse complied, and the wagon lurched forward, its rear wheel rolling over the small of Hermine's back. The weight of the wagon momentarily knocked the wind out of the child. She gasped repeatedly for air before finally pulling a breath into her lungs. Coughing and sputtering, Hermine scrambled to her feet, then stood dazed for a moment at the realization of what had happened. Tears welled up in her eyes and she ran to Papa, clutching her lower back.

Peter stopped digging and leaned on his shovel as he listened to the child spill out her story to Papa.

"You can walk? Your legs ain't numb?" Papa asked as he turned Hermine around to inspect for signs of injury.

When Papa was satisfied that Hermine's injuries were superficial in nature, he told the sniffling child, "Go see Ada."

Hermine wiped her nose on her dress sleeve and slowly headed off across the bramble patch toward the house.

"Lucky for her the soil was so loose," commented Papa as he returned to his shovel.

Peter pulled the stem of the meerschaum pipe from his mouth and called after the child, "*Fraulein!* Tell your sister to give you a half-pint of hard cider. It'll cure your ails!"

Papa shot him a withering glance, and Peter emitted a gurgling cackle as he returned the pipe to his mouth and plunged his shovel into the earth.

Hermine found Ada and Ella by the back of the house. Ella was on her hands and knees on the porch, scrubbing the floorboards, while Ada was bent over to scrub the kitchen chairs that were lined up in a spot of sun in the backyard.

Hermine sobbed out her story while clutching her back. Ada stood up from her work and placed her wet hands on her hips. "Now, Hermine. I hain't got time for tall tales," she said wearily. "If a wagon wheel had rolled over your back, it woulda crushed your spine."

"But, Ada, it's true!" Hermine protested. She looked to Ella for support.

Ella sat back on her heels and shook her head at the child. "If you got hurt doing something foolish, just say so, but don't go makin' up stories."

Hermine's shoulders drooped in defeat. Ada and Ella returned to their scrubbing, and Hermine sniffled a few more times before turning toward the bramble patch. Ada looked up to watch the child go. Across the back of Hermine's dress was a dusty track of dirt left by the wagon wheel. "*Ach der liebe!*" gasped Ada.

* * * * *

Mama's parents, John Frederick and Katherine Gasteier, usually came to visit one Sunday every month, if the weather allowed. They arrived mid-morning, after a ten-mile trip from their home in Oxford Township in Erie County. The couple drove a black horse and black buggy and dressed all in black, John Frederick with his black homburg and Katherine with her little black bonnet that all good German women wore after the age of forty.

The Gasteier grandparents spoke only German as they exclaimed over the girls. Ada, Ella, and Flora had forgotten most of the German they had spoken as children, while the younger girls knew only English. The older girls could translate a few German words now and then, but for the most part, the sisters just smiled and nodded at their grandparents, while the Gasteiers smiled and patted each granddaughter on the head.

When Katherine saw little Minola in Ada's arms, she pinched the baby's rosy cheeks and played patty-cake with her tiny hands. From his coat pocket, John Frederick pulled a small bag of hard candy that he had bought at Zipfel's store as they passed through Monroeville. He pressed it into Ella's hand with a German admonition that Ella surmised meant "Share this with your sisters."

Mama was always pleased to see her parents, and her mood was light and happy when they arrived. While she and Papa visited with their guests, the girls sat on the apple butter kettles behind the summer kitchen and shared the bag of candy. Margaret took the sour lemon ball out of her mouth and held it up to baby Minola's lips for a taste. All of the sisters laughed as Minola puckered up her little face.

Before long, Mama called to the girls to find a rooster that would like to come to dinner. Hermine, Margaret, and Martha jumped off the apple butter kettles and went in pursuit of the chicken. Ada handed baby Minola over to Mama as she, Ella, and Flora headed toward the kitchen to prepare the meal.

The girls singled out a rooster and darted after him. The rest of the chickens scattered in alarm, some hopping in short flights and others dashing in zigzag patterns in front of the girls. The designated rooster sped across the yard and darted under the fence into the barnyard, with the girls right behind him. Next, he ran between the horse and cow barns and made a wildly skidding turn when he saw Martha in front of him. Tiring, he veered between the cornbarn and chicken house and found himself in a dead-end alley. Hermine quickly grabbed him by the legs and carried him upside down toward the house, being careful to hold the angry rooster at arm's length so he would not peck her legs. She handed him off to Papa, who retrieved his hatchet from the woodshed and carried the rooster to the old tree stump used for beheading chickens.

Ada cleaned and dressed the chicken, then dredged the pieces in flour and dropped them into bubbling lard. She opened a quart jar of canned succotash and heated it on the cookstove, while Ella mashed boiled potatoes into a bowl of endive and smothered the vegetables with a mixture of hot lard and vinegar. Flora filled a large bowl with cottage cheese from the crock in the cellar and another with pickles, then sliced thick slabs of bread from a loaf that Ada had baked on Saturday. The younger girls were busied with setting the table, pumping a pitcher full of cold water, and placing a saucer of Ada's cinnamon crumb cake at each place setting.

After dinner, John Frederick and Papa strolled out to the fields to inspect the crops, while Katherine and Mama laid baby Minola in the crib for a nap, then settled in the parlor. The girls washed the dishes and tidied up the kitchen, always ending with a sweep of the floor, which was one of Mama's commands for neatness. Before long, the grandparents patted each granddaughter on the head, bid a German farewell, and climbed into their black buggy for the return trip home.

* * * * *

The younger girls spent most of the summer months outdoors, away from Mama's quick temper. When they weren't working in the fields, they played house in and around the barns or sometimes set up quarters in an abandoned pig shelter in the plum orchard. Small green apples, corncobs, and old bottles served as their makeshift dolls.

In the summer of 1905, word circulated about hobo activity in the outlying Monroeville area. The girls' imaginations ran wild with thoughts of thieving, kidnapping vagrants roaming the countryside. They found a stout tree limb and took turns swinging it in a show of bravado, while describing how they'd defend themselves by whacking any trespasser in the knees and sending him howling all the way to Mosses'.

One afternoon, while Papa was at work in the fields and Mama and Ella were paying a sick call on Dorothea Grau, Flora, Hermine, Margaret, and Martha pushed little Minola in her baby buggy out to the idle hay wagon in the farmyard. Ada remained in the summer kitchen to do the mid-week baking. The girls propped their hobo stick against the rack on the back of the hay wagon and quickly became absorbed in chalking lines on the wagon bed to designate rooms in an imaginary house for their family of apples and corncobs.

Flora lifted her head when she heard the crunch of footsteps on the graveled drive. Coming toward them was a ragged character, exactly what the neighborhood grapevine had warned about. All thoughts of self-defense were quickly abandoned. Flora screamed and leaped from the hay wagon, with Hermine, Margaret, and Martha tumbling after her. Flora wheeled the baby buggy around and bolted for the house, giving poor little Minola a bumpy ride in the wildly pitching buggy. Hermine grabbed Margaret and Martha's hands to speed them along, and the girls streaked across the yard.

At the back porch, Flora snatched the baby out of the buggy, and the sisters rushed through the kitchen door, locking it behind them. Watching from the kitchen window, the girls saw the hobo turn about and head back down the drive.

"I think he's leaving," panted Flora as she consoled baby Minola, who was crying from her rough handling.

"Maybe he'll head down to Mosses'," breathed Hermine. "He could catch Edith easy—she runs like her knees are tied together."

"I think he wanted the baby," fretted six-year-old Margaret.

Four-year-old Martha clutched a handful of Hermine's dress for security, her eyes wide with terror.

The girls crept into the living room to follow the hobo's exit. They shrieked when they saw the shadow of the man pass by the windows on the front porch. They raced for the parlor door, which could not be locked, and threw their weight against it. Flora braced her back against the door while still holding the baby, praying that the sisters' combined strength was enough to keep the intruder out. The doorknob rattled, and the girls responded with a high-pitched squeal.

They heard his footsteps walk away from the door and scuff down the front stone steps. Staying low, they crept near the window in the parlor and peered through its lace curtain. They saw the hobo headed along the south side of the house, then heard the outside cellar doors creak open.

"Why's he going in the cellar?" asked Martha, her chin quivering.

"Must be looking for food," whispered Hermine.

"The pantry door!" shrieked Flora. "If he's in the cellar, he can come up through the pantry door!"

The girls flew to the pantry and locked the door to the cellar, then held onto each other and shivered with fright as they heard the intruder's footsteps on the cellar stairs. Their eyes were round with terror as they watched the pantry doorknob jiggle. Little Minola continued to wail in Flora's arms.

The girls heard the intruder's footsteps retreat down the cellar steps. They raced to the south parlor window to see which way the vagrant headed after he emerged from the cellar. When they saw him turn east toward the plum orchard, they clambered up Stegmiller's stairs, where they could get a good view of the backyard from the window at the top of the steps.

The hobo picked a plum, scattered the chickens that were settled in the dust of the pig yard, and disappeared behind the barn.

"I think he's gone for good this time," announced Flora after she had watched cautiously for any sign of the trespasser's return. She continued to bounce little Minola in her arms, even though the child had calmed down after her rough treatment.

"Let's just stay up here and play. I don't wanna go back outside," said Margaret, her voice wavering. The sisters agreed, and they were soon engrossed in play, using some corks, clothespins, and acorn caps for dolls.

That night at supper, the girls described their frightening experience.

"What'd he look like?" Papa asked as he forked in his fried potatoes and onions.

The girls looked at each other. The panic of the moment had prevented them from retaining detailed observations of the intruder's appearance.

"He looked scary," summed up Martha.

"Did you get a look at him, Ada?" Papa questioned.

Ada shook her head and gave a slight shrug of her shoulders.

"I thought you girls had a big stick for clubbin' hoboes," commented thirteen-year-old Ella, one eyebrow raised.

"We was too scairt," confessed Flora.

Several days later, Papa sent Flora and Hermine to the barn to collect small tin cans. Bugs had invaded the potato field, and Papa's method of insect control was to have the girls walk up and down the long rows, knocking the bugs into small tins of kerosene.

As the two sisters gathered the cans, Hermine noticed some clothing hanging over the partition between two grain bins. She cocked her head and stepped closer to inspect the garments. There was a ragged old coat and pants and a battered black felt hat.

"Flora, look! It's the hobo's clothes! He left them here!" Hermine shouted excitedly.

"Why would he leave his clothes behind?" questioned Flora as she hurried to Hermine's side. Picking up the holey coat and pants, Flora announced, "No, these are just the old clothes that Papa wears when he sprays Paris Green on the cherry trees." Then, underneath the clothing, she noticed a brown paper bag with eye holes cut in it. As she fingered the bag, Flora's jaw dropped in astonishment. "There wasn't any hobo! It was Ada!" she gasped. "Ada dressed up like a hobo to scare us!"

Flora and Hermine raced to the house to tell their other sisters and to confront Ada, whose wide smile was an immediate confession.

All that afternoon the sisters walked up and down the long rows of potato plants, flicking bugs into their kerosene cans and laughing as they recounted the fright they had had at the hands of the pseudo-hobo. They threatened Ada with retaliation, but in the end, all agreed there was no way to top the trick she had played on them.

Ella, Ada, & Flora
Papa holding Minola, Mama, & Hermine
Margaret & Martha

Chapter 10
The Seibel Homestead
1906

MARGARET'S FIRST YEAR at the Plank Road school began in the fall of 1905. It coincided with Ella's final year of education. Because Ella had completed the eighth reader early in the school year, Miss Slade brought in books from her own collection as well as from the new library in Norwalk to challenge her avid student. Ella delved into works by Charles Dickens, Mark Twain, and William Shakespeare.

Miss Slade also had Ella tutor the younger students and help with school projects, referring to Ella as her "right-hand man." For the last day of school before Christmas break in 1905, Ella assisted Miss Slade in setting up an intricate maze of strings that looped over the partition dividing the schoolroom. Each string had a student's name attached to one end, and at the other end, hidden behind the partition on the boys' side of the classroom, was a Christmas gift selected for that child by Miss Slade.

The students massed in the girls' side of the room, wiggling with anticipation and barely able to contain their excitement. When a student's name was called, they eagerly stepped forward and pulled their assigned string, reeling their gift from behind the partition to a chorus of oohs and aahs from their classmates. Ella stood close by the web of strings to straighten out any entanglements.

Hermine's long-held desire was for a doll with black hair, just like her own. The few dolls *Sinter Klaus* had brought the girls on Christmas Eve were always golden-haired angels, and Hermine was convinced that dolls with black hair did not exist. However, when she tugged her string, up came a raven-haired beauty. Hermine was so overcome with surprise that she momentarily released the string, causing the doll to plummet behind the partition. Ella caught the string and untied it from the doll's body.

Hermine's blue eyes were round with disbelief as she clutched the doll to her chest. "Miss Slade, how did you know?" she gasped. Miss Slade and Ella exchanged smiles over Hermine's head.

When all of the students had taken their turn, Miss Slade peered curiously at the end of the partition closest to her desk. "Why, there appears to be one string left," she announced in mock surprise, "and it has Ella's name on it."

Ella was dumbfounded. She had helped Miss Slade set up the string maze the night before, tying each gift to one end of a string while Miss Slade attached a paper slip bearing the child's name to the other end. Ella knew there had not been a string labeled with her name.

She eagerly pulled the lone remaining string. Over the partition bumped a hardbound copy of *Little Women* by Louisa May Alcott. With trembling fingers, Ella caressed the cover before opening it. Written on the inside endsheet in Miss Slade's precise script was the quote "'He that loves a book will never want a faithful friend…' Dr. Isaac Barrow." Ella was overwhelmed; it was the first book she had ever owned.

There were no school lessons that day. Instead, Miss Slade led the students in playing games and singing Christmas carols. As she dismissed them that afternoon, she stood beside the schoolhouse door and distributed homemade popcorn balls wrapped in crinkly tissue paper.

The girls sped home with their gifts. Flora had received a tiny sewing kit, and Margaret clutched new ribbons for her curly hair. When Mama saw Ella's book, she scoffed, "Bah!" and handed Ella a pan of potatoes to prepare for supper. Ella sat at the kitchen table with the book propped on her knees, reading as she peeled and sliced.

When the school term drew to an end in May of 1906, Miss Slade asked Ella to remain inside one day while the rest of the students raced outdoors to eat their lunches. Miss Slade seated herself at her desk, straightened a sheaf of papers, then looked up at her pupil. "Ella, have you given any thought to going on to high school in Monroeville and then attending the county Normal School? I think you'd make an excellent teacher."

Ella caught her breath. The thought of further education just three miles from home was alluring, and she envisioned herself surrounded by books and a world of learning. Then, the situation at home crowded to the forefront of her thoughts. She lowered her eyes and stammered, "I can't. My Mama ... she ... well, I'm needed at home."

Miss Slade nodded her head slowly. She knew that many of the rural students dropped out after completing the eighth reader, the demand for their help at home far outweighing their need for an education, but she regretted that such a capable student as Ella would be confined to a life of housework. She reached out and clasped Ella's hands, which were nervously picking at the edge of Miss Slade's desk. "Just keep reading, Ella. Promise me that. Always, always read."

Ella nodded and blinked hard to hold back the tears that threatened to spill over her eyelids.

When school ended, Papa did not know what to do about his

bookish daughter and her longing for an education. With Ada often away at sewing lessons, he relied on Ella to oversee the household and the younger children. He couldn't spare her. In addition, attendance at the high school in Monroeville required a twenty-dollar tuition, which he could ill afford. To compensate, Papa ordered a subscription to *Ladies Home Journal*, reasoning that Ella would enjoy reading the stories and Ada could order the sewing patterns that were pictured in each issue. Rural free delivery of mail now included Townline Road, so the magazine would be brought to their doorstep. Papa knew it was a poor substitute for an education, but it was the best he could do.

Ella worked in tandem with Ada, sharing the household chores and the care of their siblings. She did housecleaning for folks in the community, which sometimes required her to be absent from home for several days at a time. But no matter where she was, Ella always ended her day by reading.

* * * * *

In May of 1906, Papa's mother Kathrina died from the lingering effects of a stroke. She was seventy-seven years old. Of Kathrina's four children, only George and Papa remained; her two daughters, Wilhelmine and Lissetta, had died when they were in their thirties.

Papa's mother,
Kathrina Scheldt Seibel Scheidt

Kathrina's death caused her surviving spouse, Old Man Scheidt, to brood about his mortality. Without children of his own to provide a generational legacy, he fretted that he'd be forgotten through the ages, his life marked only by a humble headstone in Riverside Cemetery. Old Man decided to make arrangements for a final testament that honored his existence. He selected a large upright monument and had it erected over Kathrina's grave. He instructed the engraver to carve the name "Scheid" in large arcing letters across the top of the stone, purposely dropping the "t" from "Scheidt" so that his name seemed less Germanic. This also gave the appearance that he was aligned with the socially prominent Scheid family of Monroeville. Just below the surname, the engraver etched Old Man's first name, Wilhelm, and his date of birth, leaving a space for the death date. At the bottom of the headstone, Kathrina's vital statistics were added.

Old Man was pleased with the effect. After all, he reasoned, his family had once had some modest wealth, even paying a man to serve as his replacement in the Civil War, and therefore, it was fitting for him to be commemorated by a headstone of substance. It mattered little that he had frittered away his family's funds—and Kathrina's too—on foolish investments and copious quantities of hard cider; he was satisfied that people would pass by his marker and know he was a man of worth.

Old Man was not in good health. Years of excess hard cider consumption had taken its toll, and his memory and coordination were failing. He stumbled frequently on his daily walk from the small brick house in Monroeville to the nearby creamery, where he sat for hours on a stool in the corner. The workers there began to complain about his racking cough and indiscriminate tobacco spitting. He told the same stories over and over again, always punctuated at the same point by a raspy cackle. Sometimes, he fell asleep on the stool and awoke with a jerk, his foot kicking the cider jug and sending it tumbling across the floor. Hard cider gurgled out of the jug's narrow spout and created a slippery hazard on the cement floor. Soon, the creamery workers contacted George and Papa with the request to "do something" about their stepfather.

The one thing Old Man's memory clung to was his preference for George. He emphatically stated his desire to move in with George and Bertha and to avoid "*dieses Haus mit allen Kleidern* (that house with all the skirts)," as he referred to Papa's female-dominated household.

Bertha had been the beneficiary of Old Man's influence in the house shuffle eighteen years earlier, but the dividend came with a price: she would now be the caretaker of a cranky alcoholic who was in failing health. "*Die Hühner* (The chickens) have come home to roost," Mama said with smug satisfaction.

Papa helped his brother load Old Man's few possessions into George's wagon. Old Man elected to ride in the back of the wagon, seated in his favorite rocking chair and clutching his cider jug in his lap. They left the house on the River Road and proceeded through town, with George hunched forward over the reins, his mouth set in a terse line. Old Man rocked in his chair in the wagon bed, occasionally waving at an acquaintance or taking a long draw from his jug. Papa tried to hide the smile that played about his lips as he thought of what a peculiar sight they made.

When they arrived at George's house, Bertha met them on the back porch. Her arms were crossed over her bosom and her face wore an expression of defeat. She led the men through the back door and pointed to a small room off the kitchen where they were to place Old Man's bed, dresser, and other belongings. Old Man insisted that his beloved rocking chair be placed beside the cookstove in the kitchen, along with his cider jug and an old coffee can where he could spit his tobacco juice. Bertha shuddered inwardly but held her tongue.

After the last of Old Man's effects had been moved into George's house, Papa walked home, thinking to himself that for once he had come out on the winning end of things.

* * * * *

During the berry-picking season, Mama's pent-up need for social contact reached its peak. She put little Minola in the baby buggy and walked down the road to Mosses'. Emmaline Moss found Mama to be a leaky vessel when it came to family secrets. With a little bit of probing, along with a cup of tea and a few sugar cookies, Emmaline was able to elicit an assortment of interesting tidbits from her guest. Unfortunately, she found it difficult to discern which pieces of Mama's information were factual and which were faulty.

Emmaline pointed through her kitchen window to the Seibel girls, who were bent over the strawberry rows in the field behind the barn. "My goodness! I can't imagine making my Edith work outdoors like that. Why, your girls must have appetites like field hands when they come in for meals," Emmaline sniffed.

Mama missed the implied putdown. "*Ja*," she replied, "All I do is cook, cook, cook. Morning to night, always in the kitchen I am. That, and taking care of this one," Mama waved her hand at Minola, who toddled about the kitchen unsupervised.

Emmaline clucked her tongue in sympathy. "Is it worth it? I mean, do you make much money off those strawberries?" she probed.

Mama proceeded to tell Emmaline details of Papa's income from last year's strawberry sales, his current balance at Zipfel's store, and what he still owed on his nursery stock debt. Mama finished by tipping her chin in the air and stating proudly, "But I taught him everything he knows about strawberries. I said, 'William, I know strawberries, and there's money to be made in them. You just listen to me.'" She shook her finger for emphasis and took another sip of tea.

Emmaline's eyebrows arched. She scooted forward on her chair and offered Mama another cookie. "And George and Bertha? How are they doing … financially?"

Emmaline had plumbed a deep well with the subject of George and Bertha. While Mama's mind was frequently cloudy, she had never forgotten her resentment over the house exchange. In addition, she was willing to make up any facts she didn't have.

"*Ach!*" Mama cried. "They're rich! Rich! William's mother left them everything, and Old Man's pockets are so heavy with money he don't know what to do with it all."

Emmaline's mouth formed a perfectly round circle.

Late that afternoon, while Mr. Moss was washing up for supper, Emmaline eagerly relayed the information she had gleaned from Mama. Mr. Moss grabbed the linen handtowel from the nail by the wash basin and began drying his hands and forearms. "Pffft!" he scoffed, "Don't believe a word Sophie tells you. That woman's crazy, and you know it. Hell, everybody knows it."

Emmaline flipped the hamsteaks that were sizzling in the skillet. She cocked her head and thoughtfully considered her husband's assessment of Mama. Tomorrow, she would be sharing tea and gossip with Mrs. Ordmann, who lived across the road. Emmaline saw no reason to withhold this perfectly interesting neighborhood news just because the original source was a little unstable. She decided the appropriate thing to do was to relay Mama's revelations but add a caveat about the woman's sanity.

* * * * *

The strawberry harvest overlapped the haying season by a few weeks. During the cool of the morning, the girls joined the other berry pickers in the fields. Then, after the dew had dried on the cut hay, Papa selected a trusty picker as the field boss, and the girls helped him bring in the hay.

Ella and Flora raked the hay into piles for Papa to fork onto the empty hay wagon. Ada was in charge of driving the team of horses, while Hermine distributed the hay that Papa tossed aboard. Margaret and Martha stomped from one end of the load to the other, compressing the hay and making room for more. As the pile of hay grew deeper, their short legs sometimes plunged through the mountain of timothy. They scrambled to recover their footing before the next pitchfork full of hay was tossed their way.

When the hayrack was barely visible behind the tall stack of sweet-smelling timothy, Papa took the reins and guided the horses to the barn. There, he unloaded the wagon by pitchforking the hay into a mound at the door's entrance. The girls forked the load of hay to the rear of the barn, where it grew into a mountain that nearly reached the rafters. The girls were severely taxed by such strenuous manual labor, but no protests were voiced within Papa's earshot.

At the end of the haying season, the girls enjoyed climbing to the top of the haystack and peering into the dove cotes nailed high on the barn walls. At first they spied the small white pigeon eggs; in time, these were replaced by downy chicks, which the girls watched grow and develop into fledglings.

* * * * *

When the strawberry harvest was finished, the new raspberry and blackberry bushes hung heavy with their first crop of lush, glossy black berries. A few of the faithful strawberry pickers stayed on to earn money by picking the bramble fruits, but the majority of the labor was provided by Papa and the girls.

Papa had carefully tended his new bramble crops, constructing wire trellises to confine the long canes. But still, the branches reached out with their cruel thorns, snagging clothing and tender flesh. Even though the heat of the summer was at its zenith, the girls stretched old black ribbed stockings over their arms, with holes cut out for the fingertips, to protect their arms and hands from the barbs. To shield their skin against the sun and to preserve a degree of whiteness, they donned the large straw hats used in the strawberry fields and buttoned their dress collars tight around their throats. Although they had gone without footwear all summer, there was no going barefoot in the bramble fields. Thorny canes lay like snares between the rows, providing a painful puncture to the unfortunate shoeless person.

The older girls in particular were sensitive about the dark stains left by the berries on the ends of their fingers. If the tomatoes were ripe, they soaked their fingertips in tomato juice before going to church or anywhere else that a ladylike impression was desired. Even better was the juice of one of the lemons that Papa sometimes brought home from Zipfel's store in trade for his berries.

Once again, Papa was on the road early in the morning, marketing the perishable bramble fruits in Monroeville or Chicago Junction. Occasionally, he peddled the surplus on the streets of Bellevue, but the smaller acreage of brambles meant a smaller crop to market than the abundant strawberries.

When the bramble harvest was over, Papa went through the patch, cutting out old canes, setting the new growth straight within the trellises, tying the trailing canes to the wires, and disking the ground between the rows to keep down the weeds and new offshoots.

The summer ended with a few relatively idle weeks between berry harvests and the start of school. During this time, Papa took inventory of the girls' shoes, reassigning hand-me-down footwear to fit growing feet and assessing which shoes needed new soles before the school year began.

Papa sat down on the porch steps next to seven-year-old Margaret, who was using one of Mama's sewing needles to pick a splinter out of her bare foot. She tucked the needle into the upper bodice of her dress while Papa held one of Hermine's old shoes up to the bottom of her foot to gauge the fit. Satisfied that new soles were all that were needed to adapt the footwear for Margaret's use, Papa headed off to his workshop above the cornbarn, where he kept a supply of shoe leather, a small hammer, and a wooden box of No. 2 tacks.

Hermine, Margaret, and Martha galloped off to the cornbarn, too, and set up a playhouse in one corner of the downstairs, using several upturned shipping crates from the strawberry harvest as their house. They assembled make-believe families of hollyhock blossoms and small green apples.

Margaret spotted a corncob on the other side of the upturned crate and wedged herself partway through the slats to retrieve it for her imaginary family. As she wriggled back to join her sisters, one of the slats caught the head of the needle that was still stuck in the bodice of her dress, forcing its pointed end downward into her chest. The exposed portion of the needle bent backward, ripping her dress and snapping off the imbedded piece below the surface of her skin.

Margaret gasped and dropped to the barn floor. She looked down at the growing stain of blood on the front of her dress and the broken needle that dangled from the torn fabric.

"You're bleeding!" five-year-old Martha cried. "Mama's gonna be mad 'cause you ripped your dress and broke her needle."

Margaret's hand cupped the injury as she looked from Martha's face to Hermine's. "It hurts," she choked out. "It hurts bad!" Tears spilled over her eyelids and down her cheeks.

Hermine jumped up and grabbed Margaret's hand. She pulled her sister behind her up the steps to Papa's workshop on the second floor. Martha followed, her face clouded with worry.

Papa was bent over the workbench with his back to the door, tapping small tacks into the sole of Margaret's shoe, when the girls gathered in the doorway of his shop.

"Papa, Margaret got hurt," Hermine stated.

"Go see Ada," Papa muttered around a row of tacks clenched between his lips.

"She already left for the Weber girls'," replied Hermine.

Margaret sniffled and wiped at her eyes while keeping one hand cupped over her injury.

"Ella'll take care of it," Papa replied without turning around. He took a tack out of his mouth and carefully tapped it into the margin of the sole.

"She's cleaning down at Knopfs'," Hermine responded, her voice starting to rise with concern.

"Then go see your Mama," Papa stated impatiently.

The girls looked at each other with alarm. They knew that one didn't go to Mama for comfort or first-aid. Also, she would lash out about the ripped and stained dress and the broken needle. They shifted their weight nervously in the doorway, and Margaret's sniffling crescendoed.

Still sensing his daughters' presence behind him, Papa swiveled about on his stool and looked at the three distraught girls. He pulled the tacks from his mouth and motioned Margaret forward, "Let's have a look."

Margaret crossed the room to her father and dropped her hand from the front of her dress. Between sobs, she related what had happened. Papa removed the needle that dangled from the torn fabric and inspected its broken end, gauging how much was embedded in Margaret's chest. He gently peeled back the ripped dress material and examined the wound. His brow furrowed. Swiveling about, he searched his workbench for a fine-nosed pair of pliers. "Maybe I can grab the end of it with these," he muttered as he turned back toward Margaret.

Margaret's eyes grew wide at the sight of Papa wielding the tool. "No!" she squealed, and her hand flew to cover the wound again. "No! Don't touch it!" Her sobs grew louder, which alarmed her already worried sisters. Martha threw her arms around Hermine's legs and buried her face in her skirt.

"It's gotta come out," Papa replied. "It's too close to your heart." He cocked his hands on his hips while thinking of a solution, then sighed and stood. "Come on, we'd better get you to Dr. Gilman's."

Papa hitched up Jib, then lifted Margaret onto the wagon bench. "Go tell your Mama where we're going," Papa directed Hermine and Martha as he tapped the reins on the horse's rump. The wagon rumbled down the driveway and turned onto the road. The two sisters walked slowly toward the house, not relishing their task of telling Mama about Margaret's injury.

After Dr. Gilman had removed the imbedded piece of needle and bandaged the wound, Papa and Margaret headed for home. Margaret turned her tear-stained face toward Papa and asked with concern, "What about my dress? Mama will be mad." She fingered the blood-stained rent in the fabric.

Papa swung the horse down Chapel Street toward the Weber girls' house, where Ada was having a sewing lesson.

* * * * *

Papa's auction purchases that summer included a used potato planter and digger to speed the planting and harvesting of the potato crop. While the girls were pleased with these improvements to their field work, they were overjoyed with another treasure that Papa brought home: a used treadle sewing machine. He cautioned them that it was not in working order, but with enough tinkering, he was confident he could get it running. Papa was a master with machinery, and he took delight in making repairs. If he couldn't fix something to its original condition, he could usually create a jerry-rigged mechanism that produced the desired outcome, however unconventional the moving parts.

The sewing machine was given a place of honor in the living room below one of the west-facing windows, where the light was optimal. Papa's repairs made the machine functional again, but it was not a professional job. The machine had an annoying habit of stitching along with a steady *ca-chunk, ca-chunk, ca-chunk* interrupted by a grinding noise, during which time the bobbin froze, resulting in a long span of skipped stitches. Even with this liability, the machine was a great asset, and Ada began sewing most of the family's wardrobe.

At the end of the summer of 1906, the Weber girls informed Papa that they had taught Ada everything they knew about sewing. While they would severely miss the farm produce Papa had supplied in trade for the lessons, they acknowledged that Ada's skills were now every bit as fine as their own. Ada soon began occasional work as an itinerant seamstress in the neighborhood as well as in town.

Ada, Ella, Hermine, Minola on Mama's lap, Margaret, Martha, Papa, & Flora

* * * * *

Through the fall of 1906, the girls and Papa picked apples and loaded them into baskets. Papa chose a certain time of the moon for picking "the keepers," asserting that the bruised areas on apples would dry up if picked during the right time of the moon, but if picked at the wrong time, the damaged area would cause the apple to rot. The orchard included such varieties as Northern Spy, Baldwin, Ben Davis, Wealthy, Greening, and Grimes Golden. An assortment of the apples would be used for making a kettle of apple butter, while the rest were stored in the cellar and eaten throughout the winter, with Papa urging the girls to eat the poor-keepers first. The Ben Davis apples were the best-keepers but so nearly tasteless that they were considered uninviting even in March, when they were the only apple variety that remained in the cellar.

After the better apples had been harvested, Papa pulled the wagon into the apple orchard, and the girls tossed the windfalls and damaged apples into its bed. These would be taken to Knopf's cider mill and made into vinegar for food preservation and sweet cider for making apple butter. The girls' fall afternoons and weekends were filled with the steady *thump-bump* of tossed apples ricocheting off the wagon sideboards and bouncing in its bed. When the wagon was filled, Papa led Davey into the orchard, hitched the horse to the wagon, and headed down the road to Knopf's cider mill at the corner of Townline and Everingin Roads.

Papa backed the wagon up to the chute on Knopf's scratcher, or apple crusher, and nodded his head at Mr. Knopf, who was turning the hand crank on the apple press. Fritz Mahler, from farther east on Everingin Road, leaned against the side of his wagon, which was loaded with barrels of cider that Mr. Knopf had pressed earlier.

Fritz watched as Papa stood on the tailboard of the wagon and shoveled apples into the chute of the scratcher. Nudging Mr. Knopf with his foot, Fritz crossed his arms over his chest and called to Papa, "Hey, Bill, why you doing all that work alone? Hain't you got any boys around your place to help you out?"

Mr. Knopf looked up from his press and saw Papa's jaw tighten. "Go easy now, Fritz," he cautioned quietly.

Fritz chuckled. "Oh, that's right. How'd I forget? It's all hens and no roosters in your chicken house. What you got now—seven girls?" He made an exaggerated whistle and shook his head. "Mmm, mmm, that ain't a family—that's a litter. I can just see you, Bill, when the young bucks come sparkin' at your door. You'll say, 'Why, come on in, and which one ya want? You can have the pick of the litter!'" Fritz guffawed.

A slow flush crept up Papa's face, but he continued shoveling, doing his best to ignore Fritz's needling. "Hell, Bill, at the rate you're goin', the boys in Ridgefield Township ain't got no choice in who to marry. They all gotta hitch up with a Seibel girl just so you don't get stuck with a bunch of old maids someday!"

Papa threw down his shovel in the bed of the wagon and leaped to the cider mill floor. He grabbed the front of Fritz's shirt and jerked the man close to his crimson face. "D-D-Don't you say n-n-nothin' bad 'bout my girls. You hear me? They're good girls! Good girls!" Papa gave Fritz a final shake before releasing him.

Papa walked stiffly back to his wagon and resumed shoveling apples into the scratcher. Fritz stretched his neck and rearranged the front of his shirt. "Jesus, Bill," he muttered. "Just tryin' to fun you."

Mr. Knopf shook his head at Fritz and resumed tightening the apple press. "When you gonna learn, Fritz? You don't trifle with a man 'bout his daughters."

* * * * *

When the juice came back from Knopfs' as sweet cider, the process of making apple butter began. Papa hung the copper-lined apple butter kettle from a tripod in the backyard, then hauled lengths of hardwood from the woodshed, creating a nearby pile. The girls retrieved eight or ten bushel baskets of mixed-variety apples from the cellar. They carried kitchen chairs outside and set them in the grass by the baskets of apples. Armed with paring knives, they began the long task of *schnitzing*, or coring and quartering the apples. The cut pieces of apple were tossed into the kettle, and the cores and rotten spots were dropped into a pan for the pigs and chickens.

The girls joked and laughed while they *schnitzed.* When Mama joined them, they refrained from such frivolity, knowing her low tolerance for anything but work. They settled into a steady cadence of *core, quarter, flip, thump.* When the first basket was emptied, they turned it upside-down as a small sign of progress, then stacked the subsequent emptied baskets on top of it, totem pole style.

To keep Mama from snapping at the younger ones, Ada tucked little Minola into her lap. She selected an apple, polished its surface to a high shine on her apron, then impaled it on the end of a stick. Using the tip of her paring knife, Ada quickly created a smiling face on its shiny surface. Minola eagerly reached for the stick, crying "Gimme! Gimme! Gimme!" and waved the makeshift doll about. For Martha, Ada carefully carved a long ribbon of apple peel. She poked a small hole in each end, then wrapped it around Martha's wrist and showed her how to secure the bracelet by using the apple stem as a clasp.

Early the next day, Papa started a slow fire under the kettle and added several bucketsful of sweet cider to the *Apfelstücken* (cored and quartered apples). He retrieved the long-handled spoon-bill stirrer from its pegs on the barn wall and handed it to the girls. They clutched their sweaters tight against the early morning October chill and tried to stand upwind of the fire's smoke as they took turns slowly stirring the bubbling mixture. "Remember," Papa cautioned, "it's twice around the kettle and once across. And don't stop stirring. Nothin' worse than burnt apple butter."

As the day warmed, the girls shucked their sweaters and continued to stir while Papa monitored the fire. It was a full-time job tending to the apple butter and keeping little Minola away from the bubbling cauldron. She toddled to her sisters with arms upraised, demanding to be held. The older girls propped Minola on one hip and continued to stir by tucking the paddle under their other arm. For Margaret and Martha, it was a joint effort to push the stirrer across and around the kettle as the sauce thickened.

By late afternoon, it was time for "adding the money," as Papa referred to the act of adding the sweetener. A jug of molasses, which he had set near the coals of the fire to warm, was poured over the boiling mixture, and the stirring continued. Finally, Mama emerged from the kitchen with tins of cinnamon and cloves. She spooned a generous amount of cinnamon and a lesser amount of cloves into the kettle and returned to the house, where Ada and Ella were sterilizing the canning jars.

The deep reddish-brown apple butter wafted a tantalizing spicy aroma mixed with woodsmoke toward the girls as they continued to stir. Mama returned with a wooden spoon and small saucer. She scooped up a small spoonful of the apple butter and tasted it, then pulled the tin of cinnamon from her apron pocket and added a spoonful more to the kettle. After the girls had thoroughly blended in the newest addition of spice, Mama sampled again and nodded her head in satisfaction. Next, she dipped the saucer partway into the bubbling concoction to test for consistency. When the mixture clung to the saucer, Mama announced that the apple butter was thick enough for canning.

Papa dipped the milk buckets into the kettle, filling them with apple butter, which he carried to the kitchen. There, Ada and Ella ladled the hot mixture into the sterilized jars, and Mama and Flora used cloths to wipe the rims, then placed the glass tops on the jars and snapped the wire bails in place. Hermine, Margaret, and Martha took turns stirring the still-bubbling kettle of apple butter and tending to little Minola, who had refused to nap throughout the day and was now tearful and cranky.

When the last bucket of apple butter had been ladled into jars, Ella scooped the sauce that remained at the bottom of the kettle into a bowl to be placed on the table and consumed with their supper. Ada sliced an entire loaf of bread, which she carried outdoors on the wooden cutting board. The family gathered around the kettle, using the slices of bread to clean the remaining apple butter from the bottom and sides of the cauldron. Ada swiped a slice of bread around the rim of the kettle and handed it to Minola, who held onto Ada's skirt with one hand and sniffled while she ate her apple butter treat.

After the family had daubed up the last bit of apple butter from the kettle, Papa used a handful of corncobs to scrape off the crust of baked-on sauce from around the rim and to scrub the interior of the kettle. The corncobs would not scratch the copper lining and ruin the pot. In the morning, after the kettle had cooled, the girls would wash it with soapy water, and Papa would roll it back to its usual post behind the summer kitchen.

* * * * *

As the fall days grew colder, the free-ranging chickens roosted in the lower branches of the trees for the night. If allowed to perch there overnight in frosty weather, the chickens' feet would freeze, causing them to be crippled. Each evening after dark, the girls roamed the backyard, gathering up the chickens. Flora held the lantern high above her head, while Ella, who was the tallest of all the girls, was designated as the "chicken snatcher." She plucked the chickens from the trees and handed them off to her sisters, who then ferried the outraged birds to the chicken house amid much squawking and flapping.

When winter set in, the chickens remained locked in the hen house. Ada and Ella brewed chicken mash and table scraps on the cookstove, which Papa carried out to the henhouse. Buckets of water and bushels of corn and oats were also transported across the snowy farmyard. Keeping the chickens fed and watered was a twice-a-day chore, but their eggs, and an occasional chicken dinner, were the cornerstone of the Seibel diet, along with the potatoes that the girls had harvested and stored in the cellar.

* * * * *

Ada received several sewing commissions through the winter of 1906, traveling to Milan to sew for some of Mama's relatives and spending several weeks with families in the outlying Monroeville area. During Ada's absences, Minola frequently ran to the kitchen door and looked up expectantly, asking a mournful "Mama? Mama home?" Like a duckling, Minola had imprinted Ada as her mother, and like her sisters, Minola had learned early in life not to seek mothering from her real Mama.

Chapter 11
The Seibel Homestead
1907

MONDAY WAS WASH DAY, and this spring day in 1907 promised to be particularly suitable for the task of washing and drying the nine-member Seibel family's laundry. A warm sun and a light breeze indicated rapid drying time for clothes hung on the line. Ada and Ella positioned the wash tubs—one for washing and one for rinsing—on opposite sides of the stationary wringer in the summer kitchen. They set the copper boiler on the cookstove and filled it with bucket after bucket of water from the wellstalk, then lit a blaze in the firebox.

While the water heated, the two sisters fixed a breakfast of oatmeal and milk for the younger children. After the girls had eaten, Ella washed the breakfast dishes, then dipped about half of the hot water from the copper boiler into the two wash tubs. She slivered a cake of lye soap into the remaining water on the cookstove and gathered up the scrub board and brush.

Ada's nimble fingers flew as she braided her sisters' hair, fastened the rows of buttons down the back of their dresses, and filled their lunch pails with apple butter sandwiches, a plump sugar cookie, and a long-keeper apple from the baskets in the cellar. Soon, Flora, Hermine, and Margaret angled across the yard and down the road toward George and Bertha's, where they'd follow the shortcut along the creek to the Plank Road school.

Martha scooted on her knees across the summer kitchen floor, walking her rag doll on paths she had made between the piles of clothing that Ella had sorted according to color and degree of dirtiness. Two-year-old Minola rubbed the sleep from her eyes while firmly clutching a handful of Ada's skirt in one fist. When Ada was home between sewing commissions, Minola clung tightly to her seventeen-year-old mother substitute. She toddled after Ada, never releasing the grip on her skirt, as Ada bustled between the kitchen, pantry, and summer kitchen.

Mama plopped an armload of bedding on the summer kitchen floor, then seated herself in a rocking chair in the living room. She retrieved her crocheting from a nearby basket on the floor and began to rock at a furious pace, her needlework large and loopy like the web of a drunken spider.

When the white items had been boiled, Ada used a smooth, bleached stirring stick to lift each garment from the bubbling water and transfer it to the wash tub. She and Ella took turns rasping the clothes up and down on the face of the corrugated scrub board.

After the first load was washed, rinsed, and wrung, Ada told Minola to help herself to a sugar cookie from the kettle on the pantry shelf. The toddler released her grip on Ada's skirt and scampered toward the pantry. Ada quickly lifted the wicker basket of wet laundry onto her hip, grabbed the cloth bag of wooden clothespins, and slipped out the summer kitchen door.

The dew was still wet on the grass as she crossed the yard to the clotheslines that stretched south of the house along the edge of their property. Ada set the basket of laundry on the grass and thrust a handful of wooden clothespins between her lips. She pinned up a row of the family's underclothes, followed by the more dainty female under-attire, then clamped a fresh supply of clothespins between her lips as she gave the first wet bed sheet a smart snap prior to hanging it.

A horse snorted and jingled its harness behind Ada. She turned to wave to Mr. Moss, who had also taken advantage of the warm spring morning to begin plowing the field that lay between the two neighboring farms. However, it was not Mr. Moss who returned her wave. Framed in the clearing between the Rose of Sharon and honeysuckle bushes at the edge of the yard was a tall, handsome young man. His hands rested on the plow handles, while the knotted reins were looped over his shoulders. He stood with one hip jutted out leisurely, as though he had been standing there watching her for some time. A slow smile crept upward from one corner of his mouth. For a long moment, he gazed at Ada with a bemused expression on his face, then he tipped his hat at her and gave a small nod before making a soft clicking noise that signaled the horse to resume plowing.

Ada blinked several times. Was she seeing things, or was this good-looking stranger in Mr. Moss's field a reality? Suddenly, Ada realized that she still had the row of wooden clothespins clamped between her teeth. Her hand flew to her mouth and snatched them out. No wonder the stranger had worn an expression of amusement! Her face flushed crimson with the thought of how silly she must have looked. Ada shook her head lightly to clear her thoughts. She felt slightly off-center, as though she were trying to balance herself in the back of Papa's moving spring wagon.

Ada tiptoed over to the cover of the honeysuckle bushes and peered between their branches, searching Mr. Moss's field to confirm the presence of the handsome stranger. Just then, the summer kitchen door banged open, and little Minola sped down the porch steps and across the lawn, calling "Ada! Ada!" Ada quickly stepped away from the bushes and finished hanging the laundry, with Minola's small hand once again clutching her skirt.

When Ada reached the back porch, she turned to look again in the direction of Mr. Moss's field. The laundry flapping in the breeze on the clothesline caught her attention, and Ada realized with horror that the handsome stranger had full view of the family underwear, including her own dainties, hanging on the line. She rushed back to the clothesline, Minola's little legs pumping to keep up, and quickly rearranged the drying clothes so that the bed sheets obscured the view of the unmentionables.

Ada and Ella washed, scrubbed, rinsed, and wrung a second load of laundry. As Ella carried the filled basket toward the summer kitchen door, Ada intercepted her. "I'll hang this load. You keep an eye on Minola," Ada directed as she wrested the laundry basket from Ella's hands.

Ella's brow furrowed. "But we take turns hanging the laundry. We always do."

"I don't mind. Really, I don't," called Ada over her shoulder as she shifted the basket to her hip and whirled out the door.

For the rest of the morning, Ada took command of hanging the laundry, seizing the opportunity to peer through the honeysuckle and Rose of Sharon bushes at the handsome stranger plowing the field next door.

By noon, the laundry was done. Ella pulled the corncob stoppers from the bottom of the tubs and drained the wash water into buckets. She sent Martha and Minola to the kitchen while she and Ada used the wash water to scrub the summer kitchen floor. As they progressed across the wooden floor on hands and knees, Ella cast a puzzled look at her sister. She had noticed Ada's distracted countenance and sudden devotion to hanging the laundry. "I hope you're as eager to do my share of the ironing tomorrow, too," she commented, looking sidelong at Ada.

But Ada's thoughts were elsewhere.

Later that month, the Knopf teenagers, Stella and Harry, cleaned out the upper floor of the family's apple mill and circulated word that they would hold a dance for the neighborhood young folks. Ada and Ella were invited, but by the evening of the dance, Ella had developed a raging sinus headache. She lay on the bed she shared with Ada, a warm compress over her eyes.

Ada adjusted the belt that encircled her narrow waist and gave her upswept hair a final pat as she watched out the bedroom window for the arrival of Rosie, Elmer, and Walter. The cousins planned to walk to the dance together.

"Tell me all about the dance when you get home. And don't forget a single detail," directed Ella, lifting one corner of the compress to give Ada a meaningful gaze.

"Probably won't be much to tell," replied Ada. "Just Rosie's hunt for a beau, Edwin Moss's lame jokes, and my two left feet."

"Mmm, the usual," murmured Ella as she gently replaced the compress.

As the cousins climbed the stairs to the second story of Knopfs' apple mill, they were greeted by the sound of Heber Grau's sons, Frank and Otto, tuning up their fiddles. The large room was illuminated by lanterns hung from the rafters, and a table at the back of the room held Mrs. Knopf's punch bowl set, a platter of cookies, and a deep tub of popcorn. Ada and Rosie joined a knot of neighbor girls clustered near the punch bowl, while Elmer and Walter drifted to a group of fellows milling about at the opposite side of the room.

Ada sipped her cup of punch, occasionally peering over its rim at the growing circle of young men. Her eyes grew wide when she spotted the handsome stranger chatting with Edwin Moss.

Rosie had also spotted the newcomer. She cozied up to Edith Moss, linking her arm through Edith's, and asked, "Who's that talking to Edwin?"

Edith peered over her shoulder toward her brother and his companion. "Oh, that's just Albert Gfell. He's our new hired hand."

"Hmm," murmured Rosie, "Maybe you'll introduce me?"

Edith gave a shrug of indifference. "Why would you want to meet him? He's just a farmhand."

"Looks like you're going to get your chance for an introduction, Rosie," whispered Stella. "Here he comes."

Ada choked on her sip of punch as she watched Albert and Edwin cross the room toward the cluster of girls. Rosie straightened and adopted her most coy expression, but the two young men stopped in front of Ada.

"Albert wants to meet you," Edwin said without fanfare. Waving his hand between the two, he announced, "Albert Gfell, this is Ada Seibel. Ada Seibel, meet Albert Gfell. Albert, Ada, Ada, Albert. An Aye for an Aye. A-men!" Edwin chuckled at his own thin joke and headed for the tub of popcorn.

Over her shoulder, Ada could hear Rosie's snort of disappointment.

"So, your name's Ada," Albert said softly, bobbing his chin.

Ada was sure the handsome stranger could hear her heart thumping in her chest. Despite her recent swallow of punch, her throat felt tight and unable to produce a sound. She nodded her head in response.

A slow smile curled up from one corner of Albert's mouth. "I thought your name might be George."

"George?" Ada croaked. She shook her head in puzzlement.

"Yup. George. Like George Washington. You were sportin' a fine set of wooden teeth the first time I saw you."

Ada recalled the row of wooden clothespins clamped between her lips the day she was hanging laundry in the side yard. A flush of crimson crept up her neck and flamed her cheeks.

Albert's smile broke into a full grin.

"Time to partner up for the Virginia Reel!" shouted Otto Grau. Pointing his fiddle bow at the center of the room, he ordered, "Contra form. Now, don't be shy!" He and Frank tucked their fiddles under their chins and launched into a lively rendition of "Old Zip Coon," while couples formed two lines, the men facing the women.

Albert took the cup of punch from Ada's hand and set it on the nearby table. "Care to dance?"

Ada swallowed hard. It had been years since she was a student at the Plank Road school, where Miss Slade had taught the students to dance the Virginia Reel. Her mind raced, trying to remember the steps that accompanied each call. She nodded her head at Albert, still unable to vocalize a response, and gave a quick, silent prayer that her two left feet would cooperate. They crossed the room and joined the other couples in line.

Ada concentrated with all her power on each step. She counted the beat under her breath and paid close attention to the other dancers' movements. When it was Ada and Albert's turn to sashay down the center of the line of dancers, Ada placed her hands in Albert's, looked up into his twinkling blue eyes, and promptly stepped on his foot. Her face flushed scarlet, but Albert smiled down at her and graciously responded, "Oh, pshaw! I only walk on the bottoms; you can walk on the tops."

They danced to "Turkey in the Straw" and "Arkansas Traveler" between trips to the refreshment table. Ada's heart still thumped wildly in her chest, but her throat had loosened, allowing her to carry on a conversation with Albert. He told her about his desire to eventually leave farm life and join the railroad; Ada told him about her apprenticeship with the Weber girls and her periodic sewing commissions. Before long, the Grau brothers played a sadly sweet "Good Night, Ladies," signaling the end of the dance.

As the young people edged toward the stairs, Albert asked, "Mind if I walk you home? We seem to be going in the same direction."

"I … why … yes, that would be alright," Ada stammered as she looked around for Rosie, Elmer, and Walter. "But I need to walk with my cousins, too. They're the ones I came with."

"Good practice to dance with the ones that brung you," Albert stated slyly as he plopped his hat on his head at a rakish angle.

"But I didn't dance with them," Ada replied matter-of-factly. She blushed when she saw Albert's grin and realized she had taken his teasing comment quite literally. She again felt herself slightly off-balance and wondered at the strange effect Albert had on her.

The young couple was joined at the foot of the stairs by Ada's cousins. Rosie slumped along in disappointment that the only males walking her home were her brothers Elmer and Walter. The five strolled north along the darkened Townline Road toward their respective homes.

When they reached the edge of Mosses' front yard, Albert bid the group good night. He turned to Ada, tipped his hat, and said, "See you at the clothesline … George."

Ada was glad it was too dark for her cousins to see the bloom of crimson on her cheeks.

"Looks like you've got yourself a beau," sighed Rosie wistfully.

Ada climbed the porch steps, feeling lighter than goose down, and groped her way through the darkened house. She could hear Papa's soft snore and was relieved that Mama was not having one of her nocturnal rambles. She tiptoed up the stairs, across the girls' bedroom, and into the room she shared with Ella. Ada unpinned her hair, shook it loose, and plaited it into a long braid that she tossed over her shoulder. Changing quickly into her nightgown, she slipped into bed beside Ella, only to bump into a small body occupying her side of the bed.

"Scoot over," whispered Ada, trying to nudge the sleeping form into the center of the bed.

Five-year-old Martha rolled over and mumbled, "I crawled in with Ella to wait up for you."

"Shh, I'm home now," Ada patted the groggy child and scooted in beside her.

Ella awoke and rolled onto her side, facing Ada. "How was the dance?" she asked sleepily.

"Wonderful," sighed Ada.

Ella's eyes blinked open. "Wonderful?" she repeated in disbelief. It was not the adjective she had expected to hear. "What was so wonderful?"

Ada was silent for a long moment as she stared into the darkness above her, replaying the evening's events in her mind. "I met someone. Someone special," she confided.

Ella was fully awake now and raised herself up onto one elbow. "Someone special at Knopfs'? Who?"

Ada proceeded to tell Ella all about Albert Gfell, describing his twinkling blue eyes, slow smile, their first meeting at the clothesline, and the dances and conversations they had shared that evening.

Martha listened sleepily to the conversation taking place between her two sisters. She didn't understand Ada's interest in this man named Albert, but for now, Ada was home and that's all that mattered. Martha draped her arm and leg over Ada's torso, snuggled in closer, and closed her eyes.

The next morning at the breakfast table, Papa asked Ada about the dance. "Good turnout last night?" he inquired as he spread a thick layer of strawberry preserves on a slice of bread.

"*Ja*, all the neighborhood usuals were there," responded Ada. She paused and cleared her throat. "Plus Mosses' hired man."

"Albert was there, huh?" mused Papa, wiping the blade of his knife along the bread crust. "Mr. Moss has good things to say about him."

"So does Ada!" exclaimed Martha, her blue eyes wide with innocence.

Papa noticed the scarlet flush that rose on Ada's cheeks, as well as Ella's attempt to hide a smile behind her slice of bread. He placed his knife across the top of his plate and chewed thoughtfully as he looked around the table at his seven daughters.

The following Monday, Ada carried a basket of wet laundry across the yard, ticking off a mental list of all the chores she needed to tackle that day. Little Minola tagged along behind, one hand in her usual secure grip on Ada's skirt. Ada stopped abruptly, causing Minola to bump into the back of her legs. She stared in disbelief at the clothesline. From one end of the line to the other dangled bundles of spring flowers tied with feed sack twine.

"Looky!" cried Minola, pointing at the unusual scene.

"I see," breathed Ada in response.

She slowly approached the clothesline and set the basket of laundry on the grass. Her fingers trembled as she untied the first bouquet and discovered a tiny slip of paper tucked in among the stems. It had one word written on it: "May." Slipping the note into her apron pocket, Ada turned to Minola and directed her to hold the first bouquet of flowers while she untied the second. Another note escaped and fluttered to the ground. It read "I." A smile crept across Ada's face as she untied the subsequent bouquets and read their one-word missives. The completed message tucked in with the flowers said, "May I come calling this Sunday evening? Albert."

Ada clutched the flowers to her chest and started across the lawn toward the house, fingering the eight small notes in her apron pocket. Little Minola skipped along behind her.

"*Himmel!* (Heavens!)" Ada gasped when she reached the porch steps. She had completely forgotten about the basket of wet laundry that she had left sitting in the grass. She whirled about and scurried toward the clothesline, with Minola hurrying to keep up.

Late that Sunday afternoon, Ada tapped her foot impatiently beneath the kitchen table while the family ate supper. As soon as the last morsels of food were scraped from the plates, Ada was on her feet and clearing the table. Papa was still in mid-chew when his plate disappeared from in front of him. He grabbed his coffee cup before it too was whisked away.

With the dishes washed and the kitchen straightened, Ada hurried upstairs to prepare herself for Albert's visit. Hermine and Margaret adjourned to the parlor to practice their piano duet for the upcoming recital, while the remaining four sisters trailed up the steps and gathered on Ada and Ella's bed to watch Ada's transformation.

Ada dusted herself with talcum powder from the tall rectangular tin on top of the dresser, then donned her best black lisle stockings, crisp white underskirt, and gauge vest. She sucked in her breath, pulling her corset strings as tight as possible to achieve the tiniest of waistlines, then shrugged on her corset cover. She selected her white linen shirtwaist with the cutwork inserts and slipped her dark brown walking skirt over her head. The final touch was a deep red belt to encircle her waist. Peering out the window toward Mosses' house, Ada hurriedly unpinned her hair from the low knot she wore for every day and rapidly brushed her long, thick hair with the tortoise shell brush. She piled her hair in a soft, loose bun at the top of her head and pinned it in place. Flipping open the small wooden jewelry box on top of the dresser, she retrieved the ring she had received for confirmation. Ada sat on the bed beside her sisters and slipped one foot into her shoe, working the button hook through the long row of buttons.

Minola pointed out the window toward a horse and buggy that was slowing near their driveway. "Who dat?" she asked.

Ada leaned forward and followed Minola's finger. "*Ach!* It's Albert already!" She yanked on her other shoe and hastily fastened the row of buttons. Tossing the button hook onto the dresser tray, she stood and smoothed her hands down the front of her skirt. "How do I look?" she asked her sisters.

Ella wet her fingers and corralled a few errant wisps of Ada's hair, while Flora brushed the wrinkles from her walking skirt. Martha licked her thumb and rubbed at a spot on Ada's shoe. Then Ada dashed for the stairs, her sisters scampering behind her. Ada wanted to intercept Mama before she answered Albert's knock on the door. Even though Mama was enjoying a blessedly lucid interlude right now, her conversations with visitors could still be quite unpredictable.

Ada caught her breath when she saw Albert standing in the kitchen, talking to Papa. His dark overcoat was open just enough to reveal a long, gold watch chain looped from his vest button into his pocket. His slicked-back dark hair was offset by his crisp white shirt collar.

Hermine and Margaret abandoned their piano practice to join their sisters in the kitchen doorway, gawking at the tall stranger who had come to court Ada. Mama parted the cluster of girls and greeted Albert with a wide smile. She loved company and was not going to miss an opportunity to entertain. She pulled out a kitchen chair and motioned for Albert to take a seat.

"We're not as *ausgefallen* (fancy) as the Mosses," apologized Mama, "but if you wanted *ausgefallen* (fancy), you'd be courtin' Edith instead of Ada."

Ada's face grew crimson at Mama's inappropriate comment. Papa interceded by suggesting that the young couple take a buggy ride. Ada retrieved her shawl from the peg in the summer kitchen, and Papa watched from his rocking chair in the corner as Albert held the door open for Ada.

When the kitchen door closed, little Minola realized that Ada was gone. Thinking her surrogate mother had left for another extended sewing commission, Minola flew to the door, threw it open, and raced down the porch steps after the young couple. With tears streaming down her face, the toddler bolted across the yard, crying "Ada! Ada!" Minola caught the hem of Ada's skirt just as Albert was helping her into the buggy. The distraught child clung to the fabric with both fists. Flora, who had dashed out the kitchen door in pursuit of her little sister, attempted to pry Minola's small hands loose, causing Minola's sobs to escalate into screams.

"Oh, shooks," said Albert good-naturedly. "Let her come along. Can't no one say we didn't have a chaperone."

Flora released Minola's hands, and Albert lifted the toddler onto the buggy seat. As he crossed behind the buggy, Ada settled Minola into her lap and whispered in the child's ear, "The I-dacity!"

Albert climbed onto the buggy seat beside them. Minola looked up at him with watery eyes and a trembling chin. Her small chest heaved with hiccups. When Albert smiled down at her, she buried her face in Ada's bosom. Albert gave Ada a bemused grin and tapped the reins on the horse's back.

Albert Gfell

After the horse had settled into a steady pace, Albert reached under the buggy seat, pulled out a small wicker box, and handed it to Minola.

"This is supposed to be for your sister, but I better get the chaperone's approval," he winked at the sniffling toddler.

Minola opened the lid to reveal six chocolate candies nestled in a sky-blue cloth lining. She looked up at Ada, seeking permission with her eyes. Ada nodded, and Minola selected a chocolate to pop into her mouth. She leaned back against Ada's chest and hiccupped, clutching the wicker box in her small hands as the buggy proceeded down Townline Road.

Albert soon became a regular Sunday evening caller. Ada bustled through the days of the week, hurrying them along until it was Sunday again. Occasionally, the young couple stole a few minutes to visit during the week when Albert was working in the field nearest the Seibel house and Ada was at the clothesline or in the garden.

Papa quietly observed the growing fondness between his eldest daughter and the Mosses' hired hand. He remembered his own days of courtship with a bit of wistfulness but was sobered by the present-day reality of seven daughters and a wife who was incapable of caring for them.

* * * * *

The strawberry season reached its peak yield by early June. Ada was excused from picking due to a sewing assignment from Mama. She wanted Ada to create new dresses for Ella, Flora, Hermine, and Margaret to wear for the upcoming piano recital at Mrs. Knopf's. Mama knew that Emmaline Moss's daughter Edith and Mrs. Ordmann's daughter Elsie would be attired in their finest, and she wanted the Seibel family to make an equally good showing.

Ada spread the fabric on the living room table and carefully cut out the dress pieces. She pinned and basted, then seated herself at the treadle sewing machine in front of the west windows. As she sewed, Ada thought of Albert, and a smile crept across her face. She found herself less frustrated with the sewing machine's annoying habit of skipped stitches; in fact, everything in life seemed rosier these days. She hummed lightly under her breath. Ada's thoughts turned to the future. In a year or so, Minola would be older and less dependent; Flora would be finished with school and able to assist Ella with the household tasks. Maybe she and Albert … Ada's heart flip-flopped in her chest at the thought of a future with Albert that included their own home and family.

Ada's reverie was broken by Mama dropping a bundle of skirts and a handful of fabric on the wing of the sewing machine. "Here," Mama ordered. "When you're done with the girls' dresses, sew these extensions into the waistbands of my skirts. They're getting *zu fest* (too tight)."

Ada picked up the scissors to snip a thread, then her hand stopped in midair as she spotted the maternity extensions Mama had laid on top of the pile of skirts. She blinked, certain that her eyes were playing tricks on her. "A-Another baby?" she gasped in disbelief.

Mama was headed toward the kitchen. "*Ja. Und Mein Gott*, let it be a boy this time," she muttered.

Ada sat in stunned silence, unable to complete the motion of snipping the thread. Her hands fell into her lap and tears welled in her eyes.

* * * * *

The rest of the girls were joined in the strawberry fields by pickers who ranged in age from toddlers that tagged along after their mothers to teenaged boys looking to earn just enough money to buy Fourth of July fireworks. Papa had his favorite pickers—those who worked quickly and with serious intent. This included the Burrer brothers, Phil, John, August, and Henry, who sought any means to supplement their widowed mother's income. While the Burrers were rapid, efficient workers, they also brought a level of gaiety to the fields with their friendly banter, good-natured teasing, and outbursts of laughter.

Phil Burrer could not be beaten when challenged to a berry-picking duel. His large hands moved swiftly over the tops of the strawberry plants, parting the dark green foliage and then darting in to quickly twist the ripe berry free from its stem. He dropped fistfuls of ruby-red fruit into the baskets in his six-quart carrier. When the last quart was filled, he left the heaping carrier between the rows as he moved on to a waiting empty carrier. After he had harvested enough berries to fill four carriers, he looped each arm under the handle of a carrier and grabbed the handles of the other two carriers, keeping his arms outstretched to balance the load of twenty-four quarts.

At the packing shed, Phil carefully set his abundant harvest on the counter. "There's my girl!" he greeted twelve-year-old Flora, who was in charge of the packing shed in Papa's absence. Flora blushed at the attention from the older boy as she counted out his tickets. Phil gave her braids a quick tug and hurried back to the field to boast of his berry-picking prowess while fanning his fistful of tickets like playing cards.

At noontime, the pickers gathered in the shade of the trees and spread their packed lunches on the grass beside them. The young men and boys usually retreated to the cool, dark recesses of the barn, where they lounged against the haystack and ate their lunches.

The presence of so many young males about the farm caused Papa to issue a one-sentence warning to his growing daughters: "Don't go in the barn with the boys." He offered no explanation for his rule. As the girls headed toward the house for their scant lunch, they cast wary eyes at the barn, not sure why their male co-workers were acceptable companions only while in the berry fields.

Young berry pickers on the Seibel farm

*****

On the Sunday afternoon of the piano recital, Papa and Ada stayed home to glean the remaining berries from the strawberry fields. Mama and the girls walked down the road to Knopfs', where Mrs. Knopf had arranged chairs in the parlor to accommodate the neighborhood students and their families. A large bouquet of pink and white peonies graced the back of the piano.

Each student took their turn playing a prepared piece. Ella had memorized "The Black Hawk Waltz," while Flora sped through her rendition of "The Spinning Song." Hermine and Margaret presented their duet of "The Cuckoo Waltz," with Ella turning the pages of the sheet music.

Little Minola was passed from one sister's lap to another. When she shared a chair with Martha, the two little girls stared in rapt fascination at the narrow mink stole worn by Emmaline Moss, who was seated just in front of them. The tail of each mink was clasped in the jaws of the mink immediately behind it, locking the animals in an endless chase around Emmaline's bony shoulders. Martha reached out a tentative finger to touch the yellow beaded eye of one of the minks, but her advance was met by an icy glare from Emmaline and a quick swat from Mama's hand.

At the conclusion of the recital, Mrs. Knopf invited all to partake in punch and rhubarb cobbler. The students scrambled outdoors to eat their refreshments beneath the boughs of the giant elm tree in Knopfs' backyard, while the neighbor ladies gossiped in the parlor.

Emmaline's eyes, which were always roving, locked onto Mama's expanding waistline. She cocked her head, then announced loudly, "Oh, Sophie, not again! Why, you Germans are so ... fertile!" She snorted with disgust.

The other women in the room stopped chatting and turned to look at Mama, whose cheeks grew scarlet from the unwanted attention.

"You know, not every pregnancy has to result in a baby. A well-placed hatpin would have taken care of things if you'd only intervened earlier," Emmaline scolded. The room remained uncomfortably silent, with all eyes on Mama and no one willing to rebuke Emmaline, who outranked them all on the social scale.

"But maybe this one's a boy," Mama offered meekly.

"A boy?" scoffed Emmaline, rolling her eyes. "You've tried for a boy *seven* times without success! Chances are this one's a girl too."

Mrs. Knopf broke the silence by clearing her throat and thanking the ladies for their attendance, then she gently ushered them toward the door.

Mama was quiet as she and the girls walked homeward in the company of the Mosses and Ordmanns. She listened as Emmaline carried the conversation, gushing on about how well Edith had performed her piano piece and the measures they had taken to obtain the very fashionable crosscut ruffle jabot Edith wore at her neck.

Overhead, a hawk cried a shrill *scree* as it floated on the thermal drafts above the open fields. Mama stopped in the middle of the road and looked upward, shielding her eyes against the bright sun to follow the bird.

"Someday, we'll all be flying up there like hawks," she announced.

"Flying!? Certainly you don't believe that Wright brothers nonsense will amount to anything, do you?!" Emmaline chided as she adjusted her stole. "Maybe it's your condition, Sophie, but you're talking crazy." She tilted her head toward Mrs. Ordmann and whispered loudly, "*Again!*"

* * * * *

That fall, Ada accepted several sewing commissions that took her away from home for extended periods, leaving Minola inconsolable. In addition, Martha began her first year at the Plank Road school, which robbed Minola of her at-home playmate. This sense of abandonment increased the child's tears and whining.

By mid-October, Mama was beyond ill-tempered. The sting of Emmaline's words and prediction of another baby girl had stayed with Mama throughout her pregnancy, augmenting her usual irritability. One day, when Ella and Minola were the only children at home, Minola tipped Mama's button box, sending a cascade of loose buttons clattering across the kitchen floor. Mama grabbed the scissors and chased both Ella and Minola out the door. The weather was unseasonably chilly to be outside without sweaters, so the two huddled in a shaft of sunshine alongside the house until Mama had time to cool down.

On days when the weather was too inclement for the girls to spend time outdoors, they played quietly in the room at the top of Stegmiller's stairs, tiptoeing across the floor and taking care not to raise their voices. The older girls were cautious about rattling the cookware, and they intercepted the teakettle before it started to whistle. Papa spent extra time outside, creating chores to tend to or puttering in his workshop above the cornbarn.

The added precautions made little difference in Mama's demeanor. Finally, on a Saturday afternoon when her buildup in irritation was headed for certain explosion, Papa harnessed Jib to the spring wagon and took Mama for a ride. As soon as the wagon left the drive, the girls flew out the kitchen door, allowing it to slam behind them. They ran in circles in the yard, waving their arms, clapping their hands, and yelling at the top of their lungs. They clambered into the house and played the piano loudly, keeping the forte pedal fully depressed the entire time. They sang raucous rounds of "Row, Row, Row Your Boat," each one shouting her refrain to drown out the others. While Ada and Ella made fudge, the younger girls slid down Stegmiller's stairs on a throw rug, dissolving in laughter when they crashed into the wall at the foot of the stairs. Their pent-up energy spent, the sisters collapsed on the back porch, where they nibbled fudge, dangled their legs over the edge of the porch, and drummed the heels of their shoes against the side of the house.

When Mama and Papa returned, all was calm, and things went on as before.

* * * * *

On a frosty day in late November, Ella threw open the barn door. Papa was seated on a three-legged stool, oiling the horse harness. "Papa! It's a boy! Mama had a baby boy!" she exclaimed.

Papa did not look up. After a long silence, Ella asked excitedly,

"Aren't you surprised?! A boy!"

Papa stood and looped the oiled harness over a peg on the barn wall. "Another mouth to feed," he commented soberly. Selecting a pair of harness straps, he returned to his stool.

Ella stood in perplexed silence. She watched her father work his callused hands over the worn leather. Finally, she closed the barn door behind her and walked slowly to the house.

Papa picked up a nearby cloth and wiped the oil from his hands. He rested his elbows on his knees, leaned his forehead against his clasped fists, and sighed heavily.

Late that afternoon, Papa pulled up a chair beside Mama's bed. She beamed at him. "A boy, William. I named him after you. He's William Elmer." She waved her hand at the sleeping baby in the nearby crib. "We'll call him Bill so there's no *Durcheinander* (confusion)."

Papa knew better than to inquire about Mama's choice of names, particularly her long-held preference for the name "Walter," which had been purloined years ago by George and Bertha for their second son. He had thought about suggesting the name "Millard," in honor of his long-ago friend from the days on the Mississippi River, but Mama seemed settled on the name "William," so "William" it would be.

"Now, you can start your 'Seibel and Son Orchards,'" Mama announced proudly.

Papa shook his head and looked at her in disbelief. "I'm forty-six years old. I've been carrying a debt for the past seventeen years for nursery stock that failed." Papa rose, pushing the chair out from under him. "It's too late for that, Sophie," he said with finality. "It's just too late."

Papa exited the room without stopping to look at his newborn son.

Mama's face clouded. The joy that had come with producing a male heir was short-lived. She picked at the edge of the bed covers and scowled.

That evening, Mama instructed Papa to move the baby's crib upstairs and place it next to Ada and Ella's bed. Mama finally had her boy, but it was up to Ada to raise him.

Chapter 12
The Seibel Homestead
1908

PAPA HURRIED through the morning chores. His breath hung in frigid clouds in the January air as he carried the buckets of steaming milk across the farmyard to the kitchen. It was the right phase of the moon and the right weather for the task that lay ahead: hog butchering. The day was cold enough to keep the meat from spoiling but not so cold as to freeze the carcass. Papa had many preparations to attend to before the neighbor men arrived to lend their assistance in the labor-intensive task.

A few days earlier, he had penned two select hogs, taking them off their feed and supplying only water so that their digestive tracts would be clear of waste prior to butchering. Yesterday, he had rolled the iron kettles from behind the summer kitchen and hung them from two tripods in the backyard, one of which was erected under a stout tree branch. Then he hauled lengths of hardwood from the woodshed, creating a convenient pile for feeding the fires. This morning at four o'clock, he had called "Girls! Girls!", rousing his daughters from their sleep to begin filling one kettle with bucket after bucket of water from the pump in front of the barn. Flora, Hermine, Margaret, and Martha would be kept home from school for several days to help with the preparation of the meat as well as tend to little Minola and baby Bill.

After Papa had set the milk pails inside the kitchen door, he summoned Ada and Ella to help him carry the butchering table from the wagon shed. The table was a long, thick slab of hardwood, its surface scarred by saw marks from many years of butchering. Ada and Ella huffed and puffed at their end of the heavy table, hurrying to keep up with Papa's purposeful strides as he carried the other end of the table across the farmyard.

Papa assessed the quantity of water that the girls had poured into the kettle positioned under the tree branch. Declaring it sufficient, he started a fire beneath the kettle and returned to the barn to fetch the feed sack that hung from a nail on the barn wall. It contained his butchering tools: boning knife, butcher knife, sharpening steel, and meat saw. When the water was hot enough, he'd scald the instruments, sterilizing them for the work ahead. Next, Papa retrieved the singletrees that he used to hook the horse harness to the spring wagon and farm implements. He rigged them to pulleys, which he attached to the tree branch.

As the sky grew pink with dawn, Mr. Moss and his son Edwin,

Albert Gfell, and Mr. Ordmann arrived. Heber Grau would join them later in the morning when the fat was ready for rendering, since he was known throughout the neighborhood for his expertise in producing the snowiest-white lard. Heber did not raise pigs of his own, so each neighbor gave him a ring of sausages and a crock of lard in exchange for his assistance at butchering time.

Ada peered out the kitchen window at the men clustered around the kettle, warming their hands over the steaming water. No matter how many Sunday evenings Albert had come calling, her heart still fluttered at the sight of him.

Ada's reverie was broken by Mama's complaint that she couldn't find the tin of sage they would need later for seasoning the sausage. The kitchen was a cacophony of noise, with the girls clattering breakfast dishes, Martha and Minola tussling over a rag doll, baby Bill howling from his cradle in the corner, and the teakettle whistling its alarm. Mama placed her hands on either side of her head, squeezed her eyes tight, and grimaced. Sensing Mama's tension, Ada dashed to the cookstove and moved the teakettle to the warming section, then plucked baby Bill from his cradle. Clucking soothingly to the child, she set a bottle of milk to warm in a pan of water, then hurried to the cupboard and pawed among its contents until she found the missing tin of sage. Ada settled the doll dispute between Martha and Minola and seated herself in the rocker to feed the hungry baby. It was best to mollify Mama's jagged nerves on a day that would be long and filled with hard work.

"Ready?" Papa asked as he banged through the kitchen door on his way to retrieve the gun from the bedroom closet beneath Stegmiller's stairs.

"Won't get any readier," replied Ella as she assembled the meat grinder and clamped it to the edge of the kitchen table.

When the younger girls saw Papa cross through the kitchen with gun in hand, they huddled on Stegmiller's stairs and plugged their fingers in their ears. They sang "Twinkle, Twinkle, Little Star" to block out the report of the gun or the pigs' final squeals.

Papa and the men worked quickly in the process of bleeding the pigs. They made an incision along the pigs' hind legs and inserted the gambrels, which were then hooked to the singletrees. Using the ropes and pulleys, the men hoisted the pigs until they swung freely from the tree branch. A bucket was placed beneath each slaughtered pig to catch the blood, which would be used to make *blutwurst* (blood sausage). Several of the men held tin cups beneath the incision in the pigs' abdomens, catching and drinking the warm blood.

While the pigs bled out, Papa checked the temperature of the water in the kettle, which would be used for scalding the carcasses. If the water was too cold, the dipped pig's hair would not slip when scraped; if too hot, the bristles would set and become almost impossible to remove. Papa added a small amount of wood ash to the water to soften it and aid in loosening the coarse hair, then carried the buckets of pigs' blood into the kitchen. He assigned Hermine the task of stirring it to prevent coagulation until it was time to add oatmeal and meat trimmings to make the *blutwurst.* She reserved her look of disgust until Papa had exited.

One pig was lowered into the almost-boiling water and then raised for a test scrape by Mr. Ordmann, who was a master of judging the amount of immersion needed to effect the proper slip. When he declared the hair adequately loosened, several of the men began scraping the hog from head to hoof while the other pig was lowered into the kettle. Next, the heads were removed, cut into quarters, and set in a tub of cold water to soak overnight. Mama and the girls would use them to make head cheese. The carcasses were gutted, with the entrails placed in a tub and carried into the kitchen to be used for casings in the sausage-making process. The men sloshed several buckets of hot water into the carcasses and allowed them to cool.

Ada had been keeping an eye on the men's progress from the kitchen window. While they waited for the hogs to cool, she placed some ironstone mugs in the bottom of a basket, slipped her coat on, and carried the basket and hot coffee kettle out to the idle men. Tendrils of steam curled into the air as she tipped the kettle's spout over each man's mug.

Mr. Ordmann cocked his head and watched as Ada filled Albert's cup. "Tell you what, Albert. You oughta marry any woman brung you coffee outdoors."

The men smiled and nudged each other as Ada's cheeks flushed and Albert shifted his weight from one foot to the other.

"I'll take that on good advisement, Gus," Albert replied, a slow smile creeping across his face.

"Hell, Gus, any woman'd serve *you* coffee outdoors just to keep you outta the house!" Mr. Moss teased. The men roared with laughter at Mr. Ordmann's expense.

Ada hurried back to the house, uncomfortable with the men's attention to her relationship with Albert. Papa sipped his coffee thoughtfully and watched her climb the porch steps. He liked the quiet, honest Albert Gfell and had resolved that if the young couple decided to wed, he would not stand in their way. But he could not fathom how the household would carry on without Ada's guiding hand.

Heber Grau hailed them as he angled across the snowy farmyard, carrying his large wooden paddle for stirring the melting fat.

"Don't the roosters crow in the morning over on Everingin Road?" called Mr. Moss, teasing Heber about his late arrival. Even though it had been arranged that Heber would not arrive until the fat was ready to be rendered, the men had found a new object for their joking, and they ribbed Heber that he had laid abed while they were hard at work. He took it good-naturedly as he went about building a low fire under the kettle where the fat would be melted.

Ada took a seat at the kitchen table and helped to clean the guts. It was a tedious job, turning, scraping, and rinsing the casings. Because great caution had to be taken not to pierce the casings and thus render them useless for holding the sausage stuffing, only Mama, Ada, Ella, and Flora were entrusted with the task. As they scraped and rinsed, they took turns bouncing baby Bill on their knees, while Martha and Minola played beneath the table. Hermine and Margaret kept the copper boiler filled with hot rinse water and also were given the job of blowing into the cleaned casings to turn them right-side out, after which the scraping and rinsing began anew.

Outside, the men had moved the cooled carcasses to the butchering table and began to cut the pork into useable pieces. The lean trimmings were tossed into a large pot for the sausage-making operation in the kitchen, and the feet were removed for pickling. The leaf fat from around the pigs' intestines was the first to be dropped into the heated lard kettle. After the first shallow layer of fat had started to melt, Heber carefully added small pieces of back fat, followed by other cubes of fat as they were processed. He stirred patiently and kept the fire low to prevent scorching.

Papa liked to say they used every part of the pig except the squeal. However, Albert found one last piece that went unclaimed. Glancing around, he carefully attached a pig's tail to the bottom edge of Edwin's coat and stepped quickly away. The trick went unnoticed by Edwin, who continued about his business of carving a shoulder. His sawing actions caused the tail to bounce and wiggle. The men guffawed and teased Edwin unmercifully, calling a high-pitched "*Suuu-eee!!*" and commenting that he'd be eating his dinner from a trough. At last, Edwin located the source of their amusement and the culprit who had pinned it there. He pelted Albert with snowballs in a running chase that looped around the house.

When the casings had been cleaned and thoroughly rinsed, Mama set the pot of lean pork trimmings on the kitchen table. Each of the girls took a turn feeding meat and a small amount of fat into the open mouth of the meat grinder while cranking the grinder handle in a continuous clockwise motion. It reminded them of turning the crank on Uncle Will's ice cream maker at the Gasteier reunions. Even little Minola pushed the handle around and around while Martha dropped in chunks of meat. The two girls watched in fascination as small pink tubes of meat were extruded from the many holes in the face of the grinder and fell into the pan situated below it. Ada would use this batch of bulk sausage to make a large skillet of sausage gravy for the men's noon meal.

Mama emerged from the pantry with a big bowl of curing salt. The mixture included equal parts coarse brown sugar and salt, with a measure of saltpeter for added preservative. She set the bowl on the kitchen table and crossed to the summer kitchen to spread an oil cloth on the work table, where the men would rub the salt cure into the dressed shoulders, hams, and bacon prior to hanging them in the smokehouse.

Minola stopped turning the handle of the meat grinder and peered into the bowl of salt cure. The mixture resembled the topping that Ada sprinkled on her cinnamon crumb cake. With a quick glance toward the summer kitchen door, Minola dipped her small hand into the bowl and scooped a fistful of the salt cure into her mouth. She awaited the sweet sensation of brown sugar and cinnamon. Instead, her eyes flew open and her mouth began to froth. Clawing at her tongue, she hurtled herself toward Ada's legs, spitting and retching from the intense salt taste.

"*Ach der liebe!* What happened to you?" exclaimed Ada as she steered the crying child toward the drysink and pumped a cup of water. While Minola drank eagerly, Martha explained what she had witnessed. Ada used the edge of her apron to wipe Minola's chin and dry her tears.

Mama stood in the kitchen doorway, her hands on her hips and an angry scowl on her face. "You got what you deserved, *du kleiner Dieb* (you little thief)," she scolded.

Minola hid her face in Ada's skirts and moved around to the opposite side of Ada's legs, where she was shielded from Mama's glare and possible retribution.

At noon, Flora was sent outside to stir the lard in the rendering kettle while Heber came in to eat dinner with the other men, who were seated at the large table in the living room. Mama fluttered back and forth between the living room and kitchen, apologizing that she couldn't offer them a thresherman's-style meal due to the sausage-making operation that preoccupied the kitchen. She hissed at the girls to hurry along the meal preparation.

Ella pulled a pan of hot, fluffy biscuits from the cookstove and tipped them into a cloth-lined basket. Ada sent Hermine to the table with a large bowl of sausage gravy and deftly flipped fried eggs from the bubbling lard onto a platter. She arranged slices of apple küchen on another platter and told Margaret and Martha to deliver the eggs and küchen to the men. Little Minola trailed her sisters between the living room and kitchen, while baby Bill wailed from his cradle in the corner. Mama's hands trembled from the tension and noise as she circled the table, pouring hot coffee. Mr. Moss noticed her unsteadiness and leaned to the far side of his chair as Mama tipped the hot kettle over his cup.

Albert's location at the table in the living room allowed him to catch glimpses of Ada through the kitchen doorway. He watched appreciatively as she bustled about the kitchen, preparing the food, directing her sisters in the delivery of the meal, and warming a bottle for baby Bill. The young couple occasionally exchanged glances, and Albert gave Ada a furtive wink. He ate heartily, a smile on his face.

That afternoon, the men rubbed the salt cure into the meat and hung it in the smokehouse while Mama and the girls mixed *blutwurst*, made braunschweiger, and stuffed sausages. Heber declared the lard rendering complete when the cracklings turned brown and floated to the top of the kettle. He strained the finished product into crocks and stirred it until the lard became creamy and set into a semi-soft form. The girls covered the crocks with cheesecloth and moved them to the cool cellar, leaving one for Heber to take home as payment for his skill. Papa distributed rings of sausages to the men in appreciation for their labor.

Albert looped his sausages over one shoulder, shook Papa's hand, and said, "See you Sunday evening, Mr. Seibel."

Mr. Moss nudged Papa and advised, "Don't go puttin' on your Sunday best, Bill. He ain't coming to see *you*!" The men chuckled as they ambled down the drive and turned south on Townline Road.

The next day, Mama and the girls made head cheese from the soaked hogs' heads and other scraps. They packed the mixture into loaf pans and set them in the cellar with a heavy weight on top of each pan. The girls smacked their lips at the thought of head cheese sandwiches in their school lunches.

The last task associated with butchering was the making of soap. To get the younger children out from underfoot and away from the dangerous lye mixture, Ella supplied them with scissors and some old copies of the *Monroeville Spectator.* Margaret, carrying baby Bill in the wicker basket, led Martha and Minola up Stegmiller's stairs, where they could cut paper snowflakes to their hearts' content.

Outdoors, Ada measured some of the freshly made lard into the kettle that Heber had used for rendering. She stirred the melting fat with a long-handled paddle while Flora tended the fire. In the kitchen, Ella and Hermine soaked the wooden soap molds in water and gathered up the blankets that would be used in the final stages of soap production.

Mama poured rainwater through the ash hopper in the smokehouse and siphoned off the liquid lye. She tested the strength of the caustic agent by dropping an *unglückliches Ei* (unlucky egg) into the liquid. If there was too much lye in the solution, the soap would burn the skin; not enough would prevent the soap from setting up. When only the tip of the floating egg was revealed, Mama was satisfied that the lye was at the proper strength.

She daubed her face with vinegar to prevent reddened skin from the noxious lye fumes as she heated the lye water on the cookstove, then carried it outside and carefully added it to the melted lard. The four older girls took turns in the long process of stirring the mixture until it was thickened, always trying to stand upwind of the fumes and woodsmoke. When large white bubbles began to pop over the surface, Mama announced that the soap was *unterhaltung* (talking), an indication it was ready to be "proved."

Mama retrieved an ironstone plate from the kitchen and dribbled a small amount of the soap mixture onto it. She pressed the cooled sample between her thumb and forefinger, checking that it formed shiny, translucent ribbons. As a final test, she touched the sample to her tongue. When she detected a little *Biss* (bite) to the mixture, she declared the soap ready.

Flora and Hermine arranged the soaked wooden molds on the ground, and Ella lined them with wet cloths. Ada and Mama poured the creamy mixture into the molds, which the girls carried into the summer kitchen and covered with blankets to prevent the soap's heat from escaping too quickly. After the soap had hardened for several days, they would remove it from the molds, slice it into bars, and allow it to air harden for several more weeks. Mama insisted that the soap have ample time to season so that each bar lasted longer.

The last task was to start a barrel of softsoap in the cellar. Lye and fat were added to the rainwater. Several times a day for the next three days, the girls took turns trotting down the cellar stairs to stir the mixture with a long sassafras stick cut from the trees at the ridge at the back of the farm. In about a month, the mixture would become a jelly-like, brown softsoap. The girls would dipper some into a crock for use in washing dishes and performing the endless scrubbing demanded by Mama's high standards for cleanliness.

By the end of the week of butchering and soap-making, Mama was on the brink of exhaustion. Her nerves were frayed from the long hours, hard work, and general disruption to her tidy kitchen. Then word came that her oldest sister, Maggie Gasteier Parker, had passed away at the age of forty-four. Maggie was the eldest of the Gasteier siblings and had been born at sea on the ship *Queen Victoria* during the Gasteiers' emigration to America in 1863. She had been named Margaretha Katherine Victoria but was always known as Maggie. Mama had now lost two of her sisters—Maggie and Libby—and she spiraled into a deep depression. She spent days in a grief-induced stupor in the rocking chair in the corner of the kitchen.

George & Maggie Gasteier Parker

Ada left for a week-long sewing commission in Bellevue, and Flora, Hermine, Margaret, and Martha returned to school. On the morning of Maggie's funeral, Papa gently spread a quilt over Mama's lap and knelt beside her chair, quietly asking if she wanted to attend the service. She looked at him with sad, confused eyes but gave no response. Later in the morning, Papa hooked Jib to the sleigh, and he and Ella and the littlest children headed to the funeral in Milan. He thought that time alone in the quiet house may serve as a balm to Mama's unsettled state.

At noontime at the Plank Road school, the children ate a hurried lunch, then shrugged on their coats, hats, scarves, and mittens. They sped out the schoolroom doors, rounded the corner of the building, and headed for the creek, which had frozen over. The children slid in their hard-soled shoes across the smooth sheet of ice or played a make-shift game of hockey with a frozen hedge apple and some long sticks. One of the boys retrieved a board that leaned against the back of the coal shed. The smaller children lined up for their turn to be seated on the board while the older students pushed them across the ice at a rapid speed. Upon release, the board and student shot down the ice, frequently colliding with the bank and spilling the laughing passenger onto the creek's glassy surface.

At last it was six-year-old Martha's turn to ride the board. She tucked her knees under her chin and clasped her mittened hands around her legs. She beamed with anticipation and nodded her head to signal the older students that they could begin their long, running push. Martha sailed across the ice, beaming as the wind whistled past her face. The ends of her scarf fluttered behind her, and the creek banks sped by in a blur. With her light weight and the hearty push from the older students, the board shot farther down the creek than any other rider had gone. The children clapped and cheered at her speed and distance. Then, Martha's smile vanished as she saw what lay ahead. Just before the creek curved south, it widened and deepened, causing the ice to form in a delicate crust around open patches of water. Martha dragged her heels on the ice to arrest her forward trajectory. The board spun around, ricocheted off the bank, and toppled Martha onto the thin ice, which broke under her weight. She plunged up to her chest in the frigid water. For one long moment she sat there, shocked by the icy water that seeped into her shoes and soaked through her coat, dress, leggings, and union suit. Scrambling to her feet, Martha slogged to the water's edge and clawed her way up the creek bank, the weight of her sodden clothes and shoes pulling her down.

A group of school children raced toward the struggling child and pulled her to the top of the bank. As they clustered around, Martha's body shook with involuntary waves of shivering and tears. Eight-year-old Margaret wrapped her arms around her sister and tried to comfort her, "Shhh, shhh. I'll walk home with you. You'll be alright."

Flora and Hermine sped to the circle of children on the creek bank. "Get her home as fast as you can, Margaret," Flora advised. "She's soaked to the skin."

While Hermine raced to the schoolhouse to tell Miss Slade what had happened, the other children walked with Margaret and Martha toward Plank Road, expressing sympathy and concern for their shivering schoolmate. Flora again impressed Margaret with the urgency of hastening homeward. "Don't dawdle, or she might lose her fingers or toes!"

Margaret nodded her understanding and pulled Martha along by her wet mittened hand. "C'mon, we have to run!" Margaret implored.

"But I'm s-s-so c-c-cold," Martha choked out between chattering teeth. Her toes and fingers had already gone numb, and her heavy wet clothing chafed uncomfortably as she trotted behind her sister.

Margaret elected to follow the road home, rather than risk another tumble into the water if they took the shortcut along the creek. The one-mile walk had never seemed so long. Margaret's own shoes were damp from the outdoor play, and her toes grew numb. Her mitten was wet from clutching Martha's sodden one, but she urged her sister onward. "There's Uncle George's house, Martha. We're almost home!"

Martha slowed to an agonized walk. Frigid creek water continued to squish out of her shoes at every step. A rim of frozen droplets formed along the edge of her coat, and ice crystals frosted her scarf. "I c-c-can't feel my feet no more," she sobbed. "I wanna stop!"

Flora's warning rang in Margaret's head, *"Don't dawdle, or she might lose her fingers or toes!"* Margaret held back tears of her own and pulled her sister toward home.

The girls' breath came in rasping gasps as they climbed the porch steps and entered the kitchen. Mama was still seated in the rocking chair in the corner, just where she'd been when the girls left for school that morning. They eyed her warily, not sure if the condition of Martha's clothing would set her into a tirade. Mama watched them with unseeing eyes.

Martha collapsed on the floor by the warm cookstove, and Margaret hurried to remove her sister's wet mittens and shoes, which she pushed under the cookstove to dry. Next, she pulled off Martha's cold, wet leggings, which caused the child to sob, "It hurts, M-M-Margaret, it hurts!"

Mama cocked her head and focused on the two girls. "Margaret?" she whispered to herself. "Maggie?"

Margaret laid the wet leggings across the surface of the cookstove. She pulled Martha to her feet and started to unbutton the wet coat. Martha's bare feet and hands were pale and waxy, and she whimpered in pain.

"Maggie? Libby?" Mama whispered again, her voice quaking. "*Bist du das?* (Is that you?)" Mama stared in disbelief at the two girls, then tossed aside the quilt that covered her lap and rose unsteadily to her feet. Her body shook with sobs as she clasped her hands to her face and cried, "*Oh, mein Gott! Es ist meine Schwester! Sie ist zu mir zurückgekommen! Oh, mein Gott, mein Gott!* (Oh, my God! It's my sisters! You've come back to me! Oh, my God, my God!)"

Mama rushed to the two little girls and threw her arms around them, sobbing wildly. She stroked their hair, caressed their faces, and croaked over and over again, "*Maggie! Libby! Du bist lebendig! Lebendig!* (Maggie! Libby! You're alive! Alive!)"

Margaret and Martha stood paralyzed with fear. They were not accustomed to receiving affection of any kind from their mother, so this wild display of emotion was frightening. They did not understand the German that she spoke, but even more confusing was that she repeatedly called them by names that were not their own. Martha's shivering sobs escalated, and tears rolled down Margaret's cheeks.

Mama's attention turned to Martha's coat. She frantically tugged at the coat sleeves, her mind clouded by memories of how the narrow arm openings in a cape had contributed to her sister Libby's death. "*Nein, nein, Libby! Du darfst das nicht tragen! Der Kap ist schlecht! Schmeiß es weg!* (No, no, Libby! You must not wear this! The cape is evil! We must get rid of it!)"

Mama pulled the coat off the frightened child, opened the cookstove door, and shoved the coat into the firebox. The girls gasped, and Martha sobbed louder at the realization that her only coat was about to be burned.

The wet wool coat smoldered but would not catch flames. Mama stabbed at it with the fire poker, muttering under her breath in German about the evil garment. Dropping the poker, she scurried to the summer kitchen, retrieved the tin container of kerosene, and poured a stream of flammable liquid onto the offending coat. The kerosene ignited with a "*whoosh!*" Bright orange flames leaped out of the firebox and licked at the spilled trail of kerosene on the floor. Mama stood back and watched in satisfaction, using the heels of her hands to wipe the tears from her wet face.

The girls screamed and retreated from the inferno, clutching each other as they watched the flames creep toward Martha's shoes and mittens on the floor. They edged backward toward the drysink, where Margaret stumbled over the bucket that Ella was using to soak some of baby Bill's diapers. Grabbing the bucket, she hurtled the water and wet diapers at the cookstove, dousing the fire that snaked across the floor. The cookstove door was still open, and flames from the blazing coat danced and licked outward. Margaret picked up the discarded poker and slammed the cookstove door shut, sealing Martha's coat to a fiery fate. The wet leggings draped across the top of the cookstove began to steam from the blaze in the firebox.

The acrid smell of burnt wool, singed clothing, and charred floorboards hung heavy in the air when Papa, Ella, and the little ones returned from the funeral. While Mama roamed the house, mumbling in German about her sisters, Margaret and Martha tearfully related the frightening details of the afternoon. Papa held onto the back of a kitchen chair as he listened, his legs weak from the realization of how close his family had come to tragedy. It had been a mistake to leave Mama at home alone, and he silently vowed he would never do it again.

*****

The summer brought a bumper strawberry crop. Papa had finally achieved his goal of having four berry fields in constant rotation: a newly planted field that was not ready for picking; a field in its first year of producing large berries; a field in its second year, yielding smaller but sweeter fruit; and the waning field, which was open to self-pickers and would be plowed under at the end of the season. When the harvest slackened to the point where the pickers didn't find it profitable to venture out from town, the girls fanned out in the fields, gleaning the remaining berries. With the money from the sale of the end-of-the-season berries, Papa bought the girls a varnished croquet set with brightly painted stripes around the balls, mallets, and stakes.

The old sunken croquet court that Papa and his siblings had constructed as children became the focus of Sunday afternoon entertainment. The girls delighted in inviting friends to join them for spirited croquet matches. Sometimes the neighbor children served as opponents, or friends from school or church took buggy rides and ended up at the Seibels' croquet court. Occasionally, some of the berry pickers, such as Phil Burrer and his brothers, returned for a visit and an afternoon of good-natured competition. Phil's hearty laugh rang in the mulberry trees that surrounded the court. When Flora gave his ball a "send" with her deadly accurate one-handed swing, he'd teasingly protest, "Hey, I thought you were my girl!?" Flora blushed and beamed.

On Sunday evenings, Albert and Ada played a more sedate game of croquet, interspersed with long moments of standing close together and talking quietly. Ada twirled her croquet mallet in the grass at her feet and looked up into Albert's twinkling blue eyes. He crossed his mallet over the back of his shoulders and smiled down at her. Meanwhile, Martha and Minola galloped around the perimeter of the court, and baby Bill squealed as he rocked back and forth on his hands and knees on a blanket beneath the trees.

Sunday afternoon croquet players.
Back row: Flora, Bessie Scard, Ella, & Ada
Front row: Gladys Trigg, Margaret, Fannie Scard, Martha, Hermine, & Minola

* * * * *

Papa made his usual rounds of the auctions that summer and brought home a handsome cherry bookcase. The girls helped him move it into Papa and Mama's bedroom, to the corner that had been occupied by the baby crib for over seventeen years. With the crib now upstairs next to Ada and Ella's bed, Papa finally had a corner to call his own. In the bottom of the bookcase, Papa stored the tickets that were given to strawberry pickers for each quart that they harvested. In the top, he kept his business ledger, detailing the strawberry, raspberry, and blackberry yields, the price he received per quart at various markets, and a list of pickers' names and their earnings. In the back of the ledger, he recorded a column of his debt for sundries and supplies at Zipfel's store. A second column showed his debt to Mr. Scheid for the 1890 purchase of the failed nursery stock. Several times a year, Papa penciled in a payment in each column and tallied a smaller amount of debt. With a heavy sigh and a small feeling of accomplishment, he closed the book and returned it to the shelf.

* * * * *

In the early fall, it was time to "rob the hives," as Papa referred to the harvesting of honey from the beehives that were located in the plum orchard behind the house. Papa enlisted Flora as his assistant, since her rapid, efficient work pleased him. The two spread old copies of the *Monroeville Spectator* on the butcher table in the wagon shed to catch the sticky honey after the frames were decapped. Papa loaded some punk wood into the smoker and wafted smoke over their light-colored, long-sleeved clothing. Pushing a wheelbarrow, they approached the beehives, which were nearly devoid of bees during the busy afternoon hours of nectar gathering. Papa lightly smoked the hives to calm the remaining bees, then used a hammer to gently tap a chisel around the lid of each hive, loosening the glue-like seal of propolis put in place by the bees.

He carefully lifted each honeycomb-filled frame from the hives, brushed off any clinging bees, and handed it to Flora, who placed it in the wheelbarrow. When all of the frames had been retrieved, Papa wheeled the cart to the wagon shed, where he and Flora used serrated bread knifes to decap the cells of the honeycombs. They inserted the dripping frames into a honey extractor that Papa had built from an old barrel, a discarded wheel from the potato planter, and other spare parts. They took turns whirling the crank of the extractor and allowing centrifugal force to pull the honey out of the combs. While they waited for the thick liquid to settle to the bottom of the barrel, Papa and Flora returned the frames to the hives, where the bees would begin refilling the decapped combs.

A bee sting or two was an inevitable consequence of robbing the hives, but Papa had taught Flora to quickly scrape off the stinger with her fingernail, then daub the area with honey. The antidote did not remove all of the discomfort, but it worked as well, if not better than, the messy baking soda paste that Mama recommended.

The last task was to pull the plug in the bottom of the barrel and allow the amber liquid to fill a row of small crocks. Flora plucked a piece of waxy comb from the surface of a crock and popped it into her mouth to chew like gum. The girls helped carry the crocks across the farmyard to the kitchen, where they set each crock on a step on Stegmiller's stairs. Flora secured a piece of cheesecloth over each crock to prevent the bees from flying in the open window at the top of the stairs and reclaiming the honey.

* * * * *

Later that fall, Albert had exciting news when he came to call one Sunday evening. He had gained employment on the B&O railroad. He agreed to stay on at Mosses' until the corn was harvested, but then he would be gone, traveling from the central railroad hub of Newark to Cleveland and Cincinnati and even Indiana, Michigan, and the city of Chicago. Ada listened as Albert talked excitedly about pursuing his dream of railroad work, but all she could think of was how her own dreams were crumbling.

The following week, Ada stood at her bedroom window, watching with dread as the men progressed across Mr. Moss's corn field, deftly twisting the ears of corn from their stalks and tossing them against the bang board that lined the top of the wagon bed. She willed time to slow down or stop, but soon all of the corn had been harvested. Albert's employment at Mosses' was over.

On the last Sunday evening that Albert came calling, the young couple sat side-by-side on the horsehair couch in the parlor. Ada tried without much success to hide her sadness. Albert pulled a small wooden box from his coat pocket and placed it in Ada's lap. "Just in case I prove to be forgettable," he smiled, motioning for her to open the box.

Ada gave him a puzzled look and gently lifted the lid. Coiled in the satin folds within the box was a gold locket suspended from a slender chain.

"Open it," Albert urged.

Ada unsnapped the tiny clasp and opened the locket. There was a picture of Albert, with his slicked-down dark hair and one-sided smile, gazing up at her.

"Will you wear it ... close to your heart?" Albert asked tenderly.

Ada's throat closed and she knew that if she looked up at him, she would not be able to contain the tears that welled in her eyes. She nodded her head and fastened the locket around her neck.

The next morning before the sun was up, Albert crossed Mosses' front yard and headed north on Townline Road. When he passed the Seibel residence, he detected the faint glow of lantern light coming from the kitchen. He tipped his hat in salute and continued on toward Plank Road and Monroeville, where he would catch a southbound train for Mansfield and then on to the railroad hub at Newark. Albert stepped quickly, whistling as he walked. He was looking forward to this new adventure in life.

Ada had tossed and turned all night, finally crawling out of bed hours before the rest of the household was awake. Alone in the kitchen, she heated the coffee kettle, started a pan of biscuits, and pumped water to fill the copper boiler on the cookstove. It was Monday—laundry day—but there would be no one to meet her at the clothesline.

Albert Gfell working on the railroad

Chapter 13
The Seibel Homestead
1909

AFTER THE NEW YEAR, Flora, Hermine, Margaret, and Martha returned to the Plank Road school with the knowledge that their beloved teacher, Miss Slade, had married and moved away over the holidays. Taking her place was a man by the name of Rupert Graff, the first male to assume the teaching duties at the school. As they walked north on Townline Road, the girls and their neighbors speculated about the new teacher's manner of instruction and form of discipline.

"I bet he likes to use the paddle," commented Elsie Ordmann, "especially on the big boys."

"Not on me, he won't," proclaimed Clifford Knopf, puffing out his chest. "I'll dunk his head in the water pail if he tries to whup me!" Clifford and some of the other older boys attended school regularly during the winter session, when work on the farm was slack.

"Do you think he'll have colored chalk?" asked Margaret, remembering the fat piece of yellow chalk that Miss Slade occasionally used for writing on the big slateboard. The teacher had once allowed the students to write their names in yellow chalk in the lower corner of the slateboard, indicating that that student was making a trip to the outhouse. However, the novelty of using the colored chalk had inspired a sudden and urgent need for every student in the one-room school to "make a trip out back," so Miss Slade had had to restrict the use of the chalk.

"Colored chalk? Doubt it." Elsie's braids flew as she shook her head vigorously in response to Margaret's question.

"Maybe he'll bring some new books and read to us, like Miss Slade always did," offered Martha hopefully.

"Naw, he'll be mean. I'm sure of it," affirmed Elsie.

The girls had worked themselves into a state of apprehension by the time they lined up outside their door at the Plank Road school. They waited and waited for the new teacher to emerge and swing the school bell in an arc over his head, the way Miss Slade had always signaled the start of the school day.

Soon, a tall, bespectacled gentleman hailed them as he loped across the schoolyard, carrying the freshly filled water pail in one hand. The boys murmured disappointment when they saw that the coveted job of water fetcher had been usurped by the new teacher. It had always been a privilege to be selected by Miss Slade to carry the water pail to the neighboring house, where Mrs. Lantz would sometimes wash the common dipper while the boys filled the bucket from the pump by the back porch. If they dawdled long enough or remembered to appear especially well behaved, Mrs. Lantz might hand them a sugar cookie to munch on their way back to school.

"I'm Mr. Graff," the teacher puffed as he climbed the stone steps and motioned the students to follow him through the school doors. The children were bewildered by their new teacher's casual approach to the start of the school day. Gone were the school bell and the admonition to form orderly lines as they filed in. The students crowded through the doors, hung their wraps on nails in their respective cloak rooms, and placed their lunches on the shelves above. Sliding into their seats, they waited quietly for Mr. Graff to lead them in the Pledge of Allegiance and the Lord's Prayer.

Mr. Graff seated himself on the edge of the teacher's desk, removed his glasses, and pulled a handkerchief out of his coat pocket. While he rubbed the lenses of his spectacles, he gazed about the room. "So, what do you want to do today?"

The students looked at each other in amazement. All visions of a stern-faced school master doling out harsh punishments quickly disappeared.

As the weeks passed, it became evident that Mr. Graff's method of teaching was to set the children to work on reading or ciphering something that was already familiar to them. Meanwhile, he tended to schoolhouse chores, such as carrying in a scuttle of coal from the shed, poking the fire in the potbellied stove and shaking down the ashes, winding the schoolhouse clock, refilling the kerosene lamps and cleaning their chimneys, or sweeping snow from the front steps. But Mr. Graff's favorite task was fetching water from Lantzes' well. He had taken a shine to Mrs. Lantz, and his trips to the well—and Mrs. Lantz's kitchen—were growing more frequent and longer in duration.

In the teacher's absence, the students were at first well behaved and kept to their assigned schoolwork. Then one day, Althea Fox removed the pin that secured her collar and inserted its head in the metal hinge of her seat. With one finger, she flipped the end of the pin, creating twangy musical notes. The children giggled and looked around for the source of the sound. Althea's mischievous grin gave her away, and soon the children were whispering the names of songs for Althea to play on her musical pin.

A wadded rag used for wiping slates sailed over the partition that separated the boys' side of the room from the girls' side. More giggling erupted amid cautionary shushing that Mr. Graff might be just outside the door.

"I'll see about that," proclaimed Clifford Knopf, and he strode down the aisle toward the door. All the students turned in their seats to watch as he disappeared into the boys' entryway. Clifford pressed his ear against the schoolhouse door and listened. Hearing no scuffing of footsteps outside, he grew bolder and returned to the front of the classroom, where he seated himself at the teacher's desk. The girls gasped, and the boys snickered in approval.

"I've got a perfect view of Lantzes' yard from here," he assured, pointing to the window across the room. "I'll give a holler when Ol' Graff's comin'." Clifford laced his fingers behind his head and leaned back in the chair. For added emphasis, he parked his boots on top of the teacher's desk.

The schoolroom erupted in gasps, cheers, and laughter. One of the older boys dashed to the girls' cloakroom, where he grabbed a round lunch pail and rolled it down the aisle on the girls' side of the room. Not to be outdone, some of the other boys seized lunch containers from the girls' shelf and tossed them back and forth over the partition. Girls squealed in protest when they spotted their airborne lunches. The younger boys climbed on top of their desks and leaped off, flapping their arms and crowing like roosters. Some of the girls took turns drawing on the slateboard behind the teacher's desk, while others played tag in the aisles or walked balance-beam-style on the narrow recitation bench.

"Here comes Graff!" Clifford shouted when he spotted the teacher exiting Lantzes' kitchen. His boots hit the floor, and he raced toward his assigned seat. The rest of the students scrambled to restore order to the classroom.

When Mr. Graff sauntered in, the children were bent over their books and slates—the picture of studious intent. Sly glances and concealed smiles were exchanged, but the teacher was too busy poking the fire in the potbellied stove to notice.

Mr. Graff's long absences and the ensuing chaos in the classroom continued for weeks. When the novelty finally wore off, some of the older students began to complain to their parents. Papa and the other members of the school board met with Mr. Graff, who was given a reprimand but allowed to complete the school year. For the students at Plank Road school, it was a lost opportunity for education.

* * * * *

Albert found the excitement of working on the railroad to be interspersed with long, boring hours spent at boarding houses with the other men, waiting for an outbound assignment. To pass the time, they played cards, pulled pranks on each other, explored the towns they were in, or wrote to their loved ones back home. Ada regularly received postcards and letters sent from Newark and Cincinnati, Ohio, and South Bend and Michigan City, Indiana.

Ada had to smile at one postcard showing Albert in an undersized derby with a cigar clamped between his teeth. The message scrawled on the back read "Ain't I a dandy?"

"Ain't you, though," whispered Ada as she positioned the postcard between her wooden jewelry box and the tin of talcum powder on top of her dresser.

Ain't I a dandy?—Albert

*****

In the spring of 1909, Old Man Scheidt sat at George and Bertha's kitchen table, poking at the noontime meal with his fork and grumbling that Bertha's cooking was the cause of his constant indigestion. Bertha had silently endured Old Man's presence in her house for the past three years, but listening to his complaints about her culinary skills pushed her to the edge. She knew she was talented in the kitchen, and George, Rosie, and Walter always forked in her cooking with gusto. In addition, Elmer's letters from college frequently expressed a longing for one of her delicious home-cooked meals. She set her lips in a firm line and balled her fist beneath the table.

Sensing Bertha's tension, George waved his fork at Rosie and directed, "Go play somethin' pretty on the piano for your mother."

Bertha had raised Rosie to be a lady, keeping her indoors to preserve her alabaster skin and encouraging her to spend time at the keyboard rather than in the kitchen. Consequently, Rosie had developed few life skills, but Bertha's greatest pleasure was listening to her daughter play classical arrangements. She leaned back in her chair and sighed as piano music filled the air.

"*Bah! Diese Nahrung schmeckt wie Schweine slop* (Bah! This food tastes like pig slop)," snarled Old Man, dropping his silverware on the table with a clatter. "*Und Jesus! Dieses Gott-verdammte Hämmern auf dem Klavier! Es gibt nur einen Platz auf diesem Bauernhof um diesem Geräuschen zu entgehen.* (And Jesus! That God-damned banging on the piano! There's only one place on this farm to escape from that noise.") Picking up the ever-present cider jug from beside his chair, Old Man hobbled toward the back door, stepping on the tail of Bertha's aged dog Bunda, who was stretched out in a spot of sun on the kitchen floor.

The dog yipped in protest, and Bertha glared in Old Man's direction. A lack of appreciation for her cooking was one thing, but to disparage Rosie's musical talent and hurt her beloved dog was more than Bertha could take. She pushed her chair from the table and started to rise.

George reached out and grabbed Bertha's forearm. "Now, mother," he cautioned.

The slam of the back door lent an unwanted punctuation to the middle of Rosie's "Moonlight Sonata."

"What's wrong with *him*?" asked Walter around a mouthful of apple pie.

"Probably bound up again," mumbled George. "Maybe some time spent in the outhouse will improve his disposition."

Bertha snorted her doubts as she carried Old Man's dishes to the drysink. George and Walter finished their pie, shrugged on their coats, and returned to their chores in the barn.

While she washed the dishes, Bertha suggested that Rosie should fix herself up, and the two of them would drive the buggy into Monroeville, where Rosie could order some new sheet music. The unspoken object of the trip was to advance twenty-year-old Rosie's matrimonial prospects by parading through some of the businesses along Main Street that were owned by families with eligible bachelor sons. Like a merchant, Bertha knew the only way to make a sale was to display the goods to their best advantage. "Remember, you're quality," Bertha called after Rosie as she climbed the stairs to her room to begin the transformation.

Due to Rosie's inability to make a decision, the simple act of changing clothes was a time-consuming endeavor. Should she wear her hair pinned neatly at the nape of her neck or massed high on her head and secured with combs? Which ear bobs brought out the pink in her complexion, and which hat complemented the hues of her dress? If she wore her Grandmother Loew's amethyst ring, would it give potential suitors the impression that she was putting on airs? Rosie agonized over each decision, weighing the pros and cons of her selections.

Finally primped and powdered to perfection, Rosie made one last necessary stop. When she pulled open the outhouse door, she discovered Old Man seated there in the darkness, his overalls pooled around his ankles and his cider jug tucked beside him on the wooden bench. He was slumped sideways against the outhouse wall and offered no reaction to the embarrassing interruption.

Rosie quickly shut the door and muttered an apologetic, "Oh, sorry!" She blinked several times and cocked her head, contemplating the scene on the other side of the outhouse door and trying to make a decision about its implications. Then her eyes widened and she bolted across the yard toward the house, screaming, "*M-o-t-h-e-r!!!*"

The funeral was a dry-eyed affair. Old Man was buried beside Kathrina in Riverside Cemetery, beneath the ostentatious headstone that he had carefully selected as his final testament. Although his personal worth had once totaled over $10,000, Old Man left an estate of only $615. He bequeathed $500 to George; Papa received nothing.

* * * * *

Little Bill's care was left to his sisters. Because there was an abundance of female attire in the house, they dressed him in the girls' hand-me-downs until Ada had time to sew some boy's clothes. No one thought to take Bill to the photographer's studio on Monroe Street to have his picture made, as Mama had done for many of his older sisters. The immediate needs of a large, growing family superseded any frills or special treatment for its youngest member.

Being raised by his sisters, who were children themselves, led to some less-than-beneficial experiences for Bill. Sometimes, Margaret, Martha, and Minola put him in the baby buggy with the intention of taking their little brother for a nice walk about the yard. However, the stroll usually ended in a footrace, with the buggy careening from side to side as the girls dashed across the yard and circled the house. On more than one occasion, the buggy overturned, and a howling Bill was carried into the kitchen for Ada to soothe.

As soon as he was old enough to walk, Bill toddled after Minola. The companionship of a younger brother caused Minola to release her grip on Ada's skirt, freeing Ada in her daily tasks about the kitchen. However, Minola and Bill found endless mischief that always brought them back to her for comfort, protection, or a solution.

One day, the two children lay on the summer kitchen floor with Mama's button box between them. They took turns dropping the buttons through the cracks in the planks, aiming for the open cistern below. They giggled with each *ploop!* that indicated a button had found its mark.

When Mama discovered them, she flew at the children in a rage, berating their foolishness as she swatted at them with the broom. Minola and Bill fled to the kitchen and took sanctuary behind the folds of Ada's skirts, while she defused the situation. Ada assured Mama that the children would retrieve the dropped buttons, and she marched the two outdoors, removed a piece of lattice by the back porch, and sternly motioned for them to wriggle through. Minola and Bill protested their fear of the dank, dark crawl space, but Ada could not be dissuaded. The children hurriedly gathered the buttons that were scattered on the ground beneath the house and placed them in Ada's outstretched hand.

During berry season, Minola and Bill abandoned the other pickers in the field and climbed the stairs to Papa's workshop above the cornbarn. There they made a contest of picking up as many No. 2 tacks as possible with the magnetized hammer. They tried without success to swing the huge foot-pedal lathe into action and played with all the tools scattered on Papa's workbench. When they heard the sound of the spring wagon in the farmyard, indicating Papa's return from selling berries in town, they scampered for the stairs, knowing that Papa considered his workshop off-limits to children.

In their flight, Minola stepped on a rusty tack, puncturing her bare foot. She hobbled out to the berry field to find Ada, who led the crying child, followed by little Bill, to the kitchen. Ada gently washed the wound with a bar of lye soap, then retrieved a slice of salt pork from the smokehouse and tied it to the bottom of Minola's foot with a strip of cloth. Tears dried, Minola and Bill went back outside to play, the piece of salt pork flopping with each step. By the end of the day, the slab of meat had worked its way around to the side of Minola's foot, but its medicinal qualities had had their effect.

The barn was full of places to explore, and Minola and Bill poked into every corner. One day, as they played beneath the wagon, Minola jabbed her finger into the thick, black grease rimming the axle on the wagon wheel. She wiped it on the back of her hand and marveled at how it changed her skin color. She remembered one of the adults in the berry patch had teased Papa that his deeply tanned skin made him look like a Negro.

Minola held the back of her hand toward Bill to show him its blackened appearance. "Wanna be a Negro, Bill?" Minola asked.

Bill smiled and nodded his head eagerly.

Minola liberally daubed Bill's face, neck, arms, and hands with the gooey black axle grease. Pleased with the effect, she led him to the kitchen to show Ada.

The screen door to the kitchen was locked. The children pressed their foreheads against the screen to get a better look into the kitchen, leaving a thick smear of grease where Bill's head rested. Minola spotted Ada and Ella on their knees across the room, scrubbing the kitchen floor. Ada had locked the screen door in the interest of keeping small feet from tracking dirt across the still-wet floor.

Minola rattled the door handle and pounded on the wooden frame. "Ada! Ella! Come look at Bill. He's a Negro!"

Minola heard the thump of the scrub brushes as they hit the floor and the gasps of "*Ach! Himmel!*" as her sisters spied the now-black Bill grinning at them from the opposite side of the screen door.

Ada hurriedly unlatched the door and pulled little Bill into the kitchen by the front of his shirt. Her brow was furrowed and her jaw slack.

"Minola, how *could* you!?" scolded Ella.

Judging by her sisters' angry reactions to her artistic endeavors, Minola felt it best to be as far out of sight, mind, and reach as possible. She scampered off the porch, across the yard, and down the lane to the row of sassafras trees at the back of the farm. She lingered there until she thought Ada and Ella had had time to cool down.

Meanwhile, Ella set the copper boiler on the cookstove and filled it with water, adding a scoop or two of softsoap. Ada carefully undressed young Bill, trying not to touch the black axle grease or smear any more of it on his clothes than was already present. The two sisters exchanged frustrated comments and looks of exasperation.

When Minola finally slunk back to the house, her brother's freshly washed clothes danced on the line, the screen door glistened with soap bubbles from its impromptu cleansing, and Bill had been scrubbed into a white boy again.

Like Margaret, Bill was blessed with curly hair. Ada had been reluctant to cut the pretty ringlets that fell just below his ears, but combing the mass of curls was also a daily struggle. Occasionally, the girls tied Bill's locks up in a bow and laughingly referred to him as their youngest sister. Papa chose to ignore the display.

In the fall of the year, Ada and Ella sent the girls and Bill to gather hickory nuts at the little cemetery by the bend in Townline Road. Mosses were hosting a neighborhood gathering, which included a cake walk, and Ada and Ella intended to do the family proud by submitting a triple-layer spice cake with hickory nut filling.

While the older girls gathered nuts, Minola and Bill climbed over the fence that enclosed the cemetery, which was thick with brambles, milkweed, and burdock. They crawled low to examine rabbit trails, woodchuck holes, and toppled headstones. When the two children emerged from the thicket, the girls gasped at the sight of Bill's hair. Burrs were embedded close to the scalp, and his ringlets were a matted, tangled mass of bramble stems, milkweed fluff, and more burrs. Minola's braids had saved her hair from a similar fate. "Better not let Mama see this," Flora warned the others.

The siblings headed back to the farm, where Flora delivered the hickory nuts to the kitchen and whispered the problem of Bill's hair to Ada and Ella. The others led Bill to the barn, far from Mama's disapproving eyes. Ella kept Mama busy cracking out the hickory nuts in the kitchen, while Ada tucked her sewing shears and Papa's razor into her apron pocket and headed outdoors.

"*Ach, der liebe!*" exclaimed Ada when she saw the tangled mess that was Bill's hair. Flora pulled up a milking stool and tucked Bill into her lap. She wrapped her arms around his body to hold him still, while Hermine clasped his head tightly between her hands. Ada circled the trio, carefully snipping at Bill's locks. The toddler squirmed and howled, more angry at being held down than at the makeshift haircut. The areas that were matted too near the scalp required the intervention of Papa's razor. When Ada was done, she stood back and surveyed her work.

"Eye-yi-yi!" she lamented, shaking her head. The finished product was an uneven patchwork of closely cropped hair and bald spots.

That evening as Ada and Ella prepared supper and Flora and Hermine set the table, Mama scowled in Bill's direction, "What happened to him?"

The girls exchanged nervous glances, none of them wanting to suffer the possible repercussions from Mama. Finally, Ada spoke up and told the story of little Bill's excursion in the bramble patch. Mama scoffed in disgust at Bill's appearance.

Papa pulled up his chair to the table and shook his head but couldn't hide a small smile. "Least he looks like a boy now."

* * * * *

The neighborhood gathering in Mosses' barn was an autumn festival, complete with a galvanized tub for bobbing for apples. The Grau brothers stood on overturned apple crates at one end of the barn and tuned their fiddles. The women oohed and aahed over each other's entries for the cake walk, silently judging their own creations against those of their neighbors. Mama snorted when she noticed that Bertha had brought not only a mile-high chocolate cake but also a plate of her dreamy divinity fudge. She hissed at Ada and Ella for submitting only their triple-layer spice cake with hickory nut filling, asking them if they wanted the family to look like "*üble Verwandte* (the poor relation)." Outside the barn doors, the clang of metal hitting metal and the sound of laughter reverberated through the air as the men pitched horseshoes and teased each other about an off-the-mark throw.

Edith Moss approached the Seibel girls and pointed to little Bill's unconventional haircut. "What's the matter with him? Lice?"

"Nope," replied Flora. "But whatever it is, it's contagious. Better stay away from him if you want to keep your hair."

Edith recoiled in disgust and moved away from the Seibel girls, who exchanged sly glances and tried to mask their grins.

After several rounds of the Virginia Reel, the Grau brothers took a break and headed for the jugs of apple cider being chilled in the cows' water trough. Emmaline Moss took the opportunity to step up onto one of the apple crates, clap her hands, and call in her thin, high voice for everyone's attention. "Listen, listen! I have exciting news!"

The crowd quieted and turned to hear Emmaline's announcement.

"As most of you know, telephone service is coming to those who live along Plank Road. You've probably seen them erecting the poles. But those of us on Townline Road are out of luck because the phone company will only run the lines down a side road if a stock holder lives there. Are any of you folks stock holders?" Emmaline shaded her eyes against the glare of the kerosene lanterns and looked for a positive response from her gathered neighbors.

Everyone in the crowd shrugged their shoulders, shook their heads, and mumbled, "No."

"I didn't think so. But, due to a recent generous inheritance that came my way, I am the newest telephone company stock holder!" Emmaline squealed as her hands fluttered in front of her. "The phone lines will be brought down Townline Road as far as my house. Because of my benevolence, all of you who live north of me will be able to tap in and have phone service, too!" Emmaline beamed at the crowd of neighbors as she awaited their grateful response.

"What about those of us south of you?" called out Mr. Knopf from the back of the crowd. "What are we supposed to do for phone lines?"

Emmaline's face fell at this challenge to her charity. "Why! You can't expect me to pay to run the lines all over the whole neighborhood! I'm a good Christian woman who believes in helping those less fortunate than myself, but I draw the line at handouts," sniffed Emmaline, lifting her chin.

The crowd chattered excitedly about the news. The neighbors who lived south of Mosses and could not afford the expense of extending the tantalizingly close phone service grumbled among themselves. Mr. Moss helped Emmaline down from the apple crate and listened sympathetically as she sputtered about the perceived lack of gratitude shown her.

The Seibels had their new phone mounted on the west wall of the living room, near the landing of the stairs to the second floor. This modern convenience opened up a whole new connection to the outside world. While none of the members on the party line would admit to it, all had perfected the art of "rubbering"—pressing one's cheek tightly against the mouthpiece of the telephone to muffle any background noises while holding the receiver to their ear and listening intently to the conversations of their neighbors. It was common for a neighbor woman to comment that she had "just happened to overhear" such and such when she picked up the receiver to see if the line was clear. While Ada denied rubbering, the deep, circular imprint of the mouthpiece on her cheek gave her away.

* * * * *

To Ada's surprise and delight, Albert's schedule allowed him opportunities to return to Monroeville. When work on the railroad was slack, he picked up temporary employment with Mr. Moss or other farmers in the vicinity. The Sunday night courting resumed on an irregular basis.

Mama's behavior on those Sunday evenings could be unpredictable, which caused Ada endless hours of concern. She worried that Albert would decide to find a sweetheart from a more normal family. But kind, understanding Albert took Ada's homelife in stride. One Sunday evening, his long legs carried him across the lawn and toward the back porch. "Evenin', Mrs. Seibel," he called to Mama who was clawing at the dirt in the flowerbed at the side of the house. "Makin' garden?"

Mama turned to him with a puzzled look on her face. "I can't find the *Hefekuchen* (yeast cakes), Fred," she lamented, confusing Albert with her favorite brother. "I left them right here." She pointed toward the numerous holes she had dug in the flowerbed. "Did the chickens carry them off? They're always playing tricks on me, you know," she complained.

"Can't trust them chickens," Albert commiserated as he rapped on the kitchen door.

Ada and Albert retreated to the parlor and closed the doors behind them, but their privacy was short-lived. Minola and Bill could not abide the separation from their mother figure. They rattled the doorknob, laid on the floor and wriggled their fingers under the door, and pleaded to be let in. When there was no response from Ada, the two children drummed their feet against the parlor door.

"Oh shooks," said Albert, "let 'em come on in."

Ada opened the parlor door and gave the two children a look of disapproval, which they ignored as they bolted into the room.

Albert reached into his coat pocket, pulled out a pack of chewing gum, and handed a stick to each of the children. Little Bill's eyes opened wide at his first taste of the clove-flavored gum. Albert chuckled and cautioned Bill to chew, not swallow. Bill obeyed and chewed vigorously, smacking his lips with each exaggerated motion of his jaw. He and Minola lay on the parlor rug at Ada's feet, playing with the buttons on her shoes, tracing the pattern of the rug with their fingers, and contentedly chewing their gum while they listened to the quiet conversation of the young couple. Bill occasionally pulled the wad of gum out of his mouth, placed it on the point of Ada's shoe, and examined its wrinkled surface before popping it back into his mouth.

When it was time for Albert to leave, he tousled Bill and Minola's heads. "See ya, Bill. Bye, Dick," he smiled.

Minola was too shy to speak to Albert, but she was privately pleased that he had given her the nickname of Dick.

Bill hopped to his feet and waved, "Bye-bye, Gum Man."

*****

Between Albert's visits, Ada sent postcards informing him of her travels to various sewing commissions. She frequently was employed by a widowed neighbor woman, Mrs. Kath, who had three small children. The two women developed a mother-daughter-type bond, and at last Ada had a female relationship where she could be the recipient instead of the responsible caregiver. She confided to Mrs. Kath her growing feelings of love for Albert and her conflicting sense of duty brought about by her home situation. Mrs. Kath offered a sympathetic ear and shared the details of her own romance with her suitor, Mr. Witke.

Sometimes, Mrs. Kath left Ada in charge of the three children while she went out for a few hours. On one occasion, Mrs. Kath suggested that Ada bake cookies for the children, since her sewing projects were light. Ada gathered the ingredients for molasses cookies and set the children to work measuring, mixing, and using an overturned cup to cut shapes from the rolled-out dough. Ada built a fire in the cookstove while the children transferred the cookies onto baking sheets.

When it was time to pull the cookies from the oven, Ada was perplexed that they hadn't risen. She checked the underside of several cookies and found them baked to perfection. Puzzled, she scooped the cookies onto the table to cool. The children sampled them while they were still warm and declared them delicious. They asked for seconds, and Ada granted permission.

When Mrs. Kath returned home, the children greeted their mother with smiles on their faces and cookie crumbs on their chins. They pointed to the plate of cookies on the table and proudly announced that they had helped make them. Ada confided to Mrs. Kath that she was embarrassed by the cookies' flat appearance and puzzled by what she had done to affect their outcome so drastically.

Mrs. Kath tapped her finger against her chin thoughtfully. "Show me the ingredients you used."

Ada opened the cupboard and pulled out the various tins, assembling them on the table. Mrs. Kath placed her hands on either side of her face. "Oh, Ada, I should have told you!" Picking up the tin of baking powder, she explained, "The label says baking powder, but I keep *cleaning* powder in here!"

The two women exchanged horrified glances and then looked at the three upturned faces of the children. They quickly inspected the children's mouths for signs of trauma, and Ada hastily threw the remaining cookies in the trash. For the next day or two, Mrs. Kath kept a close eye on the children, watching for any ill effects.

The Kath children weren't fazed by the tainted cookies and frequently asked Ada to bake with them again. She complied but was always careful to avoid the mislabeled baking powder tin. Long after Mrs. Kath had married Mr. Witke and moved to Mansfield, she and Ada chuckled about her special recipe for "Cleaning-Powder Cookies."

*****

The fall of 1909 brought a new teacher, Miss Eleanor Ruffing, to the Plank Road school. Despite her diminutive stature, Miss Ruffing was able to command the classroom and restore the order that had been sorely lacking under Mr. Graff's tutelage. She dressed up the schoolroom with maps of the United States and the world. But best of all, she brought with her a love of books and a small library. The Seibel girls, who dearly loved to read, were in heaven.

Plank Road school children with teacher Miss Eleanor Ruffing, center of middle row
Back row: second from left, Hermine; fifth from left, Flora
Margaret standing on steps at far right
Front row: Martha, seated and wearing checked dress

While Miss Ruffing worked diligently to advance the students' academic standing, she also believed in a sprinkling of fun. On a winter's day when the roads were covered in a solid sheet of hard-packed snow and the sun lent a hint of warmth to the otherwise frosty temperatures,

Miss Ruffing suggested that the children should test their spelling skills against those of the students at a neighboring school. Excitement rose in the classroom because this meant one thing: a bobsled ride. After lunch, two of the older boys were dispatched to the neighboring residence of Mr. Metz, who might be receptive to the idea of providing such a diversion.

The students waited anxiously, making half-hearted attempts to concentrate on their lessons. When it seemed the anticipation of the event could be endured no longer, they heard the faint sound of sleigh bells. A momentary hush overtook the classroom, and wide smiles lit every face. Nodding her head, Miss Ruffing gave the signal for them to prepare for the sleigh ride. The children scrambled to put away their books and slates. They rushed to their respective cloak rooms, hurriedly tossing on coats, scarves, hats, and mittens and making sure the youngest students were properly bundled for the exhilarating ride. The school doors burst open, and the excited children tumbled out.

Mr. Metz had tossed clean straw in the bed of the wagon box that served as the bobsled, and Mrs. Metz had thoughtfully sent along a supply of blankets. The girls and younger children burrowed into the straw and covered themselves with layers of blankets, while Mr. Metz helped Miss Ruffing onto the wagon seat and handed her the lap robe. The boys, whose energy could not be contained, elected to run alongside the bobsled. While the girls sang songs, including "Jingle Bells," the boys pummeled each other in a running snowball fight.

As the bobsled approached the Opperman Road school, the students quieted down until Mr. Metz pulled his team of horses into the schoolyard. Then, the students erupted in loud whoops and cheers. The schoolhouse door opened about six inches, and the face of Miss Hern, the school mistress, appeared. When she saw that the commotion was caused by visitors from the neighboring school, she smiled broadly and invited them in.

The students hung their wraps in the cloak rooms and scooted onto the desk seats beside their Opperman Road counterparts. The teachers conducted a joint lesson that seemed much more interesting in the new setting with fresh faces surrounding them. At last, the students lined up for a spelldown. Miss Hern selected words for the Plank Road students, while Miss Ruffing delivered words to the Opperman Road pupils. The younger students fell by the wayside fairly early, taking their seats and cheering for the representatives from their schools. When a student spelled a word correctly, he or she moved to the end of the line and awaited the challenge of a new word.

Finally, the best spellers were whittled down to three students: Hermine and two pupils from the Opperman Road school. They successfully spelled their way through "arithmetic," "spacious," "Venezuela," "receive," and "orthography." One of the two Opperman students was knocked out by the word "palatial," leaving Hermine and her final opponent, who were quite evenly matched, to battle through round after round. With each word spelled successfully, the schoolroom erupted in cheers from the visiting or home school crowd. At last, Miss Ruffing announced "Luxembourg."

The Opperman student furrowed his brow. "L-u-x-e-m-b …" The boy anguished over what letter to say next. He dropped his head and wrote the word several times with his fingertip in the palm of his hand. Shifting his weight anxiously from side to side, the boy quietly mouthed the letters as he deliberated over his choices. Finally, with cheeks flushed and eyes closed, he spelled "L-u-x-e-m-b-e-r-g."

Hermine's heart hammered in her chest. She had spent the better part of the year seated in front of the map of Europe that stretched across the wall of the Plank Road school. She knew her opponent had just misspelled the name of the country.

"I'm sorry," Miss Ruffing announced, "that is incorrect. Hermine, it's your turn. If you spell 'Luxembourg' correctly, you are the champion speller for the day. If not, the spelldown will continue with more words until one of you is eliminated."

Flora sat tensely at the edge of her seat and whispered a prayer into her clasped hands. Margaret crossed the fingers on both hands and clenched them tightly until her fingers ached, while Martha nervously chewed her lower lip.

Hermine nodded, took a deep breath, and visualized the map of Europe on the wall of the Plank Road school. She spelled carefully, "L-u-x-e-m-b-o-u-r-g."

Miss Ruffing smiled. "Congratulations, Hermine! You're the spelling champion!"

Hermine exhaled slowly, while the schoolroom erupted in cheers from the Plank Road students. Margaret couldn't contain her glee, and she leaped into the aisle beside her desk, pumping her fists in the air as she danced a little jig. Flora beamed and offered a quick silent prayer of thanks, while Martha drummed her hands on the desk she shared with a not-so-enthused Opperman Road student. Mr. Metz, who had been watching the competition from the back of the classroom, stomped his foot and let out an involuntary whoop.

The students bid farewell to the Opperman Road scholars and invited them to pay a bobsled visit before the winter was over. They shrugged on their winter wear and piled into the bed of the sleigh. The trip back to the Plank Road school was filled with happy chatter and congratulations to Hermine on her spelling prowess.

The girls sped home that afternoon, anxious to share with their siblings the news of the bobsled ride and Hermine's victory. Margaret raced ahead of her sisters, sliding and pirouetting on the icy road and calling out joyously, "Hermine is the spelling champion of the Opperman and Plank Road schools … of Luxembourg … of the world!"

Hermine puffed out her chest and adopted a regal air as she strutted along. The sisters dissolved in laughter at her haughty posture. They trotted onward, alternately running and sliding down Townline Road toward home.

The schoolgirls:
Margaret & Hermine
Martha & Flora

As they warmed themselves beside the cookstove, the girls bubbled over with details of the day, each sister interrupting the other to interject a thought or superlative about the experience. Ada and Ella listened and smiled as they bustled about the kitchen preparing supper.

Ella declared that such a momentous occasion should be celebrated with a dessert, a treat which they rarely indulged in during the week. She hurried to the cellar and returned with a jar of peaches.

After a supper of beef gravy over mashed potatoes, Ella speared the peach halves into individual saucers and ladled on a generous spoonful of warm cream. She topped each golden peach with a sprinkling of cinnamon. The girls didn't tell Mama the reason for the special dessert; they knew she would not share their enthusiasm over Hermine's academic accomplishment.

* * * * *

In the spring of 1910, word came that Mama's mother, Katherine Gasteier, was in failing health. She could no longer handle the work associated with keeping house and preparing meals for her husband John Frederick and son Will, a bachelor who lived with his parents and farmed the homestead. As the oldest surviving daughter, Mama felt it her responsibility to offer a solution. She quickly volunteered Ella as a live-in housekeeper. John Frederick insisted that he would pay Ella for her work, despite Mama's protests.

Uncle Will came to get Ella on a Sunday in April, just a few weeks before her eighteenth birthday. After a hearty dinner, he loaded Ella's small trunk into the back of his wagon and helped her climb onto the wagon bench. The girls and little Bill gathered in the side yard and continued to wave goodbye long after Uncle Will's wagon had left the driveway. Ella frequently swiveled on the bench to return their waves, then took one last wistful look at home before the wagon rounded the bend in Townline Road.

Ella's absence robbed Ada of her partner in managing the household tasks and parenting their younger siblings. Her thoughts of a future with Albert had already been complicated by his job on the railroad, but now the increased responsibility to her family presented an additional obstacle. Sometimes, her dreams seemed unobtainable.

Ada was not the only one whose future had been altered by Mama's decision to dispatch Ella to the Gasteier homestead. Papa already relied heavily on Flora for assistance with the farm chores. She helped to milk the cows before and after school, skimmed the cream and churned it into butter, and assisted with the planting and harvesting of all the farm crops, including berries, potatoes, corn, and sorghum cane. Papa called her his "right-hand man," but that was the extent of his praise, even though he found her rapid, efficient work style so pleasing. With Ella gone and Ada frequently away on sewing commissions, the yoke of household and parenting duties now fell upon Flora's shoulders. She worked harder than anyone to fulfill the expectations placed upon her and to please everyone.

That spring, Miss Ruffing began preparing her oldest students to take the Boxwell-Patterson exams, a requirement for entrance into high school. Flora diligently drilled and studied along with her classmates, but on the day of the exams, she watched silently as the others huddled over their tests. She knew it was pointless to take the exam or to hope for a higher education. Her future was tied to the farm and the family.

Chapter 14
The Seibel Homestead
1911

IN MARCH OF 1911, Hermine and Margaret were scheduled to be confirmed with seven other youths one Sunday morning at the Emmanuel Evangelical Church in Monroeville. Tensions in the family were high. For days, Mama had been roaming the house, babbling, shouting, singing, and going without sleep. Flora had cut out two skirts and blouses from white linen fabric for the girls to wear at their confirmation ceremony, but due to the extra work of attending to Mama, the pieces lay over the back of the sewing chair, untouched.

Finally, Ada was summoned to return home from her sewing commission and help to construct the girls' dresses. Time was running short for the amount of intricate needlework that needed to be done.

While Ada bent over the treadle sewing machine in the living room, Flora and the girls tended to Mama and took care of the cooking and household chores. The mood in the family began to lighten, knowing that capable Ada was in command.

On the Friday before the confirmation ceremony, the belt broke on the always temperamental sewing machine. Ada tried to remedy the situation by replacing the belt with a knotted strip of cloth, but the fix was temporary and unsatisfactory. Precious time was lost waiting for Papa to make a more permanent repair.

That night, during her nocturnal wandering, Mama tripped over Ada's sewing basket and crashed to the floor, gashing her eyebrow on the point of the rocking chair. Her wails of distress awoke the entire family.

Ada sped down the stairs in her bare feet, followed by her siblings. The girls settled Mama in a chair at the kitchen table and lit the kerosene lamp to assess the injury, while Papa slid his boots on and clumped down the cellar steps to retrieve a cold potato from the root cellar. Ada sliced the potato and held its cut surface to the welt over Mama's eye. Little Bill rubbed his eyes and clung sleepily to Ada's nightgown.

On Saturday, Mama, her eye as blue-black as a plum, roamed the house, overturning the corncob basket by the stove and ransacking her dresser drawers in an undefined search. Flora forgot about a pan of biscuits in the cookstove, until the kitchen filled with acrid smoke. Hermine and Margaret peppered Ada with anxious questions about the progress of their dresses, fretting that they'd be the only girls in the confirmation class without suitable attire if the sewing project could not be completed. Martha and Minola tussled on the living room floor behind Ada's chair, with Martha howling in indignation that Minola had torn the corner of her school map. Little Bill repeatedly tried to climb into Ada's lap for some motherly attention. Ada, whose eyes ached from lack of sleep and long hours at her needlework, broke down into uncharacteristic tears.

Bill stood by her chair and studied her face with his wide blue eyes. It was unusual to see Ada cry. Remembering the remedy for Mama's tears the night before, Bill asked innocently, "You need a potato?"

Ada wiped her eyes with the back of her hands and gently shook her head. She drew in a ragged breath, pressed the foot-powered treadle, and continued to sew.

By that evening, Mama's chaotic interlude had ended, and she slumbered in a drunken-like stupor that would last for days. The girls were silently relieved that there would be no need to dissuade her from attending church services in the morning, where her behavior and hideously purple right eye would attract attention.

After the younger family members had been bathed and sent to bed on Saturday night, Flora set a kerosene lamp beside the sewing machine and joined Ada in hand sewing the intricate tucks and edging on the confirmation dresses. Their fine, even stitches secured the rolled collars, which would be accented by oblong gold pins that Papa had bought for Hermine and Margaret as confirmation gifts.

The confirmation dresses.
Margaret: front row far left; Hermine: front row second from right

By Sunday morning, the two dresses hung in crisp, pristine readiness, belying the tension and tears that had accompanied their creation.

* * * * *

That spring, Papa did something very uncustomary—he bought an item that was brand new, not a second-hand auction find. It was a Domo cream separator. After years of difficult and inefficient hand-skimming, the Domo made separating the cream from the milk seem like child's play. The girls used the crank-driven mechanism in the evening, when Papa and Flora had finished milking the cows. The separator then stood idle until after the morning milking was done, when the equipment was disassembled and the numerous disks added to the cleanup of breakfast dishes. However, the girls soon realized that the Domo's convenience was offset by the difficulty of washing each cream-laden disk, whose slimy residue required many changes of the hot, soapy wash water.

Papa also brought home a broken push lawnmower that spring. It required some tinkering before the blade mechanism would spin into a grass-chewing whir, but Papa always enjoyed a mechanical challenge. The girls found that it took the strength of two sisters leaning their bodies against the handle to produce a meaningful swath across the lawn, which had never experienced any sort of manicuring other than Mama's fanatical weed-pulling and the scratching of the wandering chickens. After long days in the strawberry fields, the girls wearily retrieved the lawnmower from where it leaned against the house and struggled to make inroads in the ever-growing grass. They wished Mama would expend some of her boundless energy and incredible strength by tackling the lawncare.

* * * * *

In the summer of 1911, George Seibel made arrangements to have a large new barn built on his property, using the five hundred dollars left to him by Old Man. While the row of trees and hedges that divided the two Seibel farms blocked the view of the building's progress, the pounding of the carpenters' hammers echoed across the field toward Papa's property. The staccato rapping agitated Mama and served as a constant reminder of George and Bertha's ownership of the coveted house and their recent inheritance. Mama surveyed Papa's weather-beaten barns and berated him for not gaining a share of Old Man's estate.

Papa stoically replied, "George and Bertha had Old Man under their roof for more than two years. I'd say they earnt every cent they got."

Mama's response was a scowl and a brusque, "Hmph! I say only a weak man gives up without a fight."

The building project was completed in August, and George and Bertha invited all of the neighbors to attend a party in the new barn. The girls and Bill looked forward to this social event with great excitement.

Ada had gone to Grandpa and Grandma Gasteier's to help Ella cook the large noontime meals for the oat-threshing crew, leaving Flora in charge of preparing several dishes to take to the party. While Flora longed to bake a couple of tart lemon pies with mountains of lightly browned meringue topping, she could not bring herself to ask Papa for the necessary but expensive lemons from Zipfel's store. Ada would have been comfortable in approaching Papa on this matter, but Flora's avenue was to make do with what was at hand. She settled on using the fruits and vegetables that were in season on the farm.

Flora picked a large pan of green beans from the garden and set Hermine and Margaret to work snapping them at the kitchen table. Martha, Minola, and Bill were given the task of sorting through several quarts of blackberries, with Martha governing the amount of berries that found their way into the mouths of her two young helpers. Flora harvested some beets and set them to boil on the cookstove, along with a pan of eggs.

That evening, while Papa finished the chores and Mama swept the kitchen floor, the girls and Bill walked north on Townline Road toward George and Bertha's. With arms outstretched before her, Flora carried a shallow crock of pickled beets bobbing with hard-boiled eggs, trying not to lap any of the ruby red liquid onto her dress. Hermine hugged a bowl of green beans mixed with bits of fried bacon, while Margaret balanced a blackberry cobbler. Martha carried the basket with their eating utensils, and Minola and Bill darted back and forth across the road, chasing lightning bugs that blinked in the early twilight.

The barn was a long, narrow structure that faced south onto George's farmyard, exposing its impressive slate roofline to the road. Across the length of the roof marched four sentinel lightning rods, each sporting a blue glass ball. In the evening light, the barn's brilliant coat of white paint nearly glowed. Outside the open barn doors stood two sawhorses supporting long planks that groaned under the weight of a growing smorgasbord of food.

The neighbors oohed and aahed appreciatively as they toured the new building, exploring its grain bins and horse stalls and admiring its twin lofts—one for hay and one for straw. The younger children scampered up the hayloft ladder and sat on the edge of the mow, swinging their feet and occasionally leaning over their knees to drop a well-timed missile of spit toward an unsuspecting barn cat below them. Peals of laughter erupted when a torpedo found its mark. In the straw mow, some of the boys tossed around a bumpy green Osage orange fruit plucked from the hedgerow on George's farm.

The older youth, including Flora and Hermine, congregated at the back of the open floor space, where the shadows were deeper and the adults less intrusive. Some good-natured teasing, embarrassed glances, and shy smiles were exchanged.

Gus Ordmann inhaled deeply of the new lumber and paint odors and nodded as he announced, "Smells like prosperity!" He clapped a beaming George on the back.

After Papa was done with the evening chores, he set the last bucket of milk on the cellar steps for Flora to separate in the morning. He rolled up his sleeves and unbuttoned his collar to wash his arms and neck, then lathered up his face and drew the straight razor against the taut skin of his cheeks. Using the shaving mirror, Papa cast a sidelong look at Mama, who was seated in the rocking chair across the room.

Mama had been agitated all day, muttering angry comments about George and Bertha and emphatically stating that she would not attend the party to admire their spoils. But Papa noticed that she had changed into her Sunday dress topped by a long white apron of lawn worked with dainty stitches and drawn threads. Her hair, which was usually pulled into a tight knot at the base of her neck, was now piled in a softer arrangement that sat higher on her head. These were sure signs that Mama was prepared for a social outing.

After donning a clean shirt and stiff collar, Papa combed his hair and turned to Mama. "You coming?" he asked softly.

Mama gave a slight nod and rose from the chair. They crossed the yard and walked toward George and Bertha's in the growing dusk, commenting on the condition of the crops in the fields along the way. Papa was relieved to see that Mama's mood had mellowed.

When they reached the farmyard at the end of George and Bertha's poplar-lined driveway, Mama insisted on stopping first at the makeshift table to compare Flora's contributions to the dishes brought by the other women. Papa moved on to greet his neighbors and fell into conversation with a group of men.

After Mama had carefully inspected the offerings of food and felt pleased with the worthiness of Flora's fare, she turned to take in her first full view of the grand new barn. Her gaze rose above the open barn doors toward the building's peak and locked in disbelief on the open expanse of the barn face. Tall black letters marched across the shimmering white paint, spelling out "Seibel and Sons." Mama remembered the long-ago dream of having "Seibel and Sons Orchards" painted on their own barn, and the bitter failure of Papa's nursery stock, the subsequent debt, and the string of seven daughters. Her hands balled into fists, and a low guttural moan erupted from her throat.

"You … stole … EVERYTHING!" Mama growled. "*Alles! Alles das meine war!* (Everything! Everything that was mine!)"

Spying Bertha conversing with a group of women beside the open barn doors, Mama rushed forward, grabbed her sister-in-law by the arms and shook her hard. Mama's face was violent purple and contorted with rage as she screamed, "You stole it all—the house, the cupboards, the name 'Walter,' 'Seibel and Sons.' *Alles was meine sein sollte!* (Everything that was supposed to be mine!)"

Bertha recoiled in fear and confusion and retreated from Mama, only to find herself backed against the side of the barn. She tried to free her arms, but Mama tightened her grip while pressing her face closer and growling, "You took everything!"

One of the women near Bertha screamed. The crowd of neighbors that had been engaged in conversation and laughter grew deathly silent as everyone turned to locate the source of the commotion. Shocked exclamations and stifled gasps hung in the air when they spotted Mama pinning Bertha against the barn. Papa and George pushed their way through the crowd toward their wives.

Before Papa could reach Mama, her legs buckled, and she collapsed at Bertha's feet. Her arms and legs jerked rigidly, and her head twitched involuntarily in short, rapid spasms. Papa knelt beside her on the grass and rolled her gently onto her side.

The crowd pressed in around them, with someone whispering, "What's wrong with Sophie?"

"They say it's spells, but I don't know. Seems more like she's crazy, you ask me."

"Can't Doc Gilman fix what ails her?"

"Probably ain't no medicine to fix a problem like that."

"Maybe she oughta be locked up. She shook up Bertha pretty bad. No tellin' what she'll do next."

Some of the neighbor women clustered around Bertha, trying to soothe her as she sobbed into George's chest and gasped for words to express her terror.

Flora and Hermine stood on tiptoe at the edge of the crowd in the barn doorway, trying to see over the heads of their neighbors. "What is it? What happened?" Flora asked.

"It's your mother," said Mrs. Knopf softly. "She started screaming and attacked your Aunt Bertha. Next thing we knew, she was having a spell on the ground."

Flora covered her face with her hands and turned away from the crowd. Hermine's eyes welled with tears, and she brushed them away with the back of her hand.

Up in the hayloft, the younger children had a bird's-eye view of the scene. Martha stopped swinging her legs in mid-air and sucked in her breath, her eyes riveted on Mama and the crowd.

"Aint' that your mother?" asked Helen Hogard, whose family had recently moved into the community. "What's wrong with her?"

"My Ma says she's crazy," interjected Elsie Ordmann matter-of-factly. "No two ways about it, my Ma says, just plain crazy."

Martha couldn't respond. Her throat felt as dry as parchment, and her heart hammered in her chest.

Mama lay limp on the grass, her arms and legs quiet now. Her face wore a bewildered expression, and she blinked rapidly as if trying to clear her thoughts and make sense of what had happened.

Mr. Hogard pulled his horse and wagon to the area in front of the barn. Papa scooped up Mama and gently laid her in the wagon bed, then climbed in beside her. The wagon slowly turned and rumbled down the driveway in the growing darkness.

Flora could think of only one thing to do—gather her siblings and go home. Her cheeks burned crimson as she rounded up Bill and Minola, who were inspecting a nest of kittens in one of the grain bins. Hermine motioned to Margaret, who watched silently from the hayloft.

Martha felt a light tap on her shoulder. Margaret wordlessly signaled her to follow.

"I … I guess we're going home now," Martha stammered as she looked from Elsie's face to Helen's, an embarrassed flush creeping up her neck. She scrambled to her feet and hurried to follow Margaret down the haymow ladder. The two sisters rushed to catch up with their siblings.

The crowd of neighbors was breaking into small groups, their heads together as they whispered opinions about what they had witnessed or offered possible curatives for Mama's behavior.

Flora kept her eyes cast downward as she tugged Bill behind her. Hermine pulled Minola along by the hand, while Margaret and Martha followed close behind. As the girls threaded their way through the crowd, an occasional kind hand reached out to offer a sympathetic pat on the shoulder, but just as frequently, the words "crazy," "dangerous," and "those poor children" followed them.

The six siblings walked in silence down Townline Road, the only conversation being Bill's protest, "But, Flora, why can't we stay and eat?"

Mrs. Metz, who lived in an impressive brick house on Plank Road, had witnessed Mama's seizure at the party. She felt certain that she could remedy Mama through the ministrations of prayer and her Christian Scientist faith. Mrs. Metz paid several visits to Mama, reading her passages such as "Disease is an experience of the so-called mortal mind. It is fear made manifest on the body." She counseled Mama that her affliction may be the result of sin or wrong-doing or equally the result of fear or ignorance of God's power and goodness. She implored Mama to believe in the personal healing that could cleanse her body and mind if she would only prevail upon the strength of the Spirit.

Mama enjoyed the company of Mrs. Metz, and to encourage repeat visits, she happily complied with her guest's suggestion of fervent prayers for God's intercession. Before long, however, Mrs. Metz realized that her subject was showing no improvement despite the concentrated spiritual sessions. It appeared that Mama was a lost cause, and Mrs. Metz's visits dwindled to an end.

Mama did not forget the interest shown in her by Mrs. Metz. On those occasions when she felt in need of attention or a sisterly ear to bend, Mama set off across the fields toward Mrs. Metz's house. The girls knew that part of the conversation would include Mama's lament, "My girls do nothing for me," but it was better to have Mama spilling family secrets and tales of woe to Mrs. Metz than to their immediate neighbors, the Mosses and Ordmanns. They also reasoned that Mrs. Metz had initiated the contact and thereby warranted Mama's unpredictable intrusions.

Dr. Gilman, too, paid a visit to Mama. After an examination that included testing her reflexes and shining a light into her eyes, he prescribed small white pills, which Mama took faithfully at bedtime. The medication had no effect.

*****

The rural mail was now delivered by Mr. Seeley in an automobile. Each delivery day at about noon, Minola and Bill stood out in the front yard, impaling small, knotty apples on the end of wiry sticks and spinning them off into the ditch as they awaited the sound of the auto chugging its way down Townline Road. When Mr. Seeley pulled up to their mailbox, the two children stood transfixed by the sight of such a wondrous machine. They returned the postman's friendly wave and watched as the auto *putt-putted* its way toward Mosses'. When the machine was out of sight, the two youngsters sped off to explore other parts of the farm. They never bothered to retrieve the mail from the box—the real treat was in witnessing its delivery.

About once a week, the mail contained a postcard or letter from Albert. Ada slipped into the pantry to be alone while she read and reread the message, her lips moving silently as she absorbed the words. Albert told about shoveling load after load of coal to fire the boilers on a trip to Cincinnati, then shoveling more coal in the rail yards at Newark. If he was going to work so hard shoveling coal, he preferred to be out on a run, where he could occasionally view the passing scenery, listen to the steady *chuf-chuffing* of the steam engine, and feel the vibration of the huge machine down in his bones. Albert's love of the railroad was showing no signs of abating, and Ada sighed as she slipped the letters into her apron pocket.

Letters from Ella arrived regularly, too. She told of the cooking, cleaning, washing, and gardening she did at Grandma and Grandpa Gasteier's, and she requested that Ada send her a stamped piece of embroidery cloth so she could fill her lonely evenings. Grandma and Grandpa went to bed before nightfall, and Uncle Will retreated to the living room with his German newspapers. Life at the Gasteier homestead was too quiet and solitary for a nineteen-year-old girl from a large family. The overriding theme of Ella's letters was a longing for communication and visits from her sisters. The girls wrote back, using a gold fountain pen that Margaret had found in the grass along Plank Road while walking to school one day. They felt certain the pen was quite expensive, so it lent a sense of sophistication to the act of letter writing.

* * * * *

When the berry-picking season had started in May, Papa made an unusual promise: if the harvest was good, he would reward his daughters with a trip to Euclid Beach Park via the new interurban railway system. The novelty of a journey to an amusement park on the east side of Cleveland was incentive enough for the girls to return to the large strawberry fields in the evenings and meticulously glean any berries overlooked by the regular pickers. When the strawberries waned and the blackberries came on in abundance, the girls donned protective gear and carefully worked their way down the long rows, not complaining about the heat, the snagging thorns of the canes, or the yellow-bellied, brown-legged spiders that hung in webs near the largest clusters of berries.

The long-awaited day of the reward finally arrived on a Sunday in late August. Ada well understood the unspoken rule that someone must stay home with Mama, so she graciously volunteered to keep an eye on Minola and Bill, who, at ages six and almost four, were deemed too young for an amusement park. In addition, Albert was in the neighborhood on a three-day pass from the railroad, so Ada had even more incentive to stay home.

Papa, Flora, Hermine, Margaret, and Martha boarded the interurban in Monroeville. The cars were so crowded that the five could not sit together. Papa and the three younger girls found seats toward the back of the car, while Flora slid in beside a well-dressed woman near the front.

The woman smiled sweetly at sixteen-year-old Flora and studied her closely, then handed her a flower, which Flora shyly accepted. The woman chatted amicably for a while, before deftly turning the conversation toward financial opportunities for young, attractive women like Flora. She mentioned "companionship" and "parlors" in Cleveland. Flora felt uncomfortable about the direction the conversation was taking. She had heard whispers of "white slavery" and allusions to debauched young women but was unclear of the circumstances of such mysterious situations. Nevertheless, she was uneasy about the woman's intentions and nervously blurted, "I'm traveling with my father. He's right back there." She jabbed her thumb over her shoulder in Papa's direction.

The woman's painted eyebrows rose in understanding, and the two rode in silence until the next stop, when the woman exited the car.

As the interurban rocked along toward Cleveland, Papa leaned his head against the back of his seat and watched the countryside pass by outside the window. He thought of his youthful experience of riding the rails out west. He had always enjoyed the sensation of a moving train, the scenery that came in and out of view so quickly, and the anticipation of adventure that had fluttered like a moth in the pit of his stomach. Papa reflected on the changes that had befallen him in the ensuing years since his travels down the Mississippi. He thought of Mama and closed his eyes.

At the Cleveland Public Square, Papa and the girls transferred to a streetcar to take them the last eight miles to Euclid Beach Park, which was advertised as "one fare, free gate, no beer."

As they passed under the large stone entryway to the park, the girls felt like they were entering a wonderland. Everywhere they looked was something new, magical, and totally foreign to their life on the farm in Monroeville. The delicious aroma of popcorn filled the air, and Papa stopped at the Humphrey concession stand to purchase two blue-and-white-striped bags of popcorn for the girls to share. They strolled the midway, peering at the large dance floor inside the pavilion and pointing at the Velvet Coaster that clattered overhead on its wooden tracks.

Papa bought tickets for the moving picture show at the Hippodrome, a flickery film of people jerkily demonstrating the health benefits of fresh air and daily exercise. A pianist provided mood music of an appropriate tempo.

Best of all was the carousel with its forty-four horses and two chariots, which were decorated with leaf carvings surrounding a Greek god and two cherubs. Martha deliberated so long over which horse to select that the carousel jolted into motion. Its tinkling music and thumping bass drum startled her, and she scrambled atop the nearest carousel horse, an all-white steed with its head tossed back.

The girls were irresistibly drawn to the water. They hurried along the shoreline walkway to the pier that extended out into Lake Erie. Seagulls floated overhead, dipping low for an occasional bug and then wheeling off over the water with a scolding *scree*. By shielding their eyes against the sun, the girls could make out the silhouette of a distant freighter on the horizon. They turned around to admire the shoreline with its wooded picnic area and metal benches overlooking the beach. Young boys dressed in long woolen swimsuits scampered along the water's edge or bobbed in the waves.

Twelve-year-old Margaret watched enviously and announced, "I'm going to learn to swim someday."

"Where? In the cow tank?" teased Hermine.

"In the lake. Or maybe the ocean. I don't know where, but I'll do it—I'll learn to swim!" she said adamantly.

In mid-afternoon, Papa checked his pocket watch and announced that it was time to head home. There were cows to be milked and evening chores to be done. The girls reluctantly followed Papa to the streetcar, turning often for one more look at the grand and glorious Euclid Beach Park.

Ten-year-old Martha sat with Hermine on the interurban car back to Monroeville, her head propped against Hermine's shoulder and her eyelids too heavy to keep open. Her sisters were filled with happy thoughts of the wondrous things they would tell Ada, Minola, and Bill when they got home.

*****

In the fall of 1911, Minola joined Hermine, Margaret, Martha, and a group of neighborhood children on the walk to the Plank Road school. Minola was already prepared to love the teacher, Miss Ruffing, based on the adoration expressed by her older sisters. Also, Miss Ruffing was a proponent of reading and had brought to the school a small lending library, which the Seibel girls used to its full advantage. Since Ella's departure to Grandma and Grandpa Gasteier's, Minola had missed the cozy evenings of snuggling in bed with Ella and falling asleep to the sound of Dickens' stories. Occasionally, she could cajole one of her other sisters into reading to her, but they were frequently busy with schoolwork or household chores. Minola was determined that she would learn to read for herself.

On the walk to school, Minola tagged along behind her older sisters and their neighborhood girlfriends as they ambled down Townline Road toward George and Bertha's drive. The older girls assumed the roles of the Presidents' daughters, assigning themselves to be Ruth, Esther, and Marion Cleveland, Alice and Ethel Roosevelt, and the current President's daughter, Helen Taft. There were not enough important Presidential relatives to go around, so the girls kindly created a character for Minola. They chattered about attending elegant White House parties and described their pearl-, diamond-, and emerald-encrusted evening gowns as they tried to maintain high-society dignity while straddling the stile over George's fence or dodging low-lying branches along the path by the creek. At last they arrived at the Plank Road school, leaving behind the marble halls of Washington, D.C., and entering the humble one-room building.

Minola was joined on the recitation bench each day by Floyd Busch, the only other pupil her age. Both were capable students, and Miss Ruffing soon had them progressing from letter and number recognition to reading simple words and performing rudimentary math. At noontime, there were schoolyard games of "Prisoner's Goal" and "Pump, Pump, Pullaway," and at the end of the day, Miss Ruffing always read to them from a book about animal characters. Minola found the entire academic experience to be thoroughly satisfying, and she was disappointed when Friday afternoon came, signaling two days away from her beloved school environment.

Minola's attendance at school left young Bill bereft of a companion. At first, he followed after Ada and Flora in the kitchen, but the proximity to Mama and her tendency to lash out over the slightest irritation drove him outdoors. There, he sought out male companionship by traipsing after Papa, who seemed oblivious to the small shadow skipping behind him.

Bill was a keen observer, and he watched intently as Papa repaired the makeshift equipment on the farm. He peppered Papa with questions about the "how's" and "why's" of repairs, but most of the time, Papa was too absorbed in the task at hand to answer. Bill developed problem-solving skills and an easy rapport with tools as he imitated Papa's techniques.

Bill also noted Papa's ability to deftly turn his head and spit a stream of brown tobacco juice without interrupting his work. The young boy snitched a handful of raisins from the pantry and packed his cheek with them until he had achieved a bulge that suitably resembled Papa's. When enough liquid had formed in his mouth, he attempted a spitting performance, but the best he could muster was a sticky dribble down his chin and onto the front of his shirt.

When Ada saw the brown stain on his clothing, she sighed an exasperated, "Eye-yi-yi." Bill surveyed the damage to his shirt and responded by muttering something else he had learned while shadowing Papa: "*Gott* damn it!" Ada marched Bill to the drysink, where he soon became acquainted with the taste of lye soap.

When there was work to be done, Papa's call of "Girls, girls!" as he strode purposefully toward the house was meant to be an all-inclusive, gender-blind summons, but Bill was certain that Papa thought he was just one of the girls. He searched for his own identity among seven sisters by actively seeking recognition from Papa in the only way he knew how—through misbehavior.

Before supper one night, Bill unscrewed the top of the pepper shaker and lightly replaced it. When Papa reached for the seasoning and shook it over his fried potatoes, the cap tumbled off, spilling a mound of pepper onto his meal. While the girls sat in wide-eyed horror, Bill chuckled in glee. Papa plucked his young son from the table by the back of his collar and grabbed the razor strop from the kitchen wall as he headed out the door with Bill in tow.

Bill frequently unleashed temper tantrums in Papa's presence or neglected his chores. He threw mud clods at the cows when they approached the water trough or pelted Minola with rotten eggs that he discovered deep in the hay stack. Through his actions, Bill succeeded in garnering Papa's attention and more than a few spankings. Yet, while conversing with visitors, Papa often commented, "My one boy causes me more trouble than all my daughters put together." There was a slightly pleased expression on his face as he delivered this observation.

Chapter 15
The Seibel Homestead
1912

IN APRIL 1912, while the rest of the world buzzed with news about the sinking of the *Titanic*, a bout of mumps swept the Seibel family, including Papa, who first suffered with jaundice. The supply of oatmeal ran low as Papa mixed it with tepid water to bathe his itchy, yellowed skin. Ada made bowl after bowl of the bland, easily swallowed porridge to feed to the mumps sufferers. She soaked rags in cold well water to use as compresses for her feverish and achy siblings, who requested something cool against their skin, and she laid rags on the back of the wood stove to heat for Mama, Martha, and young Bill, who preferred warmth. Eventually, Ada stumbled to her bed with fatigue, a dull headache, and swollen cheeks. Since Hermine and Flora were afflicted with mumps on only one side, they carried on with the tasks of nursing the sick and tending to the daily chores.

Emmaline Moss telephoned, advising the Seibels to quarantine themselves. She pointed out that it would be terribly inconsiderate of them to expose the neighbors to mumps, especially those families that included sons. Emmaline excused herself for speaking of the indelicate subject of sterility but warned, "You wouldn't want to be responsible for denying a family their lineage, would you? I'd hate to think that a fine young man like my Edwin might be rendered barren by your carelessness." In the end, the Mosses were infected with the mumps by their hired girl, Leda, who carried the virus with her to the Moss household after a weekend visit with her family of younger siblings.

By late April, the girls had recovered enough to return to school. Hermine discovered that during her absence, the only other student in the eighth reader had dropped out. One afternoon, she tossed her schoolbooks on the table in the summer kitchen and sunk dejectedly into a chair. The rest of the younger children clattered into the kitchen where they were joined by Bill in raiding Ada's cookie kettle for an after-school treat.

Hermine watched as Flora used one hand to feed dripping wet clothing into the stationary wringer while turning the crank with the other. Ada was away on a sewing commission, so the Monday chore of laundry had fallen solely to Flora. The task this day had been interrupted by rain that prevented hanging the freshly washed clothes on the line to dry. Flora cranked furiously, trying to finish the laundry before it was time to start supper and help Papa with the evening milking.

Hermine drew circles with her fingertip on the wooden tabletop and sighed. "I've decided to drop out of school, Flora. Elna Pfaff quit, and now I'm the only one in the eighth reader. It's just … well … it just seems useless to keep going, do my recitations and a little ciphering, spell a few words. For what?"

Flora stopped cranking the wringer and turned to give Hermine a long look. She cocked her wet hands on her hips and replied, "Okay, I've got a plan. You take over my chores, and I'll go out into the world and see what I can make of myself. But you'll have to get supper every night that Ada ain't here, help Papa with the chores, and don't forget—you have to milk the one-horned cow from the right side or else she kicks. Remember to keep an eye on Mama and Bill—both can cause a lot of upsets—and don't let the fire in the cookstove go out. The tinder got a little wet in this rain, and it ain't startin' so good. There's also the cream to separate every morning, and you'll have to make garden this year and do the canning. Let's see, the rhubarb'll be ready before long, and remember when you cut it—the redder the stalk, the sweeter the rhubarb. That way you don't have to use so much sugar. Oh, and Papa'll need help with planting the new strawberry field pretty soon, so plan on fittin' that into your day, too." As Flora spoke, she untied her apron strings, folded the garment, and held it toward Hermine.

Hermine sat in stunned silence, her moment of self-pity broken by Flora's description of reality.

The school year drew to a close before Decoration Day with singing of Civil War songs and reciting poems about the great conflict. As the students exited the schoolhouse on the last day of instruction, Miss Ruffing pulled Hermine aside.

"I want to encourage you to go on to high school, Hermine. You're a fine student, and it'd really be a shame if you quit now."

Hermine dropped her eyes and gave her head a slight shake.

"Think about it, Hermine. Please. You could still take the Boxwell-Patterson entry exam this summer—they're offering it in July at Monroeville High School. Review your lessons over the next couple of months and take the test. It'd be such a waste if you didn't further your education." Miss Ruffing squeezed Hermine's arm for added emphasis before watching the teenager scamper across the schoolyard to catch up with her three younger sisters.

Miss Ruffing's words bounced around inside Hermine's head for the next several days. "You're such a fine student … It'd really be a shame if you quit … such a waste…" Hermine picked up her schoolbooks from the living room table where she'd deposited them on her final day of school and started to review them. Every day while bent over a long row in the strawberry patch, she quizzed herself on state capitals, the list of Presidents, and the countries on each continent. When rain showers forced the pickers to seek shelter in the packing shed, Hermine invited the others to pepper her with potential essay topics or ask her to explain the duties of the three branches of government.

On the day of the scheduled Boxwell-Patterson exam, Hermine rose early, walked the three miles into town, and took the test at Monroeville High School. Inwardly, she trembled at the path she had set herself upon.

When the test results arrived, Hermine was stunned and a little panic stricken to learn that she has passed and would be admitted to the freshman class at Monroeville High School that fall. The tuition was twenty dollars, and she had no idea how to approach Papa about this additional expense. She sought out Ada, who, after so many years of acting as a surrogate mother to the family, had developed an easy relationship with Papa and possessed the ability to bring the younger ones' needs to his attention.

Hermine stood nervously in the kitchen doorway one evening as Ada quietly relayed the news of Hermine's educational desires to Papa. He removed his work boots and leaned back in the rocking chair with a heavy sigh. Papa closed his eyes and was silent for such a long time that Hermine feared he had fallen asleep or, worse yet, his lack of response indicated his disapproval.

Papa knew that the educational floodgates were opening and that Margaret, Martha, Minola, and Bill would follow Hermine's lead. He thought about the cost of tuition, the debt he carried, and the unpredictability of his cash crops. Finally, Papa opened his eyes and announced, "I can pay for high school but nothing more. The rest is up to you."

Hermine's heart fluttered, and she whispered a barely audible, "Thank you, Papa."

In late July, word came of a way for Hermine to earn some money toward her tuition. Cousin Rosie, who had been caring for the Werners, an elderly couple living near Bellevue, was called home to help her mother repaper the living and dining room walls. In Rosie's absence, the Werners needed someone to help with household chores and provide companionship. Ansel Werner was an invalid, and his spinster sister, Naomi, could not manage his care in addition to all the daily tasks.

Hermine eagerly agreed to fill in for Rosie at Werners' for a week. She swelled with pride at the thought of the money she would earn, thus relieving Papa of some of the financial burden.

Ada hitched up the buggy and drove Hermine to the Werners' on a Sunday afternoon. Naomi Werner, as bent as the number seven, greeted them at the door and motioned them into the kitchen, where she offered the sisters some weak tea and an apology that she had no baked goods to serve them. She explained that with Rosie away, it was a struggle to keep up with the chores, so "the niceties" such as baking went undone. Ansel sat by the kitchen window, a shawl draped over his rounded shoulders and a blanket covering his legs despite the July heat. He slowly raised a boney hand in acknowledgment of Ada and Hermine and opened his mouth in a silent, toothless greeting.

Naomi outlined the duties that would be expected of Hermine, which consisted primarily of hauling in water and firewood, feeding and watering the chickens and the horse, gathering the eggs, washing the dishes, performing light housecleaning, and doing the laundry. Naomi would do the cooking, because Ansel required a special diet. Hermine nodded her understanding of the expectations, and Ada rose to leave, assuring Naomi that she would return in a week to retrieve Hermine and drop off Rosie.

Before Ada turned the horse toward home, she reminded Hermine, "You're getting paid for this, so make sure you earn it. Work harder than they expect you to."

Hermine was accustomed to hard work from her nearly fifteen years on the Seibel farm, so the chores at the Werners' seemed almost like a novelty. Here, she was not expected to help with making hay, tending to the field crops, or picking berries, as she was at home. In fact, at the Werners' she looked forward to feeding and watering the animals and gathering the eggs, since it afforded her the opportunity to be outdoors and away from the smell of liniment and Naomi's annoying habit of rattling her dentures.

Occasionally, Naomi prevailed upon Hermine to lend a hand with Ansel's care. Sometimes, it was nothing more than spoon-feeding the elderly fellow his meal. Other times, it involved oiling his scalp to combat the large flakes of dried skin that drifted like snow onto his shawl-covered shoulders. Hermine shuddered but complied when Naomi asked her to remove the old man's slippers and socks and trim his thick, yellow toenails.

Hermine soon realized that toothless Ansel's special diet consisted of only soft foods, such as oatmeal, scrambled eggs, mashed potatoes, or bread slices soaked in milk. With her ill-fitting dentures, Naomi also found these foods easier to digest, so the diet for all three was dictated by how little chewing a food required. Before long, Hermine was dreaming of thick, chewy bacon slices from the smokehouse back home, Papa's orchard of crisp apples, and Ada's crunchy pickles. She swallowed Naomi's bland, soft offerings, reminding herself that she would be home in time to share the Sunday dinner of fried chicken and dumplings, endive wilted with hot bacon drippings and mixed with onions and riced potatoes, cucumber slices swimming in cream and vinegar, followed by elderberry pie with its sugar-sprinkled crust.

Besides the foods of home, Hermine missed her sisters and Bill. She had never been away from them for so long, nor had she ever slept in a bed that wasn't occupied by at least one sister. The days and nights at the Werners' seemed unusually quiet and long. Hermine came to understand how lonely Ella must be at Grandma and Grandpa Gasteier's and why all of Ella's letters begged for news from home and visits from her sisters.

In the evenings, Naomi liked Hermine to sit with her in the dim living room and read aloud from the *Bellevue Gazette* while Ansel snored softly from his chair in the corner, his head collapsed on his chest and a small puddle of drool forming in the valleys of his shawl. As soon as daylight had waned, Naomi put Ansel to bed and then retired for the night, leaving Hermine with nothing to do but climb the stairs to her small, hot bedroom and lay awake for hours, listening to the crickets chirping outside. She mentally crossed off each long day, which brought her one day closer to receiving her payment and going home.

On Sunday morning, Hermine hopped out of bed, happy with the thought that Ada and Rosie would be arriving today to spring her from the tedium of the week's existence. Naomi commented that it was a shame Hermine was leaving, since there would be a special dessert for tonight's supper. Although Hermine's curiosity was piqued by what sort of no-chewing-necessary confection Naomi intended to create, it was irrelevant. She was going home today, and that's all that mattered. Hermine hurried through the outside chores, even curry-combing the horse for good measure. She carried in a fresh pail of water and two armloads of firewood, refilled the kindling basket, and voluntarily combed Ansel's wispy hair. With each completed task, Hermine rewarded herself with the thought, "And that's the last time I'll have to do *that*!"

After washing the noontime dishes and tidying the kitchen, Hermine bundled up her own clothing, straightened the room she had occupied for the week, and settled on the front porch step to catch the first sight of Ada and Rosie and the approaching buggy. Naomi had not mentioned payment, but Hermine was sure a generous sum would be offered when Ada arrived. After all, she had worked hard and done more than was expected.

The afternoon crept slowly by. At times, Hermine left her post on the step and leaned over the picket fence at the edge of Werners' yard. She squinted hard, peering as far eastward down the dirt road as possible. Whenever a buggy came into sight, her heart quickened with surety that it was Ada and Rosie, but each time she was crestfallen. The Werners did not have a telephone, so Hermine was left to wonder why no one came for her. Surely, she had been forgotten.

That evening, Hermine joined Naomi and Ansel for another bland supper, followed by a bowl of Naomi's surprise dessert—stewed prunes, which slipped easily down one's throat without the necessity of chewing. After washing the supper dishes, Hermine sat in the dim living room, reading newspaper selections to arthritic Naomi and slumbering Ansel, and tried hard to hide her disappointment at still being in their company. As she lay in bed that night, she gave in to her overwhelming sense of abandonment and allowed the tears to flow freely.

The next morning, Hermine was awakened by the presence of someone sitting on the foot of her bed.

"Ada!" Hermine bolted upright and threw her arms around her sister. "Oh, I'm so glad you're finally here!" She tumbled out of bed, trying to free herself from the tangle of bed sheets while lunging for her work dress on the wall peg.

"We can leave soon as I'm dressed. Oh, Ada, I've been so lonely, and I looked a hole in the road yesterday. Why didn't you come for me?" As she talked, Hermine pulled her work dress over her head and hastily buttoned it, not caring that the buttons and holes were misaligned.

"Hermine, you goose, slow down! You've put your dress on over your nightgown," admonished Ada.

"Don't matter," Hermine assured as her fingers raced to braid her long hair. "I just wanna go home. Where's Rosie? Downstairs?"

Ada shook her head. "Rosie didn't come. Her mother wants her to help with housecleaning, so you'll have to stay another week. I brought you some clean clothes and aprons." Ada patted the bundle in her lap.

Hermine's arms fell limp to her sides. She stared at Ada in disbelief, and then the tears welled up in her blue eyes and spilled down her cheeks.

"B-b-b-but I just wanna go home," Hermine's voice quavered. She threw herself onto the bed next to Ada and sobbed pitifully.

Ada soothed her distraught younger sister and proposed a compromise: Hermine could come home for the day but would have to return to the Werners' that evening. Hermine hiccupped her acquiescence.

Naomi agreed to the arrangement, and Hermine climbed into the buggy beside Ada. She wiped at her wet eyelashes with the back of her hand and turned her face toward home.

When the buggy reached Townline Road, Hermine strained to catch the first glimpse of home. A jubilant smile spread across her face as they rounded the curve by the cemetery and the homestead came into view. Home, with its weather-beaten barns and the house clapboards in need of paint, had never looked so beautiful.

The day whisked by with the sisters playing croquet and piano duets. They indulged Hermine with crunchy pickles and nut-studded molasses candy. Margaret, Martha, and Hermine laid on the grass in the front yard, their arms entwined as they picked out shapes in the clouds above them. When the supper dishes were washed and put away, Ada smoothed the front of her apron and exhaled a long, slow, "Well …"

Hermine knew there was no more delaying the inevitable; it was time to return to Werners'. She gave each of her sisters and Bill a hug, said goodbye to Mama and Papa, and climbed onto the buggy seat beside Ada. The tears were flowing before the buggy reached the end of the drive. At the curve by the cemetery, Hermine turned for one last look at home, but the tears in her eyes distorted the scene into a slanted, shimmering illusion.

Hermine fulfilled another week's obligation to the Werners, but when Ada came the following Sunday, she bore the news that Rosie was not through housecleaning. Hermine would have to stay for a third week. The weeping was not as desperate this time, and Naomi once again agreed to a day-long respite for Hermine.

It appeared that Rosie was enjoying her absence from the dull days at the Werners' and had no intention of hastening her return. At the end of the third week, she sent word that she was still occupied, leaving Hermine to fill in for her yet again. Hermine's one-week stay at the Werners' had stretched into four by the time Ada arrived on a Sunday afternoon with Rosie perched on the buggy seat beside her. For her month-long service to the Werners, Hermine was paid the dismal sum of two dollars, which she handed to Papa as a contribution toward her tuition.

During Hermine's absence, Papa had pondered her living arrangements for the school year ahead. A daily three-mile walk to and from Monroeville was unreasonable. He made arrangements for Hermine to board with the Derringer family, who lived a few blocks from Monroeville High School. In exchange for her room and board, Hermine would be expected to do light housekeeping and help with the young Derringer children. After her experience with the Werners, Hermine knew she was up to the task.

* * * * *

When school commenced at the Plank Road school that September, Minola raced ahead of Margaret, Martha, and the rest of the neighborhood children, eager to reunite with her beloved Miss Ruffing. She waited anxiously outside the schoolhouse doors, ignoring the other students' invitation to join them in a game of tag before school began. Minola wanted to greet Miss Ruffing and share the news that she had read all of Martha's book *Two Little Indians* during the summer, and none of her sisters had had to help her decipher any of the words. She knew Miss Ruffing would be pleased and amazed.

When the boys' door to the schoolhouse swung open, a wide smile crept across Minola's face. Miss Ruffing always opened the boys' door first, then crossed through the schoolroom to the girls' entry and emerged through their door onto the stone step, swinging the school bell over her head to summon the children. Minola hopped from one foot to the other in anticipation.

When the girls' door opened, Minola stared in disbelief. Who was this short, round woman clapping her hands for attention? Where was Miss Ruffing? Minola searched the crowd of school children for her sisters. She spotted Martha sitting on the top rail of the schoolyard fence with Elsie Ordmann, and she sped toward the two girls.

"Who's that woman? Why isn't Miss Ruffing here?" Minola demanded of her sister.

Before Martha could respond, Elsie interrupted, "That's Miss Kohl, you ninny. She's taking Miss Ruffing's place. You oughta known that—your father's on the school board."

Minola searched Martha's face, who nodded. "Papa mentioned it. I thought you knew." She hopped down from the rail fence and headed toward the schoolhouse, arm-in-arm with Elsie.

Minola could not make her feet budge. She stared after the two girls, then shifted her gaze toward Miss Kohl, who stood on the stone step clapping her hands and calling, "Boys and girls! Boys and girls! Come along."

Slowly, Minola made her way to the schoolhouse door, her enthusiasm for this day shattered by the unexpected loss of Miss Ruffing.

* * * * *

George and Bertha's second child, Elmer, graduated from Ohio University with a teaching degree. Bertha was bursting with pride at his accomplishment, since it was unusual for anyone from a German agricultural background to graduate from high school, much less from a university. She felt Elmer's educational achievement elevated her status among the neighbors. In conversation with them, Bertha liked to validate her contributions by noting, "Elmer says—he's a college graduate, don't you know …," while raising her index finger and giving a superior nod. The neighbors didn't feel they needed the frequent reminder of Elmer's higher learning, but they admired his accomplishment nonetheless.

George, however, was a little disgruntled that his eldest son had selected a career other than farming. He took great pride in his fine farm with its large new barn, stately house, tidy farmyard, and productive fields. George salved his dismay with the thought that there was still younger son Walter to carry on the family farming tradition.

* * * * *

Ada and Albert had been courting for five years, and the subject of marriage came up frequently. However, the circumstances of Ada's home life along with Albert's devotion to the railroad presented formidable obstacles. Ada did not want to be a "railroad widow" whose life revolved around whether her husband was "in" briefly or "out" for long periods of time, as the railroad schedule dictated. Better to be unmarried and remain at home with her sisters than to have a part-time husband and be left all alone for days or weeks in a far-away city like Newark or Cleveland or South Bend, Indiana. And then there was the situation of Mama and the children. Ada wrestled constantly with the consequence of marrying, which would leave only Flora to run the household, help Papa with the farm, care for the younger children, and manage unpredictable Mama as best as one could.

Sometimes, Albert grew impatient with the impasse in their relationship. He loved his job on the railroad and the exhilaration of speeding along the narrow tracks behind the chuffing energy of the mighty steam engines. The pay was good, the job honest. He couldn't understand Ada's hesitation about his employment, but he did recognize the pivotal role she played in the Seibel household. And so, he accepted the delay and continued to court by postcard or Sunday afternoon visits, always making sure he had a few sticks of gum in his pocket for Minola and Bill.

Postcard sent by Albert during a railroad layover in Cleveland, Ohio

* * * * *

In late October, Ada and Flora harvested the remaining heads of cabbage from the garden and carried them into the summer kitchen in large bushel baskets. They stripped off the dark outer leaves, carefully scrubbed the heads in a large tub of water, then set them aside to drain and dry.

Early the next morning while Flora readied the younger children for school, Ada quartered and cored each cabbage head. Mama sat at the work table in the summer kitchen with a large pan in her lap, reducing each quarter to thin ribbons on the wooden cabbage shredder. When the pan was filled, Ada thoroughly mixed in several tablespoons of salt. She set the pan aside to let the cabbage soften, which would allow packing without excessive breaking or bruising of the shreds. Meanwhile, Mama pulled another pan into her lap and continued shredding, while Flora washed and dried the large crocks that would store the sauerkraut through the long winter ahead.

When the pan of salted cabbage had softened sufficiently, Ada and

Flora packed it into a crock, pressing the cabbage down with a wooden mallet to extract the juice and remove unwanted air pockets that could lead to excessive softening of the kraut.

When the crock was filled with salted and pressed cabbage shreds, Ada spread a piece of muslin over the surface, tucking the edges down against the inside of the crock. Flora placed an overturned plate on the surface of the kraut to prevent exposure to air and added a weighting stone, causing the brine to lap at the edges of the plate. Mama was adamant about properly covering and weighting the cabbage shreds, lest the sauerkraut develop a pink tinge from a yeast invasion or a darkness due to insufficient juice and exposure to air.

When they were midway through packing the second crock, the telephone on the living room wall jangled its distinctive two long rings, the party line signal of a call for the Seibels. Flora hurried toward the phone, wiping her hands on the front of her apron.

Uncle Will's German-accented voice greeted her with, "Which girl is this?"

Mama's mother, Grandma Gasteier, had been in failing health. When the weather allowed, Mama and Papa made the long Sunday buggy ride to visit at the Gasteier homestead. If travel was prohibited and Mama was lucid, she called once a week to seek an update on her mother's condition. It did not bode well that Uncle Will was calling on a Thursday morning. Flora summoned Mama to the phone.

From the summer kitchen, Ada and Flora could hear Mama conversing in German with Uncle Will. When she returned, her expression was stoic as she picked up the half-filled pan, set it in her lap, and resumed shredding cabbage. Flora and Ada exchanged puzzled glances.

The three continued on in silence until an occasional metallic *ping* made Ada and Flora look up from their work. Mama sat with her hands limp at her sides. Tears rolled down her cheeks and *plinked* on the rim of the metal pan in her lap.

"My *Mutter* has left me," stated Mama, staring straight ahead. "My sisters Libby and Maggie, and now my *Mutter*." She shifted her gaze toward her daughters and asked, "Why did they all leave me?"

Ada and Flora sat uncomfortably for a long minute. Their usual interactions with Mama involved working hard to meet her high standards for cleanliness and order, acting as a buffer between Mama and the younger children, righting the upsets left in her wake during a spell, or avoiding her all together, which was the avenue taken by their younger siblings. None of them had any experience in providing comfort or consolation to their mother.

Mama resumed her work, the rasping of the cabbage shredder punctuated by the *plinking* of her tears on the pan rim.

The funeral was held in the parlor of the Gasteier homestead on November 2. Pastor Egli's eulogy was conducted in high German, which none of the girls understood, except for an occasional "Frau Gasteier." One Bible verse, from Revelations, was written in English on the memorial pamphlet: "For there shall be no night there." Papa translated another verse, this one from Psalms:

"Seventy is the sum of our years, or eighty, if we are strong,
And most of them are fruitless soil for they pass quickly and we drift away."

For Bill, who was almost five years old, the boredom of the service was overwhelming. He fidgeted beside Ada and tugged on her sleeve until she tilted her head toward him. He whispered in her ear, "Is she buried yet?"

Ada put a finger to her lips and gave her head a small shake.

During Pastor Egli's closing prayer, Bill pranced his fingers along the back of Grandpa Gasteier's chair, which garnered a scowl from Mama.

For the girls, the funeral brought the joy of being reunited with Ella. Following the burial in the small cemetery that surrounded the Oxford Evangelical Church, Ella gathered her sisters in the church stairwell, where she proposed that one of them spend the winter with her.

Hermine's recent experience with loneliness and homesickness at Werners' prompted her to quickly volunteer, but Ella pointed out that she would have no means of transportation to the nearest high school, which was in Milan. Neither Ada nor Flora could be spared at home, and so it was decided that after the holidays, Margaret would stay with Ella and attend the local one-room schoolhouse.

* * * * *

Christmas brought a flurry of activity at the Seibel homestead. Ada and Flora stayed up late at night to sew new dresses for Hermine, Margaret, Martha, and Minola and to embroider a pair of pillowcases for Mama. They took the interurban to Norwalk, where they met Ella, and the three sisters pooled their money to purchase a fur cap for Papa and a mouth organ and tin horn for Bill. For Ada, there would be a new hair receiver; for Ella, a sheaf of pale blue stationery; and Flora would receive a diary. Ada carefully whip-stitched the hem of a linen handkerchief and embroidered it with Albert's monogram, "AHG," in navy blue silk thread. In a shop in Newark, Albert selected a little teakettle with a painted ceramic handle for Ada.

A few days before Christmas, Papa cut a young fir tree and set it in a bucket of river gravel in the southwest corner of the parlor. The tree trimmings were simple: some gold-colored tinsel strands, ropes of popped corn, and a few French candies in colorful wrappers tied onto the boughs. Interspersed among the decorations were several small white candles in their spring-clamp holders. The doors to the parlor were then closed, capturing the brisk, clean pine scent in the room, which was now off-limits to the younger children.

Ada and Flora baked several dozen sugar cookies in the shapes of chickens, rabbits, dogs, and stars, which the children frosted with white icing and sprinkles of colored sugar.

On Christmas Eve, Ella returned home, and the family attended services at the Emmanuel Evangelical Church in Monroeville. The children presented a program of recitations and musical selections, followed by Rev. Keppel's Christmas message. Afterward, a costumed Santa Claus gave each of the children an orange and a pasteboard box containing jaw breakers and hard candies decorated with Christmas symbols in the middle.

Upon their return home, Papa carried a pail of water into the parlor and set it in the corner as a precaution while the candles on the tree were briefly lit. Minola and Bill stared in rapt wonderment at the twinkling lights, the festooned pine boughs, and the carefully wrapped packages. They were certain President Taft himself did not have a more splendid or opulent Christmas tree than the vision before them. After the candles had been extinguished, the family opened their presents.

On Christmas Day, Ada, Ella, and Flora scurried about the kitchen preparing a feast of ham, scalloped potatoes, lima beans, baked corn, applesauce, bread and apple butter, and a dessert of snow-white angel food cake topped with sour cherry preserves.

Bill marched about the kitchen, tooting his tin horn and wheezing in and out on his new mouth organ.

Mama, who was setting the table, winced at the discordant notes and barked, "*Heraus!* (Out!) *Heraus* with you and that noise! *Heraus!*" She pushed Bill toward the back door and the wintry outside.

"B-b-but I don't have my coat!" protested Bill, his eyes wide as Mama propelled him out the door.

Ella quickly grabbed an empty bowl and a wooden spoon from the pantry. "Here, Mama. We need some sauerkraut for on the table."

Mama's hands were clamped on either side of her head, as though it threatened to explode unless manually held together. Her face was contorted in a painful expression. Finally, she accepted the bowl and spoon offered by Ella and crossed to the summer kitchen where the sauerkraut crocks were kept.

Once Mama was occupied with filling the bowl, Ella pulled the shivering young boy into the house and scurried him to the foot of Stegmiller's stairs. "Now, put those toys in your pocket and no more honking them in the house. Understand?"

Bill looked up at Ella through tear-filled eyes and nodded.

"Then up with you. Hurry now." Ella pointed toward the room at the top of Stegmiller's stairs. Bill scurried up the steps to join Martha and Minola, who were engaged in cutting a flurry of paper snowflakes.

After the Christmas dinner was eaten, the girls washed and dried the dishes and swept the kitchen floor. Papa harnessed Dolly, who had replaced old Jib, to the cutter and placed Margaret's bundle of clothing on the back seat. Ada added a box of mixed nuts for Grandpa Gasteier and Uncle Will. Ella and Margaret hugged everyone goodbye, then huddled under the lap robe beside Papa on the front seat of the cutter. Margaret was exhilarated at being deemed old enough to provide companionship to Ella through the long winter months at Gasteiers'. She beamed and waved wildly as the cutter zipped down the ice-covered drive and onto Townline Road.

After the New Year, Hermine returned to Monroeville to board at the Derringers' and resume her high school classes. Ada was hired for a three-week sewing commission, which left only Flora, Martha, Minola, and Bill at home with their parents. The Seibel house seemed almost empty.

Chapter 16
The Seibel Homestead
1913

FLORA'S EIGHTEENTH BIRTHDAY fell during a bitterly cold week in early January. As a present, Papa paid for Flora to attend painting classes given by the minister's wife at the nearby Hunt's Corners Reformed Church. After her first lesson, Flora hurried home across the frozen fields, clutching her knit scarf tightly over her lower face to guard against the frigid wind. Her mind filled with creative ideas for the landscape she was painting, and a smile came to her lips as she remembered Mrs. Schumacher's glowing comment, "Flora, you have a natural-born artistic talent!" While the other students clustered around Flora's canvas, Mrs. Schumacher pointed out perspectives that only a more advanced artist, or one with native skills, would include. Flora blushed at the praise, which she was so unaccustomed to receiving. Mrs. Schumacher promised to teach the students a variety of media, from oils to chalk, and there was talk of displaying their artwork in the lobby of the interurban station in Monroeville. Despite the biting wind, Flora felt warm and happy inside.

Crossing the farmyard, she bustled toward the laundry that she had hung on the clothesline that morning. Frozen overalls and union suits jittered in the wind like stiff dance partners, but the sheets, towels, and aprons were missing from the lineup. Mama must have started bringing in the laundry in Flora's absence. As she plucked the clothing from the line, Flora glanced warily over her shoulder toward the house. Mama had been cross all day, stewing that Flora had hung the dark clothing with the light, which violated Mama's strict code of order. Flora hoped that in her absence young Bill hadn't had any problems with Mama. It was an unspoken rule that someone had to stay home to watch her and, with the girls back in school and Ada away on a sewing commission, that task fell to Bill. At age five, he was considered old enough to summon help if there was trouble.

Carrying an armload of laundry into the summer kitchen, Flora strung the stiff overalls onto clothes bars to finish drying and crossed into the kitchen with the frozen union suits, which she propped along the wall behind the woodstove so they would dry in time for the children to wear to school tomorrow. Flora always heeded the precautionary tale about Papa's sister Wilhelmine, whose untimely death had been attributed to wearing damp underwear.

Mama sat at the kitchen table, dipping her fingertips into a small bowl of water and flicking droplets onto the aprons, sheets, and towels. She rolled the damp linens tightly and tucked them into a wicker basket, to be stored overnight in the cold summer kitchen. Flora would spend the next morning ironing the clothing, rotating sadirons between the surface of the hot cookstove and the ironing board.

Mama looked up from her work and scowled. "*Ach*, you're finally done making foolishness," she scolded. "Painting while the clothing is beat to tatters by the ice and wind. *Schande auf dich!* (Shame on you!) No man wants a wife who paints but can't do laundry proper."

Flora's head bowed. Of all the siblings, she was the most susceptible to absorbing Mama's criticisms. With eyes downcast, she scurried out the kitchen door to retrieve the rest of the laundry.

* * * * *

Margaret was thoroughly enjoying her stay with Ella at Grandpa Gasteier's. Uncle Will enrolled her at the one-room Merry schoolhouse and made arrangements for her to receive the necessary schoolbooks: *Leading Facts of American History*, *A Practical Physiology*, Metcalf's *English Grammar for Common Schools*, Pattengill's *A Manual of Orthography and Elementary Sounds*, and *The Complete Arithmetic: Oral and Written*. With her warm, outgoing personality, Margaret quickly made new friends. Each morning, the neighbor girl, Katherine Crecelius, stopped by to walk to school with Margaret. The two girls linked arms and alternately ran or slid down the ice-covered road.

Margaret found the condition of the Merry schoolhouse to be quite different from the tidy, well-kept Plank Road school back home. Here, the bell was missing its clapper, the water pail was minus its handle, and the schoolhouse clock had no hands. The teacher's extreme near-sightedness limited her ability to monitor the older students at the back of the room. Soon, Margaret joined with the others in whispering, giggling, passing notes, and launching paper wads. At noontime, the shouts and laughter of the students rang in the crisp air as they played games of "Fox and Geese" and "Keep Away" in the snow-covered schoolyard.

There were many neighborhood sleigh rides, and Margaret burrowed under blankets beside Katherine and her other schoolmates, singing songs, laughing heartily, and occasionally being tossed out onto the snow when the sleigh overturned after hitting a rut in the frozen field.

Since patchwork friendship quilts were the fad with adolescent girls, Margaret spent many an evening embroidering her signature on quilt blocks, along with colorful squares featuring bushels of tomatoes, bunches of forget-me-nots, or sprigs of lily of the valley. These were exchanged with other schoolgirls, who made Margaret promise that she would return to visit them often when the school year was over.

In the evenings, after the dishes were dried and put away, Ella and Margaret spread out the sheet music to "I Am the Guy" and "Moonlight Bay" and performed duets on the out-of-tune piano. They played church hymns and classical music for Grandpa Gasteier, who was moved to the brink of tears by an overwhelming sentimentality. Sometimes they pulled taffy, mended grain sacks, or shelled nuts while challenging Uncle Will to a debate on topics such as the International Date Line, which Uncle Will had never heard of and refused to believe existed.

At night, the two sisters curled up side-by-side in the narrow bed they shared and took turns reading aloud selections from Laura Jean Libbey's dime novels that were serialized in the *Illustrated Companion* magazine. Miss Libbey's stories always included the same basic elements: A young girl, suddenly alone in the world, attracts the attention of a suitor whose social status is far above her own. After mishaps and separations, the two are finally reunited, and the young couple lives happily ever after. Even though Ella and Margaret scoffed at the predictability of the story, they couldn't resist a satisfied sigh at the outcome.

In addition to companionship, Margaret also provided a set of helping hands with the housework. When Grandpa and Uncle Will butchered a pig, she stayed home from school for several days to assist Ella with making sausage, lard, and soap. Each day after school, Margaret and Ella carried the tin milk pails across the farmyard and milked the cows, then separated the cream, which they churned into butter. They baked on Saturdays and tidied the house for Sunday company, which usually consisted of visits from one or more of Mama's brothers or sisters and their families.

Sunday afternoons found Uncle Will preoccupied with courting. Mama's sister Katie had arranged a relationship between Will and a young minister's widow named Anna Cull. As he prepared to leave the house, Ella liked to tease Uncle Will about his pomaded hair and highly polished shoes, and Margaret threatened to slip one of her monogrammed handkerchiefs into his pocket, just so he'd have some explaining to do about his familiarity with a certain "MLS." Uncle Will flushed red to his hairline as he shrugged on his coat.

* * * * *

At the tall cherry bookcase in the corner of the bedroom, Papa laid his stub of a pencil beside the ledger book and furrowed his brow. He studied the long column of figures under the heading "Owe to Mr. Scheid," searching for an error in his ciphering, then picked up the pencil and recalculated the numbers. The tally was correct. Papa leaned back in his chair and gazed at his reflection in the glass doors of the bookcase. If this year's growing season was favorable and the strawberries and other cash crops yielded a good harvest, he could pay off the debt he owed to Mr. Scheid for the money he had borrowed twenty-three years ago to start a commercial orchard.

Papa exhaled slowly. He thought ruefully of the failed fruit trees, his unfulfilled dreams of "Seibel and Sons Orchards," and the cloud of debt he had labored under for nearly half of his fifty-one years. But to be debt free! Papa rolled the concept around in his mind, scarcely able to conceive of how it would feel to no longer carry that burden. Of course, there was still the running tally at Zipfel's store, but that was manageable. He closed the ledger book with a sigh and a small shake of his head. Every berry, potato, and kernel of grain would have to be carefully nurtured, harvested, and marketed in order to achieve financial freedom. However, being a natural pessimist, Papa could not allow himself to hope for a good growing season and a bountiful harvest. Surely something would happen to dash his dreams once again.

* * * * *

The flood of 1913 began with a strong windstorm on Good Friday, March 21, which blew the door off one of Papa's barns, uprooted several trees in the area, and discouraged Ella and Margaret from attempting a trip home for the holiday. A driving rain began as the rest of the Seibel family left church following Easter Sunday services. The girls expressed much consternation about drooping Easter bonnets and mud-splashed skirts as Papa guided Dolly toward home through the growing quagmire on Plank Road.

The rain hammered on the windowpanes all through their Easter feast. After they had eaten, the girls carried the dirty dishes to the drysink, and Ada scooped softsoap into a kettle of hot dish water. She glanced out the kitchen window at the standing water in the farmyard and announced to Hermine, "It don't look like you'll be going back to Derringers' this afternoon, 'less you intend to swim."

Hermine swept the crumbs from the white linen tablecloth into her cupped hand and joined Ada at the drysink. As much as she hated to miss school, she knew the roads were becoming a sea of impassable mud.

With a sly smile, she replied, "And it don't look like Albert'll be treading water at the back door neither."

Ada flicked some soapsuds in Hermine's direction, but her response was cut short by Flora's call from the cellar. "Girls! Come help me move the apples and potatoes. The cistern's overflowed, and the bottoms of the bushel baskets are gettin' soaked. The crates of strawberry runners and seed potatoes need movin' too."

Papa, who had been keeping a glum vigil by the kitchen window, sprang into action, donning coat, hat, and boots to go outdoors and switch the direction of the downspouts that fed the cistern. The girls and Bill clattered down the cellar steps and picked their way across the muddy earthen floor. If the long-keeper apples and the last of the potato harvest were lost, their meals would be skimpy and make-do until the garden produce came in. The crates of strawberry runners and seed potatoes were the starting materials for the new crops to be planted that spring, and their value could not be overestimated. Forming a line, the siblings passed baskets and crates of rescued farm goods from sister to sister and set them safely on the cellar steps.

The pounding rain had an agitating effect on Mama. To keep the younger children from arousing Mama's ire, Ada set them to work dying Easter eggs at the kitchen table. Martha, Minola, and Bill huddled over coffee mugs filled with hot water, vinegar, and coloring agents such as beet juice, yellow onion skins, and strong black coffee. They marveled at the slow transformation of the brown egg shells into purplish-red, pale orange, and dark-brown hues. When the eggs had dried, they took turns hiding them in the summer kitchen, up Stegmiller's stairs, and throughout the kitchen and pantry. There was general dismay when Bill could not remember where he had hidden one egg. He shrugged nonchalantly and reassured his sisters, "Don't worry. We'll find it someday."

It rained unceasingly for two days, amounting to over six inches of rainfall that flooded fields, streams, and rivers. The runoff in the shallow ditch between the house and Townline Road lapped its banks and spilled onto the front lawn, submerging the sunken croquet court and edging toward the house. The farmyard was an ocean dotted with small islands occupied by the well pump and the outbuildings. Papa surveyed the water-logged scene and dejectedly uttered the old saying, "Famine and flood go hand in hand."

Papa moved the chickens to the second story of the horse barn to keep them from drowning in the low spot where the chicken coop stood.

Twice a day, he sloshed across the flooded farmyard, carrying buckets of water and chicken mash up the narrow steps to the barricaded fowl that squawked and flapped in their unfamiliar surroundings. The cows and horses could not be turned out into the flooded pastures, and they grew restless in their confinement.

In Monroeville, the damage was heavy. Outbuildings, tools, lumber, chickens, crates from the piano factory, and parts of the mill were carried away by the rampaging Huron River. Roads that weren't washed out or undermined by the floodwaters were rendered impassable by the thick mud and standing water. Mail delivery was halted, telephone and telegraph poles were down, and railroad service was disrupted statewide.

Word came that a locomotive engine on the Wheeling and Lake Erie Railroad had plunged through a flood-weakened bridge, drowning the engineer, fireman, and the young brakeman from Monroeville, August Burrer, who had picked berries with his brothers on the Seibel farm for many years. Ada shuddered at the thought of losing her beloved Albert to such a fate. She added this dreadful possibility to her growing list of reasons why Albert should abandon his job on the railroad.

Monroeville High School could not be heated due to a break in the gas lines, so classes were canceled. Hermine felt better knowing that she had not missed any days of instruction while stranded outside of town. Classes at the Plank Road school were also dismissed due to the impassable road conditions. Minola was inwardly relieved at this unexpected recess, since things had not been going well at school.

Miss Kohl exhibited an overt favoritism toward the older boys and turned a blind eye toward their increasingly aggressive misbehavior. The ringleader, Roy Haab, was an oversized adolescent whose dismal academic showing was compensated for by a manipulative mind. His two lackeys, Julius Herbst and Helmer Schoepf, took directives from Roy, partly to be members of the reigning social order and also to avoid being the objects of his bullying. Roy managed to ingratiate himself with Miss Kohl by arriving at school before her each morning and performing the daily chores. He started the fire in the potbellied stove, carried in a scuttle of coal, fetched a bucket of water from Lantzes's well, and wiped down the chalk board. However, Roy also used the solitary morning hours to deface other students' books, snap their pencils in half, pocket any trinkets he found, and leave an occasional tack on a student's seat.

When the younger schoolchildren reported being tripped, punched, or robbed of their lunches by Roy and his henchmen, Miss Kohl always sided with Roy. "I'm sure you're misinterpreting things. Roy's such a big lad, he probably doesn't know his own strength." Then she'd arch one eyebrow meaningfully and level her gaze at the complainant. "And remember, tattling is a negative character trait that *no one* likes."

During recess one day, the three bullies sprang upon a group of younger boys who were playing a game of marbles on the schoolhouse steps. Roy scooped up the glass orbs and held them hostage over his head while taunting the younger boys, who pleaded for the return of their marbles. He leaped off the school step and began walking toward the fence at the rear of the property, his hand aloft clutching the marbles. The younger boys followed, while Julius and Helmer circled them like wolves searching for a weakling in the herd.

Floyd Busch, who was in the second grade with Minola, began to cry about his loss. "Those are my marbles. I got 'em for Christmas. Give 'em back!"

Julius and Helmer sneered and called, "Baby! Baby! You're nothin' but a cryin', snivlin' baby!"

The catcalls garnered the attention of the rest of the schoolchildren, who flocked to the scene but followed at a safe distance. No one wanted to draw Roy's attention and become the next victim.

When Roy reached the fence, he lowered his hand and momentarily studied the marbles, then held them toward the boys. "You want these back?" he asked.

The younger boys nodded eagerly, thinking that perhaps Roy had had a sudden change of heart.

"Then go find 'em!" Roy shouted as he flung the handful of marbles toward the creek. A few of the marbles *plinked* into the water, but most bounced into the scrubby woodline beyond the creek bank. The three bullies guffawed and slapped their knees.

"Look at the tears on that bawl-baby's face," smirked Roy, pointing at Floyd.

The frustration of the situation overcame Floyd, and he rushed at Roy in a blind rage, hitting and kicking his much larger tormentor. The crowd of schoolchildren gasped.

Roy was initially stunned at this backlash but quickly regained his composure. He pulled his assailant away by the collar and propelled him toward the boys' outhouse. Floyd's feet barely touched the ground as Roy half-lifted, half-shoved him across the play yard. The crowd edged along behind, irresistibly drawn to witness the scene but feeling powerless to intervene.

When they neared the outhouse, Roy gave the younger boy a final push, and Floyd staggered up against the outhouse wall. Roy pressed Floyd's face against the rough wood while twisting the boy's arm tightly behind his back, producing a painful outcry.

"You ever gonna do that again?" barked Roy. He held his face menacingly close to Floyd's, his breath hot upon the younger boy's cheek. "Huh? Are you?" he demanded.

Floyd squeaked a pitiful, high-pitched "No-o-o!"

"Well, let's make sure you don't forget this lesson." Roy motioned for Julius and Helmer to keep Floyd pinned against the wall while he delivered one final humiliating blow. He stepped back a few paces and glanced over his shoulder at the cluster of frightened schoolchildren behind him. Roy fumbled with the buttons on his pants. A ripple of horrified astonishment swept through the crowd as they watched a stream of urine spray the back of Floyd's coat, pant legs, and shoes.

Roy re-buttoned his pants and turned to face the crowd. "There's worse treatment than that for any tattlers. Understand?"

The schoolchildren shrunk backward, unified in fear and silence.

One afternoon, Minola asked permission to get a drink from the common water bucket, which was kept in the boys' entryway. As soon as she took a long sip from the agateware cup, she heard snickering from the three troublemakers, who were seated just inside the door to the classroom. Minola knew instantly that they had contaminated the water, either by spitting or urinating in it. She pinched her eyes closed and forced back an involuntary gag reflex, then retreated to her seat.

Without intervention from the teacher, Roy, Julius, and Helmer rapidly escalated their mischief. The three began exposing themselves, pawing the girls, and laughing uproariously as their victims cowered or fled. They lurked around the girls' outhouse, alternately barricading a child in the privy and guffawing at her frantic pleas for release, or hiding in the darkened facility and springing upon the unsuspecting girl who entered. For protection, the girls made group trips to the outhouse, as nervous as a covey of quails. Many an afternoon, Minola watched in discomfort as the hands on the schoolhouse clock inched slowly toward the four o'clock dismissal hour, when she could speed home to the safety of her own family's outhouse.

Because their teacher failed to protect them, the children absorbed the notion that their role as victims was condoned. Their fear of reprisal from the three bullies kept them from revealing to their parents the disturbing predator/prey atmosphere that existed at the schoolhouse.

When the floodwaters finally receded and the roads became

passable, Hermine returned to board with the Derringers in Monroeville, and classes resumed at the Plank Road school. Minola awoke with a sense of dread in her heart, a knot in her stomach, and the inability to open her eyes, which had crusted shut overnight from a case of pink eye. She groped her way down the stairs and stumbled into the kitchen to find Ada, whom she knew would minister to her affliction and keep her home from school. Minola was familiar with the sick-day routine: Ada would push together two kitchen chairs and instruct her to spend the morning reclining quietly. There would be no fawning over or cosseting of the patient, other than an occasional hand upon the forehead to check for fever and the tucking of a blanket under the chin. Nevertheless, Minola looked forward to this period of convalescence, when she could absorb the inviting kitchen aromas of coffee, fried potatoes, and baking bread, but best of all, the comfort of having Ada close by.

"*Ach der liebe!*" exclaimed Ada when she spotted Minola waving her arms in front of her as she entered the kitchen. Ada wrung a soft rag in the water that was warming on the back of the cookstove and guided Minola to the daybed just inside the living room doorway.

"Lay down here, little one," Ada instructed Minola. She seated herself on the edge of the daybed and gently laid the warm wet cloth across the child's crusted eyelids. "Your eyes'll be open by the time breakfast is ready, and then you can get dressed for school."

The notion of returning to school sent a wave of panic through Minola. She threw her arms around Ada's waist and buried her face in her sister's lap, sobbing, "No! No! Don't send me to school today, Ada. Please, don't make me go. *Please!*"

Ada was stunned. Minola had always been an eager student who loved school more than anything else. With great difficulty, Ada disengaged Minola's arms from around her waist and lifted the weeping child's face.

"What's gotten into you?" she queried. "Why don't you want to go to school?"

Minola shook her head and re-buried her face in Ada's lap.

After much coaxing, Ada finally elicited the truth from Minola.

"I see," was Ada's only response as she set her lips in a thin line. She wiped the child's tear-stained face, then freshened the cloth with warm water and again placed it over Minola's eyes.

Ada bustled about the kitchen, preparing breakfast. When the table was set and the oatmeal almost cooked, she tossed a shawl over her shoulders and slipped out the kitchen door. Ada headed toward the barn where Papa and Flora were milking the cows.

Papa sat pensively through breakfast, spooning in his oatmeal and blowing on the hot coffee that he had poured into his saucer. Minola sniffled from the other end of the table, her eyes open but red rimmed. Bill commented that she looked like one of the crusty-eyed barn kittens. He reminded Ada that she always dabbed cream on the kittens' eyes to induce the mother cat to lick the infected area, and he suggested she should use the same remedy on Minola's eyes.

After breakfast, Martha and Bill trundled upstairs to get dressed, followed by Minola, whose footsteps were heavy with dread. She and Martha made the bed they shared, then Minola slowly tugged on her long, black lisle stockings. As she pulled her shepard's-check school dress over her head, she heard Papa's angry voice coming from the living room.

Martha and Minola exchanged a puzzled look and tiptoed to the top of the stairs. Papa was on the telephone, blasting away at Roy Haab's mother. Then, he demanded to speak with Roy himself. In his anger, Papa's stuttering made him sound all the more intimidating. After he hung up, the girls could hear him ringing central and asking for the Herbst and Schoepf residences. Again, Papa stuttered and blasted at the boys' mothers and then at the culprits themselves.

All during school that day and for the rest of the year, Roy, Julius, and Helmer conducted themselves as though they had experienced a religious conversion. Their sudden sanctification was a mystery to the others, but Martha and Minola knew the source of their transformation.

* * * * *

Ada and Flora carried the crates of seed potatoes up from the dark cellar and placed them in a sunny window in the summer kitchen. The girls and Bill had spent a long Saturday in March in the dank basement, knocking the growing sprouts from the potatoes to protect them from premature wilting. Now, the potatoes would spend a week warming in the thin spring sunshine, thus breaking their dormancy and ensuring rapid growth for the day when Papa hitched Dolly to the potato planter and guided her to the waiting field.

The April air was still chilly as Flora tucked the ends of a head scarf into her coat collar, pulled on a pair of work gloves, and dutifully seated herself on the back of the planter for a long day of dropping potato sections into the revolving disk of the implement. Papa tapped the reins on Dolly's back, and the trio proceeded back and forth across the wide expanse of the potato fields. The rhythmic *clack-clack-clack* of the planter and the repetitive nature of the work lulled Flora into daydreams about landscapes she would like to paint or various artistic media yet to be explored. She was frequently startled back to reality by the choking sound of the jammed planting disk, requiring her to prod the backlog with a stick she kept in her lap. Papa was more irritable than usual about these skips in plant spacing, so Flora tried to keep her mind about her business and thus avoid his frustrated outbursts of "*Gott!* What are you doing back there? Pay attention!"

As soon as the potato fields had been planted, Papa carried the crates of over-wintered strawberry runners to the barn and set the girls to work bundling them. On an overcast spring day, the familiar process of planting the year's new strawberry field began.

* * * * *

In late April, Miss Kohl led the students in transplanting a lilac bush on the school grounds to commemorate Arbor Day, followed by tilling the soil around the schoolhouse foundation and planting sweet pea and nasturtium seeds. She encouraged Martha and Minola to come to the schoolyard throughout the summer to pick bouquets of flowers. The girls knew their summer would be consumed with picking berries, not flowers.

* * * * *

Papa stood in the prime strawberry field, his hands on his hips as he gloomily surveyed the long rows of strawberry plants. A late frost had blackened the centers of the delicate white blossoms and left the leaf edges dark and curled. These early blooms represented the best and most lucrative part of his berry crop, since the first flowers to open produced the largest, most desirable fruit that commanded the highest prices at the beginning of the season, when the demand for berries was at its peak. Papa estimated the frost would reduce his total crop yield by ten to fifteen percent, a loss he could ill afford. This meant that the berries gleaned from the waning field were necessary to fill the production void. The money from the sale of the late-season berries would not be used this year to purchase a special reward for the children or pay for a trip to Euclid Beach Park.

However, the floodwaters had done some good by providing extra moisture to the compact soil, which enabled the ground to store more heat than a loose, dry soil, thereby offering a level of protection against the frost. The plants that had not yet blossomed were spared, and by the time school ended in late May, the girls were in the strawberry fields each day at dawn, filling basket after basket with plump red berries.

Hermine and Margaret had returned home for the summer, and they joined Ada, Flora, Martha, Minola, and young Bill in the fields. They were aided by the usual group of pickers from town—young, old, male, female, those who picked for financial necessity, and those who picked just enough to make jams and shortcakes. Occasionally, a picker leaned over a neighboring row to snitch the largest of berries. This behavior was viewed as thievery and prompted an angry, "Hey! Get off my row!" But the berry pickers brought a wider circle of social interaction to the Seibel farm, and the teasing, gossiping, and commiseration made the long, hot days more bearable.

By necessity, Mama was left in the house alone, with one of the younger children occasionally sent to check on her. She busied herself with her latest preoccupation—a monkey jug. Mama had salvaged a cracked brown jug from the junk pile and adhered an assortment of items to its surface: a broken stick pin, a small chain, several discarded buckles, an old locket, a nearly toothless comb, a mirror shard, a tiny ear of corn (which would in time be reduced to an empty cob by plundering mice), and several arrowheads that Bill had found at the back of the farm near the ridge where the sassafras trees grew. Bill was outraged that his arrowheads had been purloined, but the girls quickly discouraged him from voicing any protest in Mama's presence. When Mama was preoccupied with other pursuits, such as pulling weeds, Ada quietly pried the arrowheads off the jug and replaced them with river pebbles, acorns, or buttons.

One morning while Papa was away marketing the berries and the rest of the family was busy in the berry fields, Ernie the junk peddler rattled into the drive on his battered wagon piled with rusty farm castoffs. Mama was delighted at the unexpected opportunity for company. She smiled brightly as she ushered the junk man into the house and pulled out a chair for him to be seated at the kitchen table. Ernie was puzzled by this warm reception; on his rounds, he was usually relegated to waiting on the back porch steps. Most women assessed his grimy clothing and obvious disinterest in bathing and insisted he remain outdoors while they produced any discards.

Mama bustled about the kitchen, searching for something to serve her company. "*Ach!* My daughters neglect their *Hausarbeit* (housework). No baking! How can they be so *faul* (lazy)?" she complained apologetically. She rifled through the pantry, finally producing the only loaf of bread that remained. Mama set the bread, a cutting board, and a knife on the table in front of Ernie, then scurried to the cellar to retrieve the best condiment she could offer—their scant supply of butter. Mama poured two mugs of strong black coffee and settled at the table to watch Ernie heartily attack Ada's last loaf of bread, each slice spread with a generous amount of butter.

Mama was an eager conversationalist, and the two chatted about the weather, the gossip Ernie carried from his visits to neighboring farms, and finally the purpose of his visit—the procurement of junk, which he sold to a larger scrap dealer. Mama scowled and turned her hands upward. "I have nuttink. No junk," Mama lamented in her thick German accent.

"Well, then, I guess I better get my trottin' harness on," Ernie announced as he rose, patting his belly appreciatively.

Mama was not ready to lose this rare companionship. "Wait! Stay!" she ordered and rushed into the summer kitchen, scanning the room for something that would entice Ernie to linger. She grabbed the copper wash boiler from behind the cookstove and one of the milk pails from the bench beside the door.

"Here!" Mama proudly offered as she returned to the kitchen.

Ernie looked in astonishment at Mama's offerings. "Y-yer givin' those to me? You don't want nothin' for 'em?" he asked warily.

Mama shook her head vigorously. "*Nein. Nichts.* (No. Nothing)," she asserted.

Ernie couldn't believe this stroke of luck. The pail and copper boiler would fetch a good price from the scrap dealer.

"Sit! Have more bread!" ordered Mama, motioning toward the remaining half-loaf as she refilled their coffee mugs.

"Don't mind if I do." Ernie smiled a gap-toothed grin at his hostess and smacked his lips as he cut another thick slice of bread.

Late that afternoon, Bill was quizzed about his role in the mystery of the missing bread and household items. He declared his innocence with wide blue eyes, and Minola vouched that he had been with her in and about the fields all day. Mama matter-of-factly stated that she had fed Ernie the last loaf of bread and given him the copper boiler and milk pail. Papa, who was normally quite stoic about Mama's behavior, responded with an angry, "*Gott* damn it, Sophie! Why'd you do that? Now I gotta spend money I ain't got the next time the tin peddler comes around." He stiff-armed the kitchen door and stalked toward the barn, gesturing as he continued the argument with himself.

Mama flinched when the screen door slammed, and the children steeled themselves for an outburst. Instead, she busied herself with mixing a paste of flour and water to glue the cap from an old fountain pen onto her monkey jug.

The loss of the last loaf of bread was felt immediately. Supper that night consisted of milk poured over the berries that were overripe or too small for sale. It was not hearty sustenance after a long, hot day of work in the berry fields.

On Sunday afternoons during strawberry season, relatives who scarcely visited throughout the year came to renew family ties and receive quart baskets of berries—for free, of course. They chatted with Mama as though her spells and strange behavior were not the whispered topic of frequent family conversations. The younger children were patted on the head and asked, "Now, which one are you?" They clapped Papa on the back after he had helped his guests pick baskets of the nicest berries, never revealing how much the lost income from these giveaways hurt him financially.

Aunt Sadie & Uncle Charles Gasteier with Papa

* * * * *

For Ada, the spring floodwaters had had an unexpected benefit. With the statewide disruption of the railroad lines, many employees were furloughed, including Albert, who returned to Monroeville and found work on the Ben Lutz farm. Their Sunday afternoon courtship resumed, with attendance at church socials, cake walks, and the performance of two plays, "Judge Offerheimer's First Case in Court" and "Captured, or The Old Maid's Triumph," staged at Monroeville High School by a group of young people. Both comedies made Albert chuckle, but Ada spent most of the performance stealing glances at Albert's profile, his smooth shaven cheeks, and the slow smile that curled up from one corner of his mouth. She marveled at how, even after six years of courting, the sight of him still made her heart flip-flop in her chest.

Ada and Albert enjoyed croquet games in the yard, leisurely strolls down the farm lane behind the barn, and long buggy rides in the country. Minola and Bill usually accompanied the young couple, circling them on the croquet court, running ahead to chase insects along the grassy lane, or sitting between them on the buggy seat. Bill developed an easy rapport with his sister's suitor, who had been a part of family life for as long as he could remember. Minola took a more reserved approach and assumed that Albert disliked small children. It was a notion she had developed about Papa, who had little interaction with the youngest of his seven daughters. When Albert plunged his hand deep into his pocket, Bill stepped up eagerly for the much-anticipated stick of clove gum, while Minola hung back, equally expectant but hesitant to interact.

For Ada, there was always some type of small gift—a bag of lemon drop candies, a length of ribbon for around her waist, a card of ornate buttons, or a bouquet of flowers picked from Mrs. Lutz's garden. Albert understood the complexities of Ada's home situation, but she was the one for him, and so he would wait for her.

* * * * *

One evening in late July, Minola and Bill rummaged through the jelly cupboard in the cellar until they found a suitable quart jar. They raided the canning supplies in the summer kitchen for a square of cheesecloth and added a length of string from the old oatmeal tin that stored bits of twine and broken shoelaces. They raced outside through the growing twilight toward the oat field, which twinkled with hundreds of fireflies. The two children ran through the oats, capturing fireflies and imprisoning them in the jar, then capping it with cheesecloth secured by string. That night in their darkened bedroom, the two watched dreamily as the fireflies winked yellow signals from the canning jar on the dresser.

The next morning, Papa prepared for the threshers. He examined the binder, counted the grain sacks, which the girls had spent the week mending, and made sure there was enough twine to secure the sacks after they were filled with the oat harvest. He was relieved that threshing day had arrived before a windstorm flattened the field of standing grain or a rainstorm caused its moisture content to be too high for harvest. When he was satisfied all was in readiness, he walked behind the barn to survey the oat field. Papa was horrified to discover paths of trampled oats winding throughout the field, rendering the downed grain lost to the harvest. He knew if an escaped cow or horse had gotten into the field and grazed, it would not have left the numerous entrance and exit points and wildly meandering paths that lay before him.

Papa steamed angrily toward the house, where he found Minola and Bill on the back porch. They had recently been exiled from the kitchen by their sisters, who were busily preparing a huge noon meal for the coming threshermen. Minola held the glass canning jar over her head, and the two children were studying the remaining fireflies.

Papa berated both of them for their foolishness, stuttering in his rage. He grabbed the children by their forearms and marched them behind the woodshed, where they received a whipping.

For the rest of the day, Minola and Bill laid low, avoiding the house, the barns, and the hustle and bustle of what was normally one of the most exciting days on the farm.

Papa on the grain binder

* * * * *

Wednesday, September 3, brought excitement of a different nature: the marriage of forty-two-year-old Uncle Will to Anna Cull. The extended family was invited to gather at the Gasteier homestead to celebrate the nuptials. The Seibels left early in the morning for the long ride, with Mama and Papa, Flora, Hermine, Margaret, Martha, Minola, and Bill riding in the wagon. Albert and Ada traveled separately in Albert's buggy pulled by Lady, his sleek black horse. On the floorboard of the buggy, Ada clamped a crock of freshly made applesauce between her polished shoes, hoping that the cheesecloth tied tightly over the crock's opening would restrict any spills during the bumpy ride.

Aside from fretting over the potato salad, which promised to spoil in the extremely warm summer temperatures, Mama was in high spirits. She always enjoyed visiting, especially with her siblings, with whom she could reminisce. The children looked forward to interacting with their numerous cousins, and for Minola and Bill there was the lure of the railroad tracks, which ran diagonally across the Gasteier farm.

Ella was up early, too, tidying the Gasteier house for the big day and preparing a burnt sugar icing for the white cake she had baked the day before. She smoothed back a wisp of hair from her forehead and fanned her face with the dish towel as she looked around the kitchen. This was the last meal she would prepare here. After today's wedding, her services were no longer needed; Anna would become the mistress of the house, taking over from Ella the care of Grandpa Gasteier and Uncle Will.

It seemed hard to believe that her time here had come to an end. Over the past three-and-a-half years, Ella had come to know every creak and groan of the house as it settled for the night, the dusty smell of the parlor curtains as she peered through them on rainy Sunday afternoons, the angle of the sun as it slanted across the milk pails drying outside the back door, and the places in the yard where the snow drifted the deepest. She knew the schedule of the trains that rumbled across the farmyard, the songs of the birds that nested in the tree outside her bedroom window, and the somber chime of Grandpa's large Bavarian mantle clock. She had dusted and polished every piece of furniture, washed and ironed all the linens, canned and preserved every type of vegetable and fruit grown on the farm, and knew each pot, pan, and cooking spoon like an old friend. She was familiar with Grandpa and Uncle Will's dietary preferences, could differentiate the sound of their snores in the night, and knew which parts of their socks wore out first.

"And now what?" thought Ella as she swirled the icing over the surface of the cake. She pondered a nursing career, considered becoming a schoolteacher, or wondered if a good man like Albert waited in her future. She was twenty-one years old; anything was possible.

The adults at the wedding of Will Gasteier & Anna Cull, who are seated in the center of the front row.
Grandpa Gasteier is seated to the right of the bride, with Mama seated behind him and to the right. Papa is standing in the back row, the last man on the right.

The Gasteier cousins at the wedding of Uncle Will & Aunt Anna. Ella: back row, third from left, with Hermine to the left front of her. Albert: back row, fifth from left, with Ada to the right front of him. Seated from left in second row: Margaret, Flora, & Martha (face partially hidden). Bill standing in the center behind front row of boys. Minola seated at far right (with hand by face)

*****

School commenced the following Monday, and young Bill was now old enough to join Margaret, Martha, Minola, and the other neighborhood children on the walk down Townline Road, across the stile at the back of Uncle George's farm, and along the creek toward the Plank Road school. Bill stopped frequently to examine a woodchuck hole, pick up pebbles and store them in his pockets, or lift large stones in the creek bed, looking for hidden crawfish.

When he noticed that the group of older students had moved on, he raced after them, but his short legs could not keep up with the crowd. He stopped and called indignantly, "Hey! Wait up! Wait for me!"

The students were consumed with chatter about the coming school year and the new teacher, Miss Frances Cutler, who had been hired to replace Miss Kohl. They ignored Bill's pleas and continued on their way.

Bill ran again until he was out of breath, but the students were still far ahead of him and oblivious to his absence. Frustrated and angry, he stomped his foot and shouted, "*Gott* damn it! Son of a bitch! Wait up for me!"

Margaret, Martha, and Minola, who had been deep in conversation with Elsie Ordmann, stopped abruptly and whirled about to face their brother, who looked innocent enough in the Buster Brown-style suit Ada had made for him. Bill's face was clouded with outrage, and he breathed heavily from the exertion of running.

"Bill!" scolded Martha. "There's no need for talk like that!"

"Land's sakes!" clucked Elsie. "Where'd he learn such bad language?"

The girls were too chagrined to reveal that Bill had picked up more than mechanical skills from the hours spent shadowing their father.

"Go on ahead," Margaret told the others as she walked back to where Bill stood, his hands cocked on his hips and his lower lip trembling.

She wrapped her arm protectively around Bill's shoulders and said softly, "Come on, Bill. I'll walk with you. Everything'll be okay."

Bill blinked back the tears that threatened to spill over his cheeks, and he fell into step beside Margaret.

Some of the students at the Plank Road school—1913-1914.
Back row, first girl on the left is Martha.
Front row, fourth from left is Bill; beside him is Minola.

* * * * *

In October, when the weather turned cool and overcast, Papa pulled all of the children out of school for several days and summoned Hermine home from Monroeville to help harvest the potato crop. The horse-drawn potato digger was a boon, but gathering the potatoes from their overturned mounds still required hours of bending. Papa placed two empty crates on a wheelbarrow bed positioned in the center of the harvest area. The seven girls used their aprons like hammocks to carry potatoes to the waiting containers, while Bill transported his contribution by shoving potatoes into the pockets of his pants and sweater and carrying a tuber in each of his small hands.

When the crates were filled, the girls took turns wheeling the load to the barn, where the potatoes would cure in the cool darkness. The wheelbarrow was returned to the field, two more empty crates placed on its bed, and the process begun again. They flipped any potatoes that had been speared by the digger into a bushel basket, to be used for meals in the coming weeks.

The siblings sang songs, told riddles, and teased each other good-naturedly to pass the long hours. Occasionally, they stood and stretched their aching backs, taking a few moments to admire the reddish-brown leaves of the pin oak trees that ringed the fields.

When Papa finished with the potato digger, he joined his children in picking up the potatoes and filling the waiting crates. He worked quickly, reminding the girls and Bill not to rough up or bump the potatoes, which would cause bruises and lower the storage quality and appearance of the tubers. His stern demeanor caused the siblings to work quietly, certain that he had no use for frivolity. They did not know the pressure Papa felt to maximize the harvest.

Margaret harvesting potatoes

The mild weather that had prevailed during the harvest took a sudden wintry turn in early November, with a blizzard packing high winds and eighteen inches of snow. Numerous freighters were destroyed on the Great Lakes, with a large loss of cargo, including coal, iron ore, and grain. This meant short-term rising prices for consumer products. Papa had already sold his potato harvest for sixty-six cents a bushel, thus missing this narrow window of opportunity to capitalize on a spike in market demand.

* * * * *

On the last day of 1913, Papa stood before Mr. Scheid's desk and counted out the hard-earned bills that would pay off his long-standing loan.

Mr. Scheid had grown old and frail, but his mind was razor sharp. He fingered the long ledger sheet that tallied Papa's debt. "I rather hate to see this day come, Bill. You've been one of my better investments," the older man cackled. "Let's see, how many years has it been you've been paying for my pipe tobacco and a few other luxuries?" He turned the ledger page over, searching for the first entry date.

"Twenty-three years," Papa said quietly. "It's been twenty-three years since I first took out the loan."

Mr. Scheid whistled softly, running his finger along the initial entry line and noting the year "1890." He pulled out a clean slip of paper, dipped his fountain pen in the ink well, and began to write the final receipt.

"Guess it's a good thing you finally had a boy to help with the farm work and get you outta debt," Mr. Scheid mused as he wrote.

"It was my girls," Papa corrected. "My girls worked hard."

Mr. Scheid smiled, handed Papa the receipt, and leaned back in his chair. "No, Bill, you got it all wrong. Girls get you *into* debt, not outta it." Papa opened his mouth to protest but instead extended his hand for a final shake that would close the transaction.

He climbed upon the seat of the cutter, tucked the laprobe around his legs, and studied the receipt marked "Paid in Full." Mr. Scheid's handwriting had grown feeble over the years, and the words appeared wavy, as though under water. Papa shook his head at what the paper represented—both a victory and a bitter reminder of his failures. He folded the receipt and tucked it into his coat pocket. Twenty-three years of debt was behind him. He felt liberated, as though he should race the cutter up and down the streets of Monroeville, shouting his new-found freedom to all who would listen. If he were a drinking man, he'd pay a visit to one of Monroeville's many saloons and tip a glass or two in celebration. But that was not Papa's nature. Instead, he drew a deep breath of crisp December air, tapped the reins lightly on Dolly's back, and turned the cutter toward Townline Road. There was work to be done at home.

Chapter 17
The Plank Road School
1914

MISS CUTLER STOOD BY THE WINDOW in the girls' cloakroom, peering as far east as possible down Plank Road. A smile crossed her face, and she quickly turned to walk up the aisle on the girls' side of the classroom. Stepping onto the platform at the front of the room, she announced, "Now children, it's very important for a teacher to instill the qualities of honor and trustworthiness in her students so that they will become upstanding, contributing citizens of their community. As part of that exercise, I'm giving you all assignments to work on quietly at your desks. I will then exit the building and stand just outside the schoolhouse door, listening to see how well you remain quiet and industrious. I may stand out there for just a few minutes or perhaps longer—you won't know how long. This will test the degree of trustworthiness you currently exhibit. If all of you remain quiet and complete your assignments, you will be rewarded with an extra recess. If you disappoint me, I'll have to institute a program of punishment. Anyone who is out of their seat or making noise will receive a paddling, and the rest of the class will be required to write 'I Am Not Trustworthy' one thousand times."

A small groan went up from the classroom at the description of the punishment.

"We'll begin our lessons in trust and honor immediately." Miss Cutler quickly made assignments for each group of children before stepping briskly toward the schoolhouse door. Once outside, she scampered across the schoolyard toward a buggy that waited at the edge of Plank Road.

Roland Schiel grinned as Miss Cutler climbed onto the buggy seat and snuggled up next to him. He snapped the reins on the horse's back. The buggy jolted forward and proceeded at a clip down Plank Road.

The students toiled diligently at their tasks, remaining in their seats and not making a sound, other than the scratching of pencils on paper, the turning of pages in books, and the occasional scuffling of hard-soled shoes on the wooden floorboards.

When Miss Cutler returned, her face was flushed, and she swayed slightly as she walked down the aisle on the boys' side of the classroom. She stopped occasionally to perform a cursory check on the work of several of the students. When she leaned over Bill's desk, he detected a sour, almost medicinal odor about her. It reminded him of Peter Essendorf, the old neighborhood soak whom Papa had recently employed to re-plaster the kitchen walls and hang a new cupboard.

Miss Cutler stepped unsteadily onto the platform, plopped into her chair, and gave a small hiccup. "I'm pleased with the trustworthiness you've displayed. As I promised, you may all go outside for an extra recess." She waved her hand absentmindedly toward the schoolhouse doors.

The students exchanged happy smiles as they scrambled to put away their books and tablets and scurried out into the schoolyard.

Miss Cutler remained in her seat, hiccupping lightly. She pulled a small hand mirror from her desk drawer, propped it against a stack of books, and blinked at her reflection. Humming to herself, she repinned her mussed hair and checked the buttons on the front of her blouse.

Several times a week, Miss Cutler stationed herself beside the window in the girls' cloakroom, followed by the announcement of an impromptu trustworthiness exercise. The students were pleased with the extra recess they received as their reward and saw no reason to carry home reports about their frequently absent teacher.

* * * * *

In April, Papa rumbled into the farmyard with a load of new raspberry crowns in the bed of his wagon. Martha cried when she saw the cargo. With the loan finally retired, the girls had not expected an increase in crops and subsequent field work. But to Papa's way of thinking, there was financial ground to be made up and no time to waste. To assuage their spirits, he promised a trip to Cedar Point amusement park at season's end for the girls who picked the most berries.

Papa drove the wagon into the field on a Saturday morning. He, Ada, and Ella dug long rows of holes, while Margaret and Martha carried the bare bramble roots from the wagon and dropped them into the evenly spaced depressions. Flora and Hermine pressed the soft soil around the crowns and cut back the canes to low stubs. Minola and Bill were charged with occasionally wetting the burlap sacks that covered the remaining crowns on the wagon bed. However, most of their time was spent scampering on and off the wagon, searching for arrowheads in the loose soil, chasing each other up one furrow and down another, and racing back to the house to check on Mama.

As they worked, the girls chattered about the reward trip to Cedar Point, which meant a ride on the B&O railway to Sandusky, where they would board the ferry boat *G.A. Boeckling* to cross Sandusky Bay, finally reaching the amusement park at the tip of the peninsula.

Occasionally, Ada straightened from her task, scanned the field for Minola and Bill, and called out, "What have I told you two? Don't sit on the ground during a month with an "r" in it. You'll end up needing a mustard plaster for your chest."

The two children dutifully rose, assumed a crouched position to appease their older sister, and returned to their preoccupation of digging in the soil.

*****

In May, Miss Cutler suggested the students stage a program, complete with recitations and tableaux. In response to the growing military tensions in Europe, a patriotic fervor had swept the country, so Miss Cutler decided on the theme of American history.

In a scene depicting the Pilgrims, Bill would play an Indian, which his sisters agreed was a role requiring no rehearsal on his part. He plucked a long black feather from the rooster's tail, and Ella used it to fashion a headband for his stage debut. In the Revolutionary War scene, Minola would portray Betsy Ross. Flora made a mob cap out of an old doily, and Minola could lay the school's American flag across her lap and pretend to stitch. For the final tableau, Miss Cutler selected Martha to portray the Statue of Liberty, partly because of her dark-haired beauty and partly because Miss Cutler knew that Martha had several talented sisters at home who could create a suitable costume. Flora procured some stiff cardboard from her art teacher, Mrs. Schumacher, and created a semicircular headpiece for Martha. Ella glued together several layers of the *Monroeville Spectator* and cut out long triangular pieces to resemble radiating points after they were affixed to the headpiece. Flora fashioned a torch handle out of the remaining cardboard and mixed together some of her oil paints to give the headpiece and torch a realistic oxidized metal appearance. Ella topped the torch with a bit of red cloth to resemble a flame. Margaret, who was an excellent reader, was appointed as the narrator for the entire performance. During Martha's Lady Liberty scene, she would recite Emma Lazarus' poem, "The New Colossus." Meanwhile, Ada was engaged to sew a stage curtain that could be drawn between acts.

The evening of the performance was one of great excitement. The schoolhouse was crowded with adult bodies wedged uncomfortably behind undersized desks; other spectators stood along the back wall. Even community members who did not have children at the school turned out for the entertainment. Hermine walked the three miles from where she boarded in Monroeville to join Ada, Ella, and Flora in the audience. Papa stayed home with Mama, who would have eagerly attended, but the girls feared her unpredictable behavior would result in an embarrassing incident.

When the curtain parted for the first tableau, featuring Bill in the Pilgrim/Indian scene, he grinned and waved wildly at his sisters in the audience.

"Obviously no hostile Indians in Plymouth," whispered Ella to her sisters, as they stifled their chuckles.

Minola was not as comfortable with her stage presence, and she kept her eyes demurely downcast as she pretended to sew the first American flag.

The final tableau found Margaret and Martha onstage together for the Statue of Liberty scene. Martha's eyes gleamed as she proudly lifted her homemade torch aloft while Margaret recited the stanza, "Give me your tired, your poor, your huddled masses yearning to breathe free, the wretched refuse of your teeming shore. Send these, the homeless, tempest-tost to me. I lift my lamp beside the golden door!"

All of the students joined Margaret and Martha onstage and united in an *a cappella* version of "America the Beautiful." They were rewarded with thunderous applause from the appreciative audience.

The performance would prove to be the last staged in the Plank Road schoolhouse. A movement toward centralization of all the rural schools had been underway. Papa understood the benefit of better educational opportunities and circulated a petition in the neighborhood, asking parents to agree to send their children into Monroeville. He first sought out the families he knew would readily sign, saving the more obstinate parents for last. The only holdout was Adolph Lantz, who lived next door to the Plank Road school.

The schoolhouse doors were closed for the final time when the term ended just before Memorial Day. Papa and the other two members of the school board met at the empty schoolhouse one evening in late May. The students' desks, the slate board, and the American flag had been transferred to the public school in Monroeville. The men divided the remaining possessions, including the small pile of coal in the shed. One board member took the potbellied stove and the recitation bench. The other dropped the agateware drinking cup into the empty communal water bucket and loaded them onto the back of his wagon, along with the teacher's desk. Papa came home with the black-handled school bell and the schoolhouse clock, which he hung on the wall between the parlor and the downstairs bedroom. Its steady *tick-tock* now marked the rhythm of the Seibel household instead of measuring out the minutes of each school day.

* * * * *

By summer, Papa and the girls were deep in strawberries. Help was needed for haying as well as hoeing the corn, so Papa hired a teenaged neighborhood boy, Josip Hogard. In return for the manpower, Josip was provided a small weekly salary, a cot in the room at the top of Stegmiller's stairs, and a seat at the dinner table. By nature, Josip was a taciturn young man, not given to small talk, frivolity, or idleness. The girls whispered among themselves that he was a younger version of their father. Even Papa couldn't help but recognize the similarity in their traits, and he exhibited approval of Josip in several small but meaningful ways. Although Papa rarely offered praise to his own children, he was overheard to say an occasional "good work" to Josip at the end of a particularly long and laborious day. Sometimes, he even entrusted the teenager with delivery of the strawberry harvest to the railroad station in Chicago Junction.

However, Josip differed from Papa in that he had a quick and violent temper. One Sunday afternoon, the girls invited him to join them for a round of croquet. Unaccustomed to playing the game, Josip soon found his skills to be woefully inadequate compared to that of the Seibel girls. When he tapped the ball and missed the wicket, the girls teased him good-naturedly. Seizing the croquet mallet in both hands, Josip beat the head of the mallet repeatedly against the ground, his face dark and contorted with rage, and then he flung the mallet into the bushes beside the house. He stalked to the front porch and plopped sullenly on its edge, signaling the end of his involvement in the afternoon's recreation.

The girls and Bill stood on the croquet court in uncomfortable silence. Thinking to defuse the situation, Margaret handed her mallet to Hermine and headed toward the porch. "It's okay, Josip. Maybe you'd rather listen to my piece for the piano recital. It's the 'Hungarian Rag.'" She smiled warmly at Josip as she opened the porch door to the parlor. "You oughta like it, being a Hunky and all."

Josip scrambled to his feet and lunged toward Margaret. "Don't go calling me a Hunky, you damn Dutchie!" he roared.

Margaret screamed in alarm and slammed the parlor door behind her, pressing her weight against it to keep out the angry young man. The girls dropped their mallets and raced around the corner of the house toward the back door, to come to the aid of their sister. Bill remained on the croquet court, suddenly alone and quite unsure of what to make of all the commotion.

Following this incident, the Seibel siblings were cautious in their interactions with Josip. However, as the weeks progressed, the disagreeable side of his nature was exacerbated by the lack of food. With all of the girls in the field and Mama too indisposed to cook, meals during strawberry season were sketchy and make-do, usually consisting of bread slices spread with molasses or jam, a bowl of strawberries too small or overripe for marketing, an occasional skillet of fried potatoes and eggs, and a cup of buttermilk or cold coffee. It was not adequate sustenance for those who labored in the heat of the fields.

Grumbling about the meager offerings, Josip took his appetite down the road to the dinner tables of the Mosses' or Ordmanns'. There, he helped himself to heaping second portions of meat and potatoes, sopped up pools of gravy with flaky biscuits, and always enjoyed pie, cake, or cobbler for dessert. He complained openly about the scant fare offered by the Seibels and responded to the probing questions posed by Mrs. Moss and Mrs. Ordmann about life in the Seibel household. While the girls knew Josip was justified in his complaints, they were indignant and humiliated by the situation.

* * * * *

As the strawberry season waned, Papa pulled the ledger book from its shelf in the tall cherry bookcase and carefully tallied his profits. All summer long, he'd thought about ways to market his berries more efficiently. He concluded there was one investment that would have the greatest impact.

Papa went to the garage of Frank Fritz in Monroeville and paid $250 cash for a 1907 Fuller automobile. The auto—always referred to as a "machine"—had no roof or doors; black leather upholstery that gave off a lingering animal aroma in the hot sun; acetylene lights mounted carriage-style; large, wagon-like wheels with solid rubber tires; and a round rubber horn that bleated a mournful *ooogla, ooogla.*

Mr. Fritz demonstrated how to crank the machine, and after it roared to life, Papa climbed onto the front seat behind the steering wheel for his one and only driving lesson. He laid his hands loosely on his knees, as he'd done so many times while holding the horse's reins, and lightly wrapped his thumbs around the bottom of the wheel.

"Better grab the tiller tight, Bill. This ain't no horse," Mr. Fritz advised as he settled himself on the seat beside Papa. He showed Papa the proper setting for the choke and explained the timing and throttle levers, on either side of the steering wheel. Pointing to the three floor pedals, Mr. Fritz explained that one was the brake, one caused the machine to go in reverse, and the last one was the gear shifter. The lever protruding from the floor was to be used in working the brakes as well as the clutch.

With Mr. Fritz's guidance, Papa stepped on the gear shifter pedal while simultaneously moving the throttle lever to "give 'er some gas." He eased the floor lever forward. The machine lurched ahead, sending Papa and Mr. Fritz backward in their seats. Mr. Fritz shouted instructions that would keep the auto from stalling, and Papa engaged in a ballet of moving levers, shifting gears, pressing pedals, and adjusting the timing position.

As they puttered along the flat ribbon of Plank Road, Papa leaned horizontally onto the seat and stared at the floorboard, trying to determine the appropriate foot pedal to slow the machine for a turn onto Farr Road.

"Cripe's sake, Bill!" Mr. Fritz admonished, shoving Papa upright. "Gotta keep your head above the dashboard when you drive this thing!" Papa was mildly embarrassed by his novice's lapse of judgment. With all the unaccustomed coordination of hands and feet, he then forgot to keep one hand on the tiller while he worked the levers, and the machine edged toward the roadside ditch. He overcorrected, sending the car veering toward the opposite ditch before recovering his direction. The two men swerved, stalled, and jerked down country roads until, at last, Papa felt he had sufficiently mastered the intricacies of driving the machine and was prepared for his solo journey home.

Mr. Fritz stood beside the auto, patting the shiny fender, as Papa clenched the steering wheel in a death grip. "Be seeing ya soon," Mr. Fritz grinned, "since I'm the only one in town that sells gas."

The machine was a source of pride as well as chagrin for the girls. They were elated to be the first family in their immediate neighborhood to make the transition from horse and buggy to auto. Not even Emmaline Moss, always the trendsetter of Townline Road, had badgered her husband into acquiring such a status symbol. However, by 1914, the Fuller already had the taint of antiquity about it, and the girls' sensitive egos were bruised at the thought of being seen in something considered so dated. In addition, the machine had so few cylinders that it needed assistance in cresting even the smallest rise in the road. At those times, a shake of Papa's thumb indicated that the girls must disembark, gather behind the machine, and, through their combined strength, provide a fraction's worth of horsepower for forward trajectory.

Papa's first machine—the 1907 Fuller

The Fuller also had the maddening habit of stopping dead at intersections. Papa got out and cranked the machine or occasionally had to tinker with the engine. The girls could gauge the severity of the trouble by the number of knocks, pings, and "*Gott* damn it's" that emanated from under the hood. But Papa had a mechanical aptitude, and the Fuller's many breakdowns gave him an opportunity to enlarge his talent.

The machine also expanded the Seibels' horizons. There were more frequent trips to see Mama's siblings in the Bellevue-Monroeville-Milan area as well as Grandpa Gasteier, Uncle Will, and his new wife, Anna, at the Gasteier homestead. But best of all, Papa's promised trip to Cedar Point amusement park could be made by auto along the new Chaussee, a narrow road that ran down the spine of the Cedar Point peninsula.

Because the Fuller had only five seats, Papa selected four of the girls for the reward. He declared Flora, Hermine, Margaret, and Martha the best pickers. Ada was away from home anyway, wistfully working on traveling attire for Laurinda Bessel's trousseau. Ella had secretly informed Papa that she would stay home to keep an eye on Mama, Minola, and Bill, thereby allowing one of her younger sisters the opportunity for a memorable day.

On the morning of the trip, Ella and Flora packed a basket with deep-fried buttermilk chicken, potato salad, oatmeal cake, and a tall jug of lemonade, while Papa went to the barn to crank the Fuller. The girls listened anxiously for the sound of the cantankerous machine roaring to life. Only the cackling of the chickens and the occasional squeal of a pig greeted their ears. Young Bill, who was as drawn to mechanical opportunities as his father, raced from the barn to the house and provided the unwelcome news that the Fuller's engine would not turn over.

Four dispirited sisters exchanged forlorn glances. "I knew it wouldn't happen. I just knew it was too good to be true," said thirteen-year-old Martha, her lower lip quivering.

"Maybe Papa can get it fixed before it's too late to go," offered Hermine as she straightened the large white bow at the back of Martha's head. "And if we can't go today, then we'll go another day."

Bill leaned his elbows on the kitchen table and eyed the basket of picnic food longingly. "If you stay home, we could..."

The roar of the Fuller interrupted Bill's suggestion for a shared lunch. The machine hiccupped a few times as it backfired and lurched across the farmyard.

The girls rushed to the back door, almost forgetting to grab the lunch hamper in their haste.

"Get in before she conks out!" called Papa, frantically working levers, pedals, and the choke to keep the engine running.

Hermine, Margaret, and Martha scrambled into the back seat, a tangle of arms, legs, and dresses. Flora leaped onto the running board and plopped the picnic basket on the front floorboard. "Go, go, go!" she urged while gathering up her long skirt to vault into the front seat.

Papa stepped on the gear shifter pedal, adjusted the throttle and timing levers, and eased the gear lever forward. The machine lurched ahead, and the passengers' heads snapped backward in response. The machine puttered out the drive and onto Townline Road. The girls settled into their seats, straightened their skirts, and turned to wave happily at Ella, Minola, and Bill standing in the side yard.

For their route to the lake, Papa selected Ransom Road, straight north of Monroeville, because of its relatively flat terrain. He often drove this way to the Gasteier homestead, and the girls referred to it as "the Long Road" for its widely scattered houses, sparse shade, and lack of topographical interest. They motored along at a breathtaking fifteen miles per hour, with the girls smiling and waving at anyone they saw working in the fields or passing by on the roadway.

Papa pulled his tobacco pouch from an inside coat pocket and tucked a pinch into his cheek. Occasionally, he leaned over and spit out his excess tobacco juice, which flew back and spattered the three girls in the rear seat. They recoiled in disgust, but no one considered voicing an objection to Papa about this outrage.

When they reached a small incline at Bogart Road just south of Sandusky, the machine struggled to make the grade. Without waiting for Papa's signal, the girls hopped out, assembled behind the auto, and pushed until the minor hill had been crested. Papa downshifted and slowed the vehicle until the girls had caught up with the machine and scrambled aboard.

At last, they turned onto the Cedar Point Chaussee, where they were greeted by seven miles of verdant, water-filled scenery so foreign to the open farmland of their daily existence. The narrow road passed through a shade-dappled tunnel of trees and snaked between the lake on the east and small pools filled with water lilies on the west. The girls pointed at rowboats tied to fishing piers and mused about what it must be like to live in the small cottages that dotted the shoreline.

Papa parked the machine in a grove of trees across from the beach, and the girls clambered out, anxious to begin their adventure. There was much to see and do. They headed straight for the Amusement Circle, which featured rides, games, sideshows, and concessions. Papa bought the girls tickets for the merry-go-round and the House of Mirth, where they laughed at their reflections in the hall of mirrors—sometimes they were short and squat and other times elongated with giraffe-like necks. They watched others try their luck at the shooting gallery and games of skill, and they peered with a mixture of suspicion and curiosity at a fortune teller wearing a brightly colored head scarf who called to them with a thick accent and motioned them toward her stand.

At noon, the five walked back to the machine, where they spread a blanket in the grove of trees and ate their picnic lunch. Afterward, Papa stretched out on the blanket for a short nap, while the girls ambled over to the beach. They passed the bath house, where bathing suits could be rented for twenty-five cents a day, and watched bathers on the Sea Swing, which allowed riders to spin out over the water. It was said that the Lake Erie waves occasionally hit a rider with just enough force to rip or remove part of their bathing attire, thus sending the unfortunate victim swinging back to shore in an embarrassing predicament.

Margaret shielded her eyes against the sun and watched the bathers wistfully. "I wanna learn how to swim. It looks like so much fun."

"Maybe you will some day—when you marry one of the Rockefellers and have your own swimming pool and maids to wait on you hand and foot," teased Flora as she adopted an exaggerated haughty air.

The sisters walked along the shore toward the Hotel Breakers but lacked the courage to march onto the porch and into the elegant lobby, decorated with wicker furniture and Tiffany chandeliers. Instead, the girls strolled back to the grove to wake Papa. They returned to the Amusement Circle and watched a trained wild animal show, peeked inside the dance hall, gazed at the Ferris wheel rising high above the midway, and listened to the shrieks of the riders on The Racer roller coaster. They purchased tickets for the Circle Swing—six cars that spun outward from a tall tower and gave the illusion of flying. When the ride was over, they laughed at each other's wind-blown hair and Martha's cockeyed bow.

In mid-afternoon, Papa announced it was time to head home. He purchased one last treat—a pink cloud of cotton candy for the girls to share. Hermine carried it on its paper cone as the sisters strolled toward the grove, pinching off pieces of the sticky confection and allowing it to melt in their mouths.

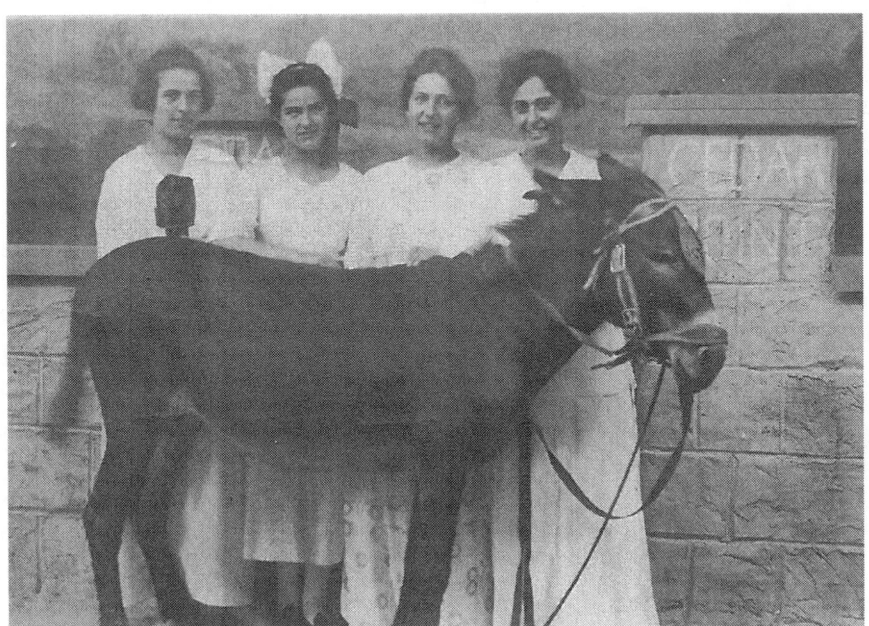

Margaret, Martha, Flora, & Hermine at Cedar Point

The next day, the girls were back in the blackberry patch, their arms and hands sheathed in long, black lisle stockings, hats pulled low over their faces, and collars pinned tight around their necks. They chattered happily as they progressed up and down the rows, describing in great detail all of the experiences of their trip so that Ella, Minola, and Bill could share in the wonder of the special day. For once, the bramble thorns didn't seem as menacing nor the work so hot and tedious.

* * * * *

That fall there were no children parading down Townline Road, crossing the stile over George Seibel's fence, and dallying along the creek that led them to the Plank Road school. Instead, siblings gathered in front of their houses and waited for one of the three horse-drawn school wagons—or "kid hacks"—that the Monroeville school system dispatched to pick up its rural students and transport them to the central school in town.

The Seibels soon adopted the ritual of posting one sibling by the south parlor window to watch for the school wagon, while the others finished their breakfast, fussed over their hair, and prodded Bill to brush his teeth. When the jingle of the approaching horses' harness gave notice that there was no time to lose, Hermine, Margaret, Martha, Minola, and Bill gathered up their school books and dashed out the front door, since anyone who kept the school wagon waiting was in for derision from the other passengers.

The students entered the school wagon through the rear door and took their seats on narrow benches that ran the length of the wagon. The most coveted seats were those near the door—away from the monitoring eye of the driver, Mr. Busch—and thus were quickly claimed by the students who were picked up first. The Seibels scattered themselves throughout the wagon to sit with neighborhood friends and classmates.

Since Minola's grade at the Plank Road school had consisted only of herself and Floyd Busch, she had no female classmates to share a seat with. Margaret noticed the lonely situation her youngest sister was enduring and motioned her to squeeze in beside her on the bench. Minola rested her head against Margaret's shoulder and listened to her sister's warm laughter and happy conversations during the long rides.

The lower grades occupied the first floor of Monroeville Central School, with the high school and County Normal School being held on the top two floors. For Minola, the transition from the small, one-room Plank Road school to the large fourth-grade classroom at the central school was a difficult one. The social order had already been set by those girls who lived in town and had been classmates for the past three years. There was no place but the bottom rung of the ladder for a shy, bookish girl from the country with no established coterie of friends.

The Ridgefield Township District #4 school wagon. Standing fourth from left is Martha; Margaret is sixth from left, with Minola in front & to the right of her.

Monroeville Central School

In addition to being a social outcast, Minola soon discovered that she was far behind in the world of arithmetic. When the teacher stood at the board and demonstrated a problem in long division, Minola was utterly lost. She had done quite well with addition and subtraction at the Plank Road school, but Miss Cutler had never taught her and Floyd these mathematical operations called "multiplication" and "division."

Up until this point, Minola had felt quite satisfied with her level of academic achievement, but now she was faced with the dreadful scourge of being labeled as stupid. Day after day, she and Floyd were kept in at recess time to work on their substandard math skills. Minola stole wistful glances out the window at her classmates frolicking on the playground, and her eyes occasionally welled with tears when she could no longer suppress the discouragement she felt. In the evenings, Margaret and Martha drilled Minola on her multiplication and division tables, when they weren't doing their own homework, helping to prepare supper, or tending to the nightly chores.

The only saving grace academically was Minola's excellent reading ability, which earned her some positive recognition from the teacher. She gathered an occasional compliment from a classmate about her attire, thanks to Flora's wizardry with a needle and thread. Minola clung to these brief moments of praise the way a drowning man grasps for a life raft.

* * * * *

Because Papa had spent his strawberry profits on the purchase of the machine, he did not have much money for auction finds that year. However, he did bring home a Victorian-era stereoscope and a series of picture cards that depicted a wealthy man in the throes of a love affair with his maid. One card showed the man sneaking into the kitchen to embrace the maid, who was kneading bread dough. The next card showed the maid with her arms wrapped around the man's neck. In the subsequent image, the man protested his innocence to his suspicious wife, despite the contradictory evidence of the maid's floury handprints on the back of his coat. The girls snickered as they viewed the series over and over again. Minola and Bill took delight in assembling the cards in the wrong order, so that the story was out of sequence. They experimented with sliding the adjustable card holder as close to the eyepieces as possible and tried drawing their own cards to test out their three-dimensional capabilities.

One rainy afternoon, the girls assembled the card series in the stereoscope for Mama to view. When she'd finished with the images, she scowled and shook her head, remembering her own years as a domestic in Mr. John Wright's mansion. "Bah!" she scoffed. "No maid has time for such *Dummheit* (foolishness)." For Mama, there was no such thing as suspension of belief.

* * * * *

When the golden days of autumn gave way to winter, Papa stored the machine in the barn. Without antifreeze, the radiator had to be drained after each use, and the engine grew even harder to crank in the cold. The roads, which were largely unimproved, became almost impassable with deep, frozen ruts. At such times, the horses were more reliable and easier to maintain. The girls resigned themselves to a decrease in weekend social outings, unless the location could be reached by foot or horse-drawn conveyance.

Albert's Sunday afternoon visits continued, and the talk of marriage began to increase. With the younger children growing up and attending school, and Flora and Ella at home to share the tasks of farm and family, Ada realized she could at last consider a life away from the Seibel household. The final obstacle was Albert's employment on the railroad, which he consented to give up if it meant having Ada by his side. After nearly eight years of courtship, the young couple could finally plan a life together.

Chapter 18
The Seibel Homestead
1915

WEDNESDAY, JANUARY 20, dawned crisp and clear, with occasional flurries of fat snowflakes in the air. After Flora had finished washing and drying the noontime dishes, she surveyed the kitchen, making sure it was tidy enough to meet Mama's strict demands for cleanliness. Flora was especially careful to placate Mama today—Ada's wedding day. It would not do to send Ada off to the church and her new life while Mama was in the midst of a tirade. Satisfied that there was nothing out of place to provoke Mama's ire, Flora checked on the bowl of bread dough she had rising on the back of the cookstove, then hurried up the steps to the bedroom where Ada and Ella were changing their clothes.

Ada smoothed the front of the long brown skirt she had made for this day and adjusted its pleats over the brown-and-white-checked inserts. She tucked in the hem of her crisp white shirtwaist, straightened its row of dainty buttons, and fastened a brown suede belt around her corseted waist.

"You sure you got everything?" asked Ella as she peered at the small bundle of clothing, the button hook, and the hairbrush nestled at the bottom of Ada's valise.

"I'm not gonna be in South Bend that long," reminded Ada, fastening the clasp on the gold locket Albert had given her when they began courting almost eight years ago. "Besides, Papa's bringing the rest of my things over to the Meyer house when we get back on Saturday."

"You mean to 'the honeymoon cottage'," smiled Flora.

Ada's cheeks flushed crimson at the name the family had given to the house Albert had rented from Mrs. Meyer north of Monroeville. The young couple planned to work the small acreage as tenant farmers.

Ada topped her upswept hair with a brown felt hat and examined her reflection in the dresser mirror. She cocked her head and listened. "Who's Mama talking to downstairs?" she asked.

"Probably herself," assured Flora. "Papa's out in the barn."

Ada gasped, "*Himmel!* She's talking to Albert! I didn't see him drive in!" She speared her hat with a jeweled pin, snatched up the valise, and whirled for the bedroom door, hoping to intercept Mama before she said something inappropriate.

The three girls reached the kitchen doorway in time to overhear

Mama proudly telling Albert, "I was twenty-two when I got married. *Nicht* a forced marriage either, like George and Bertha." She clucked her tongue in disapproval. "Sampling the cream before buying *die kuh* (the cow). *Ach!*"

Albert stood by the back door, a light dusting of snow on the shoulders of his dark overcoat and a bemused expression on his face. Flora shot Ada a look of apology and distracted Mama by enlisting her aid in transferring the bread dough to the baking pans.

Ada and Ella donned their winter coats and headed toward the back door, which Albert held open for the two sisters. Ella exited, but Ada stopped and turned to take one last look at the kitchen. Here, she had washed dishes from the time she was old enough to stand on a chair, prepared the family meals, soothed the tears and hurts of her siblings, and scrubbed the wide plank floor on her hands and knees every Saturday. Her imprint was on every inch of this kitchen, yet the next time she returned here, she would be Mrs. Albert Gfell and the responsibilities of this household would no longer be hers.

"Change of heart?" teased Albert from the doorway, breaking Ada's reverie.

"No. No ... I...," she stammered, then dashed across the kitchen and threw her arms around Flora.

Flora squeezed Ada's shoulders and whispered in her ear, "Better go. You've waited a long time for this day."

Ada, Albert, and Ella joined Albert's brother Fred in the buggy, and the four set off toward the church parsonage in Monroeville, where Rev. Keppel awaited them. Because of Albert's Catholicism, the ceremony would be held in the parsonage living room instead of the church sanctuary. Occasionally, Albert patted his coat pocket, checking to make sure the wide gold wedding band for Ada and the two train tickets to South Bend, Indiana, were still there.

The ceremony itself seemed like a dream to Ada, one that she had long anticipated but could not believe had finally come true. When she looked up into Albert's twinkling blue eyes, her heart hammered in her chest and she was barely able to respond, "I do."

Ella and Fred signed the marriage license as witnesses and drove the young couple to the B&O station in Monroeville. Albert and Ada held hands during the long train ride to South Bend, and Albert occasionally pointed out the window at sites that had become familiar to him when he traveled this route during his railroad work. At ages twenty-seven and twenty-four, they were finally embarking upon a life together.

The following Saturday, Bill rode with Papa to deliver Ada's belongings to the honeymoon cottage. In the back of the spring wagon was a trunk that contained her clothing, a few pieces of jewelry nestled in a small wooden box, the little teakettle with painted ceramic handle that Albert had given her for Christmas one year, a set of silver teaspoons, her dresser set and an embroidered dresser scarf, a quilt she had pieced, and sheets with pillowcases monogrammed with the letter "G." Bill clutched Ada's sewing basket in his lap and peppered Papa with questions about Ada's new home and if she would look different now that she was married. For the most part, Papa rode in silence.

*****

For Minola, the absence of her mother-figure coupled with her scholastic struggles had imparted a deep sense of loss. When Bill suggested that the two of them set out for Ada's after school the following Friday, she eagerly agreed. Bill proudly led the way on the mile-long walk, singing a little drum-beating song about soldiers marching that he had learned in his second-grade class.

The two youngsters never questioned their welcome at the honeymoon cottage, but quickly re-established their relationship with their surrogate mother by raiding her cookie kettle and exploring the new house and furnishings. Albert had borrowed nine hundred dollars from the husband of Mama's sister Katie. He was the son of Mr. Scheid, whom Papa had been indebted to for over twenty years. With the money, Ada and Albert purchased a team of horses and some farm machinery; a black leather couch; carpets; a table, chairs, and sideboard for the dining room; a brass bed and oak chiffonier; two rocking chairs; a cookstove; a copper wash boiler and a galvanized tub; a lantern; and various sundries.

Best of all, however, was the Edison phonograph on loan from Albert's parents. The children begged to hear it, and Ada complied by winding the motor and carefully placing the stylus onto a cylindrical disk. Bill and Minola listened in amazement as the clover-shaped horn emitted a man's operatic voice singing an aria. Ada explained that the man whose voice they were hearing was no longer alive. Minola was enraptured by the wonder of it, while Bill declared it impossible. The next song was entitled "The Preacher and the Bear," a rollicking tune about a minister who encounters a ferocious grizzly. The preacher begs for mercy from a higher power and ends his plea with "Dear Lord, if you can't help me, for goodness sake don't help that bear!" The last song included the lyrics "There'll be no one around to see, no one around to hear. We'll pull down the shades. Oh, oh, oh, don't be afraid." Minola vaguely understood that there was a naughty overtone to the song, but Bill was perplexed and asked, "What's there to be so scairt of?" Ada merely gave an enigmatic smile.

Nearly every Friday afternoon during the school year, the two youngsters set off for the honeymoon cottage and spent the weekend. It was liberating to be free of the tension associated with being around Mama. Here, they could let the screen door slam, rattle the lid on Ada's cookie kettle, play hide-and-seek indoors, and never have to worry about provoking Mama's temper. There were outbuildings to explore, an apple tree with a saddle-shaped depression on one low branch that made a perfect seat, and interactions with the young Meyer children next door, who were ideal playmates. In addition, the small farm backed up to a bluff that overlooked the Huron River, where Minola and Bill spent hours turning over rocks, skipping stones, and wading in the shallow rapids.

Ada, however, was not as fond of the proximity to the river because of the many snakes it brought to the property. One morning, Ada backed out of the kitchen door with a fresh-from-the-oven apple pie in her hands. As she turned carefully to set the pie on the porch railing to cool, she spied a large black snake sunning itself on the ledge. She shuddered and bobbled the pie, which landed face down on the porch floor. Tendrils of steam rose from the hot apple pie filling as it oozed across the floor boards. Ada fled to the safety of the kitchen, upset by the loss of the pie, consternated by her irrational fear of snakes, and yet unable to return to the porch and clean up the mess.

When Albert came in from the fields for his noontime meal, he stepped over the upturned pie on the porch. "What happened out there?" he asked as he washed his hands and forearms in the drysink basin.

Ada buried her face in her hands and shook her head, then explained the encounter with the snake and her fear of returning to the porch.

Albert wrapped his arms around her and soothed, "Don't fret. I'll clean it up."

"Do you think the snake'll be back?" Ada asked, a worried expression on her face.

"Depends. If he liked your pie well enough, he might bring his friends," teased Albert.

Ada shuddered and buried her face in his chest.

* * * * *

Sometimes while Bill and Minola were visiting, Ada and Albert became playful, with Albert chasing Ada through the house. The two youngsters were puzzled by this curious behavior. When Albert pinned Ada against the wall outside their bedroom door, Bill jumped up and down, calling, "Chase me, Albert, chase me! Betcha can't catch me!"

Albert dug his hand into his pants pocket and retrieved a penny, which he flipped to Bill. "Here. You and Minola walk down to Zipfel's store and pick out some candy. And take your time."

Bill looked at the penny in awe, then at Minola. The two children sped out the door for the mile-long walk into town.

"The Honeymoon Cottage"
Ada, Minola, Flora, Bill, Margaret, Hermine, Helen & Emma Roth, & little Florence & Raymond Meyer

Albert enjoyed the children and indulged in some good-natured teasing at their expense. At the dinner table, he'd notice the absence of the butter dish and say to Minola, "Dick, go fetch the butter. Your legs are younger than mine."

On Sunday afternoons, Albert hitched his horse Lady to the buggy so he and Ada could return the children to the Seibel homestead. Bill, who was always hungry for male companionship, scrambled onto the buggy seat and watched as Albert draped the harness over Lady's back.

When Albert climbed onto the buggy seat next to Bill, he feigned surprise to find a young boy sitting there. "Oh shooks! Where'd you come from?" he asked Bill, his blue eyes twinkling.

Guileless Bill furrowed his brow and responded, "*You* know, Albert. Home! I come from home!"

"Well, how do you get to this place called home?" asked Albert, his slow smile spreading across his face.

"Why, Albert, you oughta know. Just follow the tracks," Bill said in disbelief as he pointed at the wagon ruts in the roadway that passed in front of the house.

* * * * *

Summer brought the endless round of farm chores—hoeing the corn, cutting the sorghum canes, picking berries and cherries, weeding the garden, and haying.

In addition, a new, speedier variety of bug had invaded the potato plants. It was no longer effective for the girls to practice insect eradication by attempting to knock the bugs into half-filled cans of kerosene. Papa bought several spray pumps, and the girls marched up and down the long rows of potato plants, squirting poison at the darting insects.

* * * * *

An older itinerant worker came to the farm when Papa was overloaded with field work, and so the man was given employment and a place to sleep in the barn. He had rosy cheeks—probably from his fondness for the cider jug—and a shock of white hair that stood up in wild spikes, making him look like he was either perpetually scared or had just run the race of his life. The Seibel siblings referred to him as Old Whitey. Although not the strongest or fastest worker, he did provide additional manpower, and the girls were pleased to be relieved of some of the more strenuous tasks about the farm.

During haying season, Old Whitey took over the job of forking the hay from the doorway to the back of the barn while Papa and the girls returned to the field for another wagonload. Minola and Bill took advantage of the growing mound of hay to reach the pigeon cotes high on the barn wall, where they inspected for signs of hatchlings.

Old Whitey leaned on his pitchfork and watched the two children, then called, "Hey, you youngens. You lookin' for birds?"

When the children nodded affirmatively, he motioned them to join him on the barn floor. By manipulating his hands and fingers in a shaft of sunlight, Old Whitey made shadows of a bird in flight, a goose, and a rooster appear on the wall of the darkened barn. The children were mesmerized by the show.

"Do some more!" shouted Bill.

Old Whitey complied by creating a goat, a rabbit, and an elephant. Then, his hand gestures changed, and Minola grew uneasy at the suggestive nature of the shadows he created.

"Bill," she said warily, "I don't think..."

"Show me how to do that!" Bill interrupted, and he stepped toward the old man, eager to learn the secrets of creating hand shadows.

Minola backed away, then turned and raced out the barn door.

Old Whitey grabbed Bill in a bear hug and showered him with kisses. For a moment, Bill was frozen by this unexpected turn of events. Terrified and repulsed by the old man's actions, Bill struggled until finally managing to free himself. He sped out of the barn.

That evening at the supper table, Bill related his experience with Old Whitey. As he told about the man kissing him, Bill made an exaggerated wiping motion across his face with the back of his arm, punctuated by a resounding "Yuck!" His blue eyes were wide for emphasis as he finished, "I was scairt, that's for sure."

Papa stopped chewing and listened in silence, his jaw muscles taut. He laid down his fork, rose suddenly from his chair, and strode purposefully toward the back door.

The next day when Papa and the girls resumed haying, Old Whitey was gone.

*****

The neighborhood threshermen came in late July, along with the mighty steam-driven threshing machine that spit out a stack of golden straw into the barnyard. Minola and Bill enjoyed searching for the end of the binder twine, which was the same color as the straw.

The cows were also drawn to the tall stack, and they rubbed against the straw, ridding themselves of pesky flies and wearing a groove around the stack until it resembled a mushroom. Eventually, the cows created a winding tunnel through the center of the mound. On more than one occasion, Minola and Bill made a hasty retreat from the tunnel when they came face-to-face with the hulking body of a cow.

Albert came to assist Papa and the other threshermen in the field, while Ada tied on an apron and helped her sisters prepare a hearty noontime meal for the hungry workers. Platters of meat, bowls of gravy and fried potatoes, green beans fried in bacon grease, sauerkraut, tomato slices, spears of dill pickles, thick slabs of fresh-baked bread spread with butter, and sweating pitchers of cold well water were placed on a long table in the summer kitchen.

After the last slice of blackberry pie had been served and the dishes washed and put away, the girls swept up the old straw that had provided a measure of padding under the living room carpet. They carried the carpet outside and hung it on the clothesline, where Minola and Bill were tasked with beating the dust from it while their sisters carried armloads of fresh straw inside to scatter about on the living room floor.

After the carpet had been replaced over its fluffy new padding, the girls dragged the bed ticks outside and emptied them in the chicken yard, then overfilled them with fresh, clean straw. That night when they went to bed, it seemed as though they could touch the ceiling.

* * * * *

Since Ella's return from caring for Grandpa Gasteier and Uncle Will, she had been cleaning houses, including the parsonage occupied by Rev. Keppel and his family. The minister recognized that the bright, capable mind of his young housekeeper was not being adequately challenged. He suggested that Ella consider enrolling in the all-female Schauffler Missionary Training School in Cleveland.

A three-year course of study would qualify her for work as a missionary or a pastor's secretary, whose duties would include canvassing for new members, outreach to the poor and downtrodden, Bible instruction for the younger members, home visitations, committee work, and a variety of other church responsibilities. Reverend Keppel painted a glowing picture of life in the service of the Lord.

Ella mulled the possibility for several months. She and Flora were an efficient team when it came to handling the household tasks, and the children had become more helpful as they'd grown older. Like Ada, she wrestled with the desire for her own fulfillment versus the sense of obligation to her siblings.

That summer, Miss Hobart from the Schauffler Missionary Training School paid a visit to the Seibel homestead. She enthusiastically recruited Ella, handing her a leaflet written by a recent graduate. It was entitled "A Tribute to Schauffler" and described the homelike atmosphere of the school, the congeniality of the other students, the stimulating classwork, and the rewarding purpose of their education.

While this was all very appealing, Ella knew that Papa could not pay for education beyond high school, so the Schauffler opportunity seemed unobtainable. However, Miss Hobart overcame this barrier by announcing that students were financially responsible for only one-half of their expenses; scholarships covered the remaining half.

Ella reasoned that through careful management of her funds—the money she had saved from cleaning houses and the salary Grandpa Gasteier had paid for her years of housekeeping—she could afford to enroll at Schauffler.

When Miss Hobart left the Seibel home that day, twenty-three-year-old Ella's name was on the roster of incoming students for the fall term.

*****

By summer's end, Papa had taught Flora the intricacies of driving the Fuller, and the sisters and Bill piled into the machine for Sunday afternoon visits at Ada and Albert's. There, they made molasses taffy, listened to the phonograph, and sang and laughed. It felt good to be uninhibited by Mama's affliction.

Minola, a friend, Hermine, Margaret, Flora, & Bill in the Fuller

*****

In the fall, Papa drove Ella and her small trunk of clothing to the B&O station in Monroeville. He uttered some cautionary advice about life in the big city of Cleveland. Ella nodded her understanding and bravely took her seat upon the eastbound train.

Papa stuffed his hands in his pockets and watched as the train departed, wistfully recalling the railbound adventures of his own youth.

Ella

*****

In the absence of her two older sisters, Flora added the mantle of chief housekeeper and surrogate mother to her role as Papa's "right-hand man." She also assumed the oversight of Mama, whose mind had grown cloudier from repeated spells and seizures. At times, Mama bustled about the kitchen, preparing one meal after another—a mission from which she could not be deterred. When the rag man came to collect old newspapers and worn-out clothing, Mama attempted to give away items they were still using or wearing. One afternoon, Flora returned to the house from gathering eggs just in time to intercept a stack of quilt blocks that Mama was handing over.

*****

The return to school brought continued struggles for Minola in the mathematics realm. Night after night, Margaret sat with her, drilling her on multiplication and division tables and providing practice problems. Because Margaret's instruction at the Plank Road school had included a different method of solving the problems than was accepted at the central school, Minola became all the more confused. In her frustration, she resorted to drawing pictures while Margaret tried patiently to keep Minola academically afloat.

Hermine and Margaret were enjoying their high school experiences, especially participation in a girls' basketball league. However, following the sinking of the *Lusitania* and President Wilson's warning to Germany, the local German community found themselves the object of suspicion. These prejudices spilled over into the school population, with a superior attitude assumed by the students who resided in "New England," an English community along Plank Road on the western edge of Monroeville. There were taunts of "Damn Dutchie" and "Hey, Heinie" directed at the students of German ancestry. The Seibel siblings met the hostility with stoic resolve.

Hermine & Margaret's classes at Monroeville High School

* * * * *

Letters from Ella arrived frequently, filled with details about her busy schedule at Schauffler Missionary Training School. Classwork included Bible study, missions, church history, stenography, vocal and drawing lessons, musical sight reading, language and literature, the practical arts (hygiene, nursing, and sewing), and gymnasium. The domestic arts course would culminate with each girl being allotted $4.50 to serve a four-course meal to eight guests. The students shared the chores of cooking, ironing, and housekeeping—tasks for which Ella needed no training. She attended lectures, including one by William Jennings Bryan, and helped out at the Saturday afternoon Mizpah sewing school for young girls, which excused her from missionary visitation one day a week. Ella was invigorated by the stimulation and challenges of her new life at Schauffler, and she was surrounded by female companionship—from across the nation as well as abroad—which eased the separation from her sisters.

Ella (seated in rocking chair at far right) with other students at the Schauffler Missionary Training School in Cleveland

At Thanksgiving time, Ella invited her schoolmate, Emma Macha, to come home with her for a short stay. Ella felt it necessary to forewarn her friend about Mama's unpredictable behavior. Emma reassured Ella that nothing would strike her as bizarre after some of the strange things they had witnessed during their required calls upon the unfortunates in Cleveland institutions. Nonetheless, Ella was apprehensive about bringing home a guest.

Mama was in high spirits during Emma's visit, since she was always pleased to have company. She made only one inappropriate comment, asking if Schauffler was a home for old maids. Ella turned crimson, but Emma graciously smiled and shook her head.

As the two girls rode the interurban back to Cleveland, Emma commented, "Your mother seemed normal enough."

"She can give that impression ... sometimes," sighed Ella.

Emma Macha & Ella
at the Seibel homestead

Chapter 19
Rural Bellevue, Ohio
1916

AFTER A YEAR of working the farm at the honeymoon cottage, Albert learned of a tenant farm with more acreage at the north end of Sand Hill Road, midway between Monroeville and Bellevue. He worked out an agreement with the spinster Yingling sisters who owned the farm, and the young couple moved from the honeymoon cottage into the tenant house in early March.

The frame structure was a typical tenant's house, with a kitchen, pantry, living room, and bedroom downstairs and two bedrooms upstairs. It was in need of paint and repairs, but the Yingling sisters were not interested in investing money in the upkeep of a tenant house. Albert turned his hammer and a bag of penny nails to good use, repairing sagging porch steps, fence rails, and barn siding. He climbed the tall windmill to grease the squeaking gears of the rotor, replaced the rope on the stationary pulley in the barn, and readied a plot of ground for a garden.

The tenant house on Sand Hill Road

Ada immediately set about making the house a home. She sewed curtains out of grain sacks for the kitchen and downstairs bedroom and attractively arranged their sparse furniture in the living room. She was pleased by the long, narrow pantry with cupboards lining both walls, where she carefully placed her canning jars of pickles, jams, jellies, fruits, vegetables, and meats. Ada set a crate of seed potatoes in the pantry window to warm and situated the crock of sauerkraut on the top cellar step, where it would keep cool but be within easy reach. The perishable eggs, milk, butter, and *Hüttenkäse* (cottage cheese) were set on a shelf in the well. With her little teakettle whistling happily on the cookstove, Ada settled into her new home with pleasant thoughts about this chapter in their young lives.

Because of the increased acreage, Albert needed help with the farming. His younger bachelor brother, Alfred, came to live with the couple and farm alongside Albert, receiving a small weekly salary, all of his meals, and a bedroom at the top of the stairs. The neighbors called Alfred "Jack," Albert called him "Eee," and, in time, he would be known simply as "Unk." Alfred liked his hard cider, but Ada, following in the footsteps of her father, had no tolerance for drinking. A compromise was reached whereby Alfred always had a jug on the premises, but it remained out of the house.

Ada and Albert's new neighborhood was composed of original-settler Yankee families with commodious homes and slightly patrician attitudes. Interspersed among them were tenant farmers, mostly of German heritage. Ada felt herself to be a step better than the typical tenant farmer's wife but yet not good enough to rub shoulders with the long-established families of English heritage. Despite this curious mixture of pride and insecurity, she and Albert were welcomed into the community and regarded with esteem for their hard work and honesty.

Often, some of the neighbor men dropped by to trade seeds with Albert, propose an exchange of breeding stock, or discuss the weather and farm prices. They stood about the windmill, passing around a cup of cold well water along with the neighborhood news. During such times, Ada tiptoed from the kitchen into the bedroom, quietly laid upon the bed, and listened to their conversations through the open window. It satisfied her need for inclusion without embarrassing Albert by intruding upon what was clearly meant to be an all-male gathering.

For Minola and Bill, Ada and Albert's move from the honeymoon cottage meant less access to Ada. Instead of walking to her house after school on Friday afternoons and spending the weekend, they had to wait impatiently for Sunday afternoons, when Ada and Albert came home for a visit or the Seibel family paid a call on the young couple. The children missed the frequency of their liberating interludes at the honeymoon cottage and Ada's special mothering.

Ada enjoying a cup of water at the windmill

* * * * *

Minola's social struggles at school continued that spring. The fifth-grade girls with established circles of friends reigned mercilessly over the less fortunate ones. Each week, the ringleader singled out one girl to be ostracized, with the caste system increasingly structured by the general anti-German sentiment resulting from the military tensions in Europe. One day during Minola's turn as the outcast, she was shocked to discover she was out of paper just as the teacher began dictating their spelling test words. Esme Strohmeier, who had previously felt the sting of exclusion, noticed Minola's panic and sympathetically slipped her a piece of paper from across the aisle.

Minola learned that to fit in, one went along. On a warm spring day, the ringleader announced that they would cross the street at recess to visit in the home of Josephine Rohr, a classmate whose family was well known for its lack of hygiene. Minola tagged along with the group, despite her misgivings about stepping inside a home that was decidedly unclean.

On the second story of the school building, Hermine, Margaret, Martha, and some of their high school classmates chattered happily as they leaned out the open window during a break between classes. They enjoyed sampling the mild weather and surveying the traffic in the street below. The three sisters spotted Minola trailing behind a group of classmates crossing the street. They watched in horror as she entered the Rohr house.

Classes at Monroeville High School—Margaret & Hermine in upper row; Martha in second row from bottom

That evening, Martha admonished Minola for participating in the impromptu visitation. "You don't know what sorts of filth you could carry home from a place like that!"

Minola hung her head in shame. She lacked the words to describe the conflict of conscience versus social pressure, so she said nothing.

Several weeks later, Flora, Hermine, Margaret, and Martha found themselves beset with intensely itchy scalps. Upon close inspection, an infestation of head lice was confirmed. The girls' highly respectable sensibilities were outraged.

"How can this be happening to *us*? We're clean people! We bathe and wash our heads every Saturday night!" protested Margaret.

"Maybe it was something Bill dragged in on that baby possum he was carrying around," mused Martha. "Thank goodness he finally figured out an animal that plays dead don't make a good pet."

"Naw, it wasn't the possum," assured Hermine. "That thing woulda passed along fleas, not lice. It had to be a disgusting, filthy person that got near one of us."

Minola listened to her sisters' anguished conversation as she worked on a drawing project at the kitchen table.

"C'mere, Minola. Let's have a look at you, too," beckoned Flora as Hermine filled the copper boiler with water to heat for a hasty shampoo. Margaret scurried to the summer kitchen to retrieve a bar of lye soap.

Minola haughtily refused. "I can't have lice. I don't go near *those* kind of people."

Martha cocked her hands on her hips and snapped, "Don't you get it, Minola? We're '*those* kind of people' now!" Then her eyes widened in sudden recollection. "Wait a minute. You went over to those filthy Rohrs' house one day. We saw you from the school window. So, it was you! You brought this … this … pestilence into our house!" Martha pointed an accusatory finger at her younger sister.

Minola lowered her eyes and returned to her drawing. "I don't have lice," she asserted, scratching her scalp. A louse dropped from her head and scampered across the paper, belying her protests. Minola laid down her pencil and rose from the table. She crossed the room and humbly allowed Flora to examine her head near the sunny kitchen window.

"You're loaded with 'em," announced Flora. "Line up for a head washin'. You're not gettin' left out of *this* party."

Flora's deft fingers worked the lather from the lye soap into each of her sisters' long hair. Bill, squirming and protesting that it wasn't Saturday night, was wrangled to the drysink for his turn at sanitation. Flora finished up by scrubbing her own head.

Despite repeated shampoos and boiling of the bed linens, the girls and Bill continued to battle head lice. Finally, Papa drove into town and purchased some pure alcohol from one of Monroeville's many saloons. The lice were no match for the strength of that remedy. The girls followed up the alcohol dose with a vinegar rinse and allowed their hair to dry outdoors.

One day shortly after the lice had been vanquished, Marjorie Lowell insisted on combing Minola's hair at school. Minola resisted, knowing that some dead nits still clung to her hair. Marjorie lived in "New England" and was therefore at the top of the social strata. If Marjorie saw the nits and announced their presence to her schoolmates, Minola knew she would be doomed as the class pariah. Minola swallowed hard and quietly confessed to Marjorie about her recent infestation with head lice. Marjorie picked up the comb, began styling Minola's hair, and acknowledged that she too had recently suffered through the same affliction. It was a relief for Minola to discover that the two social circles were united through the common bond of head lice.

Margaret drying her naturally curly hair

* * * * *

Late May brought a bargain between Hermine and Flora: Hermine would take Flora's place in the strawberry fields so that Flora could spend time at the old treadle sewing machine making a dress for Hermine to wear at her high school graduation. On the night of the ceremony, Hermine clutched the diploma to her chest, filled with pride at her accomplishment and at the beautiful emerald green dress that Flora had finished hemming that very afternoon. To celebrate the first high school graduate in the Seibel family, Flora baked a fluffy angel food cake and topped it with a ruby-red sauce made from some of the culled strawberries.

Hermine

Hermine spent the summer laboring beside her sisters on the farm and pondering her future. Ella, who was home for the summer, bubbled over with enthusiasm about her first-year experiences at Schauffler Missionary Training School, which fueled Hermine's desire to continue her own education. A teacher had encouraged her to enroll in the fifteen-month secretarial course offered at the Oberlin Business College. However, without financial backing or a nest egg set aside, like Ella had, her options seemed limited.

But there was not much time to think of the future when so much work was demanded in the present. The strawberries flourished that summer, producing a bumper crop that kept the Seibels busy picking, packing, and selling the perishable fruit. Groups of strawberry pickers walked or biked out from town, with a few hitching rides on passing machines, and they joined the girls and Bill in the fields. Early in the season, the berries were large and plentiful, baskets filled quickly, and the pickers were orderly and accepted authority. However, as the season waned and the berries grew smaller, discontent often spread through the berry patch.

One morning as the crew crawled down the long rows of the waning field, a teenaged picker named Joe Kessel stood up, stretched his back, and glumly assessed the number of filled quarts in his berry carrier. The work had been slow, hot, and tedious, and Joe didn't feel that the fruits of his labor ranked in proportion to his effort or discomfort. By working in the strawberry fields this summer, he intended to earn enough money to purchase a dandy supply of fireworks for the Fourth of July, treat himself to a trip to Cedar Point, and apply the rest toward a shotgun he'd been eyeing at Zipfel's store. Earlier in the season, he had filled the baskets with ease—sometimes one hundred quarts a day—and rapidly earned tickets toward his goal. However, his progress now was hindered by the amount of time it took to fill the quart baskets with the smaller berries from the waning field. Fewer quarts meant fewer tickets earned for the Saturday payout. As Joe kneaded the knot in his back, he reasoned that the increased difficulty of picking a diminishing crop should be rewarded with a raise of a half-cent or a full cent per quart.

Joe scanned the field for Papa, who had driven the machine, loaded with crates of berries, to the railroad station at Chicago Junction. Noting that Flora, the authority in Papa's absence, was occupied in the packing house at the far end of the field, Joe began speaking loudly about his dissatisfaction and the need for a raise. He suggested the crew stage a sit-down strike until their demands were met. Some of the nearby pickers sat back on their heels, listened to Joe's rant for a few minutes, then returned to their work. Others, particularly the younger members, were easily persuaded by Joe's argument. Soon, the rows were filled with disgruntled pickers sitting cross legged on the straw, their arms folded in defiance across their chests.

The girls and Bill looked around uncomfortably but continued to pick. Martha scampered down her row to the packing house and alerted Flora to the strike. "What are we gonna do?" she asked, a worried expression on her face.

Flora chewed her lower lip and responded, "Wait for Papa, I guess. It's all we can do."

When Papa returned, he unloaded the empty shipping crates at the packing house while listening to Flora's concern about the strike in progress and Joe's demand for more money. Papa asked her to point out the strike leader and then strode purposefully down the long row, taking Joe by the elbow and pulling him to his feet.

Papa hastened Joe to the far end of the field, out of hearing range of the other workers. The girls continued to pick berries but stole occasional glances from under the wide brims of their straw hats as Papa repeatedly jabbed the stubbed index finger of his right hand at Joe's chest. They knew Papa's impatience with waste and lost time, and they cringed at the stuttered blasting he was undoubtedly delivering. Joe, however, stood with his hands on his hips and seemed unphased by the older man's outrage.

Papa had few bargaining chips. The abundance of the crop was more than he and his offspring could handle on their own. In addition, there was the haying, livestock, and other farm chores that demanded their attention. He needed the combined efforts of a large workforce to harvest the highly perishable fruit. In the end, the pickers received a raise of a half-cent per quart. Papa reasoned it was better to lose a portion of his profits than a large part of the harvest.

Margaret packing quarts of strawberries into a shipping crate

As the strawberry harvest diminished, the sour cherry crop ripened. Papa hitched Dolly and Nellie to the wagon, which carried a barrel of Paris Green fruit spray, and Flora slowly guided the team of horses along the row of cherry trees. Bill vigorously worked the pump on top of the barrel to maintain pressure to an extended sprayer that Papa waved back and forth over the ripening cherries.

By the Fourth of July, some of the youth who had picked strawberries on the farm were jubilantly spending their earnings on firecrackers, while the Seibels harvested yet another bright red fruit.

Spraying the sour cherries

Picking cherries

*****

Albert proudly surveyed his first crop of wheat on the new tenant farm. It had been an excellent growing season, and the wheat markets were good. He contracted with Papa's second-cousins, "Hoopey" and "Spider" Seibel, to provide their steam-powered threshing machine on harvest day as well as some additional manpower. Ella, Flora, and Hermine arrived to help Ada prepare the threshermen's dinner, while Minola and Bill tagged along to be part of the excitement. Margaret and Martha stayed home to keep an eye on Mama.

Papa joined Albert, Alfred, Hoopey, Spider, and several neighborhood men in the fields, feeling invigorated by the steady chuffing of the steam engine, the cascade of wheat kernels into the grain sacks, and the clean smell of the golden straw as it spewed from the thresher's chute. The work brought back many memories of harvesting wheat during his days on the Mississippi River. Papa was filled with a sense of nostalgia as well as an appreciation for the rugged physical demands of threshing, which he was still able to meet at age fifty-five.

At noon, Ada and her sisters placed a lavish spread before the hungry threshermen, who were seated at an extended table in the living room. They hungrily forked in tender roast beef, mashed potatoes and gravy, buttered lima beans, sauerkraut, sliced cucumbers and onions swimming in a cream-vinegar mixture, yeast rolls, and cinnamon-sprinkled applesauce, followed by generous wedges of elderberry pie. Between mouthfuls of food, the men teasingly referred to Albert as the "Millionaire Farmer" due to his excellent wheat crop and bountiful dinner fare.

"Oh pshaw," Albert responded, unable to hide the pleased smile that spread across his face.

Minola and Bill insisted on being seated at the dinner table with the men, partly because it meant they didn't have to wait to have their meal, like their older sisters in the kitchen, and partly because of the exciting unpredictability of Hoopey and Spider. Ada had warned the two youngsters that Papa's cousins were "rough as cobs" and not to be imitated, which only increased the children's interest in these seldom-seen relatives.

Hoopey and Spider did not disappoint. Their speech was liberally sprinkled with swear words—even a request to pass the butter was pockmarked with profanity. They teased and jabbed each other throughout the meal, constantly one-upping the other with boasts of strength and power. At one point, Spider pumped his fist twice in the air—like a locomotive engineer pulling the whistle—and belched loudly each time. Hoopey blew his nose on the edge of Ada's white linen tablecloth. Minola and Bill were thoroughly fascinated.

When the meal ended, Hoopey and Spider's boasts of physical superiority escalated into an arm-wrestling match. The other men sat back and watched, amused by the impromptu after-dinner entertainment. They laughed and hooted as the contest swayed first in favor of Hoopey and then Spider. Minola and Bill sat transfixed in wide-eyed wonderment. Ada entered from the kitchen and gave a small gasp as she saw the table tremble under the exertion of the two red-faced brothers. She scurried to retrieve her good ironstone dishes from the path of slamming fists. Albert noticed Ada's distress and suggested it was time for the threshers to get back to work.

Minola and Bill trailed the men outdoors, watching in awe as Hoopey and Spider continued to tussle, jab, and swear across the farmyard toward the fields. The youngsters had never witnessed such raw strength, crude manners, and blatant profanity. How fortunate they felt to claim these two ruffians as relatives!

* * * * *

To celebrate his excellent wheat harvest, Albert purchased a John Deere walk-behind plow for twenty-two dollars from Bessel Hardware in Monroeville. It seemed only fitting that Ada, too, should share in the bounty of their good fortune, and so he surprised her with a wringer washing machine.

Papa was also feeling benevolent. With the money from the sale of the strawberries the girls had gleaned from the fields after the pickers were gone, he bought something special—a used Kodak camera with a brown leather case. He cautioned the girls against being wasteful with the film and warned Bill not to tinker with the intricate mechanisms.

The siblings were delighted with this new acquisition, and they invited Edith Moss and Elsie Ordmann to join them for a Sunday afternoon of lemonade, cookies, and picture taking. Edith's sniff that the camera was an older model could not dampen the girls' enthusiasm. Each took a turn arranging their subject matter, holding the device at waist level, and adjusting the camera until the image lined up perfectly in the view finder. The camera could only be used outdoors, but this was a minor inconvenience. At last, the girls could document the important things in their lives.

Taking pictures with the new camera: Margaret, Martha, Elsie Ordmann, & Minola

Papa also purchased buckets of white paint. The girls, always sensitive to appearances, had expressed dismay with the weather-beaten condition of the house. They agreed that if Papa provided the paint, they would provide the labor. For several long weeks, the girls picked blackberries in the morning and took turns painting the house in the afternoon. Bill begged to paint something besides the low clapboards, but it was deemed too dangerous for an eight-year-old to balance on the boards that provided footing on the steep porch roof or to dangle precariously from the top of a ladder while reaching for a distant corner. Instead, he amused himself by writing messages in white paint on the lower clapboards—"Flora I'm hungry" and "Minola stole MY stick of gum." Satisfied with his self-expression, he covered over the graffiti with long brush strokes.

Painting the house

Not all of Papa's purchases that summer were of a frivolous nature. He bought a black horse named Jetty to pull the wagon when the machine was put up for the winter. Nellie and Dolly, the workhorses that had replaced Jib and Davey, were excellent in the field but lacked the temperament for being on the road.

The girls soon spoiled Jetty with twists of sweet clover and offerings of green apples. They rode him around the yard and brushed his sleek coat until it gleamed.

Martha on Jetty

* * * * *

In early August, there was great excitement in Monroeville. A traveling Chautauqua had arrived and set up a large tent in the schoolyard, offering five days of entertainment. There would be educational lectures about health, science, and the humanities along with political oratory, opera singers, and Shakespearean stage performances.

The Seibel girls longed to attend every day, since opportunities for entertainment and intellectual advancement were infrequent. In addition, former President Teddy Roosevelt had declared a Chautauqua "the most American thing in America." The girls knew all too well the social importance of confirming themselves as Americans, not imperialist Germans, during this time of international military tensions. However, berry picking, house painting, and other farm chores kept them at home until Sunday, when Papa said the family could attend the Chautauqua after church.

On Sunday morning, Ella tucked cold ham sandwiches, a quart jar of dill pickle spears, a crock of hard-boiled eggs, and a pan of cinnamon buns into a hamper. Flora added bottles of a new beverage she had concocted—homemade root beer that had been fermenting in the cellar. The family sat impatiently through church, trying their best to pay attention to Rev. Keppel's sermon and not grimace when Emmaline Moss warbled an off-key solo in her reedy falsetto.

After church, they hastened down the street and into the large tent pitched in the schoolyard. The girls and Mama found seats together, while Bill palled around with some of his school chums. Papa stood with the other men near the open tent flap. A hush fell over the crowd as a raven-haired singer took the stage. Soon her beautiful soprano aria filled the tent. Some members of the audience were so moved by the outstanding quality of the performance that they dabbed their eyes with hankies or clasped their hands to their bosoms. Emmaline Moss considered herself a bona-fide member of the soprano sisterhood, so her facial expression was one of superiority by association, which caused the girls to nudge each other and roll their eyes. Papa, who was never known to whistle, hum, or exhibit any musical interest, cocked his head to one side in rapt appreciation of the singer's talent.

Following the performance, the girls spread a blanket under a tree in the corner of the schoolyard, and the family enjoyed their picnic lunch. After eating, Bill sped off to reunite with his pals. Fueled by the carbonation of a half-bottle of Flora's root beer, he entertained his buddies with the belching trick he had learned from Spider at the threshermen's table. The girls strolled about the grounds, arm-in-arm with some of their friends, until the next performance, which was a dramatic reading of Shakespearean selections.

The day was thoroughly enjoyable and long remembered by the Seibel siblings. During weary afternoons of house painting, the girls chattered about the entertainment. At one point, Margaret climbed to the top of the ladder, threw open her arms, and performed her best imitation of the soprano. She was interrupted by the jangling of the telephone on the living room wall.

Martha grinned up at Margaret and said, "Better get that, *Emmaline.* It's the New York Metropolitan Opera calling for you!"

The girls dissolved in laughter as Flora hurried to answer the phone.

*****

Ella's preparations for her return to the Schauffler Missionary Training School in the fall rekindled Hermine's desire for further education. She bemoaned her lack of funds and resigned herself to a life of farm chores. However, before departing for Cleveland, Ella offered a ray of hope. She suggested Hermine approach Grandpa Gasteier about a loan.

Hermine's spirits were lifted, and she spent the fall working out the terms of a loan from Grandpa Gasteier and gaining admission to the secretarial course at Oberlin Business College, about thirty miles east of Monroeville. The school term would begin in January, and Hermine was filled with a mixture of anticipation and anxiety over the prospects of moving away from home, meeting the demands of college courses, and taking on a debt. But, the thought of turning back never crossed her mind.

*****

The change of seasons brought storms that littered the yard with sticks and downed branches, violating Mama's demand for *ordentlich und sauber* (neat and tidy). Despite the steady rains, Mama prowled the yard, picking up sticks and creating one large, neat pile to be burned at a later date. She chattered incessantly as she carried out her single-minded mission. The girls watched from the kitchen windows, wondering how they could be afflicted with colds, coughs, and sneezes, but Mama always exhibited rugged good health despite the rainwater squishing from her shoes and the lack of a head covering.

Flora harvested her small patch of pumpkins and canned the pulp for pie filling. She used the pumpkin seeds to make a tea, which she had read was a remedy for convulsions. She coaxed Mama to drink numerous cups, but there was no abatement of Mama's spells or improvement in the quality of her existence. Flora vacillated between exasperation and motherly concern for one so frustrating and yet so hopelessly adrift.

*****

Before Papa put the machine into winter storage, Flora drove into Monroeville to buy some fabric. When Hermine went away to college, she would not have ready access to her sisters' wardrobes, so Flora was prevailed upon to create several dresses that Hermine could rotate throughout the weeks before sending home a trunk of clothing to be laundered.

As Flora walked along the street toward Zipfel's store, she heard a familiar voice call out "There goes my girl!" She looked around and then tilted her head up. Strapped at the top of a telephone pole was Phil Burrer, who had picked berries for many summers on the Seibel farm. He flashed Flora his disarming grin and waved as he made repairs to the phone line.

Flora's heart fluttered in her chest and her cheeks flushed crimson. She returned a shy smile and demure wave and continued on toward Zipfel's store. Selecting the fabrics took more concentration than Flora could muster. When Mr. Zipfel totaled up her purchases, she fumbled to count out the money. Phil's words continued to tumble through her head as she drove the machine toward home. "My girl" … "My girl" … "There goes my girl!"

Chapter 20
The Seibel Homestead
1917

FOLLOWING THE NEW YEAR, Papa loaded the trunks belonging to Ella and Hermine into the back of the spring wagon and drove the two girls to the interurban station in Monroeville. The sisters traveled together as far as Oberlin, where Hermine bid Ella a misty-eyed farewell and exited the car to begin her studies at the Oberlin Business College. Ella pressed her face close to the frosty window pane and waved goodbye as the interurban pulled out of the station toward Cleveland and her return to the Schauffler Missionary Training School. Hermine watched the car rumble eastward, fighting a panicky urge to run after it and cling to the security of Ella.

Hermine

She stood alone on the station platform, clutching a valise that contained a loaf of Flora's freshly baked bread, a jar of strawberry preserves, a sheaf of stationery, and a traveling plate, cup, and cutlery that the girls had given her for her nineteenth birthday in October. Tucked into the deepest corner of the valise was a small purse of cash loaned to her by Grandpa Gasteier. She watched as people bustled past, greeting new arrivals, carrying on conversations, and displaying a familiarity with travel procedures that made Hermine feel like a foreigner. She remembered Papa's advice to locate a drayman to transport her and her trunk to the boarding house where she had secured a room. Swallowing hard, Hermine approached a burly middle-aged man leaning against a low wagon displaying the sign "Leiman Drayage." She timidly asked his price.

"Depends," the man replied around the stub of an unlit cigar. "Where you goin'?"

Hermine fumbled in her coat pocket for the slip of paper with the address of Mrs. Parrish's boarding house.

"30 Groveland Street," Hermine read aloud. "Do you know it?"

"It's my business to know *every* street in this town, little missy," Mr. Leiman assured, the corners of his eyes crinkling as he studied Hermine's anxious face. "I'll take you there for a quarter … and a smile."

Hermine gave the man a puzzled look, wondering if smiles were the typical currency for all business transactions. She guessed it was something she would learn about in her secretarial courses.

Mr. Leiman hefted Hermine's trunk onto the back of his dray as she fished a quarter from the purse at the bottom of her valise. When she extended the payment toward the drayman, he shook his head and waved his hands in front of him. "Where you come from, little missy? Didn't nobody ever tell you? Don't pay till services've been rendered."

Hermine blushed and felt every inch the country rube. She nodded her understanding and slipped the money into her coat pocket.

Mr. Leiman drove the dray through town, pointing out various college buildings, the massive Memorial Arch, and snow-covered Tappan Square. Two blocks south of the square, he turned onto Groveland Street and reined the horse to a stop in front of the narrow boarding house.

Mrs. Parrish greeted Hermine and the drayman at the door and led them upstairs to a room at the end of the hallway. Mr. Leiman lifted Hermine's trunk from his shoulder and set it on the floor at the foot of the bed. He pulled the cigar stub from his mouth, leaned toward Hermine, and whispered behind his hand, "Now's when you pay me that quarter and a smile, little missy."

A sheepish grin crossed Hermine's face, and she dropped the quarter into the drayman's outstretched mitt.

"Paid in full. Much obliged." Mr. Leiman winked at Hermine,

shoved the cigar stub into the corner of his mouth, and lumbered down the hall.

Mrs. Parish shifted a suspicious gaze between Hermine and the retreating form of the drayman. "I'd best be upfront about my rules," she sniffed. "I don't allow male callers, except on Sunday afternoons. Visits are confined to the parlor, with Mr. Parrish and myself in attendance." Shaking a finger at Hermine, she added, "I'll not have tongues wagging about improprieties under *my* roof!"

Hermine's mouth fell open, but she was too taken aback to sputter a protest against Mrs. Parrish's assumption of a budding relationship between her and the much-older drayman. The landlady didn't wait for a response but rattled off an extensive list of rules and expectations. In return for a reduced room-and-board rate, Hermine would perform household chores, including food preparation for the evening meal, washing dishes, and dusting and sweeping the entire house each Saturday. Hermine sensed that Mrs. Parrish would be a hard woman to please, but she was not overly concerned with meeting high standards. When it came to housekeeping, Hermine had been schooled by the toughest taskmaster of all—Mama.

Mrs. Parrish finished with an accounting of when meals were served and rent was due, then bustled out of the room and down the hallway. Hermine quietly closed the door and looked about her room. It was small but sufficient, with a single bed and nightstand, a highboy dresser, a table and chair, and a row of pegs along one wall for hanging her clothes. She opened the trunk lid and removed the garments that Flora had sewn for her. Holding one of the shirtwaists to her face, Hermine inhaled the familiar scent of lye soap and home before folding the shirtwaists and camisoles into the highboy and hanging the skirts and dresses on the wall pegs. She tucked the small purse of cash into the dresser drawer beneath her undergarments, reasoning that no thief would be so bold as to rifle through her dainties in search of valuables.

The view from the room's single window was of the clapboards and downspout on the neighboring house. Hermine thought wistfully of the view from the bedroom windows back home, which had been unobstructed except for the boughs of the mulberry trees. Using the travel dinnerware, she cut a slice of bread and topped it with strawberry preserves, then perched on the edge of the bed as she nibbled her sandwich. The peony-patterned wallpaper reminded Hermine of the fragrant peony bush that bloomed each spring beside the front porch steps back home. A wave of homesickness washed over her, and a lump formed in her throat, making it hard to swallow the jam and bread.

Once school commenced, there was little time for thoughts of home. Hermine's classes included penmanship, shorthand, filing, spelling, and grammar. In typing class, she learned how to center the paper in the rollers and set the margins, as well as how to clean and oil the typewriter. There were timed tests for speed and accuracy, and Hermine frequently stayed after class to practice her typing skills, then raced to the boarding house to complete her chores for the demanding Mrs. Parrish.

The secretarial students were expected to take pride in their work, and consequently, nothing short of perfection was acceptable. On Sundays, Hermine wrote long letters home expressing anxiety about meeting the expectations of the secretarial school as well as those of Mrs. Parrish. She agonized over unexpected expenses and the prospects of repaying her loan. Hermine's misgivings were palpable through the thin blue stationery.

The Seibel girls sent encouraging letters but finally decided that Hermine was in need of a visit from one of her sisters. They agreed that Margaret's outgoing personality and nurturing disposition were just the balm that Hermine needed, and so Margaret boarded the interurban to Oberlin one weekend in early March. She was met at the station by Hermine, who hugged and kissed her sister as though they had been separated for two years instead of two months.

The girls linked arms and walked about the campus, with Hermine pointing out the buildings where she took classes, the Memorial Arch, and Tappan Square, just as Mr. Leiman had done upon her January arrival in town. They stepped into a lunch counter just off the square to warm up and share a cup of hot chocolate.

At the boarding house, Margaret assisted Hermine with her kitchen chores before the two retreated to Hermine's room, where they giggled over imitations of the dour Mrs. Parrish. At night, they shared the narrow single bed and chatted until sleep overcame them.

Margaret encouraged her sister to continue as the Seibel siblings' role model in pursuing higher education. She confided her own desire to follow Hermine's lead and obtain nurse's training after graduating from high school.

For Hermine, the weekend was therapeutic, and she returned to her schoolwork and household chores with renewed confidence.

Margaret in front of the Memorial Arch during a visit to Oberlin

*****

In April, the United States declared war on Germany. The barely concealed anti-German sentiment in the community became more blatant. Those citizens who clung to the customs of their mütterland were viewed as Teutonic spies. Sauerkraut was promptly renamed "Liberty cabbage" and frankfurters became "hot dogs." At Monroeville High School, the German language class was immediately disbanded, with the female students set to work rolling bandages for the American Red Cross, while the male students drilled in military training.

Patriotism ran high, and many of the young German men were eager to prove their allegiance by flocking to the recruitment stations and enlisting as Doughboys in the "War to End All Wars." Frequent public rallies were held, featuring a rag-tag parade of the recent enlistees followed by a contingent of young women and school children, who linked arms and sang the popular tune, "Tramp, Tramp, Tramp, The Boys Are Marching."

Monroeville was plastered with posters encouraging the purchase of Liberty bonds to fund the war effort. Some bore ominous images, such as the blood-red handprint of the enemy. Others were more subtle, such as the poster of a woman dressed in white, lifting her hand skyward in a pose reminiscent of the Statue of Liberty. Below her was the simple message: "Victory—Liberty Loan." On the door of his store, Mr. Zipfel tacked "The American's Creed" poster, which ended with the declaration: "I believe it is my duty to go to my limit and invest all my surplus in 'Victory' Liberty bonds." No matter the design of the posters, all implied that if a citizen had the money to buy bonds and did not, he was a traitor. Papa participated in the bond drive to the extent his finances permitted, but inwardly he regarded the military efforts as a rich man's war. He was sure there were those who would profit from the war machine, but it would not be the farmer.

That spring, Emmaline Moss hosted a weekday afternoon gathering of the neighborhood women to knit scarves and socks for the valiant soldiers "over there." Mama and Flora were invited, as were Bertha and Rosie Seibel, Dorothea Grau, Mrs. Ordmann, Mrs. Knopf, and several other women from the community. The ladies sat in a circle in Emmaline's well-appointed parlor, knitting, gossiping, and sharing tips about "Hooverizing," the war-induced food-conservation movement named after Herbert Hoover, the chairman of the National Food Administration.

Emmaline announced that in her patriotic efforts to conserve sugar and wheat, she would be serving the ladies a concoction called "1917 Pudding," made of graham flour, bread crumbs, sour milk, and unsweetened applesauce. She delicately cleared her throat and added that she'd recently received the recipe during a visit with Mrs. Daniels of Monroeville. She looked around the room, waiting for all to appreciate her friendship with one of the town's most prominent—and English—citizens. Satisfied that her name-dropping had not gone unnoticed, Emmaline excused herself and headed to the kitchen to prepare the refreshments.

Dorothea Grau, who was seated next to Mama, dropped her knitting project into her lap and flexed her hands. "*Ach!* My fingers *sind so steif* (are so stiff)," she complained, easily reverting to her mother tongue. "*Ich möchte mein Teil tun, aber ach! meine Hände! Sie schmerzen mir.* (I want to do my part, but oh! my hands! They bother me.)"

"*Ja, meine auch* (Yes, mine too)," commiserated Mama. "*Sie nennen es knitter's-Nerven von dieser ganzen Arbeit, die Kleidung für die Soldaten herzustellen.* (They're calling it knitter's nerves from all this work making clothing for soldiers)."

Flora gave Mama an uneasy look, but before she could whisper a caution against speaking German, Emmaline entered from the kitchen and overheard the foreign conversation. She set the silver serving tray on the nearby buffet, cocked her hands on her hips, and loudly admonished, "Sophie! I won't tolerate that German gibberish in my house!" She stomped her foot for emphasis. "Don't you know we're at war with those … those barbarians from your homeland?!"

Mama's face flushed crimson, but she did not rebut Emmaline's comments by pointing out that she was a native-born American, just like Emmaline. The rest of the ladies stopped their knitting to stare at Mama. Even though each of them was of German heritage and equally guilty of slipping into their mother tongue on occasion, none dared to defend Mama and thereby invoke the wrath of Emmaline. In addition, Mama's reputation for odd behavior was a well-whispered topic behind neighborhood doors, so a mixture of cowardice and curiosity caused the women to quietly watch for Mama's reaction. Would she fly into a rage or have a spell on Emmaline's brocaded carpet? No one spoke for what seemed like an eternity. Flora chewed her lower lip and kept her eyes downcast on her clicking knitting needles.

Emmaline resumed her hostess duties by handing out individual serving dishes of the 1917 Pudding. Soon, the room was filled with the soft clink of silver teaspoons against fine bone china and the murmuring of the ladies as they complimented Emmaline on the bland dessert. Mama, however, set her untouched serving on the buffet, gathered up her knitting, and walked stiffly out the back door. Flora's cheeks burned as the knitting circle exchanged glances.

While filling teacups with unsweetened tea, Emmaline caught a glimpse of movement beyond the north parlor window. Parting the lace curtains, she exclaimed, "Why, Sophie didn't take the road home. She's walking straight across the muddy fields!" She turned to Flora and clucked sympathetically, "What a mess you'll have on your hands when you get home."

Flora shifted uncomfortably in her chair. Emmaline had no idea how correct she was. Not only would Mama track mud across the back steps, porch, and kitchen floor, but her mood would be as black as midnight following the public humiliation. What a mess indeed! Flora avoided making eye contact with the other ladies. She knew they were bursting to comment on Mama's departure. She took another bite of the tasteless dessert and studied the unfinished scarf in her lap.

*****

With Ella and Hermine home for the summer, the girls invited cousin Rosie to walk with them up to the Plank Road school one evening and have a cookout on the old school grounds. Ella carried a basket that contained the newly renamed "hot dogs" wrapped in butcher paper, slices of bread, a jar of tomato relish and one of pickles, and some "Wartime Cookies" that Flora had made using oatmeal and molasses to save on flour and sugar. Rosie, who had spent the day in great indecision over what to contribute to the picnic, finally decided on a crock of salted radishes and a jug of switchel.

The seven girls ambled north on Townline Road, stopping to pick up suitable roasting sticks along the way. Aunt Bertha's dog, Bobby, insisted on tagging along, and he darted at grasshoppers and snapped at dragonflies in the roadside grass.

When they reached the Plank Road bridge, the girls leaned over the railing and dropped pebbles into the shallow water below. They laughed in reminiscence of school days spent dawdling in just such a manner.

On the school grounds, Martha and Minola noticed that the little lilac bush Miss Kohl had led the students in transplanting for Arbor Day four years ago was thriving. The girls stood on tiptoe to peer in the windows of the now-locked school, pointing to where they had once been seated and recalling former teachers and classmates.

They selected a cooking site at the back of the school grounds not far from the banks of the creek, then combed through the adjacent tree lot for firewood. While Ella and Flora worked on starting the fire, Rosie opened the basket and arranged the picnic fare on a blanket. Hermine whittled the ends of the roasting sticks, and the rest of the girls searched along the creek to find suitable flat rocks for seating.

The firewood was slightly damp and would not ignite. Ella and Flora coaxed it by offering dry leaves they found banked against the schoolhouse's foundation. The flames flared but quickly died out. Rosie suggested they try using the butcher paper that contained the hot dogs. She tore the paper into scraps, which Hermine pushed into the heart of the weak fire with a sharpened roasting stick. The four young women were leaning over the cook site, deep in fire-starting concentration, when they heard the other girls yell from across the creek, "No, Bobby, no! Stop him!"

They whirled around to see Bobby greedily ingesting the last of the unprotected hot dogs. Rosie ran at Bobby, clapping her hands and scolding him, but the dog merely wagged his tail and swallowed the last morsel.

Margaret, Martha, and Minola came charging up from the creek bed, and the seven girls looked at each other in dismay.

"Well, forget *this*," said Hermine, dropping the now useless roasting stick beside the blackened ashes of the butcher paper.

They stood around the blanket, forlornly surveying the remains of their picnic.

"Look," said Margaret, picking up two slices of bread. "We can still have jam sandwiches."

"But I didn't bring any jam," pointed out Ella.

"Don't need it," replied Margaret. "You just *jam* two pieces of bread together—jam sandwich!"

The girls laughed at Margaret and then at themselves as they recounted the horrified looks on each other's faces when they spotted Bobby gobbling the hot dogs. In the end, they spread the tomato relish on the bread slices and saluted their meatless picnic as a very patriotic endeavor.

Ella, Minola, Margaret, Martha, Rosie, & Hermine on the Plank Road bridge

*****

To better market his strawberries, Papa decided he needed a machine with a larger carrying capacity than the Fuller, which could hold only a limited number of packing crates stacked precariously on the vehicle's seats and floorboards. Using the profits from last year's berry harvest, he purchased a used Ford truck with an open wooden bed. The increased cargo space allowed him to maximize his trips to the railroad station at Chicago Junction, which, due to confusion over mail delivery with the city of Chicago, had recently been renamed Willard in honor of Daniel Willard, the president of the B&O railroad. The Seibels were now a two-machine family, which caused neighborhood tongues to wag, although there was no denying the two vehicles were aging crates.

Papa's Ford truck beside a packing shed in the strawberry fields

Young Bill, who was not quite ten years old, was as drawn to mechanical objects as his father, and he intently observed the intricate process Papa used to operate the machine. One afternoon, when he had been assigned to keep an eye on Mama while the rest of the family was in the strawberry fields, Bill dawdled around the truck, which Papa had parked beneath a mulberry tree in the backyard upon his return from Willard. Bill ran his hands over the dusty fenders, opened the hood and inspected the engine, bounced on the leather seat with his hands grasping the wheel, and pretended to shift gears and press pedals just as he had seen Papa do.

He ached to take the machine out on the road; however, his conscience prevented him from shirking his duty of watching Mama. Bill crawled into the bed of the truck, stretched out on the wooden floorboards, and tucked his arms behind his head. He weighed his options while studying the dappled light that sifted down through the mulberry leaves. Finally, his face brightened with a solution. He leaped over the tailgate and dashed into the house.

Mama was seated at the kitchen table, gluing a broken piece of blue glass onto her monkey jug. Bill stood impatiently by her elbow, waiting to be acknowledged, but Mama did not look up from her project. Finally, he asked, "Wanna go for a ride, Mama?"

Invitations for outings were rarely extended to Mama, but she, as much as anyone, enjoyed a diversion. Without a bit of concern that her flour-and-water glue mixture would harden in its bowl, she was on her feet and headed toward the back door.

While Mama climbed into the passenger's seat, Bill cranked the machine until it roared to life. Scampering onto the driver's seat, he manipulated the choke, stepped on the gear shifter pedal, adjusted the throttle, and eased the floor lever forward, just as he'd seen Papa do. The truck popped forward, which elicited a "Woooo!" from Mama, who grabbed at the dashboard for stability.

Bill cranking the machine

Bill quickly turned the wheel to avoid colliding with the corner of the house and maneuvered the machine onto the gravel drive. His tongue was clenched between his lips in concentration. They puttered onto Townline Road and headed north, out of the line of sight of the strawberry pickers. When they reached the intersection with Plank Road, Bill's inexperience caused the truck to stall. He hopped out, gave the vehicle a crank, and the engine responded.

As they motored along Plank Road, Bill grew more comfortable behind the wheel. He stole a glance at Mama, whose face bore a pleasant, relaxed expression that he had never seen before. When they passed Mr. Busch's cow pasture, Bill leaned out the open window and squeezed the bulb on the truck's horn, eliciting a deep *a-oooog a.* The cows startled and ran, their tails lifted in curved exclamation and their udders swinging wildly from side to side. Bill and Mama laughed at the sight.

Bill downshifted and carefully executed the turn onto Farr Road, which stretched long and flat before them. Clenching the wheel with one hand, he shifted the gears and announced, "Okay, Mama, hold on tight. I'm gonna let her out w-i-d-e open!"

Mama looked at Bill, and her face split into a broad grin. She clutched the top of the door frame with one hand and used the other to brace herself against the dashboard. "On with it!" she urged.

Bill stepped on the gas, simultaneously working the clutch and the gear shifter like a seasoned pro, until the truck reached its top speed of fifteen miles per hour. He glanced over at Mama. Several strands of her hair—always so neatly gathered in a knot at her neck—blew in the light breeze. She was looking forward, with her chin slightly uplifted and a wide smile on her face.

Bill slowed the machine and turned onto Everingin Road, then completed the large rectangular driving tour around the neighborhood by turning onto Townline Road and heading for home. He pulled into the driveway and parked the truck under the mulberry tree, just where Papa had left it that morning. After killing the engine, he turned to Mama and asked, "So, what'd you think?"

"That was *gut* (good)!" confirmed Mama.

That evening at the supper table, Bill revealed the details of his motor tour with Mama and the breathtaking speeds they had achieved. The girls looked aghast at one another and waited for Papa to thunder a scolding in Bill's direction or to haul him by the shirt collar out the door and behind the woodshed. Instead, Papa slightly nodded his head and said nothing.

From that day on, nine-year-old Bill was the official driver when Papa was not behind the wheel. During berry season, he provided round-trip transportation for the pickers from Monroeville. Young and old scrambled aboard the truck, filling its open bed, perching on the side rails, sitting on each other's laps in the passenger's seat, and clinging to the running boards. Miraculously, no one ever fell off the overloaded truck or was injured.

Bill enjoyed his new role as chauffeur, particularly since it offered a valid excuse to leave the strawberry fields. Unlike his sisters, Bill was not a diligent picker; instead, he viewed the berry season as a prime opportunity for male companionship. He and the other young boys who came to the fields with their families half-heartedly filled a few quart baskets, ate more than their share of berries, and then snuck off for some free-wheeling fun. They played in the creek, looked for arrowheads along the ridge at the far end of the farm, pelted each other with dirt clods, or lolled on the huge boulder deposited in the middle of the farm during the long-ago glacial age. While Papa was not a permissive man, he gave the impression of being lenient when it came to Bill's productiveness in the strawberry fields. Besides being too preoccupied to oversee his son's work habits, Papa reasoned that Bill would grow into agrarian responsibility when he took over the farm someday.

Bill flanked by two of his buddies

For a boy who appeared to be bereft of much parental supervision or social standing, Bill managed to cultivate friendships with the sons of the better families in Monroeville. His two special buddies, Kenny and Clayton, came from good homes with attentive parents who adequately trained and supervised their offspring. Through this association with well-mannered friends, along with the tacit role model of his father and the random mothering of seven older sisters, Bill absorbed proper conduct to complement his outgoing, fun-loving nature. He quickly became a favorite of all who met him.

Mama enjoyed the presence of the young boys that came to play with Bill. It awakened the long-ago memories of her days as a domestic at the John Wright manor house and the fondness she had held for her employer's young grandson. She frequently carried the cookie kettle out to the back porch and dispensed Flora's molasses cookies to the boys, while patting each one on the head and calling him "Walter."

* * * * *

In early August, Papa announced that he intended to drive the Ford down to Columbus to attend the Ohio State Fair, which featured farmers' symposiums on new practices for increasing farm productivity. To everyone's surprise, he added that he was taking Bill with him.

Young Bill could barely contain his excitement. There would be so much to see and do at the fair—the life-sized cow and calf sculpted from butter; the exhibits, games, and sideshows; the electric lights; and sleeping overnight in the back of the Ford. While all of this was cause enough for anticipation, Bill felt there was one other site that he and Papa must see during their time in Columbus. That summer, there had been much talk about an Ohio man who had murdered his girlfriend in a jealous rage and was scheduled for electrocution at the Ohio Penitentiary in December. Like most young boys, Bill held a fascination for crime and punishment. He peppered his sisters with questions about electrocution until they grew exasperated with the morbid subject. He followed Papa about the farm like a shadow, begging him to consider a visit to the prison while they were in the vicinity. If Papa responded at all, it was with a vague, "We'll see."

Upon their return from Columbus, Bill bubbled over with details of every element of their trip. With his blue eyes wide, he described the butter cow and calf, the enormous American flag flying outside the fair's entrance gate, and the experience of sleeping under the stars in the bed of the truck. However, he saved the best description for last—that of "Old Sparky" at the Ohio Penitentiary. It had been the trip of Bill's young life, but better than any of the sites and experiences was the knowledge that Papa finally recognized him as a son, not just one of the girls.

*****

Rationing for the war effort continued to tighten the ways and means of Americans. The Food Administration declared "Food Will Win the War," "Eat All You Can't Can," and "Wheatless Days in America Make for Sleepless Nights in Germany," while advocating war gardens, food conservation, and meatless and wheatless days. All women were encouraged to sign a pledge as "kitchen soldiers" to guard against waste.

In addition to food restrictions, there were soon gasoline shortages. Papa discouraged unnecessary travel in the machine, but he was prevailed upon to make a Sunday excursion to visit Grandpa Gasteier, Uncle Will, and Aunt Anna, who had welcomed a new baby, John Louis, into the household. On the return trip home, Papa puttered the Fuller to a stop in Monroeville. Turning in his seat, he asked, "Do you want to go to the theatorium?" The response was resoundingly affirmative.

Minola had often heard her town-dwelling schoolmates talk about the picture shows during recess. The girls imitated such movie stars as Pearl White, Theda Bara, and Mary Pickford. Unable to mimic something she had never seen, Minola always stood aside and watched as the girls put on elegant airs, describing one actress' cupid's-bow mouth and another's kohl-rimmed eyes. Now at last, Minola would have a point of reference.

Papa paid a dime for each movie ticket, and the family took their seats inside the hot, stuffy theatorium. Soon the lights dimmed, a pianist began playing mood music, and a short film sputtered onto the screen. Charlie Chaplin and the Keystone Cops walked jerkily and performed with much animation. Minola and Bill laughed at their antics. The feature film followed, starring Clara Kimball Young in "The Deep Purple." As innocent country girl Doris Moore, Miss Young spent the bulk of the movie staring soulfully into the camera or trembling in terror as the villains used her as a pawn in a blackmailing scheme. The piano music swelled at the appropriate dramatic moments. Frequent static flashes and intermittent breaks interrupted the film, but the Seibel siblings barely noticed.

Before long, the film on the first reel made a rapid flapping noise, signaling that it was ready to be exchanged for the second reel. The lights came on, and a middle-aged man bounded down the aisle. He stood facing the audience.

"Who's he?" whispered Minola to Martha, who had previously attended the nickelodeon with her high school friends.

"That's a Four-Minute Man. He talks about Americanism and

supporting the war during the four minutes it takes to change the movie reels," explained Martha.

"Is he a movie star?" queried Minola.

Martha gave her younger sister an exasperated look. "No, you ninny! He's the janitor at the high school!"

*****

Since Ada and Albert didn't own a machine, their travels were not curtailed by gas shortages. They continued to journey by horse and buggy to the Seibel homestead on Sunday afternoons, where they enjoyed a fried chicken dinner, a game or two of croquet, and plenty of laughter and conversation.

Ada expressed relief that as a farmer, Albert was considered an essential worker and was therefore exempt from registering for the draft. None of the sisters noticed the blush on Flora's cheeks when she casually mentioned that she'd heard Phil Burrer had enlisted.

Papa, Mama, & Albert
Ada, Margaret, Martha, & Flora
Minola, Ella, Hermine, & Bill

*****

Rationing and conservation affected not only food and all products essential to war production, but clothing as well. High prices for material caused Flora to practice economy and creativity in sewing the family's wardrobe. She studied the current fashions shown in *The Delineator* and the *Illustrated Companion* magazines, then remade old clothing into something serviceable by changing collars, buttons, and pockets or by taking apart the garment and creating an entirely new item. Her talents kept the siblings well dressed, which earned them words of praise from their schoolmates who were forced to rely on shoddy, overpriced store-bought clothing.

Margaret was thoroughly enjoying her senior year in high school. She had many friends, participated in the class play, and joined an intramural basketball squad. Her only complaint was with Mrs. Morris, the civics teacher.

A humorless woman, Mrs. Morris demanded respect but did little to earn it. She punished indiscriminately by detaining the entire class for one student's infraction. Many an afternoon, Margaret and the rest of the class had to stay after school because someone had whispered, another hadn't turned in an assignment, or a student was late to class. This caused Margaret to miss her ride on the school wagon, and thus, she walked the three miles home through good weather and bad. The inequality of Mrs. Morris's discipline and the inconvenience of the long walk provoked a growing resentment.

Martha's beauty and intelligence made her a popular member of the high school's junior class. Friends so frequently called that at the first jangle of the phone on the living room wall, her siblings yelled, "Martha, it's for you!"

The 7th & 8th grades at Monroeville Central School.
Minola (7th grade): Second row from bottom, far left

The 4th & 5th grades at Monroeville Central School.
Bill (4th grade): bottom row, far left

*****

Life on the homefront was dominated by soaring prices, food shortages, and speculation about the suitability of horse meat for human consumption. The winter months brought bitter, subzero temperatures. Gas pressure was low and coal became scarce, causing many stores to observe heatless days and forcing the occasional closure of schools. Papa, who had enjoyed the better heat value of coal when he could afford it, returned to cutting the pin oaks at the back of the farm. The girls and Bill wrapped heated soapstones or flatirons in newspapers to tuck into the foot of their beds at night. Strong winter winds shook the house and blew snow in around the drafty window frames. By morning, there were small snowdrifts on the floor and a rime of frost on the edge of the bed quilts. However, they agreed the discomforts and sacrifices they were experiencing at home paled in comparison to those endured by the troops in the trenches of far-off France.

Troops digging trenches

Chapter 21
The Seibel Homestead
1918

FLORA PULLED BACK the kitchen curtain and peered anxiously toward Townline Road, trying to discern Margaret's form through the driving snow and growing gloom of the late January afternoon. Martha, Minola, and Bill had arrived home from school an hour ago via Mr. Busch's horse-drawn bobsled. They had been nearly frozen from the ride, even though the sides of the sleigh had provided a shield from the biting wind, and the group of school children huddled in the straw bedding had offered a small measure of combined body heat. For Margaret, alone and on foot, the three-mile walk home from Monroeville would be brutal. Heavy snows had formed deep hummocks along the ditches and in the fields, preventing any possibility of a short cut.

Martha joined Flora at the window. "It had to be Mrs. Morris keeping the class after school again. Margaret wouldn't have stayed for any other reason in weather like this," stated Martha firmly.

Finally, Flora spotted a dark outline stumbling slowly along the road between Uncle George's house and the Seibel homestead. "There she is!" Flora announced with relief. "Keep an eye on her while I raise the fire in the cookstove."

Martha assumed the watch post while Flora added more wood to the firebox, moved the teakettle from the warming ledge to the front of the stovetop, and laid two kitchen dish towels to warm on the stove's surface.

When Margaret staggered up the back porch steps, her three sisters were there to meet her. Flora and Martha each took an elbow and half-carried, half-propelled Margaret into the warm kitchen, where Minola pried the snow-covered books and ink-smeared papers from Margaret's clenched fist. Flora's fingers flew to remove Margaret's snow-encrusted mittens, scarf, and hat, then worked at the icy buttons on her coat.

Martha opened the door of the firebox and pulled a kitchen chair close to the radiant heat. With a moan, Margaret collapsed into the chair and started to sob, partly from the pain of her near-frostbitten condition and partly from the relief of finally being home. Minola and Martha quickly loosened Margaret's high-topped shoes, passing the buttonhook back and forth between them. When her feet were freed from the snow-laden shoes, the girls removed her wet stockings, rolled up the leggings of her union suit, and propped her bare feet on the open door of the cookstove.

Martha wrapped one of the warm dish towels around her sister's pale, numb feet and applied the other to her stiff fingers.

Minola draped Margaret's wet outer garments on the back of a kitchen chair and pushed the snowy shoes under the cookstove to dry. Retrieving a quilt from the foot of Mama and Papa's bed, she tucked it around Margaret's shivering shoulders.

Flora dipped a corner of her apron into the warm water of the teakettle and gently dabbed at Margaret's eyes, which were crusted with the icy remnants of tears. "Mrs. Morris again?" she asked, pressing her own warm hands against Margaret's red, raw cheeks.

Margaret nodded weakly. "Olive Schroeder's f-f-fountain pen l-l-leaked all over her desk," Margaret managed to explain between chattering teeth, "and Harlin Munger laughed at her, so the whole c-c-class had to stay after."

"In weather like this!?" exclaimed Flora. "Mrs. Morris had to know the country kids would miss their rides and face a long walk home!"

"She don't c-c-c-are about us country kids," winced Margaret as the feeling began to return to her nearly frostbitten toes and fingers. "She despises us … all of us, I swear she does!"

Flora removed the dish towel from Margaret's hands and replaced it with a cup of hot tea. "Shhhh," she soothed. "You're home now. Everything'll be alright."

"No, it won't!" protested Margaret. "You don't know the worst of it. I fell on an icy patch in the road and dropped my books. The wind—it was so fierce. It scattered my civics essay papers every which way. I tried gathering 'em up, but I got into snow above my knees, and I fell some more, and …." She dropped her chin and took a deep, ragged breath. "The essay's due tomorrow, and if I don't turn it in, Mrs. Morris'll make the whole class stay after school again, but this time, on account of *me*!" Margaret's shoulders shook as she sobbed in distress. "I've never hated anyone in my whole life," she choked out, "but I hate Mrs. Morris. I do. I just *hate* that witch!"

It was unusual to hear the happy, outgoing Margaret express such vehement dislike. The sisters exchanged sympathetic glances but felt helpless in offering a solution. Martha picked up the wet papers that Margaret had managed to salvage from the wind and snow. She shuffled through them, trying to create an order; however, the ink was blurred and illegible, and many of the pages were missing. Margaret had been working on this project for a week; it would be a huge task to reconstruct the entire essay—impossible to accomplish in a single evening. It seemed inevitable that tomorrow would bring another after-school detention for Margaret and a repeat of the long, cold walk home. In a show of solidarity, Martha announced that she, too, would stay after school so that Margaret did not have to walk alone.

In the end, Mother Nature provided a reprieve. The driving snow and fierce wind continued all night and throughout the following day, creating huge drifts that resembled pods of humpback whales at sea. All transportation came to a standstill, and school was cancelled for the rest of the week.

There was a tacit understanding in the neighborhood that each farmer would dig a path through the snow along his frontage to maintain passage for mail delivery, school transportation, and other commerce. However, Papa saw no need to battle the elements for the benefit of limited traffic when there were more essential paths to clear, such as from the house to the barns, well, and outhouse. The road in front of the Seibel homestead remained obstructed by massive drifts.

When the storm abated, Elsie Ordmann donned her galoshes and picked her way across the snowbanks to pay a call on the Seibels. Her visit was not entirely social in nature. She announced loudly that the Seibels were "dummies" for not digging out their section of the road. It was clear that Elsie was parroting an opinion she had heard expressed by her parents, or perhaps she had even been instructed to relay their message. While the sisters were mildly offended by the name-calling, Margaret remained unphased. Thanks to the weather and Papa's obstinacy, she had been able to reconstruct the civics assignment, thus avoiding a repeat of Mrs. Morris's unjust punishment.

*****

By May, the bitter temperatures and heavy snows of winter were forgotten, being replaced by Minola and Bill's struggle with measles, Ada and Albert's bout of a mild grippe, Papa's concern that a late frost would wipe out the strawberry blossoms, and Ada's failed attempt to raise young turkeys. During a Sunday afternoon visit to the Seibel homestead, Ada wondered aloud if the death of the poults had anything to do with the generous portions of soured *Hüttenkäse* (cottage cheese) she'd fed them. As her sisters pondered the dietary needs of young turkeys, Ada bashfully confided that she hoped for a more successful outcome in late October, when she and Albert would be welcoming a baby. In addition to this joyous news, the family prepared for three graduations: Margaret from Monroeville High School, Hermine from Oberlin Business College, and Ella from Schauffler Missionary Training School. There was cause for great expectations and optimism in the Seibel household, despite reports of a massive German offensive movement on the battlefront in France.

In early June, Margaret's graduating class presented their final production, a patriotic play entitled "Claim Allowed," which doubled as a fundraiser for the war effort. Margaret performed the role of Mrs. LaFohl, the wife of a munitions manufacturer. Two days later, the fourteen members of the class assembled for the evening commencement ceremonies, witnessed by their proud families. Martha and the other junior class officers were charged with serving as ushers. She escorted Ada and Albert to their seats beside Papa, Flora, and Minola; young Bill had stayed home with Mama. Margaret understood the necessity of Bill's absence as well as that of Ella and Hermine, who were finishing up school terms and preparing for their own graduation ceremonies.

The town opera hall carried out the patriotic theme of the graduating class, with red, white, and blue bunting decorating the front of the stage and the speaker's podium, which was framed by the American flag and the state flag of Ohio. A small orchestra of nervous underclassmen performed "Pomp and Circumstance" as the graduates filed in and took their seats upon the stage.

Following the Pledge of Allegiance, Mrs. Morris, who possessed a beautiful soprano voice, sang a solo. The graduates exchanged sly looks of disdain. One of the boys drew a handkerchief out of his pocket and loudly blew his nose during a hushed refrain in the music, while another noisily shuffled his feet. A female student steadily tapped the heel of her shoe on the off-beat to disrupt the soloist's timing.

Margaret refused to participate in the undercurrent of contempt or allow her dislike of Mrs. Morris to taint the happiness of this day. Instead, her thoughts drifted to the future. When the strawberry season was over, she had arranged to take a kitchen job in the farmhouse at Ruggles Beach Resort on Lake Erie, where families from Ohio and neighboring states escaped the heat and crowded cities by spending their summers along the shoreline. The income from her kitchen employment, and perhaps a loan from Grandpa Gasteier, would finance her tuition at nursing school, with classes beginning in January. However, best of all, Ada had asked Margaret to be her nurse when the baby came in the fall. Margaret felt privileged to be chosen for such an important responsibility. Besides helping Ada during her time of confinement, the experience would also provide an initiation into her chosen profession.

In the more immediate future—just five days from now—there was the class reception, where she would wear the fashionable navy blue suit Flora had created through clever reworking of existing garments, thus managing to overcome the war-induced shortages of material. There would be cake and lemonade at the reception—a real treat in these times of flour and sugar rationing—and she was sure Flora would also concoct a special dessert in her honor, which, of course, would include strawberries. Margaret squeezed her hands together in her lap and beamed out at the audience. There was so much to look forward to.

Margaret's graduation picture

Margaret wearing the graduation suit sewn by Flora

*****

To save costs during the war, the four members of Ella's class at Schauffler Missionary Training School created their own graduation announcements by typing the information on postcards. They agreed the exercise was good practice for their future roles as church secretaries, missionaries, and Sunday School leaders. At the bottom of each card, they included the class motto: "Be Strong and Very Courageous." On the announcement Ella sent to the Seibel homestead, she added a handwritten request: "Please omit present." With wartime constraints and five siblings still at home, Ella and Hermine had agreed they would discourage graduation gifts for themselves. However, they did approve of Papa's gift to Margaret—a Gruen watch, complete with a tiny second hand, to be used in her nursing profession. Because of the demands of the strawberry season, plus Margaret's concurrent commencement, none of the Seibel family was able to travel to Oberlin or Cleveland for Hermine or Ella's graduation ceremonies.

For Ella, it was a time of anticipation and sadness. She had immensely enjoyed her years at Schauffler and the many friends she had made there. With tearful goodbyes and promises to write, each graduate left the familiar surroundings of Schauffler to return to their hometowns or to begin newly landed jobs. Ella secured a position at Schifflein Christi Church in Cleveland, where she would assist Rev. Huebschmann by calling on the unwed mothers at the Maternity Hospital, visiting the wards of the Detention Home, and building up church attendance through "canvassing," which Ella soon learned meant door-to-door evangelizing. Reverend Huebschmann assured Ella that even though her salary was small, her rewards would be great.

1918 Schauffler Missionary Training School graduates.
Back row: Esther Fenwick & Lillian Digel
Front row: Ella Seibel & Emma Macha

Ella took her duties seriously and performed them to the best of her ability, although she was distressed by the falsified life stories, out-of-wedlock children, and hallucinating patients that she encountered during her institutional visits. She was particularly uncomfortable with the task of canvassing, which took her into poor as well as wealthy neighborhoods.

One afternoon, she stepped onto the wide sandstone porch of a fine-looking brick home, lifted the brass door knocker, and let it drop. She cleared her throat and smoothed the front of her skirt while waiting for the lady of the house to answer.

The lace curtains at the side window parted, and a young woman's face peered out. Ella flashed a friendly smile and did a quick mental rehearsal of the proselytizing speech Rev. Huebschmann had helped her prepare. Slowly, the front door opened, and the young woman, dressed in a stiff white maid's cap and starched apron, motioned Ella into the foyer.

Ella asked to speak with the mistress of the household, and the maid obediently disappeared into an inner room.

Ella could hear the young woman's low murmur, then the maven of the manor brusquely inquired, "Who is she? A maid looking for work? Tell her we have no openings here."

The maid's skirts rustled as she turned to relay the message to Ella.

"Zola," the woman's voice hissed. "Let this be a lesson to you. I could easily replace you with that trollop at the door or any other cinder-scraper that shows up. Heaven knows there's plenty of them flocking to the city these days, looking for work."

The maid returned to the foyer with flushed cheeks and a defeated countenance. The two young women exchanged knowing glances, but there was no need for apologies or explanations. Ella let herself out the door.

Throughout the unsettling experiences of her church work, Ella was comforted by the presence of Hermine, who had found an office job with the Crescent Paint Company in Cleveland. The sisters rented a room on the second floor of a boarding house on Crawford Road and shared the five dollar per week rent, with a dollar increase for heat during the winter months.

Across the street from the house was the Church of Christ's Disciples, where the two sisters occasionally attended services. At such times, it was liberating for Ella to be simply a member of the congregation instead of an employee of the church.

The house on Crawford Road where Ella & Hermine rented the upstairs front room

*****

At the Seibel homestead, the strawberry fields demanded their usual long, hot hours of labor. Ten-year-old Bill happily motored back and forth between Monroeville and the farm, transporting pickers and sometimes delivering crates of strawberries to Zipfel's store, where Mr. Zipfel applied the credit to Papa's running debt. Due to war-induced inflation, strawberry prices shot up to nine or ten cents per quart. Papa was delighted to have an abundant crop, with harvests of nearly seven hundred quarts per day during the peak of the season. Of course, the prices of all other goods soared in equal scale, so Papa's buying power remained stagnant.

One afternoon, as the pickers crept on hands and knees down the long rows of strawberries, an unfamiliar droning sound interrupted the tedium. Young and old sat back on their heels and scanned the fields for the source of the noise.

"Look!" shouted a young boy. "Up there! It's an aeroplane!"

All work in the fields halted as the pickers stood and shielded their eyes against the white-hot sun to watch the plane grow closer. The sound of the engine was now interspersed with sputtering, and the aircraft's bi-wings waffled back and forth. It was obvious the plane was experiencing mechanical difficulties, and the pilot was bringing it in for an emergency landing.

Bill and his buddies, who had escaped their picking duties by slipping away to the creek, spotted the airplane, too. They gazed up in awe as the plane flew over their heads toward an open hay field east of the farm. The boys scrambled up the creek banks and raced toward the landing site, shouting and waving their arms in excitement at the proximity of the plane. Many of the workers in the strawberry fields abandoned their half-filled baskets and rushed to follow the descent of the aircraft, too.

For the next three days, Bill hovered about the downed plane, watching as the pilot made repairs and learning a few new swear words that were missing from Papa's arsenal. Each evening at the supper table, Bill chattered nonstop about the plane, the pilot, and the mechanical aspects of the engine. At night, his dreams were filled with aerial stunts and the glory that would be his someday as a flying ace over enemy lines.

Bill & the airplane

*****

Mama's deep-seated need for order and cleanliness reared to the surface just as the berry season began to wane and the girls were turning their attention to the ripening cherries and bramble fruits, a second cutting of hay, and killing the potato bugs. Usually, Mama's sense of tidiness could be appeased by picking up sticks in the yard or pulling weeds around the outbuildings. This time, however, she could not be dissuaded from scrubbing walls, floors, and windows, turning mattresses, and blacking the stove. While the girls would have gladly relegated this massive undertaking to Mama, she unfortunately no longer possessed the ability to follow a logical, organized cleaning regimen. Instead, she chattered incessantly as she spun from one task to another, leaving a partially scrubbed porch floor, a half-blacked stove, pantry items stacked on the kitchen table, a coating of lemon paste wax drying on the upright piano, and stripped mattresses pulled from the beds. The girls took turns alternating between the work in the fields and the cleanup in the house, feeling bone-weary and more than a little resentful of the extra labor created by Mama.

Margaret had planned to be at her summer job at Ruggles Beach farmhouse by the Fourth of July, in time for the busy vacation season. However, she delayed leaving for a week until Mama's spell had subsided. Consequently, she worried about the reduction in her earnings and the impact on her ability to pay for nursing school.

The night before her departure, Margaret folded clean aprons at the kitchen table and rolled several pairs of stockings that Flora had recently darned. Papa eased himself into his rocking chair with a sigh. After removing his boots, he leaned his head against the back of the chair and watched as his daughter prepared for her trip. Clearing his throat, he quietly cautioned, "You're likely to meet strangers—young men, maybe soldiers—at the dance hall across the road from the farmhouse."

Margaret nodded and tucked the aprons and stockings into her valise as Papa struggled to find the words to broach a topic with which he was clearly uncomfortable.

"It's easy to … don't … well … be careful or …" Papa fumbled.

"It'll be alright, Papa," Margaret reassured. "Reverend Keppel has preached and preached about the evils of dancing. I know better than to 'trod the downward path.'" She smiled at Papa and secured the clasp on the valise before setting it beside the kitchen door, ready for her journey.

The next morning, Papa drove Margaret into town, where she caught the interurban northeast toward Ruggles Beach. The conductor punched her ticket and asked amicably, "You going to Ruggles for work or for fun?"

"Work," responded Margaret. "I've got a job in the kitchen at the farmhouse."

The conductor smiled. "Lots of young folks go to Ruggles for fun, you know—dancing and such."

"Not me," Margaret assured, and she told the conductor about her goals. "Although," she conceded, "I *would* like to learn how to swim while I'm there."

"Thatta girl," chuckled the conductor. "Can't be that close to Lake Erie without having some fun." He moved up the aisle, punching tickets and making small talk with the other passengers, then stepped into the adjoining car.

Margaret rode in silence, enjoying the scenery and thinking of the summer ahead. She would have to work very hard and perhaps pick up some extra chores at the farmhouse to make up for the wages she had already lost. But thoughts of Lake Erie's proximity and the opportunity for swimming thrilled her. She couldn't help but smile to herself in anticipation.

Before long, the conductor re-entered the car and called, "Next stop—Ruggles Beach!" He ambled down the aisle and stood next to Margaret's seat as he polished a green apple on his coat sleeve. Holding the shiny apple toward Margaret, he urged, "Better take this. You might need a little extra strength for all that workin' and swimmin'."

Margaret felt a momentary wave of homesickness sweep over her at the sight of the apple. She thought of the *thump-bump* of windfall apples hitting the sideboards as she and her sisters filled Papa's wagon, the scent of apple butter bubbling in the kettle, and the crates of "long keepers" in the cellar. Swallowing her nostalgia, she graciously accepted the conductor's offering and stepped off the interurban car at the next stop. As she walked down the road toward the farmhouse, she crunched into the apple and reflected upon how easily she had fallen into conversation with the conductor and accepted his gift. Margaret wondered if she had already defaulted on her assurances to Papa about avoiding strange men.

Upon arriving at the resort grounds, Margaret crossed the wide lawn to the back of the farmhouse and poked her head in at the kitchen door. A large black woman was rolling pie crusts at an enamel-topped table in the center of the room.

"Hello!" greeted Margaret. "Can you tell me where I can find Miss Ruggles? I've been hired to work here, and she told me to check in with her when I arrived."

"Who be you, dearie?" asked the woman, expertly fitting the crusts over filled pie pans.

"I'm Margaret Seibel."

"Lawd, Margaret, I've been waiting on you to come," the woman replied as she deftly swiped crescent-shaped vents into the pie crusts. "I'm Mrs. Davis, the cook here. You'll be workin' with me and—almighty Moses!—I can use the help. Got forty guests right now and spectin' more soon. And every one of 'em a hungry mouth." Mrs. Davis shook her head for emphasis. "There's five other girls workin' here for the summer, but mostly they help with the housekeepin' and laundry and such, although Miss Ruggles makes sure they give me a hand with servin' meals and cleanin' up. But I need me a good full-time assistant in the kitchen." She placed the pies in the large oven and wiped her floury hands on her apron. "You good with bakin', Margaret? It ain't easy concoctin' somethin' tasty, what with all this wartime rationin' goin' on, don't you know."

Margaret thought of Ada and Flora and their mastery with yeast breads, küchens, fluffy cakes, fruit pies, and cookies. She hoped she could emulate a fraction of their talents and thereby satisfy Mrs. Davis and the guests. "I know quite a few good receipts and I've …"

"Well, where's my manners?" interrupted Mrs. Davis, eyeing Margaret's valise. "Miss Ruggles is gone to Berlin Heights right now, so you'll have to square up with her when she gets back, but I can show you to your room."

She motioned Margaret to follow her out the kitchen door to an adjacent set of stairs. The cook lumbered up the steps, which opened into a small room above the kitchen. Mrs. Davis stood with her hands on her hips and breathed heavily from the exertion. After catching her breath, she instructed, "Now, you can either sleep here or over yonder where the other girls are stayin' for the summer." She pointed out the window toward a low barnlike structure across the lawn. "They call it 'The Last Resort,'" chuckled Mrs. Davis. "All five of 'em are stayin' over there, but what's one more?" she shrugged.

Margaret looked around the small room, which was more of a storage area than a bedroom. It held a narrow bed, a battered trunk, and a corner closet. A small window provided light and a measure of ventilation. The room reminded her of the area at the top of Stegmiller's stairs back home, where she and her sisters and Bill had spent many hours in play, safely removed from Mama's ire. Margaret stepped closer to the window and peered toward The Last Resort, pondering her options. Certainly, she would get to know her co-workers much better if she roomed with them, but, on the other hand, a room of her own would be a unique experience. For as long as she could remember, she had shared a room, and usually a bed, with her sisters.

Margaret set her valise upon the narrow bed. "I'll stay here," she announced, unable to pass up the opportunity to have a room all to herself for the first time in her life.

"Good 'nuf," confirmed Mrs. Davis as she eased herself down the stairs. "Now, dearie, let's get you into an apron and get workin' on dinner."

Margaret pulled an apron from her valise, took one more look at "her" room, and scampered down the stairs after Mrs. Davis.

As the morning progressed, the kitchen became a beehive of activity. The other girls on the summer staff—Gladys, Norma, Ida, Helen, and Cora—swirled through the kitchen in a careful choreography of transporting food to the dining room, serving the guests, and refilling platters, bowls, and water glasses. Margaret ran to the well pump so often to refill pitchers that she thought her arms would fail from the vigorous pumping. There was much to learn about dining room decorum—serve from the left, remove dishes from the right. This wasn't at all like serving the hungry threshermen back home, whose only concern was with the abundance of food, not how it was presented.

After the guests had eaten their last forkfuls of pie and retired to their rooms or the front porch for an afternoon nap, the girls cleared the table and carried soiled dishes and linens to the kitchen. Before beginning the cleanup, they gathered at the kitchen table with Mrs. Davis to eat their own lunch, which consisted of leftovers from the noon meal. The girls chatted about their hometowns and the plans for their summer wages. Margaret learned that a couple of the girls were recent high school graduates, just like her, while others were college coeds. All of the girls had financial intentions similar to her own, except for Helen, who was engaged to be married and was saving up some pin money.

The girls washed and dried the dishes, laundered and hung out the linens, swept the carpeted dining room, and helped Mrs. Davis with preparations for the evening meal, which would be lighter fare than the spread served at noon. By mid-afternoon, Margaret had met with Miss Ruggles to discuss her wages, which were set at ten dollars per week. With all the kitchen chores completed, the girls were free to take a break before returning to help with supper. As they exited the farmhouse, they invited Margaret to join them for a dip in the lake.

"But, I don't know how to swim," sighed Margaret.

"Gladys'll teach you," offered Cora. "I swam like a rock when I first got here," she continued, punctuating her sentence with gurgling noises, "but Gladys worked with me, and now I can even do dives off the dock."

Margaret's blue-gray eyes shown with excitement as she joined the girls at the water's edge, wearing a borrowed bathing suit and cap. Gladys led her pupil into the shallow water, which felt refreshing after the hot afternoon in the kitchen. The first lesson was how to float on one's back. Gladys instructed Margaret to kneel so that the water was about waist deep, then tip her head back into the water, point her chin toward the sky, extend her arms straight out from her shoulders, and arch her back. Gladys provided added support by holding her hands underneath her student, then slowly withdrew them. Margaret smiled up at the sun, amazed at the peaceful feeling of weightlessness. She tucked her chin to see how the rest of her body looked as it bobbed on Lake Erie's surface. However, the change in head position immediately altered the physics of flotation. To Margaret's surprise, the brilliant blue sky turned a watery green, and Gladys' reassuring voice was replaced by a muffled emptiness as her face slipped beneath the surface. Margaret flailed and swallowed lake water as she sank. Suddenly, Gladys' strong arms were there, lifting her to the surface, where she sputtered, coughed, and struggled to catch her breath. Gladys assured her that this experience was typical, and she offered reminders about keeping the back arched and chin pointed skyward. Before long, Margaret was ready for another attempt. By the time the girls reluctantly left the cool waters to return to the farmhouse, Margaret had mastered the art of floating on her back.

That night, with her hair still damp from the lake, Margaret perched on the edge of her narrow bed. By the light of a kerosene lantern, she recorded the day's events in the pocket diary she'd brought from home. Margaret's fountain pen scratched rapidly across the page as she jotted down a glowing description of her new friends, the room of her own, and the success of her first swimming lesson.

Swimming at Ruggles Beach

By the end of the week, Margaret felt like she had been friends with the other girls all her life. Sometimes, they rose early in the morning and went bathing in Lake Erie, to offset the heat of the coming day, followed by an afternoon swim and frequently an evening dip as well. They giggled over guests and silly jokes as they cleaned up after meals, and they chatted late into the night in the girls' large dormitory bedroom in The

Last Resort.

On Friday morning, as the girls prepared the dining hall for the noon meal, they buzzed with anticipation about the weekend dances held in the dance hall in the grove across the road. Margaret listened as they chattered about the young people who attended from various neighboring towns as well as those from the resort. They ticked off a list of their favorite songs and dance partners and extended an invitation for Margaret to join them at the dance that evening. Margaret resisted by pointing out that she had promised her father she wouldn't consort with strange men.

"You can dance with me," offered the engaged Helen. "After all, I'm practically a married woman. You'll be safe with me as your partner."

"C'mon, Margaret," coaxed Ida. "Dancing is good for you. It teaches you to be graceful and have good posture." She twirled across the dining room floor, using a china plate as her partner in a maxixe.

"But, I don't know any of the steps," protested Margaret weakly.

"We'll teach you!" insisted Norma. "Just like with the swimming lessons."

"Well, I guess if it teaches me to be graceful…," relented Margaret.

That evening, the girls donned their white linen dresses and eagerly crossed the road, with Margaret having second thoughts about her decision. The band was playing "In for a Penny, In for a Pound" to a crowded dance floor when the girls bought their nickel dance tickets.

"C'mon," beckoned Helen, "I'll teach you how to do the one-step." She pulled Margaret to the edge of the busy dance floor, clasped her partner's hand, placed her other on Margaret's waist, and led her in an easy four steps forward, two steps to the side, followed by a twirl, before repeating the pattern. Margaret diligently counted the steps under her breath, and by the time the song had ended, her look of concentration had been replaced by a wide smile. The two girls cashed in their tickets for another dance, to the tune of "Pack up Your Troubles." This time, the steps came more naturally.

For the next song, Margaret and Helen sat on the wooden benches that lined the walls of the dance hall and watched as Ida, Gladys, Norma, and Cora glided across the floor with their male partners. Helen slipped off her shoe and rubbed at the toes Margaret had stepped on during her dance lesson. She pointed out couples doing the fox trot, Castle walk, maxixe, and hesitation waltz.

Suddenly, a young man appeared in front of Margaret. He held out a dance ticket and invited her to join him on the dance floor. For a long moment, Margaret looked up at him with her eyes wide and mouth agape. A vision of Rev. Keppel in the pulpit, preaching about the evils of dancing, flashed before her, and she distinctly heard Papa's voice warning about the strange young men she'd meet at the dance hall. She quickly declined, causing the young man to shrug and move on.

Helen jabbed an elbow into Margaret's ribs. "You little saint," she chided.

Margaret decided she had gone against her principles enough for one evening and walked back to her room in the farmhouse. As she lay in bed, her feet tapped out a one-step to the faint strains of music that wafted across the road from the dance hall.

In early August, Margaret moved into The Last Resort with the other girls, having fully satisfied her desire for a room of her own. They immediately celebrated her nineteenth birthday by feasting on a watermelon they had chilled in a quiet cove of Lake Erie. Aside from her sisters, Margaret had never experienced such a strong kinship with other females. They traded clothes, styled each other's hair, and took turns reading their diaries aloud—an exercise that always resulted in peals of laughter and threats of editing.

To earn extra money, Margaret contracted with several of the resort's guests to do their ironing. It was a small way to offset the wages she had missed due to her delayed arrival at the grounds. Despite the added work, Margaret still found time for daily trips to the beach. Gladys continued to provide swimming instructions, and before long, Margaret could swim well enough to leap off the dock with the other girls. She wrote long letters home to her sisters, detailing her many activities. "Think of it, girls, <u>I am swimming</u>!" she penned enthusiastically.

The lure of the dance hall was a constant struggle. On several evenings, some of her former classmates from Monroeville arrived for the dance. Margaret didn't feel she was reneging on her promise to Papa by dancing with the boys she knew from home. However, there was still the nagging guilt that she had let Rev. Keppel down. She'd solemnly vow not to attend any more dances, but the sound of the laughter and music from across the road, as well as the constant coaxing from the other girls, wore down Margaret's resistance.

One evening, Margaret convinced herself there would be no moral downfall in attending the dance if she remained a spectator only. The other girls took turns dancing with each other or the young men in attendance, while Margaret sat on the bench with her feet tucked underneath, hoping no one noticed how actively she kept time to the music.

A rumble of engines from the road interrupted the music and caused everyone to rush to the wide window openings. The source of the noise was a troop convoy, which turned off the road and began setting up an encampment in the field beyond the dance hall. Some of the young men from the dance ambled over to the growing city of tents, while the girls watched from afar. The band plucked out "There's a Long, Long Trail A-Winding," and young couples once again waltzed across the dance floor. Before long, soldiers began to filter over from the encampment and mingle with the crowd. All of the girls except Margaret took turns dancing with the servicemen, even the betrothed Helen. The girls returned frequently to the bench where Margaret sat and chastised her for her lack of participation.

"You're being un-American," scolded Ida. "These boys will be shipped out soon, and who knows what horrors they'll see or if they'll even return home."

"Yes, don't you want to give them some happy memories to carry with them?" asked Gladys. "You know … the girl I left behind, tra la, tra la …" She tilted her head and framed her face with her hands.

"Oh, don't be a stick in the mud, Margaret," chided Helen. "*I'm* dancing with them even though I'm engaged to be married! It's my civic duty!"

Margaret's resolve began to soften. She reasoned that it did seem unpatriotic to merely watch from the sidelines. Dancing with the soldiers was probably an important morale-booster for them, and she acknowledged that she should do her part to support the war effort. Papa had bought war bonds with his meager funds; the least she could do was dance with one or two servicemen.

Norma worked her way toward them through the crowd, leading a handsome soldier. "Girls, this is Edmund Atherton. I knew him from college, before he enlisted," she explained. "What a surprise to run into him here!" All of the girls on the bench sat a little straighter and smiled brightly.

After the introductions had been made and some small talk exchanged, Edmund offered Margaret a dance ticket. She nervously accepted and warned, "I can only do the one-step."

"Perfect," smiled Edmund. "It's my favorite."

The band struck up "You're Some Pretty Doll." Edmund whisked Margaret onto the dance floor and held her lightly in his arms. He provided a commanding yet easy lead to follow, and the couple glided and twirled across the arena. Margaret noticed that Edmund never stepped on her feet, and he didn't work her arm like he was pumping water, the way some of her previous dance partners had. They chatted amicably as they danced, and Margaret couldn't help but admire his perfect features, gleaming white teeth, and coal-black hair. With Edmund as a dance partner, she felt a sense of weightlessness, as though she were floating across the dance floor—almost as effortlessly as she bobbed on her back in the waters of Lake Erie.

When Edmund took turns dancing with the other girls, Margaret noticed he was proficient in all the popular steps. She felt chagrined that she had limited him to the very basic one-step but was impressed by how gracious he had been in accommodating her beginner's status. Margaret accepted invitations to dance from other soldiers. Some tromped methodically across the floor as though they were marching to their drill sergeant's cadence, while others propelled her in sudden backward and forward spurts like the push and pull of a two-man bucksaw. Margaret had several more dances with Edmund, and each time she privately hoped the song would never end.

Later that evening as the girls retired to The Last Resort, the topic of conversation was the dashing Edmund Atherton.

"Oh yes, all the girls at college had a crush on him," offered Norma. "He's positively *squishy*!"

Margaret smiled to herself in the darkness. "*Squishy!*" She was delighted to be learning the college slang so that when she started nursing school this winter, she'd be up to date on the current lingo. And yes, there was no doubt about it—Edmund Atherton was "positively squishy." She made a mental note to ask Ada if she had thought Albert was "squishy" the first time she met him.

The girls found additional forms of entertainment besides swimming and dancing. One evening, Helen's fiancé drove his father's seven-passenger Paige from Lorain and took all of the girls riding. They drove to Huron and saw the movie "The Kaiser, The Beast of Berlin," then stopped for ice cream. It was the first time Margaret had been out motoring after dark. As they sped along the lakeshore road, she tilted her head against the back of the seat to watch the changing pattern of the moonlight through the leaves.

The girls also played leap frog on the beach, went rowing on the lake, enjoyed feasting on grapes they picked from the arbor behind The Last Resort, and staged a mock wedding in the farmhouse parlor one afternoon. Gladys and Cora, dressed in their dark bathing suits, served as the groom and preacher. Helen and Margaret posed as the bride and bridesmaid, wearing their long white nightgowns as wedding attire and carrying bouquets of Queen Anne's lace, bachelor's buttons, and brown-eyed Susans picked from the resort grounds. Ida and Norma wore their white linen dresses to represent the mothers of the bride and groom. The boarders were amused by the entertainment, and several of the guests took pictures of the mock wedding party. Margaret couldn't believe she was wearing her nightgown out in public, much less being photographed in it. She was certain this show of immodesty had carried her further along the downward path that Rev. Keppel had warned about in his sermons.

September 1st marked the first government-mandated gasless Sunday, a new edict to restrict travel and thereby conserve fuel for the fighting forces. While the ruling would limit the crowds at the dance hall as well as opportunities for motoring into the countryside, it had little impact on the girls. The resort had begun to empty as summer vacationers returned to their hometowns. Norma, Gladys, and Ida, the three college coeds, packed their trunks to head to their respective campuses. Helen went home to complete the plans for her upcoming wedding. The goodbye hugs were teary and heartfelt, with the girls making many promises to write and agreeing to reunite at Helen's wedding.

Miss Ruggles offered Margaret and Cora the opportunity to stay on at the farmhouse and help Mrs. Davis tend to the needs of the few remaining boarders. There was also an orchard of peaches that must be picked and canned. Margaret eagerly accepted the extension and was grateful for the opportunity to make up for the lost wages from her late arrival at the grounds back in July. She reasoned that between saving the peach pits for the government (which was burning them into charcoal for use in gas-mask filters) and dancing with the soldiers, she was doing her part to support the war effort. However, she was quite sure that Papa and Rev. Keppel would not rate dancing in the same meritorious category as peach pit collecting.

* * * * *

Martha, Minola, and Bill returned to school after Labor Day. Pretty and popular Martha held great anticipation for her senior year, although she already harbored a dislike for the harsh Mrs. Morris, based on Margaret's previous experiences. Bill viewed fifth grade as an opportunity for social outreach, with a dash of academics on the side. Minola did not look forward to a return to the eighth grade caste system and her continued struggles with math. In hopes of prying Margaret away from Ruggles Beach, Minola wrote a mournful letter imploring her sister to come home soon and rescue her from the certain fate of failing math class.

The new school year brought a familiar face to the teaching ranks at Monroeville High School. George and Bertha's eldest son, the college-educated Elmer, returned home to accept the position of high school science teacher. As a twenty-eight-year-old unmarried male, Elmer was a prime candidate for the service; however, he had not enlisted. In addition, at community gatherings Bertha was very outspoken that neither of her sons would be "sacrificial lambs." The government had escalated recruitment as more and more doughboys crossed the Atlantic, so Bertha's opposition was highly unpopular during a time of fevered patriotism. The public backlash targeted Elmer but frequently spilled over to the extended Seibel family as well.

The high school boys quickly pounced upon Elmer's status. During class, one boy feigned a head cold and sneezed out a very audible "Slacker!" It proved to be contagious, and soon other boys were either sneezing the derisive comment or coughing the sounds of a clucking chicken. The classroom tittered in response, while Martha's cheeks burned.

One morning, Elmer entered the classroom to find a mound of white chicken feathers deposited on his desk. In large letters on the chalkboard were written the initials of the American Protective League, an organization meant to locate those suspected of disloyalty. Gentle and passive by nature, Elmer merely swept the feathers into the trash can, erased the message on the chalkboard, and began his lesson.

One of the boys leaned across the aisle and hissed to Martha, "See there? You Seibels won't fight."

* * * * *

Margaret's last day at Ruggles Beach was Saturday, September 21. After tidying up the kitchen and dining room, she and Cora took one last stroll along the beach. They promised each other they would return to work at the farmhouse again next summer. Margaret packed her valise, proudly tucking her earnings into the bottom corner, and closed the door on The Last Resort, which had seemed quiet and lonely after the other girls left. She boarded the interurban for Monroeville and then walked the three miles home, where she found Flora, Martha, Minola, and Bill helping Papa harvest the sorghum cane in the field behind the barn.

When they heard Margaret call, "Hello, strangers," the siblings dropped their corn knives and ran to greet her with hugs and shouts of "Welcome home!" Papa acknowledged Margaret's arrival and continued down the long rows of sorghum, lopping seed heads from the standing cane. The siblings took a break from stripping cane leaves to sip juice from the cut stalks and listen to Margaret's happy recounting of her summer experiences. They handed her a corn knife and teased that her vacation was now over.

Bill, Margaret, & Minola sipping sorghum juice

The next day, Elsie Ordmann and Edith Moss paid a Sunday afternoon visit. The girls pulled taffy, played duets on the piano, and laughed through a round of croquet in the warm September sun. As much as Margaret had enjoyed her summer, it was good to be home, and her sisters and neighbors were equally glad to have her back in the fold.

During the following week while the younger siblings were in school, Margaret worked alongside Flora in the kitchen. She described the dining room etiquette, the challenges of wheatless and meatless days when feeding a multitude, and how she had had to multiply Ada and Flora's recipes to accommodate the farmhouse guests. After Minola arrived home from school in the afternoons, Margaret sat with her at the kitchen table and tutored her younger sister through the complexities of square roots. At night, Martha and Minola demanded that Margaret sleep with them in their bed, since she would soon be leaving again to go to Ada's. The three lay like spoons, with Margaret in the middle. They chatted in the darkness, and Margaret described her Ruggles Beach co-workers and the adventures of swimming, dancing, and motoring after dark. Minola curled into Margaret and fell asleep listening to tales of friends frolicking in the waters of Lake Erie. Martha nestled her head close to that of her older sister and envisioned dancing with dashing soldiers or gliding along the lakeshore road in the moonlight.

On Friday evening, Minola slid into her seat at the supper table. She watched with glassy eyes as a bowl of fried potatoes and onions and a platter of sliced tomatoes made their way toward her. Usually a hearty eater, Minola had no appetite. Her limbs felt heavy and achy, and it was with great difficulty that she passed the dishes to Bill, who shrugged at Minola's indifference and heaped a larger serving onto his own plate. She left the table and laid down on the daybed just inside the living room door. However, the sounds of clattering dishes and cutlery hurt her head, and before long, she crept up the stairs and into bed.

Later that night, Margaret and Martha slid into bed beside Minola and found her body uncomfortably hot with fever. Before moving to her usual bed with Flora, Margaret tiptoed downstairs to the summer kitchen, where she soaked a cloth in cold well water for Minola's forehead.

Minola was no better the next morning, and she had developed a near-constant cough and double ear aches. Flora and Margaret took turns ministering to her needs, but by Saturday afternoon, they had another patient; Martha complained of chills, a sore throat, and a pounding headache. Margaret carried a hot water bottle upstairs and tucked it under the covers beside Martha. Flora held a cup of cold water to Minola's parched lips before she slipped back into a fitful slumber.

On Sunday, Ada and Albert drove their horse and buggy to the Seibel homestead to have dinner and retrieve Margaret. Because of the gasless Sunday rule, Papa could not use the machine to deliver Margaret to the young couple's home, where she would stay to help Ada in the weeks surrounding the birth of the baby. While Papa and Albert strolled out to the corn field to examine the crop, Flora and Margaret fussed over Ada, who was now nearing the end of her pregnancy. When they told her about the ailing Martha and Minola, Ada insisted on climbing the stairs to check on her sisters. She helped Flora and Margaret gently wash the girls' faces and arms, refill the hot water bottle for Martha, and refresh the cold compress for Minola. They prepared a tea and honey mixture to soothe the girls' sore throats.

Mama had no interest in her ill offspring nor the noontime meal. Fueled by black coffee, she ransacked the cabinets in the summer kitchen, complaining that the grapes needed to be harvested, but she could find no wax for sealing the jelly jars. It was obvious Mama was ramping up for another spell, so it was pointless to try to redirect her thinking. Nevertheless, the girls flinched at the sounds of cabinet contents hitting the summer kitchen floor.

Ten-year-old Bill, who had a growing boy's ravenous appetite, picked at his food, then pushed his plate aside and laid his head on his folded arms. Flora pressed the back of her hand to his forehead and ominously announced that he felt too warm. She escorted him upstairs, tucked him into his bed near that of Minola and Martha, and draped a cool rag across his forehead.

By mid-afternoon, Albert gave a drawn out, "W-e-l-l…," which signaled his readiness to head for home and begin the evening chores. He helped Ada and Margaret onto the buggy seat, then tucked Margaret's valise behind the bench.

"You sure you can manage here by yourself?" a concerned Ada asked Flora. "She's cross as two sticks again," Ada commented, cocking her head toward Mama, who was plucking clusters of grapes from the arbor and complaining vigorously in German. "You might need Margaret more than I do right now."

"I've tended to sick ones before, including Mama," assured Flora. "Besides, you need Margaret's help if you're gonna get all your housecleaning done before the baby comes." Flora patted Ada's arm and gave a reassuring smile.

Albert pulled himself into the buggy and squeezed onto the seat beside the two sisters. He gently tapped the reins on Lady's back, and Ada and Margaret waved goodbye to Flora and Papa.

Albert drove the buggy slowly toward home, being careful to avoid any ruts or bumps that would jostle the very pregnant Ada. Margaret chattered happily the entire way, telling the young couple all about her stay at Ruggles Beach. She described dancing with the "squishy" Edmund Atherton and slyly asked Ada if that term applied to Albert.

"Oh, I'm squishy alright," agreed Albert, his blue eyes twinkling as he motioned toward the close quarters of the three adults on a buggy seat built for two.

After supper, Albert and his brother Alfred headed out to the barn to finish the evening chores. The two sisters washed and dried the dishes and discussed Ada's long list of housecleaning tasks to be tackled before the baby arrived. Margaret began sweeping the kitchen floor, then called to her sister, "Watch, Ada. I'll show you how to do the one-step." Using the broom as a partner, she glided and twirled around the kitchen table, plopping onto a kitchen chair with a laugh. She pulled the rolled-up sleeve of her dress across her brow and announced, "Mercy, it's so warm in here. Hotter than the kitchen at Ruggles Beach."

"Guess it was that dance partner of yours. Just too much of a fancy stepper," joked Ada as she folded the dish towel. When she turned to smile at Margaret, she noticed beads of sweat across her sister's forehead. Her smile faded. Even to the very pregnant Ada, the kitchen was a comfortable temperature. She crossed the room and fanned the dish towel in front of Margaret's face, creating a small breeze. "You okay?" she asked, her voice tinged with concern.

"I ... I don't know," responded Margaret. "I feel sort of funny in the head, kinda dizzy. But I never got dizzy from dancing before."

"Maybe a cup of cold water will set things right," offered Ada, and she hurried outside to the well pump.

Margaret sipped at the water and furrowed her brow. "I think I should go lay down for a while ... just until this passes. I'll feel better in a little bit, I know I will." She rose to walk toward the living room, but stumbled against the doorway.

Ada grabbed her sister's arm. "Let's get you upstairs and into bed. I think you caught what the kids have back home."

The two sisters slowly climbed the narrow staircase to the second story. Ada kept a steadying hand on Margaret's elbow as they passed through the small open area used as a sleeping room by Alfred to the adjoining front bedroom. She removed Margaret's high-topped shoes, unpinned her hair, and hurried downstairs to retrieve Margaret's valise. Ada pawed through its contents until she found a nightgown, which she helped her sister don. Margaret wearily slumped into bed, complaining of the pounding behind her eyes. Ada pulled the covers over her reclining sister and smoothed the damp tendrils of hair away from her face. She made her way downstairs again to soak a compress in cold water.

Margaret's cough began in the night. Ada awoke and slipped out of bed. She groped her way to the kitchen, lit the kerosene lantern, and carried it outside to pump another glass of cold well water. She tiptoed as gingerly as she could up the stairs and through Alfred's sleeping quarters to Margaret's room. Cradling the back of Margaret's neck, Ada lifted her sister's head and held the cup of cold water to her lips. Margaret's neck was hot and damp, an obvious sign she was burning with fever. Ada dipped the compress into the remaining well water and dabbed at Margaret's forehead and neck.

"So hot," mumbled Margaret in her delirium. "Let's go swimming in the lake for a while."

* * * * *

Early Monday morning, Papa entered the dark kitchen and lit the lantern on the kitchen table. Usually, Flora was up by this time and had breakfast started before joining him to milk the cows. It was unusual for her to oversleep. Perhaps she had not slept well with all the coughing going on upstairs. He, too, had had a fitful night, between the children's coughing and Mama's nocturnal wanderings. Papa started a fire in the cookstove and moved the coffeepot from the warming shelf to the stove's surface. It was unlikely the children would be well enough to attend school today, so there was no use starting the oatmeal that Flora usually prepared for their breakfast. He cut two fat slices of bread and laid them on the surface of the cookstove to toast. Papa pumped a basinful of water from the well stalk in the summer kitchen and splashed its contents onto his face, hoping that the brisk wakeup and a cup of strong black coffee would help him start his day.

At the sound of footsteps in the kitchen, Papa looked up from the towel as he dried his face. He expected to see Flora, hurrying to start breakfast and apologizing for her tardiness, but instead it was Mama. She had roamed the house all night, complaining in German that someone had stolen the jelly jars. She swept past him into the summer kitchen and began pulling old newspapers out of the *Mehlfach* in her search for the missing canning supplies.

Papa shook his head and flipped the bread slices, then poured himself a cup of coffee before slathering the two pieces of toast with molasses. As he chewed, he listened to the sounds of coughing from upstairs and resolved that he would check on the children and awaken Flora before he went out to milk the cows.

As Papa climbed the stairs, a soft circle of lantern light greeted him, indicating that Flora was up and getting dressed for the day. He stopped midway and cocked his head to listen for the sounds of Flora moving about over the racking coughs of the children. "Flora?" he called. "You up?"

There was silence and then a moan, followed by the persistent coughing. Papa took the remaining steps two at a time. Flora lay horizontally across her bed, still in her nightgown but with a stocking dangling from one foot. It was obvious that she had risen, lit the lamp, and attempted to dress but was unable to overcome the same symptoms that gripped the other three children. She lay with her head turned away from the lantern's light and her arm draped over her eyes.

"Ohhh, my eyes hurt," Flora whispered. "And my head. The pounding."

Papa quickly turned the lantern wick down until only a dim light remained, enough for him to examine the faces of the children. Minola had kicked off her half of the covers, and her face was waxen and glistening with sweat. On the other side of the bed, Martha clutched all the covers close around her and shivered spasmodically as each coughing spell racked her body. Bill was curled into a ball, his lips slightly parted as he panted rapidly.

Papa lifted Flora's feet onto her bed and gently maneuvered her until her head was once again on the pillow. He pulled the covers over her and hurried downstairs to refill the hot water bottle with warm water from the reservoir on the cookstove and soak some compresses in cold well water. He dashed into the bedroom, pulled the quilt from the foot of his and Mama's bed, and opened the blanket chest to retrieve two more quilts. He remembered his own bouts with river fever as a young man and how he was often all alone to battle the alternating fever and chills that had consumed his body. Carrying the bed coverings, hot water bottle, and cold compresses, Papa bounded up the stairs. Over the children's coughing, he could hear the lowing of the cows as they lined up at the barn door, waiting impatiently to be fed and relieved of their full udders.

Papa hurried downstairs to pump cold water into a milk pail, which he carried upstairs. He gave each of the children a drink and did what he could to temporarily comfort them, but the morning chores could not be put off any longer. Before leaving the house, he telephoned Dr. Gilman, who indicated he would pay a call sometime that day.

As Papa crossed the lawn toward the barn, he thought of Mama roaming about the house. He recalled her history of adding kerosene to revive a slow fire in the cookstove and how a near conflagration had narrowly been averted during one of her previous spells. Papa knew he could not jeopardize the well-being of the children by leaving them alone with Mama; they were too ill to flee if she started the house on fire. He rushed to the barn and retrieved a length of rope. Returning to the house, Papa walked quietly to the bedroom, where he could hear Mama pawing through the drawers of the tall cherry bookcase and talking nonstop about the jelly jars. He pulled the bedroom door closed and looped the rope around the knob, then tied the other end to the leg of the upright piano in the parlor. Papa tugged on the rope several times to test his security system. Satisfied that the children were protected, he hurried outside to attend to the agitated cows.

* * * * *

Before starting breakfast, Ada climbed the stairs to check on Margaret, whose night-long coughing had disrupted the sleep of all the house's occupants. Alfred was sitting on his bed, pulling on his socks. "Hell of a night," he commented as Ada passed through his sleeping quarters.

Margaret was huddled under the covers, shivering violently. Ada pressed her hand to Margaret's forehead, which was damp and feverish. She hurried downstairs to raise a fire in the cookstove so there would be some warm water for filling the hot water bottle and making tea.

Ada quickly scrambled some eggs and set a loaf of bread and a jar of elderberry preserves on the kitchen table. As she poured coffee for Albert and Alfred, she shared her concern over Margaret's condition. Albert promised he would stop in at Dr. Gilman's office when he took an implement to the blacksmith shop for repair.

When breakfast was over, Ada piled the dishes in the drysink while she carried a cup of tea and the hot water bottle upstairs. She slid the hot water bottle under the covers, and Margaret eagerly pulled it to her chest. Cradling Margaret's head, Ada carefully spooned warm tea between her patient's lips.

"Oh, Ada, my joints ache like they're broke," moaned Margaret. Her glassy blue-gray eyes searched Ada's face. "I hope you don't catch this."

Ada bit her lower lip but did not acknowledge how afraid she was that she would come down with the illness and lose the baby.

After Margaret had sipped about half a cup of tea, she dropped into slumber, still clutching the hot water bottle. Ada carried the tea cup downstairs and decided to call home before she started to wash the dishes. She wanted to get an update from Flora on the children and also inform Flora and Papa that Margaret had come down with the illness last night. The telephone rang and rang. Ada thought it odd that Flora did not answer but assumed she was outside helping Papa with the morning's chores.

* * * * *

Dr. Gilman arrived at the Seibel homestead in mid-morning. He looked weary and stooped. Before entering the house, he looped a gauze mask over his nose and mouth. Papa had never seen the doctor take such precautions before; he knew immediately that the situation was serious. Papa led Dr. Gilman to the second-floor bedroom where the four siblings lay. The doctor rapped on their chests, used his stethoscope to listen to their lungs, and took their temperatures, which was not easily accomplished because their constant coughing quickly dislodged the thermometer. He proclaimed Martha the worst, with a temperature of 103 degrees.

"It's the Spanish influenza, no doubt about it," Dr. Gilman told Papa. "Monroeville's loaded with it. In fact, it's so bad, they've closed the schools. I just came from Mosses' next door, and all but Mr. Moss are down with it. It's everywhere, Bill, and spreading faster than I can keep up."

The doctor opened wide the windows in the bedroom and encouraged the children to breathe plenty of fresh air. He suggested Papa find some additional hot compresses to draw Minola's double ear infections to a head and also to provide comfort for those suffering from chills. He left several bottles of tonics and elixirs for the children as well as some salts he recommended Papa gargle with as a preventative. Dr. Gilman inquired about Mama, but Papa merely shook his head and replied, "It ain't this illness that's botherin' her." The doctor nodded in understanding.

After Dr. Gilman motored out the drive, Papa searched through Flora's rag bag for suitable material to construct some hot compresses. He doubted his sewing abilities and was therefore relieved to find several small draw-stringed sacks that had once held bran. He carried them out to the barn and filled them with oats from the horse's bin, tied their openings securely, and placed them in the oven to warm.

The telephone on the living room wall jangled. It was Ada, who expressed surprise at hearing her father's voice instead of Flora's. Papa told her that Flora had been taken ill that morning, and he relayed the doctor's diagnosis. As he talked, he watched Mama bustling about the kitchen. She had started a kettle of water boiling on the cookstove. Into it she dropped corncobs from the kindling box beside the stove. Papa ran his hand over his eyes and listened as Ada described Margaret's condition.

"Do I need to bring her home … for your sake?" asked Papa.

"No, she's too sick to be moved," asserted Ada. "I can take care of her."

* * * * *

On Tuesday morning, Ada took down the calendar from its nail on the kitchen wall and turned the page to October 1st. Margaret had been sick for a day and a half, but it felt much longer. Ada's back and legs hurt from the many trips up and down the stairs. In addition, her abdomen felt hard and tight, and she was weary from lack of sleep.

Last night, Alfred had moved his pillow and blanket to a stall in the barn and established a makeshift sleeping quarters to escape Margaret's nonstop coughing. The new arrangements provided proximity to his cider jug, so Ada had no doubt Alfred's slumber would be deep.

After breakfast, Ada dropped into a chair at the kitchen table and scratched out a hasty letter to Ella and Hermine in Cleveland advising them of Margaret's illness and the situation at home. She implored one of them to come home and take over the care of the sick children. "You know how it is there with Mama," she stated simply, for there was no need to describe a situation so familiar to the Seibel siblings.

That afternoon, Dr. Gilman followed up on Albert's office call. He examined Margaret and advised she be taken home for Ada's sake, but again Ada refused. She quietly reminded Dr. Gilman that Papa had his hands full with the sick ones at home, including Mama. The doctor left a bottle of Foley's Honey and Tar for Margaret and a vitamin tonic for Ada.

Even though Margaret had no appetite, Ada prepared a bowl of beef broth and carried it upstairs. Margaret's arm was draped over her eyes, and she croaked, "The light hurts so bad." The brilliant autumn sunshine was streaming into the room through the westward-facing window, so Ada closed and latched the outside shutters, which fragmented the sunlight into shafts and provided a dimming effect. After spooning warm broth into Margaret's mouth, Ada went downstairs to retrieve some newspapers, which she tacked over the window frame. The room took on a sepia hue from the filtered sunshine.

* * * * *

By Thursday morning, Mama's spell was starting to crest. Papa had slept on the daybed in the living room, to be close to the stairs so he could tend to the children through the night and also to avoid falling into an exhausted slumber in his own comfortable bed. If he was deep asleep, he might not hear the children when they called out. He rubbed a hand over the rough stubble on his chin and realized he hadn't shaved since Sunday morning, the last day when things had been somewhat normal. Time seemed a blur. Without Flora to separate the cream, the buckets of milk he'd set on the cellar steps had soured. A pan of grapes Mama had plucked from the arbor was fermenting on the back porch. He couldn't remember the last regular meal he'd eaten. There was no time for anything but tending to the children, keeping an eye on Mama, and doing the very minimal outdoor chores.

*****

Ada slowly pulled herself up the stairs to check on Margaret. It seemed like the staircase was getting longer and steeper and the weight of her belly was growing heavier. She stopped at the top of the stairs to catch her breath.

Margaret's cough had developed a deep, dry rattle, and Dr. Gilman now visited every day. He had suggested that Ada consider hiring a nurse to help her care for Margaret, pointing out that Ada herself would soon be in need of postpartum assistance.

When Ada entered Margaret's room, she let out a small gasp. Margaret's pillow case, sheets, and nightgown were spattered with blood, and there were even flecks of blood on the nearby wall. Margaret's coughing had been so violent that it caused a small vessel in her nose to rupture.

"I'm so sorry," Margaret cried weakly, tears mingling with the smears of blood on her face.

Ada hurried to prop her sister upright to prevent her from choking on her own blood. She reassured Margaret that everything would be alright, that she would get things cleaned up in no time.

Ada hurried downstairs and filled a basin with warm water and a washrag. She pulled spare linens from the trunk and one of her own nightgowns from the dresser and tossed them over her shoulder. Slowly and carefully, she climbed the stairs, her center of balance displaced by the baby as well as the basin she carried in front of her.

As Ada tenderly washed the dried blood from her sister's face, arms, and hands, Margaret studied her with tear-filled eyes. "I came here to take care of you," Margaret sobbed, "but the tables got turned."

Ada clucked soothingly that Margaret would be well again in no time and able to help with the baby when it came. She changed the blood-spattered nightgown and bed linens and gave Margaret a sponge bath before easing her back onto the bed. Pulling Margaret's brush from the valise, she gently combed her sister's mass of curls. Margaret closed her eyes and sighed.

Ada emptied the bath water out of the window at the top of the steps, then carried the basin and soiled linens downstairs. At the foot of the stairs, she sagged against the wall. A cramping sensation gripped her abdomen, and she squeezed her eyes shut until the pain had passed. It was too early for the baby to be coming. Today was October 3rd, and by her own calculations, she had two or three more weeks to go. However, the exertion of multiple trips up and down the stairs was moving things along.

That noon over dinner, Ada quietly told Albert that she wanted to follow Dr. Gilman's recommendation to hire a nurse for Margaret, and she confided her own symptoms of early labor. Albert immediately agreed, telephoning the doctor and requesting he find a nurse to begin duty as soon as possible. Until help arrived, Albert insisted he would take over Margaret's care.

Through the night, Albert rose several times to carry a cup of cold water upstairs to Margaret, refresh her compresses, or refill the hot water bottle. Margaret saw the shadowy silhouette of Albert leaning over her, but in her delirium, he was Edmund Atherton asking for a dance. "I can only do the one-step," she whispered.

*****

Ella and Hermine received Ada's plaintive letter on Thursday when they returned to the boarding house after work. In short order, they decided that Ella would ask Rev. Huebschmann for a leave of absence and then travel home to care for the family. She hastily packed a bag and made plans to catch the interurban to Monroeville the next evening. The two sisters asked their landlady for permission to use her telephone to call the Seibel homestead. They wanted to advise Papa of the plan and also receive an update on the health of the children. However, they were unable to get through; connections were spotty because many telephone operators had fallen ill with the influenza and could not man the switchboards.

*****

On Friday morning, Papa awoke with a jolt. He had fallen asleep sitting upright on the daybed with his back against the living room wall. He blinked several times to clear his foggy head and identify the noise that had awakened him. It wasn't Mama; during the night, her spell had crescendoed into a seizure, and she was now lost in a stupor-like sleep that would last for days. He rubbed his hand over his weary eyes. Finally, his senses focused, and he realized the sound that had awakened him was the creaking of the stairs. On the landing stood Minola, looking thin and wan in her nightdress. She still sported the puffs of batting in her ears that Papa had found in Flora's quilting supplies. He had stoppered her ear canals with the fluffy material after both eardrums ruptured.

"Are we having breakfast?" Minola asked quietly. "I'm hungry." She had not eaten more than several spoonfuls of tea and broth in almost a week.

Papa leaned forward with his elbows on his knees. "I'll fix anything you want," he smiled with relief.

As the sun came up, Martha rolled onto her side and gazed at the golden leaves on the mulberry trees outside the bedroom window. She recalled that when she was taken ill, all of the trees were lush with the green of late summer. She felt as though an eternity had passed, and she had no recollection of the individual days. At times, she had awoken and it was daylight, but the next time her eyes opened, it was night. Her head felt fuzzy and unable to connect two thoughts. She heard Flora stirring and the patter of Bill's feet heading toward the staircase. Martha closed her eyes and drifted into slumber.

*****

Before noon on Friday, Dr. Gilman motored into Ada and Albert's drive with nurse Augusta Heyman as his passenger. Gustie was a pleasant and efficient young woman who immediately took command. After Dr. Gilman examined Ada, he recommended she rest as much as possible and absolutely avoid climbing stairs. He and Gustie then looped gauze masks over their faces and proceeded upstairs to check on Margaret. The doctor listened to her lungs, peered into her throat, and left Gustie with a new bottle of medicine and instructions to liberally dose Margaret. He was becoming concerned by her deepening cough and lack of response to any of the tonics he had previously prescribed.

Gustie bustled around Margaret's room, straightening the bed covers, refreshing the compress on Margaret's forehead, and spooning the medicine into her patient's mouth. Margaret studied Gustie's face and furrowed her brow in confusion. Gustie introduced herself and her role.

Margaret smiled. "A nurse?" she asked weakly. "Me, too."

*****

When Ella stepped off the interurban in Monroeville on Friday evening, the town appeared deserted. Due to the flu epidemic, the schools and theatorium had been closed, church services and all public meetings were banned, and even Monroeville's numerous saloons had reluctantly shut their doors. A poster on the station wall warned: "Avoid needless crowds. Don't spit in public places. Wash your hands before eating. When the air is pure, breathe all of it you can—breathe deeply."

Ella walked the three miles to the Seibel homestead, feeling uncertain of what she would find there. As she neared the farmhouse, she was relieved to see the glow of lantern light in the kitchen window. When she opened the kitchen door, Papa was washing dishes at the drysink. In all her recollections, Ella could not remember a time when Papa had washed a dish. Flora, Minola, and Bill were seated at the kitchen table, eating scrambled eggs. They looked up at her in puzzlement, as though they could not recall if she had been away for a long time or had merely stepped outside for a moment. Ella noted the dark circles under their eyes, their slow reaction to her arrival, and the eight bottles of medicine lined up on the kitchen table.

Minola and Flora grinned as they rose to greet her. Bill hurtled himself out of his chair and threw his arms around Ella's waist. "We were so sick, all of us except Papa and Mama," he explained. "Martha's still in bed 'cause her lungs hurt."

Ella tousled Bill's hair and wrapped her arms around her sisters. "Ada wrote and said you needed help," she offered.

Papa nodded as he wiped his hands on a dish towel. "The worst of it's over now, thank *Gott*."

The next morning, October 5th, Ella started the laundry, which had been accumulating for over a week. She stripped the children's beds and boiled the sheets, then hung them out to dry in the bright autumn sun. After all of the laundry was flapping on the clotheslines, she telephoned Ada. Gustie answered and explained her role at the house, then provided an update on both Ada and Margaret. She was pleased to report that Margaret was doing a little better this morning, but Ada's symptoms of early labor continued.

Ella relayed the update to the rest of the family and jotted a quick note to Hermine, whom she knew was anxiously awaiting news from home. Ella continued to put the house in order, dumping the pails of sour milk and the pan of withered grapes and putting away the contents of cupboards and drawers that Mama had scattered during her spell. Papa was relieved to return to his outdoor domain, which had been seriously neglected in the past week.

* * * * *

Even with rest, Ada's labor pains began to increase in intensity. It became obvious to Gustie that the baby's birth could not be delayed. Between her ministrations to Margaret, she phoned Dr. Gilman and sought his counsel. Albert hovered around Ada, fetching a cup of cold water, providing his hand to squeeze through the frequent contractions, and feeling helpless to alleviate her pain. Gustie suggested they walk Ada around the living room to help with the birthing process. With the nurse on one side and Albert on the other, they made a slow circle of the room.

Alfred came in from the barn and watched the three from the kitchen doorway as he peeled a hard-boiled egg. The trio's progress was interrupted by Ada doubling over in pain. "A nip of cider might take the edge off that," suggested Alfred around a mouthful of egg.

"No!" snapped Albert, instantly ashamed of his brusque response.

Alfred shrugged and returned to the chores in the barn.

Dr. Gilman arrived and took charge of the scene in the downstairs bedroom. He dispatched Albert to the kitchen and directed Gustie to help Ada onto the bed.

Albert poured himself a cup of coffee, sat at the kitchen table, then jumped to his feet and began pacing the room, listening for any sound from the bedroom. He needed to keep busy and feel useful, so he went out to the well and pumped a cup of water, which he carried upstairs to Margaret. Albert gave her a sip of water, wet his hankie in the cup of water, and dabbed at her temples as he told her all that was going on downstairs. Margaret smiled and squeezed his hand. He was relieved to see signs of improvement in his sister-in-law.

Ada rode waves of pain that blinded her to anything but her next breath. She was aware of motion in the room and the command "Push!" that came from the end of a long, dark tunnel. Just when she thought she could bear the pain no longer and would surely perish, she heard a tiny cry. Was that her own final gasp as she left this earth?

"Ada!" Gustie exclaimed. "You have a little girl!"

Ada lifted her head to see Dr. Gilman wiping off a squirming purplish-pink body. The little arms were flailing, and soon a hearty wail erupted from the baby.

"A girl," Ada murmured. "I have a daughter!" She clasped her hands to her chest and offered up a silent prayer of gratitude. She wondered how Mama could ever have been disappointed with the news of a daughter's arrival. Ada wiped at the tears spilling onto her cheeks and asked, "Is she okay, being early and all?"

"She looks just fine," assessed Dr. Gilman as he placed the baby in the blanket held out by Gustie.

Upstairs, Albert heard the first tiny cry of the baby, almost like the mew of a kitten. He froze with the wet hankie in midair over Margaret's forehead. At the second cry, he almost bobbled the cup of water onto Margaret's nightgown. Albert raced down the stairs and impatiently rapped at the bedroom door. A beaming Gustie ushered him in. Ada was propped up on the pillows with the baby tucked into the crook of her elbow.

"Congratulations, Albert," offered Dr. Gilman. "You've got a healthy baby girl."

Albert crossed the room, a slow smile creeping up from one corner of his mouth. He didn't care if Gustie and the doctor were still in the room; he leaned over the bed and kissed Ada on the lips. "You done good," he whispered.

Albert gently pulled the edge of the blanket away from the baby's face and touched his finger to her tiny pink fist. "She's perfect!" he proclaimed. He couldn't stop smiling, and he was sure that no man before him had ever felt such euphoria and pride.

Before Dr. Gilman left, he checked on Margaret and advised Albert that Ada and the baby should not be exposed to her. The influenza was highly contagious, and Ada in her weakened state would be quite susceptible. "You don't want to be raising that baby alone," he warned ominously.

Albert nodded his understanding.

Gustie left the little family of three in the back bedroom as she tended to household tasks and Margaret's care.

Albert carefully picked up the tiny bundle and cradled her to his chest. "Let's name her Mildred," he suggested. "It's my favorite name."

Ada hesitated for a moment. "I was thinking we should name her Margaret."

The couple pondered their options and finally reached a compromise. They named the baby Margaret Mildred, but she would be called Mildred.

Albert telephoned the Seibel homestead to announce the arrival of the baby. Ella smiled at her brother-in-law's exuberance and shared the joyous news with the family. Everyone was relieved that Ada and the baby were well, and all approved of the name selection.

Things were starting to look up. Margaret was showing signs of recovery; now there was just the concern that the influenza would spread to other family members.

Albert & Ada with baby Mildred

*****

By Monday morning, Mama had roused from her days of slumber and sat in a stupor in the kitchen rocking chair. She exhibited no reaction to the news that she was now a grandmother. Martha was out of bed but still had a rattle in her lungs, and she complained that her chest hurt. Dr. Gilman advised that she had been on the verge of developing pneumonia. Flora, Minola, and Bill were recovering, but each had a lingering cough and continued to feel like their heads were stuffed with feathers. They found that their sense of smell had also been affected, and they could not detect the comforting aroma of coffee brewing and bacon frying as Ella prepared breakfast.

*****

On Wednesday afternoon, October 9, Gustie carried a basin of warm water upstairs to give Margaret a sponge bath. She began to gently wash her patient's face, then stopped and cocked her head. There was a blueness around Margaret's eyes and lips, but Gustie couldn't be sure if she was seeing things in the dimmed bedroom light. She turned the lantern wick higher and bent closer. Her eyes had not deceived her.

Gustie lifted Margaret's hand to inspect her fingertips, which also carried the same blue pallor.

Margaret whispered, "I heard a baby crying." She stopped to catch her breath. "I've got to get better soon so I can help with..." Her sentence was interrupted by a racking cough. A spray of blood-tinged froth speckled the front of her nightgown.

Gustie's eyes widened over her gauze mask. She tried to keep the concern from her voice as she spoke soothingly to Margaret, repeating the story of the baby's arrival and the choice of name, even though Albert had bounded up the stairs to share the news with Margaret shortly after the baby's birth. Gustie rolled Margaret onto her side to remove the soiled nightgown and bathe her back. She was alarmed by the crackling sound made by Margaret's chest.

After dressing Margaret in a fresh nightgown and propping her up on several pillows to ease her breathing, Gustie carried the basin of water downstairs and refilled the hot water bottle. Margaret had complained that her chest felt painful, and she had teeth-chattering chills despite her fever. Gustie advised Ada and Albert of Margaret's troubling symptoms.

Dr. Gilman was summoned but could not come until that evening due to the increased number of influenza victims who needed his attention. When he arrived, Gustie and Albert accompanied him upstairs. The doctor examined Margaret's face and noted mahogany-colored spots that had formed over her cheek bones. The blueness around her eyes and lips had deepened and spread toward her temples and down her neck. In addition, her breathing was fast and shallow. The doctor tapped Margaret's chest, which responded with the crackling Gustie had heard earlier. Pulling a stethoscope from his bag, he listened to her lungs, which sounded leaden and congested.

Dr. Gilman motioned Albert and Gustie to the adjacent sleeping quarters, where he delivered the grim diagnosis: double pneumonia. He offered to stay at Margaret's bedside but acknowledged there was little more he could do; in addition, he had other flu sufferers to call on yet that evening. He assured Albert that Gustie could provide as much care as he could at this point.

Albert was stunned. He escorted Dr. Gilman to the back door and then stood in the kitchen, running his hand through his hair and wondering how to break the news to Ada. He walked slowly to the bedroom and pushed open the door. Ada looked up from nursing the baby and immediately knew the prognosis. Her chin quivered. "I have to be with her."

Albert helped Ada climb the stairs, then retrieved baby Mildred, placing her in a wicker clothes basket in the adjoining sleeping quarters. Gustie motioned Ada to sit on the bedside chair she had been occupying and excused herself to refill the hot water bottle. Albert watched as Ada tenderly stroked Margaret's face and spoke lovingly to her.

Margaret drifted in a semi-conscious fog, muttering snatches of sentences that made no sense to the young couple. She complained of the cold and mentioned papers scattered in the snow. She had to gather them or Mrs. Morris would be mad. Now she heard music. The soldiers were here, but was it alright to dance with them?

As Margaret's breathing became more labored, she stopped talking and fell into a private delirium. She was floating again on the waters of Lake Erie, with Gladys' strong arms holding her up. It was such a pleasant sensation, and a faint smile curved her lips. But the waters started to creep over her face, and the sky turned from brilliant blue to fractured shafts of yellowish green to total blackness as she sank deeper and deeper. Ada's voice was replaced by muffled emptiness. Where were Gladys' strong arms to lift her to the surface again? Now she was weightless and gliding—gliding across the dance floor, gliding along the lakeshore road under the moonlight.

Margaret

Gustie held her fingertips to Margaret's neck and with a nod confirmed that she was gone. She started to pull the sheet over Margaret's face, but Ada caught her hand. Through a veil of tears, Ada gently smoothed her hand over Margaret's mass of curls and tenderly kissed her on the forehead.

* * * * *

The telephone on the living room wall at the Seibel homestead jangled at 11 p.m. The siblings were seated around the living room table, trying to piece a puzzle. Papa answered the phone but said very little, his voice sounding raspy and strained. When he hung up the receiver, he leaned his forehead against the wall. The siblings stopped, their hands frozen in mid-air over the puzzle. No words were spoken, but they knew the unthinkable had happened.

* * * * *

Albert brought Ada and the baby downstairs and encouraged Ada to lie down on the bed. It had only been four days since she had given birth, and he was worried about her health.

The undertaker, Mr. Daniels of Monroeville, was summoned. Albert let him in the back door and showed him to the staircase but could not bear to participate in the sad scene upstairs. Gustie would have to be the undertaker's assistant. Instead, he went into the downstairs bedroom, where Ada lay on her side on the bed, the baby nestled beside her. Albert lay down next to Ada and wrapped his arms around her. Upstairs, they could hear the steady *thump-thump* of Mr. Daniels's foot as he operated the floor pump on the embalming apparatus. Tears streamed down Ada's cheeks and onto the downy hair of baby Mildred. Albert could not comprehend how they had traversed the arc from absolute joy to utter sorrow in such a short span of time.

* * * * *

The Seibel siblings went to bed, where they sobbed and sniffled quietly in the darkness. Bill drifted in and out of a fitful sleep, occasionally calling out Margaret's name. For the sisters, it seemed as if they were in a long nightmare from which there was no waking.

"It's my fault," choked out Minola. "I was the first to get sick, and I gave it to Margaret when I made her sleep with us."

Martha sniffled and reached out to squeeze Minola's arm. After a long moment, she asked, "Why couldn't the influenza have taken Mama instead of Margaret?"

None of the sisters rebuked Martha. She had verbalized an unspoken sentiment held by all.

* * * * *

The next day, Papa drove the machine into Monroeville and met with Mr. Zehnder, the clerk of Ridgefield Township. After offering his condolences, Mr. Zehnder spread the map of Riverside Cemetery on his desk.

"Did you want something near your family on the Scheidt plot?" Mr. Zehnder asked, stabbing his finger at the area where Old Man and Kathrina were buried. "There's one plot available next to them."

"No!" Papa said, a little more forcefully than intended. He cleared his throat. "I ... I don't want just one plot. I wanna buy a half a lot—six plots."

Mr. Zehnder looked up at Papa with concern. "More sick ones at home, Bill?" he asked.

"No … not yet," Papa answered. However, his confidence in the children's recovery had been shaken by Margaret's seeming improvement followed by her sudden death. And then there was Ella and Hermine, Ada and Albert and the baby, and Mama and himself who had not yet come down with the influenza. Who knew how many more times death would visit the family before this epidemic was over? Being a natural pessimist, Papa prepared for the worst by buying enough plots for several family members. If he should be the next victim of the influenza, the girls—or whoever was left—would not have to perform this heart-wrenching task of gravesite selection.

Mr. Zehnder helped Papa select a half-lot and wrote out a receipt for fifteen dollars. Papa folded the paperwork and slid it into his coat pocket as he climbed onto the seat of the machine. Pulling out his handkerchief, he sat for a long time in the brilliant autumn sunshine, dabbing at his eyes and wiping his nose. He had never expected to be burying one of his girls.

* * * * *

The funeral was set for 1:00 p.m. on Saturday, October 12, at the Seibel home. Mama's brother, Uncle Will, arrived with Albert, who explained that Ada was not up to traveling with the baby. Because the epidemic necessitated that the funeral be a private affair, the only neighbors to attend were George and Bertha. Mr. Daniels brought Margaret's body to the house and positioned her casket between the two west windows of the parlor. While the undertaker was arranging the body, the rest of the family went outdoors, unable to bear being witness to the proceedings. Hermine had been summoned, and she and her sisters stood in the yard with their arms around one another, a fresh flood of tears coursing down their faces.

There had been a hard frost during the night, and the mulberry leaves tumbled down in a golden shower. As Hermine gazed at the yellow leaves littering the ground, she recalled that, as children, she and Margaret had pocketed the leaves like gold coins, pretending to be rich. She longed for those childhood days and Margaret's companionship. Flora commented that they should be thankful Margaret's last summer was filled with so much joy and laughter at Ruggles Beach, even though it meant she had been home with them for such a brief time.

Mama seemed detached, showing no emotion over Margaret's death. She drifted about the yard, pulling a few weeds from around the foundation of the house and acknowledging Will and Albert with a nod of the head, as if they were strangers or casual acquaintances. Her recent spell had left her more confused than ever.

Reverend Keppel motored into the drive with a woman seated beside him. Through the sheen of their tears, the girls assumed it was Mrs. Keppel, until Martha gasped. The woman crossing the yard toward them was Mrs. Morris, the teacher whom Margaret had disliked so intensely. Reverend Keppel offered his condolences and explained that in honor of Margaret's love of music, he had invited Mrs. Morris to sing a solo at the funeral. The girls clutched each other and choked back their sobs. Reverend Keppel did not know that Mrs. Morris's presence only augmented their grief.

The minister led the group into the parlor and began the service. He advised them that their family circle was not broken, but that Margaret had gone ahead to heaven, where she was waiting for the day when they would all be reunited. Reverend Keppel warned that they dare not ask why Margaret was taken in her youth but remember that the fairest flowers are picked before the frost.

Mrs. Morris sang her selection, "Beautiful Isle of Somewhere," which had been sung at President McKinley's funeral. The girls were not comforted by the song or the soloist, and later they resolved there would be no music at any future time of loss. At the closing of the service, the family followed the casket out to Riverside Cemetery for interment. The slow *rum-tumming* of the machine's tires on the uneven brick roadway leading to the cemetery sounded like a muffled drum cadence.

As Rev. Keppel closed the graveside ceremony with a prayer, Minola blinked back her tears and tilted her chin skyward, unable to bear looking at the gaping hole that would soon contain the body of dear Margaret. She concentrated on the trees, which had been green and lush before the influenza descended upon them. Now, many were leafless. It struck Minola that her life had been changed in the same way; Margaret's death had left it just as barren.

For the Seibel girls, the fall season had always focused on going to school, harvesting potatoes and apples, and giving the house a thorough cleaning. They had never paused to admire the exquisite beauty of autumn, with its warm sun and bright leaves—nature's best show of the year. But the dazzling light and color that had surrounded the days of Margaret's illness and death left an indelible imprint upon the sisters. They would forever cling to those precious last days of Indian summer.

* * * * *

While over 12,000 Americans had died from the influenza epidemic during September of 1918, the cruelest month was October, with 195,000 deaths in 31 days. For the flu victims, a return to health was not the end of the pain. Martha had a lingering chest rattle and developed the need for eyeglasses. An additional indignity was that the victims' hair began to fall out by the handfuls due to their high fevers. Martha shampooed with hop tea to encourage hair growth, tried combing her hair into different styles, and finally resorted to wearing hats. Minola's hair grew back taffy colored and curly for a while.

Minola, Flora, & Bill after the Spanish influenza

Martha, Minola, and Bill were still recovering from the illness and were deep in mourning when Monroeville schools reopened on Monday, October 28, after being closed for four weeks. When Minola stepped down from Mr. Busch's wagon on the first day back at school, she felt slow and confused. Other students who had suffered through the influenza were equally gaunt and muddle-headed, and those who had also lost family members carried a haunted expression. Minola slowly made her way up the walk toward the school's front steps. Over on the playground, three elementary school girls were jumping rope. Their sing-song rhyme caught Minola's attention:

"I had a little bird,
Its name was Enza,
I opened the window,
And in-flu-enza."

Minola's eyes filled with tears. She rushed up the steps and struggled to open the heavy school door.

* * * * *

With Ella and Hermine's return to Cleveland, Flora resumed her role as keeper of the home fires as well as Papa's right-hand man. One afternoon, she cut the remaining cabbage from the garden and carried it into the summer kitchen in bushel baskets. She noticed how frequently she had to stop and catch her breath.

With only Mama to help her make the sauerkraut, the process seemed slow and tedious. Flora missed the lively conversation of her sisters. At one point, Mama set down her wooden cabbage shredder and asked peevishly, "When is Margaret coming home? We need more hands!"

Flora was speechless. Her chin quivered, and she fought back the tears. Mama frustrated her a thousand times a day, but how could she scold someone who was so mentally adrift? In addition, Mama had had her own episode during the influenza epidemic and Margaret's death and therefore had no recollection of the events. Flora put down her pan of shredded cabbage and went to the living room, where she dried her eyes before picking up the phone to call cousin Rosie. Maybe Rosie could come down and help them with the sauerkraut. While she wasn't much of an asset in the kitchen, Rosie had the gift of gab, which Flora sorely needed today.

Flora lifted the receiver to her ear and was poised to dial the operator when she heard Emmaline Moss's voice saying, "… and Albert insisted they name the baby Mildred. I heard that was the name of his former sweetheart." She clucked her tongue. "Poor Ada! To go through life calling her own daughter by the name of her husband's first true love!"

Flora felt as though someone had punched her in the stomach. She wanted to shout into the receiver, "That's not true, Emmaline! How can you spread such lies?" Instead, she quietly replaced the receiver in its cradle and slumped against the wall. She wiped at her wet cheeks with her apron and returned to the summer kitchen to shred cabbage with Mama.

* * * * *

The tide of the war had turned in the Allies' favor. Rumors of an armistice circulated on November 7, with false celebrations and optimistic predictions that the flu and the war were winding down together. Four days later, Minola and Bill were beating the parlor rug on the clothesline in the backyard when they heard the distant sound of church bells ringing in Monroeville. The war was finally over!

Unfortunately, the flu had not been vanquished. By December 6, there were still forty-three cases of the illness in Monroeville. Margaret's was not the only death in the extended Seibel family. Word came that Mama's sister, Katie, had lost her twenty-year-old son, George, to influenza while based at the Great Lakes Naval Training Station in Chicago. Flora trembled each time the telephone rang, since it always brought bad news.

* * * * *

There seemed to be countless ways throughout each day that the siblings missed Margaret. Flora had appreciated her sister's capable and cheerful assistance in the kitchen and her way of mothering the younger ones. At night, the bed she had shared with Margaret now seemed cold and empty. Because Margaret and Martha were only a year apart in school, they had enjoyed cozy chats about their common circle of friends and activities. On numerous occasions, Martha thought to herself, "I must tell Margaret about…," and then the familiar ache returned when she realized Margaret was no longer there to confide in. Without her special tutor, Minola floundered through math until Martha stepped in to provide assistance. During sibling squabbles, Minola had always had the support of Margaret; now she felt so alone. Bill had grown accustomed to Margaret's mothering—seeing that his hair was combed, teeth brushed, and lunch packed before he dashed out the front door to catch Mr. Busch's school wagon each morning. For the Seibel siblings, the separation from Ada upon her marriage three years ago had been difficult although bearable, but the daily reminders of the permanent loss of Margaret freshened their grief and deepened their longing for her.

For Ada, the tenant house on Sand Hill Road, which had once held so much promise of happy events, became a constant reminder of Margaret's death. When she went upstairs to change the sheets on

Alfred's bed, she could not bear to look into the adjoining bedroom that had been the scene of such immense sorrow.

By late fall, Albert announced that he had learned of a larger tenant home with more acreage, owned by their current landlords, the spinster Yingling sisters. The farm, located on Ridge Road, was just a short trip around the corner from their existing home; in fact, the rear acreage of the two farms adjoined. Ada promptly encouraged Albert to make the necessary arrangements.

On December 18th, Papa, Martha, Minola, and Bill arrived at the Gfell home to assist with the move. Flora, who had so desperately wanted to help, stayed home to watch over Mama, who was again in the throes of a spell. Minola and Bill raced ahead of the movers to inspect the new home. It was a stately brick, built in 1821 by two pioneer brothers, with a frame extension that housed the kitchen area. The commodious upstairs of the brick section would not be needed for now. Instead, the two front downstairs rooms, which could be heated more easily, would be used for bedrooms, with a comfortable sitting room situated behind them. Albert pointed to the south wall of the sitting room and told the two youngsters that a large fireplace had once stretched across the entire expanse. He'd heard that on cold winter nights, local Indians had let themselves into the house to sleep on the floor in front of the fireplace. Minola shivered to think she was standing on floorboards where Indians had once rested. Bill, on the other hand, smiled broadly and promptly stretched out on the floor, making loud snoring noises.

The brick tenant house on Ridge Road

Minola and Bill walked back to the tenant house on Sand Hill Road and helped pack up the young couple's limited belongings. To Minola, moving was an exciting novelty, and she envied those who were privileged to experience it. She was keenly aware that the Seibels were forever rooted on the homestead.

When the last of the household goods had been loaded onto the wagon, Ada and Minola bundled baby Mildred into her carriage and surrounded her with Ada's few precious breakables that could not be subjected to rough handling by the movers. The two sisters would push the carriage to the neighbor's house, where they'd stay until the temperature in the brick house could be made comfortable for an infant.

Ada closed the door on the tenant house for the last time, her hand lingering on the knob. She had experienced the peaks of joy and the depths of sadness in this house. As she pushed the baby carriage across the front yard to the road, Ada stole one last glance at the bedroom window that had been Margaret's.

For the Seibels, a year that had begun with bright promise and optimism had ended in quiet mourning as they learned to live without their Margaret.

Chapter 22
Seibel Homestead
1919

THE START OF THE NEW YEAR brought murmurings of further gloom. There was talk that Martha's senior class would not graduate because they had missed a month of school during the influenza epidemic in the fall. Rumors circulated that the flu would resurge in the spring. Each day was filled with uncertainty, and many nights were marked with muffled sobs as the girls buried their faces in their pillows and gave release to their lingering sorrow over Margaret's death.

In early January, Flora took the interurban to Cleveland and spent several days with Ella and Hermine, sleeping three to a bed in their chilly rented room on Crawford Road. Hermine had landed a position at the Willys-Overland Company, and between the frosty temperature of their sleeping quarters and her nerves over the new job, she had quite a case of cold feet. Upon Flora's return home, she promptly set about piecing a quilt to increase Ella and Hermine's comfort.

Flora & Hermine in front of the boarding house on Crawford Road

Despite the addition of the quilt, both Ella and Hermine came down with the dreaded influenza in February. Their landlady, Mrs. Hunt, tended to her two boarders while taking extreme precautions for herself. At times, the sisters awoke from their fevered slumber to see Mrs. Hunt wrapped mummy-like in a sheet at their bedside, a pillowcase pulled over her hair and forehead, a gauze mask covering the lower half of her face, and an old pair of riding gloves protecting her hands. The only visible human features were her concerned eyes behind gold-rimmed spectacles. After the sisters recovered, Ella rode the interurban home to spend a week rebuilding her strength before resuming institutional visits and pavement-pounding.

*****

Following Margaret's death, Martha coped by adopting a *carpe diem* mentality. Instead of studying, she went ice skating with friends on Frink's Run or walked down to Elsie's house to listen to Ordmanns' new Victrola. She attended sleepovers at girlfriends' houses, where they pulled taffy, played cards, danced to records on the Victrola, and gossiped late into the night. During school lunch breaks, Martha and her classmates hurried downtown to the drugstore and indulged in a penny game of chance in hopes of winning a box of candy. They occasionally lost track of time and were tardy returning to class. During the subsequent after-school detention, they rolled their eyes at each other in exasperation. The focus of life was having fun and living in the moment, not paying penance for harmless youthful pursuits. However, on Sundays, following Rev. Keppel's powerful sermons, Martha experienced a change of attitude and vowed to lead a humble, Christian life. Her resolve lasted until she exited the sanctuary and climbed into Papa's aging machine for the ride home. She cringed at being seen in such a relic.

Martha also resolved to be understanding with Mama, but she quickly became impatient at the constant cycling of spells. Mama wandered the house, chattering incessantly, which made it difficult to study for semester exams. To calm Mama's agitated state, Martha led her into the bedroom, where she loosened the tight knot of hair at Mama's nape and ran the old silver-plated hairbrush through her thick, waist-length hair. While the hairdressing had a soothing effect on Mama, it only served to remind Martha of the spindly remnants of her own hair. She felt like a plucked chicken, but there sat Mama, unscathed by the flu and with a glorious head of hair. Martha immediately chastised herself for such envious thoughts. After all, her hair would eventually grow back, but Mama's mental condition would never improve.

With fewer restrictions on gasoline usage, Martha and her schoolmates went on frequent outings in machines borrowed from their parents. When she heard the sputter of an engine in the drive, Martha quickly grabbed her coat and hat and slipped out the kitchen door, casting a wary look over her shoulder. She did not want Mama to follow and beckon her friends into the house for a visit. Even though Mama was always quite sociable with guests, her conversation could be unpredictable. After she had warned one of Ella's friends, "Don't ever drop your bloomers for any man," the girls made a point of keeping their friends, particularly male callers, at a safe distance from the house.

Martha & friends going for a ride

Martha and her friend Ruth Strohmeier frequently double dated with Lad Herrick and Myron Kolb. They attended parties and dropped in at the theatorium, where Elsie Ordmann played the piano for the silent movies. In the darkness, they whispered about the fate of heroine Norma Talmadge in the feature film "The Secret of the Storm Country" or blinked back tears during the wartime melodrama "The Heart of Humanity."

One evening as Lad motored the girls home in the dark, he nearly missed a curve in the road. He overcorrected and ran his father's machine into a mailbox post. Ruth was jolted forward, hitting her mouth on the dashboard. While the boys inspected the car for damage, Ruth and Martha huddled in the glow of the machine's head lanterns to assess the injury. Martha angled the mirror of her compact to reflect the light for Ruth, who used her thumb to gently nudge her incisors forward to their original position. She tapped her teeth together gingerly and gave Martha a pained expression.

"Are your teeth gonna be alright?" Martha asked, her voice tinged with panic.

"I … I don't know," stammered Ruth, pulling out a handkerchief to dab at the blood on her lips, "but I won't be eating taffy for a while, that's for certain." She touched the tip of her tongue to her repositioned front teeth and winced.

The boys reported that there was no damage to the machine, but it was a subdued ride home for the formerly carefree foursome.

* * * * *

In the post-flu months, Flora practiced prevention by cautioning her siblings to bundle up and always wear their hats when going outdoors. She endlessly reminded Bill, "Put something on your head." Since he often misplaced his knit hat, Bill grabbed the closest head covering available. Once it was an old shawl; another time it was a bonnet left behind by a berry picker. One evening, to appease as well as tease, Bill trailed Flora out to the barn with a single glove plopped on top of his head.

As Flora opened the barn door, she turned and caught sight of her brother's head gear. "Bill!" she admonished. "What'd I tell you?"

"You said to put *something* on my head," responded Bill innocently. "So, I did!"

* * * * *

As a growing boy in a house full of females, eleven-year-old Bill looked to assert his independence and identity. He expressed a longing for a space of his own, not just the bed in the room he shared with his sisters. Flora suggested he claim Ada and Ella's former room, which adjoined the girls' larger bedroom, but Bill rejected that idea. It was finally agreed that the room at the top of Stegmiller's stairs would provide the privacy and independence that Bill sought. The siblings no longer used the space as a refuge from Mama, and it had become a repository for unused crocks, Flora's soap-making supplies, Mama and Papa's old *kisten* (trunks), and a narrow cot that Papa had bought at an auction for the use of the few itinerant farm hands who had been given indoor lodging. Despite the Spartan accommodations, Bill was thrilled with his new surroundings. He arranged his few treasures—arrowheads, cicada casings, a bird's nest, and an assortment of stones, some embedded with fossils—on top of one of the *kisten*. To Bill, the room validated that he was not just "one of the girls."

* * * * *

In mid-April, the Monroeville schools adjourned for half a day so that the students could travel to Norwalk to see the trophy train—artifacts brought back from Europe by the victorious Doughboys—and a $10,000 tank purchased with Liberty bond money. There would be inspirational speeches by local dignitaries, but the crowning celebration would be the soldiers' parade to welcome home Company G of the 145th Infantry. Flora drove the aging machine to Monroeville and joined her siblings on the interurban to Norwalk. They mingled with the crowds admiring the tank and other military artifacts and then found a place along Main Street to watch the parade.

Soon, martial music filled the air as the Norwalk High School marching band led the troops down the street. The crowd whistled, cheered, and clapped for the soldiers, and office workers tossed confetti from the upper stories of the buildings that lined the street. Bill, who was shorter than the rest, stood on tiptoe and craned his neck this way and that for a glimpse over the shoulders of the bystanders before him. Having no luck at improving his view, he wormed his way through the crowd until he was on the curb, where he had an unobstructed panorama of the passing parade.

For the girls, there was a hollowness to the victory, because Margaret was not there to share in the celebration with them. She, too, had supported the war effort and endured the necessary rationing and sacrifices. How she would have enjoyed the parade, the people, and the public celebration of American triumph.

Flora felt awash with melancholy until she spotted a familiar face in the phalanx of soldiers passing by. It was Phil Burrer, an officer in Company G, leading his men in a precision drill. How handsome and dignified he looked with his crisp uniform and ramrod-straight posture! Flora's face flushed, and her eyes followed Phil until he was out of view.

On the interurban ride back to Monroeville, Flora replayed the image of Phil over and over in her mind. When Bill tugged on her sleeve and asked what she thought of this or if she had seen that, Flora responded in a vague, distracted manner. Even the Fuller's hard start and subsequent breakdown on the way home could not fluster her. The four siblings left the machine where it died on Plank Road and walked home, with Flora's head in the clouds.

Papa retrieved the worn-out Fuller and attempted to repair it, but even his considerable mechanical skills could not resurrect the derelict vehicle. The girls were secretly relieved that their days of riding in the out-of-date, backfiring old crate were over. Because Papa believed in extracting every last bit of value from an item, he stripped the Fuller of parts that could be recycled for other uses before he hauled its remains down the lane to a rusty demise at the back of the farm. The girls were mortified to discover that Papa had salvaged the front seat from the

Fuller and had converted it into a swing for the front porch. They shunned the improvised swing as a symbol of everything old-fashioned and make-do that they strived to overcome.

Their pride took another blow when they were forced to use Papa's old Ford truck as a conveyance. There was not enough room in the cab for all of the family members to have a seat in enclosed comfort, which meant that several of the siblings had to ride in the open wooden bed of the truck. The girls' tender egos were bruised by being treated as cargo. One Sunday afternoon as Papa drove the family home after a visit at Ada and Albert's, Martha, Minola, and Bill were relegated to the truck bed while Papa, Mama, and Flora shared the cab. The sisters quickly flattened themselves on the floor of the truck bed when another vehicle approached or when they passed through a populated area. Bill didn't recognize the indignity, and he waved vigorously at passers-by. To him, the truck was a mechanical marvel, and he was simply pleased to be around its gears, cylinders, cranks, and levers, whether he was the driver or the passenger. However, like the girls, he was less enthralled with the open transportation when it meant riding in the rain.

In early May, Papa bought a used Overland, which soon exhibited reliability issues. Meanwhile, George and Bertha purchased their first machine, a brand new Buick. Because the Overland was frequently out of commission, cousin Elmer kindly gave the girls a lift in the stylish, shiny Buick. When he brought them home from church choir practice after dark, Martha leaned her head against the back of the car seat, gazed at the stars above, and thought of Margaret. Was she looking at those same stars from the other side in heaven and thinking of her sisters?

Hermine, Martha, Elmer with dog, Flora, Rosie, a friend, & Walter

* * * * *

While Martha helped Papa plant the new strawberry field, her thoughts turned to the future. Graduation was but a month away, and there was much to consider. Ada and Flora had offered to collaborate on Martha's graduation outfit—an organdy shirtwaist and a khaki wool skirt—as well as her reception dress. But of more weighty concern were her educational plans. Martha had initially been swayed by visiting missionaries whose powerful sermons detailed their service in exotic lands. Reverend Keppel encouraged her interest and suggested she follow Ella's footsteps at Schauffler Missionary Training School. However, it was a different sister that Martha chose to emulate. She decided to pursue Margaret's unfulfilled dream of becoming a nurse.

Two nurses representing Mt. Sinai Hospital in Cleveland visited Monroeville High School and interviewed Martha. They suggested she pay a call at the hospital and acquaint herself with the program. In mid-May, Martha boarded the interurban for Cleveland, where she was met by Ella and Hermine. The three sisters toured the hospital and learned about the nursing program. Martha was awed by Mt. Sinai and longed to attend there. However, paying for higher education was the problem. Ella and Hermine offered to help with tuition, but their meager salaries alone could not bear the full cost. In addition, Hermine was now paying on her own college loan from Grandpa Gasteier. During the interurban ride back to Monroeville, Martha chewed her lip and weighed her options. Perhaps Papa would be willing to help, or maybe she would do like Hermine and seek financial assistance from Grandpa Gasteier.

Martha felt beset by indecision. If she was going to take on the burden of debt for her education, she wanted to be sure she enrolled in a quality program. While she was highly impressed with Mt. Sinai, she knew there must be other equally qualified nursing programs, and perhaps some that carried a lower tuition. Flora suggested Martha seek advice from Dr. Gilman. Surely, he was knowledgeable about such things and could provide some direction.

Martha timidly paid a call on the family doctor, who listened thoughtfully as she revealed her dilemma. He rubbed his hand over his chin and acknowledged that while Mt. Sinai ran a very good nursing school, he was partial to another Cleveland institution, Lakeside Hospital, which had had a nursing program since 1898. Dr. Gilman studied Martha's youthful face. "How old are you?" he asked.

"Seventeen," responded Martha. When she saw him scowl, she quickly offered, "But I'll be eighteen in just a month."

"Your age isn't going to help you," Dr. Gilman advised. He shuffled the papers on his desk into a neat stack and then peered over the rims of his spectacles at Martha. "Fill out an application for Lakeside, but put down your age as nineteen."

"You mean … I should lie?" asked Martha incredulously.

Dr. Gilman gave the papers a sharp rap on the desk and turned toward his tall wooden filing cabinet, signaling the end of the conversation.

Martha left the doctor's office feeling more confused than before. That weekend, she and Flora spent an afternoon at Ada's, putting the finishing touches on her graduation clothing. Martha stood on a stool while Ada and Flora pinned the hem of the khaki wool skirt, and she told her sisters about her dilemma.

"Nothin' good ever came of lying," advised Ada, her lips clamped around a row of straight pins. "I'm disappointed in Dr. Gilman for suggesting such a trick."

"Can't you wait and apply next year, when you really *are* nineteen?" asked Flora. "That'd give you a year to earn some money, too."

The money issue had been weighing heavily on Martha's mind. Her friend Ruth had made arrangements to spend the summer working at Ruggles Beach farmhouse, just as Margaret had done the previous summer. Ruth gently begged Martha to join her, acknowledging that Martha would have to overcome tender memories of Margaret but also reminding her of the income, the proximity to the beach, and—Ruth's voice dropped to an eager whisper—the dancing! Martha briefly considered the option but knew her longing for Margaret would only intensify if she retraced the footsteps of her sister's final summer.

* * * * *

On graduation day, the Seibel household bustled with activity. There was a clean shirt that needed to be pressed for Bill to wear to the graduation, and the evening chores had to be finished earlier than normal. Before preparing a hasty supper, Flora hurried to drizzle a sweet red sauce on a strawberry trifle she had made in honor of Martha's achievement.

In the midst of the happy commotion, Mama's growing agitation signaled an impending spell, which cast a pall on the preparations. She set a furious pace in the rocking chair by the cookstove, muttering to herself in German. Bill entered the kitchen, carrying the basket of eggs he had gathered, and failed to catch the screen door before it slammed behind him. The three sisters held their breath as they awaited Mama's angry outburst, but she only scowled in Bill's direction.

After supper, the girls hurried to wash the dishes and tidy the kitchen before changing their clothes. "I'll stay home with Mama," Minola quietly offered. "Bill stayed home last year when, when … Margaret graduated," she stammered in painful reflection. "He'd choke if he had to miss another one."

Martha gratefully accepted and whispered to her sisters, "Why can't Mama just be normal—like everyone else's mother? We can't ever take her anyplace without worrying what she'll do or say, and she can't be left alone. It's no way to live—for her or for us."

Flora patted Martha's arm in consolation. "Nothing can be done about it, so go on and get dressed, or you'll be late for your own graduation."

Martha scampered upstairs and changed into the organdy shirtwaist and khaki wool skirt. She stood before the dresser mirror, pinning her hair high on her head, then trying it low, but maintaining the part in the middle that was so popular with all her classmates. She clipped on a pair of long dangling earrings that were in vogue and turned her head from side to side, assessing the look. Wrinkling her nose and giving a small shake of the head, she deemed the ear bobs not dignified enough and slipped them back into her cloth jewelry bag. As she dropped the bag into the top dresser drawer, she spotted the small pasteboard box that had been Margaret's. Slowly tipping back the box lid, Martha stared at the mementoes of a life cut short—a dance ticket from Ruggles Beach, a celluloid trinket from Cedar Point, a red silk ribbon from a war bond parade, a dried four-leaf clover, and the oblong golden pin that was Margaret's confirmation gift from Papa.

Martha lifted the box to her nose. She could still detect the faint aroma of talcum powder and lye soap—the scent of Margaret. She gently removed the confirmation pin from the box and, through a film of tears, affixed it to the neck of her blouse. Not only would the pin serve as a small way of having Margaret with her this evening, but it would also reflect Martha's promise to fulfill her sister's educational dreams.

To distract Mama and ease tensions in the house, Minola suggested the two of them take a walk down the lane to the back of the farm, where they could pick some ferns and flowers. Mama had finished decorating the monkey jug with trinkets and treasures, and now her newest pastime was creating framed landscapes from dried foliage that she pressed between the pages of her daughters' books. The girls resented the greenish imprints left on the pages of their precious books, but they knew it was best not to express outrage.

Mama

Mama strode along the lane, chattering nonstop and pulling random weeds along the fence line. Minola pointed out some delicate pink wild roses and suggested they would make a nice addition to Mama's collection. Mama squatted beside the low vines and began pinching off the blossoms between her thumb and forefinger. She prattled on about putting flowers in her hair when she was young, during the time she had worked as a domestic at the mansion of Mr. John Wright. She complained about having to accept her pay from behind Mr. Wright's back and how the Wrights had never invited her to participate in their ballroom dances.

Minola half-listened, twirling the basket she had brought along for Mama's selections and absentmindedly gazing across the strawberry fields toward the lengthening shadows of the tree line. Suddenly, she realized that Mama had stopped chattering. Minola whirled around, panicked that

Mama might be steaming toward the house.

Instead, Mama was still crouched beside the wild rose bush, her rough hands fingering the delicate blossoms. She looked up at Minola, shielding her eyes against the late afternoon sun.

"When I worked for Mr. Wright, I never stayed away from home as long as Margaret has. *Nicht* (Never)," Mama's brow furrowed in confusion. "She should *nach Hause kommen* (come home). It's not right to stay away this long."

Minola's hand trembled as she held out the basket for the harvested blossoms. She felt pity for Mama, who had no recollection of their awful suffering with the influenza and Margaret's subsequent death. Minola wanted to tell Mama just how much she longed for Margaret to come home, too, but the lump in her throat prevented her from speaking.

* * * * *

Martha followed the procession of her classmates onto the stage at the town opera hall and beamed at the members of her family in the audience. She had reserved seats for Papa, Flora, and Bill near the front, while Ada and Albert had requested seats at the back of the hall so they could step out if baby Mildred became boisterous. Ella and Hermine could not attend since both had to work the following day, but they sent Martha a vanity bag and a pair of kid gloves as graduation gifts.

Mr. Eaton, the president of the school board, stepped up to the podium and presented the commencement address. From her vantage point, Martha noticed that his pant legs were trembling. She pondered Mr. Eaton's case of nerves and wondered if he had practiced his speech by delivering it to his herd of prize-winning Holstein cattle. Martha gazed out at the members of the audience and was struck by how similar their expressions were to that of placid-faced cows. Suddenly, the notion of cud-chewing cattle filling the seats of the opera hall and listening dutifully to the shaky-legged Mr. Eaton was overwhelmingly funny. The desire to laugh rippled through Martha's abdomen. She bit her lower lip to suppress a wide grin and felt her shoulders shake with restrained mirth. Demurely holding a hand to her mouth, Martha shot a glance toward her family and realized that her struggle had not gone unnoticed. Flora locked eyes with her and sent a message of curiosity mixed with mortification.

Martha's barely controlled giggling was short-lived, however, as Mr. Eaton took his seat and Mrs. Morris glided to the center of the stage to deliver her usual commencement solo. Martha dug her fingernails into her palms. The memories of Margaret's dislike of the teacher and Mrs. Morris's musical offering at Margaret's funeral were painfully fresh. Martha lightly fingered the golden pin at her throat and glanced toward Flora, but the anguished expression on her sister's face was more than Martha could bear. She dropped her chin to her chest. As Martha studied her lap, a single tear splashed onto the folds of her khaki skirt and slowly wicked outward in a dark stain.

Martha

* * * * *

By mid-June, Martha had mailed her application to Lakeside Hospital for admittance to the nursing program that started in October. Despite the pricking of her conscience, she had followed Dr. Gilman's suggestion to lie about her age. The other nagging problem—how to pay for her education—had not been resolved. She was reluctant to approach Grandpa Gasteier for a loan, so she circulated word among the women of her neighborhood and church congregation that she was available for such odd jobs as babysitting, housekeeping, and canning.

Emmaline Moss engaged Martha for some heavy housecleaning

services. The Mosses had recently completed an industrious updating of their home's interior, complete with replastering the ceilings, painting the woodwork, and papering the walls. Emmaline was proudest of a modern feature she had insisted be installed during the remodeling: two built-in china cabinets with leaded-glass doors on either side of the parlor archway. Now, she could properly display her heirloom Limoges china and be rid of the freestanding display cabinet that smacked of olden days. The remodeling had not been done on a whim or to impress the Mosses' easily awed neighbors. Emmaline was anticipating an important announcement from her schoolteacher daughter Edith, who had been keeping company with a beau "from a good English family." Thus, the remodeling was intended to demonstrate that the Mosses were of equal social footing with any Yankee family.

While Emmaline was happy with the outcome of the interior work, she was dismayed by the fine coating of dust that had settled on every surface. So, for two weeks, Martha left the strawberry fields each day at noon, exchanged her straw hat for a headscarf, and spent long afternoons toiling for Emmaline. Martha didn't mind the scrubbing, dusting, polishing, and sweeping. She was used to meeting the high standards of Mama, who was not an easy person to please. However, she was not accustomed to having such a vigilant and suspicious overseer.

While scrubbing the baseboards in the upstairs hallway one afternoon, Martha crept along on hands and knees, pushing the bucket of soapy water ahead of her. As she neared the stairwell, the bucket resisted her nudge. Martha stopped scrubbing and turned to free the container from the protruding nail or raised knot of wood in the floorboards that impeded its progress. She froze with both hands on the bucket when she noticed the hard toes of Emmaline's shiny oxblood shoes poking out from behind the corner of the wall near the stairwell. Martha's eyes quickly followed the wall upward until she was staring into the pinched face of her neighbor, who was peering around the corner at her.

"Do … do you need to get past me?" Martha stammered as she recovered from her surprise and scrambled to move her cleaning supplies from the center of the hallway.

For an uncomfortable moment, there was no reply. Emmaline then responded with a crisp "no" and turned abruptly to descend the stairs, which squeaked loudly with each step.

Martha sat back on her heels, wondering how long Emmaline had been spying on her and how much practice it had taken to silently ascend those creaking stairs.

Martha was also unaccustomed to Emmaline's sly comments. One afternoon, Emmaline tasked Martha with removing all of the china from the old cabinet, carefully washing and drying it, and then passing it to Emmaline to be expertly arranged in the new built-in cabinets. As Martha turned over a nearly transparent saucer in the sudsy wash water, she leaned in closer to inspect the light-blue Limoges insignia on its underside.

Emmaline noticed Martha studying the china mark and sniffed, "I'm sure you've never handled anything but sturdy old ironstone. Fine china wouldn't last in a household like yours."

Martha wasn't sure if Emmaline was making an innuendo about the size of the Seibel family and the rough handling that dinnerware would experience at the hands of numerous children, or if she was referencing the ill-kept secret that Mama was prone to throwing things, including dishes, during her fits of rage. Either way, Martha knew she was on the receiving end of a not-so-subtle putdown.

Before Martha left the Mosses' house late each afternoon, she was subjected to one final indignity. Emmaline's eyes roved over Martha's clothing, lingering in the pocket areas of her dress and apron as though she was trying to discern the outline of a pilfered silver teaspoon or a dainty pair of sugar tongs. Martha was offended by the veiled insinuation that she would steal, but she consoled herself that she was earning money toward her—and Margaret's—goal of attending nursing school.

By the weekends, Martha was bone-weary from mornings spent stooped over long rows of strawberries and afternoons spent toiling under the watchful eye of Emmaline. However, when the telephone on the living room wall jangled with evening invitations to go motoring with Lad and Myron or to join her classmates for an impromptu gathering, Martha quickly changed her clothes, repinned her hair, and flew out the back door to meet her ride. The recent graduates had vowed to enjoy as much time together as possible before many of them left for college in the fall, and Martha refused to miss a social outing just because she was fatigued. She was anxious to exchange news with the others about classmates who had sought jobs elsewhere. She sorely missed her friend Ruth, whose long letters from Ruggles Beach bubbled over with details of fun times spent dancing and swimming when she wasn't working at the farmhouse. Martha began to doubt her decision to earn money locally and felt a twinge of regret that she hadn't joined Ruth at Ruggles Beach.

One evening, Martha accompanied her group of friends to the theatorium to see a reshowing of the western film "The Narrow Trail" with William S. Hart. She sank with a sigh into the comfort of the theater chair. Soon, the theatorium lights dimmed and the film flickered to life on the screen, while Elsie set the mood with her piano accompaniment. Before long, Martha found herself fighting sleep in the darkened room. She squirmed in her seat, sat up straight, and made every effort to concentrate on the screen, but her eyelids grew heavier and heavier. Finally, Martha allowed herself to rest her head against the back of the seat. She had already seen the movie once before, so she reasoned there was no harm in briefly closing her eyes and missing a minute or two of the action. Martha quickly fell into a deep, exhausted slumber. She was startled awake when Elsie hit a series of thunderous piano chords to signify the dramatic end of the movie. Martha sheepishly looked around, hoping that her nap had gone unnoticed by her friends.

As the theater lights came on, Lad stood and stretched. "Just as good the second time around, don't you think?" he commented in Martha's direction.

"Yes, definitely," Martha agreed quickly as she furtively wiped the sleep from her eyes.

* * * * *

By early July, the strawberries had given way to cherries and raspberries, which ripened in abundance. The throngs of pickers that added an element of excitement to the harvesting had disappeared with the last of the strawberries, leaving Flora, Martha, Minola, and Bill as Papa's work crew. The days were long and the thorns punishing as the siblings carefully filled quart baskets with the tender bramble fruits or dangled from ladders to reach the highest clusters of cherries. As they worked, the sisters fretted that Papa would insist they spend the Fourth of July picking fruit, killing potato bugs, hoeing the corn, or bringing in a second cutting of hay instead of accepting Ada's invitation for a noontime picnic. Bill chimed in with his longing for a supply of sparklers and penny firecrackers, like the boys in town would be enjoying. However, he knew such a celebration was forbidden on the farm. Mama's nerves could not withstand the noise, and an errant spark may set the wheat or oat fields ablaze.

Despite his apparent detachment, Papa was aware of his children's desire to celebrate the holiday with a brief outing. He finally nodded his assent to spend the afternoon of the Fourth of July at Ada's. Flora flew into action on the morning of the holiday. Due to the demands of the fruit harvest and the other outdoor chores, she had been hard pressed to accomplish even the minimum of household duties. She wished there had been time to bake an impressive cake or a juicy fruit pie for the celebration. Flora scampered to the cellar and scanned the shelves of the storage cupboard for possible contributions. She retrieved a jar of bread-and-butter pickles and a jug of homemade root beer, then spied the cloth-covered bowl of leftover fried potatoes. Mama had been in one of her grooves lately, mindlessly frying potatoes several times a day, which forced them into a steady diet of fried potatoes at every meal. Flora grabbed the bowl and hurried upstairs to the kitchen. She added some crisp bacon and a vinegar sauce to the leftover potato slices to make German potato salad. In a salute to the red, white, and blue holiday, Flora created a dessert of red and black raspberries swimming in sweetened cream. She knew that Ada would understand her "making-do-with-what-you've-got" offerings.

Fortunately, the Overland was in one of its rare cooperative phases, and the sisters were pleased that they did not have to ride in the back of the old Ford truck. Because of the machine's reliability issues, Papa chose the most direct route to Ada's, which took the family past the little tenant house on Sand Hill Road where Margaret had spent the last weeks of her life. The girls grew quiet as the weather-beaten house came into view. Even though the property was now inhabited by another tenant family, the girls thought the structure bore an aura of abandonment and looked as hollow-eyed and empty as they felt in their lingering sorrow. They subtlety averted their gaze as they passed the house, but Bill stared longingly at the upstairs window of the room that had been Margaret's, as if he could will her to appear at the window and wave for them to stop.

Albert's Mail Pouch tobacco thermometer on the back of the house indicated the temperature was already in the mid-eighties and climbing. Ada had discovered that the old brick house retained heat like an oven, so she spread a blanket in the shady side yard next to several chairs and a table for the food. Flora added her culinary offerings to Ada's ham sandwiches, sauerkraut, calico bean salad, and large molasses cookies.

Albert's brother Alfred chose a separate way to celebrate the holiday. He hitched up Lady to the buggy and drove into Monroeville to spend the day with another sibling, Ralph, who shared Alfred's taste for the cider jug. Before leaving, Alfred placed a slab of bacon, a bottle of cream, a dozen eggs, half of Ada's freshly churned butter, and a loaf of bread into a basket beside him on the buggy seat. Although no permission was asked nor granted for this raid on the family larder, Albert never balked at the generosity, since Ralph was his brother, too.

After lunch, the family sat on the cool grass and fussed over baby Mildred. The Seibel siblings also played with Ada and Albert's dog, Bub, and bottle-fed an orphan lamb that had made itself a pet. Minola and Bill sped off down the lane to explore the woods at the back of the farm. They lay on their stomachs on the wooden planks of a narrow bridge and dropped pebbles into the creek below, counting to see who could create the most ripples. Before long, the heat of the day prompted them to scramble off the bridge and sink their feet deep in the cool mud of the creek bottom. As with the previous places Ada and Albert had lived, Minola and Bill absorbed the novelty of the new surroundings and made themselves completely at home.

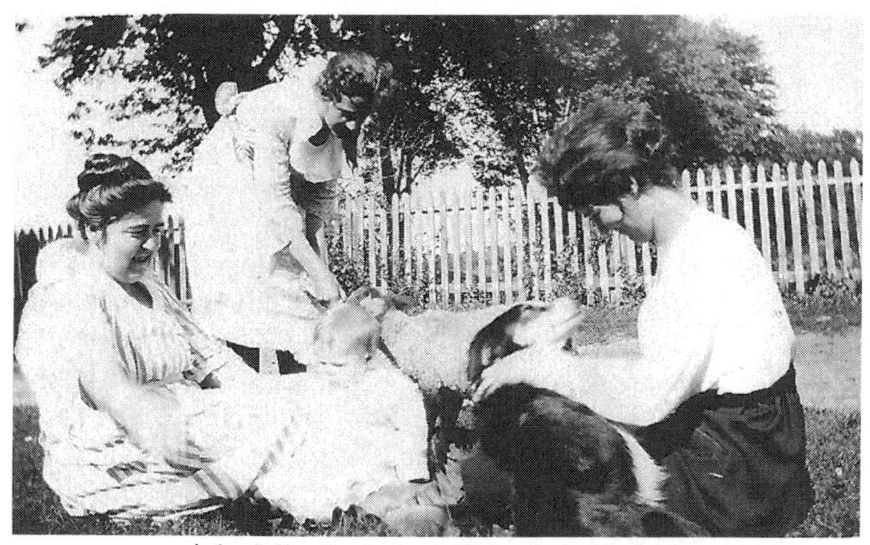

Ada, Minola, baby Mildred, & Martha

* * * * *

In Cleveland, Ella and Hermine celebrated the Fourth of July by walking to Wade Park to escape the oppressive heat of their second-story room at the boarding house. They sat on a low ledge of limestone beside the park's lagoon and ate a light lunch of cheese sandwiches and fruit. Families picnicked in the cool shade near the water's edge, while young boys bobbed miniature boats close to the shoreline. Young couples in rowboats paddled to the middle of the lagoon to enjoy the privacy and distance from their chaperones on shore.

The sisters' attention was drawn by some too-loud laughter coming from a group of young men who were clustered near the lagoon's edge. One had procured a rowboat and was demonstrating a remarkably difficult time in balancing himself as he stepped into the bow. The others roared at his unsteady stance. The girls thought he was making foolery for the amusement of his friends until they saw the men furtively pass a flask among themselves, stealing glances over their shoulders before they tipped the bottle to their lips. Ohio's Prohibition amendment to the state constitution had taken effect in late May, closing saloons and breweries and sparking a new industry of bootlegging and bathtub gin to meet the unquenched thirst for spirits. Ella and Hermine had read in the newspapers about the crush of customers five and six deep at the bars on the last day of legal sales and about the men who had carried away boxes of liquor for their personal consumption at home.

One of the young men spied the two sisters sitting on the ledge and wobbled his way toward them. He doffed his hat and made a deep, exaggerated bow. "Afternoon, ladies. Can I interest either of you in a little boat ride with me out on the lagoon?"

The girls recoiled from the smell of alcohol on his breath as he leaned in to offer a glassy-eyed grin.

Through her institutional visits for the church, Ella had witnessed the broken families, abandoned children, and destitute adults that resulted from alcohol dependence. She quickly rebuffed the man with a firm, "Certainly not!" Ella looped her arm through Hermine's, and the two sisters marched off, trailing disapproval.

* * * * *

The next morning, Flora arose at 3:30 a.m. and dressed in the dark. She tiptoed down the stairs and crossed to the kitchen, where she lit the kerosene lamp. She knew Papa would insist the siblings work all day to make up for the Fourth of July holiday. However, only one loaf of bread remained from the batch she had made last week, and Flora intended to get a head start on the baking before the day turned oppressively hot. She crossed to the summer kitchen, where the cookstove had been moved during the heat of the summer, and started a fire in its firebox. She set the coffeepot on the cookstove surface and retrieved a yeast cake from the kitchen cupboard. As she bustled between the kitchen and summer kitchen, Flora thought about the pleasant time they had had picnicking at Ada and Albert's the day before. Her thoughts drifted to what it would be like to have a home, a husband, and children of her own.

The coffeepot rattled its signal that it was about to boil, so Flora hurried to the summer kitchen and poured herself a mug before moving the coffeepot to the warming ledge. She swiped her finger across the back of the stove and shook her head, wondering when she'd last had the time to black its surface. Sipping her coffee and making a mental list of the chores to be tackled in the predawn quiet, Flora crossed to the pantry and began assembling the bread pans.

The creak of the porch steps caused her to stop and furrow her brow. Flora was certain she was the only one awake in the household. The barn lantern had been in its usual post on the bench by the back door, indicating that no one was making a nocturnal trip to the outhouse. Flora's heart pounded in her ears as the screen door slowly squeaked open. Snatching up the wooden rolling pin to defend herself, Flora cocked it above her head and stepped warily around the pantry doorway to confront the intruder.

"Hi, Flora," Bill waved nonchalantly as he eased the door closed behind him.

"Bill!" Flora gasped, awash with relief. Her legs turned to rubber, and she clutched one hand to her thumping heart as the arm brandishing the rolling pin went limp. "Wh-What are you doing?"

"Goin' to bed," Bill responded casually as he crossed the kitchen toward Stegmiller's stairs. He was dressed in the overalls and shirt he had worn to Ada's picnic, and he carried his cap in his hand.

Flora looked at her brother in disbelief, trying to comprehend why he was coming in the back door at such an early hour. "You're just goin' to bed now?" She shook her head in confusion. "What've you been doing?"

"I was in town," Bill replied matter-of-factly.

"In Monroeville?" Flora gasped. "You mean … you've been gone all night?"

Bill nodded and shrugged his shoulders as if to signal that it was completely natural for an eleven-year-old boy to slip away from the farm after the evening chores and to roam the village streets all night.

Flora was dumbfounded by the situation. Pointing the rolling pin toward the mantle clock, she weakly offered, "But, but, it's 4 a.m.!"

Bill opened his blue eyes wide and held his palms upward in a show of exasperation. "Flora, don't you know? It was the Fourth of July!" Satisfied with his explanation, Bill turned and climbed the stairs to his room, leaving Flora in the pantry doorway with her mouth agape.

Bill crawled onto his cot for a few hours of sleep before beginning another long day of farm work, but his head was filled with sparklers and firecrackers illuminated against a night sky.

Bill

*****

Despite her industriousness, Martha began to realize that her meager summer earnings would not be enough to finance nursing school. She wrestled with how to ask Papa for his assistance. Post-war inflation had brought prosperity in the form of good market prices for Papa's fruit crops. He had received thirty-five cents per quart for strawberries and paid eight cents per quart to the pickers. The prices had held for the cherries, raspberries, and blackberries, which sold for thirty cents per quart. Since the girls and Bill provided all of the labor for free on the cherries and bramble crops, Papa's profit margin soared. Martha hoped the favorable economy would make him more approachable.

One Sunday afternoon as Papa swayed gently in the old Fuller seat swing on the front porch, Martha gathered her courage and broached the topic of educational finances. From her perch on the top porch step, Martha could not see Papa's face, which was buried behind the *Monroeville Spectator*, but she rather preferred speaking to the front page of the newspaper than Papa's stoic countenance. She explained her desire to attend nursing school in Cleveland and detailed the cost of tuition, her earnings, and the offer of assistance from Ella and Hermine. Taking a deep breath, Martha then asked, "Would you help me pay for school?"

Martha

Papa did not respond. The only sounds were the squeaking of the porch swing chains and the pounding of Martha's heart in her ears. The silence was unbearable, and Martha was beginning to regret initiating the conversation. She wished she had asked Ada to intercede on her behalf, since Ada had an easier relationship with their father and could talk to him about such weighty matters. Martha was on the verge of quietly slinking away in defeat when a noncommittal "we'll see" emanated from behind the pages of the newspaper. Martha wiped her damp palms on her skirt and sighed in relief that Papa had at least acknowledged her request.

* * * * *

In mid-August, Ada asked fourteen-year-old Minola to stay with her for two weeks to watch little Mildred while Ada harvested and canned her garden's abundant produce. In return, Ada promised to sew a dress for Minola to wear on her first day of ninth grade. Minola was thrilled by the offer. Not only was it validation that she was old enough to be entrusted with the care of precious baby Mildred, but it was also an opportunity to spend one-on-one time with her mother-substitute Ada. The promise of a new dress was the icing on the cake. Minola knew just what fabric she wanted for her dress—a pine-green print she had seen at Mr. Zipfel's store. She could already envision herself wearing the new creation as she entered the doors of Monroeville High School on the first day of class in September.

When Saturday arrived, Minola happily packed her nightgown, hairbrush, book, and change of clothing into the overnight valise. That evening, she placed the bag by her feet in the back seat of the machine when the family went into Monroeville to do their weekly shopping. It had been arranged that they would meet Ada, Albert, and the baby in town, and Minola would ride home with them.

Minola eagerly led Ada into Zipfel's store and pointed out the coveted dress fabric, describing the style of the dress and the cut of the collar that she envisioned. Ada fingered the fabric, and Minola could tell by the look of concentration on her sister's face that she was mentally laying out the pattern and estimating the amount of fabric required.

"Well, if that's what your heart's set on, I 'spose we oughta get the material while we're here," Ada advised.

Minola smiled and proudly carried the bolt of fabric to the counter, where Ada told Mr. Zipfel the necessary yardage to cut. He unrolled the fabric and bounced the bolt in a muffled *thump, thump, thump* along the yardstick tacked to the edge of the countertop. Lifting the black-handled scissors that dangled from a string behind the counter, the storekeeper placed the tip of the bottom blade in a groove in the counter's surface and made a swift, clean tear across the width of the fabric. He folded the cut fabric, wrapped it in brown paper, and expertly flipped the package front to back as he tied it with string. As often as Minola had watched Mr. Zipfel cut fabric for Flora, it had never been as satisfying as today's experience. This would be a dress that she had earned—one made especially for her, not a hand-me-down from an older sister. Minola clutched the package to her chest all the way to the buggy.

The weather was oppressively hot as Ada toiled long hours canning green beans, beets, corn, lima beans, pickles, and tomatoes in the summer kitchen. A bushel basket of tart apples sat in the cool cellar, awaiting their turn to be peeled, cored, and made into sweet applesauce. While Ada worked, Minola put ten-month-old Mildred in the baby carriage and took her for long walks along the Ridge Road that ran in front of the brick house. She amused the child with nursery rhymes and simple songs she remembered from her days at the Plank Road school. Often, Minola propped Mildred on her hip and hovered about Ada in the kitchen, soaking up the comforting presence of an attentive, functioning mother, which was so lacking in her own home life.

One afternoon, Minola tucked Mildred into the corner of the couch and surrounded her with pillows. Feeling the child was satisfactorily secured, Minola darted across the room to retrieve the book *Quincy Adams Sawyer*, which the Seibel sisters had passed among themselves for literary enjoyment that summer. She had been reading passages aloud to Mildred before naptime each afternoon, both as a means of lulling the child to a drowsy state as well as satisfying her own insatiable appetite for reading.

Just as she reached the book, Minola heard a sickening thud behind her. She whirled around to see little Mildred sprawled on the hard wooden floor, her face contorted as she emitted a high-pitched scream. Scooping up the injured child, Minola was stricken by the horrible thought that her carelessness had led to Ada's daughter being maimed for life. As the baby's cries crescendoed, Ada rushed in from the kitchen. Cradling Mildred in her arms, Ada clucked soothingly as she quickly examined the child for signs of injury. An angry welt in the center of Mildred's forehead indicated the onset of a dandy goose egg. Ada tenderly kissed the injury and bounced the distressed child in her arms. Seeing the anguish on her sister's face, Ada knew that no words of reprimand were necessary. She wrapped a reassuring arm around Minola's shoulder as they headed to the kitchen to place the back of a cool spoon against the child's bruise.

That evening, Minola watched as Ada filled an oval white enamel tub with warm sudsy water and bathed little Mildred, whose wet blond hair clung to the purplish knot on her forehead.

"You used to scrub my back in the washtub on Saturday nights and call me 'Old Skinny Bones,'" commented Minola. "Remember?"

"I hain't forgot," smiled Ada.

"It's 'I haven't forgotten," corrected Minola. "There's no such word as 'hain't.'" Minola had become increasingly aware of her own flawed English and was working diligently to repair it, due in part to her admiration for Miss Mary Marvin, her eighth grade English teacher.

Ada set her lips in a firm line and did not respond.

After little Mildred was tucked in bed for the night, Ada cleared off the kitchen table and smoothed pieces of brown wrapping paper across its surface. She carefully measured Minola for her dress, then dabbed the lead tip of a pencil stub to her tongue and sketched the outline of pattern pieces on the paper. Minola hovered over Ada's shoulder, indicating where she wanted the sleeves to flare and how wide she envisioned the collar.

From time to time, Ada stepped back to assess her patternmaking. "Well, it hain't nothin' fancy," she announced.

"'Isn't anything,' not 'hain't nothing,'" corrected Minola. "Miss Marvin says, 'Never use two negatives together in the same sentence.'"

Ada arched one eyebrow and returned to her work on the unfinished pattern.

By the second week, the heat and humidity had escalated. Ada continued to toil before a hot cookstove each day, slicing, chopping, peeling, and blanching vegetables before packing them into sterilized quart jars and lowering them into a bubbling water bath on the stove's surface. Billows of steam rose from the canner, causing Ada's hair to cling in damp tendrils to her face and neck. Occasionally, she pulled a hankie from the bosom of her dress and mopped at her brow. Her feet ached from the substantial weight gain that remained from pregnancy as well as the corns that had formed from years of wearing tight, ill-fitting shoes. Ada found a measure of relief by slipping her shoes off and working barefoot.

Minola had grown bored with pushing the baby carriage on long walks and setting up towers of wooden blocks for Mildred to knock over. She had sung as many nursery rhymes as she could remember, and she had finished reading *Quincy Adams Sawyer.* To pass the time, she stood little Mildred next to a kitchen chair and encouraged her to take a step, then swooped the child up in her arms and waltzed around the summer kitchen.

"Look at us, Ada. We're dancing," Minola called as she twirled about. "What would Rev. Keppel say about that?"

"He don't seem to preach against dancin' so much anymore," Ada commented as she scooped blanched tomatoes into a tub of cold water to loosen their skins.

"He 'doesn't'," corrected Minola. "Miss Marvin's rule is: 'Don't use 'don't' with a singular noun.'"

"It's gettin' so's I can scarcely speak around you," replied Ada, a hint of irritation in her voice.

"'So's' is another no-no," responded Minola, oblivious to her sister's agitation. Minola made a grand sweep backward in her dance and collided with Ada, stepping hard on her sister's corn and causing Ada to drop a hot tomato onto the floor, where it burst into a splatter of pulp and seeds.

Hobbling on her injured foot, Ada barked, "Out of the kitchen! You're no help at all!"

Minola stared at her sister in stunned indignation. She felt her babysitting services had been vital to Ada's progress in the summer kitchen over the past ten days, and she was deeply wounded by Ada's harsh assessment. "Well then, you can take me home," sniffed Minola. "Right now."

Ada rose from cleaning up the splattered tomato and put her hands on her hips. "Is that what you want?"

Minola nodded her head in affirmation.

Ada stared at Minola for a long moment. "Get your things. I'll hitch up Lady."

Minola quickly exited the summer kitchen, still carrying Mildred.

Ada scooped the remaining tomatoes from their scalding bath, dipped them into a pan of cold water, and gingerly slipped off their skins. She set the tomatoes aside in a pan and covered them with a clean dishtowel. Hobbling to the kitchen, she found a scrap of paper and scrawled a short note for Albert, which she tucked under the sugar bowl on the table, where he'd be sure to see it if he came in from the fields and found her gone.

The ride to the Seibel homestead was long and silent except for the babbling of little Mildred. Minola kept her chin elevated in indignation and stared straight ahead. Upon their arrival, Minola quickly exited the buggy and marched to the back porch, where she plopped down on the top step and adopted her most wounded expression. Ada limped past her into the kitchen, where Martha was washing the cream separator and Flora was scrubbing a pan of cucumbers for pickling.

Minola listened through the screen door as Ada told the reason for their unexpected arrival. She waited for her sisters to scold Ada and insist that an apology was in order. Instead, Ada's voice cracked, followed by sniffling. Ada was crying! This was an unexpected turn of events. Minola had only known Ada to cry one time before, and that was when she and Bill were little children. At that time, they had been told that the source of Ada's tears was Albert's Catholicism, which stood as an impediment to their marriage plans. Minola leaned backward so she had an unobstructed view through the mesh of the screen door. The three sisters were clustered beside the kitchen table. Ada had surrendered little Mildred to Martha's care while she dabbed at her eyes with her hankie. Flora's arm was cradled protectively around Ada's shoulder.

Minola's indignation wilted. She had not considered that Ada's feelings were also hurt. She felt chagrined at her selfish and childish outlook. Minola slipped into the kitchen, quietly closing the screen door behind her. She wrapped her arms around Ada's waist in contrition. All was forgiven.

Soon, Ada and Mildred climbed into the buggy for the return trip to their home. While the incident between the two sisters had been resolved, Minola knew that she had not fulfilled the two-week obligation of assisting Ada and therefore had not earned the privilege of the new dress. She regretted her haste in demanding to be driven home and was disappointed in herself for her behavior. Wearing one of her usual hand-me-down dresses on the first day of school would be a bitter reminder of her actions.

* * * * *

As the summer waned, Martha began to monitor the mail, eagerly awaiting a letter from the nursing program at Lakeside Hospital. Mr. Seeley, the mailman, had grown accustomed to seeing her dash across the lawn toward the mailbox as he puttered onward to his next stop. On the last Saturday in August, Martha ran to the mailbox and threw open its door. Finally, there was an envelope addressed to her and bearing the Lakeside Hospital return address. Beaming, Martha ripped open the envelope as she hurried toward the house, her heart fluttering in anticipation.

Martha's brow furrowed, her smile faded, and her pace slowed. The letter thanked Martha for her application to the program, but regretted to inform her that the class roster for the 1919 program had been filled. It went on to explain that the war in Europe and the recent influenza epidemic had sparked an increased interest in the field of nursing. The hospital had received a record number of qualified applicants that year. The letter closed by encouraging Martha to apply for the October 1920 class and wishing her the best of luck in all her endeavors.

In disbelief, Martha read the letter over again, the black type slanting and blurring through her tears. She was crushed with disappointment not only for herself but also for failing to fulfill Margaret's career ambitions. With heavy footsteps, Martha climbed the front porch and entered the house to find Flora, who was on her hands and knees scrubbing the kitchen floor.

Martha wordlessly handed the letter to Flora, who sat back on her heels and read its brief message. "All things happen for a reason," she consoled. "It just means something better's meant to come your way."

Martha did not share Flora's optimism. All she could think of was her failure. She recalled how she had changed her age on the application, per Dr. Gilman's suggestion. Ada was right about nothing good resulting from a lie. She thought of all her hard work to earn money for her education, even the humiliation she had endured while housecleaning for Emmaline Moss. It all seemed like a worthless effort now. Also, there was the question of what she would do for the coming year. Flora could certainly use a helper, but Martha dreaded the thought of endless farm chores, house drudgery, and Mama's constant cycling of spells, with few opportunities for social engagements after her schoolmates left for their own educational pursuits. Martha went upstairs and flopped dejectedly on the bed she shared with Minola. She buried her face in the pillow and gave vent to her emotions. After she had cried herself out, Martha penned a long, sad letter to Ella and Hermine, telling them of her rejection.

The next day, Ada, Albert, and little Mildred came for Sunday dinner and an afternoon visit. Upon entering the kitchen, Ada set her basket on the table and began to disperse its contents. She handed Flora a jar of recently canned corn relish and a pan of cinnamon buns. There was also an issue of a farming magazine that Albert subscribed to, which was passed on to Papa. Ada lifted out a stack of snowy white diapers and placed them on the table, then turned toward Minola.

"You left this at my house when you were there," she commented, beckoning to her sister.

Minola peered into the basket. Neatly folded at the bottom was the pine-green-printed fabric that she had selected at Zipfel's store. Minola's cheeks burned as she recalled the incident that had led to the forfeiture of the dress. Obviously, Ada was returning the material for Flora's use. As Minola lifted the fabric from the basket, the bundle unfolded to reveal a fully constructed dress. She couldn't believe her eyes! Minola beamed as she held up the dress in front of her. It was styled exactly as she had described to Ada. Minola was thrilled beyond words but also deeply humbled by Ada's forgiveness and generosity.

Minola wearing the dress made by Ada

On the first day of school, Minola donned her new dress and stood eagerly at the edge of the yard, anxiously awaiting Mr. Busch's approaching school wagon. She bounded up the rear entrance steps, took a seat on one of the benches, and basked in the immediate attention that the dress garnered from the other female passengers. Bill followed, less excited about the commencement of another scholastic obligation but happy to resume his social contacts. They were trailed by Martha, who was using the school wagon as transportation into town, where she would walk to the parsonage. Mrs. Keppel had engaged Martha's services in canning peaches. Martha felt it was pointless to continue earning money through these odd jobs, since she would not be going to nursing school in October, but she had promised to assist Mrs. Keppel.

Monroeville High School's freshman class.
Minola: second row from bottom, far right

At the last stop before heading into town, Mabel Mueller, a high school senior, boarded the school wagon and took a seat on the bench opposite Martha. After complimenting Minola on her dress, Mabel expressed surprise at seeing Martha on the school wagon. "Why, I thought you'd have left for nursing school by now!" exclaimed Mabel. "Seems like everyone from your class had plans to go to college or find work in the city."

Martha dropped her eyes to her lap and didn't respond.

"So, when do you leave?" Mabel pressed.

"I'm not goin' anywhere," Martha croaked in a barely audible whisper. "I didn't get accepted."

"Oh." Mabel fidgeted for a few minutes and then tried to fill the uncomfortable silence between them. "I heard Ruth had a grand summer up at Ruggles Beach! Bet you'll miss her bunches when she leaves for college. You two were always inseparable."

Martha bit her lower lip and turned her head away, hoping to signal Mabel that the conversation was over. Through a sheen of tears, she watched the familiar roadside scenery pass by the school wagon window.

* * * * *

Martha resigned herself to being Flora's helpmate, and the two sisters toiled side by side in the kitchen or with farm chores. While she tried to adopt a pleasant façade, inwardly Martha ached with defeat and hopelessness about her life, which seemed to have settled into a rut.

One day in late September while harvesting potatoes, Martha stopped to stretch her aching back. She spotted Mr. Seeley's machine puttering away from their mailbox. Wiping her dirty hands on her apron, she slowly crossed the farmyard to retrieve the mail. Martha listlessly thumbed through the letters as she walked toward the house. To her surprise, she found an envelope addressed to her in Ella's handwriting. Usually when Ella and Hermine wrote, the envelopes were addressed to Flora and the salutation greeted all the family members. Martha was puzzled at being singled out with a missive just for her. She ripped open the envelope and scanned Ella's neat script.

Upon receiving Martha's sad letter about not being accepted into nursing school, Ella and Hermine had approached their landlady, Mrs. Hunt, whose son was the head of the collections department at the Cleveland Illuminating Company. They explained Martha's situation and asked Mrs. Hunt if she would make an inquiry through her son about any job openings at the company. At last, Mrs. Hunt relayed the news that there was a position in her son's department for someone to do filing and write statements for delinquent bill collection. Ella urged Martha to accept the job and share her sisters' room at the boarding house on Crawford Road. Not only would this allow Martha to earn money while she re-examined her life's goals, but Ella hinted that it would also be financially helpful to her two sisters, who would then be responsible for only one-third, instead of one-half, of the boarding costs. There was some urgency, however, because Mrs. Hunt's son could only hold the job for Martha until the first week of October.

Martha was stunned by the opportunity being presented to her through Ella and Hermine's kindness and initiative. For the first time in weeks, she thought of the future in a positive light, not just the endless, repetitive chores that awaited her tomorrow and the day after. Martha ran to the potato field and eagerly shared the letter with Flora.

For the rest of the afternoon, the two sisters gathered unearthed potatoes and discussed the many preparations to be made before Martha left for Cleveland. Flora was apologetic that she wouldn't have time to augment Martha's wardrobe, as she had when Hermine left for Oberlin Business College. Martha insisted she could make do with the clothing she had plus items borrowed from Ella and Hermine. There was a spring in her step as she carried an apronful of tubers to the crate in the center of the field.

"Flora, you're the first one I want to come visit us after I get settled in Cleveland," Martha invited. "We'll go shopping downtown, and I'll buy you lunch at May Company's lunch counter."

"I'd like that," smiled Flora wistfully.

That evening, Martha placed a call to Ella and Hermine at the boarding house and happily told them she was accepting the job offer and the invitation to share their rooming accommodations.

Flora sorted through the mending pile for Martha's items and moved them to the top of the stack. If she couldn't send Martha off with some new garments, she would at least make sure her clothing was repaired and serviceable.

On the first Sunday in October, Papa drove Martha and her small trunk to the interurban station in Monroeville. "Mind your sisters, and work hard," he advised.

Martha nodded earnestly and boarded the railcar toward Cleveland, where Ella and Hermine awaited her. Everything seemed possible now. One slim letter had shattered her hopes, but another had restored them.

Chapter 23
The Seibel Homestead
1920

IT WAS FRIDAY, January 9, and Flora's twenty-fifth birthday. She sat at the kitchen table, turning the handle of the glass butter churn and gazing out the kitchen window at the swirl of snowflakes against the pane. She recalled standing watch at the window on an equally snowy day two years ago, trying to catch a glimpse of Margaret who was making her way home from school on foot. How she wished she could look out the window and see the dear girl's form coming down the road once more. Flora sighed and thought to herself that perhaps it would have been better if she had been the one claimed by the influenza epidemic instead of Margaret. She had no high school education or special training, while Margaret had a diploma, a career ambition, and an outgoing personality that would have taken her places. Flora felt so discouraged with herself and wondered what she had accomplished in her quarter-century on this earth and what she would be doing in the future. Probably the same old things in the same old way, she thought with disdain.

The handle of the butter churn offered resistance, indicating the cream had transformed into butter around the dashers. Flora stopped cranking and poured the buttermilk into a crock, to be used for tomorrow's baking. She scraped the butter from the dashers and sides of the churn into a bowl and began pressing the yellowish mass with a flat wooden paddle to remove the remaining buttermilk.

Perhaps her melancholy had been sparked by the birthday present Papa had given her last night—a Gruen wristwatch very similar to the one Margaret had received for her graduation gift. Flora shook her head as if to scatter the gloomy thoughts. She must think of something positive, such as the repeat rendition of the Christmas cantata that she and the other members of the church choir would perform during a special service on Sunday evening. The program had been so well received at Christmastime that Rev. Keppel requested the choir present the musical composition again.

Flora scooped the butter into a bowl and covered it with a cloth, then tiptoed into Mama and Papa's bedroom. Mama was curled in the center of the bed, sleeping off the stupor-like effects that always followed one of her spells. Flora tucked the quilt around Mama's shoulders and gazed at her now-peaceful countenance. Although she was almost fifty-four years old, Mama had very few gray hairs, and her complexion was smooth and unlined, as though her mental affliction had spared her from life's worries. Flora hoped Mama would be awake and functional by Sunday evening so the entire family could attend the cantata.

She carried the bowl of butter to the cellar for storage and added some wood to the Homer furnace that Papa had bought with the profits from the berry crops. The boxy furnace vented to one large register in the living room floor and supplemented the heat provided by the kitchen cookstove. Although its monstrous maw begged for anthracite, a post-war coal-saving proposition caused Papa to economize by feeding it wood chopped from the pin oak grove at the back of the farm. The heat quotient was never sufficient, and in the evenings, the three Seibel siblings huddled beside the floor grate, roasting their faces and hands and freezing their backsides before retreating to their unheated bedrooms.

Flora closed the door on the furnace's firebox and dusted off her hands. The house seemed unusually quiet with Mama asleep, Papa tending to outdoor chores, Minola and Bill at school, and all her other siblings gone. Flora pulled her sweater tighter around her shoulders and tried to shake off a feeling of loneliness.

Flora

By Sunday evening, there was a foot of snow on the ground. Mama was up and functional, and Flora was silently relieved by her subdued nature. This meant the entire family could attend the cantata without fear of an embarrassing outburst.

The second presentation of the cantata was even more beautiful than the first, but when the satisfied congregation emerged from the church, they found themselves facing a nighttime snow squall. Rural families hurried to their machines, which sputtered and slid as they made their way out of town. The Seibels, however, were detained by a hastily called meeting of the Benevolence Committee, of which Flora was the secretary. By the time the meeting was adjourned and the family had crowded into the Overland, the tracks left by the other exiting vehicles had been nearly obliterated by the snow.

Papa turned the machine toward home. As the vehicle crept along Plank Road, leaving the town's illumination behind, it became increasingly difficult to distinguish the road from the snow-blanketed ditches on either side. The Overland's head lanterns cast a dim reflection in the driving snow. Eventually, one lantern sputtered and blinked out. Papa gripped the wheel and peered intently into the swirl of snowflakes. They continued on in this compromised state until the other lantern winked, flared, and died. In a tense voice, Papa commanded Bill to get out, find the track made by the last passing vehicle, and run ahead of the machine to guide them.

Bill exited the vehicle and searched for a depression in the snow that would indicate a tire track. Finding it, he waved his arms as a signal and began to jog in the track. Papa hunched over the steering wheel, his face pressed close to the windshield to discern the form of his son a few lengths in front of the machine's bumper. From time to time, he used the sleeve of his coat to clear the iced-over condensation from the glass and maintain a small circle of visibility.

Bill churned through the deep snow, his breath coming in great puffs and his lungs burning with exertion. Soon, his legs grew heavy and weak, and his feet were numb. Icy snowflakes bit at the exposed skin on his face. He pressed onward, determined to distinguish himself in this masculine role that Papa had assigned him. The soles of his shoes became caked with slippery, hard-packed snow, causing him to stumble frequently. Bill turned his head to check the progress of the family's vehicle. As he did, his feet went out from under him, and he pitched forward. Bill clawed at the drift of snow, trying to crawl out of the path of the oncoming machine, whose engine roared close behind him.

Papa scanned left and right, straining to locate Bill through the small clearing on the windshield. Suddenly, he spotted the dark form of his son lying in the snow. He slammed on the brakes, sending the Overland into a sideways skid. Minola squealed in fright and clutched for Flora's hand in the darkness of the back seat. The machine lurched to a stop, its right front wheel cocked perilously close to Bill's body.

Papa ordered Flora and Minola to get out and assist Bill with freeing the vehicle from the snow drift. The three siblings pushed as Papa rocked the machine between forward and reverse gears. Minola was wearing a pair of fashionable but impracticable slip-on shoes that had replaced the sturdier button-up variety in popularity. Their thin soles quickly became a sheet of slick, hard-packed snow, causing her to slip and fall with nearly every step. Flora, too, struggled to stay upright. The narrow profile of her silk skirt wasn't conducive to taking the large steps necessary for navigating deep snow. She felt the fabric split along the side seam as she wrestled to plant her feet and push the vehicle. Mama sat impassively in the front seat, witnessing the struggle but exhibiting no reaction. Finally, the Overland was freed from its snowy bondage, and the girls returned to their seats. Bill resumed his position as guide, although his pace had slowed.

As they inched their way along Plank Road, Minola whimpered in agony from the back seat. Her hands and feet were wet and numb, and her leggings were soaked through.

At last, they spotted the faint glow of lantern light coming from a window in the Adolph Lantz home, next door to the now-closed Plank Road school. Papa stopped the machine and instructed Bill to crawl in the back seat, where he collapsed in exhaustion, his teeth chattering uncontrollably. Papa plunged through the deep snow to Lantzes' house and banged on the kitchen door. He explained his plight to Mr. Lantz and requested a kerosene lantern to hang from the front of the machine, thus sparing poor Bill from further guide duty.

Mr. Lantz complied, and with the lantern casting a circle of light before them, Papa edged the machine onward. As he turned the corner onto Townline Road, the slick tires skidded across the snow, lodging the rear of the Overland into a drift. Once again, the three siblings exited the vehicle, waded through the deep snow, and collectively struggled to push the Overland back into the faint track left by either Mosses' machine or George and Bertha's new Buick when they had returned from the cantata earlier that evening.

The Overland now began to choke and sputter, exhibiting its reliability issues as well as problems with wind-driven snow packed around the engine. Papa eased the lurching machine along, hoping to reach home before it died. At the bend in the road by the cemetery, he released the gas pedal and let momentum guide the car, not wishing to experience another skid. They had safely navigated the curve and were just opposite George and Bertha's house when the Overland quit.

Papa let out his breath in one long *whoosh*, as if he had been holding it ever since they left the church. "I'll go up to George and Bertha's house and get George and Elmer to help me. Come in and get warmed up 'til the machine's runnin' again," he advised his family.

The three siblings began to climb out of the vehicle. However, the mention of George and Bertha had roused Mama from her stupor. Her eyes flashed and her spine stiffened. It was clear that the long-held resentment over the house shuffle had bubbled through her mental fog. "*Ach!* No!" she barked. Mama remained in the icy Overland while the rest of the family stumbled through the snow to the house.

George and Elmer shrugged on thick winter coats and pulled on their boots, while Bertha bustled about the kitchen making mugs of hot chocolate for the cold, weary siblings. Despite the friction between her and Mama, Bertha was always hospitable to the Seibel offspring.

Before long, George and Elmer returned to the house, stomping the snow from their boots and commenting on the harsh weather conditions. The Overland was once again running—perhaps temporarily—so the siblings reluctantly left the warmth of Bertha's kitchen and trudged through the driving snow to where Papa and Mama waited in the vehicle.

Papa coaxed the machine along the last stretch toward home, his hands in a vise-like grip on the wheel. In the back seat, Flora, Minola, and Bill remained rigid and tense, their bodies unconsciously leaning forward as if to will the lurching machine onward. When they reached the homestead, Papa placed the Overland in the barn, where it would be put up on blocks for the duration of the winter. The relieved family wearily crossed the farmyard toward the security and comfort of the house.

* * * * *

To ease the isolation imposed by the winter weather as well as the loss of a houseful of sisters, Flora and Minola often walked up the road to visit with Aunt Bertha and cousin Rosie. Minola frequently carried along her math assignments and enlisted Elmer's aid in explaining the concepts. She continued to struggle with math due to the poor foundation laid at the Plank Road school and the loss of Margaret and Martha as her in-house tutors. Before Flora and Minola left on these social calls, Mama always sternly reminded them, "*Halt deinen Mund* (Hold your mouth)." She did not seem to recall how freely she shared family information with Emmaline Moss or Mrs. Ordmann during her periodic flights down the road to seek out female companionship.

Both Rosie and Aunt Bertha exhibited the probing curiosity of sociable, isolated farm women. They used their high-pitched voices to ask questions—often personal ones—more than they engaged in actual conversation. When they noticed Flora or Minola wearing a new store-bought hat or pair of shoes, they'd query, "What'd you have to give for that?" The two sisters were uncomfortable with the directness of the questioning, but neither was skilled in the art of evasion.

No matter the hour of their social call, Aunt Bertha would be in the kitchen, where she dried the dishes as she peppered the sisters with questions, often wiping a single pan over and over again. She held considerable awe for the families of status, particularly her English neighbors, and she grilled Flora with, "Did you go to the choir party at the Lowells' house? Who was there? What'd they wear? What food did they serve?"

One evening, while Flora did her best to field Bertha and Rosie's interrogation, Minola wandered into the living room and distracted herself by delving into the rack of magazines beside the horsehair couch. Across the room, Elmer, who had added the role of Monroeville High School principal to his teaching duties, graded a stack of science reports. As Minola flipped through the periodicals, she noticed doodles and handwriting on the cover of one of Uncle George's agricultural magazines. She pulled the issue out of the rack for closer inspection and immediately recognized Elmer's neat penmanship. The name of Minola's beloved eighth-grade English teacher, Mary Marvin, was written over and over on the cover's margins. The profile of a pretty young woman who strongly resembled Miss Marvin was sketched beside a string of small hearts.

Minola peered at Elmer over the top of the magazine, her eyes wide with the sudden realization that he was in the early stages of romantic feelings toward her favorite teacher. She had always regarded Elmer as a cousin, teacher, neighbor, and tutor but never as the male figure in a love affair. She blinked several times and pondered this previously unconsidered aspect of Elmer. She remembered Martha's reports of how Elmer had been maligned by the young men in her class for not enlisting during the war. While Elmer was an excellent teacher, he still suffered from the community's lingering hyper-patriotism and anti-German sentiment. Minola decided that she could reveal her discovery to Flora on the walk home, but she would guard Elmer's budding romance from her peers at school.

*****

As an additional social outlet, Flora joined the National Grange of the Order of Patrons of Husbandry, or simply known as the Grange, an agricultural organization that advanced the interests of farm families. During the quiet winter months, when farm chores lessened, the Grange held a speaker's institute, which lasted several days. County extension agents spoke to the men about improved farming practices and to the women about canning methods and pattern construction. The institute culminated in a fund-raising box social, where the women brought decorated boxes containing picnic suppers, which were bid on by the men. It was customary for a married woman to pack a big box with enough food for her entire family, while a single woman typically packed a smaller box with a supper just for two. Although the contributor of each box was supposed to be a secret during the bidding, the women always described their boxes' decorations to their husbands or boyfriends so they could bid on the correct box when the auction began. At the end of the bidding, the name of the contributor was revealed, and the lucky winner had the privilege of dining with that female.

Flora used her artistic talents to painstakingly paint the Patrons of Husbandry seal—a shock of wheat overset with the letters "P of H"—on her box, surrounded by farm scenes. Into it, she carefully packed two head cheese sandwiches, two dill pickles, two oatmeal cookies studded with plump raisins, and, as a special treat, a box of Cracker Jacks. Lastly, she added a slip of paper with her name on it and tied the box with a length of royal-blue crepe paper.

The auction was punctuated with laughter, as neighbors occasionally drove up a bid before dropping out to let the intended husband or boyfriend purchase the designated box. Flora watched nervously as the auctioneer lifted her box and the bidding began. To her surprise, a spirited competition took place between two bachelor farmers. The auction price was driven to a respectable $3.50 before Earl Ensminger finally prevailed.

Flora remembered Earl from their days at the Plank Road school. Like most of the other adolescent boys, he had dropped out after he'd learned enough reading and ciphering to handle the farm business. As they shared the box supper, the two reminisced about their school days and former classmates. At the end of the evening, Earl asked if he could call on Flora. She gave her consent, but on the ride home in Mosses' bobsled, Flora thought about the difficulty of bringing a suitor into the house and thereby rousing Mama's unpredictable sociability. She began to have second thoughts about encouraging the relationship with Earl.

* * * * *

Rural electrification came to Townline Road on February 14, 1920. Papa had attended many preliminary meetings, and, of course, the Seibel siblings were very much in favor of the modern convenience. Flora and Minola were eager to do away with the messy kerosene lanterns, which had to be refilled every Saturday and their wicks trimmed and chimneys cleaned of black soot. Bill thought of the gadgets that could be powered by electricity and the new opportunities for tinkering and experimentation.

The pull-down kerosene lamps in the living room and parlor were replaced with modest chandeliers, each sporting three low-wattage bulbs. In the rest of the rooms, a single bare bulb was suspended from the ceiling by its cord, with its activation switch mounted on the wall. In his excitement over this modern feature, twelve-year-old Bill ran from room to room, turning on and off the lights. Papa warned, "Don't waste electricity." While the siblings were careful to always turn off the light switch when leaving a room, there were times when they turned on a bulb just to admire its electric glow.

One Friday evening as Flora was preparing supper, the electric light bulb in the kitchen flickered several times and went out. She turned the wall switch off and on again with no result and tried the light switch in the living room. It was no use; the lights were dead. Flora rang the operator and asked to be connected to Ordmanns'. When Mrs. Ordmann answered, Flora inquired about the status of their electricity. Upon learning that the Ordmanns' lights were on, Flora assumed there was a problem with the transmission wire between the road and the house. Knowing it would take several days for the repairs to be made, she sighed and lit one of the stand-by kerosene lamps.

Bill scampered down Stegmiller's stairs and sheepishly eyed the kitchen light bulb, then edged around the perimeter of the room and peered through the doorway toward the living room chandelier.

Flora spotted his unusual behavior and asked suspiciously, "Bill, what have you been up to?"

"I didn't do it!" Bill immediately protested.

Flora cocked her hands on her hips. "B-i-l-l… ?"

"Well, I did it, but I didn't mean to," he relented. "Kenny loaned me his toy electric motor, and when I tried to hook it up to the light in my room, the bulb went *pop*! I didn't know it would blow the lights in the whole house!"

"You and your tinkering!" scolded Flora.

She telephoned Mr. Cook, who had installed the light fixtures in the house, and explained their dilemma. He arrived the next day to replace the burned-out fuse, under the eager watchfulness of Bill. "You gonna blow 'em out, you better learn how to fix 'em," Mr. Cook advised as he detailed the intricacies of electrical maintenance to his attentive student.

* * * * *

Martha wrote long letters from Cleveland, telling that she had rented a typewriter to improve her typing skills and perhaps increase her opportunity for job advancement. She was amazed at the number of Monroeville people she saw in Cleveland. One of those familiar faces belonged to her cousin Walter, who had left the farm to find employment in the city, much to the disappointment of George and Bertha. They had hoped their youngest son would take over the farm one day, but Walter did not seem inclined to don the yoke of sunup-to-sundown chores. They consoled themselves that he was simply sowing his wild oats, and, in time, he'd come home. George pointed out that Papa had gone off adventuring down the Mississippi River for three years, but he'd returned to the family farm.

Hermine wrote about the new footwear fad. High-topped laced or buttoned shoes had been replaced by oxfords and slip-ons, but there was some frowning over the impracticability of these low-rise shoes against winter weather. No fashion-conscious young girl would be caught wearing overshoes, however, until buckled galoshes came along. The girls in Cleveland wore the galoshes open and unbuckled, and Hermine reported that this had led to the term "flappers" to describe the style of the young modern women.

*****

All winter long, Albert pondered making a major investment in modernizing his agricultural equipment. He carefully pored over his farm ledgers, ciphering debts against projected profits, and discussed the idea with Ada, whom he regarded as an equal partner in all decisions. That spring, Albert purchased his first tractor, The Happy Farmer. It was a three-wheeled design, with two large drive wheels at the rear and a single small front wheel for steering. Power was provided by a horizontal two-cylinder engine. He proudly demonstrated the modern machine to Papa and Bill. Knowing his father would never progress from horse-drawn farm equipment to mechanized methods, Bill watched with envy and awe.

Albert's brother Alfred possessed more mechanical aptitude and almost immediately adopted the used tractor as his own. Alfred tilled the fields from the relative comfort of The Happy Farmer's seat, watching the lug-studded steel wheels bite into the soil. Meanwhile, Albert continued to tread many miles behind the horse-drawn implements.

Alfred on The Happy Farmer tractor

*****

Matters at the little white church on Baker Street in Monroeville had become troubled. Reverend Keppel was pushing the church toward an independent status, which stirred a division in the congregation: one faction was in favor of leaving the Evangelical faith and becoming nondenominational; the other adamantly opposed it. Both Papa and Uncle George aligned with Rev. Keppel; the Mosses and Ordmanns were against the transition and withdrew from the church. There was poorly veiled unfriendliness in the neighborhood, but if the venom fell upon Papa's ears, he chose to ignore it. His children, however, suffered through the aftermath of the church fight.

One day, Papa instructed Bill to carry a young drake down the road to Mosses' for an exchange of breeding stock. When Mr. Moss spotted Bill crossing the farmyard, he called out derisively, "Why, here comes our little Keppel man! How many did you have in church last Sunday?"

With his guileless nature and lack of maturity, twelve-year-old Bill responded with honesty, as though Mr. Moss was entitled to elicit the information from him. "There was a lot of people there. Standing room only," Bill replied.

Mr. Moss snorted, "Won't last long. Keppel will up and leave, and then where will you traitors go? Us true Evangelicals won't take you back, that's for sure."

Minola fared no better on the school wagon, which contained several adolescents from families who were highly vocal about their unhappiness with Rev. Keppel and the church split. Until now, she had not realized the protection afforded to her by having older sisters on the school wagon. With that security system gone, Minola met the badgering with silence and retreated into reading a book. No matter how the school wagon jolted and the other students taunted, she read on and on. Her lack of defense made her a greater target, and the ridicule increased. There was no use in reporting the situation to Flora, who would be distressed but powerless to intervene. Minola kept the daily unpleasantness to herself, but her opinion of organized religion became deeply tarnished.

The church strife had taken its toll on Rev. Keppel, too. He announced his resignation that spring and accepted a call to fill the pulpit of a church in Detroit. Many years later, word came to the community that the Detroit church had suffered a similar schism.

The remaining congregation merged with the local Presbyterian

Church to form the United Christian Church. Eventually, they determined that being nondenominational was a disadvantage, because there was no seminary to supply ministers, and they aligned themselves with the Congregational faith. In less than one hundred years since settling in Ridgefield Township, the Seibels had transitioned from their original German Lutheranism to being Evangelical, nondenominational, and finally Congregational.

The unsettled situation at the Monroeville church, plus a growing sense of belonging to their current neighborhood, caused Ada and Albert to attend services and other activities at the nearby Lyme Congregational Church on the Ridge Road. At a church-sponsored pie social one evening, an elderly woman who was seated across from the young couple squinted at Albert and loudly asked her companion, "Who's that young boy?"

When informed of his identity and relationship to Ada, the old woman cackled, "Why, he's a springer, and she looks like she could be his mother!"

Albert chuckled at the woman's low-vision observation, while Ada set her lips in a firm line and plunged her fork into a slice of pie. Despite the unintentional slight, the young couple felt accepted in the congregation and soon became members.

*****

One spring day, Flora hung the last load of laundry on the clothes line and began to unpin the clean bed linens, which had dried quickly in the sunshine and light breeze. She folded the linens into the wicker basket at her feet and carried it across the yard to the kitchen, where Mama was seated at the table, busily arranging her dried ferns and foliage into a new framed landscape.

Flora removed Bill's sheets from the basket and climbed Stegmiller's stairs to make up his cot. She did the same for Mama and Papa's bed and then carried the basket upstairs to the room she shared with Minola. She smoothed the quilt over Minola's freshly made bed, then snapped a sheet in the air and let it waft down over her own bed. The clean scent of sunshine and fresh air from the crisp sheets—more pleasing than any store-bought perfume—filled her nostrils. Flora tucked the sheets in at the foot of the bed and placed the pillow at its head.

Eyeing the book *The Place Beyond the Winds* on her nightstand, Flora gave in to the temptation to lie down on the fresh linens and read a chapter or two. She stretched out on the bed and inhaled its clean aroma as she opened the book.

Flora awoke with a start to the sound of conversation downstairs. She could hear Mama talking, followed by a man's voice, but it wasn't Papa's. She hastily replaced her bookmark, scrambled off the bed, and smoothed her apron as she scurried down the stairs.

Every spring brought the return of agents who canvassed the neighborhood peddling lightning rods, patent medicines, and other overpriced nonessentials. Flora dreaded the arrival of these drummers, partly because of their pressured sales tactics and partly because Mama was so eager to engage any stranger that came to the farm. Normally, Flora heard their vehicles or buggies as they turned into the driveway, and she could divert Mama's attention before rebuffing the agent at the door. As she hurried down the stairs, Flora chastised herself for falling asleep and not hearing the peddler's arrival.

Flora stopped in the doorway between the living room and kitchen. Mama was seated at the kitchen table looking intently at a paper that the drummer held before her face. The paper was printed with rows of letters in various sizes. With his other hand, the salesman covered Mama's right eye with a square of black cardboard. He asked Mama to read the bottom row of tiny letters on the sheet. She squinted and stumbled through the task, then shrugged her shoulders in defeat.

The agent clucked his tongue in false concern as he adopted his most solicitous manner. "Ah, yes. A severe case of diminished visual acuity, but I have the solution to your affliction, Mrs. Seibel. I guarantee your eyesight will be vastly improved by wearing a pair of my patented spectacles."

He reached into a black leather bag and produced a pair of silver-rimmed eyeglasses with thick magnifying lenses. The salesman made a great show of seating the spectacles on Mama's nose and looping the thin wire stems behind her ears. He wiggled the frames this way and that as if custom-fitting them to her face. Holding the test paper within a comfortable range of Mama's face, he again asked her to read the tiny print in the bottom row. Mama complied and looked up at him, grinning with success, her eyes appearing oversized and watery blue behind the magnifying lenses.

"What a difference, don't you agree, Mrs. Seibel? Now, for only eight dollars, you can continue to have this remarkably improved vision. Doesn't that seem like a small price to pay to be able to read everything with ease?" the agent entreated.

Mama nodded her head in agreement, pleased to have the attention of the stranger.

Flora dreaded this point in the interaction with drummers. They never took "no" for an answer, and with Mama in the mix, the problem was only compounded. "We don't have the money for such things," she said flatly. Flora didn't add that even if they did, Mama was not a believer in reading, and therefore, the glasses would be a wasted investment.

The agent wheedled, "Well … how 'bout seven dollars? I'm willing to sacrifice my commission to save your mother's eyesight. Seven dollars. What a bargain, and one I don't present to too many of my customers, I might add." He flashed an unctuous grin.

Mama returned his smile. "Sounds *gut*!" she agreed.

Flora folded her arms in front of her, bit her lower lip, and shook her head "no."

"Seven dollars and we can work out a payment plan. Our spectacles are oculist-approved, top-of-the-line. You <u>do</u> want the best for your dear mother, don't you?" the salesman continued to pressure Flora.

Mama sensed that without a transaction, the visitor would soon leave, an outcome she intended to forestall. She rose from the table, still wearing the glasses, and ladled up a generous bowl of Flora's laundry-day ham and bean soup that was warming on the back of the cookstove. She set the bowl on the table in front of the visitor and poured him a cup of coffee, then returned to her seat, chattering happily to her guest.

Flora felt trapped like a prisoner in her own home, unable to control Mama or dispatch the salesman.

Soon, the agent realized that his only reward for the sales call would be the refreshments. He ignored Mama's meandering conversation and ate greedily, scraping his spoon across the bottom of the bowl and slurping coffee from the ironstone mug. His polished sales tactics now absent, the drummer snatched the spectacles from the bridge of Mama's nose and deposited them in his black leather bag. Wiping his coat sleeve across his mouth, he plucked the bag from the table and headed out the kitchen door without further regard for the two women.

Mama's face clouded over at the loss of the visitor. Flora sighed as she carried the agent's dirty dishes to the drysink.

* * * * *

After a long winter of typing collection notices for the Cleveland Illuminating Company, Martha began to re-examine her career goals. She toyed with the thought of attending college for a few years and then reapplying to nursing school.

When Ella casually mentioned her sister's tentative plan to her employer, Rev. Huebschmann, he immediately proposed Hiram College as the perfect academic destination for Martha. He spoke of the institution in such glowing terms that Ella soon encouraged Martha to visit the campus and explore the possibilities.

Before long, Flora received an enthusiastic letter from Martha, sharing the news that she would be matriculating to Hiram College in September. Martha calculated that with the money she had earned in Cleveland, the income from an on-campus job, plus occasional financial assistance from Ella and Hermine's meager salaries, she would be able to afford a year of college without taking out a loan. Flora read between the lines—while she could offer no financial support to Martha, her sewing talents would be in demand by the family's newest college coed.

Fashionable young girls wore heavy slip-over sweaters, pleated woolen skirts, woolen socks, and oxford shoes, all of which were very expensive in the post-war economy. Flora's mastery with a needle and thread would be vital in keeping Martha's wardrobe current yet affordable.

In addition, Ella and Hermine stretched their budgets by frequently sending home clothing for Flora to make over into something more becoming, or they occasionally sent lengths of fabric with a request to create a new and necessary item. However, the old sewing machine Papa had bought at auction years ago rivaled the Overland in frequency of breakdowns. It was well beyond its life expectancy, and it spent a frustrating amount of time in need of repairs. Without a reliable sewing machine, Flora did not know how she would meet the increased demands for her sewing skills, and without an income, she could not foresee a way to purchase the machine's replacement.

One spring day as Flora and Papa planted the new strawberry field, a solution came to her, and she approached Papa with her plan. Flora proposed that each evening after the chores were done, she would return to the fields to glean the berries that had been overlooked by the day's pickers. In exchange, Papa would market these remainder berries and give her the proceeds, which she would use to purchase a brand new treadle sewing machine at the end of the strawberry season. Papa approved, and the deal was struck.

The strawberry season commenced with gusto, and the large, early berries commanded thirty-five cents per quart at market. Papa was pleased with this price, and he operated under great pressure to maximize the profits from his highly perishable crop. Dawn found him on the road to the railroad hub at Willard, the bed of the old Ford truck stacked high with berry crates. Several more crates were delivered to Zipfel's store in exchange for credit, followed by a trip to Bellevue to peddle the remaining berries on the residential streets.

After a long day of picking berries, manning the packing house, and overseeing the berry fields in Papa's absence, Flora fixed a hasty supper for the family, enlisted Minola's aid with the dishes, and helped Papa milk the cows. She quickly instructed Minola and Bill to hoe and water the garden and push the lawnmower over a section of the yard. Grabbing a six-quart berry carrier, Flora returned to the fields, where she crawled up and down the rows in search of overlooked berries.

It seemed strange to be alone in the empty berry fields, which had been alive with the shouts and good-natured teasing of pickers earlier in the day. Now, there was only a light breeze to ruffle the tops of the strawberry plants and carry with it the distant sound of a barking dog. At times, Flora sat back on her heels to stretch her aching shoulders and neck and gaze across the empty fields. While the sun was not as intense in the evening hours, its lower-angled rays were unrelenting. She mopped at the rivulets of sweat that trickled down the sides of her face. Adjusting the brim of her straw hat to shield against the sun, Flora returned to her work. The enthusiastic early pickers had done a thorough job of harvesting the bright red fruit, leaving few berries to glean. Flora began to doubt her ability to earn the money for a new sewing machine.

During the height of the strawberry season, relatives who hadn't called or visited all year suddenly remembered the way to the Seibel farm. Several of Mama's siblings and their spouses arrived on Sunday afternoons, and they chatted up Mama and clapped Papa on the back. They talked about old times and childhood memories with Mama, whose mind seemed clear and her demeanor cheerful while recalling the past. When the visitors left, they reassured themselves that their sister was perhaps unpredictable but not unstable. Meanwhile, the quarts of free berries they carried homeward had diminished Flora's earnings toward her goal.

Flora, Mama's brother Charles Gasteier & his wife Sadie, Papa, and Minola

* * * * *

When the early-market demand for berries had been satiated, the prices dropped to twenty to twenty-five cents per quart. As the season wore on, the berries became smaller, the daytime temperatures grew more uncomfortable, and the novelty of picking strawberries waned for the crew that Bill transported from town in Papa's truck. Consequently, Flora's gleaning became more productive. Many evenings, it was dark before she finished packing the berry crates, loaded them onto the bed of Papa's truck, and wearily crossed the yard toward the house. Sometimes, she stopped at the well in the farmyard and splashed her face with the refreshingly cold water that gushed from the spigot with each pump of the creaking handle. As she patted her face dry on her apron, she tried to prioritize the numerous chores that awaited her in the house—the need to bake more bread, the culled strawberries waiting to be made into jam, the neglected housekeeping, the growing stack of mending. Each night, she collapsed onto her bed and quickly fell into a dreamless, exhausted slumber, only to be roused before daybreak by Papa's insistent call of "Girls! Girls! There's berries to be picked."

When Flora thought she could no longer continue her grueling schedule, the strawberry season drew to a close. Papa pulled his ledger from the cherry bookcase in the corner of his bedroom, tallied the separate column he had kept of Flora's gleanings, and counted out a stack of bills into her hand. She gazed in amazement at the hard-earned cash. Flora immediately made arrangements to purchase a 1920 Singer treadle sewing machine with attachments for hemming, binding, tucking, and darning. Its handsome oak cabinet was washed in a fashionable dark stain. The sewing machine sported a silver filigreed face plate and the "Red Eye" design of red, gold, and green decorative paint on a black background.

When the machine was delivered, Flora couldn't stop smiling. She ran her hand over its curved neck and was filled with pride and a sense of accomplishment. Never before had she made such a major purchase with money she had earned herself. She was also more than a little relieved to be freed from the frustration of operating the cantankerous old auction-find sewing machine, which Papa wheeled out to the barn to be stripped of its salvageable parts.

As an added bonus, Flora had enough money left over to purchase several rolls of wallpaper for the long wall in the kitchen. When the wallpapering project was finished, she stood back and admired the scroll-and-floral pattern. "Well, that classes the place up some," she observed.

* * * * *

With the strawberry season over, Flora resumed her dates with Earl Ensminger, who understood the seasonal demands of farm life. She followed Martha's tactic of dashing out the back door as soon as she heard his machine sputter into the driveway, thus avoiding a potential interaction between Mama and her beau. If Earl found this arrangement peculiar, he didn't voice an opinion, even if it meant that Flora was sometimes pinning on her hat as they puttered down Townline Road.

One Sunday afternoon, the couple attended a matinee of "Dr. Jekyll and Mr. Hyde" at the theatorium in Monroeville. Following the film, they drove slowly toward the Seibel homestead as they discussed John Barrymore's flair for portraying the frightening experiment gone wrong. Earl guided the vehicle into the Seibel driveway and coasted to a patch of shade in the backyard. Turning the machine off, he placed his arm across the seat back and lightly caressed Flora's shoulder. She smiled and dropped her chin.

Suddenly, the kitchen door flew open and slammed against the back of the house with a resounding *crack!* The couple's heads whipped around to locate the source of the noise. To Flora's horror, Mama sped down the porch steps, followed by a frantic Bill. Mama had tugged her hair loose from its usual taut knot, and it billowed behind her as she raced across the yard, clawing at her head and shouting, "It's in my hair! *Mein Haar*!"

Bill chased after Mama and managed to grasp her arm, but she shook him off and ran in circles, continuing to shriek and claw at her hair. Bill tried again to contain her, but Mama wrested her arm away each time, leading him on a foot chase across the backyard.

Flora threw open the passenger-side door and scrambled out of Earl's vehicle. Running toward the scene, she called, "Bill! What happened? What's wrong with Mama?"

Bill stopped chasing Mama and shook his head. "I don't know!" He shrugged his shoulders and tried to catch his breath. "She got all worked up about the kitchen wallpaper. Said there were faces whispering about her, laughing at her, 'cause she had something bad in her hair. Then she … she got like this," Bill said, motioning toward Mama. "She went for the kerosene container, but it was empty." He and Flora exchanged glances, both knowing that a house fire had been averted only by the lack of kerosene.

"Where's Papa?" Flora asked, her voice tight with concern.

"Gone. He's picking Minola up from that Sunday School picnic over at Muellers'," Bill explained. "What're we gonna do?"

Flora put her hands on either side of her face and shook her head. While Mama had exhibited an abundance of strange behavior during her spells, it had always followed a rather predictable pattern—agitation, endless chattering, and boundless energy that culminated in an explosive outburst, followed by sleep. This hallucinatory episode was something new. As Flora watched Mama's distress and contemplated how to lure her inside the house, she became aware of raucous laughter. She turned toward the source of the sound.

Earl, red-faced with uncontrollable mirth, rocked back and forth in his seat and pounded his fists on the steering wheel. "Oh, God, this is the funniest damn thing I ever seen!" he crowed between peals of laughter. "Better than the comics!"

Flora's cheeks burned with humiliation and outrage. She stalked to the car and gripped the passenger-side door, her knuckles white with tension. Thrusting her head through the open window, she pled in a low voice, "Leave, Earl. Just leave. Please."

Earl tried to contain his laughter. "But … but, Flora, you gotta admit," he waved in Mama's direction, "that's damn funny. Your mother tearing around the backyard like she's dancin' the shimmy, and your brother chasin' after her. It's a regular three-ring circus! Oh, Jesus! Never seen anything like it!" His shoulders shook uncontrollably.

"Leave," Flora commanded. "We're through."

Earl wiped his shirt sleeve across his wet eyes and gradually gained control of his laughter. He studied Flora's tense face through the open window and sputtered a few weak apologies. Flora shook her head and stepped away from the machine. Earl started the vehicle and shifted into reverse. He glanced once more at Mama, who had slowed her frantic pace to a walk and now looked confused by the unruly condition of her hair. Earl slammed the gear shifter into forward and released the brake. The machine's tires sprayed gravel as it roared down the driveway and onto Townline Road.

Flora's nerves felt raw, as though someone had rasped them with the cabbage grater, but there was no time for self-pity. "Bill, see if you can find Mama's hairpins in the grass," Flora called as she led the now-docile Mama toward the house. Perhaps a shampoo would soothe and reassure Mama that her hair was uncontaminated.

Long after she had gone to bed that evening, Flora lay awake, listening to the sounds of the house as it sighed and settled for the night. She stared into the darkness and wondered how she could have a social life or bring someone special home when Mama did such embarrassing things. Ada had been so fortunate to find Albert, who was kind and understanding when it came to Mama's affliction. Was there an Albert out there for her, and how would she ever find him?

In the morning, after she had helped Papa milk the cows, Flora began stripping the new wallpaper from the kitchen wall.

Minola was embarrassed by Mama's episode but inwardly relieved that Earl was out of the picture. After losing Ada to marriage and Margaret to influenza, Minola could not bear the thought of parting with another sister, particularly Flora, who fulfilled the role of mother, household manager, and farmhand so capably.

When Ella, Hermine, and Martha heard about the collapse of Flora's "mash up" with Earl, they immediately plotted a distraction. They invited Flora to travel to Cleveland, where the four sisters would board the lake steamer to Niagara Falls and meet a former Schauffler friend of Ella's. Flora was grateful for the opportunity to put some distance between herself and the recent disappointment.

As the interurban car rocked and swayed along the tracks toward Cleveland, Flora allowed her mind to wrestle with its usual conflict—her desire to leave home like her sisters had, contrasted with the near certainty that she could not.

Flora, Hermine, Ella, & Ella's Schauffler friend at Niagara Falls

*****

Upon her return to Cleveland, Ella learned of a higher-paying position at St. John's Evangelical Church in Dover, Ohio, a city of eight thousand. After a series of letters and telephone interviews, she was offered the job at a salary of sixty dollars per month, beginning September 1. Ella was relieved to learn that the position would not include pavement-pounding or institutional visits, but rather she would serve as church secretary, head of the Sunday School, and assistant to the minister, Rev. Schenk. She made arrangements to live with the Kloss family on Slingluff Avenue, a short walk from the church. For eight dollars per week, she would receive room, board, and laundry services. Ella felt that through frugal management of her funds, she would be able to help with Martha's college expenses, pay some personal debts, and perhaps set aside a small nest egg.

In late August, the three sisters invited a church friend, Eleanor, to travel home to Monroeville with them for one last visit before they went in their separate directions. There were many plans to be discussed about the upcoming changes in their lives, and, of course, sewing requests to be made of Flora. The young women also expressed approval of the recent ratification of the nineteenth amendment to the Constitution, granting women's suffrage. The Seibel sisters who were old enough to vote indicated their intention to cast ballots in the upcoming Presidential election that fall.

Flora proudly showed the visitors her new Singer sewing machine as well as an additional surprise. Papa was not one to verbally express approval; instead he had shown his appreciation for Flora's hard work by giving her the proceeds from the strawberry self-pickers. Flora arranged to try a Dexter twin-tub electric washing machine on a trial basis. It had two large connected tubs—one for washing and the other for rinsing—and both had agitators. Gone was the tedious regimen of rasping clothing over a corrugated scrub board until the skin on her knuckles was sore and cracked. The trial was such a success that Flora found wash day to be more like play than work. She purchased the machine and gave it a permanent home in the summer kitchen. The sisters approved of these modern appliances—anything to make Flora's life easier.

The visit home.
Flora holding Mildred, Ada, Papa, Albert
Minola, Hermine, friend Eleanor, Martha
Bill

* * * * *

Upon her arrival at Hiram College, Martha found her finances under immediate attack. Tuition was fifteen dollars more than she had anticipated, and student fees gobbled up another six dollars. She sent a frantic letter home, imploring Flora to ask Papa for the additional funds.

There were other unexpected expenses, too. The coeds were required to attend a formal reception where they would be introduced to the faculty and the 150 male students on campus. This event necessitated a request for Flora to sew a black gown. After work one day, Hermine, who wore the same size shoe as Martha, was dispatched into downtown Cleveland to purchase a pair of black satin slippers. On the night of the reception, Martha accented her outfit by tying a pink satin hair ribbon around her waist. She was relieved to hear the many compliments she received on her homemade outfit, particularly since the majority of her dorm mates were from families with stable financial situations who could afford store-bought gowns.

In addition to her courses, Martha signed up for as many extracurricular jobs as her schedule would allow. For a salary of twelve dollars per month, she washed dishes for approximately seventy people in the Hiram College dining hall every day and scrubbed the third-floor bathroom and hallway of her dormitory each Saturday. To economize, Martha packed her soiled bib aprons and other laundry into a trunk and sent it home each week. While Flora had known her sewing talents would be tapped, she had not anticipated the extra laundry, ironing, and mending that were mandated by the weekly arrival of the trunk.

Despite the demands of school and work and the concerns over her finances, Martha was thoroughly enjoying her college experience. Her outgoing personality allowed her to make friends quickly, and the coeds in the junior class voted her the best-looking freshman girl. Campus rules dictated that all women must be in their dormitories by 8 p.m., and while Martha and her friends complied, they sometimes stayed up past midnight making candy, playing cards, and gossiping about the young men who lived in the neighboring dormitory, "The Zoo." Martha's letters home were brimming with details of her new experiences but also reflected her bewilderment that no one knew of her hometown. She began to realize that while Monroeville had always been the center of her world, the little farming community was but a speck on the map to everyone else.

* * * * *

Ella was also experiencing an unexpected drain on her finances in Dover. The family she boarded with kept hours that were often in contrast to her own schedule. Because they arose at 4:30 a.m., the family ate their evening meal early and often retired to bed by the time Ella returned from church duties and after-hours meetings. Consequently, she was frequently forced to dip into her thin reserves to buy supper at a local diner. Ella purchased bags of nuts, dates, and Fig Newtons to tide her over, and she also sent a box of the treats to Martha at Hiram.

However, there was a financial benefit of living with the Kloss family. Their eldest daughter, Viola, worked as a telephone operator. Sometimes on Sunday evenings when Viola knew she would be alone at her post, she invited Ella to accompany her to work and place a free long-distance phone call to Monroeville. Ella was thrilled to make connection with Flora, and the two sisters leisurely chatted about local news and the activities of their siblings without concern for the twenty-cent-a-minute overtime rate. Ella exclaimed that such extravagance made her feel like a Rockefeller!

Ella

* * * * *

With Ella's move to Dover and Martha's matriculation to Hiram College, Hermine suddenly found herself quite alone. She could not afford to continue renting the room at the boarding house on Crawford Road, so she moved into the lodging of the Young Women's Christian Association on Franklin Boulevard. Without the companionship of her sisters, Hermine's weekends were long and lonely. She signed up for dancing and tennis lessons, participated in mixers with the YMCA, and routinely turned down advances from overeager potential suitors. Occasionally, she rode the interurban to Hiram for a weekend visit with Martha. The other coeds compared the two sisters' dark-haired beauty and announced, "We have two Martha Seibels now!" Hermine's letters home lamented over office politics at her job, where a co-worker's baby blue eyes were used to gain career advancements. She also expressed a touch of melancholy as the changing autumn leaves brought reminders of Margaret's death.

Hermine visiting Martha at Hiram College

* * * * *

A constant stream of letters flowed between the six sisters. Ada's ability to maintain a written correspondence was limited by her busy farm life, but she protested that she should not be left out of the letter exchange "even if I am married, if that makes any difference."

Post-war prosperity had vanished, with politicians preferring to call the economic downturn a "depression" rather than a "panic." Ada turned to her growing flock of chickens to make ends meet. Albert carried the eggs to town each week—sometimes as many as twenty-one dozen—where he sold them for cash or traded them for other goods. Every afternoon, Ada crossed the farmyard, trailed by two-year-old Mildred, to gather more eggs. The territorial gander did not take kindly to the trespassers, and one day he flew at little Mildred, pecking the frightened toddler and flapping her with his great wings. Ada rushed to the scene and scooped the screaming child into her arms. She stomped her foot at the hissing goose while soothing her terrified daughter. The toddler did not forget the assault, and whenever Ada stepped out the back door, Mildred warned, "Ga-ga get you!"

Little Mildred

Ada advised Flora to consider selling surplus eggs, but since Papa no longer raised pigs, the Seibels now depended heavily on the eggs as a source of protein. Each afternoon before milking the cows, Flora searched the farm buildings for fresh eggs. She slid the latch on the empty corncrib and stepped inside, knowing that one hen persistently slipped between the slats of the structure to nest in its corner. Disturbed by Flora's presence, the hen squawked and flapped its wings in protest as it scampered out the door. The dust stirred up by the fleeing chicken floated in the late-afternoon sunlight that slanted between the building's slats, creating a pattern of light and dark stripes across the wooden floor. Flora stood quietly, lost in memories of playing house with Hermine, Margaret, and Martha in the empty corncrib.

She crossed to the hen's nest and retrieved a still-warm egg, which she placed in the wire egg basket. As she turned to leave the building, Flora spotted several corncobs lying in the opposite corner. A wave of nostalgia washed over her. She and her sisters had fashioned dolls out of corncobs, green apples, and old bottles. With these crude toys, they had staged fantasy weddings and created make-believe families. Flora picked up one of the corncobs and rubbed her thumb over its rough red surface as she exited the building. Smiling wistfully, she tucked it into her apron pocket. Her childhood days seemed so long ago, and her future, well … it looked predictable—farm chores, household duties, and Mama. Flora closed the corncrib door and slid the latch.

Chapter 24
The Seibel Homestead
1921

MR. BUSCH'S OPEN BOBSLED bumped and jolted over the ruts on snow-covered Townline Road. The winter of 1920-1921 brought frequent heavy squalls that closed the area roads to travel by machines and mandated horse-drawn sleighs as the only reliable conveyance.

Minola pulled her scarf above her nose to shield her lower face from the biting wind and icy snowflakes. She stomped her feet, which had grown numb despite being burrowed beneath a layer of straw on the bed of the sleigh. Transportation to and from school via bobsled had seemed a novel lark back in November, but it had lost its element of fun after weeks of being exposed to bitter cold temperatures. The bells on the horses' harness, which once had jingled so cheerfully, now rang a harsh, annoying tone. Even seventh-grader Bill, who could find fun in any outing that involved social contact, had grown weary of the daily exposure to unpleasant conditions. He huddled in the corner of the bobsled opposite Minola with his head tucked beneath his coat collar.

Mr. Busch reined the horses to a stop near the Seibel driveway, and the two siblings stumbled out of the sleigh. As a sophomore, Minola's pride dictated that she should act with dignity before her peers who remained in the bobsled, but forsaking her self-respect, she raced after Bill and plunged awkwardly through the deep drifts that separated the driveway from the porch steps. She knew Flora would have mugs of warm milk flavored with vanilla extract for them. The thought of the steaming beverage, plus the opportunity to thaw her frozen feet beside the kitchen cookstove, caused Minola to abandon all decorum and lunge toward the comforts of home.

* * * * *

In mid-January, Martha returned to Hiram College for her second semester, unsure until only days before the start of classes if she could piece together the patchwork of her tuition funding. Expenses were higher than she had previously calculated, and Ella and Hermine's salaries were low. All involved were constantly strapped. The sisters were reluctant to ask Papa for aid unless absolutely necessary, based upon his earlier assurance that he would pay for high school but nothing more. He could be quite taciturn when approached about financial affairs, and the siblings tried to avoid the discomfort of such an interaction. Ella, Flora, and Hermine were determined to support Martha in her educational pursuit, even if it required personal sacrifice beyond their normal frugality.

Despite the financial concerns, Martha continued to flourish at Hiram. She and her friends made popcorn and the brown-sugar fudge penuche in honor of their dorm mates who were celebrating January birthdays. To lure one of the honorees upstairs to the site of the surprise feast, Martha rushed into the dormitory parlor and urged, "Doris! Come quick! Bart Chapman's getting undressed in front of his window over at 'The Zoo!'" Doris leaped for the stairwell and thundered up the stairs to the third floor, followed by Martha. She was greeted with shouts of "Surprise! Happy birthday!" and much laughter about her eagerness to enjoy the view from the window.

Martha's dormitory had a Victrola in the parlor, where her friends taught her the latest dance steps. They coached her to limber up and allow herself to "feel" the music. Perhaps it was the years of listening to Rev. Keppel rail from the pulpit about the evils of dancing, but Martha could not shimmy with abandon the way her friends did. "I guess God left the spring out of me," she offered with a shrug.

* * * * *

A love of music, more than the desire to dance, motivated Flora to try a Cheney Talking Machine on trial. It came with a sample record that included the songs "Swallow," "Gethsemane," and the toe-tapper "I'll Say She Does." Flora, Minola, and Bill took turns cranking the phonograph's side arm, activating the turntable, and lowering the needle onto the record. They marveled at the beautiful music that emanated as if by magic from the cloth-covered sound chamber.

The siblings immediately fell in love with the phonograph, playing their only record over and over again. To them, the five-dollar-a-month payment plan seemed reasonable for something that brought so much entertainment value. One evening during supper, they tentatively approached Papa with their desire to make the new-style Victrola a permanent fixture in the parlor.

At the conclusion of their sales pitch, Papa did not look up from his plate but continued to use his thumb to push the remaining beef and noodles onto his fork. He shook his head "no" and offered no reason for his decision.

The siblings knew better than to wheedle or whine. Perhaps he thought five dollars a month was too much money for an object of such frivolity. Or perhaps he recalled Mama's recent hallucinatory episode and feared that voices emanating from a box in the parlor would induce another attack. The siblings exchanged forlorn glances, their hearts shattered at the thought of giving up the Cheney they so enjoyed.

* * * * *

Ada worried about Martha's reports of frequent head colds, and she laid the blame on insufficient underattire. She sewed an underbody from pink crepe de Chine and mailed it to Martha at college, with instructions to put it on and wear it like religion.

From the remaining material, Ada fashioned a pair of pajamas for little Mildred, who struggled against donning the new nightwear. "Auntie's panties, auntie's panties!" the toddler protested when Ada attempted to dress her in the pajamas.

To coax cooperation from her niece, Flora gave Mildred her old Billiken bank. She demonstrated its purpose by dropping a penny into the top of the statue's head and made a wish while rubbing the soles of the Billiken's feet.

Mildred quickly caught on, and each time someone called at the house—whether it was a neighbor or a peddler—she ran to get her Billiken and held it up for the visitor to make a deposit. Usually she was rewarded with a penny or a nickel. Mildred would then pat the feet of the little statue and reply, "Make my wish." Ada feared she was raising a schemer.

* * * * *

To pass the long winter months and spark interest among his congregation, the new minister, Rev. Abele, initiated a friendly competition among the Sunday School classes. To win the ten-dollar prize, each class must memorize a lengthy Biblical passage that they would recite before the congregation at a special service prior to the Easter season. The class with the best delivery and percentage of participants completing the assignment would win the cash.

Flora and Minola's class was assigned all thirty-one verses of the 14th chapter of John. Flora immediately set to work on memorizing the passage. While peeling potatoes or churning butter, she consulted the open Bible on her lap as she diligently committed several lines to memory each day.

Minola, on the other hand, balked at the assignment. She was still disenchanted with organized religion following the ugly incidents surrounding the recent church split. She waved off Flora's entreaty to begin memorizing the assignment by claiming she had too much homework or was suffering from a headache. At other times, Minola abruptly marched out of the room when Flora mentioned the subject of the Sunday School competition. Exasperated, Flora called after her, "Come on, Minola. I'll coach you. 'In my Father's house are many rooms...' What comes next?"

"Probably spring housecleaning," Minola responded over her shoulder.

Flora gave up on cajoling her sister toward committing the verses to memory. She fretted as the days and weeks passed with little outward indication that Minola was making an attempt to fulfill her role in the assignment. While Flora was disappointed, she was more concerned about letting down the other members of their Sunday School class, who were counting on Minola to help them attain one-hundred-percent participation and a flawless performance.

On the morning of the competition, Flora stood before the cookstove frying eggs in the skillet and nervously reciting the assigned Bible passage. She bit her lip as Minola slid into her chair at the kitchen table, her nose buried in the book *The Patrol of the Sundance Trail.*

Bill plopped into his chair opposite Minola and tugged at the stiff collar of his Sunday shirt.

"Do you wanna practice your verses one more time, Bill?" Flora asked as she slipped a fried egg onto his plate.

"Naw, I know 'em," he assured. "You know yours, Minola?"

Flora shot a sidelong glance at her sister, who stopped reading and looked up at Bill, her finger marking her place on the page. Minola gave her shoulder a dismissive shrug as she poked a corner of toast into her egg yolk.

"I'll bet everybody in my class knows their verses 'cept for Hal Rudke. He can't be counted on for nothing—none of the Rudkes can—and he's gonna cost us the prize. Any class with a Rudke in it is doomed," Bill lamented as he buttered his toast.

Flora's appetite vanished. She pushed the egg on her plate from one side to the other, realizing that Minola's lack of cooperation would cause the Seibel name to be used interchangeably with that of the Rudkes' when it came to showcasing unreliability.

The sanctuary was packed in anticipation of the Sunday School's performance. The lower grade school class was the first to be called forward. They performed admirably, although several of the students needed prompting from their teacher to recall all the verses of the 23rd Psalm, and the littlest Rudke had failed to show up.

During the upper grade school's recitation of the Beatitudes, Hal Rudke occasionally mumbled a remembered phrase but generally looked disinterested in fulfilling the assignment, as Bill had predicted.

When the high school and young adult class took their places in front of the sanctuary, Flora looked around at the prominent families of Monroeville seated in the front pews. She twisted her hankie and prepared for their judgmental stares when Minola stood as straight and still as a corn stalk, unable to utter a single verse.

At the prompt from their teacher, Mrs. Mueller, the class began to recite in unison, "Let not your hearts be troubled; believe in God, believe also in me." Flora's ear pricked at the sound of Minola's voice beside her, reciting the verse. Her heart quickened with hope, but perhaps Minola had only learned the first few verses. Flora concentrated on making sure she did not stumble over the passages while straining to hear Minola's voice among the chorus of the other students. At one point, she stole a quick glance at Minola, who was staring straight ahead, her mouth moving in harmony with the others. As they progressed further into the recitation, Minola's voice did not falter. Flora realized that Minola had secretly memorized the entire passage during the past weeks. A flood of relief washed over her as the class finished the chapter in perfect unison and with one-hundred-percent participation.

Upon returning to their pew, Flora gave her sister's hand a grateful squeeze.

Minola leaned close to Flora's ear and whispered, "I know another Bible verse. It's 'O ye of little faith.'"

Flora mouthed an apology, and Minola settled back in the pew with a self-satisfied grin.

The victorious high school and young adult class decided to use the ten-dollar prize to indulge all the participating classes in an ice cream party. The treat would include chocolate "dope" and chopped peanuts for toppings. Bill's ecstasy over sharing in the prize was dimmed slightly by the knowledge that Hal Rudke would also be rewarded, despite his lack of effort.

* * * * *

Ella's responsibilities at St. John's Evangelical Church in Dover kept her busily serving the congregation. She called on those who were ill, decorated the Sunday School rooms, taught classes, planned programs, banked the collection moneys, conducted the church correspondence, and recorded attendance, noting that 534 of the 850 members were in church on Easter morning.

In response, the congregants placed Ella on a pedestal, thinking they could talk to her only about church matters or explain why they hadn't attended services recently. They even expected her appetite to take a saintly path. At a church supper one evening, a woman in the buffet line intercepted Ella's hand as she reached for a piece of three-layer chocolate cake. "Oh, Ella!" the woman commented in surprise, "Do you really think *Devil's* food is appropriate for someone of your stature in the church?" She gave Ella a meaningful look. Feeling that she must comply with expectations, Ella dutifully bypassed the sinful chocolate dessert and selected the apparently more worthy angel food cake.

Because she gave so fully of herself to the congregation, Ella was deeply beloved. For her twenty-ninth birthday in early May, the church members surprised her with a leather purse and a silver teaspoon with her name engraved on it. Ella was touched by their sentiment.

Ella

St. John's Evangelical Church in Dover

Life at the boarding house, however, had become problematic. Mrs. Kloss' health had deteriorated, so to ease the woman's burdens, Ella began eating all of her meals at a local diner. To economize, she purchased a ticket that allowed her a fifty-cent meal for thirty-eight cents.

The food was homemade and plentiful, including a lunch of soup, fish, mashed potatoes, coleslaw, tomatoes, bread and butter, bread pudding, banana cream pie, and coffee.

Although the meals were good, the extra expense ate into her already taut budget, particularly since the Klosses did not offer to refund a portion of Ella's rent as compensation for the services she was not receiving. Ella knew she should search for other rooming accommodations, but she was reluctant to reveal her dissatisfaction to the Klosses and possibly hurt their feelings.

When a letter arrived from Martha detailing additional financial needs, Ella pondered how she could stretch her money to accommodate the request. She wrote Martha, joking that unless she converted the church treasury into uses not intended by the good people of St. John's, the only aid she could supply was a five-dollar bill. She tucked the money into the envelope but did not reveal to Martha that it was the last of her cash. Ella resolved that henceforth she would save money by foregoing breakfasts.

* * * * *

Since her hallucinatory experience, Mama's spells had taken a different turn. It seemed to take her longer to rebound, and after rousing from her stupor-like sleep, she often went for days with very little talking or activity. When she recovered, she resumed the cyclic pattern of highs and lows that kept the family on edge.

A spring windstorm brought down many branches from the aging mulberries and launched Mama into a tidying-up frenzy. She bustled about the back and side yards creating neat piles of branches and sticks while muttering "*ordentlich und sauber* (neat and tidy)." Flora watched from the kitchen window and wished she could harness all that energy for something constructive.

Papa viewed the downed branches as a source of fuel for the cookstove. He set into a rhythm as he progressed around the yard, picking up a branch in one hand, swinging his corn knife in one or two swift chops, and tossing the stove-length sticks aside.

Minola and Bill trailed after him to gather the wood into bushel baskets. The task was monotonous and required almost as much stoop work as picking strawberries.

Bill quickly grew tired of the routine, and he used a stick to poke Minola in the back of her legs as she bent over.

Minola whirled around and scolded, "Bill! Stop it and get to work!

I'm not doin' your work <u>and</u> mine!" She lunged for his stick.

Bill laughed and leaped away from Minola's reach, taunting her with the stick.

Papa looked up at the disturbance as he swung the corn knife downward, but his aim was off. The knife slashed into his left index finger, cutting the flesh to the bone and nearly severing the finger.

"*Gott* damn it!" Papa swore as he dropped the branch and corn knife and fumbled in his pants pocket for a handkerchief to stem the flow of blood.

Bill watched in horror as Papa's white hankie quickly turned scarlet. Sensing that his tom-foolery had been the cause of the accident, Bill took off for the barn to avoid certain punishment.

Flora was leaning over the open cookstove door, removing loaves of freshly baked bread from the firebox and replacing them with pans of bread dough, when Minola burst through the kitchen door and cried, "Flora, come quick! Papa cut his finger real bad. It's bleedin' everywhere!"

Flora slammed the cookstove door and raced after Minola, still clutching the dishtowel she had been using to handle the hot bread pans.

They found Papa seated on the overturned apple butter kettles behind the summer kitchen. He was applying pressure to his wound, but the soaked hankie dripped blood. Flora quickly wound the dishtowel around Papa's hand.

"Where's Bill?" Flora frantically asked Minola. It seemed unusual that he was not at the center of such morbid activity. "He's gotta drive Papa to Dr. Gilman's office. I can't leave with bread in the oven."

Minola set off in search of Bill, passing Mama, who continued her mission of tidying up the downed limbs in the side yard. Even Papa's injury could not interrupt her single-minded task.

Upon locating Bill, Minola delivered Flora's urgent message that he must get the truck and drive Papa to the doctor's.

Bill sprang into action, relieved at the reprieve he had been granted and the possible opportunity to make amends for causing the accident. He cranked the old Ford truck to life and quickly maneuvered it to where Papa sat behind the summer kitchen.

Grimacing, Papa climbed in beside Bill, his injured hand bundled in the dishtowel in his lap.

Bill released the brake, stepped on the gear shifter pedal, and slammed the floor lever forward. The Ford momentarily coughed and then lurched forward, causing both Papa and Bill to snap backward in their seats.

"Jesus *Gott*! You tryin' to break my neck?" Papa growled between clenched teeth.

Bill clutched the steering wheel in a vise-like grip as he carefully steered the machine around ruts and potholes in Townline Road. After they had turned onto Plank Road, Bill opened the throttle all the way, and they motored toward Monroeville at the Ford's top speed of fifteen miles an hour.

Dr. Gilman tilted his head to find just the right spot in his bifocals to examine Papa's injured left hand. He motioned to the missing portions of the index and middle fingers on Papa's right hand and observed, "Well, Bill, if you're trying to get rid of all your fingers, I'd say you're doing a pretty good job." He probed the open gash on Papa's finger and announced, "Looks like I can save this one."

Papa remained stoic as the doctor stitched the deep incision, but young Bill watched in fascinated horror.

While Papa's injury healed, his ability to perform farm chores was limited, causing him to depend on Flora more than ever.

The following Saturday evening, while the family was in Monroeville to do their weekly shopping, they ran into Ada, Albert, and little Mildred in Zipfel's store.

Ada immediately extended an invitation to her siblings to ride home with her and Albert to spend the night. The three eagerly accepted and followed Ada toward the front of the store. The bell over the door rang cheerily as Albert held it open for the others to exit.

Papa stood in the center aisle and solemnly called, "Who's gonna milk the cows in the morning?"

Flora froze in the doorway. She turned and looked at Papa with his bandaged left hand. Choking down her disappointment, she apologized to Ada and told Minola and Bill to run along to Albert's buggy.

The two youngsters scampered out the door, chattering excitedly to Ada.

Flora followed Mama and Papa to the Overland and climbed into the rear seat. On the ride home, she wondered, "Must I always crawl back into my old hole?"

Flora on the front porch of the Seibel homestead

* * * * *

Ada and Albert's brick house had suffered through years of neglect at the hands of parsimonious owners and indifferent tenants. The Yingling sisters who owned the farm made it clear that they would split the cost of repairs to the outbuildings and fences, but any improvements made to the house would be borne by the young couple alone. This was a fairly common practice in the owner-tenant relationship, and Ada and Albert accepted the terms without protest. They spruced up the house's interior with fresh coats of paint and new wallpaper. Ada sewed attractive curtains for each window and braided rag rugs for the floors. Albert fixed the hinges on sagging shutters, replaced missing panes of glass, and leveled the floor boards in the summer kitchen. To them, the house was their home, and they cared for the old brick structure as if it were their own.

Ada & Albert's home

Other tenants in the neighborhood who also lived on Yingling-owned farms guffawed at the young couple for bearing the cost of home improvements without retribution. They slyly winked about how they made sure the landlord's share of the crops came up a few bushels short at harvest time, thereby offsetting any out-of-pocket repairs made by the tenant. Albert tolerated the ribbing but would not waver from his iron-clad sense of honesty. He absorbed the cost of improvements, and, in addition, each Saturday when the young couple drove the buggy into Monroeville to do their shopping, they stopped at the Yingling home to drop off a dozen eggs, a block of golden butter, a freshly butchered chicken, and a tin of thick, rich cream. Of course, Albert knew his place in the landlord-tenant relationship, and he always delivered the farm goods to the back door.

* * * * *

The fashionable home improvements instituted by Emmaline Moss had paid off when daughter Edith married Lee Addison in the renovated parlor of the Moss home. Before the ceremony, Emmaline strategically placed large standing vases of flowers beside the built-in china cabinets on either side of the parlor archway, drawing her guests' eyes to the heirloom Limoges dishes behind the sparkling leaded-glass doors. She was satisfied that the Moss family demonstrated a social status worthy of the groom and his English heritage.

In a twist of fate, the Addison family farm lay just east and across Ridge Road from Ada and Albert's home—their nearest neighbor. Lee brought his new bride to live on the family farm, and once again, Ada and Edith were neighbors, just as they had been throughout their childhood.

One afternoon shortly after the newlyweds had settled into their new home, Ada and little Mildred walked down to Addisons' to deliver a wedding gift. Edith unwrapped the deep blue teapot decorated with orange and white raised flowers and set it on the kitchen table. Two-and-a-half year old Mildred gripped the table's edge and stood on tiptoe to gain a better view. "Look at pretty!" she exclaimed.

Edith immediately moved the teapot away from the child's line of sight. "Can't you put her outside or something?" she asked, her voice tinged with annoyance. "I used to do that when I was teaching—send the troublesome ones outside to sit on the school steps." She scowled at Mildred.

Ada lifted the toddler onto her hip and replied, "Oh, I think you'll feel different once you have your own." She smiled at Mildred and ran her finger along the curve of the child's soft cheek.

Edith's silence caused Ada to tilt her head quizzically. "You … <u>do</u> want children of your own, don't you?"

Edith shrugged her shoulder dismissively. "I don't know. They make you lose your figure." She smoothed her hands down her slim hips and gazed pointedly at Ada, who still retained the weight she had gained during pregnancy.

"But, what about Lee? Won't he be wanting children?" Ada asked.

"I don't intend to be just a broodmare," Edith sniffed. "Besides, there are ways to control such things. Obviously <u>your</u> mother didn't believe in using a well-placed hatpin, but my mother told me all about it. Said it's something every married woman oughtta know."

Ada shuddered and hugged little Mildred to her.

*****

When the school year ended in June, Elmer submitted his resignation as principal and science teacher at Monroeville High School. He and Mary Marvin were wed in a simple ceremony, and the young couple moved to New York City so Elmer could pursue a master's degree in education at Columbia University. George and Bertha were overcome with mixed emotions. On one hand, they were filled with undisguised pride. Few children from German families attained such lofty educational achievements, and Bertha never missed an opportunity to share Elmer's success with the members of her community. It became a snide comment among the neighbors that one needed to stand back when Bertha was crowing about Elmer or risk being peppered by her bursting buttons.

On the other hand, George and Bertha were deeply disappointed that both Elmer and Walter had rejected life on the farm. For the German immigrants, land had been the goal, and nothing was more important than passing the hard-earned farm on to the next generation, preferably to a son. While Walter occasionally came home from Cleveland to visit, it was clear he did not intend to resume the hard work, long hours, and unpredictable income of farming. He had a good job in the city and enjoyed the numerous social outlets available in a metropolitan setting. During his visits, Walter chafed at the slow pace and inconveniences of rural life.

There would have been some consolation to losing both sons to off-the-farm careers if Bertha's maneuverings had managed to snare a husband for Rose, who could then take over the farm with her spouse. However, it appeared that thirty-two-year-old Rose was well on her way to spinsterhood.

Albert, Papa, & Walter during one of Walter's visits from Cleveland

For George, who was now sixty-four years old, the heavy farm work was becoming physically daunting. To make up for the lack of manpower, he and Bertha turned toward their German roots. They sponsored Jesse Girtz, a seventeen-year-old who was eager to emigrate from Germany and gain a toehold in America. In exchange for the sponsorship, Jesse agreed to work as a farmhand. His tenure with the Seibels would also afford him the opportunity to perfect his English while earning money to pursue his dreams.

Mr. Moss & Edwin, Papa, & Jesse Girtz

Jesse had a rich baritone voice, and he belted out songs from the mütterland as he worked in the fields. On their adjacent farm, the Seibel girls often took a break from picking strawberries and watched and listened as Jesse followed behind the horse-drawn implements, his head thrown back in song. They couldn't image anyone exhibiting so much joy—or excess energy—while doing farm work.

Bertha doted on Jesse as if he were her own son. She enjoyed cooking for his hearty appetite and conversing with him in German. After supper, she encouraged Rose to play the massive piano in the parlor so Jesse could sing along. Bertha stood in the kitchen, her head tilted in rapt admiration of the music, as she wiped a single dish over and over.

While George and Bertha were decidedly neutral about Jesse's nationality, others in the community still harbored a post-war anti-German sentiment. People remembered Elmer's lack of military service and Bertha's outspoken opinions about keeping both her sons safely at home during the war. Jesse's presence only revived old grumblings about the Seibel patriotism.

One day while Flora and Minola were purchasing fabric at Mr. Zipfel's store, a woman whose soldier son had served in France huffed past them. "I won't trade where Kraut-lovers do business!" she hissed.

The two sisters' cheeks burned and they exchanged an uncomfortable glance, knowing that their family was also being painted with the broad brushstroke of disloyalty.

* * * * *

Bertha shared the success of Jesse's arrangement with her two middle-aged bachelor brothers, Gust and Herman Loew. She encouraged them to seek out a similar sponsorship of a young German girl to cook and keep house for them on their isolated farm. The brothers saw the wisdom of this suggestion, and Gust eventually traveled to Germany to escort their new helper to the United States.

Frieda was an eager, vivacious fräulein with flaxen hair and pink cheeks. When this mismatched couple presented themselves to the authorities at the U.S. immigration port, the officials doubted their intentions. They suspected a violation of the Mann Act, which prohibited white slavery and the interstate transport of females for prostitution. Gust and Frieda were taken to a small office and grilled about their plans.

The officials were not swayed by the couple's earnest repetition of their simple but honest intentions. They began arranging transport back to Germany for Frieda and threatened Gust with charges of attempted promotion of prostitution. Things looked grim.

Suddenly, Frieda remembered her diary. With trembling hands, she pulled the leather-bound journal from the bottom of her satchel and offered it to the immigration official as proof of her intentions. After reading several entries that outlined her long-planned ambitions for gaining work and eventual citizenship in America, the authorities permitted her to enter the country. Gust was weak-kneed with relief.

When the local community learned of Gust and Frieda's interrogation, they tittered and guffawed at the notion of the staid old Loew brothers operating a brothel on their lonely country road.

* * * * *

In mid-August, Rev. Abele organized a picnic at Ruggles Beach for the entire Sunday School. Since Margaret's death, the Seibel family had purposefully avoided the popular resort, which held bittersweet memories of Margaret's last summer spent working, dancing, and learning to swim. Flora, Minola, and Bill were a bit apprehensive about attending the outing, but they resolved to overcome their melancholy and enjoy the lawn games, picnicking, and, best of all, the lake.

On the day of the picnic, Flora packed a hamper of fried buttermilk chicken, a jar of pickles, some hard-boiled eggs, a jar of honey to drizzle on fluffy biscuits, a red velvet cake with thick buttercream frosting, and a tall jug of lemonade.

With Bill behind the wheel of the Overland, the three siblings set off for the resort. Papa remained at home to keep an eye on Mama and to enjoy a quiet Sunday afternoon.

The ride seemed like a novelty, in part because the three had never traveled such a long distance in the machine without Papa at the wheel. They enjoyed the scenery, the pleasant weather, and the anticipation of the day at the lake.

As they passed over the river in Huron, Bill leaned out of the driver's seat to experience the eerie sensation of viewing the water below through the wooden slats of the bridge. While doing so, he made a disturbing discovery. The left rear wheel of the Overland had slipped to the end of its shaft and was perilously close to falling off. Alarmed, Bill coasted the machine to the end of the bridge and pulled over to the side of the road. The three scampered out of the vehicle to assess the damage.

"We won't make it to Ruggles with that wheel," pointed out Flora glumly, "and we can't make it home, either."

"So, what do we do?" asked Minola.

The siblings plopped onto the running board in defeat. They contemplated their lack of repair options and the fun they would be missing at the lake.

Suddenly, Bill brightened and bolted upright. "I know what we can do. Let's eat!"

Flora and Minola looked at each other and shrugged. "May as well," Flora agreed. She pulled the picnic hamper from the back seat, distributed pieces of cold fried chicken, and cut generous wedges from the red velvet cake.

They had finished their first course and were rummaging in the hamper for the second round when a machine motored up behind them. It was the Muellers from church. When they learned of the Overland's problem, the Muellers graciously offered to transport the three Seibels to Ruggles Beach, where Bill could place a call home.

Papa was stretched out on the Fuller seat on the front porch, his stocking feet thrust between the supporting chains of the swing. The

Monroeville Spectator, which was tented over his face, ruffled lightly as he snored.

Papa startled at the jangle of the telephone on the living room wall. "Flora, get that," he mumbled. As the phone continued to ring, Papa came fully awake and realized that Flora was not there to answer it. He reluctantly left the comfort of the swing and stumbled indoors to lift the receiver.

Bill poured out the tale of their automotive woe, while Papa rubbed his hand over his chin. He told Bill to meet him at the bridge in Huron where the Overland was parked. Papa gathered some tools and placed them in a wooden box in the back of the Ford truck. He asked Mama if she would like to go for a ride, knowing she would eagerly accept.

At the resort, families spread blankets on the grass of the shade-dappled grove, and the women proudly lifted carefully prepared lunches from their hampers. Minola shook their blanket out next to that of the Muellers, while Flora sheepishly pulled their partially devoured meal from the picnic basket. She was particularly mortified by the red velvet cake, whose large missing wedge gave evidence of their pre-emptive lunching.

After they ate, Bill hitched a ride from a passing motorist and waited on the Overland's running board for his parents to arrive. Mama remained in the truck while Papa inspected the wheel. With a bit of tinkering, he was able to perform a temporary repair. "Keep an eye on it on the way home," Papa warned as he moved the box of tools to the back seat of the Overland.

Bill nodded and eagerly drove the machine onward to Ruggles Beach, where he would still have time to enjoy the lawn games and the proximity to the lake.

Papa and Mama returned home, with Mama smiling happily at the unexpected outing.

After Flora cleaned up their picnic site, she ambled over to the empty dance hall and leaned her elbows on the sill of one of the open windows. The polished dance floor gleamed in the shafts of sun that slanted through the wide windows. Flora imagined Margaret gliding across the dance floor in the arms of the dashing soldier Edmund Atherton. Her sister's head was tilted back and a vivacious smile was upon her face as she executed a lively one-step with her partner.

Flora turned and gazed across the road toward the farmhouse and the "The Last Resort," the barnlike dormitory where Margaret had roomed with the other girls on the summer staff. Beyond the building, she could see the edge of the peach orchard, where Margaret had picked peaches only a few weeks before her death.

Flora smiled wistfully. Everywhere she looked seemed to radiate a memory of Margaret. Instead of making her sad, Flora found it comforting to be where Margaret had experienced so much joy during the last summer of her life.

On the drive home, Bill frequently leaned over the driver's side door to monitor the wheel. It occasionally edged outward on its shaft, overcoming Papa's temporary fix. However, Bill had watched each step of the repair process and knew exactly what to do. He pulled the machine off the road, and while he performed the repair, Flora and Minola walked along the roadside and picked wild chicory flowers and Queen Anne's lace.

When the siblings finally reached home, Flora set the bouquet in a vase on the kitchen table so she would be reminded of the pleasant day at Ruggles Beach.

* * * * *

By the time school started in the fall, eighth-grader Bill had gone Horatio Alger crazy, due in part to the selection of books that Ella checked out of the Dover Public Library and mailed home for her siblings' enjoyment. Bill lost himself in the rags-to-riches tales, and he gladly allowed his schoolwork and chores to suffer while eagerly reading about boys from humble backgrounds similar to his own who rose to lives of prosperity.

Because Monroeville had no public library and the high school library was severely depleted, Ella sent the classics so Minola could fulfill the required reading assignments for her junior year. Before Minola could get her hands on the books, however, Papa had his nose buried in them. She dutifully waited until he was finished.

While reading, writing, American history, and Spanish were her favorite subjects, Minola immediately regretted signing up for physics. The old specter of her weak math skills continued to haunt her. Minola approached her teacher about dropping the class, but he spoke so convincingly of her abilities that she agreed to stick with it. Her resolve lasted until class the next day, when the physics of electricity again overwhelmed her.

This time, Minola approached the school superintendent. His patience for an unsure student was limited, and he brusquely told her not to be a quitter and shooed her off to class. Minola hauled the physics book home each night and made headway in the subject through sheer determination.

*****

Ella gently told the Kloss family that she intended to board elsewhere, attributing her departure to a desire to relieve the ailing Mrs. Kloss of any extra burdens.

Ella moved in with a recent widow, Mrs. Arndt, who frequently wept over her dearly departed "poor Charlie." Ella summoned sympathy by recalling her own sorrow over Margaret's death. The two spent long, grim evenings in the parlor.

For her rooming arrangements, Ella was offered two options. She could share a downstairs bedroom with the widow, or she could have the unlit, unheated room at the top of the stairs. Ella chose the latter. In the mornings, she scooped up her clothing and dashed downstairs to dress in the cozy bathroom.

Mrs. Arndt responded to having a boarder by being oversolicitous. When Ella had a head cold, the landlady checked with her for health updates at frustratingly frequent intervals. Ella began to suspect that "poor Charlie" had died from being asked how he felt every five minutes of his life.

Before long, Mrs. Arndt had an electric light and a gas stove installed in Ella's room. Ella hoped these improvements would decrease the number of wellness bulletins she was required to deliver.

While she no longer had to buy her meals at a local diner, Ella did have to adjust to a new meal regimen. Mrs. Arndt cooked a large batch of several entrées, which the two women ate at every meal for the next three days, after which new entrées were prepared and again consumed for a monotonous stretch.

Ella quietly tolerated the peculiarities of her new boarding situation.

*****

In early October, a group outing was planned for the men and women living at the Cleveland YMCA and YWCA. It involved a daytrip to the Y's campground at Centerville Mills in Bainbridge Township, southeast of Cleveland. Twenty-four-year-old Hermine happily signed up for the outing with her friends Edna and Ruby.

Upon arriving at the campground, the young people leaped from the back of the open transport trucks and streamed toward the lake, where rowboats awaited. Edna and Ruby clambered off the truck, but Hermine called for them to wait. The heel of her shoe had become tightly wedged between the wooden slats of the truck bed. While her friends waited impatiently, Hermine tugged and twisted until the shoe was finally freed.

The three young women hurried to catch up with the others who had now reached the lake. They stood forlornly on the shore, watching as rowboats filled with young men and women began to nudge out onto the water.

"Look! There's one left!" Ruby exclaimed as she pointed in the direction of an empty rowboat bobbing beside the dock. The three hurried toward the boat to assess its availability.

"Oh, it doesn't have any oars," observed Hermine with disappointment.

"Looking for these?" a young man called as he approached from the boathouse, carrying a pair of oars over his shoulder.

"Three cheers for Ralph!" exclaimed Edna as she clapped her hands. She introduced Hermine and Ruby to her brother, Ralph Worden, who had recently moved into the Cleveland YMCA.

Ralph explained that one of the original oars was badly cracked, causing the rowboat to be rejected by the Y residents who had rushed to the dock. To prevent a mishap, he had carried the damaged oars to the boathouse to exchange for a new set, but by the time he returned, the impatient young boaters had already piled into other skiffs and set off.

Ralph offered to row the ladies about the lake, and they eagerly accepted. The four glided across the glassy surface of the water, chatting happily and admiring the autumn colors in the nearby woods.

Hermine trailed her fingers in the cool lake water and realized that for the first time since Margaret's death, she was not awash with the usual melancholy that beset her when the leaves changed color. Could it be Ralph's reassuring voice and easy-going nature?

A few weeks later, Martha traveled to Cleveland, where she and Hermine boarded the interurban for Monroeville. Martha filled Hermine's ears with details of a tricotine formal that Flora was sewing for her, and she asked her sister's opinion about whether the buttons should be cloth-covered or an accent color. After she had asked the question a second time and received no response, Martha nudged Hermine with her elbow and said, "Hey, kid, what's wrong with you? Are you in dreamland?"

Hermine returned a bashful grin. "Guess I am."

The weekend was filled with visits from Ada, Albert, and little Mildred as well as cousin Rose, but Hermine's thoughts were elsewhere.

Ada with Mildred, Flora, Martha, Minola, Hermine, & cousin Rose

*****

Early December brought Bertha's sixtieth birthday, and the neighborhood surprised her with a party. Eighty people crowded into George and Bertha's house, bringing refreshments and presents. Emmaline Moss hovered over Bertha, urging her to open the beautifully wrapped box from the Mosses. Bertha complied, and all the guests oohed and aahed when she lifted a glittering cut-glass candy dish from the folds of tissue paper. Emmaline basked in the display of her obvious good taste and generosity.

Mama stood in the corner of the parlor, ignoring the birthday action. Her eyes roamed over every aspect of the home's structure—doors, windows, woodwork, cabinets, and stairwell. With a scowl upon her face, she muttered, "This was supposed to be *mine*!"

Rose struck a chord at the piano, and Jesse Girtz led the group in hailing Bertha with a chorus of the birthday song. Mama pushed her way through the merry crowd, stiff-armed the back door, and steamed toward home in the cold night air.

Chapter 25
The Gfell Home
1922

ADA AWOKE in the thin, gray January light. She quickly reached for the two soda crackers on her bedside dresser to quell the wave of nausea that overtook her each morning. As she chewed, the aroma of coffee and frying bacon wafted from the nearby kitchen. Albert's sympathy for Ada's morning sickness had prompted him to begin cooking breakfast for himself and Alfred each day. Ada smiled at the scene she knew was unfolding beyond the closed kitchen door. Albert would be at the cookstove frying bacon and eggs on a roaringly hot surface. Alfred, oblivious to the blue-black smoke that was filling the kitchen, would be seated at the table, sipping the coffee he had poured into his saucer to cool.

The odor of the cooking food caused Ada to feel queasy, and she laid her head on the pillow until the moment passed. In the watery light, she gazed at the photo that hung on the wall at the foot of her bed. It was Margaret's graduation picture, which Ada had had enlarged and framed. She pressed her lips together as she studied the outline of Margaret's dear face. Ada would need assistance from one of her sisters when the baby came in August, but she was still haunted by the experience of losing Margaret at the time of Mildred's birth. What if another epidemic like the Spanish influenza swept through when the new baby came? Ada could not bear the thought of losing another sister or possibly Albert, little Mildred, or the baby. What if *she* was the one claimed by the illness, leaving Albert alone to raise two little ones? Or, God forbid, what would happen to Mildred and the baby if both she and Albert were taken? Ada squeezed her eyes shut and vowed she would not allow such dark thoughts to cloud her mind. Plenty of work awaited her today. Papa was coming to help Albert and Alfred shell corn, and Flora and Mama would assist her with the hearty noon meal. There would only be four men to feed, including the owner of the corn sheller—not nearly as much food to prepare as when threshers came in the summer. However, there was no time to lounge in bed. Ada gingerly swung her feet to the floor and waited for her stomach to settle before rising and dressing for the day.

After the morning chores were done and Minola and Bill had boarded the school wagon, Papa, Mama, and Flora climbed into the Overland for a chilly ride to the Gfell residence. Flora entered Ada's kitchen carrying jars of canned succotash and a pan of gingerbread with hard sauce. The two sisters worked side by side as they began preparations for the noon meal, while Mama immediately settled into the familiar groove of peeling potatoes.

Papa headed directly to the cornbarn across the road from the house, where the corn sheller had been pulled into position and would be powered by the owner's tractor. The corn had been drying in the cribs since its harvest in November, and now Albert and Alfred shoveled the ears onto a drag line that fed the sheller. Sharp wheels separated the kernels from the corncobs and sent a golden stream of shelled corn cascading into a waiting wagon, while the stripped cobs were spit into a pile. The owner of the corn sheller walked back and forth, monitoring the machinery, and occasionally climbing onto the side of the wagon to distribute the growing bank of corn kernels that Albert would sell in Monroeville or use to feed the livestock. Papa shoveled the pile of corncobs into a low trailer to be used as fuel for the kitchen cookstove or placed in a box in the corner of the outhouse. His breath hung in frosty plumes in the frigid air, and he took frequent breaks to lean upon the end of the shovel. At age sixty, Papa felt his stamina diminishing. He watched with a mixture of admiration and envy as Albert and Alfred vigorously shoveled the ear corn.

When the drone of the machinery halted, Ada crossed the kitchen, rubbed a circle in the condensation on the door glass, and peered toward the cornbarn. "They're comin'," she announced. Flora hurried to the reservoir on the side of the cookstove and filled a basin with warm water. She carried it, a bar of lye soap, and some towels to a bench in the summer kitchen where the men could wash up. Mama bustled about, tidying up things that didn't need to be tidied and lifting lids to inspect the contents of all the pans on the cookstove.

Ada ladled steaming beef and gravy into a bowl to be served over snowy mounds of mashed potatoes. Side dishes of succotash, sauerkraut, and cottage cheese were carried to the table in the adjoining dining room, along with a platter of bread slices to sop up any remaining gravy.

As the men ate, Ada and Flora circled the table, refilling platters and coffee cups and setting out generous squares of gingerbread with hard sauce. Three-year-old Mildred clutched her doll and tagged after her mother, looking shyly at the owner of the corn sheller and burying her face in Ada's skirt when the man winked in her direction.

When the men had eaten their fill and returned to the cornbarn, the women cleared the table and set a kettle of water on the cookstove to heat for washing dishes. Ada wilted onto a chair at the kitchen table and sighed, "I'm so weary." When Flora set a plate of food in front of her, Ada quickly pushed it away.

"What's wrong with you?" Flora asked as she served Mama and Mildred and then seated herself opposite Ada. Lifting a forkful of mashed potatoes, she gazed with concern at her sister. "You oughtta be starvin' by now. I know I am!"

Ada shook her head. "My stomach's a little techy these days, 'specially in the mornings. Mostly I just want to sleep."

Flora studied Ada for a moment before her face brightened with understanding. "How 'bout that? A little brother or sister for Mildred!"

Mildred looked up from her plate. "Buvver or sisser?" she asked, puzzled.

"Probably a sister," Mama replied flatly. "Always girls."

* * * * *

After years of discouraging all potential suitors due to her reluctance to expose them to the unpredictable behavior of Mama, Hermine hardly knew how to be receptive to Ralph's overtures of interest. She tentatively accepted his invitations to bowl, ice skate, attend movies, and go for long walks. Hermine found that she enjoyed Ralph's attention. No one had ever made a fuss over her or singled her out as something special, and the experience was exhilarating as well as confusing.

Hermine changed jobs and began working for the Travelers Insurance Company in the Electric Building on Prospect Avenue in downtown Cleveland. During office hours, she made a conscious effort to keep her thoughts trained strictly on her job. After hours, however, she drifted in a dreamy fog, which caused her to miss a step in the Electric Building's stairwell and ride downward on her elbows and tailbone. She quickly regained her footing, straightened her hat and skirt, and limped toward the streetcar, nursing her bruised dignity and battered elbows. If this was love's effect, she wondered how anyone survived.

* * * * *

Ella entertained the Sunday School teachers with a "backwards" party in Mrs. Arndt's parlor one winter evening. The guests wore their clothing backward and styled their hair as opposite as possible, topped by a backwards-facing hat. They were required to enter Mrs. Arndt's house backwards through the back door, greet each other with "Goodbye" instead of "Hello," and were served a meal that began with toothpicks and mints and ended with appetizers and napkins.

Mrs. Arndt stationed herself behind the narrow opening of the door to her darkened downstairs bedroom. She kept a nervous eye on her vast collection of china knickknacks and watched for any crumbs to land on the ancient carpet. In the morning, she moaned that Ella and her friends had probably run up the electricity bill by having the parlor lights on past 7 p.m. Ella quietly gritted her teeth and assumed that Mrs. Arndt had always been vigilant about turning off the lights at the chime of seven bells from the mantle clock each evening, even if "poor Charlie" had been in the middle of reading the daily newspaper.

The women of St. John's church held frequent fundraisers, earning as much as nine hundred dollars one year. In February, they sold tickets for a costume party in conjunction with Washington's Birthday. Ella and Viola Kloss pondered costume ideas and finally hit upon the ideal getup based on their disparate builds. Tall, slim Ella and short, plump Viola would make the perfect George and Martha Washington! On the evening of the party, Ella donned a pair of bloomers, borrowed Rev. Schenk's Prince Albert double-breasted frock coat, white shirt, and cuff links, and folded a lace hankie to imitate a neckerchief. She dusted her hair with talcum until it resembled a powdered wig and topped it with Viola's three-cornered hat.

At the church, Viola swept through the doorway, making a grand entrance in her petticoated skirt, while Ella waited outside. Viola clapped her hands and announced, "Ladies and gentlemen, please rise and pay respect to my esteemed husband, the honorable General George Washington!" Ella strode through the door and assumed a Presidential posture before bowing left and right. The other guests roared with approval. Ella wanted to burst with smiles and laughter but struggled to maintain the clamped-lip appearance of the General.

In early March, Ella attended the Schauffler Missionary Training School alumnae meeting in Cleveland. On the train ride back to Dover, she reflected on the pleasant weekend spent connecting with former school friends and instructors. It dawned on Ella that her outlook was much happier when she was away from Mrs. Arndt's house. The landlady's peculiarities and constant hovering were no longer affectations but growing annoyances. Ella recognized the folly of paying for lodging that she purposely avoided, so she quietly began searching for a new boarding situation within walking distance of the church. While calling on a parishioner one afternoon, she noticed a "Room for Rent" sign in the window of a house on West Fifth Street, across from Dover High School. Within weeks, she was moving her scant belongings to the Hoffmann residence.

When Mrs. Hoffmann noticed that most of Ella's personal effects were boxes of books, she inquired, "What do you want all those books for?"

Ella responded, "Why, Mrs. Hoffmann, I read them. I can't imagine being without a good book!" Ella was as puzzled by the landlady's question as Mrs. Hoffmann was by her boarder's personal library.

Ella reading a good book

When Ella accepted the boarding arrangement, she learned that Mr. Hoffmann was terminally ill. Her sisters admonished her for choosing to live with another soon-to-be widow. They reminded Ella of her recent escape from the long-faced Mrs. Arndt who shed tears and bewailed every significant anniversary related to "poor Charlie's" demise. Ella humbly accepted her sisters' scolding and fervently hoped that Mrs. Hoffmann would exhibit greater restraint in her grief than Mrs. Arndt.

In the spring evenings, Ella longed for a walking companion—someone to share observations with about budding trees and plants, the return of the robins, and the invigorating scent of a reawakening earth. She noted that most other young women her age were busy pushing perambulators for the fourth or fifth time. The congregation members assumed that Ella's world revolved only around church matters, and they never thought to enrich her existence by introducing her to eligible bachelors, even though Ella would have been embarrassed by their interest in her romantic life.

For Martha, on the other hand, there was no shortage of suitors.

While she enjoyed her active social life, she was determined to achieve her goal of becoming a nurse. Therefore, any young man who became too serious was soon set adrift.

*****

Like every teenaged girl, Minola did her best to follow the latest fashions. One spring afternoon, she walked home from Monroeville with her thick hair newly bobbed. It felt liberating to be free of the pins, nets, and ribbons required by long hair, and she enjoyed tossing her head left and right, feeling the unaccustomed swish of short hair on her face. Minola's confidence waned, however, as she crossed the farmyard and glanced toward the window in Papa's workshop above the cornbarn. She worried about his reaction to her thoroughly modern hairstyle.

Minola with bobbed hair

Minola bounded up the back porch steps and burst through the kitchen door, eager to seek Flora's input on her new style. Mama looked up from her seat at the kitchen table, where she was sprinkling laundry for Flora to press with the new electric iron. "What have you done to your hair?" gasped Mama, who continued to take great pride in her own long tresses. "Why would you do such *Dummheit* (foolishness)?" She glared at her daughter.

Minola eyed the wooden rolling pin lying within Mama's reach on the kitchen table. She recalled Mama's penchant for using anything close at hand to lash out at the object of her displeasure. "I … I like the look," Minola offered cautiously. When her response didn't cause Mama to reach for the rolling pin, she added, "Besides, bobbed hair is all the rage."

"Bah!" retorted Mama. "You'll never find a husband when you look like a … a man!" She angrily flicked water droplets onto a freshly laundered apron, rolled it tightly, and dropped it into the wicker basket at her feet. Minola gave the table and Mama wide berth as she went in search of Flora.

That night at supper, Minola waited nervously for Papa's comments. He lowered himself into his seat with a sigh and ate in silence, giving no indication that he had noticed his daughter's new hairstyle. Minola was mildly relieved, since Papa usually only expressed negative feelings—disapproval, anger, or impatience—and she had already received enough discouraging feedback from Mama.

Several weeks later, Minola overheard Papa in conversation with a group of men after church. One man announced that he'd never let his daughters trot around with shorn hair—a sure sign of waywardness. Papa quietly commented that he approved of the new style. Minola was thunderstruck.

* * * * *

Mildred began greeting all visitors—neighbors and peddlers—with the announcement, "I'm gonna have a little buvver or sisser!" Ada's cheeks flushed when such private news was shared indiscriminately. She gave her guests a chagrined smile and pulled Mildred close to her, where she could cup a hand over her daughter's mouth to check the spill of privileged information.

Ada spent many weeks pondering her need for a sister's assistance when the baby came in August. Flora was indispensable at home, and Papa would need Minola's help to pick the bramble crops. It was too soon for Hermine to ask for time off from her new job, plus she would be reluctant to spend a month away from her budding romance in Cleveland. Martha would seek full-time summer employment to help with college expenses. Ella was the only one with flexibility in her situation, so Ada wrote her sister a letter asking her to consider spending the month of August at the Gfell residence.

Ella approached the St. John's church council to request a leave of absence. After much deliberation and studying of the church activities calendar, they granted her request with the understanding that it would be a month without pay. Ella knew the leave would make finances tight for herself and would also interfere with her support of Martha's educational expenses, but she was determined to be there for Ada.

* * * * *

Mama's father, John Frederick Gasteier, passed away on April 23. At age eighty-two, he had outlived his wife by almost ten years. At his funeral, John Frederick's eight surviving offspring repeated the story of their parent's stormy six-week voyage to America aboard the *Queen Victoria.* In mid-ocean, the Gasteiers' first child, Margaretha Katherine Victoria, had been born. When the family's allotment of water was used up, the honest and principled John Frederick had been forced to surreptitiously help himself to the ship's water supply to meet the needs of his wife and newborn daughter. Upon reaching port in New York, the young family faced another long, wearisome journey—this time by train—to Erie County in Ohio. Having come to America for economic betterment, John Frederick was not content to remain a farm laborer for long. Through industry and enterprise, he eventually bought the farm on which he spent the remainder of his days.

When the estate was settled, each of John Frederick's surviving offspring received an inheritance of one thousand dollars. Uncle Will arrived one evening with the paperwork that Mama must sign before the money could be released from the bank in Milan. He did not relish this interaction with his sister due to her unpredictable nature. While Mama's grasp of recent events was shaky, Will knew that she could recall the past with clarity, so he coaxed her cooperation by tapping into their childhood memories, ending each recollection with, "Remember that, Sophie?" When Mama's signature was at last procured, Will folded the document and tucked it into his coat pocket. He hastily bid good evening and headed out the back door, exhausted from his efforts.

* * * * *

In May, Martha learned that the Cleveland Symphony Orchestra would give a concert at Hiram for the college's May Festival. Tickets for the event were $3.50, which was beyond her affordability. The thought of something so exquisite being close at hand yet unobtainable filled her with frustration and yearning. Martha sat at the desk in her room and pored over her finances, counting out every cent of her available cash and tallying her upcoming expenses. As much as she loved orchestral music and longed to attend a live symphony, she did not have the money for such an indulgence. Dejected, she scraped the coins back into her leather wallet and returned it to the top drawer of her dresser.

A few days later Doris, whose room was across the hall from Martha's, poked her head in the door and asked, "Hey, kid, what you doing Saturday night?"

"Same old thing—growing older," replied Martha glumly.

Doris crossed the room and flopped on Martha's bed. "Wendell Pollard tells me President Bates asked him to line up some kids to sell programs at the symphony Saturday night. I'm gonna do it. You interested?"

Martha was stunned by her sudden good fortune. She stared wide-eyed at Doris before squealing, "Yes! Yes! Oh, my gosh—yes!"

On the night of the concert, Martha donned the tricotine formal sewn by Flora and pinned a sprig of apple blossoms into her raven hair. After the crowd was seated and her program-selling duties were complete, Martha slipped into the darkened auditorium and stood along the back wall. At the first vibrant note of the violins, tears welled in her eyes. She was transfixed by the thundering roll of the tympanis, the commanding movements of the conductor, and the ethereal beauty of the music.

After the concert, Doris grabbed Martha's arm and whispered, "President Bates gave Wendell his machine to drive some of the orchestra members down to the train. Wendell says to meet him outside of town, and when he gets back from the train, he'll take us riding in the Prexy's car before he has to return it. You game?" Doris gave her a mischievous grin.

Martha's conscience wrestled with the appropriateness of the offer, but the thought of a night ride in the college president's car overcame her moral compass. "You bet!" she affirmed.

Wendell's roommate Paul joined the two young women, and they headed south across the campus, keeping their voices low so they would not attract attention. Leaving the illumination of Hiram behind, Doris and Martha clutched Paul's arms to steady themselves in the darkness on the uneven road surface. When they reached the appointed meeting place, the three stepped into the deep shadows of a roadside tree to wait for the oncoming headlamps of President Bates' machine. Martha shivered with anticipation.

"I see 'em," announced Paul as two pinpricks of light bobbed in the distance.

"I'm scared skinny!" confessed Martha. The thought of the illicit ride was both electrifying and panic-inducing.

"Don't worry about a thing. Wendell's a student senator. He's got pull," replied Doris with confidence.

The machine rolled to a stop, and the three clambered aboard, with Paul in the front seat beside Wendell and the two coeds in the back. The college students motored along the quiet country roads around Hiram, enjoying the novelty of a night ride and the luxury of the president's sedan. At one point, the clouds parted, revealing a luminous full moon. Wendell stopped the machine at the top of a hill, turned off the headlamps, and released the brake, allowing the car to glide down the hill with only the illumination of moonlight. Martha gasped and clung with both hands to the seat in front of her, certain they would crash headlong into an unseen obstacle.

Doris raised her arms above her head. "It's like a carnival ride! Look—no hands!" she exclaimed.

"Thanks, Prexy Bates!" Paul shouted out the window during their descent. The four students laughed until their sides hurt.

Wendell turned the car toward their meeting spot outside of town. The three exited the machine and quietly walked toward campus as Wendell drove off to return the vehicle to the president's residence. Martha reached up to re-pin the sprig of apple blossoms in her hair but found only an empty pin. With a gasp, she grabbed Doris' arm and exclaimed, "The apple blossoms! I've lost the sprig of apple blossoms from my hair!"

"So? There's more on the tree right outside the dorm," assured Doris.

"But what if they're in the back seat of President Bates' machine?" Martha asked, her voice rising in panic. "He'll know that Wendell had somebody in the machine with him!"

Paul chuckled. "Maybe the Prexy'll think Wendell had a Sheba in the struggle-buggy," he said, using the latest slang for an interlude with an appealing woman in the back seat of a vehicle. "I'd like to hear him explain his way outta *that* one!"

Doris waved off Martha's concern. "Wendell *did* have someone in the machine with him—the orchestra members he drove to the train! If the Prexy asks about the apple blossoms, Wendell can tell him one of the orchestra members left behind his Hiram souvenir." She linked her arm in Martha's and steered her toward the dormitory.

When Martha climbed into bed that night, her mind replayed the moonlit ride in the president's machine, accompanied by a backdrop of orchestral music. Despite the question of the misplaced apple blossom sprig, she couldn't stop smiling.

When the semester ended in June, Martha boarded the train toward Monroeville. She had applied and been accepted to Lakeside Hospital in Cleveland, where she intended to fulfill her and Margaret's goal of becoming a nurse. With tears in eyes, she waved goodbye to the many friends and good times she had had at Hiram College. It had been the best two years of her young life.

After a short stay at home, Martha and her high school friend, Ruth Strohmeier, took the interurban to Ruggles Beach, where they had arranged to work in the farmhouse. Martha was filled with apprehension at the prospect of working at the popular resort, knowing that memories of Margaret would surely be reawakened. However, her economic straits plus Ruth's cajoling had convinced her to seek seasonal employment where the salary was meaningful. Ruth was already a veteran of the resort, and Martha was relieved to let her take the lead upon arriving at the farmhouse. She hoped that the less interaction she had with Miss Ruggles and the black cook, Mrs. Davis, the less opportunity they would have to link her name to Margaret.

One morning a few weeks later, Martha stood opposite Mrs. Davis at the enamel-topped work table in the kitchen. Martha crimped the edges of pie shells between her fingers while Mrs. Davis kneaded bread dough. From beneath her lashes, Martha could feel Mrs. Davis studying her.

"You 'mind me of someone," the cook mused. "You ain't worked here before, has you? Cause I pride myself on ne'er forgettin' a face."

It was the moment Martha had been dreading. She continued to crimp in silence, then offered quietly, "You're probably thinking of my sister who worked here a few years ago. Margaret Seibel."

Mrs. Davis hummed under her breath as she thought. "Margaret Seibel. I do 'member her. Fun-lovin' gal. Roomed upstairs for a while, then moved over to the 'Last Resort' with the others." Mrs. Davis paused and put one floury hand on her hip as she cocked her head. "Yes … yes, she stayed on after the season and helped me can peaches! Sweet girl, that Margaret. Sweet girl. What's she doin' now?"

Martha blinked hard and her throat tightened. "Margaret … died in the influenza epidemic. Just a couple weeks after she came home from here." Martha wiped at her eyes with her shirt sleeve.

The two women fell silent, and Mrs. Davis resumed kneading the dough. "Some of the other helpers I had here that summer never come back, and I always wondered if it was the flu that took 'em." She reached across the table to pat Martha's arm, leaving a dusting of flour. "Or did they just get tired of a sassy ol' cook bossin' 'em around?"

Martha looked up at Mrs. Davis, whose kind eyes shown with sympathy. She smiled in gratitude for the cook's understanding as well as her attempt to lighten the mood.

* * * * *

In early August, Ella arrived for her month-long stay at the Gfell residence. She took command while Ada propped up her swollen feet on a kitchen chair and fanned herself with the dish towel. Even though the weather had been unseasonably cool, Ada overheated easily in her late pregnancy. After the household chores were completed each day, Ella took little Mildred for long walks or nestled the child into her lap and read to her, allowing Ada the opportunity to rest or make preparations for the coming baby.

Ada padded a wicker clothes basket with blankets and placed it in the corner of her and Albert's bedroom, along with a stack of snowy diapers. She retrieved the layette from the trunk and carefully folded the tiny items on top of her dresser.

Ella & Mildred in the front yard at Gfells'

The baby was born in the late afternoon on Friday, August 11. Nurse Holtz, who was assisting Dr. Gilman, poked her head out the bedroom door and announced over the baby's squalls, "Ella, it's a girl, and she's healthy in every way!"

While the doctor tended to Ada and the newborn, Ella took little Mildred by the hand and crossed the road to summon Albert from the barn, where he had gone to work off his nervous energy but still be close at hand. She found him on the three-legged milking stool, his head settled into the hollow of a cow's flank so he could monitor the milk bucket as he rhythmically stripped the udder.

"There's a new little someone in the house waiting to meet you," announced Ella.

"It's a sisser!" crowed Mildred.

"By de God!" Albert declared, a slow smile curling up from one corner of his mouth. "And Ada?"

Ella nodded assurance of Ada's health. Albert scooped up Mildred in one arm and grabbed the handle of the bucket, causing the milk to slosh over the rim as he hurried toward the house. Ella scampered to keep pace with his long strides.

Dr. Gilman was just leaving as Albert reached the porch. "Congratulations, Albert. Another fine, healthy daughter. Glad the circumstances were different from when *this* little lady was born," he said, giving Mildred a pat on the head.

Ella winced at the reference to Margaret's illness and subsequent death.

Albert set the pail of milk on the porch, shook the doctor's hand, and rushed inside.

"Looks like Ada's got a good start on that Seibel tradition of having girls," Dr. Gilman remarked to Ella as he eased his way down the steps toward his vehicle.

After a lifetime of hearing Mama express a preference for boys, Ella was not sure if the doctor's observation was a compliment or a curse.

Ada was propped on the bed, the baby nestled in the crook of her arm. Albert tenderly kissed Ada and gently lifted the baby. He gazed with awe at her button nose and thatch of thick, dark hair. Coming from a family of all boys, Albert could not help but be enamored by little girls.

"What're we gonna name this little stranger?" Albert asked as he stroked the baby's cheek. He tucked back the corner of the blanket and lowered the baby so Mildred could have a peek at her new little sister.

"Roberta," Ada responded with certainty. She had been reading the book *The Twenty-Fourth of June* and had admired the name of its heroine. "And 'Ella' for her middle name." It seemed fitting that Ella and Roberta—both second daughters—should share a name.

As was customary, Ada would have a two-week lying-in period after the birth of the baby, during which she was to remain off her feet and obtain proper rest. While Ella tended to the household chores and little Mildred, Nurse Holtz remained to care for Ada and the baby, particularly during the night hours. However, the nurse was young and had a boyfriend who arrived in his machine to pick her up for a date almost every evening. She returned to the Gfell home late at night and dropped into a deep slumber, failing to rouse at the wail of the baby. Ada eased herself out of bed, scooped up the crying infant, and lovingly tended to the needs of her newest daughter. At the end of the two weeks, Nurse Holtz received a payment of fifty dollars despite her negligence.

Ada & baby Roberta

The weather turned hot and sultry after the baby's arrival. Little rain had fallen in nearly a month, and the well and cistern quickly ran low, with the remaining water turning sulfur-tinged. Ella practiced water economy as best she could, but the laundry loads were large and frequent due to the addition of many diapers.

The hot weather brought Albert's oat crop to maturity, and almost as soon as Ada was on her feet, she and Ella began preparing for the threshing crew. Flora, Papa, and Bill arrived on the morning of the threshing, leaving Minola at home with Mama. The three sisters bustled about the kitchen, readying a hearty meal for the threshermen and tending to Mildred and Roberta.

At day's end, Ada was exhausted. She hung her apron on the nail by the kitchen door and gave a silent prayer of thanks for her sisters.

*****

Hermine came home for the long Labor Day weekend to see her newest niece, and Martha returned from Ruggles Beach, glowing with pride at her purse full of hard-earned cash. Flora bent over her sewing machine, making repairs to her sisters' wardrobes and hastily creating a few requested new garments. On Monday, Ella, Hermine, and Martha boarded the crowded interurban, standing in the aisle all the way to Cleveland. After Martha was settled into her new surroundings at Lakeside Hospital's nursing school, Ella returned to Dover, where she checked with Rev. Schenk for happenings within the congregation during her month-long absence. He reported that two people had died, two couples had married, and malaria was making a sweep through the community.

In October, Ella insisted that Flora come for a long weekend visit to see the splendor of fall leaves in the rolling countryside around Dover. In some small way, she hoped the getaway would atone for the many frustrations Flora experienced on a daily basis with Mama. Ella sent train fare, and the two sisters agreed that the Friday of teachers' meetings would be optimal, since Minola could stay home with Mama.

On the appointed Friday, Bill drove Flora to Monroeville, where she boarded the Wheeling and Lake Erie railcar. Bill waved from the station platform as the train slowly pulled away. He leaped behind the wheel of the old Ford truck and motored to Ada and Albert's, where he would spend the weekend helping the young couple harvest the last of their potato crop.

Flora's lack of experience in traveling alone to unfamiliar places made her nervous. For security, she clutched Ella's letter that detailed how to navigate the rail system from Monroeville to Dover. Soon, she relaxed and settled back in her seat, enjoying the novelty of being away from home and embarking on an adventure. The passing scenery grew interesting in its unfamiliarity, and she marveled at the varied palette of fall colors as the train headed southeast. When the train stopped in the towns of Orrville and Brewster, Flora consulted Ella's letter for reassurance that she should stay onboard. Upon reaching Harmon Junction, she anxiously looked out the railcar window, searching for Ella's familiar face among the crowd. Ella had instructed that if she was unable to meet the train, Flora should ask the conductor for guidance to the streetcar, which would take her on the last leg of her journey to Dover. Flora stepped down from the train and scanned the crowd waiting on the platform. Ella was nowhere in sight. She swallowed hard, feeling alone and unsure in the unfamiliar setting. As she turned to seek out the conductor, Flora heard her name. Waving her hand over the top of the crowd was Ella. Flora beamed with relief. The two sisters locked arms and chatted excitedly as they hurried to board the streetcar to Dover.

* * * * *

Minola was enjoying the opportunity to prove that she was capable of running the household in Flora's absence. At age seventeen and the youngest of the seven sisters, she felt her older siblings still viewed her as a child with limited household skills. She intended to show them that she was more mature and versatile than they thought. Without Bill there to mock her domestic efforts, Minola busied herself in the kitchen, making a kettle of potato soup for supper and an apple pie from some of the windfalls. While the food was cooking, she carried in lengths of firewood to fill the box beside the cookstove, tackled a few of the items in the mending pile, and kept an eye on Mama.

Besides managing the household tasks, Minola also gathered the eggs, carried feed and water to the chicken coop, penned the chickens before nightfall, and pumped water for the cows. One of Flora's chores that she could not fulfill was helping Papa with the milking. Minola did not want to provoke Papa's impatience by stumbling through chores that Flora performed with such efficiency.

Before retiring for the evening, Minola pumped the teakettle full of water and set it on the cookstove, ready to heat for their many warm-water needs in the morning. As she turned the kitchen wall knob to extinguish the single lightbulb, Minola made a mental note to separate the cream when she tackled the usual Saturday chores, which included baking bread and scrubbing the kitchen floor. She felt a sense of pride in her accomplishments thus far.

Minola awoke on Saturday morning to the sound of angry voices downstairs. She scrambled out of bed, hurried to the top of the steps, and cocked her head to listen. Mama was speaking in rapid-fire German, which was never a good omen. Minola could not determine the crux of the argument; however, she knew it did not take much to provoke Mama's ire. As disagreeable as Mama could be, it was unusual for her and Papa to argue. Usually when Mama got ratcheted up like this, Papa left the house, gesturing to himself as he carried his frustration with him toward the barn. Minola heard Mama's voice escalate, punctuated by Papa's shout of "Sophie, no!"

In the kitchen, Mama lifted the steaming teakettle from the cookstove and flung it in a side-armed arc toward Papa. The kitchen door hinges shrieked and the screen slammed against the back of the house as Papa dodged toward safety. However, Mama failed to release the handle of the teakettle in time to hit her intended target. Instead, the sideways trajectory of the teapot caused the lid to pop off, spewing the kettle's boiling contents onto Mama's outstretched left arm.

Minola heard the bang of the kitchen door, followed by Mama's blood-curdling scream. She raced barefoot down the steps and sped through the living room. For one moment, the scene in the kitchen was frozen before her—Papa in the doorway, Mama doubled over, and steam rising from the wet floorboards between them.

Papa sprang into action, ripping the sleeve from Mama's shirtwaist and exposing the scalded flesh beneath. Spotting Minola in the living room doorway, he ordered, "Call Dr. Gilman and get him out here right now!"

Minola dashed for the phone on the wall by the stairwell. She rang central and breathlessly told the operator she needed to be connected to Dr. Gilman's office. Minola knew the operator would listen in on the call, and she cringed at how rapidly the news of Mama's injury would circulate throughout the community. While she waited for the connection, Minola tried to calm her racing heart.

Papa led Mama to the summer kitchen, where he placed her scalded arm under the spout of the wellstalk. He pumped rapidly, keeping a continual flood of cold water pouring over the afflicted area. Mama moaned and allowed him to minister to her injury, her prior combativeness now lost in pain.

When Dr. Gilman arrived, he examined Mama's arm and determined that she had suffered a third-degree burn, which would require the removal of a large amount of damaged tissue. Carrying his black bag, he led Mama to the downstairs bedroom and called over his shoulder to Minola, "Bring a pan. I'll need you to assist me."

Minola grabbed a pan from the pantry. As she hurried toward the bedroom, she realized, much to her chagrin, that she was still barefoot and wearing her nightgown. In all the commotion, she had thought only to call the doctor, as directed, and to pick up the teakettle from where it lay on the kitchen floor. "*Ordentlich und sauber* (neat and tidy)," she thought to herself ruefully as she reflected on her Germanic need to make order in the midst of a crisis.

Papa's legs felt as though they could no longer support him, and he slumped into a chair at the kitchen table. Smoothing the checked tablecloth before him, he watched as his hands trembled.

With Mama under the influence of a sponge of chloroform, Dr. Gilman performed a debridement of the wound, passing the excised flesh to Minola to deposit in the pan. She shuddered inwardly but tried to keep her composure in front of the doctor.

When the procedure was completed, Dr. Gilman wrapped Mama's arm in white gauze and told Minola to keep her quiet and well hydrated for a few days. He handed her a packet of pills and carried his black bag and the pan of scalded tissue to the kitchen, where Papa sat with his head in his hands.

The doctor studied Papa, who was still visibly shaken. "I don't need to know, Bill," Dr. Gilman stated, "but I assume this was more than a kitchen accident."

Papa nodded. He felt inadequate to explain a wife who would hurl a kettle of boiling water at her husband. Finally he said softly, "It was supposed to be me that got burned. She was aimin' for *me*."

The doctor folded his glasses and tucked them into his inside coat pocket. Shaking his head, he let himself out the back door.

Papa carried the pan outdoors, where he buried the skin in the corner of the garden.

Minola washed Mama's shirtwaist and the detached sleeve and hung them on the line to dry. Afterward, she would repair the garment—it was what Flora would do.

* * * * *

On Sunday evening, Flora waited on the train station platform in Monroeville. She swung her valise back and forth and hummed the melody from "Ain't We Got Fun," which she and Ella had played over and over again on Mrs. Hoffman's Victrola. She thought of the motor excursions Ella had arranged with friends into the hilly countryside around Dover, where the brilliant fall colors had been breathtaking. Also, there was the pianist at The Rialto, who had entertained them with the finger-twisting song "Kitten on the Keys" before the motion picture began. This morning, the members of Ella's congregation had flocked around the two of them, extending numerous invitations to Sunday dinner. Flora smiled as she thought of every aspect of the enjoyable weekend.

The headlamps of the old Ford bobbed along the gravel drive toward the station platform. Bill brought the machine to a stop, and Flora bounded down the steps. Settling herself on the truck seat, she turned toward Bill, eager to tell him all about her weekend. Before she could begin, Bill warned, "There's been a problem with Mama."

Flora stiffened. The carefree attitude she had carried home from Dover quickly disappeared.

Mama healed rapidly, and the only physical aftermath of the incident was a web of scar tissue that prevented her from straightening her left arm.

The others, however, were now frighteningly aware that Mama's penchant for lashing out had escalated to dangerous new heights.

* * * * *

Hermine sought permission to bring Ralph home to meet the family over the Christmas holidays. Flora cast an objective eye around the homestead and fretted about what their guest would think of the draft-stopping rags stuffed along the window sashes, the cranky hen that insisted on nesting in the corner of the outhouse, the skeletal barns so badly in need of paint, and, of course, unpredictable Mama.

"He's a veteran of the Great War, so he's seen worse," fifteen-year-old Bill pointed out with a shrug.

Flora frowned at Bill's comparison but granted Hermine's request.

Everyone agreed that it was wonderful to see Hermine so happy. In addition, she revealed that Ralph had hinted of a special Christmas gift. They all smiled knowingly.

On Christmas Day, the siblings were puzzled by the large gift box that Ralph presented to Hermine, but they discreetly slipped from the parlor, allowing the young couple to be alone for this special moment.

Hermine's heart fluttered as she carefully removed the bow and tilted back the lid. She parted the crinkly tissue paper, and there before her lay a shiny new pair of ice skates.

"So you don't have to rent a pair anymore," the practical Ralph said earnestly.

Ralph Worden with Hermine, Flora, Mildred, & Minola

Chapter 26
Dover, Ohio
1923

AFTER HER BRIEF holiday stay in Monroeville, Ella returned to Dover feeling refreshed and invigorated. She hummed under her breath as her long legs carried her from the streetcar toward the Hoffmann residence where she boarded. When she entered the house, Ella discovered the sad chaos brought about by death. Mr. Hoffmann had succumbed to his illness the night before, and the house was filled with Hoffmann offspring and their families who had returned home. Neighbors slipped in and out, bringing casseroles and condolences. Ella quickly realized the necessity of overnight accommodations for the out-of-town guests. She consoled the grieving widow and offered to seek temporary lodging elsewhere so that her room could be used by the family. Mrs. Hoffmann gripped Ella's hands and mutely nodded.

Ella retrieved her valise from where she had dropped it in the entryway and eased herself out the front door. She pulled her coat tighter, not from the frosty January air but from a shiver that passed through her as she remembered her own experience with grief at the time of Margaret's death.

Ella was welcomed into the homes of various congregation members, where the women fussed and cooked as though they were entertaining the esteemed Rev. Schenk instead of his assistant. After a week of such lavish hospitality, Ella returned to her humble existence as Mrs. Hoffmann's boarder.

* * * * *

Hermine's fingers danced across the keys of her typewriter at Traveler's Insurance. Each time she paused to hit the carriage return, she stole an admiring glance at the diamond that sparkled on her left hand. She smiled with the memory of how Ralph had proposed in mid-February.

The young couple had been sitting side-by-side on a bench at the skating pond, lacing up their skates. Ralph pointed at Hermine's blades and asked, "What's that on your skates?"

Hermine held her legs out straight in front of her and turned her feet from side to side, examining her skates. "Where?" she asked, "I don't see anything."

Ralph knelt down and took the boot of one of Hermine's skates into his gloved hands. "Right here," he announced as he tugged at the laces.

"There's something stuck right here."

Hermine leaned in for a closer inspection. "Why, how'd a ring… ?" she asked, puzzled. She caught her breath with the sudden realization that the ring tucked behind her laces was a diamond, placed there by Ralph. Her blue eyes widened and she quickly looked up at Ralph, who was beaming from ear to ear. Hermine threw her arms around his neck.

For the next hour, the couple skated hand-in-hand around the pond, oblivious to the presence of others on the ice. They talked of wedding plans and agreed on a simple ceremony in the spring.

* * * * *

Letters continued to stream between the sisters, expressing happiness over the upcoming nuptials, discussing family news and local gossip, and lamenting the financial strains being experienced by all. Martha wrote about her nursing classes and the interesting case studies to which she was exposed as part of her training at Lakeside Hospital. Despite the demands of her coursework, Martha's social life did not suffer, and she detailed fun-filled experiences with her new circle of friends at nursing school. Some of her pastimes now included the newest crazes of mah-jongg games and crossword puzzles.

Martha (at right) & her nursing school friends

* * * * *

Although Ella understood Minola's lack of interest in religious affairs following the acrimonious church split, her letters subtly tried to encourage her sister to officially join the church. She pointed out that Easter would fall on April 1 that year, Minola's eighteenth birthday—the first time it would fall on that date since 1888 and the last until 1934. Ella's gentle nudging was effective. Minola approached Rev. Abele about membership classes, which culminated in joining the church on her Easter Sunday birthday.

*****

Minola's senior year of high school bumped along with academic excellence counterbalanced by social unhappiness. The class, which had started its freshman year with about thirty members, had been reduced to seventeen students—five girls and twelve boys. Minola did not have an easy rapport with many of her peers, who snickered at suggestive innuendoes or proudly announced that they never opened a book. Her small circle of female classmates, who were stratified according to long-held friendships and the superiority of in-town residency, had become increasingly interested in romantic relationships, leaving Minola with little companionship. In addition, the shame and unpredictability of Mama's affliction had long discouraged Minola from currying any relationships that would bring friends into the house. Instead, she devoted herself to her studies, which garnered recognition from the school administration. One day in assembly, the superintendent announced that there were two students in the senior class who should pursue a college education: Mary Zipfel and Minola Seibel.

The superintendent's announcement spurred Minola's thoughts to the great void that faced her after graduation in May. Several of her older sisters had paved the way toward higher education, but their choices of nursing, secretarial, and religious work did not appeal to Minola. While she was unsure of her life's ambition, she foresaw a teaching certificate as a means to a steady income until she was more certain of her future. Minola began to formulate a plan to attend the County Normal School. She knew she would have to find summer employment to finance her educational goals, since Papa had vowed he would pay for high school and nothing more.

*****

In late April, Papa pushed a wheelbarrow full of strawberry runners to the field that would hold the newest crop of berries in the annual rotation. He filled his shoulder pouch with the young strawberry plants and handed a bundle to Flora and Minola. The three set out down the long rows, following the guideline of twine that stretched from one end of the field to the other. Papa deftly sliced his spade into the soil, took two steps, and dug another hole. He made rapid progress across the field while the girls carefully set the plants into the holes, covered the roots with dirt, pressed the soil with the toe of their shoes, and moved on to the next hole.

As they worked, the sisters discussed plans for Minola's graduation dress, with Minola describing her vision of a lacey creation featuring a wide sash held by a cabbage rose over one hip. As usual, Flora expressed doubt that she had the skills to craft the envisioned garment, but Minola's confidence in Flora's creative abilities never wavered.

Behind the barn, in the field at the end of the lane, Bill followed behind the plow pulled by the mismatched team of Jetty, the sleek black buggy horse, and Tup, a young workhorse that Papa had bought at auction for a reduced price due to the horse's misshapen hips. Tup had an annoying habit of lying back in the traces, allowing the smaller Jetty to bear the load of pulling the plow. From time to time, the horses stopped dead in their tracks, unable or unwilling to work as a team. Bill slapped the reins on their backs, shouted commands, used every swear word he knew, and even resorted to pleading. Despite his exhortations, the horses stood still, flicking their tails and rattling their harnesses as if in response to Bill's commands. Finally, Bill left the field and marched to a nearby thicket to obtain a stick for prodding the beasts. As he returned, he noticed Jetty nudge Tup, and the two horses watched as Bill approached. Before he could put the stick to use, the horses leaned into the traces and resumed plowing. Their progress was short-lived, however, as Tup again shirked his share of the duties, and Jetty halted in protest.

The morning wore on in spurts of plowing, prodding, and swearing. Bill, who had no interest in farming, became increasingly disgruntled by his situation. Why did everything on their farm have to be so make-do and make-shift? Why couldn't Papa see the benefits of mechanization and buy a tractor like Albert's? Finally, in a fit of exasperation, Bill left the stalled team where they stood. He crossed the lane, marched to the middle of the adjoining field, and flopped onto the mammoth rock that had been deposited there by a long-ago glacier. It felt good to stretch his back against the warm rock face. Bill draped an arm across his eyes to block out the bright spring sun, and he propped one ankle on his bent knee. His mind wandered to thoughts of fanciful mechanisms he would invent to ease one's labor and do away with the back-breaking, mind-numbing routine of farm work.

Papa pushed the wheelbarrow to the barn to restock it with strawberry runners. After covering the tender young plants with wet burlap, he exited the barn to check on Bill's progress. As Papa neared the field at the back of the lane, he spotted Jetty and Tup standing idle at the far edge of the field, plucking shoots of grass that grew between the field and the adjoining thicket. Papa's steps quickened. Shielding his eyes against the sun, he scanned the field for signs of his son, fearing that fifteen-year-old Bill had been injured.

Papa hurried to the horses and inspected the equipment for evidence of a farming accident. He was relieved to find no traces of blood on the plow or torn clothing entangled in the harness. Papa felt the horses' sides and noted they were not lathered or blowing hard, which would have indicated the need for a well-deserved rest at the field's edge. Puzzled by their unworked condition, Papa tethered the horses' reins to a nearby sapling and continued his search. He crashed through the thicket and hurried toward the shallow creek, which had always drawn Bill like a magnet in his childhood. Papa stood on the creek bank and peered in both directions, but there was no sign of his son. Cupping his hands around his mouth, Papa called, "Bill! You here?" He listened for a response, but only the trills of spring peepers and redwing blackbirds met his ear.

Papa returned to the field, his heart pounding and his mind racing with dreadful scenarios. He decided to head back to the strawberry field and enlist the aid of Flora and Minola in continuing the search for Bill. He hurried across the field, examining the furrows for any signs he may have missed earlier. When he reached the lane, Papa stopped to catch his breath. His chest heaving, he shielded his eyes against the bright sun and scanned the adjacent fields. Papa's gaze stopped at the mammoth rock when his eye caught the motion of Bill's foot wagging atop his bent knee.

Papa steamed toward the rock, struggling to catch his breath from the recent panic, the exertion, and now his anger. "Wh-wh-what're you doing?" he bellowed as he neared the boulder.

Bill's arms and legs shot outward in surprise. He struggled to sit up on the slick rock face, but Papa's hands were on the front of his overalls, pulling him off his perch. Bill scrambled to his feet as Papa's enraged face loomed over him.

"G-g-get back to work!" growled Papa. "Laziness won't get that field plowed!" He gave Bill a shove toward the half-plowed field.

Bill sputtered a few phrases about his frustration with the mismatched team of horses, but fearing Papa's rage, he quickly gave up the explanation. Instead he scuttled toward the lane and the field beyond, anxious to put distance between himself and Papa.

"How you gonna take over this farm some day if you ain't willing to work?" Papa called after him.

There was no response. Papa watched Bill stumble over the plowed furrows toward the idle team. He shook his head in disgust and walked stiffly toward the barn.

*****

On May 19, Hermine and Ralph were wed in a quiet ceremony in Cleveland. Martha attended as her sister's witness, but distance, work obligations, and the demands of farm life kept the rest of the family away.

The young couple settled into a cottage in Bay Village that they had rented for the summer. Their furnishings were Spartan, but twenty-five-year-old Hermine felt rich beyond measure.

*****

Minola's academic excellence was rewarded when Miss Spencer, the English teacher, assigned her the role of a key character in the class play, which Minola carried off with aplomb. Miss Spencer also tasked Minola with writing the senior class history, to be read at the commencement ceremony.

On the evening of May 24, Minola processed down the aisle of the opera house with her fellow graduates and took a seat upon the stage. She smoothed her hands over the lacey layers of her white dress and straightened the streamers that flowed from the cabbage rose at her hip. Despite Flora's insistence that her sewing skills were not equal to the challenge, she had cleverly adapted two different dress patterns and spent hours huddled over the treadle sewing machine, with Minola hovering nearby to offer input on the features she envisioned for the gown. The dress was perfection, and the other girls in the class had gushed with praise when they saw it. Minola felt she had achieved her one shining moment of recognition in an otherwise dismal social existence.

She searched the audience for the familiar faces of Flora and Bill. Papa had stayed home with Mama, and Ella, Martha, and the newlyweds, Hermine and Ralph, were unable to travel to Monroeville for the Thursday evening ceremony. Even though she had hand-delivered her commencement announcement to Ada and Albert's house, Minola knew they would not attempt to attend the ceremony with their two small children. She smiled as she recalled Albert's assessment upon opening the graduation envelope as he sat at the supper table. "Why, Dick, I guess this means you're all growed up!" he announced, a slow smile curling from one corner of his mouth. "But your legs are still younger than mine," he added as he nudged the empty butter dish in Minola's direction. It was Albert's usual gentle way of sending her or Bill on a trip to the cellar to refill the butter dish.

Minola's reverie was broken by the pianist striking the prelude to Mrs. Morris's traditional commencement solo. It had been almost five years since the despised teacher had sung at Margaret's funeral, but the memory of that hurtful moment and the pain of losing Margaret had not diminished. Minola tucked her chin and studied the senior class history that lay in her lap. She willed herself to concentrate on each written word, even though the script slanted wildly through a sheen of tears.

Her solo complete, Mrs. Morris glided back to her seat. The superintendent stepped up to the podium to offer a few platitudes before introducing Minola and the reading of the class history. All eyes in the opera hall turned toward Minola. For a long moment she hesitated in her seat, blinking hard as she mentally pulled herself back to the present.

Helene Randle's elbow shot into Minola's ribs, and she leaned over to whisper, "I'll read it if you've got stage fright."

Minola rose and walked to the podium, where she rallied her composure to deliver the class history in a calm, steady voice.

Minola's graduation picture

Minola wearing the graduation dress sewn by Flora

As a graduation gift, Ella invited Minola to spend two weeks with her in Dover, during which time Minola could assist her with the church's annual Vacation Bible School. Ella added that the experience of working with young children would be good practice for Minola's future as a schoolteacher. Minola was thrilled by the invitation and the opportunity to travel alone to Dover, not to mention the two-week reprieve from the strawberry fields.

In Dover, Minola immediately recognized how beloved Ella was by the congregation she served. Children flocked to her, and adults respected her quiet, efficient manner. At the conclusion of the Vacation Bible School, Ella was approached about teaching the older students when Sunday School resumed in the fall. When word circulated among the teachers of the lower grades that Ella would no longer be their colleague, three of the women showed up at Mrs. Hoffmann's boarding house, where they cried and vowed to resign if Ella left their section. Ella was taken aback by their level of devotion and esteem, but Minola understood the high regard they held for her sister. A lifetime of selfless service to others, both in her job and with her siblings, had made Ella the ideal church employee.

Ella & a group of Vacation Bible School students

* * * * *

At summer's end, Hermine and Ralph searched for new housing arrangements. Although they were reluctant to leave their cozy cottage in Bay Village, they knew they needed more room; Hermine was expecting a baby in the spring. The couple set a self-imposed limit of forty-five dollars per month for rent but soon realized the competition for housing was fierce and their modest rent allowance would not procure anything suitable for a young family. They finally located an acceptable apartment at the corner of West 80th and Detroit Avenue on the near-west side of Cleveland, even though the rent of sixty dollars per month would leave them financially strapped. As was customary, Hermine had quit her job to await the birth of the baby, which meant that Ralph's paycheck was stretched to the breaking point.

* * * * *

In September, Minola enrolled in the one-year County Normal School, which she paid for with her earnings from the summer spent working at Ruggles Beach farmhouse. Each morning Minola boarded the school wagon with Bill and entered the massive doors of Monroeville High School, just as she always had done. However, she continued to climb the stairs past the high school classrooms on the second floor and proceeded to the third floor where the Normal School was held. Minola found it liberating to be free of the social strata of her high school days. Her fellow students in the Normal School were new acquaintances from other communities, and all were studious and like-minded in their educational pursuits.

* * * * *

Late one September afternoon, Ada unpinned the laundry from the clothesline behind the brick house and folded it into the wicker basket at her feet. She smiled as Mildred gamboled about the yard, plucking leaves from the grape arbor and tossing them into the air, then running beneath the shower of foliage. Little Roberta clutched the rim of the laundry basket and took a few unsteady steps toward the scattered leaves. She plopped onto her diapered bottom and crushed the leaves in her fists.

The clatter of bells caught Ada's ear, and she turned toward the road, expecting to see the tin peddler approaching from the west with his rattling wares. Instead, the noise emanated from a wagon drawn by a weary-looking horse. A man and a small boy sat atop the dusty cart, and two women trailed behind. One had a bright shawl bound about her shoulders that cradled an infant, and the other's head was wrapped in a colorful scarf. Both had long, flowing dark hair.

To Ada's consternation, the wagon turned into the driveway. "Gypsies," she thought to herself with a small amount of apprehension. Nomadic bands of Gypsies occasionally passed along the Ridge Road and camped for a day or two in a copse of trees on a nearby side road. They usually caused no trouble, but Ada had heard stories of trickery and theft attributed to the Gypsies. She called Mildred to her side, scooped Roberta onto her hip, and cast a nervous eye toward her prize hens scratching about in the chicken yard. Albert and Alfred were sowing winter wheat at the back of the field across the road. They would not have seen nor heard the approaching wagon. She was on her own to handle the wayfarers.

"Canna we water?" the man called over the barking of Bub, who stood defensively on the side porch.

Ada nodded and pointed toward the nearby well. She watched as the family pumped full the tin cup that hung from the well handle and passed it among themselves. After the man had quenched his thirst, he retrieved a bucket from the side of the wagon and filled it with water for the horse. The young woman climbed wearily onto the wagon seat and began to nurse the infant cradled in the shawl sling, while the little boy scampered after a cat that ambled across the drive. The older woman locked a piercing gaze onto Ada and fingered the numerous strands of beads that dangled almost to her waist.

Ada bit her lower lip as the woman headed in her direction. Was this the point when the Gypsy woman would launch into a fast, deceptive barter or, worse yet, try to distract her while the man slipped into the chicken yard and snagged several of her best hens? And what about the girls? Weren't Gypsies known to steal children? Ada tucked Mildred behind her.

"Pretty girls," the Gypsy woman commented, motioning toward Roberta and the little face peering out from behind her mother's skirt.

Ada's heart pounded, expecting the woman to lunge for her daughters at any moment. She hugged Roberta tightly and extended one arm down and slightly behind her as a protective barrier between the Gypsy woman and Mildred.

The woman fixed her dark eyes on Ada. "You wit' child again," she announced. "A boy dis time."

Ada arched an eyebrow and shook her head skeptically, relieved that the woman had no ill intent other than to prophesy nonsense.

"It true!" the woman asserted, nodding her head so vigorously that the long ends of her headscarf bobbed and the many ropes of beads rattled against each other. "I tell you truth!"

Bub left his post on the porch and stalked toward the Gypsy woman, the hair on his back bristling as his barking escalated. She nodded again at Ada before retreating across the yard to follow the wagon, which had turned and was heading out the drive. The little boy dropped the cat he had caught and raced to catch up. Ada watched as the Gypsy family proceeded eastward along the road, the clattering of the bells on their wagon slowly fading.

"Pregnant!" Ada snorted. She shook her head and wondered if the Gypsies would stop at Addisons' house and tell Edith that she, too, was pregnant with a boy. Knowing how her neighbor felt about children, Ada didn't think Edith would be the least bit receptive to the Gypsy woman's predictions.

Ada set Roberta on the ground and picked up the full laundry basket, which she propped on her hip. Holding a hand out for the toddler to grasp, she called to her daughters, "C'mon, girls. Time to start supper before Pop and Unk come up from the field."

* * * * *

The temperamental Overland's breakdowns increased in frequency until its repairs defied even Papa's mechanical abilities. After stripping it of all salvageable parts, Papa hooked Tup to the Overland's frame and hauled its remains to the back of the farm, where it joined the rusting hulk of the Fuller.

Transportation continued to be an issue, since the old pickup truck was also demonstrating unreliability. Papa finally relented and purchased his first brand-new machine, a Durant Star, which was manufactured as a competitor to the Ford Model T as the cheapest car possible. The Seibel siblings admired the neat sedan and felt they had gained some respectability, although not on the same automotive par as Mosses' upscale Dodge, Ordmanns' Paige, and George and Bertha's Buick. Bill immediately mastered the Star's modern gears, and he taught Flora the intricacies of driving the new machine.

Flora at the wheel of the Star

With reliable transportation, the siblings soon began to discuss a weekend excursion to visit Ella in Dover. When Papa learned of their plans, he quickly discouraged the motor trip, stating that the drive was too long. Ella recalled that Papa had driven to Columbus in a much less trustworthy vehicle when he and Bill had visited the state fair. She wrote him a letter, with the goal of changing his mind:

October 7, 1923
Dear Papa,

I have been wondering what arguments I could use to persuade you to let the kids come down to Dover. I would like it very much if they could come before the weather gets bad. Last summer some girls made the trip to Lakeside by way of Norwalk, and they got to the ferry in Sandusky in half a day, even after making several long stops on the way. They told me the roads were good and they had no trouble. The whole trip down here wouldn't cost as much as a single one-way train fare. Think it over and give them a chance. Flora does not have a lot of good times anyway, and the countryside is beautiful this time of year.
As ever yours,
Ella

Papa quietly considered Ella's letter, particularly her pointed comment about Flora's few opportunities for enjoyment in life. He finally set aside his misgivings and nodded his permission. Bill assured Papa that he and Flora would share the driving duties, and he also expressed confidence that he could handle any repair issues that might arise.

The following Friday, when Minola and Bill were out of school for teachers' meetings, the three siblings set off for Dover. They relished the crisp fall air, the colorful foliage, and the novelty of a carefree road trip. For Flora and Minola, the enjoyment of the trip was augmented by Bill's reaction to seeing the sights for the first time. Because they were so accustomed to the flat farmlands around Monroeville, the siblings had an almost reverent awe for the undulating topography of southeast Ohio.

With Ella, they spent the weekend motoring into the countryside, where they picnicked in an open meadow and marveled at the rolling hills. After church on Sunday morning, the three reluctantly bid farewell to Ella and began their return trip to Monroeville, subdued by the thoughts of school, farm chores, and the unpredictability of Mama that awaited them at home.

Bill, Minola, & Ella picnicking in the countryside near Dover

*****

Radio was becoming America's most popular form of entertainment, and trendsetter Emmaline Moss was the first in the neighborhood to purchase one for her well-appointed parlor. The airwaves frequently resonated with partisan political speeches, but Emmaline was partial to the hotel orchestras and organ recitals that were broadcast from downtown Cleveland. In particular, she tuned in to WTAM for the hour of music provided by Ernest H. Hunter at the State Theater's organ.

On occasion, Emmaline invited the neighbor women to join her for tea in the parlor while they listened to the recital. She enjoyed the opportunity to set the tea cart with her delicate china, knowing she was displaying a level of elegance and sophistication that was beyond her neighbors' reach. From time to time, she rose self-importantly from her chair to tune the radio's many knobs, battling static, fade-out, and strange whistling sounds.

Mama and Flora were sometimes invited to these afternoon interludes, although Flora found them anything but relaxing. There was always the concern that Mama would say something inappropriate or somehow damage Emmaline's fine china. She also noticed that the other women kept a nervous eye on Mama over the rim of their teacups, but more telling was that Emmaline took pains to position herself and the teacart at the greatest distance from Mama. Flora recognized the unspoken reason behind this maneuvering. Last year, the neighborhood grapevine had buzzed with the news of Mama throwing a teakettle of boiling water at Papa. Based on that knowledge, Emmaline was now putting a safe distance between Mama and the teapot, which was wrapped in a quilted cozy to keep its contents hot.

While it made Flora uncomfortable to witness the precautionary behavior exhibited by the neighbors, there was one positive result from the teakettle incident. Emmaline, who had always been quick to unleash her razor-sharp tongue, now displayed a less vituperative attitude toward the Seibels. When one of her delicate teacups rattled against its saucer in Mama's unsteady hand, Emmaline set her lips in a thin line but did not chastise Mama. Her restraint was surprising, but Flora knew all too well how effectively fear could modify behavior.

* * * * *

On Thanksgiving Day, all of the Seibel family gathered around Ada and Albert's dining room table, which nearly groaned under the weight of culinary abundance. Ella, Martha, and the newlyweds, who were all experiencing the restricted diets brought about by limited funds, exclaimed over the bounty.

Following the feast, the men repaired to the parlor where they discussed farm prices and the other news of the day while occasionally patting their distended bellies. In the kitchen, the women washed the dishes and started a pot of coffee to be served later with wedges of pumpkin or mince pie. As they bustled about, Ada revealed to her sisters that Hermine was not alone in expecting a baby in the spring. She related that her pregnancy had been foretold by a visiting Gypsy woman at a time when Ada herself had not known she was expecting. The sisters congratulated Ada and marveled at the woman's prescience. They wondered aloud what other events she could foretell. Ada smiled to herself but did not confide the Gypsy woman's additional prediction that the baby would be a boy. She kept that bit of prophesy tucked deep in her heart.

Chapter 27
The Gfell Home
1924

THE GFELL FARM teemed with new life in the spring of the year. Albert spent the raw days and dark nights of February and March as a midwife to his flock of sheep during the lambing season. He crawled out of bed several times each night, pulled on his boots and winter coat, and crossed the road to the sheep barn. Lifting the coal oil lantern high, he checked for any distressed ewes and carefully interceded with the delivery when it appeared that a healthy outcome was in jeopardy.

On occasion, a mother sheep rejected her tiny newborn lamb. If another ewe had recently given birth, Albert rubbed its placenta on the rejected lamb, thereby fooling the surrogate mother into adopting the orphan as her own. Sometimes the trick didn't work, so Albert dried the newborn lamb with a burlap bag and placed it in a bushel basket, which he carried across the road to the house. He tucked the basket behind the living room stove to keep the lamb warm through the night while he fell back into bed for a few more hours of sleep.

In the morning, Albert moved the tiny houseguest and its basket to the warm area behind the kitchen cookstove as he fried bacon and eggs for his and Alfred's breakfast. Insistent bleats greeted Ada when she arose. She hastily dressed and hurried to the kitchen, where she donned her apron even though its strings no longer tied around her pregnant girth. After warming a pan of milk, Ada settled onto a chair to acquaint the hungry lamb with the practice of feeding from a bottle. Little Mildred and Roberta were amused by the tapping of the lamb's tiny hooves on the kitchen floor as the wooly infant gained its strength and wobbled about on spindly legs.

After breakfast, Albert carried the lamb to the sheep barn to once again search for a receptive surrogate mother sheep. If he was unsuccessful, the lamb would be Ada's to bottle-feed until it was old enough to be reunited with the flock.

In addition to the arrival of the lambs, there were litters of new kittens tucked in the dark recesses of the barn, piles of pink piglets huddled close to their immense mother sows, a bawling calf or two, and clutches of eggs being vigilantly incubated by the geese, ducks, and hens. In the rafters near the peak of the barn, a cooing pair of pigeons took turns setting on their nest.

Late March brought new life to Hermine and Ralph's apartment, too. When the doctor announced that their newborn was a little girl, Hermine wept tears of joy. She cradled the infant in her arms, closely examining every feature of the tiny face and gazing in wonder at the perfect little hands and feet. Hermine considered only one name for the baby—Margaret Louise, after her beloved sister who had succumbed to the Spanish influenza. However, she and Ralph agreed to call their daughter Peggy, to give the child her own identity.

Hermine wished that she lived closer to her sisters, particularly Ada, so she could compare notes on the profound joy and the deep exhaustion she was discovering in new motherhood. Martha visited as her schedule permitted, offering insight gained from her classwork and hospital experience. Flora sent a box of infant dresses she had sewn, adorned with long rows of tiny buttons, as well as a hand-crocheted sweater with matching cap and booties and a knitted baby blanket. She joked that with the Seibel family's ongoing tradition of all-female offspring, she was sure to get plenty of mileage from the pink skeins of yarn she had purchased. In fact, Flora reasoned, she may as well start knitting some pink accessories for Ada's baby, which was due in May.

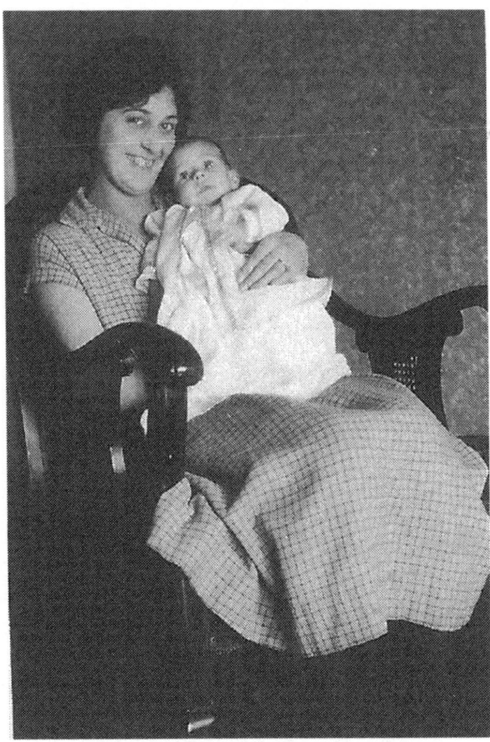

Hermine & baby Peggy

On Monday, May 12, the telephone jangled on the wall at the Seibel residence. When Flora lifted the receiver, she was astonished to hear Albert gush, "It's a boy, Flora! A boy! By de God, Ada had a boy!"

When Flora shared the news with the rest of the family, they were equally surprised and delighted, except for Mama who showed no reaction to the announcement despite her years of overt preference for male offspring.

For the past eight months, Ada had held on to the slim hope that the Gypsy woman's prediction was accurate, only half-believing that she could be so fortunate as to have a son, but it was true—the curly-haired cherub in her arms was a boy. Ada felt blessed beyond measure. Throughout her pregnancy, she had not allowed herself to think of names for little boys, and thus, she was temporarily at a loss of what to name the new arrival. She considered the name George but decided that Uncle George Seibel's offspring should have first-rights to that family name, even though Rosie was well into spinsterhood, Walter had yet to marry, and Elmer and his wife had selected the name Robert for their little boy. At last, Ada and Albert agreed upon the name Russell Albert for their son. Ada settled back on her pillow with a contented sigh. Two daughters and a son—her family was complete.

Mildred, baby Russell, & Roberta

* * * * *

The month of May continued to bring good news as Martha graduated from Lakeside Hospital's nursing school and Minola received her diploma from the County Normal School. Martha accepted a position as a private-duty nurse, usually in the homes of wealthier Cleveland residents. On one of her first assignments, she cared for a young man who was terminally ill with cancer. When the patient's mother saw Martha's youth and beauty, she expressed concern that her son would fall in love with his nurse, despite Martha's lower station in life. Martha inwardly rolled her eyes at the woman's misplaced apprehension and her obsession with the family's social status even in the face of death.

Martha graduating from nursing school

Martha in her nurse's uniform

*****

Upon graduation, Minola was hired for her first job as a schoolteacher at the one-room Laurel Hill school in Peru Township, about ten miles south of Monroeville. The County Superintendent had advised her to apply for the position because the children in that community came from respectable families and would not challenge her with behavior problems. Minola hoped this bit of advice proved more useful than the Superintendent's other cautionary gem: "Women teachers, be sure you don't fall in love with your eighth-grade boys."

All summer long, between picking strawberries and blackberries, mowing the lawn, spraying potato bugs, and helping Flora with the gardening and canning, Minola worked on lesson plans for her multi-grade classroom. In particular, she pored over the eighth-grade arithmetic book. Minola still felt dogged by the weakness in math that had resulted from her own poor preparation at the Plank Road school. She knew that students expected their teachers to have all the answers, so hesitating or stumbling over a math problem would cost her an immeasurable amount of their respect. Long after the rest of the family had settled in bed and the crickets had started their nightly cacophony, Minola worked math problems in the dim puddle of light provided by the single bulb that dangled over the kitchen table.

*****

In small ways, Papa, at age sixty-three, had begun to neglect many things around the farm. The barns, which had always been unpainted and skeletal in appearance, now lacked even the most basic repairs. The beehives had dwindled to one active hive, and the rows of brambles, which he had always kept so tidy, grew more wild and unkempt with each passing year. Besides Jetty the buggy horse and Tup the young workhorse, the livestock had been reduced to only a few milking cows and a small flock of hens—just enough to provide for the family's dietary needs. Perhaps most indicative of Papa's gradual slowing down was the hiring of a "jobber" to take over marketing the strawberries. Mr. Buckingham, from the renamed town of Willard, was about ten years younger than Papa. The two men bore a striking physical similarity and enjoyed a friendly relationship as they worked side by side to load the filled strawberry crates onto the bed of Mr. Buckingham's truck.

During his daily trips to the Seibel homestead at the height of the strawberry season, Mr. Buckingham took note of the efficient, hard-working Flora as she managed the crew of pickers and filled crates in the packing house at the edge of the field. One day, Mr. Buckingham arrived with his thirty-year-old widowed son and the younger man's two small children, who clung to their father's legs and peered shyly at the activity on the bustling strawberry farm.

After several return trips with the motherless family in tow, the elder Mr. Buckingham rather clearly indicated to Papa that he would like an alliance between Flora and his son. Papa did not respond but continued to load strawberry crates onto Mr. Buckingham's truck bed. He quietly considered how the loss of Flora would impact everything on the farm, from the management of the household to her capable assistance with the farm chores. Papa did nothing to promote the liaison, and Flora continued with her usual work, unaware that she was the object of matrimonial consideration.

Mr. Buckingham did not broach the subject again, and before long the younger Mr. Buckingham and his two children discontinued their trips to the Seibel farm.

Papa

*****

In July, Rev. Schenk asked Ella to housesit the parsonage while he and his family took a week's vacation. The Schenks provided a long list of instructions for Ella, including staying indoors in the stuffy manse as much as possible to answer any calls on the telephone or at the door, keeping the mail sorted by the date received, folding the newspapers in a particular manner on the reverend's chair-side table, and feeding Mrs. Schenk's pet parakeet. Before leaving, Mrs. Schenk draped the upholstered furniture in sheets and drew all the shades, giving the house a graveyard appearance at night. There was no offer of compensation for Ella's services, and she was too timid to point out that she was paying for unused room and board at Mrs. Hoffmann's during that week.

Almost immediately upon the Schenks' departure, there was a death in the congregation, leaving Ella to arrange a minister and music for the funeral. In addition, she made calls to the sick and shut-ins on Rev. Schenk's behalf while continuing to tend to her own duties, which included composing and mailing the church newsletter and organizing the choir's upcoming lawn fete as a fundraiser for the church's building fund. Ella preferred being busy, so the extra work did not bother her, and besides, like all the other church members, Ella's regard for the esteemed Rev. Schenk was immeasurable.

*****

On the first Saturday in September, Bill drove Minola over the dusty back roads to Mr. Vredenburg's house in Peru Township, where she would board during the school term. Bill helped carry Minola's valise and a box of books to the small room behind the kitchen that the Vredenburgs had set up for her use. A rope bed was pushed against one wall, and beside it stood a crude table and chair. A cloudy mirror hung over a small wash stand that held a ceramic pitcher and bowl for her bathing needs. The other half of the room served as the family's pantry and food storage area. While the room was sparse, it was clean and adequate. Minola knew she was fortunate to have a space of her own; schoolteachers often had to share a room and even a bed with the host family's children, who were usually pupils in the teacher's classroom.

The next day, Mr. Vredenburg, who was one of the Laurel Hill school trustees, gave Minola the key to the padlock on the school's front door. Carrying her textbooks, she walked a mile over unpaved roads to assess her working environment for the coming year. The building was shabby and ancient looking, as though it had been one of the county's original one-room schoolhouses built by long-ago pioneers. There was no shed for the coal that she would feed to the potbellied stove when the weather cooled. Instead, the fuel was piled on the north side of the building, unprotected from the weather. Minola frowned at the difficulty she would face in chipping lumps of coal from the frozen, snow-covered mound this winter.

She inserted the key in the padlock and, after a generous amount of wiggling it about, was able to spring the mechanism. The door creaked open to reveal a drab, uninspiring room. Other than a gold-framed picture of George Washington and a dusty American flag drooping from its standard in the corner, the room was devoid of ornamentation. Minola wondered if the former teacher had taken all of the decorations with her or if no one had ever made the effort to dress up this dreary center of learning. She arranged the textbooks on her desk, dusted the students' desks and the recitation bench, and swept the oiled floor, making mental notes about ways she would improve the stark surroundings. Using a piece of string, she measured the bare windows. Curtains on the lower quarter of the tall windows would make a vast improvement, she decided.

Laurel Hill school

On the first day of school, Minola arrived at 8 a.m., an hour before the start of class. She picked some flowers from along the roadside and set them in a cup on her desk, making her first attempt at beautification. About fifteen students streamed in from all directions, their bare feet kicking up puffs of dust on the dirt roads. When Minola rang the school bell, they entered the building in a quiet, orderly manner.

The day proceeded with many ten-minute recitation sessions so Minola could assess her students' abilities. They sat on the recitation bench, swinging their bare feet and huffing and puffing their way through phonics, ciphering on their slates, or demonstrating their reading skills. To Minola's delight, the students were well behaved and eager to learn, just as the County Superintendent had predicted. The only student who gave her pause was Ludwig Wolfe, a ten-year-old boy who still struggled with the rudiments of the first reader. Minola felt it would be her failure if she could not teach any child how to read, so she mentally designated Ludwig as her special project.

After the students left at 4 p.m., Minola tidied the room and swept the floor. She was amazed at the amount of debris carried in on the children's feet from the dirt roads and the schoolyard, and she fully understood the wisdom of oiling the floor to minimize the clouds of dust. Minola settled at her desk and spent an hour reviewing the lessons for the next day. Satisfied with her efforts on this first day of teaching, Minola closed the hasp on the padlock and headed to the Vredenburgs' for a hearty supper and a good night's sleep.

Late on Friday afternoon, Bill motored into the Vredenburgs' driveway to take Minola home for the weekend. She felt as though she had been gone for a month instead of a week, and she brimmed with stories to share about her students, her host family, and her new experiences as a teacher. Over the weekend, Minola enlisted Flora's assistance in painting some pictures of birds, flowers, and animals to dress up the stark school room. She vowed that with money from her first paycheck, she would buy fabric for Flora to make curtains for the schoolhouse windows. In addition, Minola asked Ella to purchase books from the Dover Library book sales in the interest of establishing a children's library at the school.

* * * * *

Despite his older sisters' excellent academic reputations, Bill made only enough scholastic effort to slide along during his junior year of high school. He derived the most enjoyment from his shop class, where he could expand upon the mechanical skills he had learned at Papa's elbow. Bill also exhibited an untapped musical talent and a remarkable memory for any melody he heard. He took up the flute and was encouraged in his endeavors by the music teacher, who recognized Bill's innate aptitude. He and his best friend, Bud Wilhelm, also carried the lead singing roles in the school's operetta, staged in the town opera hall that fall. He joined the varsity football team and spent hours away from the farm, circulating among his various social contacts in town. Bill's good looks and affable nature made him a favorite of everyone he met.

Bill (back row, left) as a member of Monroeville High School's varsity football team

*****

When the fall rains commenced, the dirt roads of Peru Township became a quagmire of mud, which the children tracked into the Laurel Hill school on their shoes. Minola used money from her paycheck to purchase a boot scraper, which she placed beside the bottom stone step and encouraged the children to use in an attempt to minimize the amount of dried mud she had to sweep up each day.

Minola continued to devote one-on-one time to her special student, Ludwig, sometimes keeping him in at recess for additional work. She recalled her own loss of recess time when the fourth-grade teacher had discovered Minola's poor math skills following the consolidation of the Monroeville schools. Therefore, she was careful to maintain a balance between Ludwig's tutoring and the time he spent in the schoolyard with the other students. Ludwig did not resent the loss of play time but instead seemed to glow under the teacher's attention.

In addition to Ludwig's academic difficulties, there were other things about the boy that puzzled Minola, for example, his very Germanic first name. Most families of German heritage had Anglicized their names following the sharp discrimination they had experienced during the recent war. She wondered why Ludwig's parents hadn't transitioned his name to Louis or Louie. As the winter months approached, Minola also began to detect an overwhelming odor of garlic about the boy. She finally realized that he was wearing an asafetida bag around his neck to ward off colds and infections, another sign of his Old World upbringing.

From time to time, Mr. Bellman, the County Assistant of Rural Schools, paid a visit to Laurel Hill school. Minola dreaded the periodic assessments by this unsmiling man. She fretted about the notes he was taking and felt self-conscious performing in front of him. One day, after the students had been dismissed, Mr. Bellman asked Minola for her opinion of young Ludwig. Minola smiled and told him about the additional instruction she was providing for the boy. She acknowledged that he was still in the first reader, his sums were erratic, and he seemed to absorb new ideas quite slowly, but he had become her special project.

"He needs to be institutionalized," Mr. Bellman interrupted curtly. "He's retarded."

"But … but how can that be? I'm making progress with him," protested Minola. "I can teach him, I know I can."

"You're a new teacher," Mr. Bellman said condescendingly. "In time you'll learn to recognize the dim-witted and the slow and not waste your time on them. They really shouldn't mix with the others, you know." He gave Minola's shoulder a solicitous pat. "I'll speak with the family about what needs to be done. If they don't see the wisdom in institutionalizing the boy, perhaps they'll agree to withdraw him from the school."

Minola watched Mr. Bellman climb into his buggy, slap the reins on the horse's rump, and trot off in the direction of the Wolfe residence. She slumped into the chair behind her desk, feeling confused and defeated.

* * * * *

Ella sat at her desk in the church office one Monday morning, counting and recounting the collection money from the previous day's worship service and frowning at the total. It did not match the sum that Mr. Burkhoff, the church treasurer, had tallied on a slip of paper, which he tucked beneath the tithing envelopes and loose coins and bills every Sunday before carrying the collection plates to Ella's office. One of Ella's Monday morning responsibilities was to count out the collection, check her total against Mr. Burkhoff's sum, and walk to the nearby bank to deposit the money in the church's account.

Ella was perplexed by the missing money, which had been occurring sporadically for several months. The discrepancies between her sums and Mr. Burkhoff's tallies had been minor in the beginning—always a matter of change—but recently had grown to a value of several dollars each time. She did not want to suspect that the earnest Mr. Burkhoff was the culprit, but for several Sundays, she casually joined him for the after-church collections count. She unobtrusively validated that the amount of money in the collection plates matched the sum he scribbled on the note, and she even volunteered to walk the money to her office. Despite these precautions, she was quite often short a few dollars on Monday mornings.

Ella did not want to raise an alarm about potential theft within the church. Instead, she was embarrassed that such discrepancies were happening on her watch, and she dug into her own purse to replace the missing money.

One Sunday after church, Ella lingered longer than usual following a meeting of the Sunday School teachers. As she made her way down the darkened hall toward her office to retrieve her coat, she heard the sound of coins hitting the linoleum floor. She quickly stepped back into the shadows of a classroom doorway. Down the hall, the door to her office slowly swung open. The face of Rev. Schenk's adolescent son, Tom, peered out. He glanced in both directions before stepping into the hallway. Ella heard the jingle of coins and the rustle of bills as Tom stuffed his fist into his pants pocket and slunk down the hall toward the outside door.

Ella put one hand over her mouth and emitted a gasp of astonishment. She never would have suspected a member of the Schenk family of stealing from the collection plates, and she was filled with disappointment and despair at the discovery. Ella hurried toward her office, flicked on the overhead light, and saw several coins scattered on the floor in front of the cupboard where the collection plates were kept. She carried the plates to her desk and counted out the money, praying silently that the total would match the sum on Mr. Burkhoff's note. It did not.

For the rest of the afternoon, Ella lay on her bed at Mrs. Hoffmann's boarding house. Her head ached and her stomach churned at the thought of having to reveal the distressing news to Rev. Schenk.

The next morning, Ella felt raw and unsettled after a sleepless night. Summoning her courage, she knocked on Rev. Schenk's office door and asked to speak with him. Her hands twisted in her lap as she told Rev. Schenk about the ongoing missing collection money, and her throat tightened as she described her certainty that young Tom was the culprit.

Reverend Schenk leaned back in his chair, tenting his fingertips before him and furrowing his brow. After a long silence, he thanked Ella for bringing the matter to his attention, assured her that he would take care of it, and asked that she keep the information confidential. Ella nodded her understanding. Reverend Schenk then offered a prayer asking for heavenly guidance in dealing with disappointment and loss of trust. He ended with a plea for God's mercy on those who commit transgressions.

Ella was relieved that the dilemma of the missing church money had been resolved. She felt as though a great weight had been lifted from her shoulders, and she threw herself into planning for the upcoming Advent season and the children's Christmas pageant.

Ella

In mid-November, Ella was asked to attend the church council meeting. In these times of financial concerns, she anticipated that she was being summoned to make cuts in the Sunday School budget. Instead, the council president apologetically explained that, upon Rev. Schenk's recommendation, Ella's services were no longer needed. The minister had convinced the governing board that they should dismiss Ella to ease their budgetary constraints. The money saved on her salary could then be put toward the church's building fund, thereby enabling the congregation to realize their dreams of expansion much sooner. While Ella's termination would increase his workload, he assured the council that he alone was quite capable of meeting the congregation's needs. Because Rev. Schenk was held in such high regard by everyone in the congregation, they followed his advice, even though they regretted the loss of their beloved church staffer. Ella was devastated.

After the shock of the news had worn off, Ella began to suspect that her dismissal was directly linked to Tom Schenk's thievery. Either Rev. Schenk believed that Ella was the culprit and had falsely accused his son, or he wished to remove anyone who knew the truth about Tom.

Ella bid a tearful farewell to Mrs. Hoffmann as well as her many friends in the congregation and the community. Her four years in Dover had been some of the happiest, most productive times of her life. She sadly boxed up her books and personal effects and boarded the train for Monroeville. Thirty-two-year-old Ella was going home to Papa and Mama, Flora and Bill, and an uncertain future. She vowed she would never again work for a church. She had trusted and revered her minister, and he had repaid her with betrayal. As the car swayed over the tracks toward home, Ella felt as hollow and empty as a corn husk.

Chapter 28
Rural Monroeville, Ohio
1925

MINOLA TUCKED HER FACE deeper into the folds of the claret-colored scarf Flora had knitted as her Christmas present. In the dim morning light, she concentrated on keeping her footsteps within the narrow track left by a passing sleigh on the snow-covered road. The bitter temperatures made the mile walk from the Vredenburg residence to the Laurel Hill school seem doubly long this morning, the first day of school after the Christmas break. Minola thought about the schoolroom chores that awaited her, and she took comfort in knowing she had left a scuttle of coal beside the potbellied stove and a filled teakettle on its broad surface. Because she did not relish starting her day by chipping away at the sometimes frozen coal pile on the north side of the building, Minola had adopted the routine of always filling the scuttle before she departed the one-room schoolhouse each afternoon. Even though the water in the teakettle would be frozen solid after the long holiday break, Minola knew she would have the copper vessel whistling happily in no time.

Minola smiled as she thought of the teakettle and the new morning ritual she intended to institute. She thrust her mittened hand into her coat pocket and patted a small tin that contained loose tea and a mesh infuser. Decorated in exotic red and gold Chinese motifs, the tin and its contents had been a Christmas gift from the Vredenburgs. Upon receiving the present, Minola decided that she would start each school day with a cup of tea after her morning preparations were complete and before the students arrived. Coming from a family of coffee drinkers who sometimes drank directly from the spout of the old graniteware coffeepot, Minola felt awash with sophistication as she envisioned herself making an individual cup of tea each morning and daintily sipping the steaming liquid. She elected to overlook the fact that the schoolhouse teacup was actually a heavy ironstone coffee mug with a chip in its rim.

As she navigated her way across the snow-filled schoolyard, Minola fumbled beneath the tin for the key to the schoolhouse door's padlock. She carefully climbed the stone steps, where a wind-driven snowdrift leaned against the door, and inserted the key into the lock. To her surprise, the key would not wiggle about, which was the usual requirement to spring the mechanism. Minola pushed the key harder in one direction and then another, but her efforts were met with icy resistance. The padlock on the westward-facing door had been fully exposed to the elements during the long school holiday. It was now frozen shut.

Minola blinked several times in disbelief. She had never considered the possibility of being denied access to the schoolhouse by a frozen lock. She banged the padlock against the doorjamb several times, confident that the blows would jar the tumblers from their icy grip. She reinserted the key, but once again it would not wiggle in the keyway despite her vigorous twisting motions. Minola pulled her scarf down below her chin, held the key directly in front of her mouth, and blew warm breath upon the metal. She did this several times and then quickly reinserted the key in the lock, holding it stationary for a moment to allow the meager heat to transfer from the metal to the tumblers. When this met with failure, Minola tried holding the keyway of the padlock to her lips and blowing into it. She repeated this method with the key, but once again, the lock would not budge.

Minola withdrew the key from the lock and shoved it in her pocket, where it clanged against the Chinese tea tin. She tugged on the lock in a vain hope that the shackle was not fully engaged and would release due to the sudden downward force of her pull, but the lock held.

Reluctantly, Minola slid off a mitten and wrapped her hand around the frozen padlock, wincing as the icy metal met her flesh. Covering her exposed hand with the discarded mitten, Minola leaned her forehead against her clenched fists and said a silent prayer that her body heat would be sufficient to warm the core of the lock. Soon, she could no longer tolerate the frostiness of the metal and her fingers' exposure to the elements. She hastily returned her bare hand to its mitten and fumbled for the key in her pocket. Once again, she blew warm breath upon the key, reinserted it in the lock, and attempted to jimmy the mechanism. The lock held tight.

In frustration, Minola slammed the palm of her mittened hand against the schoolhouse door. She stomped her nearly numb feet in place on the stone step as she considered her options, which were few. She could walk the mile back to the Vredenburgs' home and solicit the aid of Mr. Vredenburg, or she could stumble along the snow-covered road in the opposite direction to a house that was closer. Unfortunately, she did not know the occupants of this nearby house, plus she was keenly aware that no one welcomed a disruption in their morning chores, particularly from a stranger. Minola cringed at the thought of the good-natured chuckling that would take place at her expense once the story circulated throughout the community about the hapless schoolmarm who was frozen out of her schoolhouse.

Although the walk was longer, Minola elected to return to the Vredenburgs'. Because Mr. Vredenburg was a school trustee, it was within his realm to resolve school-related issues, so she would explain the situation to him and ask for his assistance. She also felt that the Vredenburgs would be discrete about her plight.

With chagrin, Minola retraced her steps across the snowy schoolyard. Not only did she dread the long, frosty walk back to the Vredenburgs', but she was disgusted by her helplessness. At nearly twenty years of age, Minola took pride in her independence and self-reliance. It was a blow to her ego to be a female in need of rescue.

When she reached the road, Minola glanced back at the school, noting the frozen pile of coal on the north side of the building. She ruefully thought of the filled scuttle that waited for her beside the potbellied stove in the locked, icy building. Little good it did her now! Minola hunched her shoulders against the cold and trundled onward.

Suddenly, her head shot upward and she whirled about. Hurriedly retracing her steps, Minola crossed the schoolyard and picked her way around to the north side of the building, using one hand against the weathered clapboards to keep her balance. Her breath hung in frosty clouds as she contemplated the snow-covered coal pile and the window above it. If she could climb the rocky mound, perhaps she could open the window sash and gain entry to the school!

Minola tentatively placed one foot on the uneven surface of the coal pile while clinging to the clapboard siding. She nosed about with her other foot, searching for a secure foothold. Slowly, she edged upward, the hard soles of her shoes slipping on the rocky mound and causing her arms to flail wildly. Abandoning all vanity, Minola pitched forward and used both hands to assist in clawing her way to the summit. There, she rose unsteadily and propped her knees against the side of the schoolhouse for support.

Minola examined the window sash, hoping to locate a finger groove in the bottom rail. Finding none, she edged the tips of her mittened fingers upward against the top rail of the lower sash and pushed with all her might. When the window did not budge, she pressed her hands forcefully against the outer stiles, hoping the pressure would liberate the sash from its bind. To her immense relief, Minola heard the crack of wood releasing. She returned her fingertips to the underside of the top rail and grunted as she shoved upward. The sash gave a tiny bit. Straining,

Minola pushed again and again. At last, she managed to elevate the window sash enough to work her fingers under its lower rail. With this improved leverage point, Minola tugged and tugged until the sash begrudgingly passed its sticking point and flew upward. She pushed aside the curtain and thrust her head through the open window. Minola glanced about the room and felt certain that Howard Carter could not have been more overjoyed at his recent discovery of King Tut's tomb than she was upon gaining entry to this humble schoolroom.

Climbing through the open window would require some unlady-like gymnastics, and Minola quickly looked around to ensure that no students were approaching on the road. She hiked her skirt and coat above her knees, while offering up thanks that she was not wearing one of the fashionable pencil skirts. She lifted her long leg until her foot slid through the open window. Again, she quickly looked toward the road for reassurance that no one would see her in such an ungainly pose. Pulling herself upward, Minola struggled to turn her body until she was hunched in a straddle on the windowsill. From this position, she was able to drop one foot to the schoolroom floor and exit the window as though dismounting a horse.

Although overcome with relief to be standing inside the little schoolhouse, Minola knew there was no time to revel in her victory. The room was icy cold and must be brought up to temperature for the students, who would be arriving soon. She rushed to the potbellied stove and shoveled sufficient coal from the scuttle into the firebox. Next, she hurried to the entryway to retrieve a stack of old newspapers to use as fire-starters. Minola's fingers were stiff from the cold and slow to cooperate as she crumpled the papers into balls and wedged them among the lumps of coal. Finally, she struck a long match against the side of the stove and held its flame to the edge of a wadded newspaper. Minola watched with satisfaction as the fire took, and she rubbed her hands in front of the stove's open door, trying to absorb the meager initial heat.

While waiting for the frozen teakettle to thaw, Minola returned the excess newspapers to the entryway, dusted the students' desks and the recitation bench, swept the room, and whisked away several spider webs that had formed during the school break. She dragged the heavy teacher's desk near the window to aid in her upcoming exit.

At last, the teakettle chirped a tremulous note, indicating that its water was on the verge of boiling. Minola retrieved the ironstone coffee mug from her desk and poured the steaming liquid into the cup. She clasped the warm mug in her mittened hands, enjoying the welcome heat as she crossed to the window.

Setting the mug on her desk, Minola again hiked her coat and skirt, straddled the windowsill, and eased outside onto the snowy pile of coal. She grabbed a reader from her desktop and propped it in the open window, to ensure that her hard-won means of entrance and exit would be maintained. Retrieving the steaming mug, Minola carefully picked her way down the rocky mound. Balance was trickier now that she was carrying the mug, and Minola edged sideways, trying to maintain stability by keeping one hand on the side of the building. She was determined not to spill a drop of the precious hot water. At last, she reached the ground and followed her footprints in the snow to the front of the building.

Minola held the mug aloft and plunged the padlock into the steaming water. When enough time had passed for the tumblers to be thawed, she fumbled in her pocket for the key. Her hand found the key and the tin of tea. She shook her head at how differently this day had started than what she'd envisioned. With great trepidation, Minola inserted the key into the lock and wiggled it about. The shackle released, and the padlock dangled from its hasp. Minola was overcome with relief. Never before had opening the door to this humble schoolroom been such a source of happiness!

Minola carried the padlock indoors to complete its thaw atop the potbellied stove. Grabbing the broom from the entryway, she swept the snow from the schoolhouse steps. By now, the chill had been dispelled from the classroom, so Minola hung her coat and scarf on the nail in the entryway. She returned her desk to its proper location, removed the reader from the open window ledge, and closed the north window. Outside, she could hear children's voices. Minola drew a deep breath, smoothed her skirt, and prepared to start the school day.

* * * * *

On January 8, the day before her thirtieth birthday, Flora boarded a B&O Pullman with her friend, Oliva Heyman. The trip had come together so quickly that Flora could not believe she was really seated on a southbound train. Oliva had often expressed an interest in going south to work for the winter. The Roaring Twenties had brought boom times to Florida, with speculators, tourists, and many new residents pouring in from the North. Oliva had read about St. Petersburg, where the construction of new hotels was surging. She felt confident that a couple of enterprising young women could easily find jobs there and earn money while enjoying the change of scenery. Oliva frequently floated this idea to Flora, who never seriously considered the proposition. She had so many responsibilities on the farm, not the least of which was Mama. How could she ever go away?

Then, Ella moved back home from Dover in November following the unhappy incident with Rev. Schenk's son. By Christmas, Ella had learned of Oliva's suggested trip to Florida and encouraged Flora to consider the opportunity. At first Flora was reluctant, but Ella countered each of her sister's "what if's" with assurances that she would manage all of Flora's chores in her absence.

"But … what about Mama?" Flora asked tentatively, her brow knit in concern.

"You forget I know a thing or two about her ways," reassured Ella.

By the time Flora grasped that she was free to travel, there was no time to do any special sewing for the trip. She quickly packed a trunk with her summer dresses and tossed in the one bathing suit and cap that all the sisters shared. If she was going to be that close to a body of water, she intended to swim!

Flora looked out the Pullman's window. The train's first stop was Washington, D.C., and Flora wanted to be sure she didn't miss seeing the mountains en route, even if it meant viewing them in the moonlight. She opened the small black "Daily Record" in her lap and fingered the miniature green pencil attached by a string. The journal had been a traveling gift from Ella, and Flora resolved to keep a log of her trip, including all her expenses and income. She didn't want to forget a thing about this momentous adventure. Flora thumbed to the poem on the opening page:

A Book of Life

A drop of ink today, tomorrow,
To tell of pleasure or of sorrow,
Of homely things so nice to know,
Also, of the fairest,
The richest, and the rarest.
A year today, what did I do?
Today I write, next year I'll know.
A little written here intensely
Will help me recollect immensely,
So that this book of little measure
Will be to me a valued treasure.

The train traveled through the night, arriving in Washington, D.C., at 9 o'clock the next morning. Oliva and Flora boarded a tour bus for some sightseeing of the nation's capital, followed by lunch at the Raleigh Hotel. They walked about the city until they were footsore and all too happy to sit in the train depot for five hours, awaiting the next leg of their journey, which would take them to Savannah, Georgia, and then to Jacksonville, Florida, where they would board a day coach for St. Petersburg.

Flora marveled at the passing scenery as the train rocked southward. The jagged slash of dark pines against the sky was so different from the stand of pin oaks at the back of the Seibel homestead. The swampland was eerie and the shotgun shacks appalling, but Flora noted the singing of birds when she transferred trains. It seemed strange to be enjoying signs of spring while the folks back home were deep in winter's icy grip.

Upon their arrival in St. Petersburg, the two young women bought a newspaper and searched its want ads for employment opportunities. They noticed an ad stating the Hollenbeck Hotel at the northwest corner of First Avenue and Second Street was seeking five waitresses. After asking for directions, Oliva and Flora arrived at the huge hotel and were interviewed by Mr. and Mrs. Bader, the proprietors of the establishment. They were hired immediately, with Oliva starting on the 14th of January and Flora on the 15th. The next task was to find lodging, and the two young women turned to the YWCA, which was within walking distance of the hotel. There, they arranged to share a small room and split the modest fee.

Flora barely slept a wink the night before she began her waitressing job. Oliva, with one day of experience under her belt, assured Flora the work wasn't much different than serving a hearty dinner during threshing season back home. However, the only compensation one received from a thresherman after the meal was a contented smile or a loud belch. Here, a friendly and attentive waitress was rewarded with tips. Oliva emphasized her success by rattling the coins in her pocket as proof that the work was both possible and profitable. She confided that the only downside was Mr. Bader, who sat on a stool in the corner of the dining room with his arms crossed over his chest and a scowl on his face. He watched every movement in the room with hawk-like attention. Oliva acknowledged that she was reprimanded by him once—for serving from the right instead of the left. "Just keep to that rule and you'll do fine," Oliva advised.

Flora's first customer kept his head buried behind the newspaper as he ordered chess pie and coffee. The butterflies were churning in Flora's stomach when she returned with his order, and she cast a wary eye toward Mr. Bader on his stool. She silently repeated Oliva's reminder: "Serve from the left, serve from the left." Her hands shook as she set the pie and beverage in front of the man, causing the coffee cup to rattle against its china saucer. The man tipped down one corner of the paper and looked at Flora, then at Mr. Bader in the corner. Returning to his reading, the man drawled from behind the paper, "Don't worry 'bout him, Sugar. I been comin' here long enough to know he's got as much bite as a toothless old dog."

Flora smiled with relief and amusement at the man's assessment and turned her attention to the other customers. When she returned to clear the man's table, she was amazed to find a tip of two quarters tucked beneath the rim of the pie plate. She gazed at the coins for a long moment. Oliva had mentioned nickels and dimes as the most common denominations left by single diners, but fifty cents was a very generous tip, particularly for a first-time waitress with shaking hands. Flora slipped the coins into her pocket and felt renewed confidence in her ability to perform the job and earn an income during this southern sojourn.

The Hollenbeck Hotel in St. Petersburg, Florida, where Flora & Oliva were employed

On their days off, Flora and Oliva went to band concerts in the park, where they bought ice cream and strolled in the sun. The two young women window-shopped, visited an orange farm, and wrote postcards to friends back home. They also took pictures of sites unfamiliar to their northern Ohio sensibilities, such as palm trees, pelicans, begonias, an alligator basking in the sun, and the two black men who worked as porters at the Hollenbeck Hotel. Best of all, they located a nearby shallow cove for swimming, where Flora could perfect her backfloat.

Flora swimming

Oliva Heyman & Flora in Florida

Flora was amazed at how much leisure time she had in Florida. There were no cows to milk and chickens to feed every morning and night, no butter to churn, bread to bake, nor meals to prepare, and no overriding dread of Mama's daily unpredictability. And yet, Flora felt a twinge of homesickness for all that she had left behind. She missed her sisters and Bill as well as the camaraderie of the neighborhood quilting bees and butchering days that would be taking place throughout the winter months. She wondered how Ella was faring with Mama's temperament. Flora was familiar with all the warning signs of Mama's impending spells and, for the most part, knew how to blunt the worst of the explosive behavior. How could anyone else read the nuances of Mama's moods? How was the family getting along without her?

* * * * *

Ella soon learned how hard Flora worked as Papa's right-hand man, keeper of the household, and caretaker of Mama. She felt as though she needed an extra set of hands to accomplish all the daily chores plus a pair of eyes in the back of her head to keep track of Mama.

One day the tinker arrived while Ella was in the cellar sorting rotten potatoes from the winter storage bins. Mama, who was unattended, warmly welcomed the man into the house and invited him to sit at the kitchen table while she gathered all the household scissors for him to sharpen. From the cellar, Ella heard the scraping of chairs on the kitchen floor and an unfamiliar male voice. She dropped the potatoes she was sorting and hurried up the steps. As she reached the pantry, Ella overheard the tinker inquire, "Where's Flora? Ain't she home today?"

"*Ach!*" Mama replied with a shake of her head. "She went over to Ada's, took sick, and died."

The tinker reared back in his chair. "No!" he exclaimed. "Why, I just seen her the last time I was 'round this way, and she was fine then." He shook his head in disbelief. "Jesus! What a shame. What a damn shame!"

Mama scowled at the tinker. Even in her clouded mental state, Mama maintained an aversion to swearing. She pushed the scissors across the table toward the peddler.

Ella stood in the pantry doorway, saddened by Mama's mixed-up reminder of Margaret's death but uncertain how to assure the tinker of Flora's well-being. Correcting the misinformation would uncomfortably draw attention to Mama's confusion, which had been worsened by Flora's absence. Yet, Ella did not begrudge her sister these months of freedom.

A box of oranges that Flora sent from Florida arrived the day after one of Mama's spells. Papa opened the crate and surveyed the neatly packed fruit. He picked up one of the oranges and held it to his nose, inhaling the citrus scent and remembering his long-ago stint with Heber Grau as laborers in the orange groves of Florida. Back then, he had been young and vigorous but burdened by financial concerns. Now his burdens were of another nature. The night before, Mama had spun into hysteria over a face she saw peering at her through the kitchen window. Papa had leaped from his rocking chair beside the cookstove and raced out into the snow in his stocking feet to apprehend the voyeur. He found no tracks in the snow to indicate someone had stood beneath the window. All was calm and still, in contrast to the unsettled situation within the house.

* * * * *

At the end of March, Flora and Oliva concluded their southern stay. They had each earned a satisfying sum of money, in addition to fond memories of their adventures. The two young women boarded a bus for Daytona Beach, where they gathered seashells along the shoreline. Flora found a bath house and changed into her bathing suit. Even though the water was cold and choppy, she wanted to seize what may be her only opportunity to swim in the Atlantic Ocean. From Daytona Beach, the women traveled by bus to St. Augustine and toured the historic city. Eventually, they parted ways so that Oliva could head west to visit relatives. For Flora, it was time to return home and resume her responsibilities. Soon it would be time to plant the new strawberry field and start the potato seedlings.

Upon arriving in Cincinnati, Flora was transferred to the B&O depot for the last leg of her journey. While inquiring about her connection, Flora missed the northbound train. Dejected, she plopped onto a bench in the empty depot for a ten-hour wait. She fought back tears of disappointment. A wave of homesickness washed over her as she thought with longing of her family, the homestead, and all that was familiar, even her many chores. To pass the long hours and to distract herself, she read, lay down and tried to sleep, then sat up and read some more. A young couple with three squalling children arrived, bringing commotion that served as a welcome distraction and a respite from the loneliness.

At last, Flora's northbound train chugged into the station and she eagerly boarded. While she had enjoyed her southern experience, Flora now had only one desire—to go home.

* * * * *

As the Seibels gathered for their Easter Sunday feast on April 12, they joked that Flora had brought the Florida weather home with her. The temperature reached an unseasonable high of seventy-one degrees that day, which prompted the family to spill out of the house after dinner. While Mama busied herself with her usual preoccupation—picking up sticks—the other family members poked about the yard, looking for signs of spring. They took advantage of the balmy weather to snap pictures of the two youngest family members, little Peggy and Russell, before Hermine, Ralph, and Martha returned to Cleveland.

Peggy with Hermine & Ada holding Russell

*****

One Friday afternoon in late spring, Bill picked up Minola at the Laurel Hill school, and the two motored along the country roads toward Ada's house. Minola held Bill's shop class project—an electric lamp—in her lap. It was only natural to seek praise and approval for one's handiwork, and the siblings always turned to Ada for such maternal feedback. Bill was unconcerned that a full demonstration of the lamp's features would be impossible at Ada and Albert's house, since the rural electrification program had yet to include their neighborhood.

Bill took the shortest route to Ada's, expertly navigating the Star around the many ruts and potholes on Sand Hill Road. As they approached a narrow bridge over a farm creek, Bill shifted the vehicle into a higher gear and pressed the accelerator to the floor. From previous solo trips, he knew that with the proper amount of speed, the machine would momentarily go airborne when it hit the approach to the bridge. He clutched the wheel in anticipation and shouted over the whine of the engine, "Get ready to fly!"

Before Minola could secure herself and the lamp, the machine bounced off the small rise at the bridge and briefly lurched into the air. It jolted back to the hard-packed surface of the road, causing the lamp in Minola's lap to fly upward and hit her in the mouth. Stunned, Minola darted her tongue across her front teeth, where she immediately detected a corner missing from one tooth. She blinked rapidly in disbelief.

Glancing over, Bill noticed his sister's wide-eyed look and laughed. "There's no feelin' like flyin', is there?"

Minola turned toward Bill and pointed in horror at her chipped tooth. Bill was immediately apologetic but tried to downplay the severity of the mishap by offering, "It ain't really so bad. It kinda … well, kinda gives you character."

When the siblings arrived at Gfells', Minola abandoned the lamp on the seat beside Bill. Her long legs were out of the machine and rushing across the yard toward the kitchen and Ada before Bill had set the brake and turned off the engine. For Minola, the purpose of the trip had now shifted from approval-seeking to a need for consolation from their mother-substitute.

* * * * *

May brought a conclusion to Bill's senior year of high school, including several major projects. He had enjoyed making the electric lamp in shop class, which expanded his love of mechanical tinkering. However, there had been tension between Bill and his Ag teacher, whose old-world outlook on agricultural technology included a decided preference for horse-drawn equipment rather than modern machinery. This only served to exacerbate Bill's lack of interest in farming. He had already spent many tedious hours walking the fields of the homestead behind a team of horses, where his view was always a set of haunches. He dreamed of the ease, efficiency, and power of mechanization. When the teacher assigned a year-end project that emphasized antiquated methods, Bill dug in his heels and refused to complete the task. The teacher had no other option than to award an "incomplete" for the term, which left Bill without sufficient credits for graduation.

Bill's sisters were extremely dismayed at his foolhardy stubbornness, but none of their reasoning or scolding could change his decision. Bill cared little for academic pursuits, deriving greater enjoyment from the social contacts offered by a scholastic setting than the educational goals to be attained. He was satisfied that the school board would allow him to participate in the graduation ceremony with his friends.

On the evening of commencement, Ella, Flora, and Minola sat in the auditorium of the opera house, fanning themselves with the graduation program against the unusually warm early-June weather. Papa had stayed home with Mama, since the heat would only exacerbate her unpredictability. Martha's private-duty nursing position in Cleveland required evening hours, and neither Ada nor Hermine would attempt to attend with their little ones in tow.

The Class of '25 processed down the aisle and took their seats upon the stage. Bill looked handsome in his suit and tie. His dark complexion and neatly combed hair were offset by the white shirt that Flora had pressed for him that morning. A smile played about Bill's lips as he leaned his elbows on his knees and glanced down the row of classmates toward his best friend, Bud Wilhelm.

The school board president offered a greeting, followed by a prelude of rolling chords from the pianist. The sisters tensed when Mrs. Morris glided toward the center of the stage to perform her usual musical offering. Inwardly, each was relieved this was the last commencement ceremony they would have to attend and thus the last time they would silently bare the hurtful reminder of Mrs. Morris's solo at Margaret's funeral. The seven years since Margaret's death had not been kind to Mrs. Morris's singing voice, which had developed a quavering reediness. However, it was obvious that Mrs. Morris did not recognize the diminished quality of her vocal abilities. When the solo concluded, she lingered at center stage, basking in the smattering of polite applause, until the school board president cleared his throat for the second time.

When it seemed that the entire audience was fluttering commencement programs before their faces or mopping their brows with already damp handkerchiefs, the superintendent began to confer the diplomas. At the announcement of his name, Bill confidently crossed the stage, accepted the ribbon-bound parchment scroll, and returned to his seat. Flora twisted her handkerchief in her lap, Minola shrank down in her seat, and Ella's cheeks flushed crimson. The sisters felt certain that everyone in the auditorium knew the shameful secret: Bill's diploma was blank.

Bill's graduation picture

*****

The unusually warm weather ripened the strawberries in a rush, causing the picking season to leap-frog its usual gradual start and gallop headlong into a harvest at its peak. Even with the marketing of the berries now being handled by the jobber, Mr. Buckingham, Papa was tense and under pressure. He sent Bill on repeated trips into Monroeville to assemble a sufficient crew to pick the perishable crop. In the fields, Papa stepped quickly across the rows, pausing occasionally to part the leafy foliage to assess the condition of the burgeoning berry crop and direct the crews accordingly. He barked stuttered reprimands when he spotted carelessness among the workers, since he could not tolerate spilled berry baskets or misplaced footing that crushed the fruit. To keep ahead of the pickers, Papa was in a constant state of knocking down the packing shed and hastily reconstructing it where the crop was ripest and the picking intense. He hurried between the barn and packing shed, transporting empty quart baskets and carriers to the field and retrieving filled shipping crates to be stored in the cool recesses of the barn until morning.

In the midst of this fevered activity, Papa lost one of his reliable, if not enthusiastic, crew members. To complete her teaching certificate, Minola was required to attend a six-week educational course at Bowling Green State University. Bill drove his sister to the interurban station one morning after the picking crew had settled in for another long, hot day in the fields. Mary Zipfel, also a County Normal School product seeking to finalize her certificate, was waiting for Minola at the station. The two young women had agreed to room together for the duration of the summer session.

Minola watched the flat, rural landscape slip past the windows of the westbound rail car. At times, she spotted laborers in the fields, and she empathized with their tired muscles, aching backs, and sweating brows under the relentless glare of the unforgiving sun. Minola was grateful for the career obligation that excused her from the drudgery of the strawberry fields.

* * * * *

The staccato of pounding hammers drifted across the fields from George and Bertha's house. Walter's recent announcement of his intentions to wed Marian Farrell, a Cleveland native, had launched Bertha into a whirl of remodeling. After assessing their comfortable but aging home through the eyes of her city-born future daughter-in-law, Bertha decried the house's lack of modern amenities, in particular, indoor plumbing. Rosie was pleased with her mother's campaign to upgrade the facilities. Ever since she had found Old Man Scheidt dead in the outhouse, Rosie had shuddered whenever she approached the privy.

In addition to a modern bathroom, the renovation included a furnace as well as a new parlor added on to the front of the house, where Rosie's massive piano would be prominently featured. The two large windows of the new parlor framed a door to the front porch. Bertha envisioned a veranda-style expanse that stretched across the entire westward face of the house. However, this grand structure never materialized, and the front parlor door led nowhere but down, since no steps were installed.

The Seibel sisters privately commented that a house without a front porch was as incomplete as the Great Sphinx of Egypt, which was missing its nose. Mama was less kind in her remarks, and she blasted Papa with reminders of George and Bertha's ownership of the house that was meant to be hers. Despite her clouded mental condition and inability to remember recent family events, Mama's mind clung to the long-ago loss of the house she coveted.

* * * * *

After graduation, Bill and his friend Bud Wilhelm pooled their meager funds and purchased a broken-down Model T Ford. They spent hours in the farmyard, propped on their elbows under the ancient relic's hood. By the end of the summer, their tinkering had produced the desired effect—an engine that would operate most of the time.

One evening after supper, Bill lingered at the kitchen table while Papa finished his coffee and Flora washed dishes in the drysink. "Me and Bud have a plan," Bill announced.

Papa studied Bill over the rim of his mug. "What kinda plan?" he asked warily as he wiped the remaining coffee from his mustache with the back of his hand.

"We're gonna drive out west. Head to California."

Papa reared back in his chair as if he had been punched in the chest. While he had been quite passive about Bill's failure to graduate, he was not receptive to his son's travel plans. "California!?" Papa thundered. "W-w-why you gotta go to California?"

"Me and Bud are gonna look up some Monroeville people, see if we can find work," offered Bill with a shrug of his shoulder.

"You d-d-don't need to go clear to California to find work—there's plenty right here on the farm," Papa stormed, drumming his shortened index finger on the kitchen table for emphasis. "This entire farm is yours to take over, and it's high time you get started!"

A look of disgust flashed briefly across Bill's face as he listened to Papa outline a destiny of unrelenting farmwork. "But I want an adventure for once in my life," Bill said with exasperation. "I ain't been anywhere but here in Ohio. I wanna see what's out there." He waved his arm expansively toward the west.

"Out there! Out there! Why you gotta have an adventure *out there*?" Papa blustered as he rose from the table, signaling the end of the discussion.

Bill had long suspected that Papa would be unreceptive to his plan, so he delivered his ace in the hole, the counterpoint he knew his father could not refute. "But Papa, *you* had an adventure. *You* took off and went down the Mississippi when *you* were my age."

Papa's face turned an angry red. He could not dispute his own youthful desire to escape the farm, although his unrest had been due to a disagreeable stepfather and not unhappiness with farm labor. Papa stalked across the kitchen floor and stiff-armed the screen door, allowing it to slam behind him.

Flora stood with her hands in the soapy dishwater and watched through the kitchen window as Papa steamed toward the barn, gesturing as he delivered a rebuttal that no one would hear. She had been a silent witness to the struggle between father and son, and she could not imagine speaking back to Papa as Bill had done. Like Ada and Ella, Bill had a more casual relationship with their father, but for Flora, it was all about striving to please.

Bill threw his hands up in the air in frustration. "You'd leave, too, if you were me, wouldn't you?" he asked Flora's back, seeking validation for his plan.

Flora did not respond.

*****

With her teaching certificate secure, Minola returned to the Vredenburgs' in early September to commence her second year of teaching at Laurel Hill school. She had come to the realization that teaching was not her life's passion, but for now she would continue to save half of her one-hundred-dollars-per-month salary until her plans for the future could crystallize.

*****

In mid-September, Bill and Bud packed the old Model T with clothing, bed rolls, tools, cooking utensils, a piece of canvas to serve as a tent or ground cover, and a crate of canning jars filled with Flora's carefully preserved garden produce. Ella tucked a sack of cold beef sandwiches, a batch of biscuits, a jar of strawberry jam, and two dozen molasses cookies under the front seat. Knowing Bill's appetite, she wondered if the two wayfarers would get beyond the county line before delving into their food stores.

Ella and Flora stood in the side yard and watched as Bill climbed behind the wheel and nodded to his fellow traveler, who was stationed in front of the aged machine, prepared to turn the hand crank. After the engine roared to life, Bud leaped into the narrow passenger's space. Bill depressed the gear shift pedal and eased the floor lever forward. The aged vehicle jerked, coughed, and died. With a look of chagrin, the two young men exited their seats, propped open the hood, and tinkered with the engine's settings. On their second attempt, the machine cooperated, and Ella and Flora waved farewell as the old Ford popped and sputtered down the drive. Papa was conspicuously absent, having elected to busy himself at the back of the farm during his son's leave-taking. The machine passed Mama, who momentarily paused in her weed pulling to stare impassively at the two young men.

Bill eased the vehicle onto the road and turned in his seat for one backward glance at the homestead. As the old Ford chugged down Townline Road, Bud whipped off his cap and waved it wildly in the air as a final salute. The sounds of the two travelers' whoops and laughter echoed across the farm fields as they embarked upon a journey of a lifetime.

Bud Wilhelm & Bill

Correspondence from Bill was exceedingly infrequent. One letter indicated they had stopped at numerous locations en route, including the Grand Canyon. Bill described how he and Bud had stood speechless on the rim of the great chasm as they surveyed the vast expanse of strange formations and colorful earth strata before them. He acknowledged that tears had filled his eyes at the impossibility of a young man from the rural flatlands of Monroeville bearing witness to such breathtaking beauty so far from home. Bill felt humbled and privileged by the overwhelming wonder of the experience.

He went on to describe how the old Model T had struggled to climb the final mountain passes between Arizona and California. However, he and Bud had discovered that by driving the machine in reverse up the steep grades, they were able to overcome the problem of insufficient gear ratio and ascend the passes in an unconventional fashion. One could sense Bill's delight in recounting this mechanical adaptation.

Another letter announced their arrival in California. They had settled in the city of Ontario, just east of Los Angeles, where Bud knew of some former Monroeville residents. Through these contacts, the two young men found employment at an electrical appliance manufacturer. When they weren't working, they explored the sights of southern California and thoroughly enjoyed their independence. Bill's few letters gave every impression that he had found his Eden at last.

*****

Since returning to Monroeville last fall, Ella had continued to correspond with her former classmates and other associates from the Schauffler Missionary Training School. Many encouraged her to reconsider her vow to never again work for a church after the disappointing betrayal by Rev. Schenk. Ella could not be swayed. However, another of Ella's correspondents was Rev. Keppel, the Seibels' former minister at the Emmanuel Evangelical Church in Monroeville who had moved to Detroit after the acrimonious church split. He expressed disappointment that Rev. Schenk, a fellow man of the cloth, had practiced such underhanded behavior, but he reminded Ella of the biblical edict to forgive one's transgressor seventy times seven. Reverend Keppel suggested a different career path for Ella, one where she could minister to the needs of others through the daily guidance of her positive presence. He was affiliated with a children's home in Detroit, and he encouraged Ella to accept a position there as a house mother.

Ella read the letter over several times and then tucked it behind a tin of talcum powder on top of her dresser. Her immediate reaction was to ignore the letter's contents and continue to help Flora with the many obligations at home. However, she wrestled with her desire for meaningful employment and a steady income. Each morning when she stood before the dresser to comb her hair or pull a pair of stockings from the drawer, her eyes gravitated toward the envelope, and her thoughts were filled with the possibilities it represented.

One afternoon in late September while she and Flora peeled pears for canning, Ella confided the contents of the letter and her subsequent indecision. She did not state the obvious—that her leaving would place the yoke of family responsibilities squarely on Flora's shoulders once again.

Flora laid her paring knife on the work table in the summer kitchen and used the dishtowel in her lap to wipe the juice that ran down her forearms. "Why, of course, you should take the job, Ella. You have training, and you ought to use it," she stated firmly.

Ella studied her sister's face, fully comprehending Flora's generosity in encouraging her to leave the homestead. "Thank you," she whispered.

Reverend Keppel was thrilled to learn that Ella had decided to accept the position, and he urged her to arrive as soon as possible to assume her new duties. The hasty departure plans created a flurry of activity at the sewing machine, where Flora produced two new shirtwaists and remade a skirt into a more fashionable style for Ella.

In early October, Papa drove Ella to the train station. "Detroit's a long way," Papa said as he gripped the wheel of the machine and stared straight ahead.

Ella understood that Papa's statement was as close as he could come to expressing his feelings of sadness at her departure. "I'll get home for visits," she reassured.

That night, Flora lay awake in bed. The light of a full moon illuminated the room. She gazed at the two empty beds across from her, which had once been shared by Hermine, Margaret, Martha, and Minola. Through the archway in the adjacent room stood another empty bed that had belonged to Ada and Ella. Even young Bill had once slumbered in these rooms with his seven sisters. Now, she was the only occupant, alone again on the homestead with Mama and Papa. Flora pulled the quilt up around her shoulders, turned her face to the wall, and waited for sleep to overtake her.

Chapter 29
Rural Monroeville, Ohio
1926

THE ONE-ROOM LAUREL HILL SCHOOL had a sense of coziness during the winter months. The aroma of pancakes wafted from the children's clothing, giving evidence of the breakfast staple prepared by the mothers of Peru Township School District No. 3. Minola found the scent reassuring, proof of the caring homes her students came from. On particularly frigid days, the students tucked their lunch pails around the base of the coal-burning stove. This practice kept the pails' contents from freezing, which would be their fate if stored on the shelves in the unheated school entryway. On such days, the fragrance of lard sandwiches, sliced dill pickles, long-keeper apples, and perhaps the hint of a gingersnap cookie mingled in the schoolroom air.

Minola found the task of tending to the coal stove to be a nuisance throughout the school day. She often became absorbed in the students' recitations and forgot to feed coal to the fire until she was alerted to her negligence by the noticeably chilly classroom temperature. Then, she hastily appointed one of the students to lead the recitation while she hurried to the stove, crouched in front of the firebox, and attempted to coax the flames back to life. This required a fifteen- to twenty-minute regimen of delicately balancing the air flow to regain momentum in the bed of coals, patiently adding thin layers of new coal to feed the flames without smothering the fire, and finally tackling the messy business of shaking down the stove and removing the ashes. By that time, her students were often finished with their assignments and sitting idle.

To minimize the interruptions in the day's lessons as well as to relieve herself of the coal-tending tasks, Minola hired Kenneth Vredenburg, the eldest son of the family with whom she boarded, to be responsible for the stove's maintenance. Kenneth was a conscientious eighth grader who was proud to be selected for the important schoolroom chore; in addition, he was thrilled with the small weekly stipend his teacher offered as compensation. While Minola remained in charge of starting the fire each morning, Kenneth arrived soon after his home chores were completed, and he confidently took command of his duties. Not only was Kenneth diligent in tending to the fire, but at the end of each school day, he refilled the scuttle with coal from the pile on the north side of the school building and placed it beside the stove for Minola's fire-starting ease the next morning. In all regards, it was a happy arrangement.

One afternoon, the students finished their lunches, returned to their seats, and began their assignments. Minola called the oldest pupils to the recitation bench at the front of the room for a reading lesson. With full bellies and a cozy-warm classroom, the teacher and students alike fought the urge for an afternoon nap. Before long, Minola was shaken from her drowsiness by the presence of a student standing at her elbow. She turned to find little Leona Fischer pulling off the thick sweater that covered her school dress.

"Miss Seibel, I'm too hot. Can I move away from the stove?" Leona asked, her cheeks flushed pink.

Minola pressed her hand against Leona's forehead and studied the child's face for signs of illness. "Are you sick? Do you need to lie down for a while?" Minola inquired.

Leona shook her head. "I'm just too hot," she replied.

When Minola turned to point out a temporary relocation for the child, she noted that some of the other students seated in the vicinity of the stove had also removed their sweaters or pushed up their sleeves. Her heart lurched in her chest. The oiled floor beneath the coal stove was starting to smoke. It was obvious that before taking his seat on the recitation bench, Kenneth had been too vigorous in stoking the coals. The excessive fire-tending had heated the stove beyond its capacity and brought the oiled floor perilously close to its flashpoint.

Minola swallowed her rising panic. "I think we all need to wake up a little bit," she said cheerfully. "Let's go outside for a game of 'Fox and Geese' in the snow. Coats on, everyone."

The students leaped from their desks and chattered with excitement as they crowded toward their cloaks in the entryway. They did not question the unexpected recess so soon after their lunch break. While the children were donning their winter attire, Minola hurried about the classroom and opened all the windows to allow cooling air to flow toward the overheated stove. She joined the children in the schoolyard, where their happy shouts indicated they were unaware of the catastrophe that had been averted.

* * * * *

Martha had found her true calling in nursing. Her patients loved her radiant smile, cheerful demeanor, and diligent concern for their comfort. In addition to the joy Martha found in patient-care, there was also the satisfaction of having fulfilled her sister Margaret's career ambition, which had been cut short by the Spanish influenza. Martha cherished this special accomplishment. She also enjoyed having her own income after years of stringing together odd jobs, begging funds from Papa, and accepting aid from her financially strapped sisters.

Besides private-duty assignments, Martha also picked up shifts at a Cleveland hospital. Her beauty did not go unnoticed by some of the hospital's physicians. After a few dates, Martha declared all doctors insufferable and swore off further social interactions with males in the medical profession. Instead she enjoyed her circle of friends, who played marathon games of bridge and sometimes went dancing. The dancehall atmosphere of furtive hip flasks circulating bootleg gin did not appeal to Martha, so she often invited her friends to Mrs. Maybaugh's house, where she boarded. The young women pushed back the furniture in the parlor and dropped the needle of the Victrola on "Yes Sir, That's My Baby." They practiced the rapid footwork, fast kicks, and swinging arms of the Charleston, which was at its height of popularity. Martha, who had always struggled with the intricacies of dance steps, found the loose and frantic Charleston easier to master. She was encouraged in her progress by her friends' comments of "Now you're on the trolley!" Mrs. Maybaugh sat on the velvet settee and laughed and clapped at the youthful exuberance displayed by Martha and her friends.

While Martha was not a practitioner of the styles worn by flappers and jazz babies, she did follow the latest fashions. To the best of her abilities, she adopted the trends into her wardrobe, including dropped waistlines, shorter hems, cloche hats, and T-bar Mary Jane shoes. She challenged Flora's sewing skills with a request to remake her winter coat into a stylish wrap-over that fastened with a huge button at the hip. It was topped with a shawl fur collar that Martha triumphantly purchased after saving her money for months.

Martha in 1920s style

*****

With all of her siblings living away from the homestead, Flora was lonely for female companionship. She and Ada chatted by phone, but Ada's busy farm life and three small children did not allow time for lengthy conversations nor frequent visits. Flora's attendance at church events, choir practice, League meetings, and Grange functions put her in the near-constant company of cousin Rose. Before long, those outside the community who did not know the Seibel families assumed the two women were sisters, much to Flora's regret.

Because the thirty-seven-year-old Rose had never learned to drive, she relied upon Flora for transportation to their mutual activities. In addition, Rose orchestrated shopping excursions to neighboring towns, with Flora as the chauffeur and reluctant companion. One day, the two women arrived in Norwalk shortly after the stores had opened. Rose insisted on visiting each establishment, where she minutely inspected the merchandise. The proprietors were quite solicitous toward Rose and patiently answered her many questions while displaying their wares for her examination. However, these lengthy interactions usually ended with Rose unable to make a decision and thus progress to the purchasing phase, much to the consternation of the exasperated shopkeepers.

Eventually, the two women entered the Woolworth store on the south side of Main Street. Rose turned her attention to a display of costume jewelry, where she peppered the young salesgirl with requests to see each bauble. Flora seized the opportunity to drift toward a distant section of the store. Eventually, Rose abandoned the jewelry and moved farther along the counter to inspect some gloves. She dismissed the clerk and bent over the glass enclosure to peer at the selection.

The young clerk hurried to the sewing department and stood at the elbow of another salesgirl, who was cutting a length of fabric for Flora. She whispered into the ear of her fellow employee, "Watch out for that woman over there. I think she's a store examiner sent by the Woolworth Company to check up on us."

Across the counter from the pair, Flora could not help but overhear the furtive conversation. Her eyes followed the direction of the salesgirl's accusatory finger, which was pointed squarely at Rose.

"And this one's a doozy!" the clerk warned. "She asks to look at *e-v-e-r-y-thing*!" For emphasis, the salesgirl added an exaggerated roll of her eyes.

Flora inwardly cringed, knowing the two clerks would eventually spot her in Rose's company as they exited the store together. She felt like a marked woman. Rose's eccentric behavior rendered her unforgettable to shopkeepers, and Flora feared the dubious distinction would soon taint her as well.

After their day-long excursion, Flora returned to the Seibel homestead, where she collapsed on the day bed in the living room with a cool compress draped over her throbbing temples.

Flora

Her respite was broken by the jangling of the telephone on the living room wall. Flora groaned but dutifully rose and crossed the room to lift the receiver from its hook. Upon her mumbled "Hello," Flora was greeted by a blistering barrage from Emmaline Moss.

"Flora? Get down here right now and take your mother home!" Emmaline hissed. "She's at my back door, and I don't know what she wants or what she'll do. How *dare* you allow that woman to terrorize the neighborhood?!"

Flora whirled around, glancing toward Mama and Papa's bedroom, craning her neck to see into the kitchen, and scanning the view from the living room windows. Mama was nowhere to be seen. Flora realized she had not checked on Mama's whereabouts upon her return from the exhausting shopping trip; she had been too consumed with relieving her aching head. Papa had gone out to the barn to start the evening chores, and in that brief lapse of attention, Mama had slipped away from the farm.

Despite her clouded mental state, Mama remembered a time when she had had Emmaline Moss's rapt attention, as well as tea and cookies, while seated at Emmaline's kitchen table. However, Mama did not recall that Emmaline's hospitality had been a means of eliciting private family information from her guest. Mama had set off down the road to seek some companionship.

Emmaline was seated in her parlor, enjoying a radio program, when she spotted Mama crossing the front lawn and marching toward the kitchen door at the rear of the house. Emmaline had not forgotten the incident when Mama threw a kettle of boiling water at Papa. It had instilled a healthy fear in Emmaline, and she subsequently avoided having Mama as an unchaperoned guest in her home.

Emmaline leaped from her chair and dashed for the kitchen door, latching it just as Mama rounded the corner of the house. Emmaline backed away from the door, hoping she had not been seen, and tiptoed to the parlor, where she secured the front door as well. The kitchen door rattled as Mama knocked, waited for a response, and then knocked again.

Emmaline's heart pounded. She felt trapped within her own home. She peered between the lace panels of the north window, hoping to see Mama marching home across the fields. The kitchen door rattled again, indicating Mama's persistence. Emmaline hurried to the phone on the parlor wall and asked the operator to connect her to the William Seibel residence.

Upon hearing Emmaline's insistent command, Flora hastily replaced the receiver on its hook, cutting off her neighbor's angry tirade, and flew out the front door. Her head pounded with each step as she ran across the yard and onto the road. Flora dreaded what she would find when she reached Mosses' house. Would Mama be rooted in Emmaline's parlor, awaiting refreshments, or, worse yet, be wandering about the house, fingering all of Emmaline's precious china knickknacks? Flora winced as she envisioned the scene that would ensue when she tried to extract Mama from Mosses' and lead her home.

In the distance, Flora spotted the small form of Mama heading toward her on the road. Out of breath and awash with relief, Flora slowed to a rapid walk. She knew she would have to be delicate in how she greeted her mother. If Mama was already agitated, an accusatory tone would make her more disagreeable and uncooperative.

"Mama," Flora forced herself to call cheerfully as she drew closer. "I've been looking for you!"

"*Ach!* I went to pay a call on Emmaline, but no one's home," Mama replied with a shrug. She shielded her eyes against the late-afternoon sun and looked up at Flora. "Strange—no one home at suppertime."

Flora sensed from Mama's wistful tone that she truly had wanted nothing more than to visit with her neighbor, but Emmaline had panicked and distorted the innocent intent of the social call. Flora knew Emmaline would soon be on the phone to Mrs. Ordmann—with all the other neighbors on the party line eagerly eavesdropping—to relate how she had feared for her safety when the unpredictable Sophie Seibel appeared out of nowhere and pounded on her door.

* * * * *

The warm days and cool nights of spring brought the two-man sheep-shearing team to Ada and Albert's farm. Albert had fenced the heavily-coated animals in the barn, to be led out one by one to an open area where the shearers awaited. They quickly maneuvered each sheep onto its side or back, thereby rendering the animals helpless and calm. The men worked their hand clippers in a rapid motion, the *click-click-click* of the shears mixing with the bleating of the sheep. As testament to their skill, the men frequently removed an entire fleece in one piece without nicking the animal's skin.

When the shorn sheep were released to the pasture, they looked thin and stark white. At first they seemed stunned by their nakedness, but before long, a sense of liberation caused the animals to become frisky. They pranced about, leaping into the air and kicking their legs out behind them.

At noon, the two shearers took a break from their labor and flexed their aching hands and backs. Albert led them across the road to the porch at the rear of the house, where Ada had set out a basin of warm water, a bar of lye soap, and a clean hand towel. After washing up, the men joined Albert and Alfred at the kitchen table. They heaped their plates with creamed chicken over buttermilk biscuits, wilted dandelion greens, and cottage cheese topped with canned pears, followed by thick slabs of chocolate cake.

By day's end, the men had sheared the fifty head in Albert's flock. All that remained was to bundle up the wool for sale. As Albert and Alfred tied the fleece with twine, Mildred, Roberta, and little Russell chased after loose tufts of wool that blew about the farmyard and caught in the fencerow like milkweed fluff.

*****

By spring, Minola's plans for the future had crystallized. While she was satisfied with the rewards of teaching, she also felt inspired to help the less fortunate in a way that was not permitted by the confines of the county school system. In addition, her life's experiences with Mama had instilled an interest in the afflictions of the mentally imbalanced. Minola set her sights on pursuing a degree from the prestigious School of Social Work at the University of Michigan.

Armed with an acceptance letter from the college and twelve hundred dollars in savings, which was one-half of her salary from two years of teaching at Laurel Hill school, Minola submitted her resignation to Mr. Vredenburg, to be effective at the end of the term in May.

Next, she announced her plans to the family during a weekend visit at home. Minola lightly cleared her throat, looked around the supper table at Mama, Papa, and Flora, and declared, "I've resigned my position at Laurel Hill. I'm going back to school—to the University of Michigan."

"School!" Mama spit out the word as though she was expelling a cherry pit from her mouth. "All a girl needs to know she can learn in *die Küche* (the kitchen)." Mama had always clung to the traditional Germanic outlook regarding the role of females, and she saw no value in higher education.

Papa raised an eyebrow at Mama's outburst, then turned his gaze toward Minola. "How you gonna pay for this?" he demanded as he swiped his fork about his plate, collecting the last bits of fried potatoes. While Papa was an advocate of education for his children, he had long ago declared he could pay for nothing beyond high school. Papa had begrudgingly provided occasional financial assistance to Martha during her two years at Hiram College, and he now was wary of being tapped by his youngest daughter for years of out-of-state tuition.

Minola mentioned her savings and acknowledged that part-time jobs as well as loans would be necessary. Papa shook his head, remembering his own nearly life-long struggle with the farm loan. "Do you want to be in debt all your life?" he sputtered. "And what if your health fails? What'll you do then?"

Minola tipped her chin upward and replied confidently, "I'm strong and willing to work, Papa. I'll make a go of it, one year at a time."

Flora reached over and patted Minola's hand. She smiled reassuringly, which belied the sadness she felt at the impending loss of another sister.

*****

On the last day of school, the students surprised Minola with a farewell party, arranged by Mrs. Vredenburg, who brought along her ice cream maker for an additional treat. The children gathered in the shade of the lone schoolyard tree and took turns cranking the handle of the ice cream churn until it could be pushed no farther. With great anticipation, they huddled around Mrs. Vredenburg as she scooped dollops of the icy confection into paper cups and handed them to the students. The children drifted to various parts of the schoolyard to consume their treat. The boys seated themselves behind the schoolhouse with their backs against its weathered clapboards, while the older girls perched on the schoolhouse steps, their heads tipped together as they giggled and gossiped. The younger girls elected to remain near Minola and Mrs. Vredenburg in the dappled shade beneath the tree.

Laurel Hill schoolgirls

After the children had eaten their ice cream, Minola herded them into the schoolhouse to prepare for departure. However, there was one more surprise. Mrs. Vredenburg marched to the front of the classroom and presented a gaily-wrapped package to Minola. The students tittered with excitement at the surprised expression on their teacher's face. "Open it, Miss Seibel! Open it now!" they clamored. Some were so overcome with anticipation that they squirmed in their seats and anxiously leaned forward on their desktops.

Minola unwrapped the present and lifted an electric travel iron from the box. Mrs. Vredenburg explained that all of the Laurel Hill families had donated money to purchase the iron, which they were certain Minola would find useful during her years as a college coed. Minola was overcome by the generosity of these families of humble means, and she profusely expressed her gratitude. The enthusiasm of the children was slightly dimmed by the fact that Minola could not demonstrate the iron's heating capacity, since the old schoolhouse lacked electricity.

After the children and Mrs. Vredenburg had departed, Minola tidied up the classroom one last time. On her desk, she neatly stacked the books Ella had procured from the Dover Library book sales. Beside them, Minola set the chipped ironstone mug, to be used by the next young schoolteacher. Straightening the curtains, she recalled enlisting Flora's aid to sew the window coverings as well as to paint the pictures that now brightened the otherwise drab room. As Minola gave the oiled floor a final sweep, she reflected on her two-year tenure at Laurel Hill. She hoped the schoolroom improvements she had instituted would not be her only legacy. Minola had strived to instill a sense of possibility in all her students, but she had particularly encouraged her female students to pursue their educational goals, whether it was an eighth-grade certificate, high school diploma, County Normal School training, or college degree.

Minola exited the schoolhouse, pulled the door closed behind her, and secured the lock. Teaching at the Laurel Hill school had been a challenging and rewarding experience; however, she was ready to begin the next chapter in her life.

* * * * *

All through the summer, as they picked and packed strawberries, Minola and Flora conferred on Minola's wardrobe needs for college. While the 1920s had brought prosperous times to the nation, the cost of living was also high. Ready-made dresses were of shoddy quality unless they carried a price tag of thirty dollars or more, which was well beyond Minola's range. Martha sent a letter suggesting her sister include casual sportswear in her wardrobe, for the long walks and other outdoor activities that Minola would participate in while at Ann Arbor, similar to Martha's own experience at Hiram College.

After long days in the berry fields, Flora bent over the treadle sewing machine late into the night to produce three mainstay dresses for Minola: a powder blue woolen dress with pleated skirt and a cowl neckline and cuffs trimmed in beige; a pleated black-and-white-checked woolen skirt topped by a black velvet bodice studded with silver buttons; and a sheer pale-green silk dress for fancier occasions. All were complemented by the popular gunmetal-gray hosiery.

On a warm September morning, Minola boarded a westbound New York Central passenger railcar for the first leg of her travels. Her stomach churned with equal parts excitement and dread at the journey she had undertaken. In Toledo, she transferred to a second train that carried her to her destination city. Upon arriving in Ann Arbor, Minola claimed her trunk and arranged transfer to the MacEachron House, one of many League Houses operating in the vicinity of the campus. Because the university was inadequately equipped with housing for its coeds, having only three dormitories for females, a Women's League was instituted to oversee the housing and living standards for the growing number of female students. The League set a 10:00 p.m. weekday and Sunday curfew, extended to midnight on Friday and Saturday nights, for all female students, while the males were allowed independence of hours. The boys were provided with linens, but the girls had to supply their own as well as arrange for laundry services, which were an added weekly expense. The Women's League also set the prevailing wage of twenty-five cents per hour for those coeds who found it necessary to fund their education through part-time employment. The League attempted to regulate the number of hours that professors and their wives could extract from the low-wage help, but rumors of abuse were rampant.

Minola struggled to pull the heavy trunk up the steps to her second-floor rooming assignment. Checking the construction-paper nametags on each door, she finally located her own name beside a tag bearing the name of her new roommate, Lillian Woodley. Minola was sweaty and disheveled from the long train ride and subsequent tussle with her trunk. She exhaled wearily, opened the door, and tugged her unwieldy trunk into the room. Seated on the bed before her was a striking young woman whose strawberry-blonde hair was cut into a sleek, short Eton crop. It was the most modern of hairstyles and accommodated the era's popular and close-fitting cloche hats. Her legs were crossed, revealing stockings rolled to just below her kneecaps. "*A jazz baby*," Minola immediately thought to herself, as she recalled Martha's description of the young women who frequented dance halls and speakeasies.

Summoning her best cheer, Minola introduced herself. "Hello! I'm Minola Seibel. You must be Lillian." She pointed to their nametags on the open hallway door. "It looks like we're roommates."

Lillian looked up from the *Photoplay* magazine in her lap. Her kohl-rimmed eyes slowly assessed Minola from head to foot. Feeling self-conscious at the inspection, Minola pushed her thick bobbed hair behind one ear and attempted to smooth her rumpled skirt.

"So it seems," said Lillian, obviously not impressed with her assigned roommate. Tossing the magazine onto the bed, she pointed to a small adjoining room. "That's your room."

Minola looked in the direction Lillian was pointing. The annex was barely large enough to contain a narrow cot, small table, and chair. Minola would have to wedge her trunk alongside the cot, where it would serve as both nightstand and dresser. The only redeeming feature of the room was a window that overlooked the street at the front of MacEachron House.

Minola glanced around the larger room that Lillian had claimed for herself. In addition to a single bed with headboard, it held a dresser, nightstand, study desk and chair, as well as access to the only closet in the two rooms and the only entry door. Atop Lillian's dresser were her carefully arranged cosmetics, including an enameled compact, as well as a candy jar filled with lemon drops, a lacquered jewelry box, and a gilt-framed photo of Lillian's family posed in front of their large, impressive city home. Artfully draped across a corner of the dresser's mirror were a colorful scarf and several long strings of beads. The wall above Lillian's headboard was peppered with pages torn from magazines featuring motion picture stars, particularly Clara Bow, the "It Girl" of the era. In all regards, it looked as though Lillian had been in residence much longer than just a day.

Minola pulled her trunk into the small adjoining room and was struggling to wedge it into the corner between the wall and cot when a fashionably dressed woman swept through the door.

"Group bathroom facilities—how I detest such things!" the woman sighed as she pulled on her gloves. "Lillian, dear, let's…" she interrupted herself when she spotted Minola in the adjacent room. "You must be Minerva," she said as she crossed the room and held out the tips of her gloved fingers for a weak handshake.

Minola complied by giving the woman's fingertips a polite squeeze. "It's Minola," she corrected.

"Yes … well! Isn't that an unusual name?" the woman stammered. "I'm Mrs. Woodley, Lillian's mother." Looking about the room, she asked, "Did your mother accompany you as well?"

A bemused expression crossed Minola's face. She wondered how Mrs. Woodley perceived that one could overlook the presence of a third person in such a microscopic room. Perhaps even more ludicrous was the thought of Mama accompanying Minola upon her matriculation to college. "No, I came alone," Minola replied.

Mrs. Woodley continued to press for more information about Minola's hometown and family while revealing that Lillian's father was a banker and they resided in an upscale suburb of Chicago. The conversation served to emphasize the wide social chasm that existed between the two roommates. Meanwhile, Lillian retrieved the *Photoplay* magazine and idly flipped through its pages.

Mrs. Woodley checked her dainty gold wristwatch and announced, "Oh my, Lillian! We have just enough time to grab a bite to eat before I catch the train back to Chicago. I know the cutest little restaurant where we can go."

Lillian rose from the bed and stood before the dresser mirror to pull on a cloche hat. She carefully arranged the fringe of hair that peeked from beneath the hat's rim. Mrs. Woodley looped her arm through that of her daughter, and the two women exited the room. Minola listened to their amicable chatter, their voices receding as they made their way toward the staircase. Down the hall, squeals of delight emanated from the girls in another room. The phone in the hallway rang, and a MacEachron resident delved into a lengthy conversation, punctuated with laughter. Minola had the unsettled feeling of being a foreigner in a land where everyone else knew the customs, the language, and each other.

Minola on the University of Michigan campus

The first week of college was a whirlwind of attending orientation sessions, planning schedules, registering for classes, and reaching out for tentative friendships. For many of the residents of MacEachron House, it was also a time of great anticipation, as the sororities held their annual rush week to select new members. Each time the phone jangled in the hallway, a girl dashed to the receiver, hoping to hear the longed-for invitation to a preliminary dinner at the sorority house of her dreams. Minola listened to her peer's prevailing conversations about the importance of establishing oneself in the right sorority and thus achieving the proper social connections. Ineligible because she lacked hometown sponsors, a family legacy in a sorority, and financial backing, Minola regarded the rush week process dispassionately. As an outsider, she knew she would not be the recipient of a telephoned invitation.

Lillian, however, was being courted by several of the most socially prominent sororities on campus. Her name was called more than any other girl's to come to the hallway phone for yet another invitation to a sorority dinner. For others, the week ended in crushing disappointment when the hoped-for call never came, or they were rushed but not accepted. One girl in particular felt the sting of rejection. She had been a sorority member the preceding two years at a small college in Pennsylvania. The University of Michigan chapter invited her to dinner, assessed her, but in the end deemed her unworthy. Minola spotted the cast-off member quietly sobbing in the corner of the darkened MacEachron parlor at the conclusion of rush week. For the remainder of the school year, the selected pledges would continue to live in the outlying League Houses, but their identity as members of the Greek order had been firmly established.

For Minola, any hopes for social outreach were quickly set aside as the need for employment took precedence. By the end of the first week of school, the Women's League had obtained a position for her in the nearby apartment of Dr. Margaret Armstrong, a pathologist in a local hospital, and Miss Nina Preston, the head of the cataloging department of the university library. Minola's assignment was to prepare suppers for the two women. Thus, her own nightly meal would be provided, which was a financial relief. In addition, she was to clean the women's apartment each Saturday morning.

Unable to afford the expensive college textbooks, Minola was forced to depend on the library copies. Thus, each evening after washing the supper dishes at Dr. Armstrong's apartment, she hurried back to MacEachron House to collect her notebooks and walk to the Rhetoric

Library in Angell Hall, where she devoted several hours to studying. One evening as she gathered her materials from the make-shift desk in her tiny room, she overheard Lillian mention to another resident that she intended to spend the evening at the Rhetoric Library. Minola suggested the two walk there together. Lillian flushed to her hairline and murmured that she had had a change of plans. Minola walked to the library alone.

After a lengthy period of study, Minola returned the textbook to its shelf and took a break by strolling about the library. As she rounded a row of bookcases, there was Lillian, seated with her sorority sisters along one side of a long study table. Minola watched the young women as they tilted their heads together and whispered furtively or passed notes to one another. When one sister rose to leave, the rest of the group followed. Minola was struck by the insecurity of such a closed circle, which forbade even the most casual contact with a "barb," as the unaffiliated were known.

Minola gathered her notebooks and returned alone to MacEachron House. Upon opening the door to her darkened room, she spotted a red-hot triangular glow atop Lillian's study desk. Minola immediately recognized the source of the brightness—the electric travel iron that the Laurel Hill school families had given her as a farewell gift. Lillian had not asked permission to borrow the iron nor had she remembered to unplug and return it after the unsanctioned use. Minola was livid. While Lillian would not associate with someone of lower social status, she obviously did not hold such lofty standards about a "barb's" possessions.

Life with Lillian became strained, as Minola no longer attempted any overtures at friendship. With her work and study schedule allowing so little time for idle chatter and social outreach, Minola had no bonds with the other residents of MacEachron House. The sportswear Martha had advised her to pack was shuffled to the bottom of her trunk, since there was no one to take hikes with nor any time for such endeavors. In addition, Minola felt sensitive about her need for part-time work and its implied inferior status during a time of such exaggerated plenty, wild parties, and carefree existence. She came and went by herself, feeling more and more isolated.

To add to Minola's misery, a small crisis developed within MacEachron House. A meeting was called by the house's elected leader, who was charged with resolving problems and conflicts. All members of the house were summoned to the meeting, except for Minola and Grace, who were the subjects of the meeting. Someone had left a soiled sanitary napkin in the bathroom, and by deduction, these two residents were singled out as the potential responsible parties. Minola was aware of the meeting and felt low. Even though innocent, what chance did she stand against petite, blonde Grace, who had been sought by several sororities? She awaited the verdict with dread.

After the meeting, Lillian returned to their room, followed by the house leader, who informed Minola that the group had decided Grace was the culprit. It was pointed out by several residents that Minola would not have done something so unhygienic, since she bathed daily and always cleaned the tub afterward. Lillian looked stunned by the exoneration of her "barb" roommate. Minola, on the other hand, was overjoyed that justice had prevailed.

Autumn in Ann Arbor was long and lovely that year; the large old trees on campus were slow to change colors and drop their leaves. It brought to mind the dazzling autumn that had coincided with Margaret's death eight years ago, and Minola frequently found herself choked with emotion. In the evenings, as she returned alone from the library, the chirping of crickets in the nearby hedges reminded her of home. Minola longed for the familiarity of the farm and her family, and she struggled with a rising desire to flee from the strange, unpleasant experiences of university life. The only thing that sustained her during these lonely times was the stream of encouraging correspondence from her sisters.

The sisters at Ada's house.
Ada, Ella, Hermine, & Martha
Russell, Roberta, Peggy, & Mildred

One recent letter from Flora included a photo taken at Ada's house that fall, when Ella had traveled home from Detroit for a weekend visit. Minola had been crestfallen that she could not attend the gathering of the sisterhood, but the small income she earned from her Saturday morning cleaning job was too vital to forego. Instead, she carried the photo with her and gazed often at the dear faces of her sisters and little nieces and nephew.

One late-autumn afternoon as she was crossing the campus, Minola spotted a familiar face. It was Frieda, the flaxen-haired fräulein whom Aunt Bertha's bachelor brothers, Herman and Gust Loew, had brought over from Germany in 1921 to keep house for them. After Gust had convinced the immigration officials that he was not violating the Mann Act by transporting a female across state lines for the purpose of prostitution, Frieda was approved for travel to Ohio. There she settled into the brothers' farmhouse on a remote country road.

Minola reintroduced herself, and the two young women enjoyed a friendly chat. Minola learned that after five years of cooking and cleaning for the two solitary men, Frieda had advanced upon her toehold in America. She had gained citizenship and saved her salary to finance a long-held goal of higher education. Armed with her earnings and a hard-won command of the English language, she had entered the University of Michigan. Like Minola, Frieda also had had to procure a part-time job to keep afloat. She worked for a professor's wife, who took advantage of the low-wage helper by readily blurring the lines between part-time and full-time work. Because of the unseasonably warm weather that fall, the fruit and vegetable harvest had continued in abundance. The tomatoes had been particularly endless, and now in November, Frieda was still canning late into the night. After she carried the filled jars of tomatoes to the professor's pantry, she was faced with stacks of dirty dishes and a daunting kitchen cleanup. Frieda described her subsequent struggle to stay awake during class and to find study time. While other students complained of fatigue after a night of wild frat parties or excess gin sipped in the backseat of a roadster, students like Minola and Frieda were exhausted from long hours of work, the pressures of school requirements, and the lack of sleep. Weariness was their constant companion.

* * * * *

In early November, Bill and Bud returned home from California. Bud had spent the past year thinking about a certain girl he'd left behind in Monroeville, and his heart called him homeward. Bill had grown tired of the monotony of the job at the appliance manufacturer. Although he enjoyed life in California, he could not afford to remain there without Bud's shared financial input. The two young men sold their derelict Model T and bought a pair of train tickets.

Flora was thrilled to have Bill home again. He eased some of her burden as Papa's "right-hand man" and helped to fill the void in the house created by the absence of her sisters. Papa was pleased that his son had returned to the farm to take his rightful place as the heir apparent.

Bill toiled alongside Papa in the fields for the remainder of the fall, once again plodding behind the mismatched team of horses while harvesting potatoes, cutting corn, taking apples to the mill, and hauling firewood. However, Bill's California sojourn had not erased his loathing for farm work, and the future stretched before him as endless days of labor with antiquated and make-do equipment. Bill felt as though he had never left the farm; in fact, he feared he never would.

Chapter 30
The Gfell Home
1927

THE LONG WINTER MONTHS offered a lull in farming activities and presented an opportunity for the Gfells to socialize with their neighbors. While threshing and butchering were community affairs, those events focused on the work to be done. Wintertime card parties, however, brought the neighbors together in a relaxed setting with plenty of time for visiting.

Ada and Albert took their turn hosting the monthly gatherings. The men played pinochle at the dining room table, which Ada had extended to its maximum seating capacity by inserting extra leaves. The women adjourned to the parlor, where their fingers rapidly plied crochet or knitting needles as they talked, since it seemed unnatural for a farm woman's hands to be idle. They shared recipes, remedies, and neighborhood gossip. Of particular interest was news about illnesses and deaths, budding romances, upcoming weddings, recently disclosed pregnancies, and new arrivals. Ada clucked her tongue in sympathy over the news of a neighbor woman who was dealing with a colicky baby. She glanced at her own three offspring, who were playing a marble game with the neighbor children in the center of the parlor floor. Ada was pleased with her little family and relieved to be done with childbirth and the demands of an infant.

A ripple of laughter from the men caused Ada to look toward the adjacent dining room. She saw Albert with his arm raised above his head, a playing card clutched tightly between his fingers. At almost forty years of age, Albert was still a handsome man, and Ada's heart fluttered at the sight of him, even after a dozen years of marriage.

With a one-sided smile, Albert brought his hand down swiftly and slapped the winning card on the table. Laughter erupted from the card players, and good-natured boasting by the victors melded with the groans of the losers. As the cards were reshuffled, the men's conversation concentrated on crops, market prices, and occasionally one player's recent purchase of a new farm implement or head of livestock. Since most of the men were tenant farmers, such acquisitions evoked endless ribbing about the good fortunes of the "millionaire farmer." The teasing was followed by sly questions regarding the number of bushels that had been held back from the harvest, referencing some tenant farmers' practice of withholding part of the crop yield to cover expenses unpaid by the landlord. Albert took more ribbing than the others on this subject, since it was well known throughout the community that his honesty was above reproach.

Midway through the evening, Ada set aside her knitting and slipped out to the kitchen to prepare refreshments. She cut inch-thick slices of homemade bread and spread them with rich, golden butter topped by slabs of headcheese. Coffee or slightly aged cider accompanied the sandwiches, with Alfred muttering that the cider was still a little sweet for his preferences.

After the guests had gone home and the Gfell family was fast asleep, Alfred arose as usual and exited his second-story bedroom. He shuffled down the narrow stairway, mumbling "God damn! Son of a bitch!" with every step. He made his way through the darkened house and down the cellar stairs. Ada's concession to Alfred's dependency was to allow his cider jug to be stored in the basement during the winter months; otherwise, she was firm that it remain in an empty horse stall in the barn across the road. After quenching his thirst, Alfred, or Unk as he was now called by his nieces and nephew, stumbled back up both sets of stairs, unspooling a ribbon of profanity throughout his travels. Of course, his nightly ramblings woke the entire household, but no one ever mentioned the disruption to their sleep. It was simply the way life was with Unk.

*****

Minola sat at her make-shift study table one Saturday evening before semester exams and watched with disinterest as her roommate prepared for a date. Lillian had been keeping company with Ted Zinn, a muscular, blond frat boy who wore a fashionable full-length raccoon coat. He zipped around campus in his sporty roadster filled with other fraternity brothers. Minola overheard Lillian happily confide to a fellow MacEachron House resident that Ted's fraternity received a standing weekend liquor order from their speakeasy source in Detroit, so his hip flask was bottomless. In all ways, Ted personified the era's "flaming youth."

Lillian carefully rolled her nylons below her knees, looped a long string of beads around her neck, and dabbed perfume on her lips. After a final inspection in the dresser mirror, she assumed her post beside the window in Minola's room, kneeling on Minola's bed to watch for the arrival of Ted's roadster. Lillian never bothered to ask her roommate's permission for such a liberty or apologize for the intrusion. Minola stared at the page before her, unable to concentrate while Lillian hummed the chorus of the popular song "Bye Bye, Blackbird" from just behind her chair.

"There he is!" Lillian squealed. Her heels tapped noisily as she sprinted across the hardwood floor, grabbed her beaded purse from atop the dresser, and slammed the bedroom door behind her.

Minola tipped backward in her chair and gazed out the window at the darkened street below. In a puddle of light from the streetlamp, Lillian skittered across the snowy sidewalk toward the roadster's open door, which Ted closed behind her. His raccoon coat swung behind him as he rounded the front of the vehicle and climbed behind the wheel. The roadster roared off into the night, and Minola returned to her studies with a sigh.

Later that evening, Minola stacked her notebooks on the corner of the study table, stretched her aching back and neck, and prepared for bed. As she buttoned the yoke on her flannel nightgown, the hallway door burst open and banged against the nearby dresser. Lillian bounded into the room just ahead of the midnight curfew. She twirled in a happy circle and grabbed Minola in a bear hug. "He kissed me! Ted kissed me—on the lips!" she gushed.

"Oh, did he?" Minola's voice was flat with disinterest as she held her arms stiffly at her side and turned her head away. Despite Lillian's perfumed lips, her breath held the unmistakable odor of gin.

Lillian was too caught up in her own tipsy happiness to recognize her roommate's lack of enthusiasm. She released Minola from the impromptu embrace and rushed out of the room, throwing open the door of the room across the hall to share her excitement with its occupants.

*****

On Saturday mornings, while her employers, Dr. Armstrong and Miss Preston, were at work, Minola let herself into their second-floor apartment to begin her weekly cleaning duties. Because the apartment was small and neither woman collected bric-a-brac, the task took only two hours, but the fifty cents that Minola earned for the job was vital to her finances. She paid special attention to tidying the women's bedrooms—straightening up the medical journals strewn beside Dr. Armstrong's bed and removing the fine layer of talcum powder that coated the top of Miss Preston's dresser. As she dusted and replaced each of the items on the dresser, Minola was reminded of how she had once stood on a chair to finger each article on Ada's dresser with childhood awe.

Occasionally, the women entertained dinner guests, with Minola acting not only as cook but waitress. Perhaps to atone for the extra work, the two women often invited Minola to join the group for their after-dinner discussions. It was an uncomfortable experience for Minola. The guests were usually much older and had intellectual interests far above the trivia that passed for discourse among the MacEachron House residents. Minola was compelled to contribute to the conversation but felt woefully inadequate. Nevertheless, at the end of the evening, her employers always thanked her for the graciousness she exhibited to their guests. They offered other favors as well, such as car rides in the countryside and invitations to worship with them at the Church of Christ on the opposite side of town. In addition, they insisted that Minola join them for their nightly meals at the gate-leg table in the dining room rather than eat alone in the kitchen, as was the usual arrangement for hired help.

One evening during supper, Miss Preston revealed to Dr. Armstrong and Minola that a treasured piece of jewelry was missing from the top drawer of her dresser. She lamented that the pin was a family heirloom and thus irreplaceable. Her heartbreak over the loss was palpable. Minola half-listened, since her thoughts were consumed by school assignments, her shrinking finances, and the ongoing challenge of juggling the demands on her time. In addition, she had never seen the missing pin and therefore did not associate herself with its loss.

As the weeks passed, Minola became aware of an undeniable change in Miss Preston's attitude toward her. While previously they had shared a warm and amicable relationship, Miss Preston now seemed cool and aloof. Minola wondered if her cooking, which had never been on the par of Ada or Flora's culinary skills, was the source of the displeasure. She was puzzled that Dr. Armstrong voiced no complaint about the fare. Slowly, the horrid realization dawned on Minola—Miss Preston suspected her of stealing the heirloom pin.

Like the incident in MacEachron House where she had been pitted against the popular Grace as the possible culprit who left a soiled sanitary napkin in the bathroom, Minola felt helpless to assert her innocence. If she insisted she knew nothing about the lost pin, wouldn't it imply that she was labeling Dr. Armstrong as culpable? Minola felt sick to her stomach over the predicament as well as her diminished esteem in the eyes of two women she greatly admired. She stumbled through the days in a tormented fog.

A few weeks later, Miss Preston invited Minola to be her guest when she and Dr. Armstrong attended the play "Hedda Gabler." Minola was surprised by the invitation and slightly hesitant to accept, but opportunities for entertainment were rare. During a break between acts, Miss Preston bent toward Minola's ear and whispered, "I have found my pin. It was wedged between two drawers in the dresser." She patted Minola's arm reassuringly, and her brown eyes crinkled as she smiled.

Miss Preston's happiness at recovering the lost heirloom was evident, but it scarcely compared with the relief that flooded Minola's body. She now understood that the invitation to the play was Miss Preston's means of atonement. Minola exalted in her restored innocence and sank back in the plush theater seat to enjoy the rest of the play.

*****

Ada bolted through the kitchen door and around the edge of the back porch so the children wouldn't see her losing her breakfast. She wiped her mouth with the edge of her apron. For weeks, Ada had tried to convince herself that her fatigue and queasiness were symptoms of a virus, but there was no denying the obvious—she was pregnant again. Ada was dismayed. At age thirty-seven, she had raised seven younger siblings and now three children of her own. Wasn't that enough? To complicate matters, Ada calculated that the baby would arrive in late September, a busy time of year on the farm. The grapes would be ripe and ready to be made into jelly, and a bounty of sweet corn and tomatoes would need to be canned. Ada shook her head and sighed. Despite the inconvenient timing, she could never resort to her neighbor Edith's solution of terminating the pregnancy with a well-placed hat pin. Dabbing at her eyes with the corner of her apron, Ada returned to the kitchen.

*****

Spring came slowly to the University of Michigan campus, with the stark trees gradually breaking forth into verdant shades of chartreuse. The incessant spring rains proved a challenge to the coeds, who had shunned any type of boots or overshoes. The impracticality of this fashion trend forced them to adopt odd walking styles to keep their footwear dry while navigating the wet sidewalks and numerous puddles on campus. However, no amount of toeing-in, toeing-out, or walking on tiptoes prevented water from splashing against the back of their legs and soiling the popular gunmetal-gray hosiery.

Eventually, the overcast skies and steady downpours gave way to a weak sun, causing the students to spill out of their residences to shake off winter's confinement and vent their youthful exuberance. At the same time, the college president, Dr. Clarence Cook Little, decreed that no vehicles, except those judged as essential, could be used by students within the auspices of the university. The affected students protested, particularly the fraternities whose social outings and furtive liquor runs were heavily dependent on their vehicles. But, youth is resourceful, and a few frat boys soon resorted to a substitute set of wheels: roller skates. The fad spread like wildfire, and before long the campus was teeming with college students roller skating to and from their classes.

Spring also brought the long-awaited May Festival—a campus-wide cultural event featuring concerts with guest soloists and noted musicians. Minola mentioned to Iris Shepherd, a pleasant young woman in her English class, that she planned to attend the Saturday afternoon concert, which showcased the classical music of Schubert. Iris commented that since she lived in Ann Arbor, her family was hosting one of the visiting symphony members. Because of this hospitality, the university had extended on-campus driving privileges to the Shepherds during the May Festival. Iris would be delivering their musical guest to Hill Auditorium and suggested she drop by MacEachron House to pick up Minola so they could attend the concert together.

On Saturday afternoon, Lillian had assumed her usual position—kneeling on Minola's bed with her elbows propped on the open window frame—as she idly scouted the street below. "Wow!" Lillian exclaimed when she spotted a shiny black Cadillac edging to the curb. "Wonder who's the lucky tomato getting picked up for a ride in <u>that</u> swanky-swell?"

Before Minola could glance out the window at the object of her roommate's envy, Lillian announced, "O-h-h-h, it's Iris Shepherd's car!" Her voice was ripe with admiration. "She must be here for Sylvia—they're both Pi Phi's."

Minola had no prior knowledge of Iris's sorority affiliation or her top-of-the-line transportation; however, she did not reveal her surprise at this information. Instead, Minola pulled on her dress gloves and stated matter-of-factly, "She's here for me."

Lillian's head whipped around. "For *you*!?" she guffawed. Minola donned her hat and turned toward the door, causing Lillian to exclaim in disbelief, "But Iris was rushed by every sorority on this campus! She's … she's a Pi Phi, for God's sake!" The implication of Lillian's statement was obvious—how could a "barb," an unaffiliated working girl, rate the friendship of one who occupied such a lofty position in the Greek social tier?

When Minola reached the street, she was warmly greeted by Iris. As the two young women climbed into the waiting Cadillac, Minola turned and waved cheerily to Lillian, who was watching from the window with her mouth agape.

The following week, the campus was abuzz with the news of Charles Lindbergh's successful nonstop solo flight to Paris. It was a heady time, fueled by a booming economy and a sense that anything was possible, even trans-Atlantic flight. America was a nation on the rise!

As the semester drew to a close, students made plans for the summer. Lillian mentioned nonchalantly that her family would be staying at their lakeshore cottage to escape the heat of the city, although it would be dreadfully boring without the excitement of dance halls, frat parties, and Ted. She was already looking forward to returning to campus in the fall, when she would move into the sorority house and resume her active social life.

The two roommates were only too happy to separate, with Minola electing to stay on campus and attend summer classes. However, she decided to vacate MacEachron House and its many unpleasant memories. Mrs. MacEachron did not take kindly to losing the income from her boarder, and she attempted to induce a sense of moral obligation to remain. Minola pled her case to the matrons of the Women's League, who reassigned her to the Mason League House, a larger home with sixteen girls on the second and third floors. Mrs. Mason and her husband prepared and served meals for the girls in a family-style setting. Minola would be employed as the house waitress, receiving meals and a reduced room rate in addition to her salary. The Women's League had also found Minola a part-time job doing the ironing for a professor's wife. Minola regretted leaving the employment of Dr. Armstrong and Miss Preston; however, her finances dictated that she seek a more profitable situation. Despite her frugality, Minola had nearly depleted the twelve hundred dollars in savings that had bankrolled her college education thus far.

Minola was assigned to share a room at the rear of the third floor with another working girl, Irene Atwell, who operated the elevator at the Betsy Barbour House. After the unpleasant experiences with Lillian, Minola was filled with trepidation about the trials she may face with a new roommate. However, tall, slim Irene was a breath of fresh air. She was open, friendly, and unconcerned by the college caste system or the trends of the day. While most coeds wore their hair in a fashionable bob, Irene piled her dark and abundant locks in an elaborate upswept arrangement. She was refreshingly independent in her social contacts as well, circulating freely among all the personalities in Mason House. She looped her arm through Minola's and pulled her along to other residents' rooms, to be included in the talk and laughter. Irene did not settle down to study until well after midnight, which forced Minola to adapt her evening schedule as well. This was a hardship, since Minola had to rise early to serve breakfast, but it was a sacrifice she was willing to make. It felt good to be included, to have friends, and to put behind her the grim, lonely days as an outcast.

Irene was a music major, and she often practiced her assignments on the piano in the reception room off the Mason House entrance hall. Despite her training, Irene loathed classical music and was much more interested in the popular tunes of the day. Consequently, she would begin the evening's concert by acquiescing to Minola's request for Brahms, Beethoven, and Liszt, but before long she had segued into something upbeat and jazzy. Often it was the popular song "Hallelujah" from the current Broadway production "Hit the Decks." As much as Minola loved the baroque requiems, she found herself humming the song's peppy refrain, "Sing hallelujah, halle-halle-lu-jah, helps you shoo the blues away."

In addition, Mr. Mason, whom the residents had dubbed "Two-Gun Charley" for his imaginative tales of the Old West, retired to the reception room each evening to smoke his pipe. There, he regaled anyone within earshot with tales of outlaws and gunslingers. His musical request was for "Lorena," which was too sad and slow for Irene's taste. Soon she had morphed the mournful song into the bouncy "Buffalo Gals," while "Two-Gun" droned on and on about shootouts, bank holdups, train robberies, and daring escapes. It made an odd mixture of nightly entertainment.

* * * * *

Mama had been on a rampage for months. In the spring, she had circled behind the barn in a weed-pulling frenzy and ripped up a swath of newly-planted strawberries before she was discovered. Papa vented his anger by mumbling to himself and occasionally gesturing in frustration as he surveyed the damage. During the height of strawberry season, Mama had purchased an overpriced and unneeded pair of scissors from a peddler who arrived when she was in the house alone. Now, on a ninety-degree day in July, the Seibels traveled to the Gfell farm to help with the threshing. While Papa and Bill toiled alongside Albert, Unk, and the neighbor men in the fields, Flora and Mama joined Ada in the kitchen to prepare the hearty noontime meal. However, Mama could not be induced to settle into her familiar groove of peeling potatoes. Instead, she wandered the yard, picking up sticks, plucking weeds, and expending her boundless energy in otherwise unproductive activities. Ada's feet were swollen and sore due to her pregnancy, the summer heat, and the long hours of standing in front of the cookstove. With regularity, she limped to the kitchen screen door to monitor Mama's whereabouts. When Mama was not within sight, Ada sent the children to check on her activities. It was an unwelcomed additional task on an already demanding day. Ada firmly understood why Flora expressed a longing for a set of eyes in the back of her head.

* * * * *

Once a week, Minola hurried to the home of Professor Anderson to do the ironing for his wife. To Minola's dismay, the stack of ironing consisted mainly of the professor's white shirts, which were the most difficult of all pressings. Too much time spent creasing the sleeve could scorch the fabric and ruin the shirt. Keeping the starched collar from wilting was also an art. Mrs. Anderson demonstrated the proper technique for producing perfectly pressed white shirts, and then she sat in a nearby chair and talked nonstop during each ironing session. Whenever she reached the climax of her stories, she opened her eyes wide to emphasize her concluding remark, "And the upshot of it was…!" Minola was uninterested in the tales and responded with a polite "I see" or "Is that so?" as she rapidly wielded the iron. She wondered why Mrs. Anderson could not do the ironing herself, since she had the skills and certainly the ample time. Minola concluded that part of the purpose for her employment was companionship. Mrs. Anderson was so pleased with Minola's efficiency and capacity for listening that she increased her wages, not realizing her employee's speed was a means of minimizing the time spent as the captive audience of an overly chatty professor's wife.

As the end of the summer session approached, Minola assessed her finances. Despite her industrious work schedule and a miser-like grip on her cash flow, she found herself without the funds to pay for the upcoming fall semester. Minola agonized over her situation and debated where she could turn for a much-needed loan. Finally, with a bruised sense of independence, Minola decided she would have to ask Papa for help.

* * * * *

On a late-August afternoon, Flora slipped a pan of sour cream cake batter into the cookstove. Minola was coming home for a two-week break from her college studies, and Flora wanted to surprise her with a special dessert. To top each cake slice, Flora planned to crush, sieve, and sweeten the last of the blackberry harvest into a deep-purple sauce. As she bustled about the summer kitchen, Flora was thankful for the unseasonably cool weather, which made cake baking a bearable task on a summer day.

Papa slowly ascended the back porch steps, stopping to pull his handkerchief from his pants pocket and mop his brow. He felt slightly nauseous and dizzy, and his legs seemed heavy. He decided he would lay down on the daybed in the living room after he delivered the quart basket of blackberries that Flora had requested. Surely these unsettling sensations would pass after a little rest. As Papa reached for the handle on the summer kitchen door, two doorknobs floated before his eyes. He blinked and shook his head to clear his vision, but a piercing pain throbbed in his temple. He pinched his eyes closed and waited for the throbbing to lessen. Groping for the door handle, Papa opened the screen door and shuffled into the summer kitchen. "Here's the last of the blackberries," he mumbled as he scraped a chair away from the work table. Before he could drop heavily onto its seat, his legs buckled beneath him and Papa collapsed to the floor. The quart basket tumbled to the rough wooden floorboards, sending blackberries rolling in all directions.

"Papa!" Flora screamed as she dashed across the room. Kneeling beside her father, Flora took his face between her hands. "Papa, what's wrong?" She lightly patted his cheeks. "Can you hear me? Papa! What happened? Please, please, talk to me," she begged.

Papa's eyelids fluttered and his mouth opened, but no words came out. He felt as though he were at the bottom of a well, where a distant voice echoed and reverberated, but he was powerless to respond. He could see the outline of a form hovered over him, but the face was indistinct. Papa closed his eyes and sank deeper into the well.

Flora scrambled to her feet and turned in a frantic circle, momentarily unable to determine the proper course of action. Thoughts crashed through her brain. *Help—I need some help! What field is Bill working in? When was the last time I checked on Mama? Dr. Gilman—I must call Dr. Gilman! Don't let the cake burn. I need to get some help!* After what seemed like an eternity of paralyzing indecision, Flora's thoughts cleared and she ran for the rope that hung from the old school bell atop the summer kitchen roof. She pulled with all her might until the old bell swung wildly in its housing, sending out peals of emergency. The only sound Flora could hear was the pounding of her heart as it thundered in her ears. *Is the bell working? Did it ring at all? Have the vines overgrown the bell and choked its movements? Why isn't Bill here yet? What is Mama getting into? Gotta keep an eye on the cake! Papa, please don't die!*

Bill was plowing down the old plants in the waning strawberry field when he thought he heard the urgent clanging of the school bell. It was a rarely-used summons, so he reined the team to a halt and listened to be sure he hadn't mistaken the jingle of the horse harnesses for the sound of the bell. As he stood with his head cocked, the distinct *clang-bang* of the Seibel alarm system floated across the fields. Bill dropped the reins and bolted for the house. "Must be a problem with Mama," he thought as he ran. "It's always Mama."

Flora rushed back to Papa's side. His limbs were moving randomly and he wore a blank expression. "Papa, don't move. Don't try to get up. I'm going to call Dr. Gilman," Flora panted, her throat tight with fear. She rose and pivoted toward the screen door, letting out a small gasp when she found Mama standing directly behind her. In the panic of tending to Papa, Flora had not heard Mama enter the summer kitchen.

Mama's brow was furrowed as she looked beyond her prostrate husband to the blackberries strewn on the summer kitchen floor. "*Ordentlich und sauber* (Neat and tidy)," she muttered. Mama hurried past Flora toward the spilled bramble fruits. Clutching the corners of her apron to create a temporary basket, Mama proceeded to pick up the errant blackberries.

Flora knew it was useless to dissuade Mama from a tidiness mission. As she threw open the screen door and scrambled across the porch to the kitchen, Flora spotted Bill racing across the farmyard. "Hurry, Bill! It's Papa! He's collapsed on the summer kitchen floor!" she shouted before continuing her dash to the phone on the west wall of the living room.

When Dr. Gilman arrived, he knelt beside his patient and performed a preliminary examination. Papa's face was ashen, and he looked older than his sixty-six years. "It's a stroke," the doctor announced. "Hard to say how damaging. Only time will tell. He'll need plenty of rest if he's to recover." The doctor cast a meaningful eye toward Mama before asking Flora, "Do you have a room where he can rest quietly and not be disturbed?"

Bill and Flora created a makeshift convalescent center in the parlor. They carried in the daybed from the living room and consciously avoided placing it between the two windows on the west wall, where Margaret's casket had stood on the day of her funeral. Papa's stroke had freshened the memories of that painful loss, and neither sibling could bear the thought of recreating a scene so reminiscent of the mournful experience. Instead, they situated the daybed beside the window on the south wall, where it would receive ample light and ventilation.

Minola's long-anticipated reunion with her siblings was tempered by watchful waiting, whispered concerns, and great uncertainty about Papa and the future. Flora had salvaged the cake she was baking for her sister's homecoming, but it was overcooked, and no one had much of an appetite anyway, even though the neighbors arrived with a bounty of food.

Minola's concern over Papa was compounded by her financial situation. She had intended to swallow her pride and ask for his help with her education funds, but now she was beset with uncertainty. Night after night, Minola tossed in her bed, thinking of the fast-approaching deadline for paying the fall tuition.

One evening, Uncle Will paid a call on the family to check on Papa's condition. He was distressed to see the incapacitated state of a man he had always admired. At the end of his visit, Minola walked with Uncle Will out to his vehicle. As Will dabbed at his eyes with his handkerchief, Minola privately confided her own dilemma. Swallowing deeply, she asked, "Would … would you co-sign a loan for me, Uncle Will? I'll pay it back—every penny—I *swear*."

Uncle Will studied the earnest face of his niece. He recognized that life with his sister Sophie had not been easy for his brother-in-law or his nieces and nephew, but the Seibel family's difficulties had now escalated. "Meet me at the Milan Bank tomorrow," Uncle Will instructed. He gave a wink of reassurance before easing the vehicle down the drive.

The next day, Bill drove Minola to the Milan Bank, where Uncle Will was waiting. When the transaction was complete, Minola climbed onto the vehicle's seat beside Bill and studied the loan papers in her hand. Papa's query from the previous summer, when she had announced her college plans, rang in her ears: "Do you want to be in debt all your life?"

In his coma-like state, Papa drifted between comforting and fright-inducing dreams. At times, he was back on the Mississippi River, with the waves lapping gently against the side of the skiff as he fished the muddy waters. At other times, he was riding the rails, his feet dangling from an open boxcar door as the countryside slipped past, or he was perched at the top of a ladder, harvesting oranges in the sunny citrus groves of Florida. He dreamt he was working in his own fields, strong and able, or peddling the unmarketed strawberries as he drove the spring wagon on the residential streets of Bellevue, calling "Str-aw-berries! Str-aw-berries for sale!" But then there were the unsettling dreams. He was ill with the river fever and parched for a cool drink of water, or he was hopelessly lost in the backwaters of the Mississippi at night, with no sense of direction and surrounded by weird howls from the unseen wildlife in the inky blackness. At times, there were leaping tongues of flames that inched in his direction as Mama poured more and more kerosene on a cookstove fire, or she threw a hairbrush, a bread pan, or a teakettle of scalding water at him. In his dreams, Papa was immobile and powerless to defend himself, and his mind echoed with unvoiced screams for help.

Dr. Gilman made daily housecalls, and, as he predicted, Papa did rouse from his stupor; however, he was weak, unable to stand without assistance, and needed round-the-clock care. Fortunately, his mental faculties remained intact. The stroke had rendered Papa's voice soft and raspy, so Flora set the old handheld school bell from the Plank Road school on his bedside table, to be used to summon her. At night, she slept on a pallet in the living room and was awakened numerous times to tend to Papa and monitor Mama's nocturnal ramblings.

Martha hurried home to help for a few days. Her expert nursing skills were invaluable, but she soon had to return to Cleveland and her busy hospital and home healthcare schedule. Hermine and three-year-old Peggy also spent time at the homestead, assisting Flora with the many concerns.

Peggy & Flora

Ada, Albert, and the children came to visit often. One day, Ada stood with her hands on her hips and assessed the situation. It was obvious that Flora could not continue to shoulder the burden of Papa's care, oversee unpredictable Mama, and manage the household as well as many of the farm chores while functioning on night after night of disrupted sleep. Flora needed the aid of a sister. Ada, heavy with late pregnancy, could be of little or no help in the demanding care of an invalid; in fact, she would soon require nursing assistance herself. Hermine was needed in Cleveland by her own little family, and Martha would soon be taking a leave of absence from her work to assist Ada with the upcoming birth of the baby. It would be unfair to ask Minola to interrupt her education to return home. There was only one thing to do: ask Ella for her assistance. Ada knew that Flora would not seek help, instead insisting that she could bear the tremendous load alone, so Ada placed the call herself. Within the week, Ella had resigned her position at the children's home in Detroit and was on a train bound for home.

Papa, who had always been so stoic and seemingly detached from his children, would not let Ella out of his sight. He cried easily and expressed great turmoil over his physical impairment, having enjoyed rugged good health for most of his life. In particular, he was tormented by a fear of Mama. He recalled the incident when she had thrown a teakettle of boiling water at him, as well as the near conflagrations caused by her penchant for reviving a slow cookstove fire with a steady stream of kerosene. Papa agonized over how he would defend himself if similar situations arose. Ella reassured her father of his safety, but this sad role reversal was unsettling for them both, and Ella struggled to hold back the tears when she relayed Papa's concerns to Flora.

As the days passed, Ella and Flora settled into a routine of working side by side to manage the household and patient care. When their chores were done, they tackled a new project: constructing a rock garden on the south side of the house and accenting it with a garden gate. This activity kept them in the vicinity of Papa's convalescent room window, so they could listen for the clang of the school handbell, and allowed them to keep an eye on Mama as she rambled about outdoors. More than anything, it provided constructive busywork that occupied their hands and minds during these troubling days.

The farm chores now fell squarely on Bill's shoulders, a development he did not welcome. In fact, Bill saw no possibility of a future for himself off the farm. Papa's incapacitating stroke had cemented him to a life of labor at a job he loathed.

Ella by a trellis in the rock garden

The rock garden & gate on the south side of the Seibel house

* * * * *

With the distraction of Papa's stroke, the onslaught of ripe grapes, tomatoes, and sweet corn to be preserved, and the daily demands of her young family, Ada had had little time to prepare for the baby's arrival. On the morning of September 24, she and Martha were in the midst of retrieving the infant's layette from the trunk when the undeniable grip of contractions signaled the baby's imminent arrival. Martha sent Mildred, who was almost nine years old, outdoors to locate Albert. Next, she phoned Dr. Gilman to let him know that his services would be needed.

Albert hurried in from the barn, with Mildred on his heels, to find Martha walking Ada in a loop between the living and dining rooms. Ada's face was pinched in pain, and her hands kneaded a knot in her lower back. Albert put his arms reassuringly around Ada and held her close before gathering the children and ushering them out the door. He loaded Mildred, Roberta, and Russell onto the back of the wagon and drove them down the road to spend the day with the neighbor, Edith, who clucked her tongue at the inconvenience of having children underfoot on a Saturday, which was baking day.

The baby arrived in the early afternoon, with Dr. Gilman announcing, "Well, Ada, you've got another girl. Plenty of helpers in the Gfell kitchen!"

Martha gently wrapped the baby in a blanket and placed her in Ada's waiting arms. While admittedly she had been less than enthused about the arrival of a fourth offspring, Ada was overcome by the immediate love that bonds a mother to her child.

Martha hurried outside to summon Albert, who was already crossing the road toward the house. He had been sitting on a stool in the doorway of the barn, mending a harness and waiting for the news, when he heard the newborn's squalls.

"It's a girl!" Martha announced. She shaded her eyes against the glare of the fall sun and tried to gauge Albert's reaction. "You're not … disappointed, are you?" Martha asked cautiously. She was well versed in Mama's oft-stated preference for boys, and she wondered if Albert, too, held the same opinion.

A slow smile curved up from one corner of Albert's mouth. "How could I be disappointed in a little girl?" he gently chided Martha. As one of six brothers, Albert took delight in the novelty of daughters.

Dr. Gilman had just closed his medical bag when Albert burst into the bedroom, followed by Martha. In two long strides, he was at Ada's side and tenderly kissed her. Albert scooped the newborn into his large hands and studied the tiny face. "And what're we gonna name this little miss?" he asked.

Ada reached out to clasp Martha's hand in hers. "Martha," she announced. "We'll name her Martha."

Albert was already accustomed to his daughters bearing the names of Ada's sisters, so he was not surprised by the choice. "What about a middle name?" he asked as he gently bounced the baby.

The adults exchanged blank expressions. No one had given any forethought to a middle name.

"Jane," stated Ada, grasping a name from thin air. "It goes well with Martha, don't you think?"

All agreed that Martha Jane was a fitting name for the newest member of the Gfell family, but she would be called Jane to differentiate her from Ada's sister.

That afternoon, Albert retrieved Mildred, Roberta, and Russell from Edith's care. They were eager to see their new sister and to escape the disapproving oversight of their neighbor. The children crowded around the wicker laundry basket where the baby slept. Five-year-old Roberta studied the infant's face. Accustomed to the closed eyes of squirming newborn kittens, she asked her father, "Is she born yet?"

During Ada's laying-in period, Ella and Flora took turns coming to the Gfell farm to help Martha with the laundry, canning, baking, meal preparation, child care, and other household chores. From her bed, Ada listened to the efficient bustle and quiet chatter in the nearby kitchen. She laid her head back on her pillow and wondered what she would do without her sisters.

* * * * *

During Martha's absence, Mrs. Maybaugh welcomed a new boarder to her rooming house. While showing the young man around the premises, she paused outside the closed door to Martha's room. Mrs. Maybaugh launched into a glowing description of her absent boarder, emphasizing Martha's beauty, intelligence, warmth, and noble vocation.

By the time Martha returned to Mrs. Maybaugh's boarding house, Ray Barth was fully prepared to fall in love.

* * * * *

For Papa, the pace of improvement was slow and discouraging. One morning, Flora and Ella sat Papa at the side of his bed to dress him for the day. While Flora lifted Papa's leg, Ella slid a pant leg over his foot, then they repeated the process with the other leg. The sisters helped Papa to his feet, and while Ella steadied him, Flora finished buttoning his shirt and tucked the shirt tail into the waistband of his trousers. Papa could not reconcile himself to this drastic change in his life, from a strong and independent man to a weak and unsteady cripple who was dependent on his daughters. He stared straight ahead and in his soft, raspy voice proclaimed, "I wish I was dead. I wish I was dead."

Chapter 31
The Seibel Homestead
1928

HEBER GRAU dropped heavily onto the chair that Flora had pulled to Papa's bedside in the parlor. The old friend and neighbor propped his crutches against the inside of his leg. Heber had recently lost a foot to the ravages of diabetes, and the two men surveyed each other quietly.

"Guess you and me won't be ridin' the rails to Florida to pick oranges this winter," Heber observed, recalling a trip they had made when both were young, strong, and financially desperate.

Papa smiled wanly. "I ain't good for much these days, Heber."

The two sat in silent reflection on the changes wrought by time.

"You try gettin' around on a set of these yet?" Heber asked, patting his crutches.

Papa shook his head.

"It ain't so bad once you get used to it. Gotten so I'm pretty good at gettin' where I wanna go. Now I ain't quite so dependent on her," Heber cocked his head toward the kitchen where his wife Dorothea was visiting with Mama, Flora, and Ella.

Papa could not remember what it was like to move about freely, to feel useful. He still relied heavily on Ella and Flora for most of his needs, including transferring him to his three-wheeled chair. Papa eyed the crutches, thinking of the relative independence they represented; however, he still felt weak as a kitten.

The two men talked about the warm temperatures during the recent January thaw, which had interrupted neighborhood plans for butchering. Heber also shared community news that would interest Papa—which neighbor had purchased a new implement, a commentary on the items being offered at a local farm auction, who had a cow suffering from milk fever. At last, their conversation turned to crops.

"Who's gonna do your plantin' this year, Bill?" Heber asked. "Your boy gonna handle it all hisself?"

Papa thought about the exhilaration of turning over a shovelful of soil in the spring and inhaling the earthy promise of another growing season—an experience he would be denied for the first time in forty years. His eyes welled with tears. In a quavering voice he replied, "I don't know."

* * * * *

As Ray Barth descended the rooming house stairs, he overheard female voices in the kitchen. He stopped and listened. Mrs. Maybaugh was usually alone as she bustled about preparing breakfast for her boarders. Ray strained to overhear the kitchen conversation.

"And now that Mr. Stollard's recovered, they won't need me for overnight duty anymore," the young woman's voice explained.

"Well, Martha, it'll be a joy to have you here for breakfasts again," Mrs. Maybaugh replied, her sentence punctuated by the creaking of the oven door.

Since his arrival, Ray had caught only fleeting glimpses of Martha, due to her erratic hospital and home healthcare hours, trips to Monroeville to check on Papa, as well as her busy social schedule. From his position on the stairs, Ray noticed that Martha had placed her gloves and nurse's cap next to a particular plate on the breakfast table. Ray straightened his tie, gave his hair a quick slick, and checked to be sure his mother-of-pearl cufflinks were prominently displayed. He descended the remaining steps and ducked into the parlor, where Mrs. Maybaugh's prized African violets lined the window sill. Snipping off a deep-purple cluster, Ray entered the dining room and placed the offering on Martha's plate. He seated himself directly across the table and waited to share breakfast with the object of his fascination.

*****

Minola, her roommate Irene Atwell, and four other residents of Mason House sat stoically on hard wooden chairs in the main office of the Women's League building. Across from them, a council of coeds charged with peer remediation listened intently to the complaint brought before them. Genevieve, the studious and prim monitor of Mason House's third floor, had accused the six young women of repeated noise violations.

"I'm in charge of maintaining order on our floor, and I take my responsibilities seriously," Genevieve began, her back ramrod straight and her hands folded demurely in her lap. "But these six residents have been extremely disrespectful of the rules, and I would like them to be formally reprimanded."

When pressed for details to substantiate her complaint, Genevieve tipped her chin skyward. "They gather in Lenore's room, next door to mine, and talk and laugh until well past 10 p.m. If I'm very still, I can hear every word they're saying," she hissed.

The council president arched an eyebrow and inquired, "Have you asked them to be quiet?"

"Oh, yes," Genevieve confirmed. "As floor monitor, I've exerted my authority many times by rapping on Lenore's door and ordering them to be quiet."

"And, do they comply?" asked a council member.

"Yes, but it doesn't take long before they start up again. And the vulgarity!" Genevieve sniffed, pursing her lips.

Minola and her friends exchanged puzzled glances, while the council president furrowed her brow and cocked her head. She quickly scanned the document before her. "Vulgarity? But your complaint mentions only repeated instances of loud talking and laughing after curfew. What's the nature of the vulgarity charge?"

Genevieve's cheeks flamed pink. She squirmed in her chair and dropped her eyes for a moment, as though searching for words to rephrase what she found too distasteful to mention. Leaning forward, she whispered, "They talk about … you know … their philosophies on … on…" Genevieve wrung her hands in her lap, reluctant to repeat what she found so offensive.

"Philosophies on what?" the council president prodded.

"On premarital … *experimentation*!" Genevieve blurted. She shuddered as though sullied by merely saying the words.

Minola watched as the council members discreetly hid their smiles behind feigned coughs or upraised documents. Some bit their lower lips to maintain earnest expressions. She felt reassured that they, too, found this trial to be a frivolous exercise in hypervigilance.

The council president leaned forward, a conspiratorial smile playing about her lips. "And, what *are* their philosophies on … the subject?"

"Well, all of them are against it except one, who says an engagement ring makes a difference. That must be Lenore's opinion, since she's the only one of them who's engaged," Genevieve offered judgmentally.

Lenore's eyes opened wide, and she emitted a small gasp. She quickly moved to cover the small diamond engagement ring on her left hand.

The council president asked the accused if any of the allegations were true. Irene stammered, "Well, yes, I guess we do talk about *all* subjects, and perhaps we don't realize how much our voices carry. But we don't mean to be disruptive."

Genevieve assumed a posture of self-righteous indignation and waited for the council of coeds to mete out justice.

After a brief adjournment for the council to deliberate—and give vent to their pent-up giggles—the hearing concluded with the council president suggesting the offenders use the Mason House parlor for their late-night gabfests. She also cautioned them to be mindful of the volume of their voices. All charges were dismissed.

Minola gazed out the window at the swirling snowflakes and pondered the irony of the moment. Based on her freshman experiences as an outcast, she never anticipated she'd one day be on trial for over-socialization.

*****

On a chilly day in mid-April, Ella pushed Papa in his three-wheeled chair to the edge of the strawberry field that Bill had prepared for planting. Papa had insisted, despite his daughters' protests, that he oversee the planting of the new field, as he had done every year since planting the first strawberries on the homestead in 1902. After wrapping a quilt around Papa's shoulders and draping a blanket over his legs, Ella positioned his wheelchair on the east side of the barn, to offer some protection from the raw spring wind.

Bill pushed the wheelbarrow of strawberry runners, overwintered from the previous season, to the waiting field. Flora inserted a stick knotted with a piece of twine into the ground and unspooled the planting guide as she marched a straight course across the length of the field. Bill set out down the row, slicing his shovel into the soil and leaving a trail of shallow holes. Flora donned Papa's shoulder pouch and loaded it with strawberry runners. Handing a bundle to Ella, the two sisters followed after Bill, dropping a runner into each hole, pressing the soil over the plant's roots with the toe of their shoes, and progressing across the new field. After each row had been completed and the planting guide moved, Ella dashed back to the house to check on Mama before returning to her duties in the field.

Papa watched from his wheelchair, a sheen of tears distorting the figures of his children in the field. He yearned to pick up a spade and a bundle of strawberry runners and participate in spring planting, just as he always had. Instead, he felt weak and useless. He dropped his chin onto his chest and closed his eyes. Despite his lack of physical exertion, Papa felt as weary as if he had planted the entire field himself. When Ella returned to the near end of the field, she noticed Papa's fatigue and wheeled him into the house for a nap. Bill and Flora would have to finish the field without her, since Papa feared being left alone with Mama.

*****

Early on May 6, a Sunday morning, the phone on the Gfells' kitchen wall jangled, startling Ada as she washed the breakfast dishes. Albert and Unk were in the barn, hurrying to finish the milking and other chores so they could return to their parents' house in Monroeville, where their mother lay terminally ill with liver cancer. Ada wiped her wet hands on her apron and crossed the room, knowing that early-morning phone calls rarely bore welcomed news. Indeed, it was her father-in-law Solomon with the sad message that Louisa's struggle was over.

As was customary, callers were received at the family home, which was on Milan Avenue. Louisa's body was laid on a board supported by cement blocks at the head and foot in a bedroom adjacent to the parlor. While Albert bounced little Jane in his arms, Mildred, Roberta, and Russell peered from behind Ada's skirt at the body of their sixty-seven-year-old grandmother, a woman they had scarcely known. Unk, the four other Gfell brothers, and their families filled the parlor and spilled into Solomon's kitchen as a stream of neighbors and relatives came to pay their respects.

For Albert and Unk, the constant demands of a farm in the spring allowed little time to mourn the loss of their mother. There were crops and several gardens to be planted, animals to be tended, and soon the clover, timothy, and alfalfa to be cut and raked in the hay field. When Albert was a young student in the one-room schoolhouse in Standardsburg, a small settlement south of Monroeville, he had learned the poem "Maud Muller." He was partial to the poem, since he readily identified with the protagonist's task of raking hay. As he pulled on his work boots on haymaking days, Albert recited the opening stanzas of the John Greenleaf Whittier poem:

"Maud Muller on a summer's day
Raked the meadow sweet with hay.
Beneath her torn hat glowed the wealth
Of simple beauty and rustic health."

Unk did not require poetry for the long day ahead. Instead, he wrapped his cider jug in wet burlap and tucked it near his feet on the haywagon as he guided the team of horses to the field.

* * * * *

Minola's hunger for music persuaded her to join the university's Choral Union as it prepared for the annual May Festival, even though she doubted the quality of her second-alto voice. The requirement that each participant wear formal attire for the spring performance presented an impediment. Minola had no funds for such a purchase, nor could she bring herself to task Flora, who was already burdened by farm chores and Papa's care, with sewing a formal. She reluctantly resigned herself to dropping out of the Choral Union.

Minola's former employers, Dr. Armstrong and Miss Preston, continued to extend invitations for Minola to join them on outings or at theatrical productions. They confided that while Minola's replacement was a better cook, they still preferred the company of their former employee. During one outing, Minola mentioned the upcoming May Festival and her decision to drop out of the Choral Union because of the dress requirement.

Dr. Armstrong reared back in her seat. "You'll do no such thing! Come round to the apartment tomorrow evening. I have a dress you can borrow."

Minola protested, but her desire to perform in the May Festival, in combination with Dr. Armstrong's firmness, quickly dissolved her resistance.

The next evening, Dr. Armstrong opened her closet and pulled out a beautiful navy-blue silk georgette with matching slip. It was obvious the dress was brand new and had never been worn. Dr. Armstrong tilted her head back to assess Minola's stature. "Five-foot-eight?" she queried.

Minola nodded her head.

"Me, too," Dr. Armstrong confirmed as she thrust the dress into Minola's arms. "This should fit you perfectly."

Indeed, the dress was a perfect fit, since the two women were so similarly built. Minola's heart swelled with gratitude to her no-nonsense but gracious benefactor.

On the afternoon of the May Festival, the Choral Union filed into Hill Auditorium and surrounded the visiting symphony. Minola watched as the well-known cellist, Alfred Wallenstein, cast his eyes longingly over the countenances of the young women around him. It was an ill-kept secret that he had been a serial dater of the Choral Union's female members during the week leading up to the performance. A few of his conquests blushed self-consciously as he swept them with a libidinous gaze.

The famous operatic coloratura soprano Amelita Galli-Curci performed a powerful solo from the deeply affective Brahms' Mass, followed by the Choral Union's contribution, which included the requiem's sweet, sad phrase, "Lord, make me to know the measure of my days on earth." Minola's mind was carried homeward to the brief, measured days of Margaret's life and now to Papa and his infirmities. Her voice choked with emotion and her eyes welled with tears. She struggled to compose herself, lest any tears course down her cheeks and stain the front of her beautiful borrowed dress.

*****

Albert and Ada made a major step toward modernization by taking out a loan to purchase a Model A Ford. Albert detested carrying a debt, but with the upward swing of the economy, including climbing crop prices and the sixty cents per dozen Ada was receiving for eggs, he anticipated paying off the loan in a timely fashion. Albert also reasoned that a machine would facilitate the frequent trips Ada and the children made to the Seibel homestead.

While Mildred oversaw her younger siblings in the house, Albert gave Ada driving lessons in the farm lane that extended to the south end of the property. However, Ada's ease with handling the reins of a horse-drawn buggy did not translate well to the machinations of driving a vehicle. She quickly became flustered by the numerous adjustments required to start the machine—make sure the parking brake was set, push the gas lever down and the spark lever up, set the throttle lever one-third of the way down, turn the carburetor adjusting rod to the right and then to the left, put the gear shifter into neutral, turn the key on, pull back on the choke, press the floor starter button, and release the choke.

When the machine's cylinders were popping and the gears were eager to engage, Ada attempted the tricky coordination of shifting the hand lever while releasing the clutch pedal. The machine lurched forward and stalled. Ada set her lips in a grim line and dropped her hands into her lap in frustration.

Albert smiled and patted her shoulder reassuringly. "It took a while to learn the tricks of running a treadle sewing machine, didn't it? Well, it's the same with driving. Just keep at it. 'Fore long, it'll be second nature."

Ada gave Albert a skeptical sidelong glance and painstakingly repeated the numerous steps to restart the engine.

With Albert's patient tutelage and many balky practice runs up and down the farm lane, Ada eventually developed an uneasy presence behind the steering wheel.

On a Saturday afternoon in June, while Albert and Unk forked a cutting of hay into the barn, Ada bustled between the kitchen and the machine, packing the vehicle for a trip to the Seibel homestead. Hermine, Ralph, and little Peggy were visiting from Cleveland, and Ada did not intend to miss an opportunity to spend time with her sister.

On the back seat of the vehicle next to the window, Ada set a basket filled with a platter of fried chicken, a crock of hard-boiled eggs, a jar of bread-and-butter pickles, and a large pan of still-warm sugar cookies. She covered the food with clean linen cloths and topped the basket with a stack of snowy white diapers for Jane.

Mildred climbed onto the front seat and held baby Jane in her lap, while five-year-old Roberta and four-year-old Russell clambered onto the back seat beside the basket. Ada carefully performed the many steps necessary to start the machine. Taking a deep breath, she slowly released the clutch while shifting the hand lever.

Across the road, Albert paused in the open barn door and watched as the machine puttered down the driveway and onto Ridge Road.

With her tense body leaning forward, Ada gripped the steering wheel and studied the road ahead. As she approached the intersection with Sand Hill Road, Ada downshifted and muscled the steering wheel to the left in a hand-over-hand turn. When the car didn't stall out in the middle of the turn, Ada breathed a sigh of relief and concentrated on coordinating her hands and feet for the next shifting of gears.

Sensing their mother's tension, the children sat quietly and enjoyed the novelty of traveling via machine. They watched the passing countryside as well as the swells of dust raised by the vehicle's hard rubber tires.

At last, Ada eased the machine down Townline Road. At the curve near the cemetery, the vehicle hit a deep rut in the road. The auto's occupants as well as the basket bounced into the air, with the children whooping in delight. The basket jolted back onto the seat and tilted against the machine's frame, causing the stack of snowy diapers to tip precariously and then tumble out the window.

Knowing her mother was too intent on driving to be alerted to the calamity, little Roberta merely watched out the rear window as the diapers fluttered into the dusty road, leaving a well-marked trail behind them.

Upon arriving at the homestead, Ada coasted to a stop under a tree in the backyard, set the hand brake, and turned off the machine. She exhaled and slumped back in the seat, awash with relief.

"Mom," came a small voice from the back seat, "Jane's diapers are in the road."

"*Ach!*" exclaimed Ada as she quickly turned in her seat to confirm the absence of diapers atop the tilted basket.

Roberta and Russell were dispatched to search the roadside and gather the missing diapers while Ada and Mildred carried baby Jane and the food into the house.

The afternoon was spent in pleasant visitation under the shade of the trees in the front yard where they could keep an eye on Mama's wandering. Papa listened to the conversation of his offspring with an open interest he had not exhibited in the years prior to his stroke. His dependency had made him more connected, and he eagerly followed the everyday occurrences of their lives. The stoic and sometimes detached father of their youth had disappeared.

While the young children were busy playing croquet, Hermine revealed the happy news that she was expecting a baby in November. The conversation turned to plans for the new arrival, and Hermine assured her sisters that she had already secured Martha as her nurse. She confided that while Martha readily agreed to assist, Hermine had detected the hint of preoccupation in her sister's demeanor that could only be explained by budding romance.

Papa in his three-wheeled chair, Ella, & baby Jane in Ada's lap

Peggy, Roberta with baby Jane, & Russell in front of the Seibel homestead

*****

Summer brought a continuation of classes and on-campus work for Minola, as well as the ongoing dread of how she would meet the next term's tuition. Uncle Will agreed to co-sign a second loan from the Milan Bank. When Dr. Armstrong learned of Minola's financial concerns, she offered a loan of three hundred dollars, with no interest and no binding signatures. Minola recognized that a verbal agreement for financial arrangements was most unusual, and she was deeply humbled by the doctor's faith in her. Minola vowed that Dr. Armstrong would be the first creditor repaid after she graduated and gained employment.

*****

Ray Barth proved to be an attentive suitor. Through his job at the Cleveland branch of his family's Henry Vogt Machine Company where he worked to perfect refrigeration equipment for oil refineries, Ray had the means to impress. He showered Martha with tokens of affection, from lace handkerchiefs and fine linen stationery to bouquets of flowers. Martha often discovered chocolate bars tucked beside her plate at the dining table or, best of all, tickets to the symphony. She was swept along by the whirlwind courtship.

*****

A cool October breeze rattled the field of dry cornstalks as Bill fitted a metal husking peg into the palm of his hand and fastened its leather strap around his wrist. Grabbing an ear of corn, he slid the peg down its length, splitting the husk. Bill gave the ear a sharp twist to remove it from its husk and tossed it against the nearby wagon's bangboard. The ear of corn fell into the empty wagon bed with a hollow *thump*. Bill reached for the next ear and continued along the row of cornstalks in a cadence of *grab, split, twist, throw, bang, thump*. When a section of cornstalks had been relieved of their harvest, Bill made a clucking noise that signaled Tup to pull the wagon forward a short distance. The big, lazy horse was only too happy to stand for long stretches of time while aimlessly stripping nearby cornstalks of their leaves and performing minimal duty.

Bill let his mind drift to the upcoming weekend. He could ask Charlotte Denhardt, a local schoolteacher, for a date. It was obvious that Charlotte was crazy about him, and she eagerly accepted his invitations for an outing. Or, perhaps he could spend some time with his friend Bud Wilhelm, if Bud hadn't already made plans with his sweetheart. Or, he could do nothing at all, which summed up his existence. Bill felt dulled by the monotony of farm chores. Why bother getting cleaned up and going into town when the only thing he had to offer in conversation was his experience with antiquated farming practices? Bill angrily hurled an ear of corn against the bangboard and watched as the cob broke in half, sending a spray of golden kernels into the air.

* * * * *

On November 15, Hermine gave birth to a baby boy, Bruce Allen. Even though the Wordens' finances would now be stretched even tighter, Hermine's heart overflowed with joy—she had the perfect family.

It was comforting to have Martha in attendance at the birth. While Hermine recuperated, Martha took command of the household. As she efficiently bustled about the apartment, Martha gushed to her sister about the decisive and driven man in her life. She wondered aloud if she was capable of bridging the chasm between her own modest roots and Ray's upbringing in a well-to-do Louisville, Kentucky, family. In addition, there was the difficulty of explaining Mama's affliction to a potential suitor, something she had always avoided by keeping her dates away from the Seibel household. If she took Ray home to meet the family, would Mama's odd behavior cause him to reject her? The shadowy shame of Mama's mental illness weighed heavily upon Martha. She peppered Hermine with questions about her own courtship with Ralph, seeking clarity on how to balance a blossoming relationship against the peculiar reality within their family.

* * * * *

In the 1928 Presidential election, Herbert Hoover had been awarded a sweeping victory for his pledge of "a chicken in every pot and a car in every garage." Although he also promised strict enforcement of Prohibition laws, New Year's Eve revelers who managed to skirt the rules of social reform offered a tipsy toast to 1929. The nation was enjoying unequaled economic prosperity; surely the good times would be even better in the coming year.

Chapter 32
The Seibel Homestead
1929

MARTHA CHEWED her bottom lip as the interurban rocked its way toward Monroeville one February afternoon, carrying her and Ray Barth to a visit at the Seibel homestead. She had delayed this trip for as long as possible, but her relationship with Ray had grown serious; it was time he met the family. While Martha had told Ray volumes about her sisters and Bill and even Papa's debilitated condition, she had deliberately referenced Mama in a most fleeting and vague manner. However, the upcoming visit had forced her to reveal the truth about Mama's mental illness. Despite Ray's reassurances that nothing could dull his love for her, Martha worried that Mama would be under the throes of a spell when they arrived. It was humbling enough to bring Ray home to the scene of her modest rural upbringing, but exposing him to unpredictable Mama caused Martha's stomach to churn.

As the interurban pulled into the Monroeville station, Martha cleared a small circle on the frosty window pane and peered anxiously toward the platform. There, hunched against the cold, was the familiar form of Bill. Martha smiled and turned to Ray. "Bill's here to meet us. Oh, you'll like him—he's such a fun-loving kid, that Bill."

After descending the steps of the interurban, Martha ran on tiptoes across the platform and threw her arms around Bill's neck. Before releasing her embrace, Martha whispered in his ear, "How's Mama today?"

"She's … alright. Nothin' unusual," Bill reassured with a flat tone as he reached to shake Ray's extended hand.

Martha chattered happily as Bill drove them out of town and westward onto Plank Road. She pointed out the homes of friends, former classmates, and neighbors, the one-room schoolhouse she had attended for seven years, and the home of Uncle George and Aunt Bertha as they rounded the bend on Townline Road.

As they exited the vehicle, Martha tucked her hand into the crook of Ray's elbow and smiled brightly, more to reassure herself than the confident Ray.

Upon entering the kitchen, Martha immediately noticed that the scarred and worn surface of the kitchen table was covered by the good linen tablecloth. In the center of the table sat one of Flora's potted African violets, providing a spot of color and cheer. Martha's heart swelled with gratitude to her sisters for their attempts to dress up the otherwise ordinary farm kitchen.

As Martha greeted her sisters with hugs and introduced Ray to the family, Mama bustled into the kitchen, still tying the strings of her best apron around her waist. She was always pleased to have company, and she welcomed Ray with a vigorous handshake and wide smile before selecting a seat of honor for him at the table.

Ella rolled Papa in his wheelchair to the head of the table. She loosely tied a dish towel bib-style around his neck to protect the front of his good shirt. Ella hurried to help Flora carry steaming platters of beefsteak and gravy, snowy mashed potatoes, succotash, freshly baked yeast rolls, and the two staples at every meal—pickles and sauerkraut—to the table.

While his daughters were distracted, Papa quietly removed the dish towel from around his neck and dropped it into his lap. The stroke had robbed him of his ability to consistently feed himself without mishap, but he still had his dignity and did not want to appear to be an invalid in front of Martha's beau.

As they ate, Mama chattered continually, regretfully acknowledging that her church attendance had been irregular lately. She pushed herself away from the table and hurried to the bedroom, returning with her small Bible.

"A Christmas present in 1886, when I was twenty. An English Bible," she noted proudly, patting the cover and looking meaningfully at Ray. "English, not German" she repeated, emphasizing the importance of assimilation.

Ray nodded appreciatively between bites, while Martha lightly furrowed her brow and shot a concerned look across the table at her sisters.

Mama opened the Bible to its salmon-colored front page, where her maiden name and the date were written in sepia-toned ink. Martha noticed that the binding on the Bible resisted opening, clearly indicating that the book had seen little use, which did not surprise her. Reading had never been a pastime that Mama encouraged, particularly if there was work to be done. Martha also doubted that Mama had had sufficient command of the English language at age twenty to read and understand the Good Book. It was obvious the Bible was a status symbol for Mama, not a well-worn and often-consulted copy of the Word.

In an attempt to redirect the conversation, Martha cleared her throat and suggested Ray tell Bill about his work with refrigeration equipment.

She was growing concerned about Bill's quiet and sullen demeanor. Perhaps a conversation about machinery would pique his interest and spark a return of the animated brother she knew.

Later in the afternoon, Ada, Albert, and the children arrived for dessert and coffee and the opportunity to meet Martha's beau. While the men gathered in the parlor and the children played with blocks on the living room floor, the four sisters bustled about the kitchen. They brewed a fresh pot of strong black coffee and set out Mama's best dessert plates.

Martha slipped into the pantry beside Flora, who was cutting two Dutch apple sour cream pies into neat wedges. "What's wrong with Bill?" Martha whispered. "He's been so quiet and just … not himself. I purposely asked Ray to talk about his line of work, but Bill never asked a question or showed any interest. Does he feel alright?"

Flora laid down the cutting knife and shook her head. "Ada, Ella, and me are worried about him, too. He's not himself anymore and, truth be told, he hasn't been since he got back from California. I know he's not happy here on the farm—he never did like this sort of work—but he just seems to be drifting along. No direction, no zest for life. It's just not our Bill!" Flora threw her hands into the air to punctuate her frustration.

Before Martha could respond, Mama bustled around the corner of the pantry doorway. She cocked her hands on her hips and hissed, "Look at you two! The minister's come to call and neither of you put on your best aprons." Mama clucked her tongue in disapproval. "Neat and tidy," she admonished as she brushed some pie crumbs into her cupped hand and whirled out of the room.

The two sisters exchanged puzzled glances. Martha poked her head around the corner of the pantry door. "Reverend Abele is here?" Martha asked Ada, who was washing forks to be used with their dessert.

"No," Ada responded. "Were you expecting him for a *particular* reason?" She plucked at her skirt and teased, "Wished I'd a known to come dressed for a wedding."

Martha flamed red to her hairline and then gasped in astonishment. "Mama thinks Ray is the minister!"

Flora's eyes widened. "That's why she kept talkin' about going to church and insisted on showing Ray her Bible!" Flora shook her head at Mama's foggy mental link between their guest and long-ago memories of church attendance. "Just be glad she didn't ask Ray to give her communion!" Flora exclaimed as she scooped a wedge of pie onto a dessert plate.

Later that afternoon as the interurban chugged toward Cleveland,

Martha confided in Ray that she and her sisters were concerned about Bill.

"Maybe I can use some of my connections to find him a job in Cleveland," suggested Ray.

"You could do that? Find Bill a job?" Martha asked in wonderment.

Ray nodded confidently as he clasped Martha's gloved hand in his own.

Martha relaxed into Ray's shoulder and considered how lucky she was to have this decisive, influential man in her life. He had been nonjudgmental of Mama, even after Martha confided the ministerial mix-up, and now he was offering to help Bill find employment and a much-needed new direction.

As the weeks went on, Ray began to press for marriage. With his persuasive and competitive nature, Ray recognized that he could leverage his efforts on Bill's behalf to his own advantage. Martha felt confused. She vacillated between her love for Ray, her concern for Bill, and her own long-held goals for the independent life she enjoyed. Martha confessed that she wanted to travel to two places—New York City and Europe—before settling down. Ray assured her he could make her travels—and other dreams—a reality if she would agree to marry him. Ray had set his sights on the beautiful, intelligent Martha, and he would not rest until she was his.

The couple's whirlwind romance culminated in marriage on April 6. The small ceremony was held in the parlor of the boarding house, with Mrs. Maybaugh alternately beaming and dabbing at tears, since she considered herself the surrogate mother of both the bride and groom.

After the ceremony, the couple left for a brief wedding trip to visit Ray's widowed mother in Louisville, Kentucky. As Martha and Ray stood upon the front porch of the Barth homestead, waiting for their knock to be answered, Martha was awed by the grand old Victorian-style residence with its arched windows, massive doors, elaborate wrought iron, and spire-topped turret.

A tired-looking middle-aged woman dressed in dark gray opened the door.

Martha thrust out her hand. "How do you do? I'm Martha, your new daughter-in-law," she said brightly.

The woman gave a bemused look as she ushered the young couple into the foyer and offered to take their coats. Ray laughed as he explained, "This is Lottie, the maid. She's been with Mother forever."

Martha blushed and stammered an apology.

"I take it you don't have household help where you come from," said a softly drawling voice from the parlor.

Martha strained to adjust her eyes to the dark interior of the house. Heavy velvet drapes at the windows, dark woodwork, and muted floral carpeting absorbed what little light was emitted by an antique lamp with ruby-colored globe.

"I … um … no," was all Martha could choke out as her embarrassment continued. Inwardly, she berated herself for forgetting that most people of means employed household help. This was a fact of life she had encountered many times while performing private-duty nursing in some of the better homes of Cleveland. How could she have made such a blunder? And why hadn't Ray forewarned her?

Mrs. Barth was seated in an overstuffed chair in the window alcove. Her diamond rings sparkled in the low light.

Ray took Martha's elbow and steered her toward his mother. In the dimly lit room, Martha's shoe caught upon the edge of a carpet runner and she lurched forward. Although she managed to remain upright, Martha was acutely aware of her ungainly entrance and poor first impression.

Ray introduced his bride, and the senior Mrs. Barth unabashedly looked Martha up and down. "So, you come from an agricultural background, I understand," she stated, tipping her head to the side. "Would that be a farm of the gentleman's variety or … of a subsistence nature?" A fleeting grimace crossed her face, as though the word *subsistence* had left a bad taste in her mouth.

"Umm…," Martha hesitated. She looked to Ray for help in fielding his mother's question, but his amused expression indicated he was enjoying Martha's discomfort. "It's a small farm. About seventy acres, mostly strawberries, potatoes, and such," Martha explained. "But Ray probably told you I work as a nurse," Martha offered as a means of deflecting attention from her rural upbringing.

"Yes, a working girl," Mrs. Barth responded with deliberation, as if pronouncing words that were foreign to her tongue. She cleared her throat and added, "That's certainly … noble," before turning her attention to Ray and engaging him in a lengthy conversation about the family business.

The next morning while Martha finished dressing, Ray joined his mother in the dining room for a cup of coffee before breakfast was served. Martha took extra pains to look presentable after yesterday's inauspicious beginnings. Perhaps she and Mrs. Barth could begin anew and forge a friendlier relationship. She gave her hair a final pat, smoothed the front of her skirt, and quietly traversed the upstairs hall to the top of the grand staircase. Wonderful breakfast aromas wafted up the open stairwell, and Martha's stomach growled in response. As she began to descend the steps, Martha could see Lottie just inside the dining room archway, where she was returning the ornate coffeepot to its warmer. Martha paused with one hand on the bannister when she overheard her name.

"And this Martha. Really, Raymond, what were you thinking?" scolded Mrs. Barth. "Marrying a girl you met in a boarding house! Why, if you wanted someone common, you could have married any of the local no-accounts. Heaven knows Lottie's family is ripe with them—you could have taken your pick of that ilk!"

Martha's knees buckled and she gripped the bannister tightly to keep from tumbling down the steps. Her cheeks flushed hot, and she swallowed hard to keep from gagging on the once-appealing cooking odors. Martha didn't know if she felt worse for Lottie, who was present while being openly disparaged, or for herself, but it was clear that the lady of the house held both women in low esteem. Martha barely breathed as she listened for Ray's rebuttal. She was confident he would come to the defense of his bride. However, the rattling of china coffee cups in their saucers, the steady metronome of the grandfather clock, and the sudden ringing of the telephone in the hallway were the only sounds emanating from the first floor.

Blinking back tears of humiliation and disappointment, Martha descended the stairs and passed Lottie, who was hurrying to answer the phone. The two women exchanged glances, but Martha found no comradeship in Lottie's tired eyes.

Martha entered the dining room and slid into a chair beside Ray. She placed the linen napkin in her lap and studied the gilt rim of the plate before her. The thought of food was now repugnant, and Martha's stomach twisted in knots. Ray passed her a tray of assorted breakfast meats, and Martha reluctantly speared a strip of sugar-cured ham.

"Well, our little family is expanding. Isn't that nice?" Mrs. Barth announced, but the flat tone of her voice belied her true sentiments. Her left hand repeatedly smoothed the white linen tablecloth beside her plate, as though sweeping away imaginary crumbs.

Lottie padded into the dining room with the message that Ray's supervisor was on the phone. Ray excused himself, leaving Martha and his mother in uneasy solitude. Lottie retrieved the coffeepot from the sideboard and filled Martha's cup. With a trembling hand, Martha lifted the china cup and sipped the hot beverage, taking pains to avoid eye contact with her mother-in-law. Only the somber *tick-tock* of the grandfather clock filled the uncomfortable silence.

Ray rushed into the room and announced that he was being sent on an emergency overnight call for his employer. He must hurry if he was to maximize his travel time, meet with the client, and return to Louisville the next day. Ray dashed through the arched doorway and bounded up the staircase.

Martha stared at the empty archway in astonishment. She couldn't believe Ray was leaving her alone with his mother during their wedding trip! He had promised they would go downtown to attend a production of one of Louisville's performing arts groups at the lavish Loew's State Theatre. This would be followed by a stop at the elegant Brown Hotel, where they would dine on the famous Hot Brown sandwich, recently created to feed the famished jazz-era dance crowd. All of their plans were suddenly dashed by Ray's call to work. Martha plucked the napkin from her lap, tossed it on the table, and hurried after her husband.

Mrs. Barth eyed Martha's chair, which she had left standing away from the dining table in her hasty retreat. She arched an eyebrow and continued sweeping her hand in small arcs across the surface of the tablecloth.

In their room, Ray was hurriedly packing his suitcase. Martha closed the door behind her and watched him. She was too bewildered to speak. Finally, she choked out, "Take me with you, Ray."

Ray didn't look up as he folded a clean shirt and placed it in his suitcase. "Wives don't accompany their husbands on business trips," he scoffed.

"Then, tell me how to get to the library or the art museum. I'll walk there—I'm used to walking—but I have to have someplace to spend my time while you're gone. Don't make me stay here with your mother. Please!" Martha begged.

Ray dropped a tie and a clean pair of socks on top of the shirt. "Why? What's wrong with mother?" he asked absentmindedly.

"She doesn't like me. I could tell it last night when we arrived, and then this morning when I was coming down for breakfast, I … I overheard what she said about me," Martha blurted, omitting how deeply hurt she was by Ray's lack of defense.

"Nonsense. You two just need to get to know each other better," Ray responded as he snapped his suitcase closed, grabbed its handle, and wheeled toward the door.

"But, Ray. Please!" Martha's voice cracked. "Don't leave me here."

Ray paused as he opened the bedroom door. "You'll be fine," he reassured. Almost as an afterthought, he leaned over and kissed his new wife before hurrying down the stairs.

Martha spent long, lonely hours reading in her bedroom and taking walks in the gardens behind the house, which were ringed by hedgerows of blooming forsythia. The bright yellow flowers, always one of Martha's favorites, normally cheered her, but now they made her feel hemmed in and further isolated.

At last, Ray returned from his business junket, filled with enthusiasm over the new challenges presented by his recent consultation. He insisted the young couple return to Cleveland immediately so he could follow up on his work assignment. There would be no visits to the art museum, attendance at a play or musical performance, or dining in fancy hotel restaurants as Ray had promised. Martha wondered if Ray's promise of employment for Bill would be unfulfilled as well.

As they left Louisville and headed northward, Martha stared out the window at the passing azalea bushes awash with brilliant pink and red blossoms. She recalled that in the Chinese culture the azalea is the "thinking of home" bush. She trained her thoughts on home—comforting memories of her sisters and Bill as well as good times with her friends in Monroeville, at Hiram College and Lakeside Hospital's nursing school, and with her work associates in Cleveland—but increasingly her mind turned to unhappy realizations about the man she had married.

* * * * *

At the end of the spring term, Minola sat at a table in the Office of the Registrar, staring at a blank yellow registration card before her. From her notebook she pulled a sheet of paper and smoothed its folds. A long list showed the courses she had taken; beside it was a short tally of those requirements that must be fulfilled to earn her college degree. Minola's pen hovered over the registration card. By carrying a full load of courses through one final summer session, she could complete her college education. Minola gripped her pen and carefully filled the card with the selected classes. She crossed the room and submitted her final course request to the registrar's clerk.

What should have been a moment of triumph was overshadowed by the specter of her financial situation. Minola's salary from her on-campus jobs, the two loans Uncle Will had co-signed through the Milan Bank, plus the generous non-binding loan of three hundred dollars from Dr. Armstrong were not enough to see her through the final eight-week session. Minola had no alternative but to burden herself with additional debt. This time, she turned to the university itself, which offered a loan with no interest or payments on the principal until the student had been employed for a year. While the loan's lenient terms were a relief, it seemed that Papa was prophetic when he had admonished Minola, "Do you want to be in debt all your life?"

*****

The strawberry season swung into high gear by mid-June. Bill, Flora, and Ella were hard pressed to oversee the pickers, move the packing house as needed, fill the shipping crates, market the berries, keep an eye on Mama, and tend to Papa's needs. In addition, most of the pickers were now schoolchildren or those interested in meeting only their personal demand for berries. The rapid and responsible pickers who once labored through the entire season had moved on to more gainful employment or were enjoying fancy profits from the Liberty Bonds they had rolled into securities during the economy's meteoric rise. Few came to the Seibel farm to earn a comparatively meager wage while toiling in the hot sun over long, low rows of berries.

Each evening after the chores were done, Flora and Ella returned to the vacant strawberry fields to glean the berries overlooked by the day's pickers. They had agreed to use the earnings from the remainder berries to purchase a radio to help Papa while away his empty hours.

*****

The first crop to fall by the wayside as a consequence of Papa's stroke was the blackberries. Without his careful maintenance of the bramble patch, the canes grew wildly, combining with the weeds that flourished between the rows to form a nearly impenetrable jungle. Flora pulled long, black, ribbed stockings over her arms and braved the perimeter of the patch to pick what fruits were easily accessible, to be used for the family's consumption.

As she carefully skirted the menacing thorns of the trailing canes, Flora recalled the days when she and her sisters had picked blackberries alongside Papa. Two sisters would team up to harvest a row, while Papa took a row to himself. The girls refrained from any idle chatter or silliness while working near their father, feeling certain that such nonsense displeased him. However, as they outdistanced him, they burst into song or storytelling. Flora now realized Papa had been aware of their every word and action, and that he had probably enjoyed it in some small way. Now, Papa followed every household development with active interest, and he openly anticipated letters from Hermine, Martha, and Minola. It had been only two years since Papa's stroke, but the days of his stern, stoic detachment and the camaraderie of the large sisterhood as they worked in the fields seemed a lifetime ago for Flora.

* * * * *

Summer on the University of Michigan campus was filled with the sweet scent of catalpa tree blossoms, the rhythmic whir of cicadas, the chirping of crickets, and the shrieks of hawks as they careened through the evening sky. Minola's senses were quickened to each sight, sound, and smell, knowing this would be her last term on campus.

As the summer session neared its close, Minola scoured the employment bulletin board outside the Office of the Registrar. She spotted an announcement that Mrs. Bristol, a supervisor from the Illinois Children's Home and Aid Society, would be on campus to interview candidates for a vacancy in her district. Minola added her name to the short list of students interested in meeting with Mrs. Bristol.

On the day of the interview, Mrs. Bristol sat with a circle of eager young applicants. She leafed through their resumés and peered over the top rim of her glasses as each applicant responded to their name and expounded on their attributes. Minola was aware that, at age twenty-four, she was slightly older than her fellow applicants. She hoped she exuded an air of maturity that masked her nervousness.

At last Mrs. Bristol announced Minola's name. "Miss Seibel, I see you have experience as a school teacher," she noted while glancing at Minola's resumé. "Tell me about that."

Minola knew the only way she would be able to land the job and begin repaying her sizable debt was to distinguish herself from the other applicants; this was no time for timidity. She cleared her throat. "Yes, ma'am. I taught in a one-room schoolhouse for two years, where I was responsible for the education of children ages five through fourteen." Minola continued to outline the Laurel Hill school experience by explaining her before- and after-school duties, detailing the musical and literary enrichment she had introduced into her students' lives, enumerating the improvements she had made to the learning environment within the schoolhouse walls, and even demonstrating her level of commitment to the job by relating the incident of climbing through the schoolhouse window when the door lock was frozen shut.

Mrs. Bristol studied Minola's earnest young face and nodded her head. She made a notation on Minola's resumé and shuffled it to the bottom of the stack before turning her attention to the next applicant.

A week later, Minola discovered a cream-colored envelope in her mail slot at the Mason League House. The return address was the Chicago headquarters of the Illinois Children's Home and Aid Society. With trembling fingers, Minola tore open the envelope and unfolded the letter. The Society was offering her the position of caseworker in the southern Illinois district. She was to meet Mrs. Bristol at her East St. Louis office on August 19, where she would learn the details of her assignment and receive orientation.

Minola's mind spun. August 19 was little more than two weeks away, but there was much to accomplish before then. She must study for and pass her final exams, pack up her belongings, travel to Monroeville to say goodbye to the family, and make arrangements for her journey west. There was no time to confer with Flora about sewing some much-needed wardrobe upgrades, but that couldn't be helped. She had a job—a job! Minola raced up the stairway to share the exciting news with her roommate, Irene Atwell.

Upon hearing the announcement, Irene grabbed Minola's arms and danced her in a circle of joy. When they stopped celebrating, Irene stated firmly, "Now, it's my turn for an announcement. You have never invited me to your home, and I don't understand why, but since this will be my last opportunity, I am going with you to Monroeville. No ifs, ands, or buts, missy."

Minola swallowed hard. While she had told Irene about her sisters and Bill, Papa's stroke, and many of her childhood memories, she had deliberately avoided discussing Mama. There was no way around the subject now. Minola seated herself on the edge of her bed, folded her hands in a tight knot in her lap, and proceeded to relate the difficult description of Mama and her affliction. When she was through, Minola waited for Irene's change of heart about her travel plans. Instead, Irene shrugged and reminded Minola that she had lost her own mother at a young age. She assured her roommate there was no shame in being motherless, either through death or because of mental illness.

Through careful management of her time and by remaining on campus to work and attend classes through the summer sessions, Minola had completed her college coursework in three years. While she had started out with the Class of 1930, she graduated with the Class of 1929. Throughout the span of her academic career she had belonged to no particular graduating class, just as she had belonged to no defined social group on campus.

The end of Minola's college experience came on Friday, August 16, with no cap and gown but merely the promise that her diploma would be mailed to her home address in the coming days. As Irene settled herself on the train seat beside her, Minola turned and stared out the window for one last glimpse of Ann Arbor. She did not want Irene to see the tears that threatened to spill down her cheeks. Minola's university days had spanned an arc from desperate loneliness to life-long friends, from aching homesickness to a great reluctance to leave.

Minola

The three days at home in Monroeville galloped by in a blur. Flora hastily stitched a go-with-everything brown skirt for Minola to wear in her new career. Mama fried pan after pan of sliced potatoes while encouraging their guest to eat heartily. She advised that a corset did wonders for robust girls, so tall, slim Irene should not hold back in her consumption. To Minola's relief, Irene handled Mama's strange behavior and outbursts with aplomb.

On Saturday evening, Minola suggested that Bill and his friend Bud Wilhelm accompany Irene and her on an outing to Put-in-Bay on South Bass Island in Lake Erie. Minola was eager to show Irene the unique features of north-central Ohio and also anxious to include Bill in any event that may restore his fun-loving ways. The four young adults took the ferry to the island, where they visited the towering Perry's Victory Monument commemorating Commodore Oliver Hazard Perry's 1813 naval victory over the British. They also toured Crystal Cave and enjoyed glasses of fresh grape juice from the island's thriving main crop.

However, the island's proximity to Canada made it a convenient stopover on the rum-running route that flourished despite the restrictions of Prohibition. When the foursome boarded the ferry to return to the mainland, they noticed their fellow passengers included a group of boisterous young men who had obviously been partaking of more potent libations than grape juice. As the boat trip progressed, the rowdiness escalated. One tipsy fellow stumbled his way across the boat deck and draped his arm across Irene's shoulders. Slurring his words, he attempted to impress her with his wit, but all that emerged was a loud belch. Repulsed by the coarse behavior, the foursome moved to a seat farther away from the scene. Before long, a fistfight broke out between two of the revelers, and much shouting, cheering, and shoving ensued. The boat's crew responded by turning a water hose upon the ruffians. Minola was abhorred by the display and apologized profusely to Irene, assuring her that such behavior was not the norm for young people in this section of Ohio.

Although Minola enjoyed her brief stay at home, the specter of her financial situation continued to haunt her. The Society made no provisions for travel expenses to her new position. She possessed a small amount of cash, which would be quickly exhausted by the purchase of her train ticket and a few meals during her travels. She would need funds to pay for lodging and to otherwise establish herself in the coming weeks until her first paycheck arrived. Minola knew she could not ask Papa for money; it was evident how financially strapped the family was, and she did not want Ella and Flora to spontaneously offer the money they had been saving toward the purchase of a radio for Papa. She had already tapped Uncle Will twice as a co-signer for college loans, and pride prevented her from returning to him for a hand-out.

On Sunday afternoon, Bill drove Minola and Irene to Ada and Albert's house for a brief farewell visit. With deep humility, Minola explained her dire economic situation to them.

"Oh pshaw, Dick. Seein's how you <u>are</u> my favorite youngest sister-in-law...," Albert responded with a slow grin. He rose and left the room. Upon his return, he handed Minola one hundred dollars that he had received from the recent sale of a cow and two old sheep.

Minola was humbled by Albert's generosity, and she gushed her thanks and a promise to repay him as soon as possible. She did not know that Albert, too, was carrying a debt and therefore ill-positioned to grant a loan.

That evening, Flora and Irene drove Minola to the train station in Monroeville. As she boarded the steps to the New York Central coach, Minola felt weighted down with dread. The new job, the relocation, and the uncertainty of what lay ahead were overwhelming. Minola's throat tightened as she waved out the window to Flora and Irene, who stood on the rail station platform. It gave Minola a strange sense of reassurance and acceptance that Irene planned to remain at the homestead for a few more days. If only she could stay there, too, and not face the new and frightening challenges before her!

In Toledo, Minola bought an *Atlantic Monthly* magazine while awaiting a transfer to the Wabash train line. Perhaps reading and the rhythmic rocking of the passenger car would lull her to some level of sleep during her overnight travels. However, despite Minola's attempts to nod off, she could not induce sleep. Acutely aware of the other passengers' stirrings, the conductor's hourly pass through the car, and her own anxiety, Minola spent a sleepless night.

At the East St. Louis station, she was met by a bright and chipper Mrs. Bristol. Minola's eyes ached and she felt like the walking dead, but she mustered all the energy she could summon. After breakfast in a local café, the two women boarded a bus for Du Quoin, Illinois, where Minola would be posted at a regional office. All through breakfast and the bus ride, Mrs. Bristol kept up a running description of Minola's duties, tidbits about her assigned territory, the paycheck schedule, and, to Minola's relief, her salary—fifteen hundred dollars a year. Mrs. Bristol stopped frequently to ask if her protégé had any questions, but Minola felt too fuzzy-headed and overwhelmed to formulate an intelligent query, so she meekly shook her head.

Despite her fatigue, Minola was able to absorb some facts about her new hometown. Du Quoin was located in the southern portion of the state in a region known as "Little Egypt." The origins of the nickname were attributed to various sources. Some said it harkened back to the 1830s when a poor harvest in northern Illinois drove its inhabitants southward to purchase grain, similar to the Biblical story of Jacob's sons going to Egypt for grain to survive a famine. There were those who said it was because the land of the great Mississippi and Ohio River valleys resembled that of Egypt's Nile delta. Still others claimed the moniker came from the abundance of settlements in the area with names reflecting Egyptian, Greek, or Middle Eastern origins. Coal mining had become Du Quoin's largest industry, but the veins of coal were shallow and quickly depleted. The mining industry's decline had left scars upon the area. On the narrow, unpaved side streets, bungalow-style houses with peeling paint clung to tiny patches of lawn. The entire town wore a tired, faded expression.

Mrs. Bristol recommended that Minola lodge in Mrs. Schaedle's house on Main Street, where she herself stayed while in the area on Society business. She assured Minola that Mrs. Schaedle was a member of one of Du Quoin's oldest families and therefore was highly respectable. The residence was several blocks from the downtown business section and Du Quoin's only restaurant, where Minola would be required to take all of her meals. The home was an excruciatingly dismal Victorian with a cheerless interior. Its austerity was matched by its widowed proprietor, whom Minola found to be vinegary and spare, with sharp eyes and a sallow complexion.

Mrs. Bristol led Minola downtown and unlocked the door to a small regional office on the second floor of the bank building. An overstuffed file cabinet faced a scarred wooden desk and wobbly chair, where Minola was expected to write reports after performing home visits or escorting children to their assigned placement homes. Minola's orientation to her new position lasted three days. With a final, "Any questions?" Mrs. Bristol whirled out the door to begin her month-long vacation.

Left alone, Minola had ample time to ponder what direction to take. She decided to familiarize herself with the stacks of files. She noted an abundance of applications from families willing to take in a child under a boarding home arrangement. However, there was a dearth of applications for potential adoptive homes. Even one as uninitiated as Minola could perceive that many in the impoverished region were interested only in the income that accompanied a state-placed child. She also suspected that applications specifically requesting an older boy were from farm families who were looking for an unpaid laborer. Many of the applications appeared to be of long standing, with no indication of home calls or investigations made to gauge the worthiness of the applicant.

Minola decided to clean out the dead wood, first in the Du Quoin area and then by train or bus trips to the surrounding communities. To reach the areas around Du Quoin, Minola hired Mr. Peterson, who delivered the rural mail, to drive her in his Model T along the dusty, unimproved roads. Their first stop was the Gilbert home, a weather-beaten frame house perched in the midst of squalor.

Mr. Peterson motored up the rutted drive, set the brake, and made an exaggerated sniff of the air as he eyed the home's sagging side porch.

"Yup, Ma Gilbert's got plans for the afternoon," he chuckled, causing his ever-present toothpick to bob.

Minola followed the jab of Mr. Peterson's thumb. The porch floor was covered end-to-end with wooden crates filled with empty long-necked bottles. A heavy-set woman shoved aside the rusty screen door that hung from one hinge. "Who you got there, Pete?" Mrs. Gilbert called warily as she stepped onto the porch, cocking her hands on her hips and using her large frame to strategically block entry into the house.

Minola's jaw went slack. While she had been aware of bootleg alcohol during her college days, she had had no contact with the illicit drink, and she certainly did not expect to interrupt a moonshiner while on her first state-authorized home visit. She mustered what she hoped was a professional demeanor, exited the machine, and climbed the porch steps, taking care to avoid a rotted-through board. Minola haltingly introduced herself and explained the purpose of her visit.

Mrs. Gilbert flashed a toothless grin, and her tone became decidedly more cordial. "Why, I'd invite you in, Miss Seibel, but I'm ... well, my house ain't fit for company today cuz I'm … uh … well, you can see I'm canning peaches," she beamed triumphantly as she waved her hand at the waiting bottles.

Clutching her clipboard to her chest, Minola bent slightly at the waist for a closer examination of what Mrs. Gilbert intimated were wide-mouthed canning jars, waiting to receive processed fruit. Row after row of what were obviously whiskey bottles stretched before her. The notion of trying to squeeze peach halves down their long, narrow necks made Minola grin involuntarily. Did Mrs. Gilbert really expect her visitor to believe such a ludicrous cover-up? Suddenly, the absurdity of the situation made Minola want to guffaw. She choked back a belly laugh while fumbling with banalities to thank Mrs. Gilbert for her time and offering to return on a more convenient occasion. Minola hastily retreated to the machine and scrambled in beside Mr. Peterson, who had overheard the brief conversation. He backed the machine down the drive while his shoulders heaved and his face contorted with suppressed mirth.

As the machine lurched forward on the rutted road, the two gave vent to their pent-up laughter. "Canning peaches!" Mr. Peterson repeatedly roared as he banged the heel of his hand upon the steering wheel. "Oh, Lordy, that's a good one!"

Drying her eyes on her handkerchief, Minola pulled out her pen and wrote in large letters across the Gilberts' application: "DENIED."

Letters flowed between Du Quoin and the Monroeville homestead.

Minola wrote volumes about her experiences in southern Illinois, describing her travels, the people, and her duties. As Ella read the letters aloud, Papa listened eagerly for the mention of familiar Illinois town names, searching his long-ago memories of threshing wheat in that area. Closing his eyes, he recalled the sights and sounds of his youthful journey down the Mississippi River nearly fifty years ago. He envied his youngest daughter's vigor as she embarked on her own adventures.

The Children's Home and Aid Society advanced no funds for travel on its behalf, and it issued expense refunds only once a month. Minola realized that she must be far more frugal with the money borrowed from Albert than she had originally anticipated. She would have to economize by always ordering her meals from the selection at the bottom of the restaurant menu, where the cheapest entrees were listed.

The days and nights in Du Quoin were oven hot, and the one comfort was a nightly bath. However, Mrs. Schaedle allotted Minola only one teakettle of hot water for bathing purposes. With a shake of her finger, the old woman admonished, "We don't have Lake Michigan to draw from like those up-staters do." She eyed Minola accusingly, as though she were a spoiled person of privilege who had just left Chicago and Lake Michigan—neither of which Minola had ever seen.

The other hardship at Mrs. Schaedle's was the feather tick on Minola's bed. Night after night, she wallowed in its suffocating grip, sweating in the terrific heat and tossing and turning endlessly.

After several sleepless nights under Mrs. Schaedle's roof, Minola began to look for other accommodations, using the excuse that it was necessary to be closer to the downtown restaurant where she ate all of her meals. Mrs. Schaedle frowned in disapproval and commented about the health benefits of walking.

Minola was surprised by how easily she found another room. The tidy white house of the Prokopfs was indeed close to downtown. A veranda, edged by large, heavily scented flowers, hugged two sides of the house. The owners were a pleasant older couple who treated Minola with kindness.

In early September, the Du Quoin State Fair opened. The Prokopfs invited Minola to accompany them on Labor Day, when the nationally known horse races would be held. Minola politely declined due to a disinterest in horse racing and a desire to spend time at the local library.

The Prokopfs packed a picnic lunch and departed for the fairgrounds, while Minola exited for the short walk to the Du Quoin Library. She hummed a little song as she strolled along, noticing that the downtown was quiet. This meant there would be less disruption at the library and fewer customers to stare at the young woman eating her meal alone at the restaurant. Upon her arrival at the library, she gave the door knob a gentle twist, expecting the door to easily swing inward. Instead, the knob didn't budge. Shocked by its resistance, Minola gave the knob a firmer turn. When the door remained closed, Minola cupped her hands on either side of her face and peered through the front window. The interior was dark and devoid of human activity. The library was closed for the Labor Day holiday! Minola was dumbfounded. The library at the University of Michigan had remained open on holidays, as did many of the Ann Arbor businesses. Minola bustled down the street toward the restaurant. A sign stating "Gone to the Fair" hung in its window. She whirled around and reassessed the downtown scene. It wasn't just quiet—it was deserted! Between the holiday and the fair, not a single establishment was open. Minola was chagrined by her latent realization that Du Quoin was far from the open and accessible college town of Ann Arbor.

She leaned against the brick wall of the restaurant. The day stretched before her in a long, lonely, and foodless span. As if on cue, her stomach rumbled with hunger pangs. There would be no meals at the restaurant—in fact, no meals at all. Minola finally resolved to slink back to the Prokopfs' house and pluck several apples off the tree in their back yard. It didn't seem right, but it felt less like thievery than if she helped herself to the food in their larder.

The rest of the day was spent in the grim second-story Society office, shuffling through files, munching on apples, and inwardly berating herself for refusing the Prokopfs' invitation.

*****

In early October, Martha sent an urgent letter summoning Bill to Cleveland. After nearly six months of refusing to discuss the topic, Ray had suddenly informed Martha that he'd found Bill a job in equipment maintenance at the Standard Oil Refinery plant in the low-lying flatlands along the Cuyahoga River. Ray cautioned that his influence could not hold the job indefinitely, so Bill must come soon if he intended to take the position.

Flora read the hastily written letter as she walked toward the house from the mailbox. She quickened her pace and detoured behind the back of the barn, where Bill was harvesting the field of corn. As he slid his husking peg down the length of an ear, Flora read the letter aloud.

Bill straightened from his task and flexed his hands. His face held a bewildered expression. "A job off the farm?" he asked. "Are you sure?"

Flora nodded and again read aloud the offer of the position in Cleveland.

"But, what happens here if I leave?" Bill asked, motioning to the fields around them.

Flora stared into her brother's eyes for a long minute. It went unspoken that she and Ella would be hard-pressed to operate the farm alone while taking care of Mama and Papa. However, she refused to hold Bill back the way she had been bound to the farm all of her thirty-four years. "We'll make some changes, but we'll manage," she replied, hoping her voice sounded more confident than she felt. "It's your choice, Bill. If it ain't what you want, though, just say so and I can write Martha and…"

"It is," Bill interrupted her. "It is what I want." He gazed beyond Flora at the weather-beaten barn with its broken lightening rod globes and drooping downspouts. He turned quickly toward the row of corn and shucked several more ears, tossing them in rapid-fire succession against the bangboard.

Flora turned to retrace her steps toward the house. Suddenly there was a halt in the steady *thump-thump* of corn tumbling into the wagon.

"You'd go, too, if you had the offer, wouldn't you, Flora?" Bill called, seeking his sister's approval of the decision, just as he had sought her input on his plans to travel to California with Bud Wilhelm four years ago.

Tup jangled his harness and snorted at the unusual amount of conversation coming from behind him in the corn field.

Flora folded the letter and tucked it inside the envelope. "I never had the chance," she murmured.

Papa was more accepting of Bill's decision than anyone had anticipated. Perhaps he recalled the futility of the argument that ensued between father and son when Bill had announced his California plans. Maybe Papa recognized the lack of zest that had settled over Bill, who labored day after day at a livelihood he loathed. Or perhaps Papa's stroke had diminished his command and rendered him a spectator to family events.

While Ella oversaw the housework, cooking, and Mama and Papa's care, Flora joined Bill in the corn field to finish the harvest so Bill could leave for Cleveland. As they worked side by side, Bill's former spirit was awakened. He called out a joke or funny thought to Flora, and for the first time in years he talked about plans for the future. It heartened Flora to see the return of Bill's long-lost vitality, although she consciously suppressed her own misgivings about what would happen to the farm and the family after his departure.

On a cool fall morning, Bill vaulted onto the front seat of the Star with a valise of clean clothes, a small sum of money, and a sack of sandwiches, apples, and cookies that Ella had packed. As Flora let the clutch out and eased the machine down the drive toward the train station in Monroeville, Bill whipped off his cap and waved it in a final salute to life on the farm. Ella waved from where she stood in the side yard, but Mama could not be distracted from her pursuit of dried corn leaves that littered the lawn and violated her sense of tidiness. From his wheelchair beside the kitchen window, Papa watched until the machine disappeared around the bend by George and Bertha's house.

* * * * *

Mr. Moss turned his Dodge northward onto Townline Road. Shrouds of early-morning fog hung low, and he commented that the autumn day would be a beauty once the sun's rays had broken through. Due to the decreased visibility, Emmaline cautioned against speed, even though she was anxious to reach the train station.

Chain stores were popping up throughout major cities, and trendsetter Emmaline was traveling to Cleveland, where she intended to shop at the J.C. Penney store. If she had enough time, she planned to visit the new self-service grocery stores, where one wandered the aisles and selected their own goods, rather than handing a list to the storekeeper. Even if she didn't purchase a single item, Emmaline relished the thought of her cutting-edge shopping experience. At the next gathering of the neighbor women, she would certainly enjoy lording over them with her revolutionary adventures.

"Jesus God!" yelled Mr. Moss as he jerked the wheel to the left and braked hard. Barely visible in the fog ahead of them was Mama walking barefoot along the roadside in her white nightgown, her long hair tumbling around her shoulders. "It's Sophie Seibel! For Christ's sake, what's she doing out in the road?"

Emmaline gasped, "And in her nightgown!"

"We better see what's wrong before…" Mr. Moss stopped speaking when he felt the iron grip of his wife's gloved hand upon his wrist.

"We'll do no such thing," Emmaline commanded. "Everyone knows that woman's crazy—you've said so yourself."

"We gotta do something! She's a danger out here on the road," Mr. Moss replied. "We could put her in the backseat and drive her home."

"And let her endanger <u>us</u>?" Emmaline's voice crescendoed. "There's no telling what she's capable of!"

The couple peered through the fog at Mama, who now appeared to be searching for something along the ditch. She was wringing her hands and seemed quite distressed.

"Drive on to the Seibels, and we'll let them know she's out here," Emmaline directed. "I am not going to miss my train to Cleveland because of her."

As the Dodge eased past Mama, Emmaline gripped the inside door handle to secure it against the possibility of Mama trying to gain entry.

Mama turned and looked at the passing machine. Her face was contorted in anguish. "*Ich habe sie nicht gefunden!* (I cannot find her!)" she wailed. "*Sie ist verloren gegangen, und ich habe sie nicht gefunden. Wo ist der Buggy? Wo ist es hin?* (She is lost out here, and I cannot find her. Where is the buggy? Where did it go?)"

Mr. Moss started honking the Dodge's horn as soon as he turned into the Seibel driveway. He circled in front of the barn and pulled to a stop adjacent to the back porch. Ella, who had been helping Papa dress for the day, dashed out the kitchen door to see what the commotion was about.

Flora was in the barn, where she had just begun the morning's milking. She bolted upright on her stool at the sound of frantic honking. The steady *ping-ping-ping* of milk hitting the bottom of the pail stopped as she listened to a man's raised voice out in the yard.

"Your mother! She's out on the road, and Jesus! I almost hit her!" Mr. Moss shouted to Ella.

Emmaline leaned across the seat, pushing her face close to her husband's, and called out the driver's side window, "Yes, and the worst of it is she's wearing her nightgown out there! It's disgraceful!"

Ella stood on the porch with her mouth agape. Mama! How could she have lost track of Mama while starting breakfast and helping Papa? She raced down the porch steps just as Flora emerged from the barn, calling, "What is it? What's wrong?"

"It's Mama. She's out in the road," Ella shouted over her shoulder as she rounded the corner of the house.

Flora's legs felt weak and devoid of function. She willed herself forward, and to her surprise, she was running, following the taillights of Mosses' Dodge down the driveway.

Emmaline settled herself into her seat and smoothed her skirt. "The Seibels are lucky they have good neighbors," she sniffed.

Dr. Gilman was called to administer to the very agitated Mama, who continued to wail about a lost soul along the roadway. While her spells usually followed a predictable pattern, this outburst was different. Mama was inconsolable. She paced, wept, and wrung her hands.

The doctor shook his head and confided that it appeared Mama had become completely untethered from reality. He removed his glasses, folded them into his breast pocket, and rubbed his eyes. "I've given her a sedative, and maybe she'll sleep long enough for this spell to pass. But it's my recommendation that she be committed to the Toledo State Hospital. It's the closest facility for those with her sort of affliction."

"A mental asylum?" croaked Ella. "You really think she belongs there?"

Dr. Gilman's gaze shifted to Papa in his wheelchair, and he recalled being summoned to the Seibel home to treat Mama after she hurled a teakettle of boiling water at Papa. "Well, she doesn't belong here," he stated flatly as he snapped shut his black leather bag. "I'll see what I can do about the paperwork."

That night as they lay in the darkness of their shared bedroom, Flora and Ella discussed the bleakness of their situation. Bill had been gone little more than a week and already they had reached a crisis point. Even if they did send Mama away, how could the two of them shoulder the heavy labor required of farming? Could they afford to employ a hired hand when the farm operated on a razor-thin margin? If they sold off the livestock, it would eliminate the need for certain crops, such as hay and oats, but without the horses there was no means of cultivating and planting the cash crops.

Both women tossed and turned through the night as they wrestled with an uncertain future.

* * * * *

Word of Mama's breakdown rippled among the siblings. Not wanting to dissuade Bill from pursuing his new life, Ella and Flora soft-pedaled the situation to him and instead sought advice from the sisterhood. No one knew what to suggest, but the family placed great faith in Dr. Gilman, and thus they thought it best to follow his recommendation. Whatever the outcome, all agreed there would be no judgment made of Ella and Flora's decision, since they were the ones most closely affected by Mama's affliction.

The farm work presented another dilemma. The sisters suggested Albert and Unk farm the homestead on a crop-share basis, while Ella and Flora oversaw the strawberry fields. After thoughtful consideration, however, Albert felt two farms—and the distance between them—would be too much for him and his brother to handle. Even though Bill's departure was undoubtedly well known throughout the community, none of the neighbor men had expressed an interest in farming the Seibel homestead on shares. In addition, the shame of Mama's recent breakdown, which had certainly been broadcast by Emmaline, kept Ella and Flora from canvasing the neighborhood in search of a possible tenant farmer. It seemed that every potential solution was fraught with overwhelming obstacles.

*****

Minola started to feel settled in Du Quoin. She was making headway on the backlog of boarding home applications, and she had learned to master the various forms of transportation necessary to accomplish her home visits. She had taken buses to small, outlying towns and hired local drivers to help her complete her journeys. She had ridden in the caboose of a freight train and with the mail on a conveyance transporting passengers and baggage in the same small car. She had used a big red flag at an unattended depot to flag down a passing train, causing her to sprint many rods to catch up to the passenger car when the train had finally screeched to a stop.

The most rewarding experience, however, was sending money to Dr. Armstrong every two weeks as partial repayment for the doctor's good-faith college loan. Minola had promised herself that Dr. Armstrong would be the first of her benefactors to be repaid, followed by Albert, and it felt good to begin the process of fulfilling that vow.

Upon her return to the Prokopfs' home one evening, Minola found a letter waiting for her on the hall table. It was a familiar cream-colored envelope marked with the Illinois Children's Home and Aid Society's return address in Chicago. Minola carried the letter upstairs to her room and plopped on her bed to read it.

The letter informed her that she was being replaced as the Du Quoin area social worker. The Society's superintendent, Mr. Wilhoit, would be arriving in Du Quoin the following week, and she was to accompany him and a sixteen-year-old ward of the state, Charlene, to Chicago, where Minola would receive further training and subsequent reassignment.

Minola was crushed. How had she failed to meet the Society's expectations when she had scarcely been given a chance to prove herself? She felt defeated and resentful, but worst of all was the looming mountain of debt she had incurred throughout college. How would she meet her obligations if she couldn't hold a job? Maybe Papa was right—

she had doomed herself to a lifetime of debt by insisting on an education at an out-of-state university. And she was being sent to Chicago—the world of Al Capone, gangsters, and the scene of the recent Valentine's Day Massacre! She couldn't imagine living in a city of such violence and vice.

Minola flopped onto her back and stared at the ceiling. Tears burned at her eyelids, but she refused to give vent to her misery. She resolved to meet this new challenge head-on—there was no other option.

On the day she was to meet Mr. Wilhoit at the Society's second-floor office, Minola arose to find her right eye red, itchy, and swollen half-shut. During the night, she had been awakened by the high-pitched whine of a mosquito in her room, and now she wore evidence of its assault. She held a cold, wet compress to her eye until it was time to leave for the meeting, but nothing improved the condition. Minola hoped Mr. Wilhoit would overlook her rather pathetic appearance.

In the office, Mr. Wilhoit greeted Minola warmly. He was a slender man with thinning gray hair and a gentle demeanor. His smile curved up slowly from one corner of his mouth, which reminded Minola of Albert. He introduced Minola to her replacement, who looked to be in her mid-thirties. It dawned on Minola that perhaps her reassignment had less to do with an unsatisfactory job performance than with the Society's desire to have a more mature and experienced person in the position. Whether this was the truth or not, Minola felt heartened by the possibility.

Mr. Wilhoit and Minola proceeded to the Du Quoin Receiving Home, where a number of the Society's wards awaited more permanent placement according to their individual needs. The staff and children greeted Mr. Wilhoit joyously, and Minola began to view the Society's Superintendent with less trepidation.

That evening, Mr. Wilhoit, Minola, and the state's ward, Charlene, boarded an overnight train to Chicago. Charlene was going to live with her older, married sister; Minola's fate seemed much less certain. Throughout the night, the teenaged girl called to Minola from her upper berth, "Honey, honey? Are you asleep?" Minola recognized Charlene's need for reassurance, and she felt a kinship with the lonely, frightened girl.

After arriving in Chicago, the trio progressed to the Society's headquarters, where Charlene was reunited with her sister, and Minola met her new supervisor, Miss Munn. The older woman immediately made Minola feel at ease with her friendly and cheerful personality. She explained that Minola would be attending some training sessions and completing special assignments. She handed Minola a list of potential boarding houses as well as a card with the word "Eleemosynary" printed in large bold letters. At Minola's puzzled look, Miss Munn explained that the word meant "relating to charity," and the card was a free pass to ride the Chicago, Burlington, and Quincy Railroad for all of her Society-related travels.

In the weeks that followed, Minola's assignments included transporting an infant to a boarding home in the city of Plano, west of Chicago. The child had been born of an incestuous relationship and was therefore deemed unsuitable for adoption. On another assignment, she took a toddler for a medical checkup at a free clinic at the University of Chicago. Minola was awed by the college's large, new gray stone buildings, recently built with Rockefeller funds. Later, Miss Munn sent Minola on an overnight journey to Marshall to investigate a large family of motherless children. The county sheriff met Minola at the courthouse and accompanied her on the call, where she found the home conditions to be indescribably filthy. The father, a wizened man reeking of alcohol, jabbed a finger in Minola's face and barked, "You take my children and I'll shoot you, the state's attorney, the sheriff, the judge—anybody who's got a hand in this!" The sheriff intervened and hustled Minola out to his waiting squad car, suggesting he return alone at a later date when the father might be sober and more receptive to the State's plan.

Minola began to understand that Miss Munn was bringing her along slowly in her training as a social worker, starting with easy assignments and building up to more complicated cases. She viewed her removal from Du Quoin as less punishment and more promotion, particularly as she began to experience the cultural attributes of Chicago—the Art Institute, Orchestra Hall, the Field Museum, and numerous libraries. It seemed like a wonderland to have so much quality entertainment for her Sunday afternoons. Minola's initial fears of Chicago as a city teeming with hoodlums and crime were swept away by the impressively tall buildings and the elegant shops along wide, windy Michigan Avenue. At times, she marveled at the improbability that she—a young woman of modest means from Monroeville, Ohio—could be living and thriving in such a cosmopolitan city.

In late October, Miss Munn recommended Minola attend the annual State Welfare Conference held at Northwestern University in Evanston, a suburb along the north shore. Minola was less than enthused, having so recently sat through years of college lectures. At the conference's end, Minola boarded the elevated train to return to her rooming house in

Chicago. As the train pulled into the station, Minola spotted a newsboy hawking copies of the afternoon paper. In bold black letters the headlines screamed "STOCK MARKET CRASH—Billions of Dollars Lost." For one who lacked the resources to invest in stocks, Minola was not overly concerned. Surely the market would yo-yo itself back to normalcy soon, and life would continue on in its usual fashion.

* * * * *

Martha sat at the kitchen table, idly pushing the last bites of dinner around her plate. She gazed across the table at Ray's empty seat. When and if Ray showed up for a meal was hard to predict—his job always received top priority. Martha missed her own job as a nurse and the sense of purpose it brought her. She sighed and listened to the silence in the small house, interrupted only by the drip of the faucet Ray promised to fix and the knock of the hot water pipes in the cast iron radiators that strived to ward off the December chill. Things would be different and better next year, Martha assured herself. She looked forward to the spring, when a little baby would arrive to fill her long, lonely days.

* * * * *

The decade of the 1920s—known for its prosperity and excess—closed with great uncertainty for all. The economy continued to spiral downward after the stunning stock market crash, and prices for farm commodities hovered at grim levels before nudging even lower. The country was on the brink of a national crisis.

The Seibels, however, were overshadowed by more-immediate concerns: what to do about Mama and how to maintain the farm.

ACKNOWLEDGMENTS

Sincere appreciation is extended to Eckhard Langer for the German translations; Dean Sterling for the formatting assistance and cover design; my friends who read, proofread, and encouraged me in this endeavor; Martha Burk, who gifted me with many old family photos and documents; my Dad, Mark Burr, who was my "go-to guy" for guidance on early-20th-century farming practices; the memory of my Mom, Martha Gfell Burr, which prompted me to fulfill the promise I made to finish writing the book; and my husband Bob, who supported me with love, laughter, and good cooking through it all.

Undying gratitude is extended to my ancestors, a family who saved everything—from buttons, fabric scraps, and berry carriers to the diaries, letters, and manuscripts that enabled me to write this story. They were a family with "deep closets," for which I am eternally grateful.

45729472R00367

Made in the USA
Charleston, SC
26 August 2015